Lecture Notes in Computer Science

Edited by G. Goos and J. Hartmanis

394

M. Wirsing   J.A. Bergstra   (Eds.)

Algebraic Methods: Theory, Tools and Applications

Springer-Verlag

Berlin Heidelberg New York London Paris Tokyo Hong Kong

Editors

Martin Wirsing
Fakultät für Mathematik und Informatik, Universität Passau
Postfach 2540, D-8390 Passau, FRG

Jan A. Bergstra
Department of Computer Science, University of Amsterdam
P.O. Box 41882, 1009 DB Amsterdam, The Netherlands

CR Subject Classification (1987): C.2.2, D.1-3, F.3

ISBN 3-540-51698-0 Springer-Verlag Berlin Heidelberg New York
ISBN 0-387-51698-0 Springer-Verlag New York Berlin Heidelberg

Printing and binding: Druckhaus Beltz, Hemsbach/Bergstr.
2145/3140-543210 – Printed on acid-free paper

Preface

A workshop on "Algebraic Methods: Theory, Tools and Applications" was held on June 9–11, 1987 in Passau, Germany. It was organized by the ESPRIT project no. 432, METEOR, in order to discuss the use of algebraic techniques for the systematic construction of software.

At the workshop, four invited talks were given by E. Astesiano, H. Klaeren, H. Partsch and H. Reichel; 15 talks were presented by members of the METEOR project. Jack Metthey, the project officer of the European Community, gave an overview on the ESPRIT projects in the area of software technology.

This volume contains the four invited contributions and 13 technical reports of the METEOR project which were selected by the program committee. 11 of them are revised versions of the talks given at the workshop. The papers by Jonkers on Cold-K and by Hussmann/Rank were added to the volume in order to complete the presentation of algebraic methods.

The program committee consisted of

> J.A. Bergstra,
> M.C. Gaudel,
> H. Obbink,
> M. Wirsing.

The program committee would like to thank J. Metthey, P. Wodon and the Universität Passau for making the realization of the workshop possible. The financial support of the following partners of the METEOR project

> Philips Research Laboratory Brussels,
> Philips Research Laboratory Eindhoven,
> Compagnie Générale d'Electricité,
> LRI – Université Paris-Sud,
> ATT & Philips Telecommunications,
> Centrum voor Wiskunde en Informatica,
> COPS Ltd.,
> TXT,
> Politecnico di Milano,
> Universität Passau

is gratefully acknowledged.

Finally, as the editors of the volume we would like to thank R. Weber for his initiative and help in preparing this volume, U. Lechner for carefully typing manuscripts and Springer-Verlag for their excellent cooperation concerning the publication of this volume.

Passau, May 1989   Martin Wirsing, Jan A. Bergstra

Table of Contents

Part III. Rapid Prototyping with Algebraic Specification

Part IV. An Algebraic Approach to Concurrency

Introduction

The proper treatment and choice of the basic data structures is an important and complex part in the process of program construction. Especially in the design phase of the development process, when the basic objects sets together with their operations have to be defined, design decisions are made that crucially influence the subsequent steps and even determine to a considerable extent the structure of the final program. Algebraic methods provide techniques for *data abstraction* and the *structured specification, validation and analysis of data structures.*

The aim of this volume entitled "Algebraic Methods: Theory, Tools and Applications" is to present a variety of experiences gained mainly within the ESPRIT project METEOR in the use of algebraic techniques for formally based software construction. The volume is divided into four parts covering different aspects of algebraic methods: algebraic specifications and their use in software engineering, a presentation of the design language COLD which integrates an imperative style of programming with algebraic specifications, experiences in rapid prototyping with algebraic specifications and the algebraic treatment of concurrent systems.

The first part contains the four invited papers (by E. Astesiano et al., H. Klaeren, H. Partsch, H. Reichel) and one METEOR contribution (by M. Bidoit et al.) dealing with different aspects of algebraic specification.

First, Partsch shows how algebraic specifications are included in the wide spectrum language CIP-L. As an example for a real-life, large-scale application he presents the development of the program transformation system CIP-S and reports the experiences gained with the formal specification of this system. In the second paper by Bidoit, Gaudel and Mauboussin, also an example for a rather complex algebraic specification is given, the specification of a subset of the UNIX file system. This specification is used for presenting and evaluating the specification language PLUSS. The third contribution by Klaeren and Indermark considers the efficient implementation of algebraic specifications. The authors define a new technique, the so-called structural recursive technique, for compiling specifications with structural recursive axioms to an appropriate stack machine code and argue that the new method has a much better performance than standard leftmost-innermost call-by-value compilation techniques.

In the paper by Astesiano, Reggio, Giovini and Zucca, concurrent processes are specified using (higher-order) partial algebraic specifications. The main idea of this approach consists in describing labelled transition systems algebraically and then to analyze the observational behaviour of the specification by defining a generalized bisimulation semantics. As a further application, some features of an object-oriented approach to programming (such as dynamic objects, classes and inheritance) are modelled with the same technique. The final paper of the chapter also deals with an observational approach to algebraic specifications. Reichel studies classes of "behavioural" models of specifications. Such models do not satisfy exactly the axioms of the specification, the axioms are satisfied up to behavioural equivalence. In the paper he shows how such model classes can be integrated in larger systems of specifications using the concept of "behavioural canon". This concept can be seen as a counterpart to the former concept of "canon" which was used by Burstall and Goguen as one of the key concepts for the semantic description of the specification language CLEAR.

In the second part the design language COLD is presented. This language has been developed in the framework of the project METEOR. It is intended to serve as the basis of a software development supporting the use of formal techniques. The attribute "design language" means that COLD can be used for describing software systems at their intermediate stage of design. As such the language includes both specification-oriented and implementation-oriented constructs. One of the most interesting features of COLD is the integration of the value-oriented world of algebraic specification with the object-oriented world of imperative languages.

In the first contribution, Jonkers gives an informal introduction to the kernel language COLD-K which is meant to be used as kernel of user-oriented language versions. All essential semantic features of COLD are contained in COLD-K. Mainly by means of examples, the paper explains the notion of "class" which is central to the language and demonstrates the algebraic, the axiomatic state-based and the algorithmic styles for describing classes. The last part of the paper is devoted to the structuring mechanisms of the language which include high-level constructs for modularization and parameterization. The second paper of the chapter by Baats, Feijs and Gelissen describes a case study in the application of COLD-K as a specification language. The subject of the case study is the INGRES relational data base system; besides an informal presentation of the main class description, a full formal design specification of (the essential features of) INGRES is given.

The three other papers of this chapter study the semantic foundations of COLD-K. The paper by Koymans and Renardel de Lavalette presents the logical framework MPL_ω, which is the basis for the semantics of classes. It is a many-sorted partial logic embodying the possibility of writing infinitary formulas. Many-sortedness and partiality correspond to the many-sortedness of (systems of) classes and the possible partiality (and/or nontermination) of functions and procedures whereas infinitary formulas allow to express explicitly inductively defined predicates and functions. A complete infinitary proof system is given and it is shown that MPL_ω satisfies the interpolation property.

The paper by Jonkers on "description algebra" presents the basis for the modularization constructs of COLD-K. Module descriptions can be constructed using operators (on classes) such as import, export, renaming and unification; each (modular) schema in COLD-K can be represented by a description, i.e. by a term built from these operators (and some other basic operators on signatures). An essential difference to comparable approaches such as Bergstra, Heering and Klint's Module Algebra is the incorporation of a special scheme of dealing with name clashes in module compositions by means of "origins". This allows to disambiguate many name clashes automatically based on knowledge about the locations of the declarations of symbols. The last paper of this chapter, written by Feijs, introduces a special version of lambda calculus called $\lambda\pi$, which is used to give a meaning to the parameterization constructs of COLD-K. Unlike in the classical lambda calculus, parameterized classes do not allow to substitute arbitrary arguments for a formal parameter but require that the actual parameter satisfies some parameter restrictions. The $\lambda\pi$ calculus formalizes the effect of such parameter restrictions. Typed and untyped versions of this calculus are studied and Church-Rosser and normalization properties are derived.

The four contributions of the part on prototyping with algebraic specifications present experiences with the RAP system, a system for analyzing, testing and executing algebraic specifications. The RAP system comprises an interpreter for specifications (combining term rewriting and resolution techniques), a compiler (translating specifications to PASCAL) and tools for checking properties such as termination or completeness of inductive function definitions.

The first contribution by Geser and Hussmann describes the system from the user's point of view. The user interface of the system and the possibilities for observation and control of the internal actions of the interpreter are illustrated by a simple example. The next three papers present non-trivial case studies with the RAP system. In the paper by Geser a formal specification of the intel 8085 microprocessor is given. The specification covers the machine instructions and their observable effect. With the help of the RAP interpreter, the specification is validated against some informal requirements. In the paper by Hussmann and Rank the compilation for a simple applicative language with recursive functions into stack-oriented target code is treated. This comprises the specification of an interpreter for the applicative language, an interpreter for the stack machine and a compiler. Different approaches to an implementation of this specification are compared: interpretation of the specification by RAP, automatic compilation with the RAP compiler to PASCAL and hand-written code in C. As a result the authors show that the RAP interpreter can solve more difficult tasks than the compilers (which are not able to solve equations) but that for pure computations of values the compilers perform much better than the RAP interpreter. Surprisingly the PASCAL code generated by the RAP-compiler (for the interpreter of the stack machine) has a performance comparable with the performance of the hand-written stack-machine interpreter. In the paper by Lavazza and Crespi-Reghizzi, an algebraic specification of the language ALGRES for expressing relations and relational algorithms is developed. ALGRES provides an extension of Codd's relational algebra. For the specification of ALGRES the RAP interpreter proves to be too slow on examples of realistic size. Therefore the authors describe also a translation of the specification to PROLOG which allows them a relatively fast execution of ALGRES programs.

The final part of this volume is devoted to the algebraic treatment of communicating processes. The three contributions focus around the approach of Bergstra and Klop to process algebra. The starting point for this approach is the axiom system ACP_τ which characterizes the basic equational properties of process combinators such as sequential, alternative and parallel composition of processes. Then this axiom system can be used for proving the equivalence of processes and for process verification. The first contribution by Bergstra and Klop gives a presentation of ACP_τ in several intermediate stages starting with a very simple axiom system. The successive axioms systems are illustrated by simple examples and their consistency is shown by the existence of graph models. The two other papers study the integration of the axiomatic approach to concurrency with specification and modularization facilities. Glabbeek and Vaandrager define a language of modules similar to the one used by Jonkers in his paper on description algebra. The language contains two additional operators for building homomorphic images and subalgebras. Using this notion of modules the combination of different versions of ACP_τ is studied and it is shown that the module operators allow to compose modules in a subtle way, when the direct combination would be inconsistent. This leads to a modular proof technique which is illustrated by the verification of the alternating bit protocol. The aim of Mauw's paper is to give an algebraic specification of process algebra in COLD and to provide facilities for describing the data types occurring in communication systems. As an application the alternating bit protocol and the one bit sliding window protocol are specified with this technique.

As help for the reader the volume contains an index of keywords and an index of examples. Each part of the volume includes at its beginning a detailed list of contents.

Passau, May 1989   Martin Wirsing, Jan A. Bergstra

PART I

Algebraic Specification

An Integrated Algebraic Approach to the Specification of
Data Types, Processes and Objects 91
E. Astesiano, A. Giovini, G. Reggio, E. Zucca

Software Specification by Behavioural Canons 117
H. Reichel

Algebraic Specification
A Step towards Future Software Engineering

H. Partsch
KU Nijmegen

Abstract

The wide spectrum language CIP-L offers, among other concepts, algebraic abstract types for the formulation of formal problem specifications. This concept has been used for a real-life, large-scale application, viz. the (formal) specification of the (kernel of the) program transformation system CIP-S. From the general experiences with formal specification and the technical experiences in using CIP-L (with all its particularities) that were gained in this project, a number of objectives are derived, both for the design of practically usable languages based on the idea of algebraic specification and their support by appropriate tools as part of a comprehensive software engineering discipline.

1. Algebraic specification in CIP-L

The wide spectrum language CIP-L (cf. [Bauer et al. 85]) has been particularly designed to support the idea of transformational programming (cf. [Partsch, Möller 87], [Bauer et al. 88]) by offering constructs that cover the wide range between descriptive (i.e. non-operational) problem specifications and low-level, machine-oriented programs. As one of the possibilities for formulating descriptive specifications, CIP-L offers hierarchical algebraic specifications (cf. also [Wirsing et al. 83]).

Instead of giving a comprehensive introduction into algebraic specification in CIP-L, we try to highlight the particularities of algebraic specifications in CIP-L in contrast to other algebraic specification formalisms by means of a simple example.

A typical algebraic specification in CIP-L is the following one (taken from [Bauer et al. 87]) that defines finite mappings (as to the use of outlined fonts, cf. below):

abstracttype MAP ≡ (**sort** index, **function** eq-i (**index, index**) : **bool, sort elem** ‖
            include EQUIVALENCE(**index**, eq-i)) ;

sort map,

Ø : **map,**

function put (m : **map** ; i : **index** ; e : **elem**) : **map,**
   laws put(put(m, i, e), j, f) ≡
         if eq-i(i, j) **then** put(m, j, f) **else** put(put(m, j, f), i, e) **endif,**

function get (m : **map** ; i : **index** ‖ isacc(m, i)) : **elem,**
function isacc (m : **map** ; i : **index**) : **bool,**
   laws isacc (Ø, i) ≡ **false,**
         isacc(put(m, i, e), j) ≡ eq-i(i, j) ∨ isacc(m, j),
         get(put(m, i, e), j) ≡ **if** eq-i(i, j) **then** e **else** get(m, j) **endif**
            provided isacc(put(m, i, e), j),

function delete (m : **map** ; i : **index** ‖ isacc(m, i)) : **map**,
   laws delete(put(m, i, e), j) ≡
       if eq-i(i, j)
         then if isacc(m, j) **then** delete(m, j) **else** m **endif**
         else put(delete(m, j), i, e) **endif**
         provided isacc(put(m, i, e), j),

function unite (m1 : **map** ; m2 : **map** ‖ unitable(m1, m2)) : **map**,
function unitable (m1 : **map** ; m2 : **map**) : **bool**,
   laws unitable (∅, ∅) ≡ **true**,
      unitable(m1, m2) ≡ unitable (m2, m1),
      unitable(put(m1, i, e), m2) ≡
        if isacc(m2, i) **then false else** unitable(m1, m2) **endif**,
      unite(∅, ∅) ≡ ∅,
      unite(m1, m2) ≡ unite(m2, m1),
      unite(put(m1, i, e), m2) ≡ put(unite(m1, m2), i, e)
        provided unitable(put(m1, i, e), m2)

endabstracttype

The type (scheme) MAP is parameterized with two sorts (called **index** and **elem**, respectively) and an equality operation on sort **index**. It defines
- a new sort of objects (here called **map**);
- a constant (denoted ∅) of sort **map**, the "empty map";
- and the operations
  - put, for associating an index in a map with a value;
  - get, for accessing the element associated with an index in a map;
  - isacc, for checking whether an element is associated with an index and a map;
  - delete, for removing the element associated with an index in a map;
  - unite, for building the union of two maps; and
  - unitable, for checking whether the union of two maps can be formed.

As in [Bauer et al. 87] the notation used here differs marginally from the one defined in [Bauer et al. 85]: rather than listing explicitly the 'visible constituents' (i.e. those constituents of the type definition that are available to its environment) in the 'head line' (after the parameters), they are simply indicated by outlining the respective identifier or symbol. Thus, the complete head line for the above example would read

   abstracttype MAP ≡ (**sort index, function** eq-i (**index, index**) : **bool, sort elem** ‖
         include EQUIVALENCE(**index**, eq-i))
         ∅, **map**, put, get, isacc, delete, unite, unitable ;

In addition, we did not give the explicit quantifications for the variables in the laws belonging to a certain function, as we used the same identifiers as in the functionality of the respective function. Thus, again, e.g., the law for the function put reads in its full form

   laws m : **map**; i, j : **index**; e, f : **elem** ‖
      put(put(m, i, e), j, f) ≡ **if** eq-i(i, j) **then** put(m, j, f) **else** put(put(m, j, f), i, e) **endif**.

This first simple example shows already some of the particularities of algebraic specifications in CIP-L.

CIP-L offers a lot of *syntactic freedom*, as there is no fixed ordering for the constituents within a type body. In this way a user may choose that ordering within a type body he considers most appropriate. Thus, e.g., it is possible to group together functionalities and axioms that characterize the respective functions (as in the example above), rather than being forced to have a strict separation between the syntactic and the semantic part of a type.

CIP-L allows the definition of *partial functions*. For defining the proper domain of such a partial function, an *assertion*, as for get in the example above can be used. There the notation

    function get (m : **map**; i : **index** || isacc(m, i)) : **elem**

indicates that the function get only yields defined values if applied to arguments that fulfil the predicate isacc. As an alternative notation also a special 'definedness predicate' (cf. [Bauer et al. 85], and also below) can be used.

CIP-L has a very *flexible parameter mechanism*. Parameters of a type scheme can be sorts, functions, and constants all of which, like functions, can be further restricted by appropriate assertions. These assertions are either formulas over the respective parameters or collections of formulas abbreviated by the name of a corresponding type scheme (without constituents). Thus, in our example above

    include EQUIVALENCE(index, eq-i)

asserts that eq-i is an equality operation on **index** where the type EQUIVALENCE is assumed to be defined by (cf. [Bauer et al. 85]):

    abstracttype EQUIVALENCE ≡ (**sort m, function** eq (m, m) **bool**) :
        laws x, y, z : m ||
            defined eq(x, y),
            eq(x, x),
            eq(x, y) ∧ eq(y, z) ⟹ eq(x, z),
            eq(x, y) ∨ eq(y, x)
    endabstracttype.

From this last example it also can be seen that CIP-L offers fairly *expressive means for formulating the axioms* of a type specification by not restricting the axioms to just equations or conditional equations. In fact, laws of a type are allowed to be arbitrary closed, well-formed, first-order formulas over (in-)equations between terms. Additionally, as a further convention, terms t of sort **bool** (as e.g. in EQUIVALENCE) are abbreviations for equations t ≡ **true**.

The semantics of a type definition in CIP-L is defined to be the family of all (isomorphism classes of term-generated, hierarchy-preserving) models of the type (for details, cf. [Bauer et al. 85], resp. [Wirsing et al. 78]). Thus, by not confining the semantics of a type definition to 'initial' or 'terminal' models, CIP-L has a *liberal semantics* (sometimes also called 'loose semantics').

A type scheme, as MAP above, also can be extended to provide further operations. An example (again taken from [Bauer et al. 87]) is

    abstracttype EMAP ≡ (**sort index, function** eq-i (**index, index**) : **bool,**
            sort elem, function eq-e (**elem, elem**) : **bool** ||
            include EQUIVALENCE(index, eq-i),
            include EQUIVALENCE(elem, eq-e)) ;

    basedon MAP(index, eq-i, elem),

    basedon (nat, eq-n, o, .≤., .-., .+.)   **from NAT**

        (sequ-of-index, nat,
            emptysequ-i, is-emptysequ-i, make-i, conc-i,
            length-i, sel-i, del-i)   **from SEQU(index, eq-i),**

        (sequ-of-elem, nat,
            emptysequ-e, is-emptysequ-e, make-e, conc-e,
            length-e, sel-e, del-e)   **from SEQU(elem, eq-e),**

(sequ-of-<index, elem>, nat,
    emptysequ-p, is-emptysequ-p, make-p,
    conc-p, length-p, sel-p, del-p)   **from** SEQU(<index, elem>,
                                                        equ-i-e),

function eq-i-e (<i1, e1> : <index, elem>, <i2, e2> : <index, elem>) : bool,
  laws eq-i-e (<i1, e1>, <i2, e2>) ≡ eq-i(i1, i2) ∧ eq-e(e1, e2),

function domain (m : map) : **sequ-of-index** ,

  laws domain(Ø) ≡ emptysequ-i,
        domain(put(m, i, x)) ≡
            if isacc(m, i) **then** conc-i(domain(delete(m, i)), make-i(i))
                         else conc-i(domain(m), make-i(i)) **endif**,

function range (m : map) : **sequ-of-elem**,
  laws range(Ø) ≡ emptysequ-e,
        range(put(m, i, x)) ≡ conc-e(range(m), make-e(x)),

function entry-list (m : map) : **sequ-of-<index, elem>**,
  laws entry-list(Ø) ≡ emptysequ-p,
        entry-list(put(m, i, x)) ≡
            if isacc(m, i) **then** conc-p(entry-list(delete(m, i)), make-p(i, x))
                         else conc-p(entry-list(m), make-p(i, x)) **endif**

endabstracttype

Like MAP, EMAP is also a type scheme. In addition to the parameters already appearing in MAP, there is also a dyadic boolean operation eq-e on elem which, like eq-i, is asserted to be an equality. In addition to the sorts, constants, and functions already provided by MAP, EMAP provides the additional new functions

- domain, yielding the sequence of all indexes in a map that have an element associated to it;
- range, yielding the sequence of all elements that are associated to some index in a map; and
- entry-list, yielding the sequence of all pairs (index, element) that are in a list.

This extension shows further particularities of algebraic type specifications in CIP-L:

In addition to parameterization, CIP-L allows to structure type definitions by building up *hierarchies of type specifications* by means of the **basedon** construct. The **basedon** construct indicates that another type definition is considered as 'primitive' and thus introduces a hierachical relation between types. For the above specification of EMAP this hierarchical relation may be graphically represented by

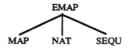

As also can be seen from the example, it is possible in CIP-L to *couple hierachical basing with type instantiation*. Thus, e.g., index, eq-i, and **elem** in

  basedon MAP(**index**, eq-i, **elem**)

refer to the parameters of EMAP, and

  MAP(**index**, eq-i, **elem**)

is an instantiation (with the formal parameters of EMAP) of MAP.

Furthermore, it is possible to *couple instantiations with renaming*. This can be seen in the above example by the three different instantiations of SEQU (denoting a type scheme for sequences) where each instantiation introduces different names for the constituents of SEQU.

From the first of these renamings it further can be seen that CIP-L also allows *operator notation* for functions. This operator notation is not just restricted to pre-fix or in-fix operators, but can be used for arbitrary "mix-fix" operators. In either case, the position of the respective arguments is simply indicated by dots. Thus, e.g., .<. from above indicates an infix operator with two arguments.

There are two more particularities which did not show up in the examples given so far.

CIP-L allows *mode definitions* as an abbreviation for certain frequently used type schemes such as direct products or direct sums. Thus, e.g., the mode definition (cf. below)

type effect ≡ make-effect **record** s : **state** ; r : **result** ; o : **output endrecord**

is (by definition) an abbreviation for

include TRIPLE(state, result, output) **as** (effect, make-effect, s, r, o)

abstracttype TRIPLE ≡ (**sort** m1, **sort** m2, **sort** m3) **triple**, c, s1, s2, s3:

function c (x1 : **m1**; x2 : **m2**; x3 : **m3**) : **triple**,

function s1 (t : **triple**) : **m1**,
   laws s1(c(x1, x2, x3)) ≡ x1,

function s2 (t : **triple**) : **m2**,
   laws s2(c(x1, x2, x3)) ≡ x2,

function s3 (t : **triple**) : **m3**,
   laws s3(c(x1, x2, x3)) ≡ x3

endabstracttype

As also can be seen from this latter example, CIP-L provides a *further means for structuring type definitions* by instantion. A type definition also may be instantiated (within the definition of a new type) by means of the **include** construct. Whereas the **basedon** construct introduces a true relation between (otherwise independent) types, the **include** construct is a simple abbreviation mechanism defined by textual substitution (for details, cf. [Bauer et al. 85]). As the hierarchical basing, **include** allows renaming too (cf. the example above).

2. A concrete software project

Differently to many other languages proposed for specification, CIP-L already has been used in a "real world" application, viz. for the formal specification of the (kernel of the) program transformation system CIP-S (cf.[Bauer et al. 87]).

The work on CIP-S not only aimed at an advanced, comprehensive tool for supporting transformational programming, it also provides a substantial case study for the application of the paradigm of formal specification and transformational programming and thus may be considered as a kind of justification that the programming methodology advocated by the CIP project indeed can be used for the development of "real software".

Furthermore a lot of experience could be gained within this project, which provided additional insight into
- the usefulness of formal methods in software engineering,
- the usability of algebraic specification techniques (as offered by CIP-L),

- additional constructs for algebraic specification languages that are desirable from a user's point of view, and
- problems still to be solved in order to make algebraic specification techniques more widely usable in practice.

These aspects will be dealt with in detail later on. However, in order to do so, some more technical information about the system project is needed. Therefore, we first give a short informal description of CIP-S (consisting of the major requirements and some of their consequences for the formal specification), and then try to convey an impression of its formal specification in CIP-L (by quoting parts from [Bauer et al. 87]).

2.1 Informal description of CIP-S

CIP-S is an interactive system intended to support

- the *derivation* of program (scheme)s from given ones by the application of transformation rules (which is to include the derivation of new rules within the system),
- the *reduction* of applicability conditions (including support for proofs by induction), and
- the *administration* of all system-specific entities (including the documentation and manipulation of program developments)

In order to meet these functional requirements the formal specification of CIP-S was conceptually based on the notion of a 'finite state machine' which led to the following system structure:

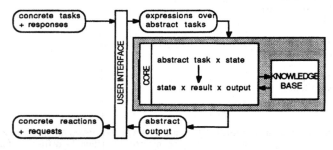

SYSTEM STRUCTURE OF CIP-S

The purpose of the different system components is as follows:

- The **user interface** is responsible for the user/system interaction. In particular, it is to manage the translation between internal and external representations and the compilation of (complex) user requests into (basic) system operations,

- The **core** is the central component of the system that provides all basic operations that are needed for each of the above-mentioned activities *derivation, reduction,* and *administration.* Additionally it controls the internal system states and prepares reactions of the system to be conveyed as output to the user by the user-interface.

- The **knowledge base** is a collection of data bases, each consisting of a number of catalogs for
  - (global or local) transformation rules,
  - (predefined or user-defined) abstract data types, realized as signatures and transformation rules that correspond to the axioms of the respective types,
  - (temporary or permanent) program schemes,
  - program developments (development trees).

In addition to these requirements on the functionality of the system, further (non-functional) requirements and constraints had to be met such as, e.g.,

- correctness,
- reliability ("foolproof system"),
- extensibility (with respect to functionality),
- language independence, and above all,
- limited manpower and resources,

all of which had additional impact on the formal specification of the system.

In order to ensure *correctness*, a calculus of program transformations was developed (cf. [Pepper 84] that provides the theoretical foundation for the system specification. The requirement on *reliability* was met by specifying all basic system operations as total functions (which implies that all error-handling is done within the sytem core) and by allowing the user to work with the system only in a very disciplined way (in restricting the access to system facilities dependent on the current kind of activity). *Language independence* is ensured by an appropriate parameterization of the system specification with all language-dependent entities (such as program schemes, transformation rules, semantic relations), and *extensibility* is provided by a clean hierarchical structure of the specification. The constraint imposed by the limitations on manpower and resources was met by restricting the activities in the CIP system poject to the essential parts of the system (which are indicated in the above graphics by the grey area).

2.2 Formal specification of CIP-S using algebraic types as provided by CIP-L

From the brief informal description above it already should have become clear that CIP-S is a fairly complex system. In order to master this complexity, the formal specification of the system consists of a rather large hierarchy of individual types each of which reflects a certain level of abstraction. In the following we will illustrate both, the hierarchy and the respective levels of abstraction, by a few representative type fragments (all quoted from [Bauer et al. 87] where the complete formal specification of the CIP-S system core can be found).

2.2.1 The system core

The abstract type SYSTEM-CORE constitutes the highest level of abstraction in the specification of the system core. It provides all (abstract) elementary operations from which the actual user commands are composed and made available to the user via an appropriate environment.

In order to meet the above-mentioned requirement of reliability, every operation in SYSTEM-CORE is total, effects a well-defined state transition (possibly the identity) , and produces a result (possibly the dummy no-result) and an abstract output (possibly an error message).

In addition to this totalization, the only purpose of the type SYSTEM-CORE is to collect those operations that shall be visible to the user environment. Hence, the specifications of the various operations essentially just "lift" the corresponding operations from other abstract types on lower levels of abstraction.

The basic operations available in the system can be grouped according to the kind of activity they support. There are two major kinds of activities, viz.

- proper transformation activities, and
- manipulations of the knowledge base.

In the following we will concentrate on the latter ones.

The (complete) type SYSTEM-CORE has a fairly simple (hierarchical) structure:

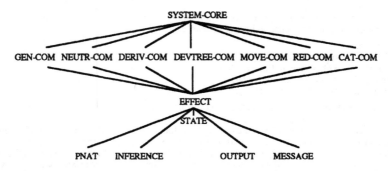

where each type SYSTEM-CORE is based on, comprises operations that are typical for a particular kind of activity. Thus, e.g., CAT-COM provides all operations that are needed to realize system commands concerning the catalogs.

Formally, the type SYSTEM-CORE is defined by

abstracttype SYSTEM-CORE ≡

basedon GEN-COM, NEUTR-COM, DERIV-COM, DEVTREE-COM,
        MOVE-COM, RED-COM, CAT-COM

endabstracttype

2.2.2 System operations concerning the knowledge base

The **knowledge base** of the system is organized into **catalogs**. Each of these catalogs contains **entries** (of the same group) which are either named or anonymous. Each **group** characterizes some system-specific entity such as terms, clauses, inferences, derivations, reductions, transformation programs, and relations on predicate symbols.

The first class of operations (on the knowledge base) concerns the generating, loading, deleting, and fusing of whole catalogs. In addition, the user can ask for the names of all currently available catalogs.

On individual (currently available) catalogs one can perform the usual operations of adding, inserting, deleting, and fetching of entries. Moreover, entries can be named and renamed. Finally, the user can ask the system to display all (all named, all anonymous) entries.

The respective formalizations of these commands mainly refer to the corresponding operations of the type CAT-BASE (cf. below). In addition, they have to take care of potential partialities. The formalization is as follows (for the complete definition, cf. [Bauer et al. 87]):

abstracttype CAT-COM ≡

basedon EFFECT,

function exists-catalog (n : name ; z : state) : bool ,
    laws exists-catalog(n, z) ≡ has-cat(n, cat-base(z)),

function generate-empty-catalog (gp : group ; n : name ; z : state) : effect,
function cat-generable (gp : group ; n : name ; z : state) : bool,

laws cat-generable (gp, n, z) ≡ ¬ exists-catalog(n, z),

    generate-empty-catalog(gp, n, z) ≡
      if cat-generable(gp, n, z)
        then replace-cat-base(new-base, z) + no-result + answer(done)
            where new-base : **cat-base** ≡ gen-empty(gp, n, cat-base(z))
      [] ¬ cat-generable(gp, n, z)
        then id(z) + no-result + answer(illegal-cat-name)
      endif,

function load-catalog (n : **name** ; c : **catalog** ; z : **state**) : **effect**,
function cat-loadable (n : **name** ; c : **catalog** ; z : **state**) : **bool**,

  laws cat-loadable(n, c, z) ≡ loadable(n, c, catbase(z)),

    load-catalog(n, c, z) ≡
      if cat-loadable(n, c, z)
        then replace-cat-base(new-base, z) + no-result + answer(done)
            where new-base : **cat-base** ≡ load(n, c, cat-base(z))
      [] ¬ cat-loadable(n, c, z)
        then id(z) + no-result + anser(not-loadable)
      endif,

  :

function add-entry (cn : **name** ; e : **entry** ; z : **state**) : **effect**,
function addable-to-cat (cn : **name** ; e : **entry** ; z : **state**) : **bool**,

  laws addable-to-cat(cn, e, z) ≡ addable-to(cn, e, cat-base(z)),

    add-entry(cn, e, z) ≡
      if addable-to-cat(cn, e, z)
        then replace-cat-base(new-base, z) + no-result + answer(done)
            where new-base : **cat-base** ≡ add-to(cn, e, cat-base(z))
      [] ¬ addable-to-cat(cn, e, z)
        then id(z) + no-result + answer(not-addable)
      endif,

function get-entry (cn, en : **name** ; z : **state**) : **effect**,
function fetchable-from-cat (cn, en : **name** ; z : **state**) : **bool**,

  laws fetchable-from-cat(cn, en, z) ≡ fetchable-from(cn, en, cat-base(z)),

    get-entry(cn, en, z) ≡
      if fetchable-from-cat(cn, en, z)
        then id(z) + ent-res(fetch-from(cn, en, cat-base(z))) + answer(done)
      [] ¬ fetchable-from-cat(cn, en, z)
        then id(z) + no-result + answer(not-fetchable)
      endif,

  :

endabstracttype

2.2.3 Effects produced by the system

The operations of the SYSTEM-CORE produce **effects** which are triples consisting of a new **state**, a (proper or improper) **result**, and an **output**. The constructor of these triples is denoted by the ternary infix operator .+.+. For accessing the components of an effect there are the operations s (state), r (result), and o (output). A further operation show-result transforms the result of an effect into output.

abstracttype EFFECT ≡

basedon STATE, OUTPUT, MESSAGE, INFERENCE, PNAT,

type effect ≡ make-effect **record** **s :** **state** ;
          r : **result** ;
          o : **output**
      endrecord,

function .+.+. (state : **state**; result : **result** ; output : **ouput**) : **effect,**
  laws state + result + output ≡ make-effect(state, result, output),

type result ≡ «supertype, comprising all system-specific entities and a new constant "no-result"»

  :

endabstracttype

2.2.4 The state

The **system state** is a triple, consisting of a current activity (neutral, derivation, or reduction), a stack of nested activities, and a knowledge base. The stack records pending activities together with those catalogs that are relevant for the respective activity. The knowledge base is a collection of catalogs. It has to contain two catalogs for the inferences and assumptions pertaining to the current activity; this condition is tested by <u>admissible</u>.

The collection of catalogs can be obtained by <u>cat-base</u> and updated by <u>replace-cat-base</u>.

Further operations are provided in connection with the <u>current activity</u> and for <u>accessing and updating the stack</u>.

In addition to these (conceptual) operations, there are further ones of a more technical nature, viz.
- id   which yields the identity on states, and
- init-state which establishes the initial state by generating an initial (neutral) activity and the empty actual catalogs.

The hierarchical structure of the type STATE is given by the following diagram:

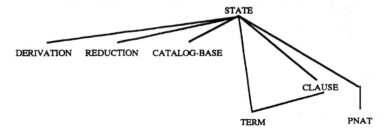

The corresponding type definition is

abstracttype STATE ≡

basedon CATALOG-BASE, DERIVATION, REDUCTION, CLAUSE, TERM,

type state ≡ make-state **record** actual-activity : **activity** ;
                                   stack   : **stack** ;
                                   cat-base   : **cat-base** ‖ admissible(cat-base)
                endrecord ,

function replace-cat-base (new-base : **cat-base** ; z : **state**) : **state**,
    laws replace-cat-base(new-base, z) ≡ make-state(actual-activity(z), stack(z), new-base),

init-state : **state**,
    laws init-state ≡ make-state(neutral, empty-stack, init-cat-base),

function id (z : **state**) : **state**,
    laws id(z) ≡ z,

    :

endabstracttype

2.2.5 The catalog base

The **knowledge base** of the system is structured into two levels:
- the basic level are catalogs that consist of named as well as anonymous entries;
- the collection of these catalogs, i.e. a mapping from names to catalogs, forms the overall knowledge base.

The hierarchical structure of the catalog base is as follows:

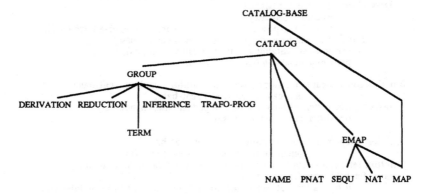

The corresponding type definition is

abstracttype CATALOG-BASE ≡

basedon CATALOG,

basedon (cat-base, empty-collection, put, **select-cat**, isacc, del, unite, unitable)
≡ MAP(name, eq-n, **catalog**),

function admissible (cb : **cat-base**) : **bool**,
   laws admissible(cb) ≡ has-cat(inf-actual, cb) ∧ has-cat(cls-actual, cb),

init-cat-base : **cat-base**,
   laws init-cat-base ≡
       gen-empty(inf-grp, inf-actual, gen-empty(cls-grp, cls-actual, empty-collection)),

function has-cat (cn : **name** ; cat-base : **cat-base**) : **bool**,
   laws has-cat(cn, cat-base) ≡ isacc(cat-base, cn),

function gen-empty (gp : **group** ; cn : **name** ; cat-base : **cat-base** ‖
             ¬ has-cat(cn, cat-base)) : **cat-base**,
   laws gen-empty (gp, cn, cat-base) ≡ put(cat-base, cn, empty-cat(gp))
      provided ¬ has-cat(cn, cat-base),

function load (cn : **name** ; cat : **catalog** ; cat-base : **cat-base** ‖
           loadable(cn, cat, cat-base)) : **cat-base**,
function loadable (cn : **name** ; cat : **catalog** ; cat-base : **cat-base**) : **bool**,
   laws loadable(cn, cat, cat-base) ≡ ¬ has-cat(cn, cat-base),
      load(cn, cat, cat-base) ≡ put(cat-base, cn, cat)
      provided loadable(cn, cat, cat-base),

function add-to (cn : **name** ; e : **entry** ; cat-base : **cat-base** ‖
           addable-to(cn, e, cat-base)) : **cat-base**,
function addable-to (cn : **name** ; e : **entry** ; cat-base : **cat-base**) : **bool**,
   laws addable-to(cn, e, cat-base) ≡
      if has-cat(cn, cat-base)
          then adding-possible(select-cat(cat-base, cn), e) **else false endif**,
      add-to(cn, e, cat-base) ≡ replace-cat(cn, new-cat, cat-base)
      where new-cat : **catalog** ≡ add(select-cat(cat-base, cn), e)
      provided addable-to(cn, e, cat-base),

function replace-cat (cn : **name** ; new-cat : **catalog** ; cat-base : **cat-base** ‖
           has-cat(cn, cat-base)) : **cat-base**,
   laws replace-cat(cn, new-cat, cat-base) ≡ put(cat-base, cn, new-cat)
      provided has-cat(cn, cat-base),

function fetch-from (cn, en : **name** ; cat-base : **cat-base** ‖
           fetchable-from(cn, en, cat-base)) : **entry**,
function fetchable-from (cn, en : **name** ; cat-base : **cat-base**) : **bool** ,
   laws fetchable-from(cn, en, cat-base) ≡
      if has-cat(cn, cat-base) **then** contains(cn, en, cat-base) **else false endif**,
      fetch-from(cn, en, cat-base) ≡ select(select-cat(cat-base, cn), en)
      provided fetchable-from(cn, en, cat-base),

   :

endabstracttype

2.2.6 Catalogs

Catalogs serve for storing the system-relevant entities, i.e. inferences, clauses, terms, transformation programs, derivations, and reductions. These various entities are subsumed under the common type **entry**. However, a catalog may only contain entries of the same kind (referred to as **group**). Therefore, a catalog also possesses a group component against which the groups of all entries are matched.

Catalogs are formally defined by

abstracttype CATALOG ≡

basedon GROUP, NAME, PNAT,

type catalog ≡ make-cat **record group** : **group**,
                  named : **map**,
                  anonymous : **sequ-of-entry** ‖
                  compatible-map(named, group)
                  ∧ compatible-sequ(anonymous, group)
          endrecord,

basedon EMAP(**name**, eq-n, **entry**, eq-n),

function compatible-map (m : **map** ; gp : **group**) **bool**,
function compatible-sequ (sq : **sequ-of-entry** ; gp : **group**) : **bool**,
   laws compatible-map(m, gp) ≡ compatible-sequ(range(m), gp),
      compatible-sequ(emptysequ-e, gp) ≡ **true**,
      compatible-sequ(conc-e(s, make-e(e)), gp) ≡
         compatible-gp(group(e), gp) ∧ compatible-sequ(s, gp),

function empty-cat (gp : **group**) : **catalog**,
   laws empty-cat(gp) ≡ make-cat(gp, ∅, emptysequ-e),

function add (cat : **catalog** ; e : **entry** ‖ adding-possible(cat, e)) : **catalog**,
function adding-possible (cat : **catalog** ; e : **entry**) : **bool**,
   laws adding-possible(cat, e) ≡ compatible-gp(group(e), group(cat)),
      add(cat, e) ≡ make-cat(group(cat), named(cat), conc-e(anonymous(cat), make-e(e)))
        provided adding-possible(cat, e),

function select (cat : **catalog** ; n : **name** ‖ has-name(cat, n)) : **entry**,
   laws select(cat, n) ≡ get(named(cat), n)
     provided has-name(cat, n) ,
   ⋮
endabstracttype

3. Experiences

The complete formal specification of the system core of CIP-S covers 140 pages and consists of

- approximately 120 basic system operations,
- approximately 30 new types (in addition to some basic ones),
- approximately 60 new object kinds,
- altogether, approximately 900 operations.

Hence, it is to be considered at least a medium-size, if not a large-scale application, from which valuable experiences in using algebraic specification techniques could be gained. For any other realistic practical application similar figures will have to be faced.

A detailed treatment of these experiences can be found in [Möller, Partsch 86]. In the following we will therefore confine ourselves to only a few aspects of these experiences, in particular those which we consider to have impact on future work in the area of algebraic specification.

Practitioners are still suspicious about the use of formal methods in software engineering. Our experience, however, shows that there is no reason for doing so. On the contrary: both formal specification and formal development, turned out to be less complicated than expected, and could be done with an effort that is well comparable with the one the "conventional" software engineering approach would have needed (thus, e.g., the first nearly complete draft of the specification took about 3 man months). In addition we could benefit from the advantages of these formal approaches.

In particular, we found out that formal specifications

- are a good basis for communication (independent of intuitive (mis-)interpretation),
- may serve as an (objective) yardstick for design decisions,
- help avoiding lots of problems induced by "hand waving" argumentation by enforcing clarity and precision,
- provide a sound basis for formal validation, and
- allow a clear modularization (e.g., by strict hierarchical design).

However, we also experienced that for using formal specification techniques in "real world applications" computer support is absolutely mandatory (cf. below).

In addition to the experiences concerning formal specification techniques in general, specific experience in using the algebraic specification constructs of CIP-L has been made. The following concepts and "features" turned out to be particularly useful:

• *modes*

Nearly half of the object kinds that appear in the CIP-S specification are defined using the mode mechanism. This not only contributed to cutting down the length of the specification, it also helped in the perception of structural similarities.

• *predefined basic types*

The specification also makes extensive use of predefined basic data types, such as maps, sets, stacks, and sequences, in particular of the possibility of renaming coupled with instantiation (in connection with the **basedon** construct). In this respect the type EMAP (cf. section 1) provides a representative example.

• *operator notation*

In connection with the basic types, we also used operator notation whenever appropriate. In addition to the obvious advantage of brevity, symbols that are already well-known from mathematics could be used, which certainly increased the readability of the specification.

In a first attempt to the system specification we even tried to use operator notation for most of the newly defined types, in order to keep the specification as short as possible. However, very soon we contritely returned to ordinary function notation, simply because we had enourmous difficulties in understanding our own specification. For newly defined types, the function notation has the advantage of conveying at least a bit of meaning, if the respective identifiers are carefully chosen. It is particularly for this latter reason, that identifiers can be found in the specification that consist of up to 30 characters.

• *partial operations*

A great deal of the "internal" operations of the system are partial operations by nature. Having available the concept of partial operations in CIP-L allowed us to model these operations adequately. In particular, error-handling could be specified (explicitly) at the appropriate level of abstraction, rather than (implicitly) by, e.g., error-propagation (as it is usually done in a specification formalism allowing only total functions).

- *expressiveness in the axioms*

   Although most of the axioms in the specification are simple equations or conditional equations, there are some axioms where we could benefit from the possibility of having first-order formulas (including existential quantifiers) as axioms. In these particular cases the respective first-order formulas also provide a formalization that is much more adequate and natural than an equivalent one which uses auxiliary operations and only (conditional) equations.

- *hierarchical structuring*

   A concept that allows to express (hierarchical) structure in a formal specification seems to be absolutely mandatory, in order to master complexity. In fact, we made heavy use of hierarchical structuring, as already can be seen from the short excerpt of the specification given in section 2.2. In particular we tried hard to build up the hierarchy in such a way that any type only uses operations from types that are directly subordinate (with repect to the hierarchy). Although this caused the introduction of several operations just for "passing information", and thus a certain increase in the length of the specification, there was the obvious advantage of "local modifiability", which was particularly important in the early phases of writing up the specification.

- *syntactic freedom*

   A large specification (as the one of CIP-S) usually contains types that (by nature) have a fairly large number of operations. In such a case it is particularly important that the syntax of the specification formalism allows as much freedom as possible. Thus, e.g., being able to group functionalities and corresponding axioms together, contributed substantially to a nice optical structuring of the specification, which in turn supports readability and understandability.

   We also rather frequently made use of the "traditional" comment construct. In particular, this provided a simple means for being able to include additional information (to support understanding) and to express (within the formal specification) underlying design decisions.

4. Implications for the practical use of algebraic specifications

The formal specification of CIP-S provided one of the first 'non-toy' applications of the algebraic specification technique as offered by CIP-L, and thus turned out to be a valuable source for getting some real experience about additional 'syntactic sugar' that is especially needed for large specifications, but also about further desirable constructs which are not of a purely syntactic nature but require semantic additions. Of course, this one experience is certainly not comprehensive, and further experiments of the same kind are needed.

4.1 Additional syntactic sugar

Within the specification of CIP-S a few additional constructs were used which, although not directly available in CIP-L, simply could be defined as (syntactic) abbreviations by appropriate transformations.

Large hierarchical specifications very often involve axioms that are composed of rather complex terms consisting of a fairly large number of 'nested' function calls. In order to master this kind of complexity (which only appears in large specifications) we introduced *let/where clauses* in axioms that allow to the abbreviation of subterms. In this way, understanding of the axioms is eased not only by the decomposition of complex terms into simpler ones (which a reader of a specification would do anyhow), but also by giving meaningful names to the respective subterms and the obligation of augmenting each term with its type.

Examples of this kind can be found in the extract of the CIP-S specification given above, e.g. (cf. type CATALOG-BASE),

   add-to(cn, e, cat-base) ≡ replace-cat(cn, new-cat, cat-base)

where new-cat : **catalog** ≡ add(select-cat(cat-base, cn), e)

    provided addable-to(cn, e, cat-base).

Here, the unabbreviated form would read

    add-to(cn, e, cat-base) ≡ replace-cat(cn, add(select-cat(cat-base, cn), e), cat-base),

which, although only showing a nesting depth of 3, is harder to understand, since the reader has to know (or to look up) that the operation add produces a (new) catalog (which is made explicit in the abbreviated form by the type information). It is certainly not hard to imagine the gain in understandability that is obtained, if this simple mechanism is used for terms showing nesting depths up to 10 (which appeared quite often in the specification of CIP-S).

Also for reasons of readability, sometimes *'descriptive constructs'* (cf. [Bauer et al. 85]) such as **some** (denoting a choice), **that** (denoting unique description), or set comprehension were used in the specification of CIP-S. These constructs are defined for the 'scheme language' (cf. [Bauer et al. 85]), but they are not available in the algebraic sublanguage of CIP-L, because in full generality they do not fit into the semantic definition of algebraic types. However, they have the advantage of allowing aspects to be expressed more adequate than in the pure "algebraic language".

Examples are axioms such as

    t ≡ **that** x : **m** ‖ p

which abbreviates the axioms

    p[t **for** x] ≡ **true**,

    ∀ x : **m** ‖ (p ⇒ eq-m(x, t))

(where eq-m is reqired to be an equality predicate on **m**), or axioms such as

    t ≡ { x : **m** ‖ p }

which abbreviates the axioms

    basedon (mset, .∈ ., ..) **from** SET(**m**, eq-m),

    t ≡ **that** s : mset ‖ (∀ x : **m** ‖ (x ∈ s ⇔ p)

In connection with the abbreviation of certain type schemes we also found out that frequently, in additon to construction and selection operations, at least an equality test for the new object kind is needed. To avoid loss of the notational advantage of mode definitions by being forced to give an explicit definition for a new equality test, we introduced an abbreviation for the *combined definition of variant record types with elementwise equality*.

Using this mechanism, under the additional assuption that eq-s, eq-r, and eq-o are equality tests on states, results, and outputs, respectively, e.g., an "induced" equality test eq-e for effects (cf. section 2.2.3) could be introduced simply by

    type effect (eq-e) ≡

        make-effect **record** s : **state** (eq-s) ; r : **result** (eq-r) ; o : **output** (eq-o) **endrecord**.

Finally, in connection with basic types such as sequences or sets it also turned out to be very convenient to have *standard denotations* available, in more or less the same way as they are used in mathematics. Thus, e.g.,

    { t_1, ..., t_n }

was used rather than

    {t_1} ∪ ... ∪ {t_n},

again for reasons of better readability.

4.2 Further desirable constructs

In addition to the above-mentioned "constructs" which just add some syntactic flexibility, other constructs were identified that also would have improved readability and comprehensibility of the specification. In contrast to the former ones, however, the latter ones could not be used, since they require certain additions on the semantic side.

Although CIP-L provides fairly rich concepts for introducing structure (parameterization, hierarchical basing, textual inclusion), which proved to be sufficient for the formal specification of CIP-S, it might be useful to have additional means, e.g., for being able to express 'modularity' in a more straightforward way.

Thus, e.g. the type SYSTEM-CORE (cf. section 2) simply consists of an aggregation of seven "sub-types" that are not related. In the formal specification this was modeled "indirectly", viz. via additional, "artificial" levels of abstraction using the **basedon** mechanism. For the particular application CIP-S this "trick" was sufficient due to the independence of the respective components. In general, however, situations will have to be encountered where a type should consist of several types which are loosely coupled, but conceptually not hierarchically depending on each other. For these situations *further means for expressing structural relations between types* (in addition to the hierarchy relation) are needed. Examples in this direction already can be found, e.g., in COLD [Jonkers et al. 86], [Feijs et al. 87], ASF [Bergstra et al. 87] or ASL [Wirsing 83].

The current specification formalism available in CIP-L allows operations to have several arguments and one result, all of (simple) object kind only. In practical applications, however, very often operations are needed that yield more than one result. Typical examples of this kind are all the operations in the system core that produce effects. Of course, by introducing tuples, operations with multiple results already can be dealt with in the currently available language. However, if these results are to be used as arguments of other operations, these tuples first have to be decomposed into their constituents before they can be used, which introduces a certain kind of notational overhead. Therefore, an extension of the algebraic formalism allowing *operations with multiple results* would be desirable.

One even should go a step further in weakening the current restrictions on arguments and results of operations defined within an algebraic type. However, whereas multiple results probably could be introduced on the current semantic basis, allowing *higher-order operations in types*, i.e., operations having operations as arguments and/or results, needs a true extension of the semantic basis. A corresponding approach is worked out, e.g., in [Möller 86]. One of the examples dealt with there is a description of the catalog base of CIP-S in terms of higher-order operations. Compared with the description given above, the description using higher-order operations has not only the advantage of being considerably shorter (by about one third), but also of exhibiting explicitly similarities between the different operations on the catalog base and the individual catalogs (for details, cf. [Möller 86, 87]).

In the previous subsection we already commented on certain syntactic extensions that were introduced in the specification of CIP-S by suitable transformation rules. However, these transformation rules had to be given "on the meta-level", i.e., outside the algebraic specification formalism. What one rather would like to have, is a true extension mechanism (within the algebraic formalism) for introducing 'local formalisms' (in the sense of [Neighbors 80], [Wile 86], or [Heering, Klint 87]). Again, the motivation here is to improve readability and comprehensibility of algebraic specifications by supporting the introduction of special notations that are most adequate for a particular application. In the same context efforts to combine the notations provided by algebraic types and Petri nets (cf. e.g. [Krämer 87]) on the common semantic basis of algebraic specifications have to be seen.

5. Directives for future research

In addition to the aspects mentioned in the previous subsection, for which at least pioneering theoretical results are already available, there are further important aspects (for making algebraic specifications practically usable) which still deserve basic research. We will divide them into the categories theory, language, methodology, and tools.

5.1 Theoretical problems still to be solved

There are certainly a lot of theoretical aspects in connection with algebraic specifications that still are to be solved, among which the following ones, on the basis of the CIP-S experience, are considered rather important:

- the *transition from underspecification to explicit non-deterministic constructs*, and

- a *constructive way of getting implementations* for algebraic types.

There seems to be a general agreement (cf., e.g. ,[London, Feather 82]) that formal specifications should leave as much freedom for implementation as possible. This in particular means that in a specification only those requirements should be listed explicitly which are absolutely mandatory.

One way of providing this kind of implementation freedom is by "underspecification" which means that certain operations are specified in such a way that the properties explicitly stated do not uniquely determine the respective operation. Within the available algebraic formalism this means that the respective operations are not 'sufficiently completely' specified. So far there is not yet a problem. Problems, however, may arise afterwards in connection with implementation, especially if an implementation is aimed at that still reflects the underspecification in terms of explicit non-deterministic constructs, since nearly all of the available notions of 'correct implementation' of an algebraic type do not take non-determinism into account.

Implementation freedom also may mean that the specification formalism should allow the explicit specification of non-determinism. Again, however, the respective theoretical foundation is not sufficiently explored yet.

There are a number of (different) notions of 'correct implementation' available (cf., e.g., [Broy et al. 86], also for further references), all of which have in common that they provide conditions to be verified for an implementation, but do not tackle the problem of how to find such an implementation. For working practically with algebraic specifications, however, more constructive ways of getting implementations, e.g., in the form of transformation rules, should be explored.

Within the CIP methodology, an implementation of an algebraic type usually starts by a transition to an equivalent 'computation structure' (cf. [Bauer et al. 85]), i.e. an 'applicative counterpart' of an algebraic type where object kinds are defined in terms of 'mode definitions', and each operation has an individual definition. It is furthermore assumed that this computation structure is then subsequently transformed into an efficient implementation. However, there is not yet a general transition from algebraic specifications to "computation structures" available, although for the specification of CIP-S this was not a problem due to the particular form of the specification.

5.2 Design of a suitable language to cover also non-functional requirements

In the previous section we already commented on additional language constructs desirable for an algebraic specificaiton formalism. The aspects mentioned there, however, all more or less aimed at increasing the expressibility of the language with respect to "functional requirements", i.e. requirements that specify what a system is supposed to do. In practice, however, functional requirements are only part of a problem description, since there are other kinds of requirements to be formulated, e.g. (cf. [Kühnel et al. 87]):

- requirements with respect to the quality of the final product
  - performance (*time, storage*)
  - maintainability
  - reliability
  - portability
  - adaptability
  - user comfort
- requirements for the implementation of the final product
  - devices to be used (existing software/hardware)
  - interfaces to be obeyed
  - coexistence with or use of existing tools
  - documentation
- requirements for testing, installation and maintenance
- requirements for the development process
  - strategies to be followed
  - methods, languages, tools to be used
  - available resources (*manpower, budget, deadlines*)
  - standards to be obeyed.

Since algebraic specification formalisms provide a reasonable means for expressing functional requirements, it seems worthwile to investigate more thoroughly which of these additional kinds of requirements can be expressed within the algebraic formalism and how this could be done. It even should be explored which kind of extensions are needed to be able to cope with the other ones, too.

5.3 Increased methodological support

Any new approach such as the algebraic specification technique, will only be really accepted, if a user sees any advantage in using it. This means, in particular, that this new formalism has to be accompanied by sufficient methodological support for its use.

In addition to more general aspects, e.g., giving hints on how to suitably structure the specification of a complex system (cf. e.g. [Parnas 72]), or how to formulate axcioms in order to ensure sufficient completeness of the specification (cf. e.g. [Guttag, Horning 78]), a suitable methodology for algebraic specifications should mainly provide a reasonable basis to start with (i.e. not to require from any user to always start from scratch) and some kind of support for combining existing parts into new specifications.

Earlier we already mentioned that the CIP-S specification made extensive use of basic data types. In fact, we are convinced that there should be a rich set of predefined basic data types (e.g. *numbers, chars, sets, sequences, trees, bags, maps*, etc.) that exist in different extensions each of which provides different sets of operations so that the user is able to choose the one which fits his particular purposes best. In addition, each of these basic data types also should provide the following "advanced" features:

- *higher-order operators*

  Available practical experiences with algebraic specifications have shown that the size of a specification can be reduced substantially, if higher-order operators (such as, e.g., *comprehension, filter, apply-to-all, reduce*) are available (cf. [Möller 87]). In addition to this economic advantage there is also the even more important aspect that higher-order operations provide very often a more appropriate level of abstraction such that, e.g., certain similarities in specifications can be expressed much more adequately.

- *induction principles and other derived properties*

  With respect to program development starting from algebraic specifications it is important to have available as much information about some data type and its operations as possible. This means in particular that, in addition to the basic axioms of some type, further derived properties should be available, too (an early attempt in this direction can be found, e.g., in [Gerhart 81]). It also means that for each basic data type the respective different instances of the principle of structural induction (such as, e.g., term induction, stepwise Noetherian induction, or decomposition induction, cf. [Pepper 84]) should be available. Thus, in the very end, the entire available infomation on each of the basic data types should amount to something comparable to Bird's "theory of lists" (cf. [Bird 86]).

- *sets of different implementations*

  Also with respect to an economic program development, it is important that the basic data types should be further equipped with sets of different, correct implementations so that the effort of implementing such a type is reduced to simply choosing among these implementations the one which is most appropriaste. Particularly for this latter aspect it is therefore also desirable that each of the implementations is furthermore augmented with information about the efficient use of the respective implementations.

- *pre-defined conversion operators*

  It also seems worthwile to have available pre-defined conversion operators between the basic types. This not only opens new ways to implementations of algebraic specifications, but also gives additional flexibility in writing up formal specifications.

- *comfortable operators to combine specifications*

  Flexibility in writing up specifications could be further increased by having available comfortable operators to combine existing specifications into new ones and by mechanisms to adapt available specifications to particular situations. Obviously, these operators and mechanisms also would contribute to the goal of "re-use", that is aimed at in practical software development. A promising approach in this direction is provided, e.g., by ASL (cf. [Wirsing 83]).

- *constructive rules for finding implementations*

  Although most of the practical work in connection with implementing an algebraic specifcation should already be covered by the above-postulated sets of "standard implementations", there still will remain situations where an implementation for a so far unknown type has to be found. For these latter situations constructive rules, similar to transformation rules, or at least methodological hints (on how to find an implementation) should be envisaged.

5.4 Development of suitable tools

For the practical use of algebraic specifications suitable software tools are indispensible. For a number of individual aspects (such as e.g. term-rewriting, derivation of additional properties, translation of algebraic specification into natural language, or checking of certain semantic properties) experimental tools exist for several years (cf., e.g., [Bartels et al. 81], [Ehler 85], [Gerhart et al. 80], [Hußmann 85], [Lescanne 82], [Leszcylowski, Wirsing 82]). In the meantime more comprehensive systems, i.e., systems covering several aspects, either have been implemented (cf. e.g., [Botma 87], [Bidoit, Choppy 85], [Bidoit et al. 87]) or are under construction.

Based on the experiences gained in the CIP system project a good tool to support the algebraic specification technique should comprise the following components:

- *a knowledgable editor* that
  - in a comfortable way produces and maintains a flexible layout of a specification
  - allows the incremental build-up of structured specifications
  - helps in writing a specifcation (e.g. by automatically creating keywords, left-hand sides of axioms, conditons w.r.t. partialities, etc.)
  - detects and resolves name clashes
  - supports global changes to a given specification, such as, e.g.,

- decomposition/amalgamation of types
- hiding of constituents
- lifting of operations (with partial hiding)
- supports the adaptation of given types by
  - enrichment
  - restriction
  - additional parameterization
  - (partial) instantiation
- performs (automatically) consistent renaming of identifiers
- adapts (automatically)
  - interfaces of a hierachical specifcation in case of structural modifications
  - applied occurrences of constituents in case of redefinition

- *an advanced documentation facility* for the
  - generation of dictionaries, indexes, and cross-references
  - generation of (various) graphical representations (e.g. structure diagrams, signature diagrams, diagrams exhibiting control and data flow in hierarchical specifcations, etc.)
  - re-translation into "informal language"
  - tracing of individual operations through a hierarchy (both downwards and upwards)

- *an analyzer* that
  - performs the usual syntactic checks
  - performs static semantic checks (such as, e.g, type conformity, hierarchy constraints, interface completeness and redundancy for types and type hierarchies)
  - supports semantic checks (such as, e.g., sufficient completeness, consistency, existence of particular models, shielding of partialities)
  - helps in completing/correcting axioms
- *a validation component* for
  - term-rewriting and/or other ways of simulation
  - the (automatic or interactive) derivation of additional properties.

6. Perspectives

There is an increasing agreement from the practitioners' side that the "traditional" appropaches to software engineering could not satisfy the high expectations with respect to solving the problems of software development. There also seems to be a strong evidence that this goal never can be achieved by improving "traditional" SE approaches. The time is ripe for a radical change by introducing formally based methods to be used in software engineering

Algebraic specification is a most promising step in this new direction. Since the first publications on the basic idea in the mid seventies, a lot of progress has been made, in particular also with respect to the practical use of the algebraic specification idea. Examples are

- algebraic specification lamguages such as, e.g., ACT ONE [Ehrig et al. 83], ASF [Bergstra et al. 87], ASL [Wirsing 83], CIP-L [Bauer et al. 85], CLEAR [Burstall, Goguen 80], COLD [Jonkers et al. 86], LARCH [Guttag, Horning 83], OBJ [Goguen, Tardo 77], [Goguen, Meseguer 81], [Futatsugi et al. 85], PLUSS [Gaudel 85], RAP-2 [Hußmann 87]
- an extension of the theory that includes higher-order operations (cf. [Möller 86, 87])
- incorporation of aspects of real-time and parallel processing (cf. [Broy 83, 84, 85]).

Although still more work in the area of algebraic specification needs to be done (cf. section 5), especially more substantial case studies with "real-world applications" are necessary to prompt the experiences gained so far, the results obtained by now are truly encouraging. In particular, they support our initial claim that algebraic specification is a reasonable step towards future software engineering.

References

[Bartels et al. 81]
Bartels, U., Olthoff, W., Raulefs, P.: APE: An expert system for automatic programming from abstract specifications of data types and algorithms. Fachbereich Informatik, Universität Kaiserslautern, MEMO SEKI-01-81, 1981

[Bauer et al. 85]
Bauer, F.L., Berghammer, R., Broy, M., Dosch, W., Geiselbrechtinger, F., Gnatz, R., Hangel, E., Hesse, W., Krieg-Brückner, B., Laut, A., Matzner, T., Möller, B., Nickl, F., Partsch, H., Pepper, P., Samelson, K., Wirsing, M., Wössner, H.: The Munich project CIP. Volume I: The wide spectrum language CIP-L. Lecture Notes in Computer Science 183, Berlin: Springer 1985

[Bauer et al. 87]
Bauer, F.L., Horsch, A., Möller, B., Partsch, H., Paukner, O., Pepper, P.: The Munich project CIP. Volume II: The transformation system CIP-S. Lecture Notes in Computer Science 292, Berlin: Springer 1987

[Bauer et al. 88]
Bauer, F.L., Möller, B., Partsch, H., Pepper, P: Programming by formal reasoning - an overview of the Munich CIP project. To appear in: IEEE Transactions on Software Engineering, 1988

[Bergstra et al. 87]
Bergstra, J.A., Heering, J., Klint P.: ASF - An algebraic specification formalism. Centre for Mathematics and Computer Science, Amsterdam, Technical Report CS-R8705, 1987

[Bidoit, Choppy 85]
Bidoit, M., Choppy, C.: ASSPEGIQUE: an integrated environment for algebraic specifications. Proc. International Joint Conference on Theory an Practice of Software Development, Berlin 1985. Lecture Notes in Computer Science 186, Berlin: Springer 1985, pp. 246-260

[Bidoit et al. 87]
Bidoit, M., Capy, F., Choppy, C., Choquet, N., Gresse, C., Kaplan, S., Schlienger, F., Voisin, F.: ASSPRO: an interactive and integrated programming environment. Technology and Science of Informatics 6:4, 259-278 (1987)

[Bird 86]
Bird, R.S.: An introduction to the theory of lists. Oxford University Computing Laboratory, Programming Research Group, Technical Monograph PRG-56, 1986

[Botma 88]
Botma, B.: AXLAB: A specification environment for algebraic types. Dept. of Computer Science, University of Nijmegen, Master thesis, 1988

[Broy 83a]
Broy, M.: Fixed Point theory for communication and concurrency. In: Bjørner, D. (ed.): IFIP TC2 Working Conference on Formal Description of Programming Concepts II, Garmisch-Partenkirchen, June 1982. Amsterdam: North-Holland, 1983

[Broy 83b]
Broy, M.: Applicative real time programming. In: Mason, R.E.A. (ed.): Information Processing 83. Proc. 9th IFIP World Computer Congress, Paris, Sept. 19-23, 1983. Amsterdam: North-Holland 1983, pp. 259-264

[Broy 84]
Broy, M.: Semantics of communicating processes. Information and Control 61, 202-246 (1984)

[Broy 85]
Broy, M.: Specification and top down design of distributed systems. In: Ehrig, H., et al. (eds.): Formal methods and software development. Lecture Notes in Computer Science 186. Berlin: Springer 1985, pp. 4-28

[Broy et al. 86]
Broy, M., Möller, B., Pepper, P., Wirsing, M.: Algebraic implementations preserve program correctness. Science of Computer Programming 7, 35-53 (1986)

[Burstall, Goguen 80]
Burstall, R.M., Goguen, J.A.: Semantics of CLEAR, a specification language. In: Bjørner, D. (ed.): Abstract software specifications. Lecture Notes in Computer Science 86, Berlin: Springer 1980, pp. 292-332

[Ehler 85]
Ehler, H.: Making formal specifications readable. Institut für Informatik, TU München, TUM-I8527, 1985
[Ehrig et al. 83]
Ehrig, H., Fey, W., Hansen, H.: ACT ONE - an algebraic specification language with two levels of semantics. Fachbereich 20, TU Berlin, Technical Report 83-03, 1983
[Feijs et al. 87]
Feijs, L.M.G., Jonkers, H.B.M, Obbink, J.H., Koymans, C.P.J., Renardel de Lavalette, G.R., Rodenburg, P.H.: A survey of the design language COLD. In: ESPRIT '86: Results and Achievements. Amsterdam: North-Holland 1987, pp. 631-644
[Futatsugi et al. 85]
Futatsugi, K., Goguen J.A., Jouannaud, J.P., Meseguer, J.: Principles of OBJ2. Proc. 12th Ann. ACM Symp. on Principles of Programming Languages, ACM, 1985, pp. 52-66
[Gaudel 85]
Gaudel, M.C.: Toward structured algebraic specification. In: ESPRIT '85: Status Report of Continuing Work. Part I. Amsterdam : North-Holland, 1986, pp. 493-510
[Gerhart et al. 80]
Gerhart, S.L., Musser, D.R., Thompson, D.H., Baker, D.A., Bates, R.L., Erickson, R.W., London, R.L., Taylor, D.G., Wile, D.S.: An overview of AFFIRM: a specification and verification system. In: Lavington, S.H. (ed.): Information Processing 80, Amsterdam: North-Holland, 1980, pp. 343-347
[Gerhart 81]
Gerhart, S. (ed.): AFFIRM - type library. USC/Information Sciences Institute, Technical report 1981
[Goguen, Tardo 77]
Goguen, J.A., Tardo, J.: OBJ-0 preliminary users manual. Computer Science Department, University of California at Los Angeles, 1977
[Goguen, Meseguer 81]
Goguen, J., Meseguer, J.: OBJ-1, a study in executable algebraic formal specifications. SRI International, Technical Report 1981
[Guttag, Horning 78]
Guttag, J.V., Horning, J.J.: The algebraic specification of abstract data types. Acta Informatica 10, 27-52 (1978)
[Guttag, Horning 83]
Guttag, J.V., Horning, J.J.: Preliminary Report on the LARCH shared language. Technical Report CSL 83-6, Xerox, Palo Alto, 1983
[Heering, Klint 87]
Heering, J., Klint, P.: A syntax definition formalism. In: ESPRIT '86: Results and Achievements. Amsterdam: North-Holland, 1987, pp. 619-630
[Hußmann 85]
Hußmann, H.: Rapid prototyping for algebraic specifications. RAP-System User's Manual. Fakultät für Mathematik und Informatik, Universität Passau, Report MIP-8504, 1985
[Hußmann 87]
Hußmann, H.: RAP-2 User Manual. Fachbereich Mathematik und Informatik, Universität Passau, Technischer Bericht 1987
[Jonkers et al. 86]
Jonkers, H.B.M., Koymans C.P.J., Renardel de Lavalette, G.R.: A semantic framework for the COLD-family of languages. Logic Group Preprint Series No. 9, Department of Philosophy, University of Utrecht, 1986
[Krämer 87]
Krämer, B.: SEGRAS - a formal language combining Petri nets and abstract data types for specifying distributed systems. Proc. 9th International Conference on Software Engineering, Monterey, Ca., 1987, pp. 116-125
[Kühnel et al. 87]
Kühnel, B., Partsch, H., Reinshagen, K.P.: Requirements Engineering - Versuch einer Begriffsklärung. Informatik-Spektrum 10:6, 334-335 (1987)
[Lescanne 82]
Lescanne, P.: Computer experiments with the REVE term rewriting system generator. Centre de Recherche en Informatique de Nancy, Technical Report, 1982

[Leszcylowski, Wirsing 82]
Leszcylowski, J., Wirsing, M.: A system for reasoning within and about algebraic specifications. In : Dezani-Ciancaglini, M., Montanari, U. (eds.): 5th Int. Symp. on Programming, Turin, Italy, 1982. Lecture Notes in Computer Science 137, Berlin: Springer 1982, pp. 257-282

[London, Feather 82]
London, P., Feather, M.S.: Implementing specification freedom. Science of Computer Programming 2, 91-131 (1982)

[Möller 86]
Möller, B.: Algebraic specifications with higher-order operations. In: Meertens, L.G.L.T. (ed.): Program Specification and Transformation. Amsterdam: North-Holland 1986, pp. 367-392

[Möller 87]
Möller, B.: Higher-order algebraic specifications. Fachbereich Mathematik und Informatik, TU München, Habilitation thesis, 1987

[Möller, Partsch 86]
Möller, B., Partsch, H.: Formal specification of large-scale software: objectives, design decisions, and experiences in a concrete software project. In: Meertens, L.G.L.T. (ed.): Program Specification and Transformation. Amsterdam: North-Holland 1986

[Neighbors 80]
Neighbors, J.M.: Software construction using components. Ph. D. dissertation, Technical Report 160, University of California at Irvine, 1980

[Parnas 72]
Parnas, D.L.: On the criteria to be used in decomposing systems into modules. Comm. ACM 15:12, 1053-1058 (1972)

[Partsch, Möller 87]
Partsch, H., Möller, B.: Konstruktion korrekter Programme durch Transformation. Informatik-Spektrum 10:6, 309-323 (1987)

[Pepper 84]
Pepper, P.: A simple calculus for program transformations (inclusive of induction). Institut für Informatik, TU München, TUM-I8409, 1984

[Wile 86]
Wile, D.S.: Local formalisms. In: Meertens, L.G.L.T. (ed.): Program Specification and Transformation. Amsterdam: North-Holland 1986

[Wirsing 83]
Wirsing, M.: A Specification Language. Fachbereich Mathematik und Informatik, TU München, Habilitation thesis, 1983

[Wirsing et al. 83]
Wirsing, M., Pepper, P., Partsch, H., Dosch, W., Broy, M.: On hierarchies of abstract data types. Acta Informatica 20, 1-33 (1983)

HOW TO MAKE ALGEBRAIC SPECIFICATIONS
MORE UNDERSTANDABLE ?

An experiment with the PLUSS specification language

(Preliminary Version)[1]

M. Bidoit[2,3], M.-C. Gaudel[2]
A. Mauboussin[3]

Abstract: This paper relates an experiment in writing an algebraic specification of a rather complex example, namely a subset of the UNIX[4] file system. The PLUSS specification language, which is used for this experiment, provides a set of linguistic features which allow the modularization of such specifications and the definition of a flexible and convenient syntax for expressions and axioms (such as mixfix operators, overloading, coercions, ...). This experiment was a way for evaluating the adequacy of these features to several criteria: mainly legibility and understandability, but also reusability of specifications. The paper presents the specification and discusses it with respect to these important points.

1. INTRODUCTION

A specification is supposed to describe a future or existing system in such a way that the properties of the system (*what* the system does) are expressed, and the implementation details (*how* it is done) are omitted. Thus a specification language aims at describing classes of possible implementations. In contrast a programming language aims at describing specific implementations.

Among the current formal approaches for specifications, algebraic specifications are especially appropriate: an algebraic specification defines a class of *algebras* (also called *models*), i.e. *a set of operations on various sets of values*. An algebra is just a possible *implementation* of the sorts and operation names which occur in the specification.

Often, algebraic specifications are written using notations that are very close to the mathematical notations for functions. A first minor consequence is a proliferation of parentheses. Besides, the combination of this mathematical notation with the axiomatic way of writing specifications frighten the non mathematicians.

[1]A revised version of this paper will appear elsewhere.

[2]LRI, Bat. 490, Universite de Paris-Sud, 91405 Orsay Cedex, FRANCE.

[3]Laboratoires de Marcoussis, CR-CGE, Route de Nozay, 91460 Marcoussis, FRANCE.

[4]UNIX is a trademark of Bell Laboratories.

This work is partially supported by ESPRIT project No. 432 METEOR and CNRS GRECO de Programmation.

Moreover, most of the time, there is an implicit requirement that these specifications must be executable, i.e. that the axioms must be written in such a way that they can be used as rewriting rules (when oriented from left to right), and that the resulting rewriting system is noetherian (term rewriting terminates after a finite number of rewriting steps) and confluent (any terminating sequence of rewriting steps applied to the same term lead to the same result). Our claim is that executable specifications are very useful, especially to detect design errors as soon as possible, but we strongly feel that executability is not (and should not be) the main goal of a specification process. Legibility is another very important criteria, among many other ones.

In this paper we took as a choice to focus on legibility. Thus some of our specifications are not directly executable: we think it is better to cope with one problem at the same time. Legibility is a fundamental requirement for industrial applicability of formal specification methods. In this paper we discuss the possibility of writing legible algebraic specifications and we illustrate our claim by a complex example.

Just as any complex document, a large specification must be structured in order to be understandable. Moreover, the so-called "syntactic sugar" can be of first importance in this case. In Section 2 we briefly present these two aspects of the PLUSS specification language which is used in the rest of the paper. Besides, the relations between PLUSS and the design language COLD are discussed. The choice of the example is discussed in Section 3: we wanted a sufficiently large and complex example in order to be credible, but then there is a risk to loose the reader in the description of the example. This is why we chose a system which is well-known by most of the computer scientists: the UNIX file system. The overall structure of the specification is given at the end of Section 3. Sections 4 to 7 are presentations of various modules of the specification. Each of them focus on a specific structuring concept such as: the role of drafts, the use of other specification components, parameterization.

2. THE PLUSS ALGEBRAIC SPECIFICATION LANGUAGE

PLUSS means "a Proposition of a Language Usable for Structured Specifications". This language provides a way of structuring algebraic specifications, i.e. any kind of specifications for which a formal semantics can be given in terms of a signature and a class of algebras (we shall see later that the user needs little knowledge of algebra). PLUSS is the result of numerous experiments in writing large specifications: Pascal Compiler [Des 83], Telephone Switching System [Bie 84, BH 85, B2G3 84], Protocols [BCM 84] and an interpreter of conditional rewrite rules [Cho 86]. An important aspect of PLUSS is that it is, to some extent, a *meta specification language*, since the structuring features are not (or little) dependent on the kind of basic algebraic specifications under consideration. In this paper we consider classes of partial algebras [BW 82], but one could also consider standard algebras, E,R-algebras [Bid 84] (such as in the $ALEX_{PLUSS}$ variant [BC 86]), exception-algebras [BBC 86], etc.

2.1. Basic concepts

This part of the paper aims at defining, *in an informal and (as far as possible) intuitive way*, the main concepts of algebraic data types which are needed to read the rest of the paper. For a formal and complete presentation of these concepts see for instance [Wir 83, AW 86].

A *signature* (usually denoted by Σ) defines a set of sorts and operation (function) names; in PLUSS a signature also defines a set of predicate names. Some examples of usual sorts are: *Integer, Bag...* Each operation name comes with a list of sorts which states the sorts of its arguments and of its result. Each predicate name comes with a list of sorts which states the sorts of its arguments. According to the PLUSS syntax (see Section 2.2.), examples of usual operation definitions are:

> _ + _ : *Integer * Integer -> Integer*
> _ *plus the element* _ : *Bag * Integer -> Bag*

examples of usual predicate definitions:

> _ *is empty* : *Bag*
> _ *belongs to* _ : *Integer * Bag*

Constants are just a special case of operations, without arguments. For instance:

> *zero* : *-> Integer*
> *the empty bag* : *-> Bag*

A *term* (more precisely a Σ-term) is any valid composition of sorted variables, predicates and operations of Σ, for example: *B plus the element x*. If there is no variable in a term, it is a *closed term* or a *ground term*, as in the example: *the empty bag plus the element zero*.

Using the names of Σ, it is possible to build Σ-terms from Σ-terms. According to the leading symbol (when the term is viewed as a tree), Σ-terms are of two kinds: functional terms such as *the empty bag plus the element zero* (the leading symbol is an operation name, e.g. *plus the element*) and predicative terms such as *x belongs to the empty bag plus the element x* (the leading symbol is a predicate name, e.g. *belongs to*).

Axioms describe the required properties for the operations and predicates. They are first-order formulae built from functional and predicative terms, and logical connectors.

An *algebra* is characterized by one or several *sets of values* and some *operations* and *predicates* on these sets. An example of algebra is: the set of integers, addition, multiplication and comparison predicates (less than or equal) between integers. Given a signature Σ, a Σ-algebra is an algebra where sets, operations and predicates are named following the names of Σ. Saying it in another way, it is any implementation of the names of Σ. Since we consider partial algebras, operations and predicates are partial ones.

Among all the Σ-algebras, one distinguishes those satisfying a given set A of axioms (see fig. 1). Furthermore, it is often sound to limit the set of values to be computable using the names of Σ. Such algebras are called *finitely generated*. That means that any value of the algebra is denoted by a ground Σ-term. There are no junk among the values. The intersection of these two classes of algebras leads to the class $GEN_{\Sigma,A}$ of finitely generated algebras satisfying a given set A of axioms (see fig. 1). Under some assumptions w.r.t. the kind of axioms used in the specification (e.g. if one restricts to equations or Horn clauses), this class $GEN_{\Sigma,A}$ contains a distinguished element, defined up to isomorphism, the so-called *initial algebra* $I_{\Sigma,A}$ [ADJ 78]. This algebra is characterized by the fact that two ground terms denote the same value in $I_{\Sigma,A}$ if and only if it is the case for all algebras in $GEN_{\Sigma,A}$. There are no additional properties (i.e. properties that are not logical consequences of the axioms) verified by $I_{\Sigma,A}$. The initial algebra is isomorphic to the *quotient* of the ground term algebra by the smallest congruence relation compatible with the axioms.

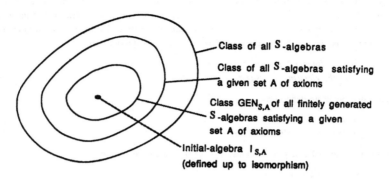

Class of all S-algebras

Class of all S-algebras satisfying
a given set A of axioms

Class $GEN_{S,A}$ of all finitely generated
S-algebras satisfying a given
set A of axioms

Initial-algebra $I_{S,A}$
(defined up to isomorphism)

Figure 1 - Inclusion of some useful classes of algebras

Very often, the initial algebra $I_{\Sigma,A}$ (or more precisely, the class of isomorphic initial algebras) is considered as the semantics of an algebraic specification. However in a specification language, it is of first importance to consider the whole class of all possible implementations. Thus the semantics of a specification must not be restricted to be initial algebras, but it seems more natural to consider some *class of (non-isomorphic) algebras*. This takes into account the fact that a specific implementation may have more properties than those strictly required by the specification. Such a semantics is said to be *loose*, and the PLUSS specification language follows this approach.

2.2. Syntactical aspects

The current PLUSS concrete syntax is defined in [CGHM 86]. The main aspects of this concrete syntax are given below.

2.2.1. Signature

To increase the legibility of the specifications, the PLUSS syntax offers the possibility of choosing complete sentences as operation names or predicate names, with arguments inserted anywhere; this is illustrated in the following examples:

> _ is an existing path of _ : Path * Tree
> _ plus the file _ added under _ : System * File * Path -> System

Overloading and *coercion* are allowed. Generally, overloading is used through different specifications to define operations with similar meanings on different sorts. It can also be used as in the following example to express that a path can be viewed either as a name followed by a path or as a path followed by a name:

> _ / _ : Name * Path -> Path
> _ / _ : Path * Name -> Path

Coercion can be used in two ways:

– to express a conversion, as in: _ : *Integer -> Real*

– to express the inheritance for sub-types, as in: _ : *System -> Directory*
   (see Section 5 for more details on this example).

Union of sorts is allowed in domain and range of operations. The use of the union symbol in the domain may be thought of as an abbreviation for an overloaded operation. Thus the following definition:

$$\_ \ plus \ \_ \ : \ Forest * Leaf \ \mathbf{U} \ Tree \ -> \ Forest$$

is an abbreviation for:

$$\_ \ plus \ \_ \ : \ Forest * Leaf \ -> \ Forest$$
$$\_ \ plus \ \_ \ : \ Forest * Tree \ -> \ Forest$$

The use of the union in the range of an operation may also be thought of as an overloading, but in this case the overloaded operations are partial operations and their domains are disjoint, as in:

$$the \ object \ at \ \_ \ in \ \_ \ : \ Path * Tree \ -> \ Leaf \ \mathbf{U} \ Tree$$

In this case, *the object at p in T* is either of sort *Leaf* or of sort *Tree*, depending of the specific value of the path argument *p*.

When the range of an operation is a union of sorts, a characteristic predicate _ *is a <name-of-sort>* is automatically defined for each sort in the union. In the example above, the two following predicates are defined: _ *is a Leaf* and _ *is a Tree*. Predicative terms such as *the object at p in T is a Tree* can therefore be used in the axioms and in the preconditions.

2.2.2. Axioms

Axioms are first order formulae built from atomic formulae and the following connectors &, **OR,** =>, iff. Atomic formulae are either equations between functional terms as in: *the last name of (p / n) = n,* or assertions on predicative terms using the meta-constructions **is true** and **is false** as in: *n is a name* **is true,** or *(p / n) is a name* **is false;** when there is no ambiguity **is true** can be omitted. The sorts of the variables occurring in the axioms must be declared, e.g. *p : Path, T : Tree.*

As a syntactical convenience, it is possible to use the union of sorts to define the sort of a variable as in: *LT : Leaf* **U** *Tree.* We will use it as an abbreviation when the set of axioms defining an overloaded operation is the same for all the possible sorts occurring in the union field of the domain, as for example in:

$$(F \ plus \ LT) \ is \ empty \ \mathbf{is \ false}$$

The axiom above is just an abbreviation for the two following axioms:

$$(F \ plus \ L) \ is \ empty \ \mathbf{is \ false}$$
$$(F \ plus \ T) \ is \ empty \ \mathbf{is \ false}$$

where *L : Leaf* and *T : Tree.*

2.2.3. Preconditions

When some operations are defined under some conditions, these conditions are expressed as logical expressions, and these expressions are listed in the **precond** part using the **is defined when** construction. For example, in the *PATH* specification, a path is never empty since there is at least one name in a path, therefore the operation *the first part of*, which gives the original path but its last name, is not defined when a path is just a name. This will be expressed by:

the first part of p **is defined when** *p is a name* **is false**

The preconditions (suitably instantiated) are implicit premises for each of the axioms where the partially defined operation occurs.

Besides, when an operation depends on another operation defined in another specification component, and when the domain of this operation is restricted by a precondition, the condition is repeated for the new operation. As a syntactical convenience, when the preconditions are identical, we will use a construction: *term1* **is defined when** *term2* **is defined**, to avoid the repetition (this will be illustrated in the specification *ONE-USER-VIEW*: see Section 7).

2.3. Structuring features

The main characteristics of PLUSS are described in [Gau 84, Gau 85, BG 85]. We briefly recall here the different constructs available in the language, they are detailed and illustrated on the UNIX specification through Sections 4 to 7.

The main originality of PLUSS is to state a careful distinction between completed specification components and specification components under design. By completed specification components we mean the following strong property: the class of possible implementations is fixed. Practically that means that such a specification component is either already implemented or may be implemented without taking care of its context (for instance the other components of a specification where this completed specification component is used). By specification component under design we mean a preliminary specification component where the signature and the axioms are not fully fixed and may be further refined: at this early stage, implementing the specification component is premature since the implementation choices may have to be reconsidered later, depending on the further refinements of the specification. These two kinds of specification components are differentiated by the keywords **spec** and **draft**.

Completed specification components (introduced by the keyword **spec**) are either obtained by an enrichment of already defined specifications by new sorts and/or new operations and/or new axioms, or as an instance of a parameterized specification or as the fixed form of a draft. Thus the primary specification-building primitives are enrichment and instantiation. In the next subsection we describe (un-parameterized) completed specifications and enrichment, i.e. the **spec** and **use** constructs. Parameterization and instantiation (**proc**, **param** and **as** constructs) are described in 2.3.2. **drafts** and the way they are fixed into **specs** are presented in 2.3.3.

2.3.1. The spec and use constructs

Standard specification components are introduced by the keyword **spec**. A **spec** associates with an identifier a signature and a class of models, and is characterized by the other used specs, the sorts, operations and predicates defined, the constructors of the defined sorts and the preconditions and axioms.

The use construct is a means for incrementally adding new features (sorts, operations, predicates) to already existing specifications. It is the most used construct of the PLUSS specification language and is used to put specifications together and to develop specifications step by step. The following *COLLECTION-OF-NAMED-OBJECTS* specification (see fig. 2) is a typical example of a spec built on top of another one, the *NAMED-OBJECTS* spec (which is not given here, but is itself based on the *NAME* spec).

By convention, using a spec must not change the class of its models. This fundamental property will be referred to as **hierarchical constraints**, and corresponds to the fact that, in order to be able to write modular specifications, it is necessary to abstract from the various possible implementations of the used specifications (hence from their models). For instance, using the *NAMED-OBJECTS* spec in the *COLLECTION-OF-NAMED-OBJECTS* spec should not lead to introduce new values in a sort which is defined elsewhere (e.g. the sorts *Object* or *Name*) or to identify some values. However, it is possible to introduce a new operation (**func**) on the sorts of the used specifications, and to specify it in terms of already defined operations and/or recursively.

Thus, when working with specs, new values can be specified only when new sorts are declared. For each new sort some constructors must be given. All the values of the corresponding set are denotable as some composition of the constructors. Formally speaking that means that the models associated with a spec are finitely generated models with respect to the constructors of the new sorts.

By default, the use specification-building primitive is transitive and transparent, i.e. all the sorts and operations that are visible from *NAME* or *NAMED-OBJECTS* are visible from *COLLECTION-OF-NAMED-OBJECTS*. Visibility can explicitly be controlled by means of the **export** and **forget** primitives of PLUSS when necessary.

In order to avoid trivial models, i.e. models where all values are collapsed together, *basic specification components* (i.e. those who do not use any other specs) are specified with a specific construct **basic spec**, the semantics of which is restricted to the initial model (hence, axioms are restricted to equations or Horn clauses for these basic specifications). An example of this construct is given in Section 4.

The specification *COLLECTION-OF-NAMED-OBJECTS* displayed in fig. 2 (which is an obvious candidate for parameterization, see Section 2.3.2.) is not part of our UNIX case study, but is used here as a tutorial example of the use construct, and also as an introductory example for the *TREE* specification (see Section 6). This *COLLECTION-OF-NAMED-OBJECTS* specification introduces a new sort *Collection* generated by the operations *the empty collection* and *plus*.

2.3.2. Parameterization and instantiation

Parameterization allows the use of generic specifications, hence saves writing as many specifications as instances of a given specification are required. For instance, writing a parameterized specification of *SEQUENCE* would save writing various specifications such as *SEQ-OF-INT*, *SEQ-OF-CHAR*, etc.

Parameterization involves three different entities: a parameterized specification (introduced by the keyword **proc**), some formal parameter specifications (introduced by the keyword **param**), and an

```
spec COLLECTION-OF-NAMED-OBJECTS
      use NAMED-OBJECTS  "this spec uses the spec NAME"
   sort Collection
   cons
      the empty collection :        -> Collection
      _ plus _      : Collection * Object  -> Collection
   func
      _ less the object named _      : Collection * Name  -> Collection
   pred
      _ is empty  : Collection
   axiom forall n : Name , C : Collection , O : Object
   ( less1 : C is empty => C less the object named n = C
     less2 : n = the name of O => (C plus O) less the object named n = C less the object named n
     less3 : n # the name of O => (C plus O) less the object named n = (C less the object named n) plus O
     ise1 : the empty collection is empty is true
     ise2 : (C plus O) is empty is false  )
end COLLECTION-OF-NAMED-OBJECTS
```

Figure 2 - The COLLECTION-OF-NAMED-OBJECTS specification

instantiation mechanism (as construct). Parameterized specifications share most syntactical aspects with ordinary specifications, e.g. they can use other (previously defined) specifications, they must include a declaration of the constructors of the new sorts introduced, etc.

The *COLLECTION-OF-NAMED-OBJECTS* introduced in the previous subsection can be parameterized, since we may want to parameterize it by the kind of named objects to be added to the collection, and then specialize the corresponding parameterized version depending on the specific kind of objects to be considered. This may be achieved by defining, instead of the spec *COLLECTION-OF-NAMED-OBJECTS* displayed in fig. 2, a (similar) proc *COLLECTION*, parameterized by the param *NAMED-THINGS* which is a formal parameter specification (see fig. 3). This parameterized specification *COLLECTION* can be later instantiated by the *NAMED-OBJECTS* spec to obtain a specification equivalent to the original *COLLECTION-OF-NAMED-OBJECTS* spec.

The aim of a formal parameter specification is to describe the minimal requirements actual parameter specifications must fulfill in order to be considered as appropriate candidates for instantiation. In our case, the only requirement is that things are named. Thus, the formal parameter specification *NAMED-THINGS* will be defined as an enrichment of the *NAME* specification, and introduces a new sort *Thing* and an operation *the name of* that, given some argument of sort *Thing*, returns its name (see fig. 3). It should be noted that formal parameter specifications, described separately from the parameterized specification, are not linked to a specific parameterized specification and can therefore be reused in other ones. Thus it is possible to have a library of params, including *ORDERED-THINGS, THINGS-WITH-EQUIVALENCE*, etc.

Now that we have the parameterized specification *COLLECTION*, we can instantiate it using the *NAMED-OBJECTS* spec as an actual parameter for the *NAMED-THINGS* param. Basically, instantiation is no more than the substitution of the actual parameter specifications to the formal parameter ones in the parameterized specification. This "substitution" is specified by a parameter

```
proc COLLECTION ( NAMED-THINGS )
  sort Parameterized-Collection

      ... similar to the spec COLLECTION-OF-NAMED-OBJECTS ...

end COLLECTION


param NAMED-THINGS
      use NAME
  sort Thing
  func
    the name of : Thing  -> Name
end NAMED-THINGS
```

Figure 3 - The COLLECTION parameterized specification and
the NAMED-THINGS formal parameter specification

passing mechanism called "fitting morphism". This fitting morphism explains in which way the sorts and operations of the actual parameter specification (here, the sort *Object* and the operation *the name of* of the spec *NAMED-OBJECTS*) correspond to the sorts and operations of the formal parameter specification (here, the sort *Thing* and the operation *the name of* of the param *NAMED-THINGS*). Most of time no ambiguity arises [Pro 82] and the fitting morphism is left implicit, as is the case here (see fig. 4).

Once parameter passing is achieved, it is often convenient to rename sorts and/or operations following one's own conventions or wishes. For instance we decide here to rename the sort *Parameterized-Collection* into the sort *Collection*, which leads to the spec *INSTANTIATED-COLLECTION* of fig. 4. This later specification is equivalent to the *COLLECTION-OF-NAMED-OBJECTS* specification defined in the previous subsection.

It should be noted that renaming is a general feature of the PLUSS specification language and its use is not limited to specifications obtained as an instance of a parameterized specification. Renaming can be combined with any of the PLUSS constructs.

```
spec INSTANTIATED-COLLECTION as COLLECTION ( NAMED-OBJECTS )
      renaming Parameterized-Collection into Collection
end INSTANTIATED-COLLECTION
```

Figure 4 - The INSTANTIATED-COLLECTION specification

2.3.3. The draft construct

In the previous subsections we have emphasized the fact that reusing some piece of specification should not modify its class of models (i.e. implementations). This property, that we have called **hierarchical constraints**, makes it possible to develop an implementation of some spec while reusing it in another spec at the same time. In that sense, spec and use are definitely good linguistic tools for structuring specifications which are already stated and which are supposed to be fixed.

However, this is not what is needed at the beginning of a specification process. At this early stage, hierarchical constraints may be too constraining, since they prevents any modification of the constructors or of the properties these constructors must fulfill. Most of the time, the set of values is not fixed at the beginning of a specification process, but the specifier only knows that some sorts and some operations are required, without further knowing which ones among these operations should be the constructors (it may even be the case that the constructors are not all present in the set of required operations and that they will be introduced later, during the specification process...).

In order to take into account this methodological distinction between achieved, fixed specifications (specs) and specifications under development, the PLUSS specification language provides a specific construct which allows modifications of the implementation class and which makes it possible to add new values, for instance by introducing new operations. These specifications of a new kind are called **drafts** and have a more flexible semantics than specs.

The semantics of a **draft** is *any model which satisfies the axioms*. There are no constructors associated with defined sorts. Thus there is no more limitation to the set of values computable by the constructors. All the models are considered, even the non finitely generated ones. Such a concept fits quite well with the idea of a preliminary specification: at this stage, the class of possible implementations is very large and all values or operations are not expressed yet.

As a consequence, PLUSS is more permissive with the way **drafts** are reused than for specs. Enrichment of a **draft** is done using the **enrich** construct, which is similar to the use one from a syntactical viewpoint, but is much more flexible from a semantical one, since any kind of new operations and new axioms can be added (as there are no constructors). However, strict hierarchical constraints apply as soon as a **draft** uses some spec.

When the development of some set of **drafts** is considered to be completed, these **drafts** can then be converted into specs by specifying, for each sort, the corresponding set of constructors. This process is illustrated by the development of the *FILE* specification (see Section 4).

2.4. PLUSS versus COLD

PLUSS is a specification language, COLD is a design language. Thus COLD has a wider scope than PLUSS and it is possible to start a design in COLD from a specification in PLUSS since these languages are compatible. The *classes* of COLD, when they do not contain imperative-like constructs such as states, procedures or algorithms, are equivalent to specifications in PLUSS. In the following we call such COLD classes *"COLD specifications"*.

The semantics of a non parameterized *COLD specification* and of a **draft** in PLUSS coincide. However, the COLD semantic definition is theory oriented [FJKR 87] and the PLUSS semantic definition is model oriented [Gau 85]. These definitions are complementary and compatible: the models of a PLUSS **draft** satisfy all the theorems of the similar *class* in COLD.

For the PLUSS spec construct, the main difference with a *COLD specification* comes from the distinction of constructors among the functions. Thus there is an implicit *"no-junk"* (cf. [Fei 87]) set of axioms, w.r.t. the constructors, and accordingly, an implicit induction scheme based on these constructors. Moreover, in the case of a PLUSS basic spec, there is an implicit *"no-confusion"* (cf. [Fei 87]) set of axioms.

In COLD there is no distinction between use and enrich as in PLUSS. The enrichment of drafts in PLUSS corresponds to the *import* in COLD. However the use composition of specs in PLUSS is a very restrictive version of the *import* in COLD, which ensures exactly the *"substitution property"* mentioned p.40 in [FJKR 87].

The parameterization mechanisms are similar for both languages. However the second order paramterization of COLD does not exist in PLUSS. Besides, there are some differences at the syntactical level: in COLD, the declarations of the parameters are embedded in the parameterized specification; in PLUSS, the declarations of parameters are independent, and there is just a reference to the parameter name in the header of the parameterized specification.

There are other minor syntatical differences in the way the bodies of the specifications are written. However a more significant one is that the definition conditions of partial functions are specified apart in PLUSS as preconditions; in COLD, they are specified within the axioms.

3. DESCRIPTION OF THE SUBSET OF THE UNIX FILE SYSTEM TO BE SPECIFIED

3.1. The subset to be specified

In order to have a real and still reasonable sized example, the specification of the UNIX file system is restricted to the viewpoint a "standard" user have on it[5]. From a user's viewpoint, the UNIX file system is a single tree made of files and directories, where the user can move from place to place, display information, add and suppress subtrees or leaves (directories and files). The system and the directories have the same structure, i.e. they are trees whose nodes are directories and whose leaves are either files or directories (in fact empty directories are rather nodes than leaves), but other directories than the system itself belong to the system[6].

Considering the whole system, the access path to a file or a directory is the absolute path from the root; considering the user's viewpoint, a path may be absolute (from the system root) or relative (to the working directory). Besides, at login time the working directory is automatically set to the home directory. At the system level, commands need absolute paths as arguments, while, at the user level, absolute or relative paths can be used for these commands. This is summarized in fig. 5.

For the purpose of our example, it was not necessary to specify all the UNIX commands. Therefore only few representative commands have been expressed: one to change the working directory (*cd*), another one to display the content of a directory (*ls*) and some commands to create, modify or remove

---

[5]This subset is different from the one specified in [Jon 84] and [TS 84] using respectively the COLD design language and the Z specification language.

[6]Even if Files and Directories are implemented in the same way in UNIX, some commands that can be used with files cannot with directories and vice versa (e.g. *rm* and *rmdir*). Thus Files and Directories are considered as different abstract data types in our specification.

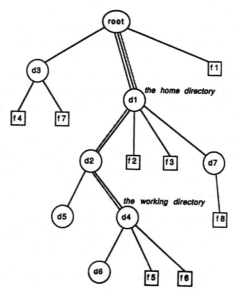

Figure 5 - A single-user viewpoint on the UNIX file system organization

files and directories (*mkdir, rm, rmdir*[7]). Access rights and dates of last modification are not specified, neither are the capability of linking files or directories. To stay at a high level of specification, the options of a command are not either specified, however the signatures of *ls, rm* and *rmdir* make it possible to further define the recursive option for these commands.

3.2. Some remarks on the specification

In this paper, we have deliberately decided to write a high-level specification. The resulting specification is not directly executable, but it expresses, in a concise way, the essential properties we wanted to describe. Besides, elementary specifications such as *NAMELIST, NAME, TEXT* and *BINARY-CODE* are not given in this paper.

Using the capabilities offered by the syntax and to help reading and understanding the specification, the names have been chosen as close as possible to common English sentences, except for the functions that are well-known UNIX commands.

---

[7]It should be noted that our specification of the *rmdir* command is slightly different from its implementation in the UNIX environment: our specification is consistent, but the UNIX implementation is not; *rmdir /.* is not allowed, but *rmdir ../name-of-the-current-directory* is allowed and let the system in an inconsistent state!

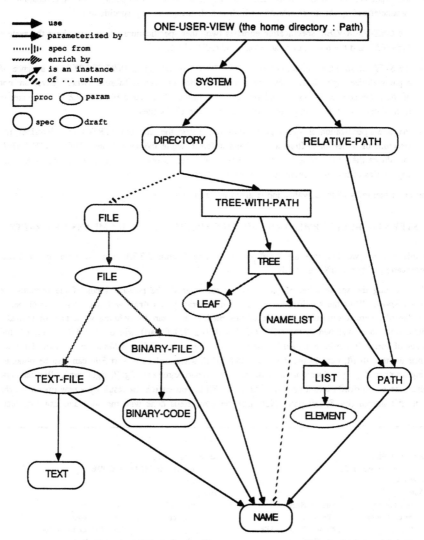

Figure 6 - The hierarchical organization of the UNIX specification

3.3. Hierarchy of the specification

Considering the above remarks on the subset to be specified, the hierarchical organization of the specification is easy to understand:

- the specification *ONE-USER-VIEW* defines the user's viewpoint; this specification is parameterized by *the home-directory* which is a characteristic of a specific user,

- the *ONE-USER-VIEW* specification enriches two other specifications: those describing the system (*SYSTEM*) and the notion of relative path (*RELATIVE-PATH*),

- the *SYSTEM* specification enriches the *DIRECTORY* specification; *DIRECTORY* is an instance of a parameterized specification describing a special kind of trees and forests (where leaves are not of the same sort as the nodes, and are described in the *LEAF* parameter), the *LEAF* parameter is instantiated by *FILE*, a simplified specification of the UNIX files,

- the tree specification is decomposed into two parts: the first one (*TREE*) just describes the structure of a tree built from a name and a forest, while the second one (*TREE-WITH-PATH*) introduces the notion of a path from the root of a tree to one of its sub-trees or leaves and the capabilities of adding or pruning sub-trees or leaves.

The exact hierarchy of the specification is given in fig. 6.

4. STEPWISE DEVELOPMENT OF THE FILE SPECIFICATION BY MEANS OF DRAFTS

In this section, we illustrate the **draft** construct (see Section 2.3.3.) with the help of the *FILE* specification of our UNIX case study.

When starting the specification of files it is not sure that all the possible kinds of file contents are already known. Thus the specification of files can be written as a draft with successive enrichments. We describe here a simplified example of this method and start by defining what files of text are. This can be done as shown by the *TEXT-FILE* draft (fig. 7, left part), where a sort *File* is defined, and values of sort *File* can be obtained by the < _ . _ > operation coupling a *Name* and a *Text*. Then we define another draft, namely the draft *BINARY-FILE*, where values of sort *File* can also be obtained using another < _ . _ > operation with *Bincode* as second argument (fig. 7, right part). We can now merge these two drafts into a new one, the draft *FILE*, and enrich the result by a new operation, *the empty file named* (fig. 8, left part). Note that the same steps done with the spec and use constructs

---

```
draft TEXT-FILE                              draft BINARY-FILE
    use NAME, TEXT                               use NAME, BINARY-CODE
  sort File                                    sort File
  func                                         func
    the name of      : File -> Name              the name of      : File  -> Name
    the content of   : File -> Text              the content of   : File  -> Bincode
    < _ . _ >        : Name * Text -> File       < _ . _ >        : Name * Bincode -> File
  axiom forall n : Name , t : Text             axiom forall n : Name , b : Bincode
  ( na : the name of < n . t > = n            ( na : the name of < n . b > = n
    co : the content of < n . t > = t  )        co : the content of < n . b > = b  )
end TEXT-FILE                                 end BINARY-FILE
```

Figure 7 - The TEXT-FILE and BINARY-FILE drafts

```
draft FILE                                    spec FILE from FILE
        enrich TEXT-FILE, BINARY-FILE             func
    func                                              file : File -> { empty, ascii text, executable }
        the empty file named : Name -> File           cons
    axiom forall n : Name                                 the empty file named , < _ . _ >
    ( na : the name of the empty file named n = n )   precond forall f : File
    end FILE                                          ( co : the content of f is defined when file f # empty )
                                                      axiom forall n : Name , t : Text , b : Bincode ,
                                                      ( file1 : file (the empty file named n) = empty
                                                        file2 : file < n . t > = ascii text
                                                        file3 : file < n . b > = executable )
                                                  end FILE
```

Figure 8 - The FILE draft and the FILE spec

would be meaningless, since the hierarchical constraints would be violated. Assuming, for sake of simplicity, that we do not want to define any other kind of files, the draft *FILE* can now be fixed and turned into a spec by stating the set of constructors of the sort *File*: the two overloaded operations < _ . _ >, and the operation *the empty file named* (fig. 8, right part). In the same step, a new operation *file* is defined, which allows to distinguish the various kinds of files. Note that this operation is defined using an **implicit sort definition**: { *empty, ascii text, executable* }. This concise notation is especially convenient for defining enumerated types, and is just an abbreviation for the following **basic specification** (see Section 2.3.1.) *FILE-TYPES*, which is implicitly used by the spec *FILE*:

```
basic spec FILE-TYPES
sort File-Types
cons
    empty      : -> File-Types
    ascii text : -> File-Types
    executable : -> File-Types
end FILE-TYPES
```

This overall development of the *FILE* specification is reflected by fig. 9, and an equivalent version of the *FILE* specification of fig. 8, where the spec **from draft** construct is *unfolded* [CLP 86], is displayed in fig. 10.

5. THE PATH AND SYSTEM SPECIFICATIONS

In this section, we illustrate the use of the spec and use constructs through the *PATH* and *SYSTEM* specifications of our UNIX case study.

The *PATH* specification is built on top of the *NAME* spec (see fig. 11), and introduces a new sort *Path*. The associated constructors are a coercion from names to path and the / operations (which are overloaded). Thus paths are defined as non empty lists of names. It is clear that one of the two overloaded / operations, together with the coercion from names to paths, will be sufficient to denote all possible paths, but nevertheless we have chosen to consider both of them as constructors in order to increase the legibility of the specifications: any path (of length greater or equal to two) can

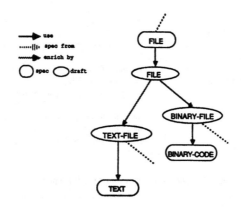

Figure 9 - Development of the FILE specification

spec FILE
        use NAME, TEXT, BINCODE
  sort File
  cons
    the empty file named : Name -> File
    < _ . _ >   : Name * Text -> File
    < _ . _ >   : Name * Bincode -> File
  func
    the name of   : File -> Name
    the content of   : File -> Text
    the content of   : File -> Bincode
    file : File -> { empty, ascii text, executable }
  precond forall f : File
  (co : the content of f **is defined when** file f # empty)
  axiom forall n : Name , t : Text , b : Bincode
  (na : the name of the empty file named n = n
    na1 : the name of < n . t > = n
    na2 : the name of < n . b > = n
    co1 : the content of < n . t > = t
    co2 : the content of < n . b > = b
    file1 : file (the empty file named n) = empty
    file2 : file < n . t > = ascii text
    file3 : file < n . b > = executable)
end FILE

Figure 10 - The spec FILE (unfolded)

```
spec PATH
      use NAME
   sort Path
   cons          " there is at least one name in a path "
     _    : Name -> Path
     _ / _       : Path * Name -> Path
     _ / _       : Name * Path -> Path
   func
      the first name of    : Path -> Name
      the last part of     : Path -> Path
      the first part of    : Path -> Path
      the last name of     : Path -> Name
   pred
      _ is a name : Path
   precond forall p : Path
   ( fp : the first part of p is defined when p is a name is false
     lp : the last part of p is defined when p is a name is false   )
   axiom forall n, n1, n2 : Name , p, p1, p2 : Path
   ( ep : n1 / p1 = p2 / n2  iff  n1 = the first name of p2 & p1 = the last part of p2 / n2
     fn1 : the first name of n = n
     fn2 : the first name of (p / n) = the first name of p
     fn3 : the first name of (n / p) = n
     lp1 : the last part of (p / n) = the last part of p / n
     lp2 : the last part of (n / p) = p
     fp1 : the first part of (p / n) = p
     fp2 : the first part of (n / p) = n / the first part of p
     ln1 : the last name of n = n
     ln2 : the last name of (p / n) = n
     ln3 : the last name of (n / p) = the last name of p
     isn1 : n is a name is true
     isn2 : p / n is a name is false
     isn3 : n / p is a name is false   )
   end PATH
```

Figure 11 - The PATH specification

equivalently be denoted by *n1 / p1* or by *p2 / n2*. This equivalence is stated by the axiom *ep* and is also reflected in some redundancies in the axioms that specifies the operations and predicates.

The *SYSTEM* specification (see fig. 12.b) is defined as an enrichment of the *DIRECTORY* specification (see fig. 12.a), and introduces a new sort *System* with the operations *root, _ plus the file _ added under _* and *mkdir* as constructors. It is at this level that, using appropriate preconditions, we introduce some basic distinctions between files and directories inherent to the UNIX philosophy (from some naive user viewpoint). One can compare for instance the preconditions *plus* and *mkdir*, or *rm* and *rmdir* respectively.

The crucial point about the *SYSTEM* specification is the role of the coercion from the sort *System* to the sort *Directory*. This coercion reflects the fact that a UNIX file system is no more than a directory, the root of which is *root*, and allows us to apply all operations defined on directories to a system. Therefore, all *SYSTEM* operations are defined by means of the similar operations defined at the

---

sort Forest, Directory
cons
   the empty forest   :   -> Forest
   < _ . _ >   : Name * Forest -> Directory
   _ plus _   : Forest * File U Directory -> Forest
func
   the name of   : Directory -> Name
   the content of   : Directory -> Forest
   the name list of   : Forest -> Namelist
   _ less the object named _ : Forest * Name -> Forest
   the object at _ in _ : Path * Directory -> File U Directory
   _ plus _ added under _   : Directory * File U Directory * Path -> Directory
   _ pruned at _   : Directory * Path -> Directory
   file : Directory -> { directory }
pred
   _ is an existing path of _ : Path * Directory
   _ is empty   : Forest

Figure 12.a - Main operations of the DIRECTORY signature

DIRECTORY specification level. Thus this coercion from a new sort (*System*) to an old one (*Directory*) corresponds to the inheritance of the properties of the old sort by the new one[8].

6. THE PARAMETERIZED SPECIFICATIONS TREE AND TREE-WITH-PATH

In this section, we illustrate the use of parameterized specifications through the *TREE* and *TREE-WITH-PATH* specifications of our UNIX case study.

Due to the simplifications made on our UNIX subset (see Section 3), a UNIX file system can be viewed as some kind of tree. The nodes of this tree may have an arbitrary number of sons, which may be of two kinds: either directories or files. It is therefore natural to specify a UNIX file system as (roughly speaking) an instance of a general-purpose, parameterized specification of trees. Among the various parameterized specifications of trees one can imagine to be present in a library of standard, commonly used specifications, we have to choose a specification of trees where a node may have an

---

[8]Due to this coercion from *System* to *Directory* and the hierarchical constraints, the preconditions *plus* and *mkdir* can be reduced to the part strictly devoted to the basic distinctions between files and directories, i.e. one could have specified these preconditions as follows:

plus : *S plus the file f added under p* **is defined when**
        the name of f belongs to the name list of the content of the object at p in S **is false**
        OR *the object at (p | the name of f) in S is a File* **is true**

mkdir : *mkdir (S, p, n)* **is defined when**
        n belongs to the name list of the content of the object at p in S **is false**

without changing the meaning of the specification (since the parts omitted in the preconditions above must hold for directories, they are induced by the coercion from *System* to *Directory* for systems). We introduced some redundancies for understandability reasons.

```
spec SYSTEM
      use DIRECTORY
  sort System
  cons
    root        :    -> System
    _ plus the file _ added under _        : System * File * Path  -> System
    mkdir       : System * Path * Name  -> System
  func
    _                        : System  -> Directory
    ls          : System * Path  -> Forest
    rm          : System * Path * Name  -> System
    rmdir       : System * Path * Name  -> System
  precond forall  p : Path ,  n : Name ,  S : System ,  f : File
  ( plus : S plus the file f added under p is defined when
                  p is an existing path of S & the object at p in S is a Directory
                  & ( the name of f belongs to the name list of the content of the object at p in S is false
                        OR the object at (p / the name of f) in S is a File is true )
    mkdir : mkdir (S, p, n) is defined when
                  p is an existing path of S & the object at p in S is a Directory
                  & (n belongs to the name list of the content of the object at p in S is false)
    ls : ls (S, p) is defined when p is an existing path of S
    rm : rm (S, p, n) is defined when
                  p / n is an existing path of S & the object at p / n in S is a File
    rmdir : rmdir (S, p, n) is defined when
                  p / n is an existing path of S & the object at p / n in S is a Directory
                  & the content of the object at p / n in S is empty   )
  axiom forall  p : Path ,  n : Name ,  S : System ,  f : File
  ( root : root = < 'root' . the empty forest >
    plus : S plus the file f added under p = S plus f added under p
    mkdir : mkdir (S, p, n) = S plus < n . the empty forest > added under p
    ls1 : the object at p in S is a Directory  => ls (S, p) = the content of the object at p in S
    ls2 : the object at p in S is a File  => ls (S, p) = the empty forest plus the object at p in S
    rm : rm (S, p, n) = S pruned at p / n
    rmdir : rmdir (S, p, n) = S pruned at p / n   )
  end SYSTEM
```

Figure 12.b - The SYSTEM specification

arbitrary number of sons and where nodes and leaves are named (since directories and files are).

A suitable specification is provided by the parameterized specification *TREE* (see fig. 14). This specification is parameterized by the *LEAF* formal parameter specification, which is intended to be later instantiated by some *FILE* specification (in our case).

Here, the only requirement about the formal parameter *LEAF* is that leaves are named. Thus, the formal parameter specification *LEAF* will be exactly the same param as *NAMED-THINGS* up to renaming (see fig. 13).

The proc *TREE* (see fig. 14) introduces two new sorts *Tree* and *Forest* that will be mutually

```
param LEAF
      use NAME
   sort Leaf
   func
      the name of : Leaf -> Name
end LEAF
```

Figure 13 - The LEAF formal parameter specification

recursively generated by the operations < _ . _ >, *the empty forest* and *plus*[9]. Note that the overloading of the *plus* operation as well as the use of the overloaded variables *LT1*, *LT2* allow us to write the axioms in a very concise way. Note also that at the level of this general-purpose parameterized specification, no further distinction is made between trees (directories) and leaves (files). Appropriate distinctions will be introduced later, once the proc *TREE* will be instantiated, by means of preconditions (see the preconditions *plus* and *mkdir*, or *rm* and *rmdir* of the specification *SYSTEM*, fig. 12.b, Section 5).

We now need to introduce some notion of path in order to be able to access to or modify some sub-tree (possibly restricted to a leaf) of a given tree at some address (i.e. path). This is the purpose of the *TREE-WITH-PATH* parameterized specification, which is designed as an enrichment of the *PATH* specification and of the *TREE* parameterized specification, and introduces three new operations: *the object at path _ in _, _ plus _ added under _*, and *_ pruned at _* (see fig. 15). All these operations are defined only if the given path is correct, i.e. if *p is an existing path of T*. This predicate is defined by the four axioms *exist1-4*. The first one comes from the natural convention that a path in a tree starts with the root of the tree. The second one expresses the fact that a path *n1 / n2 is an existing path of* a tree *T* if and only if *n1* is *the name of T*, and there exists a son of *T* (leaf or tree) named *n2*. The next two express that a path of length greater than two *n1 / n2 / p is an existing path of T* if and only if: *n1 is the name of T*, it exists a son *T1* of *T* named *n2*, and *n2 / p is an existing path of T1*.

As *the object at path p in T* may be of sort either *Leaf* or *Tree*, we use in the axioms and preconditions the characteristic predicates *is a Leaf* and *is a Tree* when necessary (see Section 2.2).

The operations *_ plus _ added under _* and *_ pruned at _* are mutually recursively defined. In order to better understand how this is specified, we explain the axioms *plus3* and *prun2* with the help of the example in fig. 16 (axioms *plus1*, *plus2* and *prun1* are just special cases when paths are made of one or two names).

Assuming the initial state of the tree *T* is the tree shown in fig. 16.a where a subtree *LT* (fig. 16.b) has to be added at path *n1 / n2 / n3* (*p = n3*), the result is the tree *T3* shown in fig. 16.c. Following the right hand side of the axiom *plus3*, this result is obtained by replacing the subtree *T1* (fig. 16.a) by the subtree *T2* (fig. 16.c), informally speaking this could be expressed (without taking care of the exact location for pruning and grafting) by: *T3 = T - T1 + T2*, where *T2 = T1 + LT* (*LT* added at the right

---

[9]It is clear from the remarks above that this specification is similar to the *COLLECTION-OF-NAMED-OBJECTS* specification defined in Section 2.3.1., but we can not directly reuse this specification since our proc introduces two mutually recursively generated sorts. However, we reuse an important part of its text up to renaming.

proc TREE (LEAF)
      use NAMELIST
  sort Tree, Forest
  cons
    < _ . _ >   : Name * Forest -> Tree
    the empty forest   :   -> Forest
    _ plus _   : Forest * Leaf U Tree -> Forest
  func
    the name of   : Tree -> Name
    the content of   : Tree -> Forest
    the name list of   : Forest -> Namelist
    the son of _ named _   : Tree * Name -> Leaf U Tree
    _ less the object named _   : Forest * Name -> Forest
  pred
    _ is empty : Forest
  precond forall T : Tree , n : Name
  (son : the son of T named n **is defined when** n belongs to the name list of the content of T)
  axiom forall n, n' : Name , F : Forest, LT : Leaf U Tree
  (na : the name of < n . F > = n
    co : the content of < n . F > = F
    less1 : F is empty => F less the object named n = F
    less2 : n = the name of LT => (F plus LT) less the object named n = F less the object named n
    less3 : n # the name of LT => (F plus LT) less the object named n = F less the object named n plus LT
    nl1 : the name list of the empty forest = the empty list
    nl2 : the name of LT belongs to the name list of F => the name list of (F plus LT) = the name list of F
    nl3 : the name of LT belongs to the name list of F **is false**
                => the name list of (F plus LT) = the name list of F plus the name of LT
    son1 : n' = the name of LT => the son of < n . F plus LT > named n' = LT
    son2 : n' # the name of LT => the son of < n . F plus LT > named n' = the son of < n . F > named n'
    ise1 : the empty forest is empty **is true**
    ise2 : (F plus LT) is empty **is false**)
end TREE

Figure 14 - The TREE parameterized specification

place in *T1*, i.e. at *n2 / n3*).

Similarly, assuming the initial state of T is the tree *T3* shown in fig. 16.d and we want to remove the subtree *LT* at path *n1 / n2 / n3 / n4* (here *p = n3 / n4*), the result will be the tree *T* shown in fig. 16.a. Informally, the axiom *prun2* expresses that: $T = T3 - T2 + T1$ where $T1 = T2 - LT$.

Since the operation *the son of _ named _* is a special case of *the object at _ in _*, it is hidden outside of the *TREE-WITH-PATH* specification (see fig. 15 the forget clause and Section 2.3.1).

7. THE DIRECTORY AND ONE-USER-VIEW SPECIFICATIONS

Now that we have the parameterized specification *TREE-WITH-PATH*, we can instantiate it using the *FILE* specification (introduced in Section 4) as an actual parameter for *LEAF*. Once parameter passing is achieved, we rename the sort *Tree* into the sort *Directory*, which leads to the spec *DIRECTORY* of

proc TREE-WITH-PATH (LEAF) **forget** the son of _ named _
      use TREE (LEAF) , PATH
func
    the object at _ in _   : Path * Tree -> Leaf U Tree
    _ plus _ added under _   : Tree * Leaf U Tree * Path -> Tree
    _ pruned at _   : Tree * Path -> Tree
pred
    _ is an existing path of _ : Path * Tree
precond forall p : Path , T : Tree , LT : Leaf U Tree
(obj : the object at p in T **is defined when** p is an existing path of T
    plus : T plus LT added under p **is defined when** p is an existing path of T & the object at p in T is a Tree
    prun : T pruned at p **is defined when** p is a name **is false** & p is an existing path of T **is true**)
axiom forall n1, n2 : Name , p : Path , T : Tree , LT : Leaf U Tree
(exist1 : n1 is an existing path of T **iff** n1 = the name of T
    exist2 : n1 / n2 is an existing path of T **iff** n1 = the name of T & n2 belongs to the name list of T
    exist3 : n2 belongs to the name list of T **is false** => n1 / n2 / p is an existing path of T **is false**
    exist4 : n2 belongs to the name list of T => n1 / n2 / p is an existing path of T **iff** n1 = the name of T
                                  & n2 / p is an existing path of the son of T named n2
    obj : the object at n1 in T = T " *due to the preconditions, n1 is the name of T* "
    obj2 : the object at n1 / p in T = the object at p in the son of T named (the first name of p)
    plus1 : T plus LT added under n1 = < n1 . the content of T plus LT >
    plus2 : T plus LT added under n1 / n2 = T pruned at n1 / n2
                                  plus (the object at n1 / n2 in T
                                          plus LT added under n2)
                                  added under n1
    plus3 : T plus LT added under n1 / n2 / p = T pruned at n1 / n2
                                      plus (the object at n1 / n2 in T
                                            plus LT added under n2 / p)
                                  added under n1
    prun1 : T pruned at n1 / n2 = < n1 . the content of T less the object named n2 >
    prun2 : T pruned at n1 / n2 / p = T pruned at n1 / n2
                                plus (the object at n1 / n2 in T
                                    pruned at n2 / p)
                              added under n1)
end TREE-WITH-PATH

Figure 15 - The TREE-WITH-PATH parameterized specification

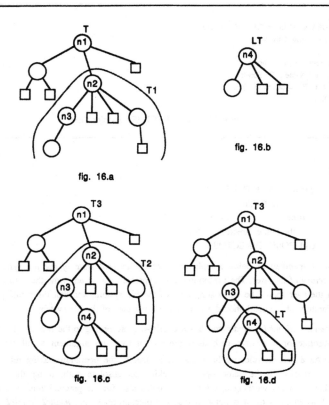

fig. 16.a

fig. 16.b

fig. 16.c

fig. 16.d

Figure 16 - How the TREE-WITH-PATH operations are defined

fig. 17. This renaming automatically induces a renaming of the characteristic predicate *is a Tree* into *is a Directory*, while the fitting morphism induces a renaming of the characteristic predicate *is a Leaf* into *is a File*. Then we enrich the result by a new operation *file*, which is overloaded with an operation on files, and states that a directory is of "type" *directory* (while files may be of "type" *empty*, *ascii text* or *executable*, see Section 4, fig. 8). Remark that we have used again an "implicit" sort { *directory* } to define this operation.

The *ONE-USER-VIEW* specification is now defined as an enrichment of the *SYSTEM* specification and of the *RELATIVE-PATH* specification (which is itself defined as an enrichment of the *PATH* specification by adding the notion of relative paths). This *ONE-USER-VIEW* specification is the topmost one of our case study, and this is at this level that all "UNIX-like" operations are defined.

The *ONE-USER-VIEW* specification (see fig. 18) is parameterized by *the home directory* of the user, which is a constant operation of sort *Path*. For such a simple formal parameter specification, the concise notation used here (see fig. 18) is just an abbreviation for the following formal parameter

```
spec DIRECTORY as TREE-WITH-PATH ( FILE )
  renaming Tree into Directory
  func
    file : Directory -> { directory }
  axiom forall n : Name , F : Forest
  ( file : file < n . F > = directory  )
end DIRECTORY
```

Figure 17 - The DIRECTORY specification

specification:

```
              param HOME-DIRECTORY
                  use PATH
              func
                  the home directory :  -> Path
              end HOME-DIRECTORY
```

A user-view is specified as being a tuple made of *the current state of the file system* and of *the working directory of* the user. The precondition *uv* expresses that at any time the path to the working directory of the user should be an existing path of the file system, and that the actual parameter (i.e. the home directory of the user) should also be an existing path of the file system.

All the operations *cd*, *mkdir*, *rmdir* and *ls* are overloaded, according to the fact that the user may use either an absolute or a relative path as argument (or even no argument at all for the *cd* or *ls* commands). As a general rule, we have chosen to specify the operations taking relative paths[10] as arguments by means of the same operation taking an absolute path, using the straightforward conversion based on the working directory. This holds also for the preconditions, where we use the ... is defined when ... is defined notation (see the preconditions *cd2*, *mkdir2*, *rmdir2* and *ls2*). The operations taking absolute paths as arguments are themselves defined by means of the similar operations defined at the *SYSTEM* specification level. The axiom *cd1* states that when used without argument, the command *cd* go back to the home directory. In what concerns the *ls* command, however, providing no argument is just equivalent to providing the working directory as argument (axiom *ls1*).

8. DISCUSSION

The PLUSS specification of our UNIX case study may be considered from three main viewpoints. The first one is the relevance of the PLUSS specification-building primitives, the second is the legibility aspects and the third one is the reusability aspects. In the following subsections we successively examine these three topics.

---

[10]The specification *RELATIVE-PATH* is given in the appendix.

proc ONE-USER-VIEW (the home directory : -> Path)
     use SYSTEM, RELATIVE-PATH
 sort User-view
 cons
   < _ . _ >   : System * Path -> User-view
 func
   the system of : User-view -> System
   pwd   : User-view -> Path
   cd : User-view -> User-view
   cd : User-view * Path -> User-view
   cd : User-view * Displacement -> User-view
   mkdir   : User-view * Path -> User-view
   mkdir   : User-view * Displacement -> User-view
   rmdir   : User-view * Path -> User-view
   rmdir   : User-view * Displacement -> User-view
   ls : User-view -> Forest
   ls : User-view * Path -> Forest
   ls : User-view * Displacement -> Forest
                 " Add here other UNIX commands. "
 precond forall S : System , p, p' : Path , dp : Displacement
(uv : < S . p > **is defined when** p is an existing path of S & the object at p in S is a Directory
                              & the home directory is an existing path of S
                              & the object at the home directory in S is a Directory
  cd1 : cd (< S . p >, p') **is defined when** p' is an existing path of S & the object at p' in S is a Directory
  cd2 : cd (< S . p >, dp) **is defined when** cd (< S . p >, p ‖ dp) **is defined**
  mkdir1 : mkdir (< S . p >, p') **is defined when** p' is a name **is false**
                                & mkdir (S, the first part of p', the last name of p') **is defined**
  mkdir2 : mkdir (< S . p >, dp) **is defined when** mkdir (< S . p >, p ‖ dp) **is defined**
  rmdir1 : rmdir (< S . p >, p') **is defined when** p' # p & p' is a name **is false**
                                & p' is an existing path of S **is true**
                                & the object at p' in S is a Directory **is true**
                                & the content of the object at p' in S is empty **is true**
  rmdir2 : rmdir (< S . p >, dp) **is defined when** rmdir (< S . p >, p ‖ dp) **is defined**
  ls1 : ls (< S . p >, p') **is defined when** p' is an existing path of S
  ls2 : ls (< S . p >, dp) **is defined when** ls (< S . p >, p ‖ dp) **is defined**)
 axiom forall S : System , p, p' : Path , dp : Displacement , n : Name
(sys : the system of < S . p > = S
  pwd : pwd < S . p > = p
  cd1 : cd < S . p > = < S . the home directory >
  cd2 : cd (< S . p >, p') = < S . p' >
  cd3 : cd (< S . p >, dp) = cd (< S . p >, p ‖ dp)
  mkdir1 : mkdir (< S . p >, p' / n) = < mkdir (S, p', n) . p >
  mkdir2 : mkdir (< S . p >, dp / n) = mkdir (< S . p >, p ‖ dp)
  rmdir1 : rmdir (< S . p >, p' / n) = < rmdir (S, p', n) . p >
  rmdir2 : rmdir (< S . p >, dp / n) = rmdir (< S . p >, p ‖ dp)
  ls1 : ls < S . p > = ls (< S . p >, p)
  ls2 : ls (< S . p >, p') = ls (S, p')
  ls3 : ls (< S . p >, dp) = ls (< S . p >, p ‖ dp))
end ONE-USER-VIEW

Figure 18 - The ONE-USER-VIEW parameterized specification

8.1. Adequacy of the PLUSS specification-building primitives

In the UNIX case study developed in this paper, all the specification-building primitives of PLUSS have been used in the various parts of the whole specification. This is a first argument in favor of the expressiveness power of the PLUSS specification language, and this observation is strengthened by the other experiments performed with the PLUSS specification language [Cho 86, Bie 84, B2G3 84, BCM 85].

Visibility control is clearly needed as a feature of the language, since specifying in the large raises the same problems as programming in the large, but was not much used here due to the self-contained aspects of our case study. Embedding this UNIX specification in a larger one would probably require the use of the visibility control primitives in order to avoid name clashes.

The way the various specification-building primitives may be combined in a both flexible and rigorous manner makes it possible to structure large specifications in a convenient way. This is reflected by the relatively small size of each of the specification components necessary to the whole specification.

8.2. Legibility aspects

The main goal of the experiment reported here was to show that formal specifications can (and should) be legible, even by someone who is not too familiar with the underlying formalism. The points we would like to discuss here are how far the resulting specification is legible or not, how far legibility considerations interact with the specification process or the specification design, and what are the methodological or linguistic tools necessary to achieve legibility.

We feel that the resulting specification is fairly legible. Most of the axioms (especially the preconditions) contained in the specifications can be read (hence, understood) as english sentences; each specification piece is quite small and its meaning and role can therefore be easily figured out. However, it is clear that the whole specification cannot be understood without a minimum knowledge about algebraic specifications or about the semantics of the PLUSS specification-building primitives. But once this minimum knowledge is acquired, understanding the UNIX specification is fairly easy. To be honest, some axioms remain difficult to understand: most of the time, it comes from the systematic use of recursive definitions for enumeration purposes; as a remedy, we consider the possibility to introduce "enumerators" similar to the CLU iterators [LG 86] into axiomatic specifications.

Another conclusion drawn from this experiment is that having legibility considerations in mind has strongly influenced the specification design. For instance, the choice of having redundant constructors in the *PATH* specification was only motivated by legibility considerations. Thus, taking legibility into account led us to numerous modifications of earlier design decisions until we feel a satisfactory enough result was obtained.

Legibility was obtained both by means of linguistic tools and by methodological considerations. Some of the linguistic tools were already present in the PLUSS language, such as the user-defined flexible syntax for operations or the capability of overloading operations, others were the result of minor modifications of the concrete syntax: outlining of the constructors clause, much expressive syntax for predicates (is false, is true) and preconditions (is defined when), use of overloaded variables to obtain more concise axioms, characteristic predicates.

Following an idea of P. Mosses [Mos 86], we have deliberately chosen a verbose style for operation names. In order to have English sentences when composing the operations in the axioms, the names are chosen following few simple rules: when an operation expresses the evolution of an object (the same sort occurs in the domain and range of the operation) the sort of this object should be the first one in the domain (in case of cartesian product), the operation name should contain the participle of a verb describing the operation and the first operand should be the subject (e.g. *T pruned at p, T plus LT added under p*); for predicate names we choose assertions (e.g. *p is an existing path of T*); for such operations as projections on a previously defined sort, we choose a nominal group followed by some appropriate preposition (e.g. *the name list of F, the object at p in T*). It is clear that this verbose style could be inconvenient for a specialist working on the specification: this lead to the classical idea of verbose and concise versions of the same specification.

We have systematically preferred predicates to boolean functions, and last but not least we were not concerned with the executability of our specifications (since we claim that specifications describe classes of implementations, they should not necessarily be executable; this contrasts with specifications written in a high-level executable specification languages, such as OBJ [FGJM 85] or RAP [GH 85, Hus 85]). Anyway, it turns out that all our specifications may easily be transformed into executable ones.

8.3. Reusability aspects

As explained in Section 3, the case study specified in this paper has been simplified in order to be small enough to be completely specified. However, a subsidiary question is how far the specification given here can be extended in order to take into account e.g. links, access rights, etc... A nice answer would be that the specification-building primitives are the right way to ensure component reusability, and that it is sufficient to embed our simplified specification in a richer one to take into account the simplifications we have made so far (i.e. to write specifications enriching the *ONE-USER-VIEW* specification and defining links, access-rights, etc...). Unfortunately, it turns out that specifying links deeply change the underlying structure, since we no more need trees but dags (directed acyclic graphs). As soon as *TREE* is used in *ONE-USER-VIEW*, this change cannot be introduced afterwards: hierarchical constraints prevent the user from changing the properties of the constructors. The only way is to replace *TREE* by a *DAG* parameterized specification, then to make a *DAG-WITH-PATH* parameterized specification, etc.: the components used by *TREE* can be reused and the components which reuse *TREE* must be modified. A similar conclusion holds for the addition of access rights.

These conclusions are not surprising, they are natural consequences of the semantics of the spec and use constructs: the semantics of a spec is the class of all possible implementations of this specification; in order to allow independent program developments for the various spec components of a specification, the use construct does not modify this class of implementations. Obviously, the modifications above introduce important changes in the class of possible implementations of *ONE-USER-VIEW* and its components. However, some parts of the text of the specification remain unchanged or slightly modified: the conclusion above does not prevent textual reusability. Even if it is necessary to rewrite the specification to take into account links and access rights, this rewriting will strongly benefit from the previous specification process and will therefore be much more easy and fast.

9. CONCLUSION

There is an old suspicion about algebraic specifications: are they applicable to large and complex examples? This paper, together with previous case studies already mentioned, definitely gives a positive answer.

Another reproach against this kind of specification is that they are difficult to understand. Our position on this point is that understandability and legibility can be significantly improved as soon as they are stated as a main objective of the specification process and that specific linguistic tools are provided. After all, efficient programs are generally not easy to understand, and programmers have often to choose between efficiency and clarity (among many others criteria). From the experiment reported here, we think that similar dilemmas occur when writing specifications. Our claim is that when dealing with formal specifications, understandability and legibility should prevail, which may imply to give up, in some cases, executability aspects.

REFERENCES

[ADJ 78] J. Goguen, J. Thatcher and E. Wagner,
"*An Initial Algebra Approach to the Specification, Correctness and Implementation of Abstract Data Types*", Current Trends in Programming Methodology, Vol.4, Yeh Ed., Prentice Hall, 1978.

[AW 86] E. Astesiano and M. Wirsing,
"*An Introduction to ASL*", Proceedings of the IFIP WG 2.1 Working Conference on Program Specifications and Transformations, Bad Toelz, FRG, 1986.

[BBC 86] G. Bernot, M. Bidoit and C. Choppy,
"*Abstract Dat Types with Exception Handling: An Initial Approach Based on a Distinction between Exceptions and Errors*" Theoretical Computer Science, Vol. 46, No. 1, pp.13-45, 1986.

[B2G3 84] M. Bidoit, B. Biebow, M-C. Gaudel, C. Gresse and G. Guiho,
"*Exception Handling: Formal Specification and Systematic Program Construction*", Proceedings of the 7th International Conference on Software Engineering, Orlando, March 1984.

[BC 86] M. Bidoit and C. Choppy,
"*The ALEX-PLUSS Specification Language*", ESPRIT Project "FOR-ME-TOO" Report, January 1986.

[BCM 84] B. Biebow, N. Choquet and A. Mauboussin,
"*Specification par Types Abstraits Algebriques de Fonctions Caracteristiques d'une Unite de Raccordement d'Abonnes Telephoniques*", Rapport de Contrat DAII 84.35.087, Sept. 1985.

[BG 85] M. Bidoit and M.-C. Gaudel,
"*PLUSS: Proposition pour un Langage de Specifications Structurees*", Actes des Journees AFCET "Nouveaux Langages pour le Genie Logiciel", Evry, France, October 28-29, 1985, BIGRE+GLOBULE No.45.

[BH 85]   B. Biebow and J. Hagelstein,
           "Algebraic Specification of Synchronisation and Errors: A Telephonic Example",
           Proceedings of TAPSOFT, Berlin, March 1985, Vol. 2, pp.294-308, LNCS 186,
           Springer-Verlag.

[Bid 84]   M. Bidoit,
           *"Algebraic Specification of Exception Handling and Error Recovery by Means of
           Equations and Declarations"*, ICALP Proceedings, LNCS, Springer Verlag, 1984.

[Bie 84]   B. Biebow,
           "Application d'un Langage de Specification Algebrique a des Exemples Telephoniques",
           These de 3e Cycle, Universite Paris 6, Feb.1984.

[BW 82]   M. Broy and M. Wirsing,
           "Partial Abstract Types", Acta Informatica 18, pp.47-64, 1982.

[CGHM 86] M-A. Choquer, M-C. Gaudel, Y. Holvoet and A. Mauboussin,
           "A Concrete Syntax for PLUSS", METEOR Report, Task 10 and 11, March 1986.

[Cho 86]   M.-A. Choquer,
           *"Specification of the Evaluation Tool: Leftmost Outermost Reduction Strategy in the
           Equational Case"*, METEOR Report, November 86.

[CLP 86]   CGE-LRI-Passau Teams,
           "A Proposed List of Components for a Specification Development Environment",
           METEOR Working Document, September 1986.

[Des 83]   J. Despeyroux-Savonitto,
           "An Algebraic Specification of a Pascal Compiler", SIGPLAN 18(12), pp34-48, 1983.

[Fei 87]   L.M.G. Feijs,
           "Systematic Design with COLD-K–an annoted example–", METEOR Report,
           METEOR/t8/PRLE/3, Philips Research Laboratories Eindhoven, December 1987.

[FGJM 85] K. Futatsugi, J. A. Goguen, J-P. Jouannaud and J. Meseguer,
           "Principles of OBJ2", Proceedings of 12th ACM Symposium on Principles of
           Programming Languages, New-Orleans, Louisiana, Jan.14-16, 1985, pp.52-66.

[FJKR 87] L.M.G. Feijs, H.B.M. Jonkers, C.P.J. Koymans and G.R. Renardel de Lavalette,
           "Formal Definition of the Design Language COLD-K", METEOR Report,
           METEOR/t7/PRLE/7, Philips Research Laboratories Eindhoven, Preliminary Edition,
           April 1987.

[Gau 84]   M.-C. Gaudel,
           "A First Introduction to PLUSS", METEOR Report, December 1984.

[Gau 85]   M.-C. Gaudel,
           "Toward Structured Algebraic Specifications", Conference Preprints of Esprit Technical
           Week '85, Brussels, September 23-25, 1985, also in ESPRIT'85 Status Report of
           Continuing Work, Edited by The Commission of the European Communities, Brussels.

[GH 85]   A. Geser and H. Hussmann,
           *"Rapid Prototyping for Algebraic Specifications, Examples for the Use of the RAP
           System"*, MIP - 8517, Universitaet Passau, Dec. 1985.

[Hus 85] H. Hussmann,
"Rapid Prototyping for Algebraic Specifications – RAP-System User's Manual", MIP - 8504, Universitaet Passau, Mar. 1985.

[Jon 84] H.B.M. Jonkers,
"Specification of a UNIX like File System in COLD-S", FAST Working Document, Philips Research Laboratories Eindhoven, 1984.

[LG 86] B. Liskov and J. Guttag,
"Abstraction and Specification in Program Development", MIT Press, 1986.

[Mos 86] P. Mosses,
"Action Semantics", 4th Workshop on Abstract Data Types, Burg Warberg, G.R.D., 1986.

[MS 84] C. Morgan and B. Sufrin,
"Specification of the UNIX Filing System", IEEE Transactions on Software Engineering, Vol.SE-10, No.2, pp.128-142, Feb. 1984.

[Pro 82] K. Proch,
"ORSEC: Un Outil de Recherche de Specifications Equivalentes par Comparaison d'Exemples", These de 3e Cycle, CRIN, Nancy, France, Dec. 1982.

[Wis 83] M. Wirsing,
"Structured Algebraic Specifications: A Kernel Language", Habilitation Thesis, Techn. Univ. Munchen, 1983, to appear in TCS, also Univ. Passau, MIP-8511.

APPENDIX. The UNIX Specification

proc ONE-USER-VIEW (the home directory : -> Path)
    use SYSTEM, RELATIVE-PATH
  sort User-view
  cons
   < _ . _ > : System * Path -> User-view
  func
   the system of : User-view -> System
   pwd   : User-view -> Path
   cd   : User-view -> User-view
   cd   : User-view * Path -> User-view
   cd   : User-view * Displacement -> User-view
   mkdir : User-view * Path -> User-view
   mkdir : User-view * Displacement -> User-view
   rmdir : User-view * Path -> User-view
   rmdir : User-view * Displacement -> User-view
   ls   : User-view -> Forest
   ls   : User-view * Path -> Forest
   ls   : User-view * Displacement -> Forest
             " *Add here other UNIX commands.* "
  precond forall S : System , p, p' : Path , dp : Displacement
(uv : < S . p > **is defined when** p is an existing path of S
                           & the object at p in S is a Directory
                           & the home directory is an existing path of S
                           & the object at the home directory in S is a Directory
  cd1 : cd (< S . p >, p') **is defined when** p' is an existing path of S
                           & the object at p' in S is a Directory
  cd2 : cd (< S . p >, dp) **is defined when** cd (< S . p >, p ‖ dp) **is defined**
  mkdir1 : mkdir (< S . p >, p') **is defined when** p' is a name **is false**
                   & mkdir (S, the first part of p', the last name of p') **is defined**
  mkdir2 : mkdir (< S . p >, dp) **is defined when** mkdir (< S . p >, p ‖ dp) **is defined**
  rmdir1 : rmdir (< S . p >, p') **is defined when** p' # p & p' is a name **is false**
                          & p' is an existing path of S **is true**
                          & the object at p' in S is a Directory **is true**
                          & the content of the object at p' in S is empty **is true**
  rmdir2 : rmdir (< S . p >, dp) **is defined when** rmdir (< S . p >, p ‖ dp) **is defined**
  ls1 : ls (< S . p >, p') **is defined when** p' is an existing path of S
  ls2 : ls (< S . p >, dp) **is defined when** ls (< S . p >, p ‖ dp) **is defined**   )
  axiom forall S : System , p, p' : Path , dp : Displacement , n : Name
(sys : the system of < S . p > = S
  pwd : pwd < S . p > = p
  cd1 : cd < S . p > = < S . the home directory >
  cd2 : cd (< S . p >, p') = < S . p' >
  cd3 : cd (< S . p >, dp) = cd (< S . p >, p ‖ dp)
  mkdir1 : mkdir (< S . p >, p' / n) = < mkdir (S, p', n) . p >
  mkdir2 : mkdir (< S . p >, dp / n) = mkdir (< S . p >, p ‖ dp)

rmdir1 : rmdir (< S . p >, p' / n) = < rmdir (S, p', n) . p >
rmdir2 : rmdir (< S . p >, dp / n) = rmdir (< S . p >, p ‖ dp)
ls1 : ls < S . p > = ls (< S . p >, p)
ls2 : ls (< S . p >, p') = ls (S, p')
ls3 : ls (< S . p >, dp) = ls (< S . p >, p ‖ dp)   )
end ONE-USER-VIEW

spec RELATIVE-PATH
    use PATH
  sort Displacement
  cons
    the empty displacement :   -> Displacement
    _   : Name -> Displacement
    _ / _   : Displacement * Name -> Displacement
    ../ _   : Displacement -> Displacement
  func
    _ ‖ _   : Path * Displacement -> Path
  axiom forall p : Path , n : Name , dp : Displacement
  (cat1 : p ‖ the empty displacement = p
    cat2 : p ‖ n = p / n
    cat3 : p ‖ (dp / n) = (p ‖ dp) / n
    cat4 : n ‖ ../ dp = n ‖ dp   " *as there is at least one name in a path*,"
    cat5 : (p / n) ‖ ../ dp = p ‖ dp   )   " *it is impossible to remove the first name* "
end RELATIVE-PATH

spec DIRECTORY **as** TREE-WITH-PATH (FILE)
  renaming Tree **into** Directory
  func
    file : Directory -> { directory }
  axiom forall n : Name , F : Forest
  (file : file < n . F > = directory   )
end DIRECTORY

spec SYSTEM
      use DIRECTORY
   sort System
   cons
     root   :   -> System
     _ plus the file _ added under _ : System * File * Path -> System
     mkdir   : System * Path * Name -> System
   func
     _   : System -> Directory
     ls   : System * Path -> Forest
     rm   : System * Path * Name -> System
     rmdir : System * Path * Name -> System
   precond forall p : Path , n : Name , S : System , f : File
  (plus : S plus the file f added under p is defined when
                        p is an existing path of S & the object at p in S is a Directory
                  & (the name of f belongs to the name list of the content of
                                 the object at p in S is **false**
                OR the object at (p / the name of f) in S is a File is **true**)
     mkdir : mkdir (S, p, n) is defined when
                     p is an existing path of S & the object at p in S is a Directory
                  & (n belongs to the name list of the content of
                              the object at p in S is **false**)
     ls : ls (S, p) is defined when p is an existing path of S
     rm : rm (S, p, n) is defined when
                  p / n is an existing path of S & the object at p / n in S is a File
     rmdir : rmdir (S, p, n) is defined when
                  p / n is an existing path of S & the object at p / n in S is a Directory
                  & the content of the object at p / n in S is empty   )
   axiom forall p : Path , n : Name , S : System , f : File
  (root : root = < 'root' . the empty forest >
     plus : S plus the file f added under p = S plus f added under p
     mkdir : mkdir (S, p, n) = S plus < n . the empty forest > added under p
     ls1 : the object at p in S is a Directory
                    => ls (S, p) = the content of the object at p in S
     ls2 : the object at p in S is a File
                    => ls (S, p) = the empty forest plus the object at p in S
     rm : rm (S, p, n) = S pruned at p / n
     rmdir : rmdir (S, p, n) = S pruned at p / n   )
end SYSTEM

proc TREE-WITH-PATH (LEAF) forget the son of _ named _

      use TREE (LEAF) , PATH

func

   the object at _ in _   : Path * Tree -> Leaf U Tree

   _ plus _ added under _ : Tree * Leaf U Tree * Path -> Tree

   _ pruned at _   : Tree * Path -> Tree

pred

   _ is an existing path of _ : Path * Leaf U Tree

precond forall p : Path , T : Tree , LT : Leaf U Tree

(obj : the object at p in T is defined **when** p is an existing path of T

  plus : T plus LT added under p is defined **when** p is an existing path of T

                                    & the object at p in T is a Tree

  prun : T pruned at p is defined **when** p is a name is false

                                    & p is an existing path of T is **true**   )

axiom forall n1, n2 : Name , p : Path , T : Tree , LT : Leaf U Tree

(exist1 : n1 is an existing path of T **iff** n1 = the name of T

  exist2 : n1 / n2 is an existing path of T **iff** n1 = the name of T

                               & n2 belongs to the namelist of T

  exist3 : n2 belongs to the namelist of T is false

                             => n1 / n2 / p is an existing path of T is false

  exist4 : n2 belongs to the namelist of T =>

                n1 / n2 / p is an existing path of T **iff** n1 = the name of T

                        & n2 / p is an existing path of the son of T named n2

  obj : the object at n1 in T = T *" due to the preconditions, n1 is the name of T "*

  obj2 : the object at n1 / p in T =

                      the object at p in the son of T named (the first name of p)

  plus1 : T plus LT added under n1 = < n1 . the content of T plus LT >

  plus2 : T plus LT added under n1 / n2 = T pruned at n1 / n2

                               plus (the object at n1 / n2 in T

                                      plus LT added under n2)

                               added under n1

  plus3 : T plus LT added under n1 / n2 / p = T pruned at n1 / n2

                                   plus (the object at n1 / n2 in T

                                      plus LT added under n2 / p)

                               added under n1

  prun1 : T pruned at n1 / n2 = < n1 . the content of T less the object named n2 >

  prun2 : T pruned at n1 / n2 / p = T pruned at n1 / n2

                             plus (the object at n1 / n2 in T

                                pruned at n2 / p)

                            added under n1   )

end TREE-WITH-PATH

```
proc TREE ( LEAF )
     use NAMELIST
   sorts Tree, Forest
   cons
     < _ . _ >          : Name * Forest -> Tree
     the empty forest :                  -> Forest
     _ plus _           : Forest * Leaf U Tree -> Forest
   func
     the name of      : Tree -> Name
     the content of   : Tree -> Forest
     the name list of : Forest -> Namelist
     the son of _ named _   : Tree * Name -> Leaf U Tree
     _ less the object named _ : Forest * Name -> Forest
   pred
     _ is empty       : Forest
   precond forall  T : Tree ,  n : Name
   ( son : the son of T named n is defined when
                                        n belongs to the name list of the content of T   )
   axiom forall  n, n' : Name ,  F : Forest,  LT : Leaf U Tree
   ( na : the name of < n . F > = n
     co : the content of < n . F > = F
     less1 : F is empty => F less the object named n = F
     less2 : n = the name of LT
             => (F plus LT) less the object named n = F less the object named n
     less3 : n # the name of LT
             => (F plus LT) less the object named n = F less the object named n plus LT
     nl1 : the name list of the empty forest = the empty list
     nl2 : the name of LT belongs to the name list of F
             => the name list of (F plus LT) = the name list of F
     nl3 : the name of LT belongs to the name list of F is false
             => the name list of (F plus LT) = the name list of F plus the name of LT
     son1 : n' = the name of LT => the son of < n . F plus LT > named n' = LT
     son2 : n' # the name of LT
             => the son of < n . F plus LT > named n' = the son of < n . F > named n'
     ise1 : the empty forest is empty is true
     ise2 : (F plus LT) is empty is false   )
   end TREE
```

spec PATH

    use NAME

  sort Path

  cons   " *there is at least one name in a path* "

    _   : Name -> Path

    _ / _   : Path * Name -> Path

    _ / _   : Name * Path -> Path

  func

    the first name of : Path -> Name

    the last part of : Path -> Path

    the first part of : Path -> Path

    the last name of : Path -> Name

  pred

    _ is a name : Path

  precond forall p : Path

  (fp : the first part of p is defined when p is a name is false

    lp : the last part of p is defined when p is a name is false   )

  axiom forall n, n1, n2 : Name , p, p1, p2 : Path

  (ep : n1 / p1 = p2 / n2 **iff** n1 = the first name of p2 & p1 = the last part of p2 / n2

    fn1 : the first name of n = n

    fn2 : the first name of (p / n) = the first name of p

    fn3 : the first name of (n / p) = n

    lp1 : the last part of (p / n) = the last part of p / n

    lp2 : the last part of (n / p) = p

    fp1 : the first part of (p / n) = p

    fp2 : the first part of (n / p) = n / the first part of p

    ln1 : the last name of n = n

    ln2 : the last name of (p / n) = n

    ln3 : the last name of (n / p) = the last name of p

    isn1 : n is a name is **true**

    isn2 : p / n is a name is **false**

    isn3 : n / p is a name is **false**)

end PATH

param LEAF

    use NAME

  sort Leaf

  func

    the name of : Leaf -> Name

end LEAF

draft TEXT-FILE
    use NAME, TEXT
  sort File
  func
    the name of   : File -> Name
    the content of : File -> Text
    < _ . _ >   : Name * Text -> File
  axiom forall n : Name , t : Text
  (na : the name of < n . t > = n
    co : the content of < n . t > = t)
end TEXT-FILE

draft BINARY-FILE
    use NAME, BINARY-CODE
  sort File
  func
    the name of   : File -> Name
    the content of : File -> Bincode
    < _ . _ >   : Name * Bincode -> File
  axiom forall n : Name , b : Bincode
  (na : the name of < n . b > = n
    co : the content of < n . b > = b)
end BINARY-FILE

draft FILE
    enrich TEXT-FILE, BINARY-FILE
  func
    the empty file named : Name -> File
  axiom forall n : Name
  (na : the name of the empty file named n = n)
end FILE

spec FILE **from** FILE
  func
    file : File -> { empty, ascii text, executable }
  cons
    the empty file named , < _ . _ >
  precond forall f : File
  (co : the content of f is defined when file f # empty)
  axiom forall n : Name , t : Text , b : Bincode ,
  (file1 : file (the empty file named n) = empty
    file2 : file < n . t > = ascii text
    file3 : file < n . b > = executable)
end FILE

Efficient Implementation of an Algebraic Specification Language

H. Klaeren
K. Indermark
Lehrstuhl für Informatik II , RWTH Aachen
Büchel 29–31, D-5100 Aachen, West Germany
e-mail: klaeren@rwthinf.uucp

Abstract

We consider the implementation of SRDL, a small algebraic specification language with particular emphasis on *structural recursion* which is for abstract data types the analogue of primitive recursion. We demonstrate how the regular behaviour of structural recursion can be exploited for generating better code. Technically, this is achieved by generalizing loop iteration on integers to bottom-up iteration on trees. Here, it is possible to replace the function stack of activation records by simpler *control stacks*. On the machine level, this tree walk is performed by a generalization of the Schorr-Waite algorithm to n-ary trees, causing only a small overhead in execution time but no additional memory requirements. The resulting code is faster and requires less storage than usual *call by value* code.

1 Introduction

There are (at least) two kinds of algebraic specification languages: those with constructive and those with non-constructive definition of operations. Non-constructive languages use sets of (possibly conditional) equations or rewrite rules for defining the semantics of abstract data types whereas constructive languages distinguish between *constructors* and *defined functions* and use recursive definitions for functions on the free algebra generated by the constructors. Among the constructive languages are SRDL [6,7], OBSCURE [11] and ORS [12]. In a certain sense, also HOPE [1] and ML [2] can be viewed as constructive algebraic specification languages.

In this paper, we shall consider only the constructive case. Here, efficient implementation of recursive function definitions is of central importance. Typically, recursive function definitions in programming languages are implemented using a *run time stack*. Functional programming systems such as ML [2] generally can only provide an economic iterative implementation for the simplest case of recursion (so-called *tail recursion*).

In this paper, we propose a different implementation strategy based on the *structure of the underlying data type*. Our research on algebraically specified abstract data types [7] and compiler descriptions [4] has led to the observation that many recursive definitions occurring in practice operate on inductively generated data types such as lists or trees in a rather disciplined way comparable to primitive recursion on non-negative integers. The regularity of *structural recursion* allows compile time knowledge about the sequence in which computation will visit the nodes of the argument tree. This eliminates the need for a run time stack of activation records. We show how structural recursive definitions can be implemented by iterative programs and what kind of performance improvements can be expected. The algorithm presented has been implemented in a compiler for SRDL [8]; it could be adapted to e.g. HOPE or ML compilers with not too much effort.

This paper is an elaboration of [10].

```
MODULE PseudoLISP =
SORTS list, smallchar ;
CONSTRUCTORS smallchar = (a,b,c,d,e,f,g);
                 list = ( NIL , " smallchar " , CONS list list ) ;

OPERATIONS
    (append v:list w: list): list =
        CASE v OF
            NIL: w;
            " a1 ": CONS v w;
            CONS hd tl: CONS hd (append tl w)
        END
END
```

Figure 1: A fragment of pure LISP in SRDL

2 SRDL

SRDL is a small algebraic specification language; it has been intentionally restricted to the most essential concepts because the relevant phenomena can then be easier studied. An SRDL specification starts with a specification of a *signature* sig = $\langle S, \Sigma \rangle$ of an *abstract data type* consisting of a set S of SORTS and a set Σ of CONSTRUCTORS. Standard data types BOOLEAN and CARDINAL (= non-negative integers) with the obvious constructors and basic operations are predefined and therefore implicitly contained in every signature. We assume for the present that all user-defined data types correspond to *free algebras* (i.e. their carriers can be tought of as sets of *terms*) although in [7] we offer opportunities for a more general framework. The main part of an SRDL specification defines OPERATIONS over this signature using recursion and case distinction on constructors of the recursion argument sort. This is done using pattern match syntax much in the spirit of HOPE, the main difference being that SRDL insists on a *complete* case distinction on all constructors and that only *one-level* constructor terms are allowed in patterns. *SRDL* has a very flexible *distributed fix* notation for terms. Details about SRDL can be found in [6,7,8].

SRDL presently contains no mechanism for higher type functions although it would be relatively simple to introduce functional parameters of the same kind as in the LISP function MAPCAR; the essential property is that the functional parameter is passed unchanged from one function call to the next. Functions that return functions as values or specify a recursion on a functional type contradict the current SRDL philosophy.

Just to give a familiar example, figure 1 shows a fragment of pure LISP in SRDL. The SORTS clause declares two sorts list and smallchar for use in this specification. The CONSTRUCTORS clause declares the constructing operations for every sort of the SORTS clause. Usually, there is at least one nullary constructor (e.g. NIL $\in \Sigma^{(\epsilon,list)}$) together with some non-nullary constructors (e.g. CONS $\in \Sigma^{(list\ list,list)}$). The CONSTRUCTORS clause for list can be interpreted as a definition of all well-formed terms denoting elements of sort list: 1) NIL is such a term, 2) if x has sort smallchar then "x" is a list-term and 3) if v and w are list-terms, then CONS v w is a list-term.

The OPERATIONS clause in figure 1 defines a single binary operation append on lists. The first line defines the *type* of append and, at the same time, the syntactic form of an append-term, which we have defined to agree with standard LISP syntax. Different syntax would be possible with the same effort, e.g. infix notation (v:list append w:list):list or standard mathematical notation append(v,w: list):list or whatever. In the definition of append, its first argument (v) is *decomposed* into its outermost constructor and its arguments (if any). The pattern match syntax introduces local names for these arguments which we call *formal predecessors* and whose scope is just the term after the corresponding ":". While it is possible to specify *general recursive* operations in SRDL, the main intent of the language and its implementation is to encourage use of *structural recursion*, which in our terminology means the analogue of primitive recursion. The notion of structural recursion shall be explained below. The operation **append** as specified in figure 1 is indeed structurally recursive, because the recursive function call refers only to the formal predecessor of the recursion argument v: (append (CONS hd tl) w) = (CONS hd (append tl w)). For primitive recursive (arithmetic) functions it is well-known that they can be computed by iterative programs; in this paper, we extend this technique to arbitrary algebraic data types.

One standard technique for the implementation of recursive function definitions is the so-called *call by value* (cbv) technique (see section 4), also denoted as *leftmost-innermost* technique. This technique is used by the compilers for most programming languages although it is not strictly correct. For the evaluation of, e.g. (append (CONS " b " (CONS " a " NIL)) (CONS " c " (CONS " d " NIL))), the call by value technique would build a run time stack containing return adresses and the respective arguments of every recursive call of append, i.e. (CONS " b " (CONS " a " NIL)), then (CONS " a " NIL) and finally NIL. When the innermost call is active, the run time stack therefore would contain a *complete decomposition* of the recursion argument in a rather redundant form together with additional information. On the other hand, the program generated by our *structural recursive* (sr) technique has a single loop which performs a bottom up walk in the input tree without using a run time stack. It starts from the leftmost leaf (i.e. NIL) and, in 3 iterations of the loop, proceeds to the root. Our SRDL compiler [8] automatically selects *cbv compilation* or *sr compilation* (with recursion elimination) depending on the properties of the respective function definition.

We shall now specify syntax and semantics of defined functions in SRDL for the simple case where there is only a single function definition in the present specification.

Let $\#(f)$ denote the arity of f. Let **sig** denote the signature determined by the standard data types (primitive sorts) with the obvious operations and the SORTS–CONSTRUCTORS clause of the present specification, $T_{\text{sig}}(X)$ the free term algebra of sig with generating set X. We call sig an *admissible signature*; an *admissible algebra* has the usual interpretation for the primitive sorts whereas all other sorts are assumed to be *free*.

We then consider a function definition (in standard mathematical notation, w.l.g.) of the form

$$F(x_1 : s_1; \ldots; x_n : s_n) : s = \tau \ .$$

This is syntactically correct if either $\tau \in T_{\text{sig}}(\{x_1, \ldots, x_n\})$ or

$$\tau = \ \text{CASE} \quad x_j \ \text{OF}$$
$$p_1 : \tau_1;$$
$$\ldots$$
$$p_k : \tau_k$$
$$\text{END}$$

where $p_i = c_i(z_1, \ldots, z_{\#(c_i)})$ and $\tau_i \in T_{\text{sig} \cup \{F(w,s)\}}(\{x_1, \ldots, x_n, z_1, \ldots, z_{\#(c_i)}\})$.

In this paper, we therefore shall assume that the function to be considered is named F with formal parameters $x_1, ..., x_n$ where the recursion variable (i.e. the variable which is decomposed in the CASE clause, if any) is x_j. The type of F is (w, s) where $w = s_1 \ldots s_n$. The "formal predecessors" in constructor patterns are always $z_1, ..., z_m$ and relevant constructors are named $c_1, ..., c_k$.

We distinguish several *recursion types* of F where **recType**$(F) \in \{none, virtual, algebraic, structural, general\}$ means the following:

$$
\mathbf{recType}(F) \;=\; \begin{cases}
\textit{none :} & \text{The right hand side of the definition of } F \text{ is a simple term} \\
& \tau \in \mathcal{T}_{\mathbf{sig}}\{x_1,\ldots,x_n\}. \\[4pt]
\textit{virtual:} & \text{The right hand side is a CASE clause which in none of its} \\
& \text{branches } \tau_i \text{ has an occurrence of } F. \\[4pt]
\textit{algebraic:} & \text{The respective right hand side is a CASE clause which in some} \\
& \text{of its branches has subterms } F(t_1,\ldots,t_n). \text{ In these terms we} \\
& \text{have } t_i = x_i \text{ for } i \neq j \text{ and } t_j = z_l \text{ for some formal predecessor} \\
& z_l \text{ occurring in the corresponding constructor pattern } p. \text{ These} \\
& \text{are the only occurrences of formal predecessors.} \\[4pt]
\textit{structural:} & \text{like } \textit{algebraic}, \text{ but with occurrences of formal predecessors out-} \\
& \text{side recursive calls.} \\[4pt]
\textit{general:} & \text{The respective right hand side is a CASE clause with no restric-} \\
& \text{tion on } F\text{-terms.}
\end{cases}
$$

The semantics of $F^{(w,s)}$ in $\mathcal{A}$ is defined as a function $[\![F]\!] : \mathcal{A}^w \to \mathcal{A}^s$ with

$$
[\![F]\!](a_1,\ldots,a_n) = \mathbf{Pol}_n[\![\tau]\!](a_1,\ldots,a_n,\varepsilon)
$$

if $\mathbf{recType}(F) = \textit{none}$, where $\mathbf{Pol}_n[\![\;]\!]$ is the *polynomial semantics* to be defined below and

$$
[\![F]\!](a_1,\ldots,a_n) = \mathbf{Pol}_n[\![\tau_i]\!](a_1,\ldots,a_n,z_1\ldots z_m)
$$

if $\mathbf{recType}(F) \neq \textit{none}$ and $a_j = c_i(z_1,\ldots,z_m)$.
Polynomial semantics $\mathbf{Pol}_n[\![\;]\!]$ is defined as follows:

$$
\begin{aligned}
\mathbf{Pol}_n[\![\;]\!] : \mathcal{A}^n \times \mathcal{A}^* &\to \mathcal{A} \\
\mathbf{Pol}_n[\![z_i]\!](a_1,\ldots,a_n,w) &= a_i \\
\mathbf{Pol}_n[\![ct_1\ldots t_l]\!](a_1,\ldots,a_n,w) &= c_{\mathcal{A}}(\mathbf{Pol}_n[\![t_1]\!](a_1,\ldots,w),\ldots,\mathbf{Pol}_n[\![t_l]\!](a_1,\ldots,w)) \\
\mathbf{Pol}_n[\![Ft_1\ldots t_n]\!](a_1,\ldots,a_n,w) &= [\![F]\!](\mathbf{Pol}_n[\![t_1]\!](a_1,\ldots,w),\ldots,\mathbf{Pol}_n[\![t_n]\!](a_1,\ldots,w)) \\
\mathbf{Pol}_n[\![z_i]\!](a_1,\ldots,a_n,b_1\ldots b_k) &= b_i
\end{aligned}
$$

3 The abstract stack machine

When compiling *SRDL*, we use an *abstract stack machine* on an intermediate level because this facilitates compiler correctness proofs and the portability of the compiler to a variety of machines.

Stack machines are a rather natural tool for implementation of programming languages, where stacks are used in two contexts:

1. expression evaluation can take profit of a stack for managing temporary locations needed for subexpression values *("data stack")*,

2. (recursive) function calls are implemented using a stack whose *activation records* contain return adresses, function arguments and local variables *("run time stack")*.

Our abstract stack machine ASM($\mathcal{A}$) is a compromise between the usual run time stack technique and the necessary mechanism for iterative implementation of structural recursion. Besides that, we have designed it in such a way that it can be easily implemented on conventional processor architectures. The only unrealistic feature of ASM($\mathcal{A}$) is that it can store an arbitrarily large term (or tree) in a single stack location, but this is convenient for mathematical treatment of programs. For the iterative computation of structural recursive functions, the abstract machine must be able to invert an input tree. This is done by a single instruction CDEC using two further stacks; both of these and the unrealistic instruction CDEC which inverts a tree in a single step will disappear when the abstract machine is implemented on a practical processor (see section 5). In this paper, the run time stack is called *function stack*.

The abstract machine presented in this paper is slightly simpler than the one in [8] since here we consider only a single function definition.

Definition: Let **sig** $= \langle S, \Sigma \rangle$ be an admissible signature, $\mathcal{A}$ an admissible algebra of sig. The *abstract stack machine for the algebra* $\mathcal{A}$ is given by the set of states

$$\text{ASM}(\mathcal{A}) := \text{IP} \times \text{DS} \times \text{CC} \times \text{FS} \times \text{IS} \times \text{PS}$$

where

IP	$:= \mathbf{N}$	(=non-negative integers, instruction pointer)
DS	$:= A^*$	(data stack)
CC	$:= \Sigma \cup \{\mu\}$	(condition code)
FS	$:= (\mathbf{N} \times A^*)^*$	(function stack)
IS	$:= \Sigma^*$	(iteration stack)
PS	$:= A^*$	(predecessor stack)

and the following set of instructions:

$\Gamma(\Sigma) := \{$ EXEC f	$(f \in \Sigma,$ execute operation f on DS),
DEC	(decompose top element of DS),
LODA i	$(i \in \mathbf{N},$ load i-th argument from FS to DS),
LODR r	$(r \in \mathbf{N},$ load relative from DS to DS),
CDEC n	$(n \in \mathbf{N},$ complete decomposition),
LOOP n	$(n \in \mathbf{N},$ loop iteration),
BRANCH	(branch according to CC),
CALL $F^{(w,s)}$	$(w \in S^*, s \in S,$ call function recursively),
RET	(return from function),
IPOP	(pop CC from IS),
LODP r	$(r \in \mathbf{N},$ load relative from PS to DS),
POPP n	$(n \in \mathbf{N},$ discard n elements from PS) $\}$.

The *data stack* DS is the central computational facility of ASM($\mathcal{A}$). The operations of the primitive sorts can be performed on DS and trees of free sorts can be constructed there from other trees. Furthermore, trees can be *decomposed* into the constructor at their root and its immediate subtrees which we call *predecessors*. For sake of uniformity, also the usual *tests* on primitive sorts are subsumed under the notion of decomposition. The *function stack* FS serves for management of return adresses and function arguments in the standard way. *Iteration stack* IS and *predecessor stack* PS serve for the implementation of structural recursion; IS will contain sequences of constructors and PS sequences of subtrees which altogether describe an input tree in a "bottom up" way.

ASM($\mathcal{A}$) *programs* are sequences of (possibly labelled) ASM($\mathcal{A}$) instructions. We use constructor symbols $f \in \Sigma$ as labels. We shall now describe the semantics of the instructions. Most of the instructions are only partially defined; we do not care about the undefined cases since our compiler will only generate code that does not lead to undefined instructions. Our stack notation separates stack locations by a period and has the top of stack to the right hand side.

EXEC f and DEC are the operations dealing with the underlying algebraic data type. Their semantics is defined as follows:

EXEC f: This executes operation f on the topmost elements of DS. For basic sorts this is the usual arithmetic/logical operation, for free sorts it is a tree-building operation. Let $f_{\mathcal{A}}$ denote the interpretation of operation f in $\mathcal{A}$.

$$\left[\begin{array}{l} DS = ds.d_1.d_2 \ldots d_n \\ f \in \Sigma^{(s_1 \ldots s_n, s)} \\ d_i \in A^{s_i} \text{ for all } i \end{array}\right] \longrightarrow DS = ds.f_A(d_1, \ldots, d_n).$$

DEC: When $DS = ds.x$ and $PS = p$, then DEC has the following effects, depending on x:

1. $x \in \{\text{true, false}\}$: $DS = ds$ and $CC = \text{true}$ or false, respectively.

2. $x = 0 \in \text{CARDINAL}$: $DS = ds$ and $CC = \text{zero}$.

3. $x = n+1 \in \text{CARDINAL}$: $DS = ds.n$ and $CC = \text{suc}$. (Note that this decrements a non-zero top of DS.)

4. $x = ft_1...t_n$ of a free sort: $DS = ds$, $PS = p.t_n \ldots t_2.t_1$ and $CC = f$. (Note the reversion of order of the t_i.)

DEC is undefined for empty DS.

CALL $F^{(w,s)}$ and RET are the operations dealing with subprograms for defined functions. We assume that, given the *name* $F^{(w,s)}$ of a defined function, the abstract machine $\text{ASM}(A)$ knows the entry point i_F of code for this function. Of course, this kind of *function table* is handled by the back end of our compiler. In this paper where we consider only a single function $F^{(w,s)}$, the entry point i_F will always be zero.

CALL $F^{(w,s)}$: Provided that there is a sufficient number of arguments of the appropriate sorts on DS, CALL $F^{(w,s)}$ moves these to a new activation record on the function stack FS, at the same time saving the return address there. Let $w = s_1 \ldots s_n$; then:

$$\left[\begin{array}{l} DS = ds.d_1 \ldots d_n, \\ d_i \in A^{s_i} \text{ for all } i \\ FS = f \\ IP = ip \end{array}\right] \longrightarrow \left[\begin{array}{l} DS = ds \\ IP = i_F = 0 \\ FS = f.(ip+1, d_1 \ldots d_n) \end{array}\right].$$

RET: This pops an activation record from FS and returns to its return address:

$$FS = f.(i, w) \longrightarrow \left[\begin{array}{l} IP = i \\ FS = f \end{array}\right].$$

When FS is empty, the machine stops.

LOOP n and CDEC n are special instructions for implementation of structural recursive functions by iterative programs. CDEC n does a *complete decomposition* of the n-th function argument. The constructor symbols in the input tree are pushed to IS and the respective subtrees to PS. The main purpose of LOOP n is a jump backwards to the nearest IPOP or DEC instruction, thus entering the next loop iteration. However if $n > 0$, it first saves the current function value at the top of DS to a place deeper in DS and removes some other entries in DS which are not longer needed. The precise description follows:

CDEC n: For an algebra A and $s \in S$ define

$$\begin{array}{rcl} \text{COps}_s : A & \longrightarrow & \Sigma^* \\ \text{COps}_s(a) & := & \left\{\begin{array}{ll} a & \text{if } a \notin A^s \\ F.\text{COps}_s(a_n) \ldots \text{COps}_s(a_1) & \text{if } a = Fa_1 \ldots a_n \in A^s \end{array}\right. \\[2mm] \text{CArgs}_s : A & \longrightarrow & A^* \\ \text{CArgs}_s(a) & := & \left\{\begin{array}{ll} \varepsilon & \text{if } a \notin A^s \\ a_n \ldots a_1.\text{CArgs}_s(a_n) \ldots \text{CArgs}_s(a_1) & \text{if } a = Fa_1 \ldots a_n \in A^s \end{array}\right. \end{array}$$

Then CDEC n works as follows:

$$FS = fs.a_1 \ldots a_n \ldots a_m \longrightarrow \begin{bmatrix} \text{IS} = \text{COps}(a_n) \\ \text{PS} = \text{CArgs}(a_n) \end{bmatrix}$$

LOOP n: Let i_0 be the instruction address of the nearest IPOP or DEC instruction before i. Then:

$$\begin{bmatrix} \text{IP} = i \\ \text{DS} = ds.d_n \ldots d_1.x \end{bmatrix} \longrightarrow \begin{bmatrix} \text{IP} = i_0 \\ \text{DS} = ds.x \end{bmatrix}$$

The remaining instructions are rather simple:

LODA i pushes the i-th argument from the topmost activation record of FS to DS:

$$\begin{bmatrix} \text{DS} = ds \\ \text{FS} = fs.(ip, d_1, \ldots, d_n) \end{bmatrix} \longrightarrow \text{DS} = ds.d_i$$

LODR r pushes the r-th element from the top of DS to DS:

$$\text{DS} = ds.d_r \ldots d_1.d_0 \longrightarrow \text{DS} = ds.d_r \ldots d_1.d_0.d_r$$

BRANCH jumps to the instruction whose label is f if $\text{CC} = f \in \Sigma$. If $\text{CC} = \mu$, it simply skips to the next instruction.

IPOP copies the top of IS to CC and pops IS; when IS is empty, it sets CC to μ:

$$\text{IS} = is.F \longrightarrow \begin{bmatrix} \text{IS} = is \\ \text{CC} = F \end{bmatrix}$$

$$\text{IS} = \varepsilon \longrightarrow \text{CC} = \mu$$

LODP r ($r \geq 1$) pushes the r-th element from the top of PS to DS.

$$\begin{bmatrix} \text{DS} = ds \\ \text{PS} = ps.p_r \ldots p_1) \end{bmatrix} \longrightarrow \text{DS} = ds.p_r$$

POPP n pops n elements of PS and discards them:

$$\text{PS} = ps.p_n \ldots p_1 \longrightarrow \text{PS} = ps.$$

4 Compilation of SRDL to stack code

The main idea in the sr compilation of SRDL is the inversion of a tree walk: Instead of decomposing an input tree recursively ("top down") and pushing subtrees onto a function stack of activation records, we invert the input tree with a CDEC instruction and traverse it "bottom up". The inversion of the tree walk is nontrivial since the abstract machine stores an arbitrarily large tree in a single location of DS.

The program generated from a structural recursive function definition starts with a CDEC instruction. We then enter a single loop during which both IS and PS are popped and function results are accumulated in the data stack DS until the whole input tree has been traversed and the function result can be found on top of DS. The arguments for a function are evaluated and pushed onto DS before calling the function; they are moved from DS to FS by the CALL instruction. Recursive calls which conform to the rules of structural recursion are not translated to CALL instructions of the abstract machine, but to LODR instructions referring to results of the preceding loop iteration. This saves a considerable amount of memory and speeds up execution, because no handling of activation records and no parameter passing is required.

In this paper, we consider only the translation of a single function, assuming that there is a main program calling this function properly. The general case is treated in [8].

We use the terminology of section 2. Let Π denote the set of ASM($\mathcal{A}$) programs. In the following description of the compiler functions we use self-explaining structuring syntax. Our compiler functions shall generate parts of ASM($\mathcal{A}$) programs which shall be concatenated by ";". We first describe *cbv* compilation.

$$COp : \text{operation} \to \Pi \quad \text{(compilation of operations)}$$
$$CV : \text{expression} \to \Pi \quad \text{(compilation of expressions)}$$

$$COp(F(x_1 : s_1; \ldots; x_n : s_n) : s = \alpha) := \begin{cases} CV(\alpha); \text{RET} & \text{if } \text{recType}(F) = none \\ CV(\alpha) & \text{otherwise} \end{cases}$$

The translation of $F^{(w,s)}$ is a subprogram starting at address 0. A 'main program' computing $F(a_1, \ldots, a_n)$ first pushes the values $a_1, \ldots, a_n$ onto the data stack and then executes a CALL $F^{(w,s)}$ instruction. The subprogram returns to its calling place by means of the RET instruction after $CV(\alpha)$ if $\text{recType}(F) = none$; otherwise RET is contained in $CV(\alpha)$ (see below).

$$CV(x_r) := \text{LODA } r$$

The argument x_r can be found on the function stack.

$$CV(c_r(\alpha_1, ..., \alpha_{\#(c_r)})) := \quad \textbf{FOR } i := 1 \textbf{ TO } \#(c_r)$$
$$CV(\alpha_i);$$
$$\textbf{ENDFOR}$$
$$\text{EXEC } c_r$$

A constructor term is evaluated by first evaluating its arguments and then executing the corresponding constructor on DS.

$$CV(z_r) := \text{LODP } r$$

A predecessor value is found on PS where ist has been left by a DEC instruction.

$$CV(F(\alpha_1, ..., \alpha_{\#(F)})) := \quad \textbf{FOR } i := 1 \textbf{ TO } \#(F)$$
$$CV(\alpha_i);$$
$$\textbf{ENDFOR}$$
$$\text{CALL } F^{(w,s)}$$

This is similar to the translation of a constructor term. The recursive call is translated into a recursive call on the machine level; it is treated there by means of the function stack.

$$CV(\textsf{CASE } x_j \textsf{ OF}$$
$$p_1 : \alpha_1;$$
$$\ldots$$
$$p_k : \alpha_k$$
$$\textsf{END}) := \qquad \text{LODA } j;$$
$$\text{DEC};$$
$$\text{BRANCH};$$
$$\textbf{FOR } i := 1 \textbf{ TO } k$$
$$c_i : \quad CV(\alpha_i);$$
$$\text{POPP } \#(c_i);$$
$$\text{RET}$$
$$\textbf{ENDFOR}$$

In the compilation of the CASE construct, the cbv schema does a simple decomposition of its argument pushing the predecessor values to PS, evaluates the corresponding CASE branch (possibly calling F recursively) and afterwards removes the predecessor values from PS.

The inductive correctness proof for cbv compilation is almost trivial: We have to prove that an instruction CALL $F^{(w,s)}$ at location ip in an ASM($\mathcal{A}$)-program leads from a state of ASM($\mathcal{A}$) with DS $= ds.a_1 \ldots a_n$ and IP $= ip$ to a state with DS $= ds.\llbracket F \rrbracket(a_1, \ldots, a_n)$ and IP $= ip + 1$ where FS, PS and IS are as before:

The parameters $a_1, \ldots, a_n$ are moved from DS to FS by the CALL instruction and IS is never used by a cbv program. Since either $COp(F \ldots) = CV(\alpha); \text{RET}$ or $CV(\alpha)$ itself contains a RET instruction and since RET clears the function stack and returns to $ip + 1$, it remains to show that the code $CV(\alpha)$ leaves PS as it is and pushes $\mathbf{POL}_n\llbracket \alpha \rrbracket(a_1, \ldots, a_n, -)$ to DS. We prove this by induction on α:

1. $\alpha = x_r$: trivial.

2. $\alpha = c_r(\alpha_1, \ldots, \alpha_{\#(c_r)})$: assuming correctness of $CV(\alpha_i)$ for the relevant i's, this is also trivial.

3. $\alpha = z_r$: according to syntax rules, this is only possible in a branch of a CASE statement; in this case, PS $= ps.p_{\#(c_m)} \ldots p_1$ because of the DEC instruction of 5. The LODP instruction generated by $CV(z_r)$ therefore pushes p_r onto DS. On the other hand, we have $\mathbf{POL}_n\llbracket z_r \rrbracket(a_1, \ldots, a_n, p_{\#(c_m)} \ldots p_1) = p_r$ which proves the correctness of this case.

4. $\alpha = F(\alpha_1, \ldots, \alpha_n)$: similar to 2.

5. $\alpha = \text{CASE } x_j \text{ OF} \ldots$: the corresponding code loads argument x_j, decomposes it such that it vanishes from DS, leaving constructor information in CC and predecessors in PS. Afterwards, a BRANCH to the corresponding code piece is performed, the predecessors on PS are removed (leaving PS as it was before DEC, and a RET instruction terminates execution of this function call.

Structural recursive (sr) compilation of SRDL is described by the following translation functions; it is correct only if the function F to be compiled is indeed structurally recursive, i.e. $\mathbf{recType}(f) \in \{algebraic, structural\}$. Note that we shall define these functions with a maximal similarity to the corresponding cbv functions. For instance, the function stack is not strictly necessary for sr functions.

$$COp : \text{operation} \to \Pi \qquad \text{(compilation of operations)}$$
$$CS : \text{expression} \times \mathbf{N} \to \Pi \qquad \text{(compilation of expressions)}$$

The integer parameter to CS serves to keep track of offsets of function values on DS from the previous loop iteration to be accessed in relative load and store operations.

$$COp(F(x_1 : s_1; \ldots; x_n : s_n) : s = \alpha) := CS(\alpha, 0)$$

As in the case of cbv compilation, the translation of $F^{(w,s)}$ is a subprogram starting at address 0. The initial offset (second parameter) is 0.

$$CS(x_r, \text{offset}) := \text{LODA } r$$

$$CS(c_r(\alpha_1, ..., \alpha_{\#(c_r)}), \text{offset}) := \ \mathbf{FOR}\ i := 1\ \mathbf{TO}\ \#(c_r)$$
$$CS(\alpha_i, \text{offset} + i - 1);$$
$$\mathbf{ENDFOR}$$
$$\text{EXEC } c_r$$

These cases are identical to cbv compilation except that we have to increment offsets before evaluating every α_i.

$$CS(z_r, \text{offset}) := \text{LODP } r$$

A predecessor value is found on PS where ist has been left by the CDEC instruction.

$$CS(F(...z_r...), \text{offset}) := \text{LODR offset} - r \ ,$$
$$\text{if this is an admissible recursive call (primitive recursion!)}$$

The translation of the admissible recursive call shows that it does not lead to recursion in the abstract machine since there we have a bottom up computation which guarantees that the required value has already been computed and can be found somewhere on DS.

$$CS(\text{CASE } x_j \text{ OF}$$
$$\qquad p_1 : \alpha_1;$$
$$\qquad \cdots$$
$$\qquad p_k : \alpha_k$$
$$\text{END}, 0) :=$$

$$\qquad\qquad \text{CDEC } j; \quad (\text{decompose } x_j)$$
$$\qquad\qquad \text{IPOP}; \quad (\text{next node in input tree})$$
$$\qquad\qquad \text{BRANCH};$$
$$\qquad\qquad \text{RET}; \quad (\text{this occurs when } CC = \mu)$$
$$\qquad \textbf{FOR } i := 1 \textbf{ TO } k$$
$$\qquad c_i : \quad CS(\alpha_i, \#(c_i));$$
$$\qquad\qquad \text{POPP } \#(c_i);$$
$$\qquad\qquad \text{LOOP } \#(c_i)$$
$$\qquad \textbf{ENDFOR}$$

This is the crucial point in the definition of sr compilation: The recursion argument is first completely decomposed to IS and PS; we then enter a loop without recursive calls of F. At the beginning of the loop, IS is popped and a conditional jump according to the top element is performed. The body of the loop contains the translations of the CASE branches. At the end of the loop, a proper number of predecessors is removed from top of PS.

The inductive correctness proof for sr compilation is slightly more complicated than for the cbv case. Again we want to prove that an instruction CALL $F^{(w,s)}$ at location ip in an ASM($\mathcal{A}$)-program leads from a state of ASM($\mathcal{A}$) with DS $= ds.a_1...a_n$ and IP $= ip$ to a state with DS $= ds.[\![F]\!](a_1, ..., a_n)$ and IP $= ip + 1$ where FS, PS and IS are as before:

The parameters $a_1, ..., a_n$ are again moved from DS to FS by the CALL instruction. Since $COp(F...) = CS(\alpha)$ and since the RET contained in $CS(\alpha)$ clears the function stack and returns to $ip + 1$, it remains to show that the code $CS(\alpha)$ leaves PS and IS as they are and pushes $\text{POL}_n[\![\alpha]\!](a_1, ..., a_n, -)$ to DS. We prove this by induction on α:

1. The cases $\alpha = x_r$ and $\alpha = c_r(\alpha_1, ..., \alpha_{\#(c_r)})$ are treated like in the cbv case.

2. $\alpha = F(x_1, ..., x_r, ..., x_n)$: This can only be proved correct in connection with treatment of the CASE construct; see lemma 2.

3. $\alpha = \mathsf{CASE}\ x_j\ \mathsf{OF}\ldots$: The main task in this case is the proof of proper dependencies between DS, IS and PS. First we show the following lemma:

Lemma 1: Let $b_r = [\![F]\!](a_1, \ldots, a_{j-1}, b'_r, a_{j+1}, \ldots, a_n)$, α' a subexpression of α_i, $k = \#(c_i)$ and let ip be the address of the first instruction in $CS(\alpha', k + \text{offset})$. Then an $\mathrm{ASM}(\mathcal{A})$-configuration with

$$
\begin{aligned}
\mathrm{IP} &= ip, \\
\mathrm{DS} &= ds.b_1, \ldots, b_k, u_1, \ldots, u_{\text{offset}}, \\
\mathrm{IS} &= is.c_i, \\
\mathrm{FS} &= fs.(r, a_1, \ldots, a_n) \text{ and} \\
\mathrm{PS} &= ps.b'_k \ldots b'_1
\end{aligned}
$$

will lead to a configuration with

$$
\mathrm{DS} = ds.b_1, \ldots, b_k, u_1, \ldots, u_{\text{offset}}.\mathrm{Pol}_n[\![\alpha']\!](a_1, \ldots, a_n, b'_1 \ldots b'_k)
$$

We prove this by induction on α':

(a) The case $\alpha' = x_r$ is again trivial.

(b) $\alpha' = c_r(\ldots)$: This is proved by the induction hypothesis that the lemma already holds for the arguments of c_r.

(c) $\alpha' = z_r$: This is correct due to the premise on PS.

(d) $\alpha' = F(x_1, \ldots, x_{j-1}, z_r, x_{j+1}, \ldots, x_n)$: This is translated to a $\mathsf{LODR}\ k + \text{offset} - r$ instruction which in this case will push b_r onto DS. Due to our premise on b_r, this case is also correct.

Up to now we have proved that the assumption of proper contents of IS and PS and of the existence of k correct function values on DS from the preceding iteration of the loop (where k is the arity of the current constructor) implies that a proper new function value is computed on top of DS. The LOOP instruction at the end of the code $CS(\alpha_i)$ will guarantee that this value is stored back to that location in DS where the next iteration shall expect it; irrelevant data are removed from DS. The proof is then completed by proving proper treatment of IS and PS. Since every iteration of the loop removes exactly one constructor from IS and a corresponding number of arguments for this constructor from PS, all that has to be done is a proof that the *leftmost-innermost* rule (=cbv rule) for function evaluation is correct, i.e. that the following holds:

Lemma 2: Let $b_r = [\![F]\!](a_1, \ldots, a_{j-1}, b'_r, a_{j+1}, \ldots, a_n)$ and let ip be the address of the IPOP instruction in $CS(\alpha, 0)$. Then an $\mathrm{ASM}(\mathcal{A})$-configuration with

$$
\begin{aligned}
\mathrm{IP} &= ip, \\
\mathrm{DS} &= ds, \\
\mathrm{IS} &= is.\mathrm{COps}_s(a_j), \\
\mathrm{FS} &= fs.(r, a_1, \ldots, a_n) \text{ and} \\
\mathrm{PS} &= ps.\mathrm{CArgs}_s(a_j)
\end{aligned}
$$

will lead to a configuration with

$$
\mathrm{DS} = ds.[\![F]\!](a_1, \ldots, a_n) .
$$

This is proved by structural induction on a_j:

(a) $a_j = c_i$ for a nullary constructor c_i: In this case, $\text{COps}_s(a_j) = c_i$, $\text{CArgs}_s(a_j) = \varepsilon$ and lemma 1 (with $k = \text{offset} = 0$) completes the proof.

(b) $a_j = c_r(d_1, \ldots, d_k)$: In this case, $\text{COps}_s(a_j) = c_r.w_l \ldots w_1$ where $w_i = \text{COps}_s(d_i)$ and $\text{CArgs}_s(a_j) = d_l \ldots d_1 v_l \ldots v_1$ where $v_i = \text{CArgs}_s(d_i)$. Assume that the assertion holds for $d_1, \ldots, d_l$. Then we will arrive at a state with

$$
\begin{aligned}
\text{DS} &= ds.\text{Pol}_n[\![\alpha]\!](a_1, \ldots, a_n, v_1) \ldots \text{Pol}_n[\![\alpha]\!](a_1, \ldots, a_n, v_l) \\
\text{IS} &= is.c_r \\
\text{PS} &= ps.d_n \ldots d_1 \\
\text{IP} &= ip
\end{aligned}
$$

The IPOP and BRANCH instructions therefore have the effect that we will get into the branch belonging to constructor c_r; lemma 1 guarantees then that this will lead us into the final state mentioned in the assertion. Note that this also completes the proof of (2) from above since we see that the structure of the data stack is such that the LODR instruction refers to the correct function value on DS.

For the case of CARDINAL as recursion sort (i.e. that sort to which the recursion parameter belongs) an even better translation schema can be used. A *complete decomposition* is here in fact superfluous because there is only a single non-nullary constructor (the suc function). On the other hand, since the suc-terms have only a single predecessor, it is not necessary to accumulate function results from the previous loop iteration in DS; instead, a single register suffices [5]. We therefore add two registers V (= value) and C (=counter) to ASM($\mathcal{A}$) with the instructions LODV, STOV, RESET, INC and LODC being defined as follows:

$$
\text{LODV} : \begin{bmatrix} \text{DS} = ds \\ \text{V} = v \end{bmatrix} \longrightarrow \text{DS} = ds.v
$$

$$
\text{STOV} : \text{DS} = ds.x \longrightarrow \begin{bmatrix} \text{DS} = ds \\ \text{V} = x \end{bmatrix}
$$

$$
\text{RESET} : \longrightarrow \text{C} = 0
$$

$$
\text{INC} : \text{C} = c \longrightarrow \text{C} = c + 1
$$

$$
\text{LODC} : \begin{bmatrix} \text{DS} = ds \\ \text{C} = c \end{bmatrix} \longrightarrow \text{DS} = ds.c
$$

The *sr* compiler functions are then changed as follows:

$CS(z_1, \text{offset}) := \text{LODC}$

There can only be one predecessor z_1. Its current value is the value of the counter C.

$CS(F(\ldots z_r \ldots), \text{offset}) := \text{LODV}$,
        for the admissible recursive call.

$CS(\text{CASE } x_j \text{ OF}$
        $0 : \alpha_1;$
        $z_1 + 1 : \alpha_2$
    $\text{END}, 0) :=$
                $CS(\alpha_1, 0);$
                $\text{STOV};$
                $\text{RESET};$

```
        LODA j;
        DEC;
        BRANCH;
   0:   RET;
  +1 : CS(α₂, 0);
        INC;
        STOV;
        LOOP 0
```

RESET and INC in the last definition can be dropped if **recType**(F) = *algebraic* because in this case there can be no explicit reference to predecessor values. Note that what we have done here is about the same technique a programmer would probably do when implementing a primitive recursive function by a loop.

For the compilation of general recursive definitions, we use the standard *call by value* technique. In other words, the complete translation function of our compiler is given by

$$COp(F(x_1 : s_1; \ldots; x_n : s_n) : s = \alpha) := \begin{cases} CS(\alpha, 0) & \text{if } \textbf{recType}(F) \in \{algebraic, structural\} \\ CV(\alpha); \text{RET} & \text{if } \textbf{recType}(F) = none \\ CV(\alpha) & \text{if } \textbf{recType}(F) \in \{virtual, general\} \end{cases}$$

Of course, the *cbv* technique is always (partially) correct, not depending on the recursion type of the compiled operation. It is therefore possible to compare both compilation methods for the case of structural recursion. As an example, we consider the *factorial* function (figure 2).

```
(x : CARDINAL !): CARDINAL =
    CASE x OF
        0: 1;
        n +1: (n +1) * (n !)
    END
```

Figure 2: The factorial function

```
      loda   1  ;x                    const   1
      dec                             reset
      branch                          stov
                                      loda    1  ;x
0:    const  1                        dec
      popp   1                        branch
      ret                      0:     ret

_+1:  lodp   1  ;n            _+1:     lodc       ;n
      suc                             suc
      lodp   1  ;n                    lodv       ;n!
      call   _!                       mul
      mul                             sucp
      popp   2                        stov
      ret                             loop    0
```

Figure 3: *cbv* code for factorial   Figure 4: *sr* code for factorial

Figure 3 shows the *cbv* code generated for this function, figure 4 the *sr* code. Table 1 and table 2 show the corresponding complexity data, viz. space and time. For space, we count all locations

space: 2n locations on function stack
      n locations on predecessor stack
      2 locations for expression evaluation
time: 10 instructions in a call with "$n+1$"
      6 instructions in a call with "0"

Table 1: *cbv* complexity of factorial

space: 2 locations on function stack
      1 location on predecessor stack
      3 locations for expression evaluation
time: 4 instructions initialization
      $9n$ instructions in main loop
      2 instructions for exiting loop
      1 instruction for return

Table 2: *sr* complexity of factorial

needed on all stacks of the abstract machine; for time, we simply count executed instructions of the abstract machine.

Table 3 summarizes complexities for both compilation methods and an input n to factorial. As we can see, the *sr* technique reduces memory usage from a linear factor to a constant, and run time is also slightly reduced. It is a rather popular opinion that recursion is "slow" and iteration is "fast"; as a matter of fact, this depends strongly on the efficiency of activation record handling and function parameter passing in the target machine. On the abstract machine level, where activation records can be created at no cost, this is almost irrelevant. The slight improvement in run time in this example is only due to missing code for parameter passing.

```
one(x: CARDINAL): CARDINAL =
    CASE x OF
        0: 1;
        n +1: one(n) * one(n)
    END
```

Figure 5: A function with exponential *cbv* behaviour

	cbv compilation	*sr compilation*
space	$3n+2$	6
time	$10n+6$	$9n+7$

Table 3: Complexity of factorial

	cbv compilation	*sr compilation*
space	$5 \cdot 2^{n+1} - 5$	6
time	$10 \cdot 2^n - 10$	$6n+5.$

Table 4: Complexity of one

There are, however, more drastical effects if the recursive definition leads to multiple computations for the *cbv* technique, as in figure 5 and table 4. Of course, the exponential *cbv* behaviour in this example occurs only when there is no common subexpression elimination. A truly exponential behaviour occurs in functions similar to the *Fibonacci* function. In [5] we show how this class of functions can be handled by our technique (for recursion sort CARDINAL). This also reduces run time from exponential to linear.

As an example with free sorts, consider now the append function of figure 1. Complexity of append is determined by the complexity of the first argument v. We consider some kind of worst case by letting $v = l_n$ where $l_0 = $ NIL and $l_{n+1} = $ CONS l_n l_n. Table 5 shows the complexity of append for $v = l_n$. The *cbv* program has 5 instructions in a call with NIL and 10 instructions in a call with CONS. For input l_n there are $2^n - 1$ calls with CONS and 2^n calls with NIL which gives the stated time complexity. Every call of the *cbv* program needs 3 locations on FS, at most 2 locations on PS and 5 locations on DS, but at any time there are at most n active calls, which leads to the stated space complexity.

There are two columns for *sr* complexity: In the first column, total memory usage on DS, IS and PS is counted. Decomposition of l_n needs $2^{n+1} - 1$ locations on IS and $2^{n+1} - 2$ locations on PS; furthermore there are 3 locations on FS for the one and only call of append and 2 locations on

	cbv	sr (abstract)	sr (concrete)
memory	$10n$	$2^{n+2} + 2$	5
run time	$15 \cdot 2^n - 10$	$5 \cdot 2^n - 3$	$5 \cdot 2^n - 3$.

Table 5: Complexity of append

DS for expression evaluation. We have already mentioned that IS and PS are not required for the realization of the abstract machine on a target processor, so the third column shows complexity without counting IS and PS locations, which is closer to realistic data.

Summing up, we can see that also in this case a linear amount of auxiliary storage can be reduced to a constant and that run time can be reduced to one third, which again is due to missing code for parameter passing in a recursion.

5 Generation of machine code

Generating machine code means implementing the abstract stack machine of the preceding section. The difficulty of this task depends on the properties of the target processor. We have chosen the *8086* processor for collecting first practical experience with *sr* compilation, because the SRDL compiler was developed also on this kind of machine. Implementations for the *68000* and for *Celerity*, a 32 bit RISC machine, are under development. We shall therefore not discuss details of the *8086* implementation but rather keep the presentation independent of any processor. The only relevant feature here is the hardware stack.

When implementing the abstract machine $\mathrm{ASM}(\mathcal{A})$, we have to implement

1. the data types of $\mathcal{A}$,

2. the state components of $\mathrm{ASM}(\mathcal{A})$, and

3. the instructions of $\mathrm{ASM}(\mathcal{A})$.

The first task is essentially solved by providing a representation for elements of free sorts, i.e. trees, since BOOLEAN and CARDINAL are more or less given by the machine architecture. We implement trees by so-called *plexes*, i.e. *tuples of machine words* where the first word always contains a characterization of the corresponding constructor including further technical information and the following words contain (short) pointers to the plexes corresponding to immediate subtrees. This means that we do not follow the standard LISP practice of turning all trees into binary trees. Of course, subroutines for decomposition of plexes and for dynamic storage allocation must be provided. The *state components* of $\mathrm{ASM}(\mathcal{A})$ are implemented by taking the hardware stack as data stack DS *and* function stack FS at the same time, following the conventions of higher programming languages. All other components are held in machine registers. Iteration stack IS and predecessor stack PS were needed for the iterative computation in the abstract machine because it can store an arbitrarily large tree in a single location of DS and therefore must invert a tree before entering the iteration. It cannot be expected that a realistic machine can store a whole tree in a single location, so IS and PS need not to be implemented. Instead, it suffices to have a single machine register pointing to the *actual plex* of a tree traversal algorithm; then the header word giving constructor information ($\approx$ IS) and the immediate subtrees ($\approx$ PS) are always accessible without further complication.

We will specify the tree traversal algorithm in a Modula-2 like syntax. Assuming that a *plex* p has (among other information) the fields conArgs (number of arguments of this constructor), predInfo (a SET OF 0..conArgs containing the indices of those arguments of the constructor belonging to the recursion sort) and Arg (an ARRAY [0..conArgs] OF Plex containing pointers to the predecessors), a *postorder* tree traversal limited to nodes of the recursion sort and performing a certain *action* on the nodes of the tree is described by the recursive algorithm of figure 6:

```
PROCEDURE visit (p: Plex; action: PROCEDURE(Plex));
VAR i: CARDINAL;
BEGIN
    FOR i:= 1 TO p.conArgs DO
        IF (i-1) IN p.predInfo THEN
            visit(p.Arg[i])
        END (*IF*);
        action(p)
    END (*FOR*)
END visit
```

Figure 6: Recursive tree traversal

Note that the *postorder* tree traversal corresponds exactly to the *call by value* strategy. It would, of course, not make too much sense to implement the iterative computation using this recursive algorithm. We therefore use a generalization of the *Schorr-Waite graph marking algorithm*. The main idea here is

1. to implement the local variables i needed in every call of visit using a certain working field *within* the tree to be traversed and

2. to implement the return to the father of a certain node by *pointer reversal*.

For the case of LISP where there are only binary trees, a working field of two bits is sufficient; for the general case, we need a working field of $n+1$ bits where n is the maximal constructor arity. (See, e.g. [3])

As a first step, we show that a working field SWF in every plex can be used for an iterative implementation of visit, assuming that there is a function parent yielding the father of a certain plex and returning NIL if there is no father. Under the further assumption that all SWF fields are initialized with 0, the iterative implementation of visit is given by figure 7:

As already mentioned, the fields SWF in the data structure take the role of the distinct instances of the variable i. Consequently, the initialization of them ("FOR i:= 1" in the recursive algorithm) is also done in the data structure. Since we always need i-1 for the predInfo test, it is more economic to initialize p.SWF with 0 and to increment it only after the predInfo test. Note that we reset the SWF field of a node before going back to its parent; this is done for proper treatment of trees with "structure sharing". The recursive call visit(p.Arg[i]) is here realized by the assignment p := p.Arg[p.SWF], the corresponding return jump by p := parent(p). visit itself returns to its calling place if parent(p) = NIL, i.e. if the root of the input tree is reached. In the recursive version, the call of action(p) is the last thing that visit does before returning; therefore in the iterative version this call occurs immediately before p := parent(p).

The function parent of this algorithm can of course be implemented by a backward pointer in every node of a tree, but this would mean more space requirements and more administrative effort in creating nodes. The second fundamental idea of the Schorr-Waite algorithm is that at any time we are only interested in the parent of the current node p. After the assigment p := p.Arg[p.SWF], this field (i.e. p.Arg[p.SWF] is temporarily redundant because its content is now in p. On the other hand, the former content of p is exactly the pointer to the wanted parent. Assuming a procedure Exchange which exchanges two pointers, the Schorr-Waite implementation of visit is given by figure 8:

```
PROCEDURE visit (p: Plex; action: PROCEDURE(Plex));
BEGIN
    WHILe p # NIL DO
        IF p.SWF < p.conArgs THEN
            IF p.SWF IN p.predInfo THEN
                INC(p.SWF);
                p := p.Arg[p.SWF]
            ELSE INC(p.SWF)
            END (*IF*)
        ELSE p.SWF := 0;
            action(p);
            p := parent(p)
        END (*IF*)
    END (*WHILE*)
END visit
```

Figure 7: Iterative tree traversal

```
PROCEDURE visit (p: Plex; action: PROCEDURE(Plex));
VAR parent: Plex;
BEGIN
    parent := NIL;
    WHILE p # NIL DO
        IF p.SWF < p.conArgs THEN
            IF (i-1) IN p.predInfo THEN
                INC(p.SWF);
                Exchange(p,parent);
                Exchange(p,parent.Arg[parent.SWF])
            ELSE INC(p.SWF)
            END (*IF*);
        ELSE p.SWF := 0;
            action(p);
            Exchange(p,parent);
            Exchange(parent,p.Arg[p.SWF])
        END (*IF*)
    END (*WHILE*)
END visit
```

Figure 8: Schorr-Waite tree traversal

We therefore have (in addition to the working field SWF in the header word of every plex) to reserve two devoted registers (for parent and p) . As a matter of fact, we need to break up the procedure visit such that we have a procedure SWA going to the next node in *postorder*. The implementation of CDEC is then a certain initialization of the Schorr-Waite algorithm and IPOP is translated to a call of SWA.

```
ONE(_):        PUSH      BP
               MOV       BP,SP
               SUB       SP,4
               const     1
               MOV       AX,1
               stov
MOV            [BP-2],AX
               loda      1                        ;x
               MOV       AX,[BP+4]
ONE(_)LOOP:
               dec
               OR        AX,AX
               branch
               JNZ       ONE(_)_+1
               POP       AX
ONE(_)0:       ret
               MOV       SP,BP
               POP       BP
               RET       2

ONE(_)_+1:
               DEC       AX
               lodv                               ;one(n)
               PUSH      AX
               MOV       AX,[BP-2]
               lodv                               ;one(n)
               MOV       BX,[BP-4]
               mul
               MUL       BX
               stov
               MOV       [BP-2],AX
               POP       AX
               loop      0
               JMP       SHORT ONE(_)LOOP
```

Figure 9: 8086 *sr* code for one

As a modest example not involving tree traversals, we shall show the *sr* code (figure 9) generated for the one function (figure 5). This is a real output from the SRDL compiler showing the interme- diate instructions in lower case and the corresponding *8086* instructions in upper case. Instruction labels are prefixed with the name of the compiled function. Note that the relative load and store instructions are somewhat clumsy to implement since the *8086* has no addressing mode relative to the stack pointer SP.

For the one function, we shall also present some execution times (table 6) on the IBM AT, comparing SRDL using cbv compilation with HOPE (specifically: IC-HOPE from Imperial College

n	SRDL cbv	SRDL sr	IC-HOPE	Modula-2
15	1.3	0	111.11	1.1
16	2.3	0	222.06	2.0
17	4.2	0	444.02	3.7
...	...	...	...	...
65535	$\approx 2^{65499}$	2	???	???

Table 6: Execution times in seconds for one

London) and an imperative programming language, Modula-2 (specifically: LOGITECH Modula-2/86 with run-time checks off).

All three *cbv* compilations show the typical exponential growth. It would be unrealistic to expect an answer for *one*(65535) within reasonable time. The SRDL cbv time for *one*(65535) has been extrapolated from the measured times. Note that this is more than 10^{19000} years. The relatively bad performance of IC-HOPE is caused by the fact that this is an interpreting system; Modula-2 performs better than SRDL due to expression evaluation in registers without using a stack.

Similar results were obtained for list operations (such as append) and for general tree operations, provided that the structural recursive definition is *complete* in the sense that all recursion arguments are needed. Otherwise, there may be redundant computations in the bottom up tree walk, wasting execution time. In this case, it would be easy to derive *need information* from a structural recursive definition in form of boolean vectors, which would allow proper reduction of the argument tree yielding optimized code. We did not implement this more general schema up to now; it could be done by passing this *need information* to the code generator which in this case could either generate different code for the abstract CDEC instruction or pass this need information to the backend which would use it in tree traversals. Note that already a simple-minded *sr* compilation has the important property of saving memory. In fact, we frequently could not measure execution times for *cbv* compilations in IC-HOPE because memory was exhausted before reaching the end of recursion.

6   The ModAs/86 System

We have implemented a system [13,8] for modular development of software systems using algebraic specifications in SRDL. The system allows editing, compiling and interactive testing of algebraic specifications.

The main idea is that, when developing a large system, abstract data types and all other modules of a functional nature should be specified in a functional, algebraic language (in this case: SRDL). Here, all advantages of the functional language and of abstract algebraic data types (including the possibility of iterative *sr* computation) can be realized. Other modules which are not as easily described in a functional way (such as, e.g., I/O) should be written in a conventional (imperative) programming language (in this case: Modula-2). Our experience in practical software projects using a former system of a similar kind showed that algebraic specification can only hope to gain practical importance if the algebraically specified parts of the system do not have to be re-implemented in a conventional language at later stages in the software development process. On the other hand, we did not want to employ a standard *transformational* approach where the algebraic specifications are semi-automatically transformed to efficient programs. The main drawback of this approach is (besides the additional energy to be invested in the interactive transformation) that programmers learn to think too bad about recursive definitions: Even if they are used in the early stages of specification, they are all too soon replaced by iterative algorithms.

We think that recursion is in quite a large number of cases a natural means of expression and that it should not be visibly removed in these cases where it has advantages with respect to understandability and correctness proofs. A very natural class of recursive definitions is—from the algebraic pont of view—the class of structural recursive definitions. Besides that, also pratical observations indicate the importance of this class. The SRDL compiler of the ModAs/86 system detects structural recursion and implements it by iterative programs. The compiler operates in two distinct phases, the first phase generating abstract stack code in the sense of section 4 and the second phase translating stack code to 8086 code.

The ModAs/86 system has an interface to LOGITECH Modula-2/86 in the sense that it is possible to call SRDL functions from a Modula-2 program. As a matter of fact, Modula-2 is also the implementation language of ModAs/86, and the *test processor* for interactive testing of an algebraic specification has completely equal rights with every other Modula-2 module using this specification. To our knowledge, this interface to an imperative programming language distinguishes ModAs/86 from other systems dealing with algebraic specifications. We think that this is better than augmenting a functional language by imperative concepts, as has been done in the case of LISP or ML, because then the imperative concepts can occur everywhere and the advantage of the functional approach is lost. In our philosophy, functional and imperative parts of a system are strictly separated.

We will briefly comment on some problems with the integration of SRDL into Modula-2:

1. For the translation of a module with IMPORT declarations, the Modula-2 compiler needs a compiled version of a corresponding DEFINITION MODULE for syntax and type checks across compilation unit boundaries. This so-called *symbol file* also contains a *version number* generated during compilation and used for consistency checks. Treating SRDL modules and Modula-2 modules in completely the same way would therefore imply that the test processor mentioned above would have to be recompiled after every change in the interface description of the SRDL module being tested, which surely is unbearable.

2. The test processor and other Modula-2 programs using an SRDL specification must be able to read terms of the user-specified abstract data types. This is most easily done by importing a parser procedure from the SRDL compiler itself. For output of terms, an inverse procedure ("deparser") is needed. Also these input/output procedures should be independent of an SRDL module.

The solution to these problems is to generate a binary core image file (.COM file) and a symbol table file from an SRDL specification. There is a special Modula-2 module SRDLInterface which exports procedures LoadModule, ReadTerm, WriteTerm and a data type EvalProc for interfacing an SRDL specification. LoadModule searches for core image and symbol table of an SRDL module and loads the core image into memory if consistency checks are passed; it returns a value of type EvalProc using which the loaded SRDL functions can be called. ReadTerm and WriteTerm use the symbol table organization and internal expression representation of the SRDL compiler to translate external representation of terms over arbitrary signatures to internal representation and vice versa. This means that the flexible distributed fix notation can also be used in the test processor and other programs importing an SRDL module.

ModAs/86 was originally implemented on a SIRIUS-1 under MS-DOS 2.11 and is now running on an IBM AT03 under PC-DOS 3.20.

7 Conclusion

When we consider abstract data types as algebras which are inductively generated by some set of constructor operations, it is very natural to consider functions over these data types which are recursively defined using a case distinction on constructors. Among such functions, a very canonical class is the class of *structural recursive* functions. Here, the recursion structure is such that for evaluation of a function F at the root r of an argument tree t it suffices to know the values of F at the immediate subtrees of r. Other recursive calls are not allowed.

We have shown that this class of recursively defined functions can be implemented by iterative programs which reduces the (usually) exponential memory requirements of the standard implementation method to a constant. Furthermore, if the recursive definition leads to multiple computations in the standard implementation, there may be run time savings of the same kind. Although our discussion here and the implemented system refer only to SRDL, the same technique could be carried over to e.g. HOPE or ML compilers.

We thank Axel Schubert [13] for implementing the front end of the SRDL compiler.

References

[1] R.M. Burstall, D.B. MacQueen, D.T. Sannella, *HOPE — An Experimental Applicative Language*, Univ. Edinburgh, Dept. of Comp.Sci., Report CSR-62-80

[2] M.J.C. Gordon, A.J.R.G. Milner, L. Morris, M. Newey, C. Wadsworth, *A Metalanguage for Interactive Proofs in LCF*, 5th ACM Symp. Princ. of Prog.Lang., Tucson 1978

[3] D. Gries, *The Schorr-Waite Graph Marking Algorithm*, Acta Informatica 11 (1979), 223-232

[4] K. Indermark, *Functional compiler description*, Banach Center Publications 21 (1988), Polish Academy of Sciences, Warsaw

[5] K. Indermark, H. Klaeren, *Compiling Fibonacci-like Recursion*, SIGPLAN Notices 22 (1987), No. 6, 101-108

[6] H. Klaeren, *Algebraische Spezifikation — Eine Einführung*, Springer Lehrbuch Informatik, 1983

[7] H. Klaeren, *A Constructive Method for Abstract Algebraic Software Specification*, Theoretical Computer Science, 30 (1984), 139-204

[8] H. Klaeren, *Ein algebraischer Ansatz zur Rekursionselimination*, Habilitationsschrift, RWTH Aachen, 1988

[9] H. Klaeren, *ModAs/86 User Manual*, Berichte des Lehrstuhls für Informatik II, RWTH Aachen, 1988

[10] H. Klaeren, K. Indermark, *A New Implementation Technique for Recursive Function Definitions*, Aachener Informatik-Berichte Nr. 87-10

[11] J. Loeckx, *A Formal Description of the Specification Language OBSCURE*, Universität des Saarlandes, FB 10, Bericht A85/15

[12] H.C. Mayr, P.C. Lockemann, K.R. Dittrich, *Operational Replacement Schemes — A Practice-Oriented Approach to the Specification of Abstract Data Types*, Universität Karlsruhe, Fakultät für Informatik, Bericht 11/80

[13] A. Schubert, *Modularisierung algebraischer Spezifikationen zum Einsatz im System- und Programmentwurf*, Diplomarbeit, RWTH Aachen, 1986

AN INTEGRATED ALGEBRAIC APPROACH TO THE SPECIFICATION OF DATA TYPES, PROCESSES AND OBJECTS

E. Astesiano, A. Giovini, G. Reggio, E. Zucca

Department of Mathematics, University of Genova, Italy

Introduction

The abstract specification of a data type is one of the concepts which have deeply influenced computer science in these last years and which is now widely accepted and understood. The basic idea underlying this approach is specifying an entity in terms of the properties that it must satisfy, instead of giving one particular concrete model which in general would be overspecified. This is done using algebraic techniques (properties are defined by axioms). This framework has proven to be adequate in many situations for the description of "static" properties (properties related to the functional behaviour of an entity). Less clear until recently was the possibility of extending this approach to handle properties related to the "dynamic" behaviour of an entity. Such properties become very important in many situations; we just mention a few. The specification of a concurrent system requires the specification of various data types; this is also the case of the formal semantics of a language including concurrency (eg, Ada). In some concurrent systems (eg, operating systems), processes can be exchanged between processes as data. For the description of concurrency we need to specify not only typically "active" objects as processes (whose behaviour cannot in general be described just as functional), but also which is the behaviour of usual static entities (whose static properties are known) when inserted in a concurrent environment: eg, what happens (which properties are true) when a queue is shared by many processes. Finally, in the object-oriented programming paradigm, which is now becoming of increasing importance, programming is presented as concreting at the programming level basic ideas from abstract data types theory, like data encapsulation (in the following "abstract data type" is abbreviated to adt); nevertheless the actual relationship between the usual adt framework and the object oriented vision is not completely understood since, for example, objects are dynamic entities (new objects be created, objects can change and also have an inner thread of control), and so also in this context the integration of data types and process specifications plays a central role.

Since some years we are developing (partly in cooperation with M.Wirsing) a method for tackling some of the mentioned problems ([AR1, AMRW, AR2, AR3]) which has also been applied in some important projects ([CRAI-DDC]). This method is based on an algebraic description of concurrent systems and allows an homogeneous handling of active and passive entities.

In our specification technique processes/concurrent systems are special abstract data types, modelling transition systems with possibly the specification of a parallel structure (see, eg, [AMRW, AR2, AR1]). Our technical framework looks naturally apt to accommodate data type specifications. Indeed all the components of a concurrent system are specified as adts. Moreover, since processes are themselves specified as adts, they can be treated as data. As we permit the specification of functions (we use higher-order algebraic specifications), we can thus specify data of any complexity and also model systems where processes are exchanged between processes, stored and so on.

This work has been partly carried out with the financial support of CNR-Italy (Progetto Strategico "Software: ricerche di base ed applicazioni") and of the Esprit project n. 1550 DRAGON.

The aim of this paper is to present an overview of the technical principles of our approach with some recent new developments.

In the first section the idea and technique of a process as an abstract data type with an appropriate semantics is given. We emphasize in particular the notion of observational semantics and present a general setting for defining generalized bisimulation semantics associated with an observational setting. The second section presents essentially an example schema in order to illustrate the principles of section 1 and to give some concrete examples of specifications. The third section, with the help of some examples, gives an overview of some issues related to data type specification in a concurrent environment; in particular we discuss the specification of usual data types and of dynamic data types, ie, data types accessed in parallel by some processes. This is a topics considered by various authors [B, GV, HJ, KP]; our presentation here is a condensed summary of a deeper technical treatment given in [AGR2], where we also compare our viewpoint with those presented in the mentioned papers.

The fourth and final section is an attempt at applying our technique to model some concepts typical of an object-oriented approach. After a brief discussion of the notion of object, we suggest, with the help of some examples, an approach for modelling classes of objects. Essentially we associate with a class an object system, which is a particular concurrent system whose components are dynamic entities and which is specified following the techniques of the first three sections. Issues like using and inheriting classes are also considered.

The algebraic framework of this paper is somewhat new with respect to the previous presentations of our approach. Instead of relational specifications (see, eg [ARW]) we use (higher order) partial algebras with predicates; the related technical concepts and results needed throughout the paper are condensed in the Appendix.

1 PROCESS SPECIFICATION

We outline in this section the methodological principles underlying our approach to the specification of concurrency.

1.1 Processes as Abstract Data Types

We adopt the well-known and accepted technique which consists in viewing a process as a labelled transition system and we extend to this framework the algebraic techniques of the specification of abstract data types, as stated in the following principle.

> A process is specified as an abstract data type representing a labelled transition system.

So we first recall the set-theoretic definition of (labelled) transition system.

Def. 1.1 A *labelled transition system* is a triple (STATE, FLAG, —>), where STATE and FLAG are sets, whose elements represent respectively the *states* and the *flags* (or *labels*) of the system and —> $\subseteq$ STATE × FLAG × STATE is the *transition relation*. In the rest of the paper a labelled transition system is simply called a *transition system*. A triple (s,f,s') belonging to —> is called a *transition*; we usually write s —> s' for (s,f,s') $\in$ —>. $\square$

The intuitive meaning of a transition s $\xrightarrow{f}$ s' is that a process which is in the state s can evolve into the state s' performing an action whose interaction with the outside world is represented by the flag f. In other words f embodies both information on the condition required on the environment for that transition to be possible and information on the effect caused on the environment by that transition. This interpretation of transitions has become classical after its use in [M1] and [Pl]. Usually, the transition relation —> is given in terms of inference rules of a rewriting system.

A transition system can be also specified algebraically. The algebraic framework we adopt in this paper is that of *partial algebras with predicates* (abbreviated to *ppa*); shortly, a *ppa specification* is, as in the usual partial algebras framework, a couple consisting of a *ppa signature* and *axioms*; but in the ppa signature we have, beside sorts and operation symbols, also predicate symbols and the axioms may involve also these predicates; so a ppa on a signature of this kind has also to satisfy axioms related to predicates (predicates are interpreted as subsets of products of appropriate carriers). A quick technical summary of ppa's can be found in Appendix; there also a brief list of the notations used in writing specifications can be found. In previous papers we have used, instead of partial algebras with predicates, relational specifications (see [ARW]), which are a subclass of partial algebras. It is easily seen that relational specifications can be mapped into partial algebras with predicates. The new setting of ppa's is more convenient for a number of reasons; its use has been suggested by the work of Goguen and Meseguer [GM], who also a wealth of motivations for this choice (but they use total algebras).

A transition system TS is specified algebraically by giving the specifications STATE of the states of the system and FLAG of the flags of the system and adding the predicate $\longrightarrow$: state × flag × state (representing the transition relation of the system) and a set of axioms Ax_{TS} defining the predicate $\longrightarrow$ (ie, Ax_{TS} is a set of positive conditional axioms whose consequences have form $s \xrightarrow{f} s'$.

TS = **enrich** STATE + FLAG **by**
   preds
      $\longrightarrow$: state × flag × state
   axioms
      Ax_{TS}

Hence, more generally, a transition system can be algebraically specified as an instantiation of a parameterized specification which takes as parameters STATE, FLAG and Ax_{TS}; such an instantiation is called an *algebraic transition system*.

Def. 1.2 An *algebraic transition system* is an instantiation of the following parameterized specification:

TS(STATE, FLAG, Ax_{TS}) =
   enrich STATE + FLAG **by**
   preds
      $\longrightarrow$: state × flag × state
   axioms
      Ax_{TS}. $\square$

Since every part of the specification of a transition system is given algebraically, we have an important difference from the classical CCS-like approach, where, for example, labels are elements of a fixed alphabet (or of a fixed structure, say a monoid, a group and so on).

> **Labels can be any data types, including processes and functions from processes into processes.**

For example, a process can be exchanged as a value between processes, processes (and functions from some data into processes) may be stored in memory and, in general:

> **Processes are data.**

The complete power of this approach is needed, for example, to model Ada tasking ([CRAI-DDC]): the denotation of a task type is modelled as a function from some parameters into the process modelling the activity of the task; the action of adding in the environment this denotation takes as parameter this function and as effect stores this function *as a value* into the (shared) environment, so that the creation of a new task of that type consists in adding to the concurrent system an instantiation of the denotation on some appropriate parameters. Examples of applications of the last two principles can be found in sections 2 and 3.

1.2   Semantics

An abstract data type specification can be a variety of semantics. When the adt specifies a process it is essential to capture its potentially infinite behaviour. Here we show that the initial semantics associates a labelled transition system with an algebraic transition system, and hence with each state a possible infinite labelled tree. Then we show how to characterize the process behaviour in dependence of some observations, in particular emphasizing bisimulation semantics, a special class of observational semantics.

1.2.1   Initial Semantics

Since we use only ppa specifications with axioms in positive conditional form, it is always possible to associate with each algebraic transition system an initial model. This initial model has the usual properties, which have in this case a particular significant interpretation: the initial model I_{TS} of an algebraic transition system $TS = TS(STATE,FLAG,Ax_{TS})$ can be viewed as (*is*) a classical set-theoretic transition system (state^I, flag^I, $\longrightarrow^I$), where state^I and flag^I are the carriers of sort state and flag respectively and the transition relation $\longrightarrow^I$ is defined by interpreting the axioms related to the transition relation (the set Ax_{TS}) as inference rules defining a rewriting system. Notice that this is possible only because of the particular form allowed for these axioms.

Prop. 1.3 Let TS be an algebraic transition system; then there exists the initial model I_{TS} satisfying the following properties:
- $TS \vdash D(t') \wedge D(t'')$ implies ($I_{TS} \vDash t'=t''$ iff $TS \vdash t'=t''$);
- for all $p \in$ Preds(TS) $I_{TS} \vDash p(t_1,...,t_n)$ iff $TS \vdash p(t_1,...,t_n)$;
  in particular:
  - $TS \vdash s \xrightarrow{f} s'$ iff $I_{TS} \vDash s \xrightarrow{f} s'$;
  - $TS \vdash D(t)$ iff $I_{TS} \vDash D(t)$. $\square$

1.2.2   Observational Semantics

When dealing with concurrency, there is no common agreement on what should be reasonably taken as *the* semantics of processes; the consensus is growing on recognizing rather that there is no semantic definition which can be used in every situation. It seems indeed that the starting point for defining the semantics of a concurrent system is that of specifying what is *observable* of its behaviour. Different observational criteria correspond to different semantic viewpoints. Processes identified by some viewpoints might be distinguished by others and it is now clear that there cannot be a unique observational criterium better than the others; each criterium catches instead some particular characteristics of the system. In our approach we do not fix a particular semantic schema, so that in principle in every particular situation we can adopt the definition of semantics corresponding to the kind of observations we make.

The semantics of an algebraic transition system is observational.

Even in this respect we keep our approach fully general, not fixing any particular equivalence on an algebraic transition system, but providing a way of inducing this equivalence by means of a standard mechanism starting from the definition of some predicates which catch our intuition of "what we want to observe" of the system. Given an algebraic transition system $TS = TS(STATE,FLAG,Ax_{TS})$, an *observational setting* for TS is an observational specification (see Appendix) OBS-TS, with TS as a subspecification and with state as observed sort. An observational specification is a triple (A, O, OB), where A is a ppa specification, O a subset of the sorts of A (the observed sorts) and OB a subset of the predicates of A (the observing predicates); intuitively, the observed sorts correspond to the sorts of the objects about which we make observations, while the observing predicates represent the observations we make.

For example, if we take the setting BIS_TS = (TS, {state}, { $\longrightarrow$: state × flag × state}), we intend to observe the states of TS using the transition relation. Another example is given by the observational setting defined below, where RESULT is a ppa specification defining the possible results of the executions of the system.

RES_TS = (RES, {state}, {Result: state × result})

RES =
    enrich TS + RESULT **by**
        preds
            Result: state × result
        axioms
            $s \xrightarrow{f} s' \wedge \text{Result}(s',r) \supset \text{Result}(s,r)$
            (other axioms defining Result on states with no transitions)

In this case the setting RES_TS corresponds to observe the final results produced by the processes regardless of their intermediate transitions and states.

1.2.3 Generalized Bisimulation

There are several ways to associate an observational semantics with a particular observational setting OBS-TS for an algebraic transition system TS. A fundamental kind of observational semantics is the one which forgets the intermediate states, while keeping the labelled transition structure. This semantics can be obtained in our setting as a generaliztion of the strong bisimulation of Park [Pa] and Milner [M2]. However we are also able to define a variety of bisimulation semantics, one for every observational setting. First we recall the definition of strong bisimulation for transition systems.

Def. 1.4 Let TS = (STATE,FLAG, $\longrightarrow$) be a transition system; then a binary relation R on STATE is a *bisimulation* for TS iff for all $s_1, s_2 \in$ STATE

  $s_1 R s_2$ implies
    i) $s_1 \xrightarrow{f} s'_1$ implies $\exists s'_2$ s.t. $s_2 \xrightarrow{f} s_2'$ and $s'_1 R s'_2$,
    ii) $s_2 \xrightarrow{f} s'_2$ implies $\exists s'_1$ s.t. $s_1 \xrightarrow{f} s_1'$ and $s'_1 R s'_2$. $\square$

Prop. 1.5 Given a transition system TS, there exists the maximum bisimulation for TS $\cup \{R \mid R$ is a bisimulation$\}$, which is indicated by ~ and called *the strong bisimulation.* $\square$

Several adjustments and extensions are needed in order to generalize this definition to our framework:
- the definition has to be rephrased in the framework of algebraic transition systems;
- we do not restrict ourselves to considering the transition relation as the only means for observing a state (as for example in the previous example, where we observe results);
- we do not want to consider the states the only observed objects, since we could have several observations on different sorts (this is mandatory if we have to handle complex systems with many transition relations defined on different kind of states);
- we need to consider equivalent not only states, but also flags (and in general, objects of all other sorts of the specification of the system: for example, two flags which differ only for process subcomponents which are equivalent should be in turn equivalent).

A more technical discussion of the motivations for a suitable definition of generalized bisimulation can be found in [AGR1]. It turns out not only that this generalization is possible, but also that the resulting technique can be successfully used in the more general framework of observational specifications, hence without constraining us to observational settings for algebraic transition systems. To generalize the original notion of bisimulation we need to consider not only relations on states, as in the original definition. So a bisimulation for an observational specification consists of a family of relations on *all* its observed sorts, and takes also into account the existence of its operations and predicates.

First we need the following technical definitions.

Def. 1.6 Let OS = (A, O, OB) be an observational specification.

- A family $\{Q_o\}_{o \in O}$, where for all $o \in O$ Q_o is a binary relation on $W_{Sig(A)|o}$ is called an OS-*family*.

- OS + $Q \vdash$ indicates the deductive system $Ax_{OS} \cup Gt_Q \vdash$, where:

    Ax_{OS} indicates the set of axioms of the specification A;

    Gt_Q indicates the following set of formulas (the ground theory associated with Q):

    $\{ t_1 = t_2, \mathbf{D}(t_1), \mathbf{D}(t_2) \mid t_1, t_2 \in W_{Sig(A)|o} \text{ s.t. } <t_1,t_2> \in Q_o, o \in O\}$.

- E(Q) indicates the strict congruence over Sig(A) defined by:

    for $s \in$ Sorts(Sig(A)) $E(Q)_s = \{ <t_1,t_2> \mid OS + Q \vdash t_1 = t_2 \text{ and } OS + Q \vdash \mathbf{D}(t_1) \}$;

    for $p \in$ Preds(Sig(A)) $E(Q)_p = \{ <t_1,...,t_n> \mid OS + Q \vdash p(t_1,...,t_n) \}$. $\square$

If Q is an OS-family, then the deductive system OS $+Q \vdash$ puts together the provable equality and truth of predicates in OS with the equalities on the elements of observed sort in Q, and E(Q) is the congruence over the signature of A which is generated by Q.

Def. 1.7 An OS-family $Q = \{Q_o\}_{o \in O}$ is a *bisimulation* for OS iff

for all $o \in O$, for all $t_1, t_2 \in W_{Sig(A)|o}$,

$t_1 Q_o t_2$ implies that

$\forall$ ob: $o \times srt_1 \times ... \times srt_n \in$ OB:

   i) $OS \vdash$ ob($t_1,s_1,...,s_n$) implies

      $\exists s'_1, ..., s'_n$ s.t. $OS \vdash$ ob($t_2,s'_1,...,s'_n$) and for $i = 1, ..., n$ $s_i E(Q)srt_i s_i'$;

   ii) $OS \vdash$ ob($t_2,s'_1,...,s'_n$) implies

      $\exists s_1, ..., s_n$ s.t. $OS \vdash$ ob($t_1,s_1,...,s_n$) and for $i = 1, ..., n$ $s_i E(Q)srt_i s_i'$. $\square$

Prop. 1.8 There exists *a maximum bisimulation* for OS given by

   $\sim_{OS} = \cup(Q: Q$ is a bisimulation for OS$)$. $\square$

For all $s \in$ Sorts(Sig(A)) two terms $t_1, t_2 \in W_{Sig(A)|s}$ are said *in bisimulation* iff $t_1 E(\sim_{OS}) t_2$.

Prop. 1.9 The ppa $W_{Sig(A)}/E(\sim_{OS})$ is a term generated model of A. $\square$

We have that $W_{Sig(A)}/E(\sim_{OS}) = I_{A\sim}$, where A$\sim$ = **enrich** A **by axioms** $Gt_{\sim_{OS}}$.

Note that, as for the Park's and Milner's definition of bisimulation for transition systems, we have a technique for proving that two terms t_1, t_2 of sort s are in bisimulation: it is necessary and sufficient to find a bisimulation Q such that $t_1 E(Q)_s t_2$.

In this paper, when no confusion arises, we write simply $\sim$ in place of $\sim_{OS}$ and of $E(\sim_{OS})$.

Some examples of the use of this definition are shown in the following sections.

2 AN EXAMPLE SCHEMA

In any approach to the specification of concurrency an important problem is how to construct the specifications of processes and how to combine them together; in particular, in the case in which one has to model large and complex systems, the capability of doing this in a modular way is very relevant.

Our approach is constructive and splits the problem as follows: first we fix a suitable set of operations which allow to express all the "basic" processes, ie the processes which have no local state (called *behaviours* following the terminology introduced by Milner [M]). Behaviours are completely determined by their possible transitions: they correspond from an abstract point of view to trees in which only the arcs are labelled. We choose a set of operations (called *behaviour combinators*) which suffices to express all finite labelled trees and all infinite labelled trees which can be expressed as least fixed points of computable functions; moreover we add some derived combinators as syntactic sugar for the description of complex processes. This particular choice has proven to be flexible and expressive enough during our experience in the formal definition of Ada [CRAI-DDC].

We consider then the problem of combining together specifications of processes, in particular the problem of modelling the parallel composition of many processes in what we call a *concurrent system*. The basic idea is that of not fixing a particular parallel combinator but giving instead a parametric schema, which allows us to handle in a very flexible way many different concrete situations. This leads to the following additional principle of our approach:

> **A concurrent system is specified as an instantiation of a parameterized ADT.**

In this section we give an example of a parameterized schema for defining basic processes and composing processes following the principles of section 1. The main purpose is to provide some concrete examples of process specifications as instantiations of a parameterized adt.

2.1 Process Combinators

Before giving formally the specification of behaviours we give an intuitive explanation of the main behaviour combinators; the axioms which formalize this description form the set Ax_{BH} and are given below. Notice that since our algebraic framework includes automatically in every ppa specification also the higher-order sorts (those of the form $(s_1 \times ... \times s_n \to s)$) and operations for building higher-order terms, we have also a set of implicit functional behaviour combinators (eg, λ-abstractions, **fix, if then else**).

The specification of behaviours is parameterized on a ppa specification DATA defining which are the values which can be handled by the behaviours and the actions which the behaviours can perform; Sorts(Sig(DATA)) must include the sorts behaviour and of sort act and the operation CREATED_BH: behaviour $\to$ act (the elements of act correspond to the possible actions of the behaviours).

In what follows Sorts indicated the set of soerts Sorts(Sig(DATA)).

Note that since DATA includes the sort behaviour, then it is possible to define behaviours which communicate, store, exchange behaviours in the same way of the other data.

Action prefixing

- $\square \, \Delta \, \square$: act $\times$ behaviour $\to$ behaviour

   The behaviour a Δ bh can perform the action a and then become the behaviour bh; this is the basic combinator for expressing the activity of a behaviour in terms of a sequence of actions; it corresponds to the dot "." in CCS.

Nondeterministic choice

- **choose**$_{srt}$ $\square$: (srt $\to$ behaviour) $\to$ behaviour   for all srt $\in$ Sorts

   The behaviour **choose**$_{srt}$ bhf can (nondeterministically) behave as each bhf(t) for every defined term t of sort srt; in a CCS-like framework this behaviour corresponds to a process of the form Σ_t bh(t). We usually write the behaviours **choose**$_{srt}$ λt.bh and **choose**$_{bool}$ λb. **if** b **then** bh$_1$ **else** bh$_2$ respectively as **choose** t: srt **in** bh and bh$_1$ + bh$_2$.

Sequential composition

- **def**$_{srt}$ $\square$ **in** $\square$: behaviour $\times$ (srt $\to$ behaviour) $\to$ behaviour   for all srt $\in$ Sorts
- **return**$_{srt}$ $\square$: srt $\to$ behaviour   for all srt $\in$ Sorts

   The activity of **def**$_{srt}$ bh **in** bhf consists in the activity of bh until it terminates; if bh terminates returning a value t of sort srt, then bhf(t) follows, otherwise the behaviour returns the value to an outer frame. The behaviour **return**$_{srt}$ t represents a terminated activity returning the value t of sort srt. The combinator **def**$_{srt}$ bh **in** bhf represents a very general and powerful form of sequential composition, since it allows a form of value passing between bh and bhf, whenever bh terminates returning a value of sort srt; if the value returned by bh is not of sort srt, then the activity represented by bhf is skipped. We usually write the behaviour **def**$_{srt}$ bh **in** λt.bh' as **def**$_{srt}$ t = bh **in** bh'.

In what follows we assume that DATA has a sort null and a total operation Null: $\to$ null (which is the only operation of sort null); **return**$_{null}$ Null is simply written **skip**. The behaviour **skip** is unable to perform any action

We also define the derived combinator

$\square \; \overset{\bullet}{\square}$: behaviour $\times$ behaviour $\to$ behaviour

as follows

bh$_1$ **;** bh$_2$ = **def**$_{null}$ bh$_1$ **in** λx.bh$_2$;

this combinator has the usual properties of the sequential composition without value passing.

Recursively defined behaviours

- **rec**: (behaviour $\to$ behaviour) $\to$ behaviour

  This combinator allows us to define behaviours with nonterminating activity; for example **rec** λx.a Δ x represents the behaviour which performs the action a forever.

seed is an auxiliary combinator which is only used for describing the creation of new behaviours (see section 2.1).

Formally the specification of behaviours (ie, the algebraic transition system describing their activities), indicated by BEHAVIOUR, is defined as follows.

The behaviour states.

```
BH_STATE =
    enrich DATA by
        opns
            □ Δ □: act × behaviour → behaviour
            rec: (behaviour → behaviour) →  behaviour
            {   choose_srt: (srt → behaviour) → behaviour,
                def_srt □ in □ : behaviour × (srt → behaviour),
                return_srt □ : srt → behaviour              | srt ∈ Sorts }
            seed: → behaviour.
```

The flags of the algebraic transition system describing the behaviours are given by the specification DATA.

BEHAVIOUR = TS(BH_STATE, DATA<act>,Ax$_{BH}$)

being Ax$_{BH}$ the following set of axioms:

$\{$ a Δ bh $\xrightarrow{a}$ bh $\} \cup$

$\{$ bhf(t) $\xrightarrow{a}$ bh $\supset$ **choose**$_{srt}$ bhf $\xrightarrow{a}$ bh $\qquad\qquad$ | srt $\in$ Sorts $\} \cup$

$\{$ **def**$_{srt1}$ (**choose**$_{srt}$ bhf) in bhf$_o$ = **choose**$_{srt}$ λt. (**def**$_{srt1}$ bhf(t) in bhf$_o$)

$\qquad\qquad\qquad\qquad\qquad\qquad\qquad\qquad$ | srt, srt1 $\in$ Sorts, t not free in bhf, bhf$_o$ $\} \cup$

$\{$ **def**$_{srt}$ a Δ bh in bhf = a Δ **def**$_{srt}$ bh in bhf,

$\quad$ **def**$_{srt}$ (**return**$_{srt}$ t) in bhf = bhf(t),

$\quad$ bh $\xrightarrow{a}$ bh' $\supset$ **def**$_{srt}$ bh in bhf $\xrightarrow{a}$ **def**$_{srt}$ bh' in bhf $\qquad$ | srt $\in$ Sorts$\} \cup$

$\{$ **def**$_{srt}$ (**return**$_{srt1}$ t$_1$) in bhf = **return**$_{srt1}$ t$_1$ $\qquad$ | srt, srt1 $\in$ Sorts, srt1 $\neq$ srt$\} \cup$

$\{$ **rec** bhf = bhf(**rec** bhf),

$\quad$ **seed** $\xrightarrow{\text{CREATED BH}}$ bh $\}$

Notice that the specification defined above is parameterized on DATA also on act; thus in the following we write

BEHAVIOUR(DATA,act)

when we want to emphasize these parameters.

Example. We give here an instantiation of the parametric schema **BEHAVIOUR**, describing processes which can perform internal actions, exchange values with other behaviours (natural numbers and processes), read and write a shared buffer (containing natural values) or create new processes.

In this case the parameter DATA will be instantiated with the following specification.

```
ACT&VALUE =
    enrich NAT by
        sorts   behaviour, act
        opns    TAU:   → act                              (total)
                SEND, REC: nat   → act                        "
                SEND, REC: behaviour   → act                  "
                CREATE, CREATED_BH: behaviour  → act          "
                WRITE_BUF, READ_BUF: nat   → act              "
```

PROC = **BH_SYST(ACT&VALUE, act)**

The term of sort behaviour

choose bh: behaviour **in**
REC(bh) Δ CREATE(bh) Δ CREATE(bh) Δ CREATE(bh) Δ **skip**

represents a process which could receive a process, say bh, from some other process and then create three instances of bh.

Given the term of sort (nat → behaviour)

Reg = **fix** λ fun . λ n .
(SEND(n) Δ fun(n)) + (**choose** m: nat **in** REC(m) Δ fun(m));

for all terms n_0 of sort nat Reg(n_0) represents a process realizing the well-known register containing the value n_0.
End example.

2.2 Composing Processes

The schema presented here as an example is the SMoLCS schema, already presented elsewhere and used in the formal definition of Ada.

A concurrent system is viewed as a particular kind of labelled transition system, in which a state has an internal structure built starting from the specification of the process components modelled themselves as labelled transition systems; in particular, in the standard SMoLCS, a state consists of a multiset of processes and a global information (a global object which represents information shared between processes). The transitions of the whole system are derived from the transitions of the process components following a three-steps approach in which at each step a new transition system is obtained from the previous, as shown below. The parameterized SMoLCS schema is hence obtained combining three parameterized subschema, each one corresponding to a step of the methodology.

Synchronization

In the *synchronization step* a transition models a synchronization between processes (eg, handshaking) and/or interaction with the global object (eg, a process reads a shared variable). Formally:

STS(CTS,INF,SYNC_FLAG,Ax$_{SYNC}$) = TS(SSTATE,SYNC_FLAG,Ax$_{SYNC}$)

where

* CTS is an algebraic transition system with transition relation

$$\square \xrightarrow{\square} \square : \text{state} \times \text{flag} \times \text{state}$$

and an operation **seed**: → state (in particular it can be an instantiation of the parametric specification **BEHAVIOUR** given in the preceding section, after having renamed the transition relation ──> by ⟹).

- INF (the *global information*) and SYNC_FLAG are two ppa specifications with main sort respectively inf and sflag;
- SSTATE =
  enrich MSET(CTS) × INF by
  axioms seed I mps = mps
  where MSET and × are the parameterized specifications of multisets (multiset union is denoted by I) and of cartesian products respectively;
- Ax$_{SYNC}$ is a set of positive conditional axioms of the form:

$$\bigwedge_{1 \leq j \leq n} p_j \xoverset{f_j}{\Longrightarrow} p'_j \wedge cond(f_1,...,f_n,i) \supset <p_1 I ... I p_n,i> \xrightarrow{sf} <p'_1 I ... I p'_n,i'>;$$

each axiom having this form can be interpreted as follows: if each of the processes p_j can perform an action f_j and if the condition $cond(f_1,...,f_n,i)$ is true (it can be viewed as an "enabling condition"), then the state of the concurrent system consisting of only those processes can perform the action sf and evolve consequently. Notice that all the processes in the state $<p_1 I...I p_n,i>$ take part to this action (this is what it is called *synchronous transition*); the possibility for some process to stay idle or to move independently (not synchronized) is taken into account in the following steps.

Example. Here we describe the synchronous interactions of the processes defined by the algebraic transition system PROC (given in section 2.1) by means of the following instantiation of the schema STS.

SYNC = STS(PROC[⟹/──>], NAT, **sorts** act, SYNC_AX)

where:
- NAT is the global information (it represents the state of the shared buffer);
- the synchronous actions are labelled by the same flags of PROC;
- SYNC_AX =
  { $bh \xRightarrow{TAU} bh' \supset <bh,i> \xrightarrow{TAU} <bh',i>,$
  $bh_1 \xRightarrow{SEND(x)} bh'_1 \wedge bh_2 \xRightarrow{REC(x)} bh'_2 \supset <bh_1 I bh_2,i> \xrightarrow{TAU} <bh'_1 I bh'_2,i>,$
  $bh \xRightarrow{READ\_BUF(n)} bh' \wedge i = n \supset <bh,i> \xrightarrow{READ\_BUF(n)} <bh',i>,$
  $bh \xRightarrow{WRITE\_BUF(n)} bh' \supset <bh,i> \xrightarrow{WRITE\_BUF(n)} <bh',n>,$
  $bh_1 \xRightarrow{CREATE(bh)} bh'_1 \wedge seed \xRightarrow{CREATED\_BH(bh)} bh \supset$
  $<bh_1 I seed,i> \xrightarrow{TAU} <bh'_1 I bh,i> \}$

End example.

Parallelism

In the *parallel step* a transition models the parallel composition, when possible, of many transitions obtained in the preceding step (eg a transition in which many processes move independently without problems of multiple synchronous access to a same resource). Formally:

PTS(STS,Ax$_{PAR}$) = TS(STS, PAR,Ax$_{PAR}$)

where:
- STS is an instantiation of the schema STS with transition relation ──>: state × sflag × state;
- PAR =
  sorts sflag
  opns □//□: sflag × sflag → sflag (comm., assoc., total)

  the operation // is used to represent the flags of the parallel composition of synchronous transitions;
- Ax$_{PAR}$ is a set of positive conditional axioms having form

$$\bigwedge_{1 \leq j \leq 2} <ms_j,i> \xrightarrow{sf_j} <ms'_j,i'_j> \wedge cond(sf_1,sf_2) \supset <ms_1 I ms_2,i> \xrightarrow{sf_1//sf_1} <ms'_1 I ms_2',i'>$$

these axioms specify which are the allowed parallel executions of the actions resulting from the independent activity of two multisets of processes and what is their effect on the global information. Notice that the global information i'_1 and i'_2, resulting after the execution of sf_1 and sf_2 respectively, can be different from the global information i', resulting after the parallel execution of sf_1 and sf_2. This feature can be used for example to model the fact that two simultaneous updatings of a same variable result in an undefined value associated with that variable.

Example. Here we describe, by means of the schema **PTS**, which are the synchronous interactions of the processes defined by the algebraic transition system PROC (given in section 2.1) which can be performed contemporaneously.

$$PAR = \mathbf{PTS}(SYNC, PAR\_AX)$$

where:

$PAR\_AX =$

$\{$ $<mbh_1,i> \xrightarrow{\text{TAU}} <mbh'_1,i> \wedge <mbh_2,i> \xrightarrow{a} <mbh'_2,i> \supset$

$\qquad\qquad <mbh_1 \mid mbh_2,i> \xrightarrow{\text{TAU} \;// \; a} <mbh'_1 \mid mbh'_2,i'> \} \cup$

$\{$ $<mbh_1,i> \xrightarrow{\text{READ\_BUF(n)}} <mbh'_1,i> \wedge <mbh_2,i> \xrightarrow{\text{n-TAU}} <mbh'_2,i> \supset$

$\qquad\qquad <mbh_1 \mid mbh_2,i> \xrightarrow{\text{READ\_BUF(n)} \;// \; \text{n-TAU}} <mbh'_1 \mid mbh'_2,i'>,$

$<mbh_1,i> \xrightarrow{\text{WRITE\_BUF(n)}} <mbh'_1,i> \wedge <mbh_2,i> \xrightarrow{\text{n-TAU}} <mbh'_2,i> \supset$

$\qquad\qquad <mbh_1 \mid mbh_2,i> \xrightarrow{\text{WRITE\_BUF(n)} \;// \; \text{n-TAU}} <mbh'_1 \mid mbh'_2,i'>$

$\qquad\qquad\qquad\qquad$ | for all terms n-TAU of the form TAU// ... // TAU $\}$

The above axioms formalize the requirement that at most one process at once can access the shared buffer, while there are no constraints on the other actions; it is easy to see that different assumptions on the access policy for the shared buffer can easily formalized by changing some of the above axioms. End example.

Monitoring

In the *monitoring step* a transition models a move of the whole system, ie, a transition obtained in the preceding step and is allowed by some global policy of processes scheduling (eg priorities). Formally:

$$MTS(PTS,EXT\_FLAG,Ax_{MON}) = TS(PTS,EXT\_FLAG,Ax_{MON})$$

where:

- PTS is an instantiation of the schema **PTS** where the transition relation $\longrightarrow$ has been renamed by $\Longrightarrow$;
- EXT_FLAG is a ppa specification of the external flags (flags of the actions of the concurrent system) whose main sort is extflag;
- Ax_{MON} is a set of positive conditional axioms of the form:

$$< ms, i > \xrightarrow{pf} < ms', i'> \wedge cond(pf, < ms \mid ms_1, i >) \supset < ms \mid ms_1, i > \xrightarrow{ef} < ms' \mid ms_1, i ' >;$$

an axiom having this form can be interpreted as follows: if a group of processes (ms) has the possibility of performing a transition (labelled by pf) and if this transition is enabled by the global condition cond(...) (on the whole state of the concurrent system), then a corresponding transition of the final concurrent system labelled by ef is allowed; note that the other processes (ms_1) do not take part in this transition.

Example. Here we describe which are the parallel composition of synchronous interactions of the processes defined by the algebraic transition system PROC, that can be performed as actions of the whole system by means of the following instantiation of the schema **MTS**.

$$SYST = \mathbf{MTS}(PAR, \mathbf{sorts\ flag\ opns\ TAU:} \to flag\ (total), MON\_AX)$$

where:

$MON\_AX =$

$\{$ $<mbh, i> \xrightarrow{a} < mbh', i'> \supset < mbh \mid mbh_1, i > \xrightarrow{\text{TAU}} < mbh' \mid mbh_1, i ' > \}.$

The above axiom formalizes the requirement that all parallel compositions of synchronous actions defined in the parallel step become actions of the whole system. It is easy to see that different assumptions on the global control on the process activities can be formalized by changing the above axiom. End example.

In summary the SMoLCS three steps schema is described in the following way:

$$\text{SMoLCS(CTS,INF,SYNC\_FLAG,Ax}_{\text{SYNC}}\text{,Ax}_{\text{PAR}}\text{,EXT\_FLAG,Ax}_{\text{MON}}) =$$

> MTS(
>> PTS(
>>> STS(CTS, INF, SYNC_FLAG, Ax$_{\text{SYNC}}$),
>>
>> Ax$_{\text{PAR}}$),
>> EXT_FLAG,Ax$_{\text{MON}}$).

Example. The concurrent system SYST, defined above, can also be given as an instantiation of the SMoLCS schema:

> SYST =
>> SMoLCS(PROC[$\Longrightarrow$/$\longrightarrow$], NAT, **sorts** act, SYNC_AX,
>> PAR_AX,
>> **sorts** flag **opns** TAU: $\to$ flag (total), MON_AX).

End example.

Now using the techniques introduced in section 1.2.2 we give SYT some observational semantics.

Example. In the case of SYST the semantics given by observing the state by means of the transition relation is not very interesting; indeed this semantics distinguishes only the number of moves the states of SYST can perform. Let SYST_BIS be the observational specification (SYST, {state}, {$\longrightarrow$}) and ~SYST_BIS be the bisimulation associated with SYST_BIS. For example, we have that

- all normal states, ie states which cannot perform any activity, are semantically equivalent

> (eg,   <return$_{\text{nat}}$ 0 I return$_{\text{nat}}$ 1, i > ~$_{\text{SYST\_BIS}}$
>
>   <SEND(3) Δ **skip** I REC(5) Δ **skip**, i > ~$_{\text{SYST\_BIS}}$ < **skip** , i >)

- < TAU Δ **skip**, i > $\nsim_{\text{SYST\_BIS}}$ < TAU Δ TAU Δ **skip**, i >>

More interesting for SYST is, instead, the result semantics, where the results of states, which correspond to correct termination, are given by the values returned by the terminated behaviour components; formally:

> SYST_RES = (SYST^{R}, {state}, { Results: state × mset(nat) })

> SYST^{R} = **enrich** SYST + MSET(NAT) **by**
>> **preds** Results: state × mset(nat)
>> **axioms**
>>> { Results(<return$_{\text{nat}}$ n$_1$ I ... I return$_{\text{nat}}$ n$_k$ I n-**skip**, i >, n$_1$ I ... I n$_k$)
>>>
>>>   I for all terms n-**skip** of form   **skip** I ... I **skip** }
>>>
>>> s $\xrightarrow{\text{TAU}}$ s' $\wedge$ Results(s',mn) $\supset$ Results(s',mn).

Notice that only the normal states corresponding to correct terminations have associated a result; for example <SEND(3) Δ **skip** I REC(5) Δ **skip**, i > has not associated a result.

Given the following states of SYST

> s$_1$ = < return$_{\text{nat}}$ 0 I rec λ bh . (return$_{\text{nat}}$ 1 + TAU Δ bh), i >,
>
> s$_2$ = < return$_{\text{nat}}$ 1 I return$_{\text{nat}}$ 0, i >,
>
> s$_3$ = < SEND(0) Δ return$_{\text{nat}}$ 1 I TAU Δ **choose**$_{\text{nat}}$ λ n . REC(n) Δ return$_{\text{nat}}$ n, i >,
>
> s$_4$ = < return$_{\text{nat}}$ 0 I return$_{\text{nat}}$ 0 + return$_{\text{nat}}$ 1, i >;

we have that s$_1$ ~$_{\text{SYST\_RES}}$ s$_2$ ~$_{\text{SYST\_RES}}$ s$_3$, since all of them have associated the unique result 0 I 1; while s$_4$ $\nsim_{\text{SYST\_RES}}$ s$_1$, since s$_4$ can produce also the result 0 I 0.
End example.

3 DATA AND CONCURRENCY

In this section we show how the principles and techniques introduced in the section 1 allows us to integrate the specification of classic abstract data types with the specification of processes. We focus our attention on three aspects:

- some values used by processes are specified as a usual adt (eg, the values which are exchanged between processes, stored in local and global memories, or exchanged with the world outside the processes);
- some values used within a concurrent system are specified by an adt having subcomponents which are processes (eg, processes defining and using process types, processes communicating processes, storing processes in shared memories, and so on);
- some object of an abstract data type is concurrently accessed by processes in a concurrent environment.

In all cases we aim at giving results showing that the proposed procedure is consistent in the sense that is does not destroy either the semantics of the adt or the semantics of the concurrent system.

For lack of room we illustrate the technique by examples, but in all cases it should be clear that the approach is fully general. A deeper discussion and a technical presentation for the general case can be found in [AGR2].

Static Data Types

In section 2 we have given the specification of a concurrent system SYST where the component processes handle natural values defined by the specification NAT; it is clear that in the same way it is possible to specify concurrent systems where the component processes use whichever data.

Consider a variation of SYST. Suppose that the data used by the component processes can be integer numbers or arrays with indices ranging over natural numbers and whose elements can be either integer numbers or, in turn, arrays of the same kind (a data type found in various programming languages). These data are defined by the following specification VALUE:

> **enrich** NAT + INTEGER[value/integer] **by**
> **sorts** value
> **opns** { ($\square$,..., $\square$): value × ... × value → value (total) | n ≥ 2 } -- array constructors
>   (n times)
> $\square$ ($\square$): value × nat → value -- components selector
> $\square$ [$\square$ / $\square$]: value × value × nat → value -- components updating
> **axioms**
>   { $(v_1,...,v_{n-1},v_n,v_{n+1},...,v_m)(n) = v_n$,
> $(v_1,...,v_{n-1},v_n,v_{n+1},...,v_m)[v/n] = (v_1,...,v_{n-1},v,v_{n+1},...,v_m)$ | m ≥ 2, 1 ≤ n ≤ m }.

Let $SYST^{VALUE}$ be the concurrent system defined as SYST except that now NAT has been replaced by VALUE and $SYST^{VALUE}\_RES$ be the observational specification, defined as SYST_RES (see section 2.2), formalizing the result semantics for $SYST^{VALUE}$.

We have that the ppa $W_{Sig(SYST^{VALUE})/\sim SYST^{VALUE}\_RES}$ restricted to Sig(VALUE) is the initial model of VALUE, ie, the embedding of VALUE into the concurrent system SYST has preserved its semantics. Under some reasonable conditions (see [AGR2]), this result holds for a generic concurrent system CS with an associated observational semantics and for a generic subspecification of CS.

Processes as Data

Here we show how in our framework it is also possible to define data types based on processes, eg, functions into processes, cartesian products where some components are processes or functions returning processes and so on.

Consider for example the case of functions from integer numbers into the processes specified by PROC (given in section 2.1). Assume that PROC has been given the so called strong bisimulation semantics (see section 1.2.1); this semantics can be formally defined, in our framework, as the bisimulation associated with the observational specification

$$\text{PROC\_BIS} = (\text{PROC}, \{ \text{ behaviour } \}, \{ \longrightarrow: \text{behaviour} \times \text{flag} \times \text{behaviour} \}).$$

In the framework of ppa specifications there are sorts and operations for handling functions, but if we want two functions to be equated iff they are extensionally equivalent, then their semantics has to be given observationally, as it is shown by the following observational specification:

PROC_FUNCT_SEM =
    (PROC_FUNCT, {behaviour, (integer → behaviour) },
               { ⟶: behaviour × flag × behaviour, Oappl: (integer → behaviour) × integer × behaviour })

PROC_FUNCT = **enrich** PROC + INTEGER **by**
               preds Oappl: (integer → behaviour) × integer × behaviour
               axioms $D(bhf(i)) \supset Oappl(bhf,i,bhf(i))$

Let FPS be the algebra $W_{Sig(PROC\_FUNCT)}/{\sim}\text{PROC\_FUNCT\_SEM}$. We have that

- FPS restricted to Sig(PROC) is isomorphic to $W_{Sig(PROC)}/{\sim}\text{BIS-PROC}$;

- for all bhf_1, $bhf_2 \in W_{Sig(PROC\_FUNCT)|(integer \to behaviour)}$
    FPS $\models bhf_1 = bhf_2$ iff for all $i \in W_{Sig(PROC\_FUNCT)|integer}$ FPS $\models bhf_1(i) = bhf_2(i)$
(ie, (integer → behaviour)^{FPS} is truly a set of functions).

Under some reasonable conditions (see [AGR2]), this result holds for a generic specification A with an associated observational semantics (s.t. the only observed sort is the main sort of A) based on an algebraic transition system TS whose semantics is also given observationally.

Dynamic Data Types

Here we show by a simple example of a stack of natural numbers a possible canonical way of modelling the concurrent access to a data type in a concurrent environment. The specification of such a data type is given following the usual techniques:

STACKN =
    enrich NAT **by**
        sorts stack
        opns Empty: → stack   (total)
                Top: stack → nat
                Pop: stack → stack
                Push: stack × nat → stack   (total)
        axioms
            Top(Push(st,n)) = n
            Pop(Push(st,n)) = st.

Our technique consists in putting a stack of natural number in parallel with the component processes of the concurrent system SYST (defined in 2.2) replacing the shared buffer containing only one natural number with a stack of natural number, obtaining a new concurrent system indicated by SYST^{STACKN}.

We can define a standard mechanism for handling a stack of natural numbers when put in parallel with several processes accessing it concurrently. First we classify the operations on stacks in three classes:

- creating operations
    Empty: → stack

- modifying operations
    Pop: stack → stack
    Push: stack × nat → stack

- observing operations
    Top: stack → nat.

The intuitive meaning of the names associated with the above sets of operations should be clear. Note that this classification of the operations can be applied to any abstract data type.

Now we can associate with every of such operations an action of the component processes with the same name (but capitalized, to distinguish it) and with each of these action flags a synchronous axiom defining the effect of the action in terms of the corresponding operation of STACKN. Thus the specification ACT&VALUE has to be enriched by the following total operations (clearly the actions for handling the buffer are eliminated):

$$\text{EMPTY:} \rightarrow \text{act}$$
$$\text{PUSH: nat} \rightarrow \text{act}$$
$$\text{POP:} \rightarrow \text{act}$$
$$\text{TOP: nat} \rightarrow \text{act;}$$

and the set of axioms defining the synchronous actions of $\text{SYST}^{\text{STACKN}}$ is given by replacing in SYNC_AX (the axioms defining the synchronous actions of SYST) the axioms corresponding to the interactions with the shared buffer with:

(a) $bh \xrightarrow{\text{EMPTY}} bh' \supset < bh, st > \xrightarrow{\text{EMPTY}} < bh', \text{Empty} >$

(b) $bh \xrightarrow{\text{PUSH(n)}} bh' \supset < bh, st> \xrightarrow{\text{PUSH(n)}} < bh', \text{Push(n,st)} >$

(b) $bh \xrightarrow{\text{POP}} bh' \wedge D(\text{Pop(st)}) \supset < bh, st > \xrightarrow{\text{POP}} < bh', \text{Pop(st)} >,$

(c) $bh \xrightarrow{\text{TOP(n)}} bh' \wedge \text{Top(st)} = n \supset < bh, st > \xrightarrow{\text{TOP(n)}} < bh', st >.$

It is easy to verify that these axioms reflect our intuition that the synchronous transitions have the correct effect. Note that for a generic data type the synchronous rules for the actions corresponding to the creating, modifying and observing operations have respectively the form (a), (b) and (c).

The parallelism of $\text{SYST}^{\text{STACKN}}$ can be defined by replacing PAR_AX with the following set of axioms:

$\{ <mbh_1,st> \xrightarrow{\text{TAU}} <mbh'_1,st> \wedge <mbh_2,st> \xrightarrow{a} <mbh'_2,st> \supset$
$\qquad <mbh_1 \mid mbh_2,st> \xrightarrow{\text{TAU} // a} <mbh'_1 \mid mbh'_2,st> \} \cup$

$\{ <mbh_1,st> \xrightarrow{\text{EMPTY}} <mbh'_1,st'> \wedge <mbh_2,st> \xrightarrow{\text{n-TAU}} <mbh'_2,st> \supset$
$\qquad <mbh_1 \mid mbh_2,st> \xrightarrow{\text{EMPTY} // \text{n-TAU}} <mbh'_1 \mid mbh'_2,st'>,$

$<mbh_1,st> \xrightarrow{\text{TOP(n)}} <mbh'_1,st> \wedge <mbh_2,st> \xrightarrow{\text{n-TAU}} <mbh'_2,st> \supset$
$\qquad <mbh_1 \mid mbh_2,st> \xrightarrow{\text{TOP(n)} // \text{n-TAU}} <mbh'_1 \mid mbh'_2,st>,$

$<mbh_1,st> \xrightarrow{\text{PUSH(n)}} <mbh'_1,st'> \wedge <mbh_2,st> \xrightarrow{\text{n-TAU}} <mbh'_2,st> \supset$
$\qquad <mbh_1 \mid mbh_2,st> \xrightarrow{\text{PUSH(n)} // \text{n-TAU}} <mbh'_1 \mid mbh'_2,st'>$

$<mbh_1,st> \xrightarrow{\text{POP}} <mbh'_1,st'> \wedge <mbh_2,st> \xrightarrow{\text{n-TAU}} <mbh'_2,st> \supset$
$\qquad <mbh_1 \mid mbh_2,st> \xrightarrow{\text{POP} // \text{n-TAU}} <mbh'_1 \mid mbh'_2,st'>$

$\mid$ for all terms n-TAU of the form TAU// ... // TAU $\}$

The above axioms formalize the requirement that at most one process at once can access the stack; it is easy to see that different assumptions on the access policy for the stack can easily formalized by changing some of them.

The monitoring of $\text{SYST}^{\text{STACKN}}$ can be left as before, ie, there are no global restrictions on the activities of the component processes at all.

This technique can be applied in general for defining a system having as global information a generic dynamic data type (see [AGR2]).

Consider now the following sequence of transitions of a state of $\text{SYST}^{\text{STACKN}}$:

$$< \text{EMPTY } \Delta \text{ PUSH(3) } \Delta \text{ POP } \Delta \text{ skip, st} > \xrightarrow{\text{EMPTY}} < \text{PUSH(3) } \Delta \text{ POP } \Delta \text{ skip, Empty} >$$

$$\xrightarrow{\text{PUSH(3)}} < \text{POP } \Delta \text{ skip, Push(3,Empty)} > \xrightarrow{\text{POP}} < \text{skip, Empty} >.$$

Intuitively, executing the sequence of actions EMPTY, PUSH(3), POP should have the effect of leaving the queue with the value Pop(Push(3,Empty)) = Empty, and indeed the sequence of transitions above has this effect. Moreover, if we replace in the example above the behaviour

EMPTY Δ PUSH(3) Δ POP Δ **skip**

by the behaviour EMPTY Δ **skip**, it is intuitively clear that we get an "equivalent" state. There seems to be a correspondence between terms and sequences of actions, which in some sense preserves the semantics: in particular there are two properties which seem to hold, at least under suitable conditions:

- if a process performs a sequence of actions corresponding to operations of the data type STACKN (it is a process which can be seen as a *translation* of a term t) then the value of the stack object should change accordingly (ie, should change to a value "strictly related to t");

- if we exchange within a given state of SYST^{STACKN} a process with another process which can perform "equivalent" sequences of actions (ie, the two processes are "translation of provable equal terms in STACKN") then we expect to obtain an equivalent state.

Indeed these properties hold for all processes which are "translation of terms" and for all contexts which "do not interfere" with their activity. The formalization of these requirements and the proof of the above properties require some technical definitions which we do not give here and which can be found in [AGR2], together with some generalizations.

4 MODELLING AN OBJECT ORIENTED APPROACH

In recent years object oriented (shortly o-o) programming (whose roots are found in the language Simula) has been moving out of the experimental corner and it is used more and more often to program large systems. While the object oriented paradigm appears in its purest form in Smalltalk-80 ([GR]), there is a number of proposed notations in which it plays a significant role (for example [Me]). The main concept in object oriented programming is obviously the concept of *object*t: indeed in object oriented programming a whole system is described as a *collection of objects*. As a first approximation an object can be described as an integrated unit of data and procedures acting on these data. Objects are *dynamic entities*; they can be *created* dynamically during the execution of a program, the data they contain can *be modified*, and in connection with parallelism they can have an *internal activity* of their own. Internal data of an object cannot be accessed directly by other objects; objects interact instead by calling *methods*. From the user's point of view the object oriented approach offers a completely new way of thinking about problems and solutions; this approach has proven to be very powerful and, in some sense, corresponding to a model of the "real world"; basically the programming emphasis is no longer in finding algorithms but in defining objects, where an object is an entity which offers some services to the outside (hiding its internal structure) and in turn uses other objects. Thus a situation is modelled by a collection of objects (what we call in this section an *object system*) which communicate via their interfaces (sending *messages* each other, in the Smalltalk terminology). From the theoretical point of view, it is not clear whether the o-o approach is just a methodology (even if innovative and powerful) or it corresponds to some new concept or framework at the foundational level.

In this section we present an attempt at inserting some basic o-o concepts in an algebraic framework, on the basis of the ideas and techniques described in section 1. Note that our aim is not to give the formal semantics of a particular o-o language; we provide instead a formal schema for modelling classes of objects; this schema should serve as a basis for the definition of a formal semantics of o-o notations. In section 4.1 we discuss the concept of object; and in section 4.2 we present the schema with the help of some significant examples.

4.1 Different Views of Objects

Since in the algebraic framework the emphasis is on data structures, the problem of handling single "instances" of some data type is something quite unusual. Let us outline some different viewpoints that are useful for the following technical proposal.

In some cases we can model objects as values of a data type; hence an *object as a value* would be modelled as a couple, say

t **with** S

where t is a term on the signature of the specification S. Accordingly to the semantics chosen for S (say initial, terminal, observational, loose) we get a corresponding semantics for the objects: if A is a semantic algebra for S, then (t^A, A) is the corresponding semantics for t **with** S. For example, S could be the specification of natural numbers and t could be a particular number. So two semantically equivalent couples represent the same natural number, hence the same object.

With the above schema we can model also *dynamic objects as values*. Indeed, as shown in section 1, we can model dynamic aspects by algebraic techniques, leading to specifications of processes. Hence a *dynamic object as value* is a couple, say

t **with** S

where S is a process specification in the sense of section 1 and t is a term of a sort corresponding to a sort of processes (eg a term of sort behaviour or a term of sort state). Notice that the semantics associated with the specification S embodies our observations about processes and hence the value of t embodies the semantics corresponding to the observable interactions with the environment. For example this is the way we can model the values of procedures and functions in a concurrent language (eg Ada), where they may involve the activity of some tasks.

In the O-O terminology objects are seen as entities and viewing objects as values does not always capture the intuitive idea of "object as an entity". We can explain the difference between a "value" and an "entity" by the familiar example of a stack of natural numbers. The couple

Push(3,Empty) **with** STACKN

represents a *particular configuration* of a stack, but a stack as an entity is none of these particular configurations. Indeed:

- during its lifetime the same stack can evolve, starting from an initial configuration, through several different configurations, hence two different couples could correspond to intermediate configurations in the evolution of the same stack entity;

- conversely, a couple does not identify uniquely a stack as an entity, since different stack entities could have the same configuration value at some stage of their execution;

- moreover the history of the entity, ie, the concatenation of the different configurations, is determined usually by the interaction with the environment.

All the above remarks points towards defining a stack as a dynamic entity with an initial state; however it may happen that in the same environment two different stack entities are active with the same initial state and have to be addressed individually by other entities. Hence we need names for identifying objects as entities and so we can model one of them by a couple

(n, t_0 **with** S)

where t_0 **with** S is a dynamic object corresponding to the initial state of the object entity identified by n. Of course two entities

(n_1, t_0 **with** S)   and   (n_2, t_0 **with** S)

have the same semantics modulo the name for any chosen semantics for S; but the individual histories of n_1 and n_2 in a particular context may be different. In the next section we will relate the different views of objects to the formal modelling of o-o descriptions of objects.

Two important remarks are in order here. First, the notion of object as entity seems associated with the existence of a dynamic interacting environment: for example, in the example a configuration of the stack can be modified because some agents have the ability to do so. Secondly, notice that whenever the object value t **with** S associated with the name n is invariant and we do not need different copies of it, then the notion of object coincides with that of object value. For example, this is the case of an object corresponding to a number k unless we need different copies of it for, say, a multiple simultaneous access to a device storing that constant k, in which case we would need two locations for containing the value k and, as usual, we would model the two locations by two object variables. This distinction between object as value and object as entity and the role of dynamics for qualifying entities is already clear, in our opinion, in CCS [M1], where for example a variable is modelled by a memory register which is a process.

4.2   Classes of Objects

In an object oriented framework, it seems hard to describe objects without describing *object systems*.Indeed, objects are characterized by the way they interact with the environment, and this description is given in what we call a *class specification*.

An *object system* is a concurrent system which is used to describe the evolution of an object; at each stage of the evolution it is possible to retrieve from the system the components of the object. A generic state of an object system is a parallel composition of *dynamic entities*. A dynamic entity is a couple n: c, where n is a *name*, ie a (possibly compound) identifier, and c can be either a *basic value* (eg, behaviours, stacks) or another name (ie a reference to another object). The first kind of dynamic entity is used to model objects which are directly modelled as values, while the second kind is used to record the associations of an object with its components. For example, if st_1 and st_2 are two terms of sort stack, then

dst.s_1: sn_1 | dst.s_2: sn_2 | sn_1: st_1 | sn_2: st_2

represents a state of an object system describing the evolution of an object named dst whose two components are identified by s_1 and s_2, and are the two stack objects named sn_1 and sn_2 (sn_1: st_1 and sn_2: st_2). The evolution of the state of an object system is described in our example using a SMoLCS-like style; note that the only dynamic entities which are able to perform actions are those representing a basic value of type behaviour.

Basic Objects

A specification of a class of objects can be either the specification of *basic objects* or of *compound objects*. The specification of a class of basic objects whose values are represented by an adt A has in general the following form:

A_CLASS =
    enrich A + "states and transitions of the object system" **by**
    opns
        "dynamic entity constructor"
        "method declarations"
    axioms
        "method definitions"

Each class specification includes the declaration of the following standard methods: A_CLASS.**new** (for the creation of new instances of the class) and A_CLASS.**assign** (for changing the value of an object).Following the guidelines of section 3 it is easy to associate canonically with every observing and modifying operation of A a corresponding method.

Let us explain this idea by means of an example. Consider the specification STACKN given in section 3. Then the specification of the class having stacks as basic values can be given as follows:

STACKN_CLASS =
    enrich STACKN + DYNAMIC_STRUCTURE_STACKN_CLASS **by**
        opns
            $\Box : \Box$: name $\times$ stack $\rightarrow$ dynamic-entities (total)
            STACKN_CLASS.**new**: behaviour
            STACKN_CLASS.**assign**: (name $\times$ name $\rightarrow$ behaviour)
            STACKN_CLASS.**push**: (name $\times$ nat $\rightarrow$ behaviour)
            STACKN_CLASS.**empty**: (name $\rightarrow$ behaviour)
            STACKN_CLASS.**pop**: (name $\rightarrow$ behaviour)
            STACKN_CLASS.**top**: (name $\rightarrow$ behaviour)
        axioms
            STACKN_CLASS.**new** = **choose** n: name **in** CREATE(n: Empty) Δ **return**$_{name}$ n
            STACKN_CLASS.**assign** = $\lambda n_1, n_2$. STACKN_CLASS.ASSIGN(n_1, n_2) Δ **skip**
            STACKN_CLASS.**push** = λn, v. STACKN_CLASS.PUSH(n,v) Δ **skip**
            STACKN_CLASS.**empty** = λn. STACKN_CLASS.EMPTY(n) Δ **skip**
            STACKN_CLASS.**pop** = λn, v. STACKN_CLASS.POP(n) Δ **skip**
            STACKN_CLASS.**top** = λn. **choose** n: nat **in** STACKN_CLASS.TOP(n, v) Δ **return**$_{nat}$ n

where:

- DYNAMIC_STRUCTURE_STACKN_CLASS is the specification of the concurrent system describing the object system associated with the class STACKN_CLASS

    DYNAMIC_STRUCTURE_STACKN_CLASS =
        enrich STANDARD_DYNAMIC_STRUCTURE + STACKN^{ACT} **by**
            axioms

$$de \xrightarrow{\text{STACKN\_CLASS.ASSIGN}(n_1, n_2)} de' \supset$$
$$de \mid n_1: st_1 \mid n_2: st_2 \xRightarrow{\text{TAU}} de' \mid n_1: st_2 \mid n_2: st_2$$

$$de \xrightarrow{\text{STACKN\_CLASS.PUSH}(n,v)} de' \supset \quad de \mid n: st \xRightarrow{\text{TAU}} de' \mid n: \text{Push}(v,st)$$

$$de \xrightarrow{\text{STACKN\_CLASS.POP}(n)} de' \supset \quad de \mid n: st \xRightarrow{\text{TAU}} de' \mid n: \text{Pop}(st)$$

$$de \xrightarrow{\text{STACKN\_CLASS.EMPTY}(n)} de' \supset \quad de \mid n: st \xRightarrow{\text{TAU}} de' \mid n: \text{Empty}$$

$$de \xrightarrow{\text{STACKN\_CLASS.TOP}(n,v)} de' \wedge \text{Top}(st) = v \supset \quad de \mid n: st \xRightarrow{\text{TAU}} de' \mid n: st$$

- STANDARD_DYNAMIC_STRUCTURE is the specification of sorts, operations, predicates and axioms which are common to all object systems:

    STANDARD_DYNAMIC_STRUCTURE =
    enrich NAME **by**
        sorts
            dynamic-entities -- states of the object system
            sflag   -- flags of the synchronous and parallel actions of the object system
        opns
      -- action for creating new dynamic entities
            CREATE: dynamic-entities $\rightarrow$ act
      -- constructors for dynamic entities
            $\Box : \Box$: name $\times$ name $\rightarrow$ dynamic-entities -- dynamic entities used to record
                                     the values of the components of the objects
            $\Box \mid \Box$: dynamic-entities $\times$ dynamic-entities $\rightarrow$ dynamic-entities
                                -- operation which combines various dynamic entities

- the flag of synchronous and parallel actions corresponding to interactions
  with (non behaviour) dynamic entities
  TAU: $\to$ sflag   (total)

-- parallel compositions of synchronous interactions between dynamic entities
  $\square \mathbin{//} \square$: sflag $\times$ sflag $\to$ sflag   (total)

preds

-- transition relation of single dynamic entities
  $\to$: dynamic-entities $\times$ act $\times$ dynamic-entities

-- parallel compositions of synchronous interactions of dynamic-entities
  $\Rightarrow$: dynamic-entities $\times$ sflag $\times$ dynamic-entities

-- transition relation of the whole object system
  $\sim$>: dynamic-entities $\times$ sflag $\times$ dynamic-entities

axioms

- the following set of axioms ensures that in an object system there cannot be
  different entities with the same name
  $\{\bigwedge_{i,j=1,\ldots,k,\,i\neq j} \text{Equal}(n_i, n_j) = \text{False} \supset D(n_1\!: c_1 \mid \ldots \mid n_k\!: c_k) \mid k \geq 1\}$

-- the transition relation "$\to$" is only defined for dynamic behaviour entities
  (see BEHAVIOUR_CLASS in the following)

-- definition of the synchronous actions related to the creation action which is the same for all class
  $\text{de} \xrightarrow{\text{CREATE}(de_1)} \text{de}' \wedge D(\text{de}' \mid de_1) \supset \text{de} \xxrightarrow{\text{TAU}} \text{de}' \mid de_1$

-- definition of the parallel actions
  $de_1 \xxrightarrow{\text{TAU}} de'_1 \wedge de_2 \xxrightarrow{\text{TAU}} de'_2 \supset de_1 \mid de_2 \xxrightarrow{\text{TAU } // \text{ TAU}} de'_1 \mid de'_2$

-- definition of the actions of the whole object system
  $\text{de} \xxrightarrow{\text{sf}} \text{de}' \supset \text{de} \mid de_1 \xxrightarrow{\text{sf}} \text{de}' \mid de_1$

- **STACKN**^{ACT} is the specification of the actions related to basic interactions with objects of class
  STACKN_CLASS:

  STACKN^{ACT} =
    enrich STACKN + NAME **by**
      sorts
        act
      opns
        STACKN_CLASS.PUSH: name $\times$ nat $\to$ act   (total)
        STACKN_CLASS.POP: name $\to$ act   (")
        STACKN_CLASS.TOP: name $\times$ nat $\to$ act   (")
        STACKN_CLASS.EMPTY: name $\to$ act   (")
        STACKN_CLASS.ASSIGN: name $\times$ name $\to$ act   (")

  where NAME is a specification of names with a total boolean equality operation (Equal) and an operation for building compound names ($\square . \square$: name $\times$ name $\to$ name).

Compound objects

The specification of a class of compound objects which have the components, identified by $cn_1, \ldots, cn_k$,
consisting of objects described by the (not necessarily different) class specifications $CLASS_1, \ldots, CLASS_k$
has in general the following form:

    C_CLASS =
      enrich $CLASS_1 + \ldots + CLASS_k$ **by**
      opns
        "additional actions for assignment and component selections"
        "method declarations"

axioms
"additional axioms for synchronous actions involving the actions
for assignment and component selections"
"method definitions"

Each class specification includes the declaration of the standard methods (as for basic objects); moreover in these cases there are also the standard methods **get_c_j** for $j = 1, ..., k$ used to access the components of the objects of the class.

Notice that C_CLASS is a specification still defining an object system. Indeed since each of the specifications CLASS$_i$ has the sort dynamic-entities and the predicates $\to$, $\Rightarrow$ and $\leadsto$, C_CLASS has also that sort and predicates; the terms of this sort can be built with all the operations appearing in all specifications CLASS$_1$, ..., CLASS$_n$ and C_CLASS; the truth of the above predicates is defined by considering the union of all axioms of the specifications CLASS$_1$, ..., CLASS$_n$ and C_CLASS.

Let us explain this idea by means of an example. Consider the class DOUBLE_STACKN_CLASS of objects having two components named s_1 and s_2 which are objects of the class STACN_CLASS. The specification of this class can be given as follows:

DOUBLE_STACKN_CLASS =
   enrich STACKN_CLASS **by**
      opns
         DOUBLE_STACKN_CLASS.ASSIGN: name $\times$ name $\to$ act
         DOUBLE_STACKN_CLASS.GET_S_1: name $\times$ name $\to$ act
         DOUBLE_STACKN_CLASS.GET_S_2: name $\times$ name $\to$ act
         DOUBLE_STACKN_CLASS.**new**: $\to$ behaviour
         DOUBLE_STACKN_CLASS.**assign**: (name $\times$ name $\to$ behaviour)
         DOUBLE_STACKN_CLASS.**get_s_1**: (name $\to$ behaviour)
         DOUBLE_STACKN_CLASS.**get_s_2**: (name $\to$ behaviour)
         DOUBLE_STACKN_CLASS.**push1**: (name $\times$ nat $\to$ behaviour)
         DOUBLE_STACKN_CLASS.**push2**: (name $\times$ nat $\to$ behaviour)
      axioms
   -- synchronous actions related to the assign action

$$de \xrightarrow{\text{DOUBLE\_STACKN\_CLASS.ASSIGN}(n_1,n_2)} de' \supset$$

$$de \mid n_1.s_1: x_1 \mid n_1.s_2: x_2 \mid n_2.s_1: y_1 \mid n_2.s_2: y_2 \xRightarrow{\text{TAU}}$$
$$de \mid n_1.s_1: y_1 \mid n_1.s_2: y_2 \mid n_2.s_1: y_1 \mid n_2.s_2: y_2$$

   -- synchronous actions related to the access to the components

$$de \xrightarrow{\text{DOUBLE\_STACKN\_CLASS.GET\_S}_1(n_1,n_2)} de' \supset de \mid n_1.s_1: n_2 \xRightarrow{\text{TAU}} de \mid n_1.s_1: n_2$$

     ...

   - axioms defining methods
     DOUBLE_STACKN_CLASS.**new** =
        def sn_1 = STACK_CLASS.**new** in
        def sn_2 = STACK_CLASS.**new** in
           choose n: name in CREATE(dsn.s_1: sn_1 | dsn.s_2: sn_2) Δ **return**$_{name}$ dsn

     ...

     DOUBLE_STACKN_CLASS.**get_s_1** =
        λn. **choose** n':name in
           STACKN_CLASS.GET_S_1(n,n') Δ **return**$_{name}$ n'

     ...

     DOUBLE_STACKN_CLASS.**push1** =
        λn, v. **def** n' = STACKN_CLASS.**get_s_1**(n) in
           STACKN_CLASS.**push**(n',v)
     DOUBLE_STACKN_CLASS.**push2** =
        λn, v. **def** n' = STACKN_CLASS.**get_s_2**(n) in
           STACKN_CLASS.**push**(n',v)

It is easy to generalize the above technique to define a parameterized schema which allows the definition of classes of objects based on other objects.

Inheritance

We show now by an example how it is possible to model *inheritance* between object classes. Let us consider a class inheriting components and methods from the class DOUBLE_STACK_CLASS and adding a method **emptyBothStacks** which empties both stack components and a behaviour component.

We first give the specification of a class of behaviour objects:

    BEHAVIOUR_CLASS =
        enrich BEHAVIOUR(CONC_ACT + STACK_CLASS) by
            opns
                □: □: name × behaviour → dynamic-components
                BEHAVIOUR_CLASS.new: (behaviour → behaviour)
                BEHAVIOUR_CLASS.assign: (name × name → behaviour)
            axioms
                BEHAVIOUR_CLASS.new =
                    λ bh. choose n: name in CREATE(n: bh) Δ return$_{name}$ n
                    ...
                bh $\xrightarrow{a}$ bh' ⊃ n: bh $\xrightarrow{a}$ n: bh'
                – axioms related to synchronous, parallel and monitoring transitions of the actions
                  in CONC_ACT
                ...

where CONC_ACT is the specification of the actions of the behaviours not related to object handling.

Then the class DOUBLE_STACK_HANDLER_CLASS obtained by inheritance from the class DOUBLE_STACK_CLASS is defined as follows:

    DOUBLE_STACK_HANDLER_CLASS =
        enrich DOUBLE_STACK_CLASS + BEHAVIOUR_CLASS by
            opns
                DOUBLE_STACK_HANDLER_CLASS.new: (behaviour → behaviour)
                DOUBLE_STACK_HANDLER_CLASS.assign: (name × name → behaviour)
                DOUBLE_STACK_HANDLER_CLASS.get_handler: (name × name → behaviour)
                DOUBLE_STACK_HANDLER_CLASS.push1: (name × nat → behaviour)
                DOUBLE_STACK_HANDLER_CLASS.push2: (name × nat → behaviour)
                DOUBLE_STACK_HANDLER_CLASS.emptyBothStacks: (name → behaviour)
                ...
            axioms
                DOUBLE_STACK_HANDLER_CLASS.new = λ bh.
                    def dsh = DOUBLE_STACK_CLASS.new in
                    def bn = BEHAVIOUR_CLASS.new(bh) in
                        CREATE(dsh.handler: bn) Δ return$_{name}$ dsh
                DOUBLE_STACK_HANDLER_CLASS.get_handler =
                    λn. choose bhn: name in
                        DOUBLE_STACKN_CLASS.GET_HANDLER(n, bhn) Δ return bhn
                DOUBLE_STACK_HANDLER_CLASS.push1 = DOUBLE_STACKN_CLASS.push1
                DOUBLE_STACK_HANDLER_CLASS.push2 = DOUBLE_STACKN_CLASS.push2
                ...
                DOUBLE_STACK_HANDLER_CLASS.emptyBothStacks =
                    λn. def n$_1$ = DOUBLE_STACK_HANDLER_CLASSget_s$_1$(n) in
                        def n$_2$ = DOUBLE_STACK_HANDLER_CLASSget_s$_2$(n) in
                            DOUBLE_STACK_HANDLER_CLASS.empty1(n$_1$) ;
                            DOUBLE_STACK_HANDLER_CLASS.empty2(n$_2$)
                    ...

Thus from the above example we can argue that inheritance can be modelled as follows:

- the components of objects of class DOUBLE_STACK_HANDLER_CLASS are the ones of DOUBLE_STACK_CLASS plus the additional component of class behaviour identified by handler;
- for each method
  DOUBLE_STACK_CLASS.methodName
  of class DOUBLE_STACK_CLASS, there is a corresponding method
  DOUBLE_STACK_HANDLER_CLASS.methodName

defined to be equal to the previous. Other methods are simply added (as eg. emptyBothStacks). Overriding of methods can be modelled by explicitly giving an axiom for the method instead of copying it from the homonymous one of the class from which we are inheriting.

Some Final Comments. It is natural at this point to ask which is the formal counterpart of an object associated with a class. It seems to us that it is rather inappropriate to think in general of objects associated with a class as dynamic entities with an initial state. Indeed in our model the instantiation of a class, which is an instantiated object in the object oriented terminology, is nothing more than a call of a method initializing a class instantiation (the method **new** in our examples) and giving it a name, the name of the instantiated object, within an object system of a bigger class. Of course at every intermediate stage of that object system it is possible to individuate, by means of its name, the components of that object, and hence the value of that object in that intermediate stage. This value is clearly a cartesian product of either basic or object values and seems to correspond to the model of object values given by Cardelli in [C]. Also his model of inheritance fits nicely into our overall algebraic specification schema.

Acknowledgment. Thanks to Maura Cerioli for her cooperation on ppa stuff.

REFERENCES

LNCS n. x stands for Lecture Notes in Computer Science, Springer-Verlag, Berlin, n. x.

[AGR1]   E. Astesiano, A. Giovini, G. Reggio, *Generalized Bisimulation in Relational Specifications*, in Proc. STACS '88, LNCS n. 294, pp. 207–226, 1988.

[AGR2]   E. Astesiano, A. Giovini, G. Reggio, *Data in concurrent environment,* to appear in Proc. Concurrency '88 , (F. Vogt ed.), LNCS n. ... , 1988.

[AMRW]   E. Astesiano, G. F. Mascari, G. Reggio, M. Wirsing, *On the Parameterized Algebraic Specification of Concurrent Systems,* Proc. TAPSOFT Conference, Vol.1, LNCS n. 186, pp. 342–358, 1985.

[AR1]   E. Astesiano, G. Reggio, *An Outline of the SMoLCS Methodology*, in Mathematical Models for the Semantics of Parallelism, Proc. Advanced School on Mathematical Models of Parallelism, (M. Venturini Zilli ed.), LNCS n. 280, pp. 81-113, 1987.

[AR2]   E.Astesiano, G.Reggio, *SMoLCS-Driven Concurrent Calculi*, (invited paper) in Proc. TAPSOFT'87, vol.1, LNCS n. 249, pp. 169–201, 1987.

[AR3]   E. Astesiano, G. Reggio, *Direct Semantics for Concurrent Languages in the SMoLCS Approach*, IBM Journal of Research and Development, vol. 31, n. 5, pp. 512–534, 1987.

[ARW]   E. Astesiano, G. Reggio, M. Wirsing, *Relational Specifications and Observational Semantics*, in Proc. MFCS'86 (Symposium on Mathematical Foundations of Computer Science, Bratislava), LNCS n. 233, pp. 209-217, 1986.

[B]   M. Broy, *Views of Queues*, technical report Universität Passau, MIP-8704, February 1987.

[BW]   M. Broy, M. Wirsing, *Partial abstract types*, Acta Informatica 18, 47-64, 1982.

[C]   L. Cardelli, *A semantics of multiple inheritance*, in Semantics of Data Types, proc. of International Symposium Sophia-Antipolis (G. Kahn, D. B. MacQueen, G. Plotkin editors), LNCS n. 173, pp. 51 - 68, 1984.

[CRAI-DDC] E. Astesiano, C. Bendix Nielsen, N. Botta, A. Fantechi, A. Giovini, P. Inverardi, E. Karlsen, F. Mazzanti, J. Storbank Pedersen, G. Reggio, E. Zucca, *The Draft Formal Definition of Ada*, Deliverable of the CEC MAP project: The Draft Formal Definition of ANSI/STD 1815A Ada, 1986.

[GM] J. A. Goguen, J. Meseguer, *Models and equality for logical Programming*, in Proc. TAPSOFT'87, vol.2, LNCS n. 249, pp. 1, 22, 1987.

[GR] A. Goldberg, D. Robson, *Smalltalk-80 The language and its implementation*, Addison-Wesley, 1985.

[GV] R. van Glabbeek, F. Vaandrager, *Curious Queues*, in: Proc. METEOR 1987 Workshop, (M. Wirsing ed.), LNCS, 1988.

[HJ] C. A. R. Hoare, H. Jeifeng, *Algebraic specification and proof of properties of a mail service*, in Program Specification and Transformation (Proc. of IFIP TC2/WG 2.1 Working Conference on Program Specification and Transformation, Bad Tölz, 1986), North-Holland, 1987.

[KP] S. Kaplan, A. Pnueli, *Specification and Implementation of Concurrently Accessed Data Structures: an Abstract Data Type Approach*, in: Proc. STACS '87 (F. J. Brandenburg, G. Vidal-Naquet, M. Wirsing eds.), LNCS n. 247, 1987.

[M1] R. Milner, *A calculus of communicating systems*, LNCS n. 92, 1980.

[M2] R. Milner, *Calculi for synchrony and asynchrony*, TCS 25, 267-310, 1983.

[Me] B. Meyer, *Eiffel: Programming for reusability and extendibility*, SIGPLAN Notices, V. 22 # 2, February 1987.

[Pa] D. Park, *Concurrency and Automata on Infinite Sequences*, in Proc. 5th GI Conference LNCS n. 104, 1981.

[Pl] G. Plotkin, *A structural approach to operational semantics*, Lecture notes, Aarhus University, 1981.

Appendix: Higher Order Partial Algebraic Specifications with Predicates

Here we briefly report the main ideas about *higher order partial specifications with predicates* (shortly ppa specifications, for partial predicates specifications), which are derived by the partial abstract specification of Broy Wirsing (see [BW]) and by the specification with predicates of Goguen (see [GM]); a complete treatment will be the subject of a forthcoming full report.

A *ppa signature* is a triple $\Sigma = (S,F,P)$, where

- S is the set of sorts; satisfying the property

  for all $n \geq 1$ if $s_1, ..., s_n, s \in S$, then $(s_1 \times ... \times s_n \to s) \in S$

  (ie, S includes also the *higher order sorts*);

- $F = \{F_w\}_{w \in S^* \times S}$ is the family of the sets of *operation symbols* satisfying the properties:

  - if $(s_1 \times ... \times s_n \to s) \in S$, then

    Apply $\in F_{(s_1 \times ... \times s_n \to s)\, s_1\, ...\, s_n. s}$;

    these operations correspond to the functional applications (usually the terms Apply$(f,t_1,...,t_n)$ are simply written $f(t_1,...,t_n)$);

  - if t is a term of sort $s \in S$ built with the operation symbols in F, and for $i = 1,..., n$ x_i is a variable of sort $s_i \in S$, then

    $\lambda x_1, ..., x_n.t \in F_{\Lambda,\, (s_1 \times ... \times sn \to s)}$;

    these operations correspond to the λ-abstractions.

- $P = \{P_u\}_{u \in S^+}$ is the family of the sets of *predicate symbols*, s.t. for all $s \in S$ $D_s \in P_s$; the predicates D_s will be used for expressing the requirements on the definedness of the elements of the specification.

Given a ppa signature $\Sigma = (S, F, P)$, Sorts(Σ), Opns(Σ) and Preds(Σ) indicate respectively S, F and P.

Given a ppa signature $\Sigma = (S, F, P)$, $W_\Sigma(X) = \{W_\Sigma(X)_{|s}\}_{s \in S}$ denotes the family of the sets of *terms* built on Σ with variables in X, where $W_\Sigma(X)_{|s}$ is just the set of terms of sort s built on the usual signature (S, F); if $X = \varnothing$, then $W_\Sigma(X)$ is simply written W_Σ.

A *higher order predicate partial algebra* A on a signature $\Sigma = (S,F,P)$ (shortly a Σ-ppa) is a triple $(\{s^A\}_{s \in S}, \{op^A\}_{op \in F}, \{p^A\}_{p \in P})$ consisting of the *carriers*, the *interpretations of operation symbols* (partial functions with appropriate arity) and the *interpretations of predicate symbols* (relations on the cartesian product of appropriate carriers, with the usual convention of writing $p^A(t_1,...,t_n)$ for $<t_1,...,t_n> \in p^A)$, such that for all $s \in S$ $D_s^A = s^A$.

Given a ppa signature $\Sigma = (S,F,P)$, a *strict congruence* $\equiv$ over Σ is a couple
$$(\{\equiv_s\}_{s \in S}, \{\equiv_p\}_{p \in P})$$
where (note that in the following we omit the obvious quantifications over sorts)
- for all $s \in S$ $\equiv_s \subseteq W_\Sigma|_s \times W_\Sigma|_s$ and if $p \in P_{s_1 ... s_n}$, then $\equiv_p \subseteq W_\Sigma|_{s_1} \times ... \times W_\Sigma|_{s_n}$.
  In the following we denote by Dom($\equiv_s$) the set $\{a \mid (a,a) \in \equiv_s\}$ and $\equiv^D_s$ denotes the relation defined by $a \equiv^D_s a'$ iff either $a \equiv_s a'$ or a, a' $\notin$ Dom($\equiv_s$).
- $\equiv_s$ is symmetric, transitive and relatively reflexive (ie if $(a,a') \in \equiv_s$, then $(a,a) \in \equiv_s$);
- $\equiv$ is a family of congruences, ie:
  for any $op \in F_{s_1 ... s_n,s}$, $p \in P_{s_1 ... s_n}$ and $a_i, a_i' \in W_\Sigma|_{s_i}$, for $i \in \{1,...,n\}$,
  if $(a_i \equiv_{s_i} a_i'$ for $i = 1, ..., n)$, then
    $$op^A(a_1,...,a_n) \equiv^D_s op^A(a'_1,...,a'_n)$$
    and
    $$(<a_1,...,a_n> \in \equiv_p \text{ iff } <a'_1,...,a'_n> \in \equiv_p);$$
- operations and predicates are strict w.r.t. $\equiv$, ie:
  for any $op \in F_{s_1 ... s_n,s}$, $p \in P_{s_1 ... s_n}$ and $a_i, a_i' \in W_\Sigma|_{s_i}$, for $i \in \{1,...,n\}$,
    (if $op^A(a_1,...,a_n) \in$ Dom($\equiv_s$), then for $i=1,..., n$ $a_i \in$ Dom($\equiv_{s_i}$)) and
    (if $<a_1,...,a_n> \in \equiv_p$, then for $i=1,..., n$ $a_i \in$ Dom($\equiv_{s_i}$)).

If $\equiv$ is a strict congruence on Σ, then it is possible to define canonically the Σ-ppa $W_\Sigma/\equiv$.

A Σ-ppa A is said term generated iff there exists a strict congruence $\equiv$ s.t. $A = W_\Sigma/\equiv$.

Let A and B be two Σ-ppa's; a family of total functions $\varphi = \{\varphi_s\}_{s \in S}$, where for all $s \in S$ $\varphi_s: s^A \to s^B$, is an *homomorphism* (of ppa's) iff
- for any $w = (s_1...s_n,s) \in S^* \times S$, $op \in F_w$ and $a_1 \in s_1^A, ..., a_n \in s_n^A$
  $op^A(a_1,...,a_n) \in s^A$ implies $\varphi_s(op^A(a_1,...,a_n)) = op^B(\varphi_{s_1}(a_1),...,\varphi_{s_n}(a_n));$
- for any $u = s_1... s_n \in S^+$, $p \in P_u$ and $a_1 \in s_1^A, ..., a_n \in s_n^A$
  $<a_1,...,a_n> \in p^A$ implies $<\varphi_{s_1}(a_1),...,\varphi_{s_n}(a_n)> \in p^B$.

A Σ-ppa I is *initial* in C iff $I \in C$ and $\forall B \in C$ $\exists!$ homomorphism $\phi: I \to B$.

A *positive conditional axiom* on a ppa signature is a formula having the form
$$\bigwedge_{i \in I} p_i(t^i_{k1},...,t^i_{ki}) \bigwedge_{j \in J} (D(r_j) \wedge r_j = q_j) \supset e$$
where e has form either $r = q$ or $p(t_1,...,t_k)$; I, J are countable sets (possibly empty), p, p_i $(i \in I) \in P$; r, q, r_j, q_j $(j \in J) \in W_\Sigma(X)$.

The interpretation of the terms and the validity of the formulas in a ppa A are defined in the usual way; only remember that:
- being A an algebra with partial operations, the interpretation t^A of a term t in A could be undefined;

- a formula $r = q$ is valid in A iff

  r^A, q^A are both defined and equal or both are undefined ($=$ denotes strong equality);
- a formula $p(t_1,...,t_i)$ is valid in A iff $<t_1{}^A,...,t_n{}^A> \in p^A$.

A ppa *specification* (also called *type*) $T = (\Sigma, E)$ consists of a signature Σ and of a set E of positive conditional axioms over Σ such that

$$\{ (\lambda y_1...y_n . t)(t_1,...,t_n) = t[t_1/y_1...t_n/y_n] \mid t, t_i \in W_\Sigma(X), i=1,...,n \} \subseteq E,$$

these formulas define the λ-operations; in this paper we denote Σ by $Sig(T)$.

For every specification $T = (\Sigma, E)$, $PMod(T)$ is the class of all Σ-ppa's, called the *models* of T, which satisfy every formula of E.

We assume that each ppa specification T considered in the paper includes the following operations:
for all $s_1, ..., s_n, s \in Sorts(Sig(T))$

    fix $\square$: $((s_1 \times ... \times s_n \to s) \to (s_1 \times ... \times s_n \to s)) \to (s_1 \times ... \times s_n \to s)$

    if $\square$ **then** $\square$ **else** $\square$: $bool \times s \times s \to s$

defined by the axioms

    fix $f = f(\textbf{fix}\ f)$ **if** True **then** t_1 **else** $t_2 = t_1$ **if** False **then** t_1 **else** $t_2 = t_2$.

The *partial conditional system* associated with $T = (\Sigma, E)$ is defined as usual. If ϕ is a provable formula we write $T \vdash \phi$.

We have the following existence theorem: for every specification T there exists an initial model I in $PMod(T)$ characterized by the following properties:

- $\forall t_1, t_2 \in W_{\Sigma|s}$ s.t. $I \vDash D(t_1) \wedge D(t_2)$, $(I \vDash t_1 = t_2$ iff $T \vdash t_1 = t_2)$;
- $\forall p \in P_{s1...sn}$, $t_i \in W_{\Sigma|si}$, $i = 1, ..., n$, $(I \vDash p(t_1,...,t_n)$ iff $T \vdash p(t_1,...,t_n))$.

An *observational specification* OS is a triple (A, O, OB) where A is a ppa specification, O is a subset of the sorts of A (the *observed sorts*), OB is a subset of the predicates of A s.t. if $ob \in OB$ then $ob: o \times s_1 \times ... \times s_n$ with $o \in O$ (the *observing predicates*).

In the paper we use also the following notations.

Let S, F, P, Ax be respectively a set of sorts, of operations, of predicates and of positive conditional axioms and let $A = (\Sigma_A, F_A)$, $B = (\Sigma_B, F_B)$ be two specifications; then:

- **sorts S preds P opns F axioms Ax** denotes the specification having for signature (S, F, P) and axioms Ax.

- $A + B$ denotes the specification having for signature

  $(Sorts(\Sigma_A) \cup Sorts(\Sigma_B), Preds(\Sigma_A) \cup Preds(\Sigma_B), Opns(\Sigma_A) \cup Opns(\Sigma_B))$

  and for axioms $F_A \cup F_B$.

- **enrich A by sorts S preds P opns F axioms Ax** denotes the specification

  $A + (\textbf{sorts } S \cup Sorts(\Sigma_A) \textbf{ preds } P \cup Preds(\Sigma_A) \textbf{ opns } F \cup Opns(\Sigma_A) \textbf{ axioms } Ax)$.

- $A[op_1/op_2]$ denotes the specification A where the operation op_2 is renamed op_1.

- To improve readability we use signatures with operations having a distributed infix syntax; for example, terms built using the operation $\square$ Op $\square$: $srt \times srt \to srt$ have form t_1 Op t_2, where t_1 and t_2 are terms of sort srt (ie, subterms of appropriate sorts replace boxes).

- We often abbreviate a set of axioms concerning an operation by adding a corresponding attribute in the operations part (we have used the attributes total, comm. and assoc. [the last twos for commutative and associative]). For example, adding "(total)" after the declaration of the operation Op: $s_1 \times ... \times s_n \to s$ indicates that we implicitly assume the axiom "$D(Op(t_1,...,t_n))$".

SOFTWARE SPECIFICATION BY
BEHAVIOURAL CANONS

by Horst Reichel
Informatik-Zentrum , TU Dresden
Mommsenstrasse 13
Dresden DDR-8027
German Democratic Republic

This paper is an extended survey of the basic concepts of *behavioural canons*. Behavioural canons are characterized by
- the use of partial algebras, where the domains of the fundamental operations are defined as sets of solutions of term equations, phrased *equationally partial algebras*;
- the use of observability concepts as well on the level of elements of algebras as well on the level of algebras, generalizing similar notions of the theory of automata;
- addressing the semantical model classes of algebraic specifications, which are closed under behaviourally equivalent algebras, by means of free constructions (left-adjoint functors).

The main point of this approach is to keep up the advantages of free constructions with respect to operational semantics of algebraic specifications, to sort out the controversy between initial and final semantics, and to make the resulting semantics more suitable for practical needs and for the definition of the concept of abstract implementations.

In the second half of the paper consequences for the generalization of the Conditional Narrowing Algorithm of Hussmann to behavioural canons are discussed in greater detail.

1. Basic notions

Software specifications by behavioural canons in the sense of [Rei 86] are based on the notion of equationally partial algebras, where

$$SIG = (SORT,OP)$$

is a signature consisting of a finite set SORT of sort names and of a finite set OP of operation names, operators for short, and each element of OP is of the form $op:w \longrightarrow s$, $w \in SORT$, $s \in SORT$.
A partial SIG-algebra A consists of a SORT-indexed family of sets A_s, $s \in SORT$ and of an OP-indexed family of fundamental operations

$$op_A : A_{s1} \times ... \times A_{sn} \quad o \longrightarrow A \quad \text{for } op:s1...sn \longrightarrow s , op \in OP$$

P_ALG(SIG) denotes the class (or category) of partial SIG-algebras, where a SIG-homomorphism $h: A \longrightarrow B$, for $A,B \in$ P_ALG(SIG), is given by an SORT-indexed family of mappings

$$h_s : A_s \longrightarrow B_s , s \in SORT$$

such that $(a1,\ldots,an) \in dom(opA)$, $op:s1\ldots sn \longrightarrow s \in OP$ implies

(i) $(h_{s1}(a1),\ldots,h_{sn}(an)) \in dom(op_B)$

(ii) $h_s(op_A(a1,\ldots,an)) = op_B(h_{s1}(a1),\ldots,h_{sn}(an))$.

$X,X1,\ldots,Xn,Y,\ldots$ denote sorted sets of variables, where each sorted set of variables is a set of elements of the form $x:s$ with $s \in$ SORT for some set SORT. Any $w=s1\ldots sn \in SORT^*$ will also be interpreted as a set of variables $w = \{1:a1,\ldots,n:an\}$.

For any set X of variables $T(SIG,X)$ denotes the total SIG-algebra of SIG-terms on X. An assignment $\underline{a}:X \longrightarrow A$ of a set X of variables in A $\in$ P_ALG(SIG) is a mapping assigning a value in A_s to each $x:s \in X$.

For any homomorphism $h: A \longrightarrow B$, $A,B \in$ P_ALG(SIG), and any set X of variables we define the mapping $f_X: A_X \longrightarrow B_X$ by $f_X(\underline{a}) =$ $f_s(\underline{a}(x:s))$ for each $\underline{a} \in A_X$ and $x:s \in X$, where A_X ,B_X denote the sets of assignments.

Inductively one can define for each $A \in$ P_ALG(SIG) the partial term function

$$t_A: A_X \text{ o} \longrightarrow A_s$$

for each $t \in T(SIG,X)_s$, $s \in SORT$, where

$\underline{a} \in dom(op(t1,\ldots,tn)_A)$ iff $\underline{a} \in dom(ti_A)$ for $i=1,\ldots,n$ and

$(t1_A(\underline{a}),\ldots,tn_A(\underline{a})) \in dom(op_A)$.

For each term equation $X:l=r$ with $l,r \in T(SIG,X)$, $s \in SORT$, and each $A \in$ P_ALG(SIG) we define the set of solutions

$$A_{\{X:l=r\}} = \{\underline{a} \in A_X \mid \underline{a} \in dom(l_A) \cap dom(r_A) \text{ and}$$

$$l_A(\underline{a}) = r_A(\underline{a}) \}$$

and we define the identical validity of a conditional equation

$$A \models X. \ l1=r1 \& \ldots \& ln=rn \longrightarrow l0=r0$$

where $li,ri \in T(SIG,X)_{si}$ for $i=0,1,\ldots,n$, $n \geq 0$, and

$A \in$ P_ALG(SIG) by

$$A_{\{X.l1=r1,\ldots,ln=rn\}} = A_{\{X.l0=r0\}}$$

where

$$A_{\{X.l1=r,\ldots,ln=rn\}} = \cap \{A_{\{X.li=ri\}} \mid i=1,\ldots,n\}$$

and

$$\cap \{A_{\{X.li=ri\}} \mid i \in \emptyset \} = A_X.$$

A theory representation TREP = (SIG,AX) is given by a signatur SIG = (SORT,OP) and by a finite set AX of conditional equations.

An algebra $A \in P\_ALG(SIG)$ is called a TREP-algebra or (SIG,AX)-algebra if $A \models eq$ holds for each conditional equation $eq \in AX$.

It is worth to mention that conditional equations for partial SIG-algebras do not only express interdependences of the fundamental operations but also express definedness conditions. Thus

$$A \models X. \emptyset \longrightarrow l=r ,$$

where $l,r \in T(SIG,X)_s$, $s \in OP$ holds if and only if

$l_A: A_X \longrightarrow A_s$ and $r_A: A_X \longrightarrow A_s$ are total and identical mappings. In the following conditional equations with empty premises will simply be written $X. l=r$.

We will illustrate the introduced notions by the following example:

<u>stack</u> = SORT: value, state
        OP: EMPTY: ---> state
           PUSH: value state ---> state
           TOP: state ---> value
           POP: state ---> state
        AX
                  . EMPTY = EMPTY
         x:value, s:state. TOP(PUSH(x,s)) = x ;
         x:value, s:state. POP(PUSH(x,s)) = s ;

The first conditional equation, having empty premise, guarantees the existence of $EMPTY_A \in A_{state}$ for each <u>stack</u>-algebra A , the second and third conditional equation makes $PUSH_A$ to a total operation for each <u>stack</u>-algebra A , whereas POP_A, TOP_A need not be total operations. But POP_A, TOP_A have to be defined for each $s \in A_{state}$ being a result of $PUSH_A$.

2.Behavioural validity

The usual realization of stacks by pointer-array-pairs does not satisfy the third conditional equation, since in such an algebra A the operation POP_A does only reduce the pointer value by one and does not change the content of the array at the previous pointer position.

This observation proves the inadequacy of the traditional validity concept of equations and conditional equations used in Universal Algebra. To overcome this lack we use a concept of the theory of automata motivated by the fact that in a realization A of stacks by pointer-array-pairs the third conditional equation is behaviourally satisfied which means that the values of the left-hand side and of the right-hand side are not equal but behaviourally equivalent states.

To formalize this idea we need a modified notion of a signature which will be called I/O-*signature*. An I/O-signature

$$I/O\text{-}SIG = (I/O\text{-}SORT, SORT, OP)$$

is a signature together with a distinguished subset I/O-SORT of SORT of so-called *I/O-sorts*. Any sort s ∈ SORT not contained in I/O-SORT is called a *hidden sort* or also a *state sort*. Based on this devision of the sort names in names of I/O-sorts and state sorts we generalize the concept of equivalent internal states of abstract automata to I/O-SIG-algebras.

In order to do that we need some notations for systems of variables and for assignments. If X is any set of variables and x:s in X then X-{x:s} denotes the set of variables that results from X be the indicated removal. If $\underline{m}' \in M_{X-\{x:s\}}$ and $m \in M_s$, then $\underline{m}+(x=m) \in M_s$ denotes the corresondingly extended assignment.

I/O-SIG-algebras are nothing else SIG-algebras where SIG results from I/O-SIG by forgetting the distinguished set of I/O-sorts.

Now let be given an I/O-SIG-algebra A , a finite set of variables X , a variable x:s1 in X, an element $a \in A_{s1}$, and a term t in $T(SIG,X)_{s2}$. From this we construct the *partial derived polynomial function*

$$t_{A,x=a} : A_{X-\{x:s1\}} \xrightarrow{o\text{---}>} A_{s2}$$

with $\underline{a} \in dom(t_{A,x=a})$ iff $\underline{a}+(x=a) \in dom(t_A)$ and
and we set

$$t_{A,x=a}(\underline{a}) = t_A(\underline{a}+(x=a)).$$

Based on this notation one can define the *behavioural equivalence of elements* a1,a2 ∈ A_{s1} for any I/O-SIG-algebra A , in symbols

$$a1 = a2 \bmod I/O\text{-}SORT ,$$

if for each term t ∈ $T(SIG,X)_{s2}$, such that X is a finite set of variables with x:s1 in X and s2 in I/O-SORT, the partial derived polynomial functions $t_{A,x=a1}$ and $t_{A,x=a2}$ are equal, i.e. if

(1) $dom(t_{A,x=a1}) = dom(t_{A,x=a2})$ and

(2) $(t_{A,x=a1})(\underline{a}) = (t_{A,x=a2})(\underline{a})$ for all $\underline{a}$ in $A_{X-\{x:s1\}}$ if both sides are defined.

In the following a term t in $T(SIG,X)_s$ will be called an *output term* if X is finite and s is in I/O-SORT.

In [Rei 85] this concept has been introduced and some basic facts have been proved. One can for instance easily see that

(2.1) The behavioural equivalence modulo I/O-SORT is an equivalence relation in each carrier set A_s , $s \in$ SORT, for each I/O-SIG-algebra A .

(2.2) For $a1,a2 \in A_{s1}$ and $s1 \in$ I/O-SORT

a1 = a2 mod I/O-SORT holds if and only if a1 = a2.

Elements $a1,a2 \in A_{s1}$, $s1 \in$ SORT, are called *distinguishable* if there is an output term $t \in T(SIG,X)_{s2}$, $s2 \in$ I/O-SORT, $x:s1 \in X$ and $\underline{a} \in dom(t_{A,x=a1}) \cap dom(t_{A,x=a2})$ with $t_{A,x=a1}(\underline{a}) \neq t_{A,x=a2}(\underline{a})$.

One has to notice that distinct from the situation of total I/O-SIG-algebras as concidered in [GGM 76] the concepts of equivalence and distinguishability are not complementary.

In [GM 82] the concept of observability, or behvioural equivalence, and its relations to software specification has been thoroughly investigated for total I/O-SIG-algebras. But Goguen and Meseguer have not concidered the behavioural equivalence of elements in I/O-SIG-algebras. They concidered only the behavioural equivalence of I/O-SIG-algebras. The corresponding concept for partial I/O-SIG-algebras is as follows:

A homomorphism f: A ---> B between I/O-SIG-algebras A,B is called a *reduction* if

* $f_s: A_s ---> B_s$ is surjective for each $s \in$ SORT;

* $f_s: A_s ---> B_s$ is injective for each $s \in$ I/O-SORT;

* If op: w ---> s and $f_w(\underline{a}) \in dom(op_B)$ then

   $\underline{a} \in dom(op_A)$ for all op:w ---> s in OP and $\underline{a} \in A_w$.

I/O-SIG-algebras A,B are called *equivalent modulo* I/O-SORT if there are reductions g: F ---> A, h: F ---> B.

Since the pullback construction preserves reductions the equivalence modulo I/O-SORT between I/O-SIG-algebras is transitive. Reflexivity and symmetry are evident.

How do fit together the concepts of behavioural equivalence modulo I/O-
SORT on the level of elements and on the level of algebras?

To answer this question we extend the notion of term equation and
conditonal term equation to the notions of equivalence and conditonal
equivalence as follows:
For any I/O-signatur I/O-SIG = (I,SORT,OP), where I = SORT denotes
for short the distinguished subset of I/O-sorts,

$$X. \; l=r \; mod \; I \; , \quad with \; l,r \in T(SIG,X)_s, \; s \in SORT$$

denotes an *equivalence* and for any I/O-SIG-algebra A we set

$$A_{(X.l=r mod I)} = \{\underline{a} \in A_X \; : \; \underline{a} \in dom(l_A) \; \cap \; dom(r_A) \; and$$
$$(l_A)(\underline{a}) = (r_A)(\underline{a}) \; mod \; I \; \}.$$

By

$$X. \; l1=r1\&...\&ln=rn \; ---> \; l0=r0 \; mod \; I,$$
with li,ri in $T(SIG,X)_{si}$, $si \in SORT$ for $i=0,1,...,n$, we denote a *conditional equivalence* and we say that an I/O-SIG-algebra A satisfies a
conditional equivalence, in symbols

$$A \; \models \; X. \; l1=r1\&...\&ln=rn \; ---> \; l0=r0 \; mod \; I \; ,$$
if $A_{(X.l1=r1,...,ln=rn \; mod \; I \;)} = A_{(X.l0=r0 \; mod \; I \;)}$.

Because of (2.2) above, the concepts of equivalence and conditional
equivalence coincide with equations and conditional equations
respectively, if I/O-SORT = SORT, i.e. if any sort is an I/O-sort and
no one is a state sort.

A first answer to the question rised above is given by the following
theorem proved in [Rei 85]:

Theorem 2.3: If h:A ---> B is a reduction and (X:G mod I) is any set
of equivalences, then for each $\underline{a} \in A_X$ the assignment $\underline{a}$ is in
$A_{(X.G \; mod \; I)}$ if and only if $f_X(\underline{a})$ is in $B_{(X.G \; mod \; I)}$.

This theorem implies that reductions preserve and reflect solutions of
equivalences. Another consequence of the theorem is:

Corollary 2.4: Let r:A ---> B be any reduction of I/O-SIG-algebras,
let I denote the distinguished subset of I/O-sorts, and

$$X. \; l1=r1\&...\&ln=rn \; ---> \; l=r \; mod \; I$$
may be any conditional equivalence. Then

$$A \; \models \; X. \; l1=r1\&...\&ln=rn \; ---> \; l=r \; mod \; I$$
if and only if

$$B \; \models \; X. \; l1=r1\&...\&ln=rn \; ---> \; l=r \; mod \; I \; .$$

According to the introduced notions a *behavioural specification* of
stacks would be obtained if one specifies in <u>stack</u> the sort 'state' as
a state sort and 'value' as an I/O-sort and if all axioms are interpreted as conditional equivalences modulo (value), each with empty
premise. The resulting class of models is then closed with respect to
behaviourally equivalent I/O-SIG-algebras and so the realization of
stacks by pointer-array-pairs becomes a model of the corresponding
behavioural theory.

In [Wol 87] it is proved that behavioural theories are a proper extension of identical theories. In more detail it is proved in this paper
that there is no finite set of conditional equations which defines
under identical satisfaction that class of models defined under behavioural satisfaction by the three conditional equivalences modulo
(value) described above.

However, these *behavioural quasi-varieties* are not yet sufficient to
present those classes of I/O-SIG-algebras which can be used to define
the semantics of behavioural specifications of software modules. One
possibility to restrict behavioural quasi-varieties to suitable classes
of models will be defined in the following section.

3. Behavioural Canons

There are several possibilities to restrict behavioural quasi-varieties
of I/O-SIG-algebras to suitable model classes. One way is the use of
hidden sorts and hidden operations together with conservative
extensions, where some fundamental data types like truth values,
natural numbers, etc are assumed to be given once for ever. This
approach is used by Wirsing et al, [W... 83].

We will go another way and we will use initiality to pick of the right
class of behaviourally equivalent I/O-SIG-algebras. For that reason we
have to guarantee the existence of initial I/O-SIG-algebras in
behavioural quasi-varieties. This problem has been solved in [Rei 85].
In the terminology of abstract automata initial I/O-SIG-algebras are
automata of maximal redundancy, which means that for each element of
a state sort its complete genesis is inherent.

But the existence of initial I/O-SIG-algebras needs a slight
restriction of the conditional equivalences defining the behavioural
quasi-variety. A conditional equivalence
      X. l1=r1&...&ln=rn ---> l=r mod I
will be called *proper* if each of the terms li, ri for i=1,...,n is
an output term. We assume that all conditional equivalences used in the
following are proper ones.

For any representation of a behavioural theory (I/O-SIG,AX) the corresponding behavioural quasi-variety will be denoted by ALG(I/O-
SIG,AX).

A *theory morphism*
        F: (I/O-SIG_1,AX_1) ---> (I/O-SIG_2,AX_2)
is given by a signature morphism F: SIG_1 ---> SIG_2 such that

(i) F_{SORT}(I/O-SORT_1) = I/O-SORT_2 ;
(ii) For each A ∈ ALG(I/O-SIG_2,AX_2) and each conditional
      equivalence ceq ∈ AX_1 it holds A != F(ceq) mod I/O-SORT_2.

In the following T,T1,...,Tn,... will be used as variables for representations of behavioural theories and
        I/O-SIG(T), I/O-SORT(T), AX(T), OP(T), SORT(T)
denote the I/O-signature, the set of I/O-sorts, the set of conditional
equivalences , the set of operators, and the set of sorts respectively.

Let F:T1 ---> T2 be a theory morphism and A ∈ ALG(T2), then A↓F
denotes that T1-algebra defined by
        (A↓F)|s = A|F(s)   for each s in SORT(T1) and
        op|(A↓F) = (F(op))|A for each op in OP(T1).

The existence of initial I/O-SIG-algebras in ALG(I/O-SIG,AX), where
AX consists of proper conditonal equivalences, implies the existence
of a left-adjoint functor
        _↑F: ALG(T1) ---> ALG(T2)
for each forgetful functor
        _↓F: ALG(T2) ---> ALG(T1),
where F:T1 ---> T2 is any theory morphism. If F:T1 ---> T2 is the
inclusion of a subtheory T1 into T2 , then we will also use the
notation A↓T1 and B↑T2 instead of A↓F and B↑F respectively.

Now we are able to introduce the notion of an *initial restriction* of
behaviour in a representation of a behavioural theory T .
An initial restriction of behaviour in T , denoted
        (T2, F:T1 ---> T),
is given by a theory morphism F:T1 ---> T and by a representation of
a behavioural subtheory T2 of T1 . For each A in ALG(T) we set
        A != (T2, F:T1 ---> T)
if
(i)   ((A↓F)↓T2)↑T1 is an extension of (A↓F)↓T2 , i.e.
      (((A↓F)↓T2)↑T1)↓T2 = (A↓F)↓T2 ;
(ii) The unique extension of the identity homomorphism of (A|F)|T2
      to a T1-homomorphism f: ((A↓F)↓T2)↑T1 ---> A↓F is a reduction.

A *behavioural canon*

        BC = (I/O-SIG,AX,RES)

consists of an I/O-signature, of a finite set AX of proper
conditional equivalences, and of a finite set RES of initial restrictions of behaviour in (I/O-SIG,AX). The single constituent's of a
behavioural canon BC will also be denoted by I/O-SIG(BC), AX(BC),
RES(BC), T(BC).

ALG(BC) denotes the class of all I/O-SIG-algebras satisfying each
conditional equivalence in AX(BC) and each initial restriction of
behaviour in T(BC) specified in RES(BC).

We illustrate the notions introduced so far by a behavioural specification of the set of finite and cofinite subsets of an arbitrary parametric set. This example is inspired by [GM 85].

<u>f-c-set</u> <u>IS DEFINITION</u>
        <u>I/O-SORT:</u> bool
        <u>OP:</u>   TRUE ---> bool
               FALSE ---> bool
        <u>AX:</u>
            TRUE = TRUE
            FALSE = FALSE   __↓__ T1
        <u>WITH REQUIREMENT</u>
        <u>I/O-SORT:</u> elem
        <u>OP:</u> EQ: elem elem ---> bool
        <u>AX:</u>
            x,y:elem. EQ(x,y) = EQ(y,x);
            x,y:elem. <u>IF</u> x≐y <u>THEN</u> EQ(x,y)=TRUE;
            x,y:elem. <u>IF</u> EQ(x,y)=TRUE <u>THEN</u> x=y;   __↓__ T2
        <u>WITH DEFINITION</u>
        <u>STATE-SORT:</u> set
        <u>OP</u>   0,1 ---> set
             {_}: elem ---> set
             _+_: set set ---> set
             _∈_: elem set ---> bool
        <u>AX</u>
            s:set.   s+s=0;
            s1,s2:set.   s1+s2=s2+s1;
            s1,s2,s3:set.   (s1+s2)+s3=s1+(s2+s3);
            s:set.   0+s=s;
            x:elem.   x∈1=TRUE;
            x:elem.   x∈0=FALSE;
            x,y:elem.   x∈{y}=EQ(x,y);
            x:elem, s1,s2:set.
                <u>IF</u> x∈s1=TRUE, x∈s2=FALSE <u>THEN</u> x∈(s1+s2)=TRUE;

```
        x:elem, s1,s2:set.
          IF x∈s1=TRUE, x∈s2=TRUE THEN x∈(s1+s2)=FALSE;
        x:elem, s1,s2:set.
          IF x∈s1=FALSE, x∈s2=FALSE THEN x∈(s1+s2)=FALSE;
      END f-c-set
```

This textual representation of the behavioural canon 'f-c-set'
represents two initial restrictions of behaviour in T(f-c-set):

$$(\emptyset, \text{inclusion}: T1 \dashrightarrow T(f\text{-}c\text{-}set)),$$

where $\emptyset$ denotes the empty theory, and

$$(T2, \text{id}_{T(f\text{-}c\text{-}set)})$$

The correspondence between an initial restriction of behaviour

$$(T2, F: T1 \dashrightarrow T)$$

and its textual representation works well in the case where
$F: T1 \dashrightarrow T$ is the inclusion of a subtheory of T, but in all known
examples of specifications this condition is satisfied. In this case we
say that each sort name $s \in \text{SORT}(T1)-\text{SORT}(T2)$ and each operator
$op \in OP(T1)-OP(T2)$ is subject to that initial restriction of behaviour
in T. Correspondingly in the textual representation a sort name and an
operator name is subject to an initial restriction of behaviour if they
follow the key word WITH DEFINITION and go ahead to a key word WITH
REQUIREMENT. Thus in the example above only 'elem' and 'EQ' are not
subject to one of the two initial restricitions of behaviour.

Since behavioural equivalence coincides with identity in carriers of
I/O-sorts, each sort name $s \in \text{I/O-SORT}(BC)$ specifies in a
behavioural canon BC a data type uniquely up to isomorphism if this
sort name is subject to any intial restriction of BC. But this is not
so for sort names which are state sorts. Since 'bool' is an I/O-sort,
for any two models A,B in ALG(f-c-set) it holds $A_{bool} = B_{bool} = \{TRUE, FALSE\}$.

The effect of the second initial restriction of behaviour, which
defines a new data type by means of a state sort, is illustrated by the
fact that the following algebras A,B,C are models in ALG(f-c-set):

$A_{bool} = B_{bool} = C_{bool} = \{TRUE, FALSE\};$

$A_{elem} = B_{elem} = C_{elem} = M$ an arbitrary set;

$EQ_A = EQ_B = EQ_C =$ characteristic function of the identity relation
of M ;

$A_{set} =$ set of all terms build up of elements of M and of the
operators $0, 1, \{\_\}, \_+\_;$

$\_\in\_{A}: A_{elem} \times A_{set} \dashrightarrow \{TRUE, FALSE\}$ is any mapping which satisfies
the last three axioms;

B_{set} = $(A_{set})/R$ where R is the congruence relation generated by the first four equations, i.e., B is the algebra freely generated by M but with respect to identical satisfaction of all axioms;

C_{set} = set of all finite and cofinite subsets of M with 0_C = $\emptyset$,

1_C = M, $(m)_C$ = (m) and $s1+_C s2$ = $(s1 \cup s2)-(s1 \cap s2)$.

The model A is the model of maximal redundancy and C is the model of minimal redundancy, i.e., any two elements in C which are behaviourally equivalent modulo (bool,elem) are equal.

One can generally prove that models of maximal and minimal redundancy always exist. With respect to the subcategory of reductions these models are initial and terminal, respectively within an equivalence class of I/O-SIG-algebras modulo I/O-SORT. In our opinion this fact repeals the contest of initial and terminal semantics of algebraic specifications using isomorphism classes only. The semantics should be defined by means of an behavioural equivalence class and it is a question of taste which special algebra is used for the identification of that behavioural equivalence class.

In the example f-c-set one can interpret the *subcanon*
    elem = (T2,{(∅,inclusion:T1 --->T2)})
as the specification of a parameter part. Intuitively one wants only to specify those parameterized data types which yield a computable I/O-SIG-algebra for each parameter instantiation by a computable actual parameter. Here we understand by a computable I/O-SIG-algebra an algebra with recursively enumerable carriers and with partially recursive fundamental operations. As discussed in [Rei86] this requirement is not yet satisfied if one requires the existence of at least one computable I/O-SIG-algebra in the semantical model class, since the model of maximal redundancy is always a computable one, but in general the behavioural equivalence of elements in this model is not necessarily decidable. Exactly this situation happens in the example f-c-set.

In the following we will not deal with the concept of initial computability in behavioural canons and we will also not present the formalization of the idea of 'parameterized software modules or 'generic modules', see [Gog 83] and [EW 86], on the basis of behavioural canons. Readers interested in this topic are refered to [Rei 86].

In our opinion the concept of behavioural canons together with the notion of canon morphisms form a suitable algebraic framework to treat the problems of 'Programming in the Large' on the level of model class

semantics. We will direct our intention at problems of operational
semantics of behavioural canons. We will investigate the effects of two
peculiarities of behavioural canons with respect to operational
semantics, namely

- equational partiality of fundamental operations, and
- behavioural semantics.

4. Rewriting and narrowing in equationally partial algebras

In this section we extend the Conditional Rewriting Calculus of
H.Hussman, see [Hus 85], from total SIG-algebras to equationally
partial SIG-algebras. This extension is based on a complete system of
derivation rules for conditional equations given in [HKR 80] and [Rei
84]. Notice that we deal in this section with conditional equations and
not with conditional equivalences. In the next section we will see that
this restriction will not harm.

For a given signature SIG, for a system $(X:G)$ of SIG-term equations,
and for any set AX of conditional SIG-term equations we define
$$AX*(X.G) = \{(X.l=r) \mid AX \mid= (X.G \dashrightarrow l=r)\}$$
and call this set of SIG-term equations the 'AX-closure of $(X.G)$,
where $AX \mid= (X.G \dashrightarrow l=r)$ means that for each (SIG,AX)-algebra A
it holds $A \mid= (X.G \dashrightarrow l=r)$.

According to [Rei 84] the AX-closure of $(X.G)$ is the minimal fixed
point with respect to the following closure operations:

(i) $(X.t1=t2) \in (X.G)$ implies $(X.t1=t2) \in AX*(X.G)$;

(ii) $(X.t1=t2) \in AX*(X.G)$ implies $(X.t1=t2) \in AX*(X.G)$;

(iii) $(X.t1=t2) \in AX*(X.G)$, $(X.t2=t3) \in AX*(X.G)$ implies
        $(X.t1=t3) \in AX*(X.G)$;

(iv) $(X.t1=t2) \in AX*(X.G)$ and t subterm of t1 or t2 implies
        $(X.t=t) \in AX*(X.G)$;

(v) $(X.t1=r1),...,(X.tn=rn) \in AX*(X.G)$ and
        $(X.f(t1,...,tn)=f(t1,...,tn)) \in AX*(X.G)$ implies
        $(X.f(t1,...,tn)=f(r1,...,rn)) \in AX*(X.G)$;

(vi) $(Y.H \dashrightarrow r1=r2) \in AX$, sub:Y $\dashrightarrow$ T(SIG,X) a substitution
        such that sub(y) in X or sub(y) is a subterm of a term in
        AX*(X.G), and sub(Y.H) = AX*(X.G) implies
        $(X.sub(r1)=sub(r2)) \in AX*(X.G)$.

It is worth to mention that this calculus is sound and complete also
for signatures which are not necessarily sensible.

In analogy to Hussmann we introduce two binary relation symbols '-->'
and '<-->', where --> stands for the transitive-reflexive closure of
the term replacement relation and the relation t1<-->t2 holds if and

only if t1 and t2 have a common -->-reduct, i.e. there is a term t
with t1-->t and t2-->t .In the following we define both relations in
a mutually recursive manner:

(i) Base-rule

$$\frac{(X;t1=t2) \in (X;G)}{AX,G \;!- t1-->t2 \text{ on } X}$$

(ii) Reflexivity

$$\frac{AX,G \;!- t1-->t2 \text{ on } X}{AX,G \;!- t-->t \text{ on } X}$$

if t is a subterm of t1 or t2 or if t is a variable in X;

(iii) Transitivity

$$\frac{AX,G \;!- t1-->t2 \text{ on } X, \quad AX,G \;!- t2-->t3 \text{ on } X}{AX,G \;!- t1-->t3 \text{ on } X}$$

(iv) Rule application

$$\frac{\begin{array}{l}(Y.t1=r1\&...\&tn=rn ---> l=r) \in AX \\ sub;Y ---> T(SIG,X) \text{ and} \\ AX,G \;!- t1<-->r1 \text{ on } X \;,..., AX,G \;!- tn<-->rn \text{ on } X \;, \text{ and} \\ AX,G \;!- y<-->y \text{ on } X \text{ for all } y \in Y\end{array}}{AX,G \;!- l-->r \text{ on } X}$$

(v) Congruence

$$\frac{\begin{array}{l}AX,G \;!- ti-->ri \text{ on } X \\ AX,G \;!- f(t1,...,ti,...,tn)-->f(t1,...,ti,...,tn) \text{ on } X\end{array}}{AX,G \;!- f(t1,...,ti,...,tn)-->f(t1,...,ri,...,tn) \text{ on } X}$$

$$\frac{\begin{array}{l}AX,G \;!- ti-->ri \text{ on } X \\ AX,G \;!- f(t1,...,ri,...,tn)-->f(t1,...,ri,...,tn) \text{ on } X\end{array}}{AX,G \;!- f(t1,...,ti,...,tn)-->f(t1,...,ri,...,tn) \text{ on } X}$$

(vi) Equivalence

$$\frac{AX,G \;!- t1-->t3 \text{ on } X, \quad AX,G \;!- t2-->t3 \text{ on } X}{AX,G \;!- t1<-->t2 \text{ on } X}$$

As in classical rewriting theory the confluence (or Church-Rosser)
property is needed to prove soundness and completeness.

Definition 4.1. A set AX of conditional equations is called G-confluent, where (X.G) denotes a finite set of equations, if for all t1,
t2,t3 ∈ T(SIG,X) the following holds:

   AX,G ¦- t1-->t2 on X,   AX,G ¦- t1-->t3 on X
implies the existence of a term t4 in T(SIG,X) such that
   AX,G ¦- t2-->t4 on X   and AX,G ¦- t3-->t4 on X .

Theorem 4.2. If (X.G) is any set of equations and AX is a G-confluent
set of conditional equations, then for each t1,t2 ∈ T(SIG,X)
   (X.t1=t2) ∈ AX*(X.G) iff AX,G ¦- t1<-->t2 on X .

The proof is a straightforward generalization of the corresponding
proof in [Hus 85] and is therefore omitted here.

The main difference with respect to total algebras is the invalitity of
the reflexivity rule. In the case of equational partiality t--->t
does not hold for each term. Now the relation t--->t has to be proved
individuelly for each term.

The extension of the conditional narrowing algorithm from totoal
algebras to partial algebras requires modifications of both of the
narrowing step and of the unification step. Futhermore an additional
step is necessary which may be called 'reduction'. By means of the
reduction step a so-called 'existence equation' t=t can be reduced to
a finite set of equations using an axiom (Z.H ---> l=r) ∈ AX in the
case that t can be unified with a subterm of l or of r . This
reduction step is necessary to guarantee that the computed answer
consits of evaluable terms. As distinct from total algebras now the
unification step can not only be used as final step, since it remains
to prove that the most general unifier produces evaluable terms. That
difficulty arises from the fact that the most general unifier of two
terms may be a substitution that produces non-evaluable terms, although
if there exists a unifier which produces evaluable terms, but this
unifier may not be the most general one. Contrary to the situation of
total algebras one would not obtain an algorithm consisting of an
iteration of the narrowing step followed by a final application of the
unification step. Now one would obtain only a semi-algorithm which consists of a mixed iteration of modified narrowing, modified unification
and reduction. A precise description of these steps is given in
[Rei 87].

Since the result is not very satisfying, we suggest another way to overcome the difficulties. We transform the equationally partial algebras in a uniform way to total algebras, apply the conditional narrowing algorithm of Hussman to that canonically constructed total algebra, and reconstruced the original equationally partial algebra by means of a suitable forgetful functor.

For a given theory representation TREP = (SIG,AX) we construct the following theory representation
        OK-TREP = (OK-SIG,OK-AX)
in such a way that

        OK-SORT = SORT ∪ {heap};

        OK-OP = OP ∪ {OK: ---> heap}
                ∪ {s-TEST: s ---> heap ¦ s ∈ SORT };

        OK-AX = AX ∪ {w. s-TEST(op(x1,...,xn))=OK ---> si-TEST(xi)=OK ¦
                    op: w ---> s ∈ OP, w=s1...sn, i=1,...,n }
                ∪ {X. G {s-TEST(x)=OK ¦ x:s ∈ X} ---> s-TEST(l)=OK ¦
                    (X. G ---> l=r) ∈ AX }
                ∪ {X. G {s-TEST(x)=OK ¦ x:s ∈ X} ---> s-TEST(r)=OK ¦
                    (X. G ---> l=r) ∈ AX }.

ALG_t(OK-TREP) denotes the class of all total OK-SIG-algebras which satisfy each conditional equation of OK-AX.

For any total algebra A ∈ ALG_t(OK-TREP) we derive an equationally partial algebra OK-A by the following construction:

        $(OK-A)_s$ = {a ∈ A_s ¦ $(s-TEST_A)(a)$ = OK_A };
        op_{OK-A} = restriction of the total operation op_A to
                $((OK-A)_s$ ¦ s ∈ SORT).

This construction yields a forgetful functor
        OK-_: ALG_t(OK-TREP) ---> ALG(TREP)
which produces partial algebras from total ones. The value of this con-struction for operational semantics of equationally partial algebras result from the following theorem.

Theorem 4.3: If A is initial in ALG_t(OK-TREP) then OK-A is an initial algebra in ALG(TREP).

The proof requires only technical considerations and is therefore not given here.

In this approach a term t represents an evaluable term in the OK-

part of the total term algebra if the term s-TEST(t) can be reduced
to OK by means of the axioms in OK-AX.

It is not hard to prove that the forgetful functor which associates
each total OK-TREP-algebra with its OK-part has a left-adjoint functor
       COMP: ALG(TREP) ---> ALG_t(TREP)
such that OK-COMP(B) is isomorphis to B for each equationally
partial algebra B ∈ ALG(TREP). Thus the OK-part of the universal
completion of an equationally partial algebra reconstructs the given
equationally partial algebra.

In the preceding approach it is important that the definedness is not
expressed by means of a two valued predicate since in this case it
would be impossible to deal with partial operations with recursively
enumerable domains which are not recursively decidable. On the other
side, it may happen that the set OK-AX of conditional equations will
no more satisfy the termination condition. The problems arised by
undecid-able domains can not be removed, it is only possible to push
the problems in a corner instead of putting them in the centre. This
way of dealing with partiality is similar to that used by Drosten, see
[Dro 88] and [GDLE 84].

5. Interconnections of behavioural and operational semantics

The intention which underlies behavioural semantics implies that one
only wants to evaluate terms producing results of I/O-sorts. Only
elements in carriers of I/O-sorts represent values, whereas elements in
carriers of state sorts do not represent values but internal states. If
operationl semantics is aimed to make algebraic specifications executable, then this implies that only output terms will be evaluated. One
consequence is that operational semantics need not be compatible with
exactly (up to isomorphism) one algebra, especially not with the
algebra of minimal redundancy. It is for instance not necessary to
reduce two terms to a common one which represent behaviourally
equivalent terms.

In the following we suggest an operational semantics which is deduced
from the algebra of maximal redundancy, i.e. from the algebra with
minimal identification of behaviourally equivalent internal states.To
be more precise we will give an complete description of the algebra of
maximal redundancy. For that reason let be given an I/O-signature I/O-
SIG, a set AX of proper conditional equivalences, a set (Y:G) of
equivalences, and finally let I denote the set of I/O-sorts in I/O-
SIG.

Now we set

AX*modI(Y.G) = { (Y.l=r) $\in$ AX*(Y.G) | l and r are equal or
            l,r $\in$ T(SIG,Y)$_s$ with s $\in$ I }.

An algebra F $\in$ ALG(I/O-SIG,AX) is called *freely generated by (Y.G) in ALG(I/O-SIG,AX)* if there is an assignment $\underline{e}$ $\in$ F$_X$ such that:

(i) $\underline{e}$ $\in$ F$_{(Y.G)}$, i.e. $\underline{e}$ is a solution of each equivalence
      (Y.t1=t2 mod I) in (Y.G);
(ii) For each algebra A $\in$ ALG(I/O-SIG,AX) and each solution
      $\underline{a}$ $\in$ A$_{(Y.G)}$ there is a unique homomorphism
      h: F ---> A with h$_Y$($\underline{e}$) = $\underline{a}$, where
      h$_Y$: F$_Y$ ---> A$_Y$ denotes the componentwise application, so
      that ((h$_Y$)($\underline{e}$))(y:s) = (h$_s$)($\underline{e}$(y:s)) for each y:s $\in$ Y.

In [Rei 85] it is proved that for each set AX of proper conditional equivalences and each set (Y:G) of equivalences in ALG(I/O-SIG,AX) there is an algebra F freely generated by (Y:G). Since that algebr is unique up to isomorphism it will be denoted by F(AX,G,Y,I).

For the problems of operational semantics the construction of F(AX,G,Y,I) relevant. It is interesting that this algebr can be constructed within the approach of identical satisfaction. On can prove that the algebra
      F(Ø,AX*modI(Y.G),Y,SORT)
is equal to F(AX,G,Y,I), where SORT is the set of all sort names of I/O-SIG and AX*modI(Y.G) as defined above.

Thus, F(AX,G,Y,I) can be constructed as the algebra which is freely generated in the class of all SIG-algebras, where SIG results from I/O-SIG by anuling the separation in I/O-sorts and state sorts, by the infinite set AX*modI(Y.G) of equations.

The elements in F(AX,G,Y,I)$_s$ for s $\in$ I are terms t $\in$ T(SIG,Y)$_s$ with (Y.t=t) $\in$ AX*modI(Y.G). Any two terms t1,t2 $\in$ T(SIG,Y)$_s$ with s $\in$ I represent equal internal states in F(AX,G,Y,I) if they are instances of one and the same term t $\in$ T(SIG,X)$_s$ where X is a finite set of variables of I/O-sorts, such that there are substitutions sub1: X --->.T(SIG,Y), sub2: X ---> T(SIG,Y) with (Y:sub1(x)=sub2(x)) $\in$ AX*modI(Y.G), for each x:s $\in$ I, and with t1=sub1(t), t2=sub2(t). In the last two equations sub1 and sub2 also denote the unique extensions to homomorphisms sub1: T(SIG,X) ---> T(SIG,Y), sub2: T(SIG,X) ---> T(SIG,Y).

This characterization of $F(AX,G,Y,I)$ implies for the operational semantics the following restriction of the narrowing step:

Any rule

$(Z. \; l1=r1\&...\&ln=rn \; ---> \; l=r \; mod \; I)$

with $l,r \in T(SIG,Z)_s$, such that s is not in I/O-SORT, can only be applied if l can be unified with a subterm inside an I/O-subterm.

Thus, any term $t \in T(SIG,\ddot{Y})_s$ is in normal form if s is not in I/O-SORT and t has no proper I/O-subterms.

Compared with other algebras of the same behavioural equivalence class the algebra of maximal redundancy leads to a minimal number of applications of the narrowing step and represents therefore an optimal choice.

REFERENCES:

[Dro 88] Ueber Erweiterungen in Termersetzungssystemen und deren Anwendung zur Prototyp-Generierung algebraischer Spezifikationen. Dissertation, TU Braunschweig

[EW 86] Ehrig,H.and Weber,H.: Programming in the Large with Algebraic Module Specification. Proc.IFIP-Congress, Dublin 1986,North-Holland.

[GDLH 84] Gogolla,M.,Drosten.K.,Lipeck,U.,and Ehrich,H.-D.: Algebraic and Operational Semantics of Specifications Allowing Exceptions and Errors. TCS 34(3),1984

[GGM 76] Giarratana,V.,Gimona,F.and Montanari,U.: Observability concepts in abstract data types. In: Proc. MFCS'76, Springer-Verlag, LNCS 45,1976.

[Gog 83] Goguen,J.A.:Parameterized Programming. In: Biggerstaf,T. and Cheatham,T.(eds),Proc.Workshop on Reusability in Programming pp.138-150,ITT,1983.

[GM 82] Goguen,J.A.and Meseguer,J.: Universal realization, persistent interconnection and implementation of abstract modules. In: Proc. ICALP'82, Springer-Verlag, LNCS 140, 265-281, 1982.

[HKR 80] Hupbach,U.L.,Kaphengst,H.and Reichel.H.:Initial specification of abstract data types, parameterized data types and algorithms. VEB Robotron, ZFT Dresden, Techn.Rep.WIB 15, 1980.

[Hus 85]   Hussman.H.: Unification in conditional-equational theories.
           MIP-8502, University of Passau, 1985.

[Rei 84]   Reichel,H.:Structural induction on partial algebras.Akademie-
           Verlag, Berlin, 1984.

[Rei 85]   Reichel,H.: Behavioural validity of conditional equations in
           abstract data types. In: Contributions to General Algebra 3,
           Proc. Vienna Conf.,June 1984, Verlag Hoelder-Pichler-Tempsky,
           Wien, 1985.

[Rei 86]   Reichel,H.: Behavioural Programm Specification. In: Category
           Theory and Computer Programming.Pitt,D.,Abramsky,S.,Poigne,A.
           and Rydeheard,D.(eds),Springer-Verlag, LNCS, 240, 1986.

[Rei 87]   Reichel,H.:Narrowing in Partial Algebras.In:Proc.EUROCAL'87,
           Leipzig, June 1987, Springer-Verlag, LNCS, to appear.

[W...83]   Wirsing,M., Pepper,P., Partsch,H., Dosch,W.,and Broy,M.: On
           hierarchicies of abstract data types.
           Acta Informatica 20,1-33, 1983

[Wol 87]   Wolter,U.: The Power of Behavioural Validity, Preprint 1-87,
           TU Magdeburg, Sektion Mathematik, 1987.

PART II

The Design Language COLD

An Introduction to COLD-K

H.B.M. Jonkers*

Philips Research Laboratories
P.O. Box 80000, 5600 JA Eindhoven, The Netherlands

Abstract

An introduction to the formal design kernel language COLD-K is given. After discussing the notion of class underlying the language, various styles of describing classes are presented ranging from algebraic to state-based techniques on the one hand, and axiomatic to algorithmic techniques on the other hand. The last part of the paper is devoted to the structuring mechanisms provided by the language, which include high level modularisation and parameterisation techniques as well as mechanisms to construct complete *designs*.

1 Introduction

The language COLD-K has been developed in the framework of ESPRIT project 432 (METEOR). It is intended to serve as the basis of a software development method supporting the use of formal techniques.

COLD-K is a *design language*, meaning that it can be used for describing (sequential) software systems in intermediate stages of their design. As such the language includes both specification-oriented and implementation-oriented constructs. One of the main aims in its design has been to unify the value-oriented world of algebraic specification languages with the object-oriented world of imperative programming languages.

COLD-K is a *kernel language*, implying that it is meant to be used as the kernel of user-oriented language versions (attuned to e.g. different implementation languages), to be derived from it by syntactic extensions. All essential semantic features are contained in the language, as well as high level constructs for modularisation and parameterisation and a number of general purpose constructs of a syntactic nature. It is for example fairly easy to define a Pascal-oriented version of the language, allowing one to develop modular, parameterised Pascal programs using algebraic and pre/postcondition specifications.

COLD-K is a *formal language*, which means that the well-formedness and semantics of the language constructs are defined mathematically [2]. This guarantees that descriptions in the language leave no room for ambiguity and that a high level of tool support can be provided. The use of formal techniques in the design process is one of

---

*This work has been performed in the framework of ESPRIT project 432 (METEOR).

the key factors (though certainly not the only) in increasing the quality of the software development process.

This paper provides an introduction to the language COLD-K, mainly by means of examples. In Section 2 the notion of a class is introduced, which plays a central role in the language. Sections 3, 4 and 5 demonstrate three different styles of describing classes and the language constructs associated with them: the algebraic, axiomatic state-based and algorithmic styles. In these sections the example of a first-in first-out buffer is used as a leitmotiv. Section 6 is devoted to the structuring mechanisms provided by the language, which include high level modularisation and parameterisation techniques as well as mechanisms to construct complete *designs*.

The COLD-K language constructs are represented in this paper in terms of the concrete syntax defined in [5], which is a rather direct mapping of the abstract syntactic structures of the language to strings with almost no syntactic sugaring. The use of this spartan syntax may easily give the language a flavour of impracticality, but we hope the reader can see through this. The use of a properly syntactically sugared version of the language is essential for the practical applicability of the language, but syntactic sugaring is not the topic of this paper. The subject here is the *kernel language* COLD-K. When we use the name COLD in the sequel, it should usually be interpreted in the broader sense of some syntactically sugared version of the language.

2 Classes

As explained in the introduction, COLD is meant as a language for describing software systems at various levels of abstraction. It should help the software developer in traversing the path from an abstract system specification to a running application in a smooth and systematic way. A key role in this is played by the notion of a *class*, which is the uniform model of software systems underlying the language. The notion of a class in COLD can be compared with that of a module in Modula-2, a package in Ada or a class in Smalltalk (though there are important differences between the latter and former notions of class).

Classes are mathematical abstractions of software systems and as such they do not really exist: They are in the mind of the COLD software developer who can only *describe* them. The ultimate goal will generally be to bring a description into such a form that it can be *executed* by a machine so that we can do something useful with it. It is the job of the machine to make sure that the execution shows a behaviour in accordance with the description. It is essential to keep the difference between these three things in mind from the beginning: classes, their descriptions and their executions. To begin with, let us discuss the notion of a class and the intuition behind it.

A class can be viewed as an abstract machine having a collection of *states* and one *initial state*. The state of a class can be changed by means of *procedures*, which act as the 'instructions' of the machine. A very simple example is that of a 'counter', which can be modelled as a class as follows. There is a state for every possible value of the counter, the initial state is the state corresponding with the initial value of the counter and there are procedures to increment and decrement the value of the counter.

```
SORT Nat
FUNC zero:          -> Nat
FUNC succ: Nat  -> Nat
FUNC pred: Nat  -> Nat
PRED less: Nat # Nat
SORT Cell
FUNC size: Cell -> Nat
FUNC cont: Cell -> Nat
```

Figure 1: State signature of *CELL*

2.1 States and state signatures

As sketched above there does not seem to be anything special about classes. The differences between classes and, e.g., finite state machines stem from the structure associated with the states of classes. The states themselves are considered primitive (like the states of a finite state machine), but they have a number of *state components* attached to them. The state components are identified by a fixed set of names associated with the class, called the *state signature* of the class. There are three kinds of state components with the following names:

1. *Sort names*: In each state a sort name denotes a *sort*, which is a collection of *objects*. The objects are said to *exist* in the given state.
2. *Predicate names*: In each state a predicate name denotes a *predicate*, which is an ordinary mathematical predicate defined on the sorts of the given state.
3. *Function names*: In each state a function name denotes a *function*, which is a partial function from sorts to sorts of the given state.

As a simple example, consider the class *CELL* of 'bounded cells' of natural numbers, which can be described intuitively as follows. A bounded cell is a container which can hold natural numbers up to a certain given size associated with the cell. In any given state of *CELL* a number of these containers exist. The state of *CELL* can be changed by creating new cells or by changing the contents of existing cells. The state components of *CELL* can be characterized by the state signature given in Figure 1. It indicates that each state of *CELL* has eight state components associated with it. Below we sketch the intended intuition of these state components:

Nat : the set of natural numbers,
zero: the natural number zero,
succ: the successor function on natural numbers (adding 1),
pred: the predecessor function on natural numbers (subtracting 1),
less: the 'less' predicate on natural numbers,
Cell: the set of cells,
size: the function associating a size with a cell,
cont: the function recording the contents of cells.

Note that the state signature says something about the structure of state components only. It says nothing about their mutual relation nor about the way they may change.

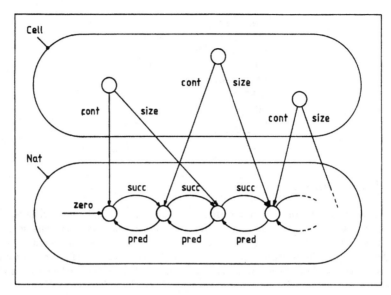

Figure 2: A state of *CELL*

There is for example no way to derive from the state signature that the natural number **zero** is the same object in every state, or that the contents of a cell may vary from state to state (which is probably what we want).

In Figure 2 we have visualized a possible state of *CELL*, where we have omitted the predicate **less**. In this picture sorts are represented by ovals, the objects in a sort by small circles and the values of functions by labelled arrows. The picture shows the natural numbers and three objects of sort **Cell** and captures the intuition sketched above. For example, we can see that no cell contains a value larger than or equal to its size. Note also that the predecessor function **pred** is a true partial function: there is no arrow labelled **pred** emerging from **zero**.

One way to look at Figure 2 is to view it as the picture of an *algebra*. An algebra is nothing but a collection of sets with a number of functions (and in this case also predicates) defined on them and that is essentially what Figure 2 amounts to. More precisely we can say that, in every state, the state components of a class constitute a so-called *many-sorted algebra* with a signature equal to the state signature of the class. This fact constitutes the basis for the use of COLD as an algebraic specification language (see Section 3).

If we are somewhat sloppy (as we will be in the sequel) we say that a state of a class *is* an algebra. Strictly speaking this is not correct since there is no way to derive from the semantics of the language that states with identical state components are identical. In other words, states are *non-extensional*. The reason for this has to do with the composition mechanisms for class descriptions and will not be further discussed here. Yet it cannot do much harm to identify states with identical state components and view them as many-sorted algebras, just as it cannot do much harm to identify equivalent states of a finite state machine.

```
SORT Nat
FUNC zero  :           -> Nat
FUNC succ  : Nat  -> Nat
FUNC pred  : Nat  -> Nat
PRED less  : Nat # Nat
SORT Cell
FUNC size  : Cell -> Nat
FUNC cont  : Cell -> Nat
PROC create: Nat           -> Cell
PROC store : Nat # Cell ->
```

Figure 3: Signature of *CELL*

2.2   State transitions and class signatures

After having associated more structure with states we are able to say more about the possible state transitions of a class as established by its procedures. As is the case with state components, the procedures of a class are identified by a fixed set of names, called *procedure names*, associated with the class. Each procedure name denotes a state transformer, which may take objects as its parameters and return objects as its result. The procedure names together with the state signature constitute the *class signature*, or *signature*, of the class. For the *CELL* example the class signature is given by Figure 3. Note that, for clarity, we have separated the state part from the state transition part of the class signature. In this signature we see two procedure names with the following intended intuition:

create: the procedure creating a new cell of a specified size,
store : the procedure storing a natural number in a cell.

Procedures transform states by *modifying* state components. We can distinguish between modifications of sorts, predicates and functions.

Modification of a sort amounts to the creation of new objects of that sort, thus extending the collection of existing objects of that sort. Once created an object can never be deleted, so sorts can only grow. For example, the procedure create of *CELL* when called with parameter n will create a new cell object of size n. It will not affect any of the already existing cells.

Modification of a predicate or function amounts to modifying its result value for certain (and possibly all) arguments. An example is provided by the procedure store of *CELL*. It takes a natural number n and a cell c and stores n in c by modifying the value of cont(c) to n while not affecting anything else.

Combinations of modifications of sorts, predicates and functions are possible. So a procedure may create a new object of a certain sort and at the same time modify a function. This situation already seems to occur in the procedure create, which adds a new object to the domains of the functions size and cont. However, we shall *not* consider this a modification of size and cont since the values of these functions for their original arguments are not affected (see Figure 4). Only if create would also

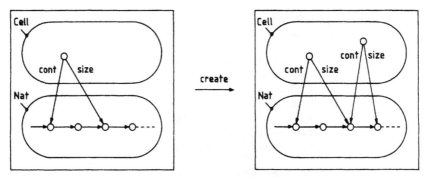

Figure 4: `create` does not modify `size` or `cont`

change the contents of an existing cell would we say that `create` modifies cont. This liberal notion of modification, which may seem strange at first sight, is quite essential, as will be explained later.

A question that may arise in connection with the *CELL* example is what the contents of a newly created cell is. We could assume that the content of a cell is automatically initialized with some fixed value, e.g., `zero`. Another option is to assume that immediately after its creation, a cell contains an unpredictable value (less than the size of the cell). This indicates that procedures are *nondeterministic* state transformers: neither the effect nor the result of a procedure need be uniquely determined by the arguments of the procedure and the state in which the procedure is applied. So, a random number generator could be modelled by a procedure of the following form:

```
PROC random: -> Nat
```

When applied twice in the same state this procedure may yield different natural numbers, in contrast with a function such as:

```
FUNC notrandom: -> Nat
```

which will always yield the same value when applied in the same state, although the value of the function may differ from state to state.

2.3 Relating class concepts to programming concepts

So far we have been discussing the notion of class underlying COLD. We have stated that classes are used as uniform models of software systems, but it may by now not be fully clear what the relation is between the concepts introduced above and the more familiar concepts from the world of programming languages. In order to explain this relation, we shall take Modula-2 as a concrete example of a programming language and discuss how COLD concepts correspond with Modula-2 concepts (see Figure 5).

The notion of class as incorporated in COLD closely corresponds with that of a module in Modula-2. Just like classes, modules have an internal state which can be changed by means of procedures. Sorts correspond with types in Modula-2, except that all sorts are 'opaque'. This implies that the objects of a given sort are considered primitive values

COLD	Modula-2
class	module
sort	type
object	value
	dynamic variable
function	function
	(array) variable
predicate	boolean function
	boolean variable
procedure	procedure

Figure 5: Corresponding concepts of COLD and Modula-2

and there is no way to access their internal representation. The only way to manipulate objects of a certain sort is by means of the predicates, functions and procedures of the class. Furthermore, there is no difference in COLD between 'simple values' such as booleans and integers, 'structured values' such as arrays and records, and 'dynamic objects' as used for building pointer structures: all are treated equally as objects.

Functions in COLD correspond to some extent with functions in Modula-2, except that we are very strict about side-effects, which are forbidden. This implies that in each state of a class, a function can be viewed as a true mathematical (partial) function, which will have no effect on the state when called. Another aspect of functions in COLD is that they can play a role similar to variables in modules. So the way to model an integer variable declared in a module would be to define a variable nullary function f: -> Int in a class, with the value of f representing the value of the variable.

The basic idea behind this seemingly ambivalent role of functions is simple. When, as an external user, we want to 'read' information from a state component of a class we are not interested in the way this information is represented. So whether the information is represented by a variable or by a piece of code computing the information (as in a Modula-2 function) is irrelevant. Variables and code are just one way of representing the same thing, and this representation should be shielded from the user of the class. This becomes particularly clear with array variables, which can be viewed as tabular representations of functions. If we have a way to compute the value of an array element from its index we could just as well represent the array by a piece of code. From the abstract point of view, both representations represent functions, which is the reason to treat them as such in COLD.

In COLD there is no built-in notion of 'variable' in the traditional sense of a box in which a value can be stored (by means of an 'assignment') and from which a value can be retrieved (by 'dereferencing'). By using functions in combination with dynamic object creation, such variables and the operations on them can be defined as objects in the language itself. How to do this is in fact already indicated by the *CELL* example. Each object of sort Cell can be viewed as a variable (in the sense of a box). The store procedure acts as the assignment and the cont function acts as the dereferencing operation. So dereferencing is treated as normal function application and not as some implicit operation as in most programming languages. In practice it may be a nuisance to write down such explicit dereferencing operations (or, more generally, to perform explicit type conversions), but at the user level of the language there are simple ways to remedy this.

Predicates in COLD correspond to a certain extent with boolean functions and boolean variables in Modula-2, with the same restrictions as indicated above for functions. There is one important difference, though. In each state of a class a predicate represents a true mathematical predicate which for a given argument is either true or false. There is no such thing as a predicate being undefined, in contrast with functions and variables. As a matter of fact, predicates do not yield a value at all: they either hold or do not hold for a given argument.

3 Algebraic class descriptions

3.1 Flat class descriptions

In the previous section we focused on the notion of class. In this section and the following ones we shall discuss how to describe classes, i.e., how to construct *class descriptions*. For the time being we shall restrict ourselves to so-called *flat class descriptions*, which describe a class by a *signature* and a linear list of *definitions*. A flat class description has the following structure:

```
EXPORT
    signature
FROM
CLASS
    definition₁
      ⋮
    definitionₙ
END
```

The signature after the keyword EXPORT specifies the class signature. Each definition introduces specific components (sorts, predicates, functions, procedures) or certain properties of the class being described. Each name in the signature should have a definition associated with it but the converse need not hold. Those components which are defined but not exported (i.e., not mentioned after the keyword EXPORT) are called *hidden*. We shall come back to the role of these hiddens later.

A sort, predicate, function or procedure definition consists of a header, which is identical to the header used for the component in the class signature, followed by a *body*. So a definition of the cont function of *CELL* class would have the following form:

```
FUNC cont: Cell -> Nat body
```

As in mathematics, there are two basic ways of defining the components of a class. The first is to give an *explicit definition*, which uniquely characterizes the component in terms of other components. This characterization is given in the body of the definition. The second is to give an *implicit definition*, which defines the component (in a not

```
SORT Nat
FUNC zero:        -> Nat
FUNC succ: Nat -> Nat
FUNC pred: Nat -> Nat
PRED less: Nat # Nat
```

Figure 6: Signature of *NAT*

necessarily unique way) by properties postulated in other definitions. In that case the body of the definition may be empty.

The definition of a property is called an *axiom* in COLD. Indeed this notion of axiom is very much like the notion of axiom in mathematics: it introduces properties of (the components of) a class without proof. An axiom definition in COLD-K has the following form:

AXIOM *assertion*

Here *assertion* is a statement about the components of the class, which should be interpreted as a property holding in *all* states of the class (and not just in, e.g., the initial state). For the time being, we can think of assertions as formulae in typed first order predicate calculus, examples of which we will see in the next subsection.

Another restriction that will be made in this section is to limit ourselves to classes without procedures. In a class without procedures there is no way to change the state, so the class will always remain in its initial state. Hence we can identify the class with its initial state and view it as a many-sorted algebra. We shall therefore denote descriptions of such classes as *algebraic class descriptions*. The main reason for starting with the above restrictions is of a pedagogical nature: we want to start with a simple subset of the language and gradually introduce new language features.

3.2 Defining the class *NAT* of natural numbers

As a first simple example let us discuss how to describe the class of natural numbers, which is one of the most frequently occurring algebraic structures. It is always a good idea to start with the signature of the class. We choose the signature given by Figure 6, which is a subset of the signature of the *CELL* class. The intended interpretations of the class components are the same as in the *CELL* example. We shall first focus our attention on the definition of the sort Nat and the functions zero and succ. We intend to define them implicitly (in fact, we have no other choice since nothing has been defined yet). The following (incomplete) class description reflects this intention:

```
EXPORT
  SORT Nat,
  FUNC zero:        -> Nat,
  FUNC succ: Nat -> Nat,
  FUNC pred: Nat -> Nat,
  PRED less: Nat # Nat
```

```
FROM
CLASS
  SORT Nat
  FUNC zero:      -> Nat
  FUNC succ: Nat -> Nat
  ...
END
```

In this class description we first of all see the signature, which consists of the headers of the sorts and operations of the class, separated by commas. Furthermore, we see three definitions with empty bodies. A sort, predicate or function definition with an empty body defines a *constant* entity: it is the same in all states of the class. So, Nat denotes the same fixed collection of objects in every state, and zero denotes the same object in every state. This is the case irrespective of what will follow at the '...'. Even if we would add procedures modifying the state (which we will do later on), Nat, zero and succ would still mean the same things in all states.

In order to make sure that Nat, zero and succ get their intended meaning we have to add axioms to the description of *NAT*. A first thing to consider is that functions in COLD-K are partial. This implies that the result of applying a function may be undefined. Of course we want zero and succ(n) to be well-defined objects for every n. This can be expressed by means of the built-in *definedness predicate*, represented by the postfix operator !:

```
AXIOM
{NAT1} zero!;
{NAT2} FORALL n:Nat ( succ(n)! )
```

The semicolon used in this axiom is the same as logical conjunction, except that it has lower precedence than the more usual propositional connectives (NOT, AND, OR, => and <=>, in decreasing order of precedence). The curly braces act as comment brackets.

At this point it is appropriate to say something about the way we deal with partiality in COLD, which has been inspired by [7]. If a function f: A -> B is undefined for a certain argument, it can be considered to yield a special object of sort B, called an *undefined object*. An undefined object yielded by f in a certain state is considered not to exist in that state (so definedness is equivalent to existence). Although the occurrence of undefined objects is not forbidden in the language, the general philosophy is that such objects correspond with erroneous situations and therefore it should be made impossible to say something interesting about them, which is achieved as follows.

Functions and predicates are *strict*: if we pass an undefined object as an argument to a function, the result of that function will also be undefined. If we pass it to a predicate, the truth value of that predicate will be false. (Note that, as stated earlier, predicates in COLD are true predicates which cannot be undefined, in contrast with boolean functions.) The strictness property also holds for the built-in predicates of the language, in particular for the definedness and equality predicates. So we have for all x and y that:

```
x = y => x! AND y!
```

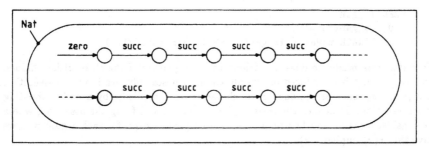

Figure 7: A non-standard model

Note that this implies that an undefined object is not equal to any other object, including itself, and that definedness can be expressed in terms of equality:

```
x! <=> x = x
```

In accordance with the philosophy indicated above, all quantifiers in the language range over defined objects. So the following tautology holds:

```
FORALL n:Nat ( n! )
```

If we speak about 'objects' in the sequel we shall always mean defined (= existing) objects, unless explicitly stated otherwise.

Returning to the definition of *NAT*, we note that we also have to express that there are no duplicates in the infinite sequence zero, succ(zero), succ(succ(zero)),..., which is expressed by the following axiom(s):

```
AXIOM  FORALL m:Nat,n:Nat (
{NAT3} NOT succ(n) = zero;
{NAT4} succ(m) = succ(n) => m = n )
```

3.3 Inductive definitions

It is a well-known fact that the axioms NAT1–NAT4 are not sufficient to characterize the natural numbers. There are classes, corresponding with so-called *non-standard models* of the natural numbers, which satisfy NAT1–NAT4 but which do not correspond with our intuition about the natural numbers. Such 'non-standard classes' are characterized by the fact that they contain objects of sort Nat which are not elements of the set {zero, succ(zero), succ(succ(zero)),...} (see Figure 7). We therefore have to add another axiom stating that there are no other natural numbers than those contained in this set. In other words, we have to state that the sort Nat is *generated* by the functions zero and succ.

It is also a well-known fact that the closure property we want to express cannot be expressed in a first-order framework. However, in COLD-K it is possible to define predicates and functions *inductively*, which gives us the opportunity to characterize the set {zero, succ(zero), succ(succ(zero)),...} rather directly by means of an auxiliary predicate. For that purpose we introduce the following auxiliary definition:

```
PRED is_gen: Nat
IND  is_gen(zero);
     FORALL n:Nat ( is_gen(n) => is_gen(succ(n)) )
```

Note that this predicate does not belong to the signature of the class: it is a hidden predicate, which is introduced for specification purposes only. An inductive definition of a predicate, such as the one above, characterizes a predicate by a body consisting of an assertion. It defines the *least* (strict) predicate satisfying the assertion, where we consider a predicate r less than or equal to a predicate q if for each argument x we have that $r(x)$ implies $q(x)$.

Similar to inductive definitions in mathematics, there is no a priori guarantee that an inductively defined predicate really exists. We have the obligation to prove that there exists a least predicate satisfying the given assertion and only then the definition is correct. Fortunately we can make life easy on ourselves since there are syntactic conditions which, when satisfied, automatically guarantee the existence of the least predicate. These conditions amount to the requirement that the assertion in the body of an inductively defined predicate r has 'Horn-clause' form. This implies that the assertion should have the form of a conjunction, where each conjunct is a universally quantified assertion of the form:

$$t_1 \text{ AND } \ldots \text{ AND } t_m => r(x_1, \ldots, x_n)$$

Here $x_1, \ldots, x_n$ are logical variables (introduced by the universal quantifiers) and each t_i is either an assertion not containing r or an assertion of the form $r(y_1, \ldots, y_n)$ where $y_1, \ldots, y_n$ are logical variables. It is easy to check that if we have two predicates r_1 and r_2 satisfying a Horn-clause A, then also the conjunction $r_1 \wedge r_2$ satisfies A. In other words, the set R of predicates satisfying A is closed under conjunction. Moreover, this set is non-empty since the predicate r which is true for all of its arguments satisfies A, hence there is a least predicate satisfying A.

We note here that an inductive definition may be correct even if it is not in Horn-clause form. In practice, the fact that we are not able to rewrite the body of an inductive definition to Horn-clause form is usually an indication that there is something wrong.

Now let us return to the definition of the predicate is_gen. This definition does apparently not satisfy the Horn-clause condition, but we can easily rewrite it into a form that does:

```
PRED is_gen: Nat
IND  FORALL m:Nat,n:Nat
     ( n = zero => is_gen(n);
       is_gen(m) AND n = succ(m) => is_gen(n) )
```

Note that we have to prove that the assertion in the body of this inductive definition is equivalent with the assertion in the body of the definition given before. This proof is simple, but requires the use of axioms NAT1 and NAT2.

In order to express that there are no other natural numbers than those generated by zero and succ we merely have to add the axiom:

```
AXIOM
{NAT5} FORALL n:Nat ( is_gen(n) )
```

This axiom, together with the definition of is_gen, gives us an *induction principle* for the natural numbers: in order to prove that a certain assertion A(n) holds for all natural numbers n, it suffices to prove that A(zero),A(succ(zero)),A(succ(succ(zero))), etc. hold. In other words, it suffices to prove that A(zero) holds and that A(n) implies A(succ(n)) for all n. Note that there is a one-to-one correspondence of axioms NAT1–NAT5 with Peano's axioms for the natural numbers.

What remains to be done in order to complete the definition of *NAT* is to give definitions of the predecessor function pred and the predicate less, for which we also use the inductive style of definition:

```
FUNC pred: Nat -> Nat
IND  FORALL n:Nat
     ( pred(succ(n)) = n )

PRED less: Nat # Nat
IND  FORALL m:Nat,n:Nat
     ( less(m,succ(m));
       less(m,n) => less(m,succ(n)) )
```

The definition of pred is an example of an inductive definition of a function. It defines the *least defined* (strict) function satisfying the assertion in the body of the definition, provided there is at least one function satisfying the assertion. In order to make this more precise, we shall explain inductive definitions in terms of inductive definitions of predicates, using the definition of the function pred as an example.

First we associate an inductively defined predicate is_pred with pred, with the intended meaning that is_pred(m,n) holds iff pred(m) = n. The definition of this predicate can be obtained by rewriting the definition of pred in a straightforward way:

```
PRED is_pred: Nat # Nat
IND  FORALL n:Nat
     ( is_pred(succ(n),n) )
```

This is again not strictly in Horn clause form, but can easily brought into it. Now pred(m), as defined above, is the unique object n such that is_pred(m,n) holds. If this object does not exist or if it is not unique, the function is undefined. This implies that pred(zero) is undefined, since there is no n such that is_pred(zero,n) holds.

Note that if the associated predicate of an inductively defined function is not functional in a certain argument, the function is undefined for that argument. So, in that case, the inductive definition still defines a function, but this function does not satisfy the assertion in the body of the definition. This situation should generally be avoided, and therefore it should be checked for each inductive function definition that the associated predicate is indeed functional.

```
SORT Nat
FUNC zero :                      -> Nat
FUNC succ : Nat                  -> Nat
FUNC pred : Nat                  -> Nat
PRED less : Nat  # Nat
SORT Item
SORT Queue
FUNC empty:                      -> Queue
FUNC put  : Item # Queue -> Queue
FUNC geti : Queue                -> Item
FUNC getq : Queue                -> Queue
FUNC len  : Queue                -> Nat
```

Figure 8: Signature of *QUEUE*

3.4   Defining the class *QUEUE* of queues

As another simple example of an algebraic class description we shall now discuss a specification of the class *QUEUE* of first-in first-out queues, for which we choose the signature given by Figure 8. The intended intuition of the sorts and operations is indicated below (except for the natural numbers and their operations, which we have already seen):

Item : the set of items to be stored in queues,
Queue : the set of queues,
empty : the empty queue,
put   : the function yielding the new queue obtained by
        putting an element in a queue,
geti : the function yielding the item obtained by
        getting an element from a queue,
getq : the function yielding the new queue obtained by
        getting an element from a queue,
len   : the function yielding the number of items in a queue.

The fact that we view the put operation as a function yielding a queue as its result and that the get operation is split into two functions, one yielding the item removed from the queue and the other yielding the queue after removal of the item, is a consequence of the algebraic approach used where we lack a notion of 'state'.

The definition of *QUEUE* will have the following structure:

```
EXPORT
  SORT Nat,
  FUNC zero :                 -> Nat,
  FUNC succ : Nat             -> Nat,
  FUNC pred : Nat             -> Nat,
  PRED less : Nat   # Nat,
  SORT Item,
```

```
    SORT Queue,
    FUNC empty:                -> Queue,
    FUNC put  : Item # Queue -> Queue,
    FUNC geti : Queue          -> Item,
    FUNC getq : Queue          -> Queue,
    FUNC len  : Queue          -> Nat
  FROM
  CLASS
    Natural number definitions
    Item definitions
    Queue definitions
  END
```

We assume that the definitions of the natural numbers are given (as discussed in the previous section), so we restrict ourselves to the parts indicated by *Item definitions* and *Queue definitions*. We start with introducing the sort Item for the objects that will be stored in queues. No assumptions will be made about the operations available for objects of sort Item, except that we have equality and definedness (which are always available). So the part denoted by *Item definitions* consists of only one definition:

```
  SORT Item
```

Next we introduce the sort of queues:

```
  SORT Queue
```

Since we use an algebraic style of definition, we have defined Queue as a constant sort, so all queues are assumed to exist beforehand. Next we introduce the empty queue and the put and get operations:

```
  FUNC empty:                -> Queue
  FUNC put  : Item # Queue -> Queue
  FUNC geti : Queue          -> Item
  FUNC getq : Queue          -> Queue
```

The axioms specifying these operations are given below, following the same pattern as with the natural numbers:

```
  AXIOM
  {QUEUE1} empty!;
  {QUEUE2} NOT geti(empty)!;
  {QUEUE3} NOT getq(empty)!;
          FORALL i:Item,j:Item,q:Queue (
  {QUEUE4} geti(put(i,empty)) = i;
  {QUEUE5} geti(put(i,put(j,q))) = geti(put(j,q));
  {QUEUE6} getq(put(i,empty)) = empty;
  {QUEUE7} getq(put(i,put(j,q))) = put(i,getq(put(j,q))) )

  PRED is_gen: Queue
  IND  is_gen(empty);
```

```
       FORALL i:Item,q:Queue
       ( is_gen(q) => is_gen(put(i,q)) )

  AXIOM
  {QUEUE8} FORALL q:Queue ( is_gen(q) )
```

Note that we have left axiom QUEUE1 outside the scope of the FORALL quantor: otherwise we cannot derive that there exists even a single queue!

What may seem to be missing are axioms stating that put(i,q) is always defined and that geti(q) and getq(q) are always defined if q is not empty, but these properties are derivable from the axioms. First of all, it follows from the strictness of equality and axiom QUEUE5 that geti(put(j,q))! for all j and q. Using the strictness of functions we derive put(j,q)! from this. Similarly we can derive from QUEUE7 that getq(put(j,q))!.

Axiom QUEUE8 implies that all queues are generated by the empty and put functions, thus giving us an induction principle for queues. Using this induction principle we can prove that each application of put generates a 'new' queue, i.e., that:

```
       FORALL i:Item,j:Item,q:Queue,r:Queue
       ( NOT put(i,q) = empty;
         put(i,q) = put(j,r) => i = j AND q = r )
```

This implies that each queue can in fact be viewed as a sequence of items.

We can use the same induction principle to give an inductive definition of the length function for queues:

```
       FUNC len: Queue -> Nat
       IND  len(empty) = zero;
            FORALL i:Item,q:Queue
            ( len(put(i,q)) = succ(len(q)) )
```

Note that the fact that there is a one-to-one correspondence between queues and sequences of put operations implies that the predicate associated with len is functional in its first argument, and thereby len is a total function.

As a final remark we note that we could also have defined a single get operation, combining the functions of geti and getq:

```
       FUNC get: Queue -> Queue # Item
```

This function yields a tuple of two objects as its result, thus making it possible to formulate axioms QUEUE2 and QUEUE3 as a single axiom:

```
       {Q2&3} NOT get(empty)!;
```

Here we see the definedness operator applied to a tuple of objects. Definedness of a tuple means definedness of all of its constituents. This implies that axiom Q2&3 expresses that at least one of the two constituents of the tuple yielded by get is undefined, which may seem insufficient: we want them both to be undefined. However, it is an inherent property of functions yielding tuples of objects in COLD that either all constituents of the result tuple are defined or all are undefined.

We can also combine axioms QUEUE4 and QUEUE6 into a single axiom:

```
{Q4&6} get(put(i,empty)) = (empty,i);
```

Here we see tuples at the left and right hand sides of the equality. Equality of two tuples means equality of the corresponding constituents of the tuples. We note that the comma, which is used here as the tuple-building operator, is in fact the sequential composition operator (see Subsection 5.1).

Axioms QUEUE5 and QUEUE7 cannot be so easily combined as the other axioms. We first have to take the result of get(put(j,q)) apart:

```
{Q5&7} FORALL r:Queue,k:Item
       ( (r,k) = get(put(j,q)) =>
         get(put(i,put(j,q))) = (put(i,r),k) );
```

4 Axiomatic state-based class descriptions

4.1 Variables, dependencies and modification rights

So far we restricted ourselves to classes without procedures. Such classes are always in the same (initial) state, which makes it possible to identify them with many-sorted algebras. Procedures (see Subsection 2.2) provide mechanisms to change the state of a class, so in classes with procedures we generally have to deal with a collection of states. An important element in the description of such classes is the description of the state transformations established by the procedures. Such class descriptions are called *state-based class descriptions*.

As before, we shall restrict ourselves to flat class descriptions. The main addition with respect to the previous section is the introduction of procedure definitions in class descriptions. Only implicit procedure definitions will be considered here, which implies that the properties of procedures are given by axioms. Such class descriptions with only implicit procedure definitions will be called *axiomatic state-based class descriptions*. Explicit procedure definitions will be discussed in Section 5.

One of the problems in axiomatic specifications of procedures is the *framing problem*: If we want to specify a procedure modifying only a few of a large number of state components, we also have to specify that the procedure leaves all other state components unmodified. Though this can be expressed by means of (a large number of) axioms, it leads to problems when adding new state components to the description. We would have to add an axiom for each procedure that leaves the new component unmodified. Apart from being a nuisance, this would make it effectively impossible to work in a modular way. This can be remedied by associating a set of *modification rights* with each implicit procedure definition, consisting of exactly those state components that are supposed to be modified by the procedure. When specifying the procedure by axioms, we only have to indicate how it modifies these state components; the other state components are by definition left unmodified.

The approach indicated above is still problematic if we want to add a new state component f that is characterized in terms of some old state component g. If g belongs to the modification rights of p, we would also have to add f to the modification rights of p (since a modification of g will generally imply a modification of f), which is again in conflict with the modularity principle. The way out here is to divide the state components into *variable* and *dependent* state components. The variable state components can be viewed as independent variables spanning the state space of the class. The dependent state components depend on these variables in the sense that they are left unmodified if the variables are left unmodified (so they cannot vary independently of the variables). If we specify the dependency of each dependent state component on the other state components explicitly, then it suffices to mention the modified variables in the modification rights of a procedure. The other state components modified by the procedure can be reconstructed by means of the specified dependencies. If we add a new dependent state component, we need only specify its dependencies and no old definitions have to be modified. Note that in explicit definitions of state components (such as inductive predicate and function definitions), there is no need to specify the dependencies: they can be derived from the body of the definition.

A consequence of the above approach is that we have to add two new forms of implicit definition of sorts, predicates and functions. The first is the *variable definition*, which consists of a header followed by the keyword VAR. For example, in the class *CELL* we could choose the function cont as a variable and define it by:

```
FUNC cont: Cell -> Nat    VAR
```

The second new form of implicit definition is the *dependent definition*, which consists of a header followed by a body of the form DEP $e_1, \ldots, e_n$, where $e_1, \ldots, e_n$ are other state components (not necessarily variables). It introduces the state component described by the header as a dependent state component which will not be modified unless the state components $e_1, \ldots, e_n$ are modified. For example, if we would want to add a predicate expressing that the contents of a cell in the class *CELL* is zero, this can be done by the following definition:

```
PRED null: Cell   DEP cont
```

This expresses that the predicate null will be left unmodified as long as the function cont is left unmodified. Note that creation of a new cell leaves the function cont unmodified (see Subsection 2.2), hence it also leaves the predicate null unmodified. Note also that constant definitions as introduced in Subsection 3.2 are in fact special cases of dependent definitions, in particular of dependent definitions with an empty set of dependencies. So a constant definition such as:

```
FUNC succ: Nat -> Nat
```

is in fact syntactic sugar for:

```
FUNC succ: Nat -> Nat    DEP NONE
```

The keyword NONE is the standard way in COLD-K to denote an empty list of anything.

Finally, we discuss what an implicit procedure definition looks like, where we restrict ourselves to its basic form. An implicit definition of a procedure p consists of a header followed by a body of the form MOD $v_1, \ldots, v_n$, where $v_1, \ldots, v_n$ are the modification rights of p, i.e., the variables that may be modified by p. For example, the procedure **store** from the class *CELL* could be defined implicitly by:

```
PROC store: Nat # Cell ->     MOD cont
```

This definition implies, among other things, that **store** will not create new cells.

4.2 Defining the class *CELL* of bounded cells

As can be inferred from the previous subsection, the construction of an axiomatic state-based class description can be described by the following conceptual steps:

1. Definition of the class signature.
2. Selection and definition of a basis of variable state components.
3. Definition of the other state components together with their dependencies.
4. Definition of the procedures together with their modification rights.
5. Specification of the static and dynamic properties of the class by axioms.

As a first example we shall follow the above scheme to construct an axiomatic description of the *CELL* class described intuitively in Sections 2.1 and 2.2. The signature of *CELL* has already been given in Figure 3. As we did before, we shall assume that the definitions of the natural numbers are given. So the definition of *CELL* will have the following structure:

```
EXPORT
  SORT Nat,
  FUNC zero  :         -> Nat,
  FUNC succ  : Nat  -> Nat,
  FUNC pred  : Nat  -> Nat,
  PRED less  : Nat # Nat,
  SORT Cell,
  FUNC size  : Cell -> Nat,
  FUNC cont  : Cell -> Nat,
  PROC create: Nat         -> Cell,
  PROC store : Nat # Cell ->
FROM
CLASS
  Natural number definitions
  Cell definitions
END
```

where we restrict ourselves to the part indicated by *Cell definitions*.

The choice of a basis of variables of *CELL* is rather obvious. We want to create new cells and change their contents independently, so we choose the sort Cell and the function cont as the variables spanning the state space of *CELL*, and introduce the following definitions:

```
SORT Cell              VAR
FUNC cont: Cell -> Nat VAR
```

Clearly, the function **size** should not be chosen as a variable, since we want the size of cells to be fixed. In other words, the function **size** is not dependent on any other state component. It should be defined as a constant entity:

```
FUNC size: Cell -> Nat
```

One may be tempted to replace this definition by:

```
FUNC size: Cell -> Nat   DEP Cell
```

since creation of a new cell will extend the domain of the function **size**. This in itself, however, is not considered a modification of **size** (see Subsection 2.2). It would be a modification of **size** if the size of *existing* cells would be modified by the creation of a new object, but that is not the case.

This completes the introduction of the state components. We have two procedures, one for creating cells and the other for changing the contents of cells, as defined by:

```
PROC create: Nat           -> Cell   MOD Cell
PROC store : Nat # Cell ->           MOD cont
```

Note that the function cont is not mentioned in the modification rights of the procedure **create**: the creation of a cell should leave the contents of existing cells unmodified.

The above indicates that the notion of modification as used in COLD-K reduces the number of dependencies and modification rights. Yet there is a more fundamental reason for using the liberal notion of modification as we do. Suppose that, at some later stage, we would want to associate an 'address' (of a location in memory) with each cell. This can be done by introducing the variable:

```
FUNC address: Cell -> Nat   VAR
```

If we had used the strict notion of modification, in the sense that creation of an object of a certain sort T modifies all predicates and functions defined on T, then we would have to add the function **address** to the list of modification rights of the procedure **create**, which is in conflict with the modularity principle. Using the liberal notion of modification we can leave the definition of **create** as is and the only thing we have to do is specify what the address of a newly created cell is.

We now arrive at the last step in the construction of the axiomatic description of *CELL*, which amounts to specifying the static and dynamic properties of cells. First of all, we have to consider the fact that functions are partial. Since we want **size** and cont to be total functions, we introduce the following axiom:

```
AXIOM   FORALL c:Cell (
{CELL1} size(c)!;
```

```
{CELL2} cont(c)! )
```

This axiom might be called a static property since it specifies properties of **size** and cont that hold in *all* states.

Before dealing with the dynamic properties, it is generally a good idea to first formulate a *class invariant*. A class invariant, or invariant, is an assertion A that holds in the initial state of the class and that is left invariant by each procedure p of the class. That is, if A holds in a certain state s and p transforms s to t, then A will also hold in t. Consequently, an invariant will hold in all states that can be reached from the initial state by means of procedure calls. It need not hold in all states, since it might be violated temporarily by a procedure.

We shall choose the following invariant for *CELL*, expressing that cells can contain only natural numbers less than their size:

```
{INVAR} FORALL c:Cell ( less(cont(c),size(c)) )
```

Note that this invariant implies that the size of a cell is greater than zero. We shall use this invariant as a guide in deriving the axiomatic characterizations of the procedures **create** and **store**. Before doing this, we should first consider the initial state of *CELL* and make sure that the invariant holds there. The simplest and most natural way to make INVAR hold in the initial state is to assume that there are no cells in the initial state, as specified by:

```
AXIOM
{CELL3} INIT => NOT EXISTS c:Cell ()
```

Here we see the built-in nullary predicate INIT, which is true iff we are in the initial state. The 'empty assertion' () is equivalent to TRUE.

4.3 Specifying state transformations

In trying to characterize the procedure **create** we arrive at the fundamental problem of how to describe the effect of a procedure or, more generally, the effect of an expression. Up till now we have only seen very simple expressions, such as logical variables and function applications. These expressions have no 'side effect' on the state: they are only meant to denote objects. A procedure application is an example of an expression that will generally have an effect on the state as well as yield a certain result. The procedure **create** will change the state by adding a new object and will yield that object as its result. Expressions will be discussed in detail in Subsection 5.1. For now it suffices to consider expressions as nondeterministic state transformers which may yield a result.

In order to characterize the effect of an expression, we must be able to express a relation between the states before and after the evaluation of an expression. What we need for this, first of all, is some way of formulating assertions about the state *after* the evaluation of an expression. For that purpose two special assertions are introduced, which are closely related to the box and diamond operators of dynamic logic [3]:

$[X]A$
$\langle X \rangle A$

The assertion $[X]A$ expresses that the assertion A holds in all possible final states of the evaluation of the expression X. The assertion $\langle X \rangle A$ expresses that the assertion A holds in at least one possible final state of the evaluation of X. Note that we use the word 'possible' since expressions are nondeterministic state transformers and therefore the final state of the evaluation of an expression need not be uniquely determined. Note also that, just like all other assertions, the above assertions should be interpreted relative to a given state and that the operators may be applied repeatedly. So an assertion such as $[X][Y]A$, interpreted in a state s, implies that if we evaluate X in s reaching a final state t, and subsequently evaluate Y in t reaching a final state u, then the assertion A will always hold in u.

The above two operators are called the *always* and *sometimes* operators. As is the case with universal and existential quantification, the operators can be expressed in terms of each other, i.e., we have the following tautologies:

```
([X]A) <=> NOT (<X> NOT A)
(<X>A) <=> NOT ([X] NOT A)
```

The assertion $\langle X \rangle$ TRUE expresses that there is at least one final state in the evaluation of X. In other words, it expresses that the expression X *terminates*. So the fact that the create operation terminates in all states can be expressed by:

```
FORALL n:Nat ( < create(n) > TRUE )
```

We shall come back to the notion of termination in Section 5.4.

In order to specify the effect of the create operation by means of an assertion of the form:

```
[ ... create(n) ... ] A
```

we need some way of denoting the result of the create operation in the assertion A. This is provided by the *declaration* and *binding* constructs of COLD-K, which may be used in assertions and expressions to introduce names and bind objects to them. These names can then be used to refer to the objects. A declaration has the following form:

```
LET x:T
```

It introduces the object name x with associated type T. After this declaration we are supposed not to refer to x until a binding of x to the result of the evaluation of some expression Y has been performed:

```
x := Y
```

From then on x denotes the object(s) yielded by Y. No other bindings to x should be performed after this. The scope of an object name declared in an assertion or expression X can be closed by means of the *block* construct, which has the following form:

```
BEGIN X END
```

This assertion or expression is semantically equivalent to X. It has the syntactic effect of making the names declared in X invisible to the outside world. The fact that create(n) yields a cell of size n can now be expressed as follows:

```
[ LET c:Cell; c := create(n) ] size(c) = n
```

Here we use the fact that the scope of object names introduced in the expression X in the assertions $[X]A$ and $<X>A$ extends to the assertion A. The semicolon used between the declaration and the binding of c is the sequential composition operator.

We note that declaration and binding need not follow one another immediately, though in practice they often will. Furthermore, the variables introduced by declarations should be interpreted as *logical variables* and not as programming variables (in the sense of imperative programming languages). From the operational point of view they can be considered *single assignment* variables (cf. variables in functional programming languages).

The fact that create yields a new object could be expressed by the following assertion:

```
FORALL d:Cell ( [ LET c:Cell; c := create(n) ] NOT c = d )
```

Here we use the fact that the FORALL quantifier ranges over the objects existing in the state prior to the evaluation of create(n). Another aspect of the create operation that we want to specify is that it creates exactly one new object, but here we run into a problem. What we have to express in the assertion following [...] above is that, if we have another 'new' object d, then it will be equal to c. But how do we express that d is new? We need some way to go back to the 'previous state', i.e., the state before the evaluation of the expression in [...], in order to state that d did not exist there. The mechanism to go back to a previous state is provided by the *previously* operator, denoted by the keyword PREV, which has two variants, one for assertions and one for expressions:

```
PREV A
PREV X
```

The assertion PREV A expresses that the assertion A holds in the previous state, while PREV X refers to the result of the expression X in the previous state. When used in the assertion immediately after the $[X]$ and $<X>$ operators, the PREV operator will refer to the state before the evaluation of X. The fact that a cell d is new with respect to some given previous state can now be expressed by:

```
d! AND PREV NOT d!
```

The use of the PREV operator is allowed only in a context where a previous state exists. In particular, such contexts are created by the always and sometimes operators. We can also say this in another way: each assertion and expression has a *history* associated with it, which is a sequence of previous states. The length of the history and the correspondence of the states in the history with places in the COLD-K text is statically determined. At the outermost level where assertions and expressions occur (in axioms and the bodies of operations) the length of the history is 0. So an axiom such as:

    AXIOM PREV TRUE

would be syntactically incorrect. The always and sometimes operators add a new state to the history, while the PREV operator reduces it by one. Hence repeated application of the PREV operator is allowed provided that the history has sufficient length.

The importance of the PREV operator goes further than the fact that we need it for specifying certain properties in connection with dynamic object creation. The use of the PREV operator makes it possible to specify the relation between two states rather directly in a single assertion, which will generally lead to more readable specifications and simplify reasoning about state transformations (cf. Jones' 'hooking operator' [4]).

We give the full characterization of the create operation below, where we remark that the always, sometimes and previously operators have precedences lower than all propositional connectives and higher than the semicolon:

```
AXIOM    FORALL n:Nat ( less(zero,n) => (
{CELL4} < create(n) > TRUE;
{CELL5} [ LET c:Cell; c := create(n) ]
         ( c! AND PREV NOT c!;
           FORALL d:Cell ( (PREV NOT d!) => d = c );
           size(c) = n;
           less(cont(c),size(c))
         ) ) )
```

Here we see a 'precondition' (the condition less(zero,n)) in the specification of create, which is necessary because it would otherwise be impossible to keep INVAR invariant. Note that we have indeed made sure that INVAR is not violated, but that we did not specify what the contents of a newly created cell should be: we only required that it should be defined and less than the size of the cell, the rest is left as freedom to the implementer. Note also that the modification rights of create as specified in its definition make sure that we do not have to say anything about the contents of the other cells.

Finally, we give the characterization of the store operation:

```
AXIOM    FORALL n:Nat,c:Cell ( less(n,size(c)) => (
{CELL6} < store(n,c) > TRUE;
{CELL7} [ store(n,c) ]
         ( cont(c) = n;
           FORALL m:Nat,d:Cell
           ( NOT d = c => cont(d) = PREV cont(d) )
         ) ) )
```

Here we also see a 'precondition' (the condition less(n,size(c))), necessary to make it possible to keep INVAR invariant. We have specified explicitly that store(n,c) leaves the contents of all cells other than c unmodified. This is necessary because the 'grain

```
SORT Nat
FUNC zero:                    -> Nat
FUNC succ: Nat                -> Nat
FUNC pred: Nat                -> Nat
PRED less: Nat  # Nat
SORT Item
SORT Buffer
FUNC len : Buffer             -> Nat
PROC new :                    -> Buffer
PROC put : Item # Buffer  ->
PROC get : Buffer             -> Item
```

Figure 9: Signature of *BUFFER*

size' of modification rights is that of complete state components, so **store** might in principle modify the contents of all cells. Note that this specification, as well as that of **create**, is in fact stronger than required (since we could, without penalty, add the invariant INVAR as a conjunct to the precondition of the operations). Note also that we have said nothing about the behaviour of **create** and **store** if their 'precondition' is not satisfied. This is left as freedom to the implementer.

4.4 Defining the class *BUFFER* of buffers

In Subsection 3.4 we saw an algebraic class description specifying the class *QUEUE* of first-in first-out queues. One of the problems with this specification is that it does not really correspond to our intuition about queues. Intuitively, a queue is an object with an internal state that can be changed by means of put and get operations. Also, it may seem a bit counterintuitive that all queues exist beforehand. More natural would be an approach where we can create a new queue dynamically if we need one.

We shall now give an axiomatic state-based class description specifying this more intuitive notion of first-in first-out queues. In order to distinguish the latter kind of queues from the former, we shall call the latter *buffers*. The class of buffers will be called *BUFFER*, for which we choose the class signature given by Figure 9.

The intended intuition of the sorts and operations in this signature (excluding the natural numbers and their operations) is as follows:

        Item   : the sort of items to be stored in buffers,
        Buffer : the sort of buffers,
        len   : the function yielding the number of items in a buffer,
        new   : the procedure creating a new empty buffer,
        put   : the procedure putting an element in a buffer,
        get   : the procedure removing an element from a buffer.

Note that there is no operation to determine the contents of a buffer. The only means we have to get something in or out of the buffer are the procedures put and get. The actual contents of a buffer is hidden and can only be accessed indirectly through these procedures. However, in order to specify the behaviour of a buffer we need some representation for its contents. This can be done by adding a hidden function that maps a buffer to its contents. This hidden function is only introduced for specification purposes (cf. the is_gen predicates) and is not physically part of any class described by the class description. To be more precise, the set of classes specified by a flat class description EXPORT Σ FROM CLASS *D* END is the set of all classes specified by the description CLASS *D* END with all hidden sorts and operations removed from them.

We shall represent the internal contents of a buffer as a sequence of items, which seems a rather natural choice. This implies that we also have to give definitions of sequences and their operations (as hidden sorts and operations), so the definition of *BUFFER* will have the following structure:

```
EXPORT
  SORT Nat,
  FUNC zero:                  -> Nat,
  FUNC succ: Nat              -> Nat,
  FUNC pred: Nat              -> Nat,
  PRED less: Nat  # Nat,
  SORT Item,
  SORT Buffer,
  FUNC len : Buffer           -> Nat,
  PROC new :                  -> Buffer,
  PROC put : Item # Buffer -> ,
  PROC get : Buffer           -> Item
FROM
CLASS
  Natural number definitions
  Item definitions
  Sequence definitions
  Buffer definitions
END
```

We shall restrict ourselves to the item, sequence and buffer definitions. First we give the definitions associated with sequences, where we have the following intended intuition:

```
Seq   : the sort of sequences of items,
empty : the empty sequence of items,
cons  : the function adding an item to the front of a sequence,
cat   : the function concatenating two sequences,
len   : the function yielding the length of a sequence.
```

We use the algebraic style of definition for defining the above sort and operations, adding the definition of the sort Item at the same time:

```
SORT Item
SORT Seq
FUNC empty:              -> Seq
FUNC cons : Item # Seq -> Seq
```

```
AXIOM
{SEQ1} empty:Seq!;
{SEQ2} FORALL i:Item,s:Seq ( cons(i,s)! )

AXIOM  FORALL i:Item,j:Item,s:Seq,t:Seq (
{SEQ3} NOT cons(i,s) = empty;
{SEQ4} cons(i,s) = cons(j,t) => i = j AND s = t )

PRED is_gen: Seq
IND  FORALL i:Item,s:Seq
     ( is_gen(empty);
       is_gen(s) => is_gen(cons(i,s)) )

AXIOM
{SEQ5} FORALL s:Seq ( is_gen(s) )

FUNC cat: Seq # Seq -> Seq
IND  FORALL i:Item,s:Seq,t:Seq
     ( cat(empty,s) = s;
       cat(cons(i,s),t) = cons(i,cat(s,t)) )

FUNC len: Seq -> Nat
IND  FORALL i:Item,s:Seq
     ( len(empty) = zero;
       len(cons(i,s)) = succ(len(s)) )
```

We have included the definition of sort Item (with no operations associated with it) in the sequence definitions, since items are the elements of sequences. Note that the names empty and len are overloaded: empty is used for denoting the empty sequence as well as the empty buffer, and len is used for denoting the length of a sequence as well as the length of a buffer. Overloading of names is allowed in COLD-K, provided no amibguities arise (which will be signalled by the syntax checker). If ambiguities occur, they can be resolved by using a *cast*. This is an expression of the form:

$$X:T_1\#\ldots\#T_n$$

where X is an expression and $T_1,\ldots,T_n$ are sorts. It forces the type of X to $T_1\#\ldots\#T_n$. An example of the use of this operator can be found in axiom SEQ1. The cast operator ":" has the highest priority of all operators.

We are now ready to give the buffer definitions. The choice of a basis of variables for the class *BUFFER* is more or less obvious. We want to independently create new buffers dynamically and change their contents by means of the put and get operations, so we define:

```
SORT Buffer               VAR
FUNC items: Buffer -> Seq  VAR
```

Here the items function associates a sequence of items with a buffer, representing the contents of that buffer. This is all very similar to the *CELL* example, except that we

want the contents of a buffer to be hidden, in contrast with the contents of a cell. The
length of a buffer depends on its contents, so we define:

```
FUNC len: Buffer -> Nat    DEP items
```

The three procedures associated with buffers are introduced by the following definitions, with obvious choices for their modification rights:

```
PROC new:                   -> Buffer   MOD Buffer
PROC put: Item # Buffer ->              MOD items
PROC get: Buffer        -> Item         MOD items
```

Finally, we give the axioms characterizing the static and dynamic properties of buffers.
First we give the 'static' properties:

```
AXIOM  FORALL b:Buffer (
{BUF1} items(b)!;
{BUF2} len(b) = len(items(b)) )
```

Note that axiom BUF2 uniquely characterizes the len function for buffers. It also
implies that the length of a buffer is always defined. Next we characterize the initial
state:

```
AXIOM
{BUF3} INIT => NOT EXISTS b:Buffer ()
```

Finally, we give the specifications of new, put and get:

```
AXIOM
{BUF4} < new > TRUE;
{BUF5} [ LET b:Buffer; b := new ]
       ( b! AND PREV NOT b!;
         FORALL c:Buffer ( (PREV NOT c!) => c = b );
         items(b) = empty
       )

AXIOM  FORALL i:Item,b:Buffer (
{BUF6} < put(i,b) > TRUE;
{BUF7} [ put(i,b) ]
       ( items(b) = cat(PREV items(b),cons(i,empty));
         FORALL c:Buffer ( NOT c = b => items(c) = PREV items(c) )
       ) )

AXIOM  FORALL b:Buffer ( NOT len(b) = zero => (
{BUF8} < get(b) > TRUE;
{BUF9} [ LET i:Item; i := get(b) ]
       ( (PREV items(b)) = cons(i,items(b));
         FORALL c:Buffer ( NOT c = b => items(c) = PREV items(c) )
       ) ) )
```

Note that we did not specify what should happen if a get operation on an empty buffer is performed.

5 Algorithmic class descriptions

5.1 Expressions

Before discussing algorithmic class descriptions, we shall go more deeply into the notion of an *expression*, which plays a central role in algorithmic class descriptions. So far we have only seen simple forms of expressions such as function and procedure calls. In its most general form, an expression describes a nondeterministic state transformation delivering a (possibly empty) sequence of objects as its result, where the length of the sequence is statically determined. Put more formally, an expression X is a *relation* between two states and a sequence of objects. If $\langle s, t, x_1, \ldots, x_n \rangle$ is an element of that relation, we say that X *terminates* in s, *transforms* s to t and *yields* $x_1, \ldots, x_n$. If for a given s there are no $t, x_1, \ldots, x_n$ such that $\langle s, t, x_1, \ldots, x_n \rangle$ is an element of the relation, we say that X *does not terminate* in s.

The notions of termination and non-termination of expressions can be expressed in terms of the sometimes and always operators discussed in the previous section. The fact that an expression X terminates in a state s is equivalent to the assertion:

<X> TRUE

because this assertion expresses that there is a state t and objects $x_1, \ldots, x_n$ such that $\langle s, t, x_1, \ldots, x_n \rangle$ is an element of the relation denoted by X. The fact that an expression X does not terminate in a state s is equivalent to the assertion:

[X] FALSE

because this assertion expresses that for all states t and objects $x_1, \ldots, x_n$ such that $\langle s, t, x_1, \ldots, x_n \rangle$ is an element of the relation denoted by X, the assertion FALSE holds. In other words, there are no such states t and objects $x_1, \ldots, x_n$.

Expressions are *strict*: if X transforms s to t yielding objects $x_1, \ldots, x_n$, the $x_1, \ldots, x_n$ are *existing* objects in t. This implies that an expression cannot yield an undefined object, so the following tautology holds for all expressions X of type T:

[LET x:T; x := X] x!

Note that this fact could be used to simplify axioms CELL5 and BUF5 in the specifications of the classes *CELL* and *BUFFER* in the previous section.

We emphasize that expressions in COLD-K are strictly interpreted as relations in the sense discussed above. They should *not* be interpreted as instructions of some kind of machine that can 'execute' the expression. We simply assume that, if an expression X terminates in a state s, there is some magic way of finding a state t and objects $x_1, \ldots, x_n$ such that X transforms s to t yielding $x_1, \ldots, x_n$. The question how to turn this magic into an effective procedure (for a subset of all expressions) is discussed in Section 5.4.

In addition to the simple expressions we have seen before, we shall discuss a number of expressions that might be called *basic control structures*. These expressions can be used, among other things, as building blocks of compound control structures such as the classical if-then-else construct, the while loop, guarded commands, etc. In the discussion below, A stands for an assertion, X, Y for expressions, $v_1, \ldots, v_n$ for variables and $T_1, \ldots, T_n$ for types.

1. Skip expression: SKIP

   Terminates in every state, transforming a state s to itself and yielding the empty sequence of objects. An alternative notation for SKIP is (), which can be used to provide calls of nullary functions with an empty parameter list:

   zero()

2. Guard expression: A?

   Terminates in a state s iff A holds in s. If it terminates, it transforms s to itself yielding the empty sequence of objects. For example, the following expression terminates iff the buffer b is not empty:

   NOT len(b) = zero ?

   The following expression does not terminate in any state:

   FALSE ?

3. Composition expression: $X;Y$

   Transforms a state s to a state t yielding objects $x_1, \ldots, x_n$ iff there is a state u such that X transforms s to u yielding $x_1, \ldots, x_k$ and Y transforms u to t yielding $x_{k+1}, \ldots, x_n$. For example, the following expression puts the items i and j in the buffer b in the given order:

   put(i,b); put(j,b)

   An alternative notation for $X;Y$ is X,Y. The latter notation is usually used in the actual parameter lists of predicates, functions and procedures. So a procedure expression such as put(i,b) consists of the composition expression (i,b) (yielding a pair of objects) and the actual application of put to the result of this expression.

4. Choice expression: $X|Y$

   Transforms a state s to a state t yielding objects $x_1, \ldots, x_n$ iff X transforms s to t yielding $x_1, \ldots, x_n$ or Y transforms s to t yielding $x_1, \ldots, x_n$. For example, the following expression puts the items i and j in the buffer b in arbitrary order:

   (put(i,b); put(j,b)) | (put(j,b); put(i,b))

5. Repetition expression: $X*$

   Transforms a state s to a state t iff there is a sequence of states $s_0, \ldots, s_n$ such that $s_0 = s$, $s_n = t$ and X transforms s_i to s_{i+1} ($i = 0, \ldots, n-1$). It yields the empty sequence of objects. For example, the following expression removes an arbitrary number of items from a buffer b:

```
(FLUSH get(b))*
```

Here we see the FLUSH operator, which throws away the result of get(b). This is necessary because the expression before the * should yield the empty sequence of objects.

6. Modification expression: MOD $v_1, \ldots, v_n$ END

Transforms a state s to a state t iff t is obtained from s by modifying the variables $v_1, \ldots, v_n$, leaving all other variables unmodified. It yields the empty sequence of objects. For example, the following expression sets the value of the variable function v: -> Nat to some arbitrary (and possibly undefined) natural number:

```
MOD v END
```

7. Selection expression: SOME $x_1 : T_1, \ldots, x_n : T_n$ A

Terminates in a state s iff there are (existing) objects $x_1, \ldots, x_n$ in s such that A holds. If it terminates, it transforms s to itself yielding (arbitrary) objects $x_1, \ldots, x_n$ satisfying A. For example, if add and exp are the addition and exponentiation functions for natural numbers, gtr is the 'greater than' predicate and the following expression terminates, we have a counter example of Fermat's last theorem:

```
SOME k:Nat,m:Nat,n:Nat,p:Nat
( gtr(m,0) AND gtr(n,0) AND gtr(k,2) AND
  add(exp(m,k),exp(n,k)) = exp(p,k) )
```

As to the priorities of the operators introduced above we remark that | has the lowest priority of all operators, immediately followed by ; and ,. The operators ? and * have equal priorities higher than [...] and <...> but lower than PREV. FLUSH and SOME... have the same priority as FORALL... and EXISTS..., which is immediately higher than the priority of !.

The usual control structures from sequential programming languages can be viewed as abbreviations for expressions built from the basic control structures. For example, the if-then-else construct:

```
IF A THEN X ELSE Y
```

can be viewed as an abbreviation for:

```
(A?; X | NOT A?; Y)
```

The while construct:

```
WHILE A DO X
```

can be expressed in terms of the basic control structures by:

```
(A?; X)*; NOT A?
```

A final point to be discussed in connection with expressions is what happens if an expression is used as an argument to a built-in or user-defined predicate. This is not obvious since expressions may be nondeterministic and have side effects. For example, we may wonder whether the following assertion is true or false:

```
(zero | succ(zero)) = (zero | succ(zero))
```

We cannot define this assertion to be undefined since in COLD-K we stick to traditional two-valued logic, so assertions are either true or false. Note that up till now we carefully avoided questions such as the one above by only using deterministic expressions without side effects as arguments to predicates.

The way we deal with the above problem in COLD-K is to interpret an expression acting as an argument to a predicate in a special way, as a so-called *term*. If X is an expression, then the term interpretation of X in a state s denotes the *unique* sequence of objects $x_1, \ldots, x_n$ yielded by X, if it exists, otherwise it yields a sequence of *undefined* objects. Note that the objects $x_1, \ldots, x_n$ are interpreted as objects in s, so any side effects of X are undone and, if one of the x_i is created dynamically by X, the result of X becomes undefined.

For example, the result yielded by the following expression is not unique:

```
(zero | succ(zero))
```

so, interpreted as a term, it is undefined and the following assertion is true:

```
NOT (zero | succ(zero))!
```

Consequently, we also have that:

```
NOT (zero | succ(zero)) = (zero | succ(zero))
```

On the other hand, the result of the following expression is unique for all natural numbers n:

```
(n = zero ?; zero | NOT n = zero ?; succ(zero))
```

so we have that:

```
(n = zero ?; zero | NOT n = zero ?; succ(zero)) =
(n = zero ?; zero | NOT n = zero ?; succ(zero))
```

Note, by the way, that there are only two built-in predicates in the language: definedness and equality. An example of an expression with a side effect occurs in the following assertion:

```
new!
```

where new is the operation creating a buffer. This assertion is false in any state s, because the newly created buffer is interpreted as an object in s (where it is undefined) and not as an object in the state t to which s is transformed by new. On the other hand, the following assertion is true for all defined items i and buffers b:

```
len(b) = zero => (put(i,b); get(b)) = i
```

The reason is that the result yielded by the expression (put(i,b); get(b)) when evaluated in a state s is unique and defined in s. Hence (put(i,b); get(b)), interpreted as a term, is a defined object (i.e., it is i).

5.2   Algorithmic definitions

After this excursion to expressions we are now ready to discuss algorithmic definitions. What we have seen so far were flat class descriptions, where all components were defined either axiomatically or by means of inductive definitions. Such kinds of descriptions are appropriate in the specification phase of a system, but on our way to an implementation of a system we generally want to express components more directly in terms of each other. In particular, we want to define operations explicitly in terms of a parameter list and a defining body, similar to the way we do this in programming languages. The ultimate goal, of course, is to bring the class description into such a form that it can be fed into a machine and run. Yet such explicit definitions also make sense in specifications since they can considerably improve the readability of specifications (if properly used). For example, it is more natural to explicitly define the length of a buffer to be equal to the length of its contents than to do this by means of an axiom.

An *algorithmic definition* is an explicit definition of a predicate, function or procedure in terms of a parameter list and a defining assertion or expression. An algorithmic definition of a predicate has the following form:

```
PRED  r: T₁ # ... # Tₘ
PAR   x₁:T₁,...,xₘ:Tₘ
DEF   A
```

where A is an assertion in terms of the object names $x_1,\ldots,x_m$. It defines the least (strict) predicate r such that, for all defined objects $x_1,\ldots,x_m$, $r(x_1,\ldots,x_m)$ holds iff A holds (note the difference with inductive definitions). An example is the definition of the following predicate that expresses that a buffer is empty:

```
PRED  is_empty: Buffer
PAR   b:Buffer
DEF   len(b) = zero
```

An algorithmic definition of a function has the following form:

```
FUNC  f: T₁ # ... # Tₘ -> V₁ # ... # Vₙ
PAR   x₁:T₁,...,xₘ:Tₘ
DEF   X
```

where X is an expression in terms of the object names $x_1,\ldots,x_m$. It defines the least defined (strict) function f such that, for all defined objects $x_1,\ldots,x_m$, $f(x_1,\ldots,x_m) = X$ (with equality in the COLD-sense). Note that this implies that the expression X in the body of the definition is interpreted as a term. An example is given by the following algorithmic definition of the function **reverse** that reverses the contents of a queue (see Subsection 3.4):

```
FUNC reverse: Queue -> Queue
PAR  q:Queue
DEF  ( len(q) = zero ?    ; q
     | NOT len(q) = zero ?; put(geti(q),reverse(getq(q)))
     )
```

This definition shows that recursion in algorithmic definitions is allowed (even mutual recursion in algorithmic *and* inductive definitions).

An algorithmic definition of a procedure has the following form:

```
PROC  p: T₁ # ... # Tₘ -> V₁ # ... # Vₙ
PAR   x₁:T₁,...,xₘ:Tₘ
DEF   X
```

where X is an expression in terms of the object names $x_1,\ldots,x_m$. It defines the least procedure p such that, for all defined objects $x_1,\ldots,x_m$, $p(x_1,\ldots,x_m)$ transforms a state s to a state t yielding objects $y_1,\ldots,y_n$ iff X transforms s to t yielding $y_1,\ldots,y_n$. Note that, in contrast with a function definition, the expression X in the body of a procedure definition is interpreted as a true expression and not as a term. The following is an example of an algorithmic definition, defining a procedure that removes the most recently added element from a buffer using an auxiliary cell object (see Subsections 4.4 and 4.2):

```
PROC pop: Buffer -> Item
PAR  b:Buffer
DEF  NOT len(b) = zero ?;
     LET c:Cell; c := create(len(b));
     store(pred(len(b)),c);
     ( NOT cont(c) = zero ?;
         put(get(b),b);
         store(pred(cont(c)),c)
     )*;
     cont(c) = zero ?;
     get(b)
```

There are no explicit definitions of sorts such as cartesian products, unions, etc. The motivation for this is that the same effect can be obtained by means of the parameterisation mechanisms of the language as we shall see later (see Subsection 6.3).

5.3 Algorithmic description of *BUFFER*

Any flat class description in COLD-K will generally contain non-algorithmic parts. This is so, not only because there are no algorithmic sort definitions, but also because COLD-K has no built-in sorts and operations whatsoever. Operations can be defined algorithmically only if we a priori have a number of primitive building blocks, and such building blocks can be defined axiomatically only. The notion of an *algorithmic class description* is therefore something that is relative to a given set of components considered primitive. It refers to a class description in which all non-primitive operations are defined algorithmically. If it is clear from the context which components are considered primitive we shall simply speak about an 'algorithmic description' of a class.

As an example, we shall give an algorithmic description of the class *BUFFER*, where the buffer operations are defined in terms of operations on linked lists. We begin with discussing what sorts and operations are considered primitive. First of all, we shall assume that the natural numbers are primitive. Secondly, in order to algorithmically describe the creation of new buffers, we need some primitive mechanism for creating objects or *instances* (in classical object-oriented terminology). For that purpose we introduce the following template of definitions, describing a variable sort T and one operation **create** to create instances of sort T:

Instance definitions(T):

```
SORT T    VAR

AXIOM
{INST1} INIT => NOT EXISTS x:T ()

PROC create: -> T    MOD T

AXIOM
{INST2} < create:T > TRUE;
{INST3} [ LET x:T; x := create ]
        ( x! AND (PREV NOT x!);
          FORALL y:T ( (PREV NOT y!) => y = x )
        )
```

This template can be viewed as a kind of macro from which definitions can be generated by supplying a concrete identifier for the macro parameter T. All definitions generated by means of this macro will be considered primitive, which is motivated by the fact that object creation is a truly fundamental operation with a straightforward implementation. We note that the above macro mechanism is only a notational convention and is not part of COLD-K. We shall see later how the same effect can be achieved by means of the constructs of the so-called scheme language of COLD-K.

It is not sufficient to have the natural numbers and object creation as primitives, since we must have some way of associating information with objects and modifying this information. For that purpose we shall introduce a second template of definitions, describing a variable function a, mapping objects of a sort T to objects of a sort V, together with a procedure **set_a** to set the attribute associated with an object to a given value. In more classical object-oriented terminology, these attributes would be called *instance variables*. The operation **set_a** corresponds with assignment to instance variables.

Attribute definitions(a, T, V):

```
FUNC a    : T      -> V      VAR
PROC set_a: T # V ->         MOD a
```

```
AXIOM    FORALL x:T,v:V (
{ATTR1} < set_a(x,v) > TRUE;
{ATTR2} [ set_a(x,v) ]
        ( a(x) = v AND
          FORALL y:T,w:V ( NOT y = x =>
          ( a(y) = w <=> PREV a(y) = w ) )
        ) )
```

We shall generate definitions from this macro by providing concrete identifiers for the macro parameters a, T and V. The motivation for considering the above definitions primitive is, again, that they define quite fundamental operations (from an implementation point of view). Note that we did not require that the value of the attribute a for a given object is always defined, since this could lead to inconsistency. The point is that there need not exist objects of sort V, in which case $a(x)$ for an object x of sort T cannot be but undefined.

As already said, we intend to implement buffers as linked lists. The basic idea is to represent each buffer as a circular linked list of dynamic size. That is, if there is danger of overflow, the circular linked list is dynamically extended with a new list element. The correspondence between the abstract contents of a buffer as given by the function **items** from the axiomatic specification and the linked list representation is indicated by Figure 10. From this picture can be derived that we need a new sort for the list elements, called 'links', and the following attributes:

```
FUNC item : Link   -> Item
FUNC next : Link   -> Link
FUNC first: Buffer -> Link
FUNC last : Buffer -> Link
```

This leads to the following structure of the algorithmic description of *BUFFER*:

```
EXPORT
   ...
FROM
CLASS
   Natural number definitions
   Item definitions
   Instance definitions(Link)
   Attribute definitions(item,Link,Item)
   Attribute definitions(next,Link,Link)
   Instance definitions(Buffer)
   Attribute definitions(first,Buffer,Link)
   Attribute definitions(last,Buffer,Link)
   Buffer definitions
END
```

where the signature at the ... is the same as in the axiomatic description of *BUFFER*. The part to be algorithmically described is denoted by *Buffer definitions*.

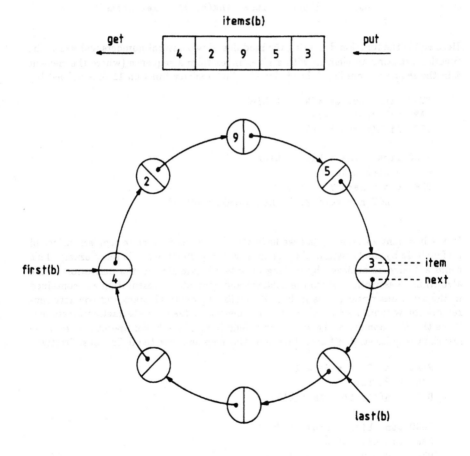

Figure 10: Linked list implementation of a buffer

In order to develop the algorithmic description of the buffer operations systematically from the axiomatic specification, we express Figure 10 somewhat more formally by formulating the *representation invariant* that we want to maintain. This invariant expresses (among other things) the relation between the abstract and concrete representations of buffers:

```
{REPR} FORALL b:Buffer EXISTS s:Nat FORALL m:Nat,n:Nat
       ( less(len(b),s);
         link(b,m) = link(b,n) <=> mod(m,s) = mod(n,s);
         last(b) = link(b,len(b));
         less(n,len(b)) => item(link(b,n)) = sel(items(b),n)
       )
```

Here mod is the function delivering the modulus of two natural numbers and sel is the function selecting an element with a given index from a sequence (where the element i in the sequence cons(i,s) has index 0). The auxiliary function link is defined by:

```
FUNC link: Buffer # Nat -> Link
PAR  b:Buffer,n:Nat
DEF  link(first(b),n)

FUNC link: Link # Nat -> Link
PAR  u:Link,n:Nat
DEF  ( n = zero ?    ; u
     | NOT n = zero ?; link(next(u),pred(n))
     )
```

In the invariant we assume that we have the abstract and concrete representations of buffers 'side by side' (instead of using an abstraction function, as is more usual). This could actually be achieved by making an intermediate step in the derivation of the algorithmic description where the abstract and concrete representation are contained in the same description, thus making it possible to relate abstract and concrete representation without having to resort to the meta-level (as with abstraction functions). Since the development of the algorithmic definitions of the buffer operations from the invariant is quite straightforward we omit this step and give the definitions directly:

```
FUNC len: Buffer -> Nat
PAR  b:Buffer
DEF  len(first(b),last(b))

FUNC len: Link # Link -> Nat
PAR  u:Link,v:Link
DEF  ( u = v ?    ; zero
     | NOT u = v ?; succ(len(next(u),v))
     )

PROC new: -> Buffer
DEF  LET b:Buffer; b := create;
     LET free:Link; free := create;
```

```
            set_next(free,free);
            set_first(b,free);
            set_last(b,free);
            b

    PROC put: Item # Buffer ->
    PAR  i:Item,b:Buffer
    DEF  LET first:Link; first := first(b);
         LET last:Link; last := last(b);
         set_item(last,i);
         ( next(last) = first ?;
             LET free:Link; free := create;
             set_last(b,free);
             set_next(last,free);
             set_next(free,first)
         | NOT next(last) = first ?;
             set_last(b,next(last))
         )

    PROC get: Buffer -> Item
    PAR  b:Buffer
    DEF  LET first:Link; first := first(b);
         LET last:Link; last := last(b);
         NOT first = last ?;
         set_first(b,next(first));
         item(first)
```

The claim is that the above algorithmic description of *BUFFER* is an *implementation* of the axiomatic description presented in Subsection 4.4 (see Subsection 6.3).

5.4   Executability

What we have seen so far were a number of ways of describing classes. Constructing class descriptions and reasoning about them is a mathematical activity that makes sense in itself. Yet, in practice, we shall generally want to make class descriptions useful in a more direct sense by *executing* them. By execution of a (flat) class description we mean that we feed the class description into a machine and that the machine will automatically construct a class in accordance with the description and will allow us to play around with the class (which is kept in the internals of the machine).

In order to make this 'playing around' more precise we imagine that we have a terminal connected to the machine, allowing us to give commands to and receive output from the machine. The output of the machine will consist of true/false answers and objects. We assume we have some way of collecting the output objects such that we can use them as arguments to subsequent commands. At the start of the session we begin with an empty collection of objects and the class C animated by the machine is in its initial state. The following commands can be given to the machine:

1. *Predicate command:* Requests the machine to evaluate a predicate r of C for given arguments in the current state of C. This always results in a true/false answer while not affecting the state of C.

2. *Function command:* Requests the machine to evaluate a function of C for given arguments in the current state of C. If the function is defined for the given arguments, it will pass the result of the function as output while not affecting the state of C. If the function is not defined, the machine will hang.

3. *Procedure command:* Requests the machine to evaluate a procedure of C for given arguments in the current state of C. If the procedure terminates for the given arguments, transforming the current state of C to a state t, the result of the procedure will be passed as output and the new state of C will become t. If the procedure does not terminate, the machine will hang.

Note that the predicates, functions and procedures of C correspond with the operations exported by the description of C together with the equality predicates on all exported sorts, hence these operations do not include auxiliary operations from the description.

As an example, consider the algorithmic description of buffers. This description does not contain constructor operations for objects of sort Item, which would make it impossible for us to ever lay our hands on an object of that sort and do anything useful with buffers. Let us therefore remove the definition of sort Item from the description and rename Item to Nat everywhere. Thus we obtain a description of buffers that can contain natural numbers. If we feed this description into a (sufficiently clever) machine, it will generate a class *BUFFER* in accordance with the description. At the beginning of the session *BUFFER* will be in its initial state and our collection of objects is empty. Hence the only thing we can do is call a parameterless operation. For example, as a first command we could call the new operation creating a new buffer object and store this object in our collection of objects under the name b. We shall use the following notation to indicate this step in our dialogue with the machine:

```
{0} b := new
```

The number between the curly brackets is the sequence number of the command. We now have a buffer object which can be used for queueing natural numbers, yet we have no natural numbers around. We add the first three natural numbers to our collection by the following commands:

```
{1} 0 := zero
{2} 1 := succ(0)
{3} 2 := succ(1)
```

We could go on as follows:

```
{4} put(b,2)
{5} put(b,1)
{6} i := get(b)
{7} m := len(b)
```

We now have the objects denoted by 0, 1, 2, i and m in our collection and we could check that indeed $i = 2$ and $m = 1$ by giving the following predicate commands to the machine (where we have indicated the answer of the machine after the "->"):

```
{8}  i = 2 -> true
{9}  m = 1 -> true
```

Note that in progressing this way we can never lay our hands on an undefined object. Any attempt to obtain such an object would make the machine hang, as will happen when we give the following command:

```
{10} h := pred(0)
```

The machine will also hang if, instead of the above command, we try to execute a non-terminating procedure call such as the second call of get below:

```
{10} get(b)
{11} get(b)
```

Note that if we would have executed the axiomatic description of buffers (for which we need a quite clever machine), then it might be the case that the last get command indeed terminates. This is caused by the fact that the axiomatic description does not specify what should happen if a get operation is applied to an empty buffer. Executing a class description implies that a class satisfying the description is constructed by the machine and if there is more than one such class (which is often the case) the machine has the freedom to pick one arbitrarily.

In order to facilitate communication with the machine, we could add all kinds of syntactic sugar, such as the ability to have more complex expressions as commands. For example, we could allow a command such as:

```
{i} put(b,succ(zero))
```

instead of the more cumbersome:

```
{i  } 0 := zero
{i+1} 1 := succ(0)
{i+2} put(b,1)
```

In practice, of course, it makes sense to identify special I/O objects (such as printers) and I/O operations (such as print commands), which can be defined as normal sorts and operations in a description, but that is not the issue here. The above suffices as an intuitive notion of execution.

It would be nice if a machine could be constructed that can execute all COLD-K class descriptions. Due to the expressive power of the language it is obvious that this is impossible. What we can do is identify a subset of the language for which such a machine can be constructed. Such a subset will be called an *executable subset* of the language. Descriptions and constructs which belong to a given executable subset will be called *executable*. Note that algorithmic descriptions and executable descriptions are two different things. An algorithmic description need not be executable and vice versa.

Several different executable subsets can be identified such as the subset of equational algebraic specifications, the subset of logic programs (based on the use of inductive definitions) and the subset of plain imperative programs. With each of these subsets an underlying machine can be associated (such as a rewrite machine for equational algebraic specifications). In general, the definition of an executable subset of COLD-K will consist of two parts:

1. Definitions of primitive (usually axiomatically specified) sorts and operations which are executable by definition, because they have a direct translation to executable code. Typically, these definitions will belong to the COLD-K *standard library*. Examples are the instance and attribute definitions in the algorithmic description of buffers.
2. Schemes for building executable constructs from other executable constructs. Associated with these schemes are *translation schemes* which make it possible to compile constructs built this way to executable code. Examples are the schemes for constructing compound control structures discussed in Subsection 5.1.

We shall not define a particular executable subset of COLD-K here. Once we have defined an executable subset (together with an underlying machine) we can conceptually view the design process as a process of transforming a (probably non-executable) system specification to an efficiently executable description in a correctness-preserving way.

We shall conclude this subsection with a discussion of the notion of termination, as promised in Subsection 4.3. As explained before, each expression X in COLD-K is interpreted as a relation between two states and a sequence of objects. The fact that X terminates in a certain state s implies that there are a state t and objects $x_1, \ldots, x_n$ such that $\langle s, t, x_1, \ldots, x_n \rangle$ is an element of that relation. This notion of termination is independent of any underlying machine. If X terminates in a state s and X is an *executable expression* (with respect to some executable subset and underlying machine) we consider it the duty of the machine to find a state t and objects $x_1, \ldots, x_n$ as indicated before when evaluating the expression X in state s. We may write down expressions which will make it quite hard for a machine to find such t and $x_1, \ldots, x_n$ for a given s. For example, if p and q are two procedures modifying a variable integer function v with the following property (holding in all states):

< p | q > v = zero

then we know that the following expression always terminates:

(p | q); v = zero ?

If we have a machine that evaluates this expression by arbitrarily and irreversibly selecting p or q, evaluating the procedure call and testing the guard v = zero, it may discover that the guard is false and hence it will hang. Apparently this is the wrong way of executing the expression. In order to evaluate an expression such as the one above the machine should have a *backtracking* capability: it should be able to undo the state transformations up to the point where the choice between p and q was made and subsequently try the other alternative. Such machines are certainly not unrealistic. The operational semantics of logic programming languages and certain string processing languages is based on them. Indeed we can interpret the above expression as a kind of logic programming: we set the goal v = zero, to be reached by means of either the procedure p or q.

If we want to have a simpler underlying machine (e.g., corresponding to the operational semantics of classical imperative programming languages) the solution is simple: expressions such as the one above should not be defined as being executable. We could restrict ourselves then to expressions which require no bactracking (i.e., no undoing of state transformations) during their execution. Suppose, for example, that we also know that the following property holds in all states:

```
a    => ([ p ] v = zero) AND ([ q ] FALSE);
NOT a => ([ q ] v = zero) AND ([ p ] FALSE)
```

where a is a nullary predicate, then the following expression requires no backtracking:

```
( a ?; p | NOT a ?; q )
```

while being semantically equivalent to the expression we saw before. The choice to be made in the execution of this expression can be made on the basis of the mutually exclusive guards (which do not change the state), hence the expression is *deterministic*.

One may be tempted to define one fixed executable subset together with an underlying machine for COLD-K and forbid expressions which are not executable altogether, which would make the notion of termination of expressions coincide with the operational notion of termination. This would not be a sensible decision for at least two reasons. First of all, we want to be able to use the language for developing descriptions that can be translated automatically to different programming languages. Choosing one underlying machine would rule out large classes of possible implementation languages. Secondly, it generally makes sense to use non-executable expressions as intermediate steps in deriving efficiently executable descriptions. For example, due to the fact that expressions need not be executable, it is often possible to derive an algorithmic description of a class from an axiomatic description by a very simple and obviously correct transformation. This algorithmic description can then be the starting point of a transformation process ending up in an executable description. For example, the expression (p | q); v = zero ? we saw above is a perfectly valid expression in an abstract algorithmic description, that could later be transformed into the executable expression (a ?; p | NOT a ?; q).

6 Modularisation, parameterisation and designs

6.1 Modularisation

Up till now we have restricted ourselves completely to flat class descriptions, i.e., descriptions of the following form:

```
EXPORT
    signature
FROM
CLASS
```

definitions
END

Such a description describes a class by a linear list of definitions of its external and internal components. It is clear that this monolithic approach becomes prohibitive as soon as we are dealing with systems of a realistic size. What we need are ways of *structuring* large class descriptions into independent parts and ways of *reusing* parts that have already been defined. The modularisation and parameterisation mechanisms of COLD-K provide powerful ways to do so, where in this subsection we shall restrict ourselves to the former.

Modular (and also parameterised) class descriptions in COLD-K are called *schemes*. They are built from basic building blocks of the form CLASS ... END and a number of *modularisation operators* for combining schemes into new schemes. There is nothing mysterious about schemes in that they are simply a way of writing down a flat class description in a more structured way. In other words, each scheme is a *denotation* of a flat class description. For example, the basic scheme:

CLASS $D_1, \ldots, D_n$ END

denotes the flat class description:

EXPORT Σ FROM CLASS $D_1, \ldots, D_n$ END

where Σ is the signature consisting of all names defined in the definitions $D_1, \ldots, D_n$. In other words, the scheme CLASS $D_1, \ldots, D_n$ END describes a class without hidden components. In the sequel we shall use the notation $\langle \Sigma, D \rangle$ to denote the flat class description consisting of the set of definitions D and the export signature Σ. We shall use the letters K, L to denote schemes and Σ to denote a signature. Note that the definitions in a flat class description indeed constitute a set rather than a sequence since their order is irrelevant.

The first modularisation operator to be discussed is the *export* operator, which provides the basic means of information hiding. In fact we have already seen this operator in the standard form of a flat class description (see above). An export scheme (i.e., a scheme built by means of the export operator) has the following form:

EXPORT Σ FROM K

If K denotes the flat class description $\langle \Sigma_K, D_K \rangle$, then the above scheme denotes the flat class description $\langle \Sigma \cap \Sigma_K, D_K \rangle$. In other words, it makes all names in the signature of K that are not in Σ invisible to the outside world, while all names in Σ that are not in the signature of K are simply discarded. So, the following scheme:

```
EXPORT
  SORT A,
  FUNC a: -> A,
  FUNC b: -> A
FROM
CLASS
  SORT A
```

```
    FUNC a: -> A
    FUNC c: -> A
END
```

is equivalent to the following flat class description:

```
EXPORT
  SORT A,
  FUNC a: -> A
FROM
CLASS
  SORT A
  FUNC a: -> A
  FUNC c: -> A
END
```

where the function c is hidden.

The second modularisation operator is the *import* operator, which makes it possible to combine two class descriptions into a new one. An import scheme has the following form:

```
IMPORT K INTO L
```

If K, L denote the flat class descriptions $\langle \Sigma_K, D_K \rangle, \langle \Sigma_L, D_L \rangle$, then the above scheme denotes the flat class description $\langle \Sigma_K \cup \Sigma_L, D_K \cup D_L \rangle$. This indicates that the import operator is symmetric and indeed *semantically* it is. However, in order to avoid the redefinition of names exported by K in L we assume that all names exported by K and used in L are implicitly defined in L, thus making the operator *syntactically* asymmetric. This implies that, in order to determine the denotation of L, we first have to add to L the definitions of the names exported by K and used in L. For example, in the following scheme:

```
IMPORT CLASS
          SORT A
          FUNC a: -> A
       END
INTO   EXPORT
          SORT A,
          SORT B,
          FUNC f: A -> B
       FROM
       CLASS
          SORT B
          FUNC b: -> B
          FUNC f: A -> B
       END
```

the first argument of the import operator denotes the flat class description given by $\langle \{A, a\}, \{D_A, D_a\} \rangle$ (where D_A denotes the definition of A, etc.). In order to determine the denotation of the second argument, we first have to add the definition of sort A to the text (*not* the definition of a, which is not used). Hence the above import scheme denotes the flat class description $\langle\{A, B, a, f\}, \{D_A, D_B, D_a, D_b, D_f\}\rangle$. Note that the implicit definition convention implies that the set of names defined between the brackets CLASS and END need not necessarily constitute a signature. They should constitute a signature after adding the implicit definitions provided by imports.

The third modularisation operator is the *renaming* operator, which allows us to adapt a class description by changing names in it. The general form of a renaming scheme is as follows:

```
RENAME ρ IN K
```

where ρ is a *renaming*, denoting a mapping from names to names. If K denotes the flat class description $\langle\Sigma_K, D_K\rangle$, then the above scheme denotes the flat class description $\langle\rho(\Sigma_K), \rho(D_K)\rangle$. In other words, this scheme denotes the same flat class description as K, except that each name u in $\langle\Sigma_K, D_K\rangle$ has been replaced by $\rho(u)$. A renaming is described by a list of *pairs*, each pair consisting of a sort, predicate, function or procedure name and an identifier, as in the following scheme:

```
RENAME
   SORT A        TO C,
   FUNC f: A -> B TO g
IN
EXPORT
   SORT A,
   SORT B,
   FUNC f: A -> B
FROM
CLASS
   SORT A
   SORT B
   FUNC f: A -> B
   FUNC h: B -> A
   AXIOM FORALL a:A ( h(f(a)) = a )
END
```

The result of applying a renaming to a name u is determined as follows. If u is a predicate, function or procedure name occurring at the left hand side of a pair, the identifier of the name is changed to the identifier at the right hand side of the pair. Then, all identifiers of sort names occurring at the left hand sides of pairs are changed in the name, in accordance with the corresponding right hand sides of the pairs. In the case above, SORT A would be changed to SORT C and FUNC f: A -> B would be changed to FUNC g: C -> B. So the above class description is equivalent to:

```
EXPORT
   SORT C,
   SORT B,
   FUNC g: C -> B
FROM
```

```
CLASS
  SORT C
  SORT B
  FUNC g: C -> B
  FUNC h: B -> C
  AXIOM FORALL a:C ( h(g(a)) = a )
END
```

The fourth and final modularisation operator to be discussed is the *abbreviation* operator, providing a mechanism to give names to schemes. An abbreviation scheme has the following form:

LET x := K; $L(x)$

where x is an identifier (a *scheme name*) that may be used in $L(x)$. It is equivalent to the scheme $L(x)$, where all occurrences of the name x in $L(x)$ have been replaced by K. In other words, the name x may be used in $L(x)$ to denote the scheme K. So the following scheme:

```
LET X := CLASS SORT A END;
IMPORT X INTO
CLASS
  FUNC a: -> A
  AXIOM a!
END
```

is equivalent to:

```
IMPORT CLASS SORT A END INTO
CLASS
  FUNC a: -> A
  AXIOM a!
END
```

We note that the modularisation operators discussed here may be combined in arbitrary ways since they can be viewed as algebraic operations on schemes (cf. [6,1]). This approach gives us a way to *normalize* each (modular) scheme to a unique flat class description (its *normal form*).

As an example of the use of the operators we give a modular description of the class of buffers, described as a flat class description in subsection 4.4.

```
LET NAT    := EXPORT
                SORT Nat,
                FUNC zero:              -> Nat,
                FUNC succ: Nat          -> Nat,
                FUNC pred: Nat          -> Nat,
                PRED less: Nat # Nat
              FROM
              CLASS
```

```
                    Natural number definitions
                  END;
       LET ITEM    := EXPORT
                      SORT Item
                  FROM
                  CLASS
                    Item definitions
                  END;
       LET SEQ     := EXPORT
                      SORT Nat,
                      SORT Item,
                      SORT Seq,
                      FUNC empty:                -> Seq,
                      FUNC cons : Item # Seq -> Seq,
                      FUNC cat  : Seq  # Seq -> Seq,
                      FUNC len  : Seq        -> Nat
                  FROM
                  IMPORT NAT  INTO
                  IMPORT ITEM INTO
                  CLASS
                    Sequence definitions
                  END;
       LET BUFFER := IMPORT NAT  INTO
                  IMPORT ITEM INTO
                  EXPORT
                      SORT Nat,
                      SORT Item,
                      SORT Buffer,
                      FUNC len : Buffer          -> Nat,
                      PROC new :                 -> Buffer,
                      PROC put : Item # Buffer -> ,
                      PROC get : Buffer          -> Item
                  FROM
                  IMPORT SEQ INTO
                  CLASS
                    Buffer definitions
                  END;
   BUFFER
```

Note how we can control the visibility of imported names by putting the import operator before or after the export operator. When put before (e.g., "IMPORT NAT" in BUFFER) all imported names are exported. When put after (e.g., "IMPORT SEQ" in BUFFER) the imported names are not automatically exported.

6.2   Origin consistency

What we told about the modularisation operators in the previous subsection is not the whole story yet. In particular, we did not discuss which approach we take with respect to name clashes when combining schemes into new schemes. Consider for example the following scheme:

```
LET X  := EXPORT Σ_X FROM
          CLASS ... FUNC f: A -> A ...... END;
LET Y  := EXPORT Σ_Y FROM
          CLASS ...... FUNC f: A -> A ... END;
LET Z  := IMPORT X INTO
          IMPORT Y INTO
          CLASS ... f ... END;
Z
```

Let us assume that both X and Y export the function name f, i.e., that $f \in \Sigma_X$ and $f \in \Sigma_Y$. The scheme Z contains a reference to the function f, but which f do we mean, the one from X or the one from Y? In the previous section we explained that import amounts to taking the union of the signatures and sets of definitions, so we could answer: "both". If the definitions of f (including all axioms characterizing f) are indeed the same in X and Y this could be accepted as an answer. If, however, both definitions are not the same there is a fair chance that f from X and f from Y are different functions, leading to an inconsistency in Z.

Therefore, in COLD-K, we take the point of view that the following is a reasonable methodological requirement:

> *It should be possible to trace down every applied occurrence of a name to a unique definition.*

In other words, each applied occurrence of a name should have a unique *origin*, hence this requirement is called the *origin consistency requirement*. This requirement becomes essential if we want to generate executable code. Code generation from an (executable) scheme in COLD-K amounts to normalizing the scheme to a flat class description and translating all definitions in the description to executable code. In order to translate the calls of operations, it should be possible to uniquely identify the defining code of the operations.

Clearly, the scheme Z above does not satisfy the origin consistency requirement. If the reason is that we by accident defined two different functions with the same name f, we have to resolve the ambiguity by hiding or renaming the 'wrong' f. For example, if we mean the second f we can satisfy the origin consistency requirement by:

```
LET X  := EXPORT Σ_X FROM
          CLASS ... FUNC f: A -> A ...... END;
LET Y  := EXPORT Σ_Y FROM
          CLASS ...... FUNC f: A -> A ... END;
LET Z  := IMPORT EXPORT Σ'_X FROM X INTO
          IMPORT Y INTO
          CLASS ... f ... END;
Z
```

where Σ'_X is the same as Σ_X except that it does not contain f.

If the reason for the origin inconsistency is that we really mean the same function f in both cases, we have to put the definition of f in a single class description, e.g:

```
LET W := CLASS ... FUNC f: A -> A ... END;
LET X := EXPORT Σ_X FROM
         IMPORT W INTO CLASS ... END;
LET Y := EXPORT Σ_Y FROM
         IMPORT W INTO CLASS ... END;
LET Z := IMPORT X INTO
         IMPORT Y INTO
         CLASS ... f ... END;
Z
```

Here we see that the LET construct is more than just an abbreviation mechanism. What we also see is that the origin consistency requirement leads to a natural way of enforcing modularity of a scheme. It requires that definitions of the same thing be put in the same description instead of being spread over different descriptions.

Schemes that satisfy the origin consistency requirement will be called *origin consistent*. Though origin consistency of schemes is not strictly required by the language definition [2] (where origin inconsistent schemes also have a meaning), it is a fact that only origin consistent schemes can be brought into normal form at the COLD-K level (rather than at the semantic level). Hence we have to revise the simple procedure, described in 6.1, for calculating the flat class description corresponding with a scheme. The basic normalization procedure for an origin consistent scheme works as follows:

1. Assign values to the defining occurrences of names, uniquely identifying their definitions. The value associated with a name is called its *origin*.
2. Assign origins to all applied occurrences of names by tracing them down to their definitions.
3. Normalize the scheme as before, treating identical names with different origins as different symbols.
4. Eliminate all name clashes of hidden names with other (visible and hidden names) by suitable renamings of the hidden names.
5. Remove all origins from the names.

Note that renamings of hidden names can do no harm, since we cannot refer to these names anyway. As an example, consider the following origin consistent scheme:

```
LET X := EXPORT
            SORT A
         FROM
         CLASS
            SORT A
            SORT B
```

```
                FUNC f: B -> A
                AXIOM EXISTS b:B ()
                AXIOM FORALL b:B ( f(b)! )
              END;
      IMPORT X INTO
      RENAME FUNC g: B -> A TO f IN
      CLASS
        SORT B
        FUNC g: B -> A
        AXIOM FORALL a:A EXISTS b:B ( g(b) = a )
      END
```

After origin assignment (using integer indices as origins) this scheme becomes:

```
      LET X := EXPORT
                  SORT A₁
               FROM
               CLASS
                 SORT A₁
                 SORT B₂
                 FUNC f₃: B₂ -> A₁
                 AXIOM EXISTS b:B₂ ()
                 AXIOM FORALL b:B₂ ( f₃(b)! )
               END;
      IMPORT X INTO
      RENAME FUNC g: B -> A TO f IN
      CLASS
        SORT B₄
        FUNC g₅: B₄ -> A₁
        AXIOM FORALL a:A₁ EXISTS b:B₄ ( g₅(b) = a )
      END
```

Note that no origins are assigned to the names in a renaming: they are not considered applied occurrences of names since they are only used to define a mapping from names to names. Normalization of the scheme leads to:

```
      EXPORT
        SORT A₁,
        SORT B₄,
        FUNC f₅: B₄ -> A₁
      FROM
      CLASS
        SORT A₁
        SORT B₂
        FUNC f₃: B₂ -> A₁
        AXIOM EXISTS b:B₂ ()
        AXIOM FORALL b:B₂ ( f₃(b)! )
        SORT B₄
        FUNC f₅: B₄ -> A₁
```

```
    AXIOM FORALL a:A₁ EXISTS b:B₄ ( f₅(b) = a )
END
```

Note that renamings leave origins unaffected. Finally, elimination of name clashes and removal of origins results in the following normal form of the scheme:

```
    EXPORT
      SORT A,
      SORT B,
      FUNC f: B -> A
    FROM
    CLASS
      SORT A
      SORT B'
      FUNC f': B' -> A
      AXIOM EXISTS b:B' ()
      AXIOM FORALL b:B' ( f'(b)! )
      SORT B
      FUNC f: B -> A
      AXIOM FORALL a:A EXISTS b:B ( f(b) = a )
    END
```

where we use the fact that identifiers in COLD-K may contain quotes.

In the above examples it was clear where each name was defined. Sometimes, however, it is necessary to use names that have an origin that is as yet unknown (we shall see examples of this in the next subsection). Such names can be introduced by means of a so-called *free definition*, which consists of a header followed by the keyword FREE. For example, the following definition:

```
    SORT A    FREE
```

introduces a sort A with an unknown origin. No a priori assumptions about the sort A thus introduced are made (such as the fact that the sort is constant or variable), except that definedness and equality are available as operations on objects of sort A. Names defined by a free definition can be viewed as a kind of parameters of the description they are defined in. This is reflected in the origin assignment process, where a unique *origin variable*, instead of an origin constant, is associated with a free name. If, during the normalization process (step 3 above), such a free name happens to clash with another name, the origin variable will be replaced (everywhere in the text) by the origin of the latter name, while the free definition 'disappears'. More generally, name clashes lead to the *unification* of the origins of the clashing names. This unification mechanism is described in detail in [6]. A simple example is provided by the following scheme:

```
    IMPORT CLASS
              SORT A    FREE
              FUNC a: -> A
           END
    INTO   CLASS
```

```
        SORT A
        AXIOM a!
    END
```

After origin assignment we obtain:

```
IMPORT CLASS
        SORT A_x    FREE
        FUNC a_1: -> A_x
        END
INTO    CLASS
        SORT A_2
        AXIOM a_1!
        END
```

where x is an origin variable. In the normalization process this variable is unified with origin 2, making the free definition vanish:

```
CLASS
    SORT A_2
    FUNC a_1: -> A_2
    AXIOM a_1!
END
```

Thus we obtain the following normal form:

```
EXPORT
    SORT A,
    FUNC a: -> A
FROM
CLASS
    SORT A
    FUNC a: -> A
    AXIOM a!
END
```

We note that, using free definitions, we could reconstruct the symmetric nature of the import operator even in the syntactic sense. If we would simply require that each name used in a class description but not defined there is declared by a free definition, then IMPORT X INTO Y is syntactically and semantically equivalent to IMPORT Y INTO X.

6.3   Parameterisation

One could think that the modularisation mechanisms discussed in the previous subsections provide sufficient structuring facilities for class descriptions and that there is no need for a separate parameterisation mechanism. For example, we could define once and for all the scheme SEQ of sequences of items:

```
LET SEQ := EXPORT ... FROM
```

```
CLASS
   SORT Item
   SORT Seq
   FUNC empty:                -> Seq
   FUNC cons : Item # Seq -> Seq
   ...
END;
```

and use renamings to derive descriptions of different kinds of sequences from this. E.g., a definition of sequences of natural numbers could be constructed like this:

```
LET NAT_SEQ := RENAME
                  SORT Item TO Nat,
                  SORT Seq  TO Seq_Nat
               IN SEQ;
```

However, when we import the scheme NAT, defining the sort Nat, and the scheme NAT_SEQ into the same class description, we get a conflict with the origin consistency requirement. The reason is that the sort Nat in NAT and the sort Nat in NAT_SEQ have different origins, since the origin of the latter sort is that of Item. We can remedy this by defining the sort Item to be FREE, but that is only a patch: it would make it impossible to reuse the scheme SEQ a second time since the origin variable of Item would be unified with the origin of Nat in NAT, making it impossible to unify the origin variable with any other origin. Another problem with the approach is that all definitions of 'sequence sorts' we can derive from the above description have the same origin, while the sorts of sequences of objects of two different sorts are clearly different and should therefore have different origins.

What we need are *generic* or *parameterised* class descriptions, from which new class descriptions can be generated by *instantiating* them with actual parameters. A parameterised class description in COLD-K is called an *abstraction scheme* and has the following form:

LAMBDA x : K OF $L(x)$

where x is a formal parameter (a scheme name), K is a scheme (not containing free occurrences of x) and $L(x)$ is a scheme which may contain free occurrences of x. It can be viewed as a partial function mapping a scheme x to the scheme $L(x)$. The domain of this partial function is defined by the *parameter restriction K* and consists of the set of all *implementations* of the scheme K. A scheme A is an implementation of a scheme B if the signature of A includes that of B and if each class satisfying A also satisfies B. The simplest case (to which we shall restrict ourselves here) is that where B is an axiomatic class description without hidden names. Checking that A is an implementation of B then amounts to verifying that the axioms of B are theorems in A.

A parameterised scheme P can be instantiated by providing it with an actual parameter A satisfying the parameter restriction. The corresponding construct is called an *application scheme* and has the following form:

APPLY P TO A

In order to explain the meaning of this construct, let us take for P the parameterised scheme from the previous paragraph:

APPLY (LAMBDA x : K OF $L(x)$) TO A

Provided that A is indeed an implementation of K, we can (as a first approximation) consider this scheme to be equivalent to the scheme $L(A)$, i.e., the scheme $L(x)$ with A substituted everywhere for x. We shall come back to the meaning of this scheme later on.

Parameterised schemes would not make much sense if they could not be given names, hence the abbreviation mechanism we saw before is extended to parameterised schemes. We can now define the *parameterised* scheme SEQ of sequences of items:

```
LET SEQ := LAMBDA X : CLASS SORT Item    FREE END OF
           EXPORT ... FROM
           IMPORT X INTO
           CLASS
             SORT Seq    DEP Item
             FUNC empty:              -> Seq
             FUNC cons : Item # Seq -> Seq
             ...
           END;
```

In the parameter restriction we see that the parameter X should contain a sort by the name of Item in its visible signature, on which no a priori requirements are put. That is, there are no axioms to be satisfied by Item and the sort may be either constant ('static') or variable ('dynamic'). In the body of the parameterised scheme the scheme name X behaves as a scheme with a signature equal to that of the parameter restriction, so importing X into a class description makes the name Item visible in that description. In the case that Item is a variable sort, the creation of objects of sort Item will make the set of sequences of objects of sort Item grow, which explains why the sort Seq is defined to be dependent on Item.

In order to derive a class description defining sequences of natural numbers from SEQ, we have to provide the description NAT of the natural numbers as an actual parameter to SEQ. Unfortunately, the names in the formal and actual parameters do not 'fit'. In order to satisfy the parameter restriction, the sort name Nat from NAT should match with Item. This can be achieved by applying a suitable renaming (a 'fitting morphism') to SEQ before applying it to NAT. For that purpose, renamings are extended to parameterised schemes in the obvious way. We rename Item to Nat and, in order to avoid any future origin consistency problems, we also rename Seq to Seq_Nat, leading to the following definition of the class of sequences of natural numbers:

```
LET NAT_SEQ := APPLY
                  RENAME
                    SORT Item TO Nat,
                    SORT Seq  TO Seq_Nat
```

```
IN SEQ
TO NAT;
```

Note that the actual parameter NAT of (the renamed version of) SEQ satisfies the parameter restriction of SEQ in the obvious way.

In order to explain what the meaning of an arbitrary scheme containing applications of parameterised schemes is, we shall extend the normal form reduction procedure discussed in the previous subsection. The normalization procedure can be left as is, except that the origin assignment process has to be refined and that a new reduction rule has to be added. The refinement of the origin assignment process (step 1 in the normalization procedure) has to do with the definitions in the body of a parameterised scheme. The names introduced by these definitions cannot be assigned a fixed origin since their meaning depends on the actual parameters of the scheme. In other words, their origin itself is parameterised. This is modelled by associating a unique 'origin parameter' (i.e., an origin variable) with each (visible) name in the parameter restriction and assigning an origin of the form $\langle c, x_1, \ldots, x_n \rangle$ to each name u defined in the body of the parameterised scheme. Here c is a unique value identifying the definition of u and $x_1, \ldots, x_n$ are the origin parameters of the scheme. When the parameterised scheme is instantiated, the corresponding origins $a_1, \ldots, a_n$ of the names in the actual parameter are substituted for the origin parameters $x_1, \ldots, x_n$, thus turning the origin of u into $\langle c, a_1, \ldots, a_n \rangle$. The meaning of the following scheme (after origin assignment) can now be precisely defined:

```
APPLY (LAMBDA x : K OF L(x)) TO A
```

Provided that A is an implementation of K, it is equivalent to the scheme $L(x)$ with A substituted for x and the origins of the names in A substituted for the corresponding origin parameters of the names in K (everywhere in $L(x)$). The reduction rule of the above type of scheme should be added as a rule to step 3 of the normalization process described in the previous subsection.

We shall exemplify the extended normalization procedure by showing how the definition of the class of sequences of natural numbers as given before is reduced to normal form. First we give the 'complete' definition:

```
LET NAT := EXPORT ... FROM
           CLASS
             SORT Nat
             ...
           END;
LET SEQ := LAMBDA X : CLASS SORT Item   FREE END OF
           EXPORT ... FROM
           IMPORT X INTO
           CLASS
             SORT Seq   DEP Item
             FUNC empty: -> Seq
             FUNC cons: Item # Seq -> Seq
             ...
           END;
```

```
LET NAT_SEQ := APPLY
                  RENAME
                     SORT Item TO Nat,
                     SORT Seq  TO Seq_Nat
                  IN SEQ
               TO NAT;
     NAT_SEQ
```

Using x as the origin parameter associated with the name Item in the parameter restriction of SEQ, this leads after origin assignment to:

```
LET NAT := EXPORT ... FROM
             CLASS
               SORT Nat₁
                 ...
             END;
LET SEQ := LAMBDA X : CLASS SORT Itemᵧ    FREE END OF
             EXPORT ... FROM
             IMPORT X INTO
             CLASS
               SORT Seq₍₂,ₓ₎    DEP Itemₓ
               FUNC empty₍₃,ₓ₎: -> Seq₍₂,ₓ₎
               FUNC cons₍₄,ₓ₎: Itemₓ # Seq₍₂,ₓ₎ -> Seq₍₂,ₓ₎
                 ...
             END;
LET NAT_SEQ := APPLY
                  RENAME
                     SORT Item TO Nat,
                     SORT Seq  TO Seq_Nat
                  IN SEQ
               TO NAT;
     NAT_SEQ
```

Note that the origin of Item in the body of SEQ is the origin parameter associated with Item and *not* the origin of Item in the parameter restriction. Expanding all abbreviations and applying the renaming leads to:

```
APPLY
  LAMBDA X : CLASS SORT Natᵧ    FREE END OF
  EXPORT ... FROM
  IMPORT X INTO
  CLASS
    SORT Seq_Nat₍₂,ₓ₎    DEP Natₓ
    FUNC empty₍₃,ₓ₎: -> Seq_Nat₍₂,ₓ₎
    FUNC cons₍₄,ₓ₎: Natₓ # Seq_Nat₍₂,ₓ₎ -> Seq_Nat₍₂,ₓ₎
      ...
  END
TO EXPORT ... FROM
  CLASS
```

```
SORT Nat₁
  ...
END
```

In order to further reduce this scheme we have to check that the actual parameter is an implementation of the parameter restriction. For that purpose, the actual parameter and the parameter restriction should first be reduced to normal form. Since origins are removed in the last step of the normalization procedure, this implies that origins do not play a role in checking the implementation relation, except for the fact that actual parameter and parameter restriction should be origin consistent. The check of the implementation relation is simple in this case and the subsequent reductions bring the scheme into the following flat form:

```
EXPORT ... FROM
CLASS
  SORT Nat₁
  ...
  SORT Seq_Nat₍₂,₁₎
  FUNC empty₍₃,₁₎: -> Seq_Nat₍₂,₁₎
  FUNC cons₍₄,₁₎: Nat₁ # Seq_Nat₍₂,₁₎ -> Seq_Nat₍₂,₁₎
  ...
END
```

Steps 4 and 5 of the normalization procedure (name clash elimination and origin removal) are simple now and will be omitted. We can see that the origin consistency problems referred to earlier do no longer occur here: the origin of Nat in this description is that of the original sort Nat and the origin of Seq_Nat will be different from the origin of any other sequence sort derived from SEQ. On the other hand, if we would instantiate SEQ in exactly the same way at some other place, the sort Seq_Nat would get the same origin as before. This is precisely what we want, since we should be able to combine descriptions containing their own instantiations of SEQ to obtain the sort Seq_Nat without running into origin consistency problems.

The parameter restriction in the definition of the parameterised scheme SEQ consists of a single sort definition, which is a frequently occurring case. Yet there are many situations where it is essential to use operation definitions and axioms in the parameter restriction as well. Suppose, for example, that we want to define a scheme containing a sorting operation. Such an operation will in general work for any sort with an associated linear order, hence it makes sense to parameterise the scheme over a sort and a binary predicate. In order to express the requirement that the predicate is a linear order, an axiom to that effect should be added to the parameter restriction. Since a linear order is a rather fundamental notion, it makes sense to define it in a separate scheme, the name of which can be used as the parameter restriction:

```
LET ORDER := CLASS
                SORT Item    FREE
                PRED order: Item # Item
                AXIOM  FORALL i:Item,j:Item,k:Item (
                {ORD1} NOT order(i,i);
```

```
              {ORD2} order(i,j) AND order(j,k) => order(i,k);
              {ORD3} order(i,j) OR i = j OR order(j,i) )
           END;
LET LSORT := LAMBDA X : ORDER OF
           EXPORT
             SORT Seq,
             FUNC sort: Seq -> Seq
           FROM
           IMPORT X INTO
           IMPORT (APPLY SEQ TO X) INTO
           CLASS
             FUNC sort: Seq -> Seq
             ...
           END;
```

This way of definition clearly shows that the scheme containing the sort operation is parameterised over a complete linear order (rather than a single sort and predicate). In instantiating the scheme LSORT, any scheme A can be provided as an actual parameter that is an implementation of ORDER. This implies that A should contain a sort by the name of Item and a predicate on Item # Item by the name of order satisfying the axioms in ORDER. Besides Item and order, A may contain many more sorts and operations. For example, instantiating LSORT so as to obtain a sorting routine for the natural numbers could be done as follows:

```
LET SORT_NAT := APPLY
                 RENAME
                   SORT Item              TO Nat,
                   SORT Seq               TO Seq_Nat,
                   PRED order: Item # Item TO less
                 IN LSORT
               TO NAT;
```

Note that using less as the sorting order is just one way of sorting sequences of natural numbers. Other sorting routines can be obtained by renaming order to another predicate satisfying the linear order axioms (such as the 'greater than' relation).

Above we have already seen one application of the use of free definitions in parameter restrictions. Another application is seen in the following example defining tuples of objects of two arbitrary sorts:

```
LET TUP :=
LAMBDA X : CLASS
               SORT Item1    FREE
               SORT Item2    FREE
           END
OF
EXPORT
  SORT Tup,
  SORT Item1,
```

```
   SORT Item2,
   FUNC tup  : Item1 # Item2 -> Tup,
   FUNC proj1: Tup          -> Item1,
   FUNC proj2: Tup          -> Item2
FROM
IMPORT X INTO
CLASS

   SORT Tup   DEP Item1,Item2
   FUNC tup  : Item1 # Item2 -> Tup
   FUNC proj1: Tup          -> Item1
   FUNC proj2: Tup          -> Item2

   AXIOM  FORALL i1:Item1,j1:Item1,i2:Item2,j2:Item2,t:Tup (
   {TUP1} tup(i1,i2)!;
   {TUP2} tup(i1,i2) = tup(j1,j2) => i1 = j1 AND i2 = j2;
   {TUP3} EXISTS t1:Item1,t2:Item2 ( t = tup(t1,t2) );
   {TUP4} proj1(tup(i1,i2)) = i1;
   {TUP5} proj2(tup(i1,i2)) = i2 )

END;
```

The use of free definitions for the sorts Item1 and Item2 in the parameter restriction is necessary here, because it would otherwise be impossible to instantiate the scheme for identical sorts Item1 and Item2 without causing origin inconsistency in the parameter restriction, as in the following example defining tuples of natural numbers:

```
APPLY
  RENAME
    SORT Item1 TO Nat,
    SORT Item2 TO Nat,
    SORT Tup   TO Tup_Nat
  IN TUP
TO NAT
```

Another approach to avoid this problem is to use a double lambda abstraction in TUP (one abstracting over Item1 and the other abstracting over Item2).

The TUP example also demonstrates why we do not need explicit sort definitions in COLD-K. Tuples (and many other data structures such as sets, records, arrays, etc.) can be defined axiomatically in the language. When we need tuples somewhere, they can be obtained by instantiating TUP with the proper parameters and importing the scheme thus obtained. Taking tuples of natural numbers as an example (see above), such an instantiation together with an import is equivalent to something that could be written in some other language (e.g., a user-oriented version of COLD) as:

```
SORT Tup_Nat = Tup(Nat,Nat)
```

We finish this subsection with two remarks. The first is that parameterised schemes may have parameters that are themselves parameterised. The use of these 'higher order' parameters requires an extension of the implementation relation to parameterised schemes, which will not be discussed here due to the fact that higher order parameters have limited practical applicability. The second remark is that not only the renaming and abbreviation operators have extensions to parameterised schemes, as we have seen, but also the other two modularisation operators (export and import), as indicated by the following reduction rules:

EXPORT Σ FROM LAMBDA $x:K$ OF L $\rightarrow$ LAMBDA $x:K$ OF EXPORT Σ FROM L
IMPORT LAMBDA $x:K$ OF L INTO M $\rightarrow$ LAMBDA $x:K$ OF IMPORT L INTO M
IMPORT M INTO LAMBDA $x:K$ OF L $\rightarrow$ LAMBDA $x:K$ OF IMPORT M INTO L

In the last rule, the assumption is that M is not a parameterised scheme.

6.4 Designs

When designing a system it does not suffice to view the system under development as a single scheme being transformed from some abstract to a concrete (executable) form. It is of prime methodological importance that during the design process a clear distinction is made between the internal and external aspects of the components from which the system is built. The internal aspects should be described in the *implementation* of the component, defining the realization of the component. The external aspects should be described in the *specification* of the component, which acts as a contract between the user and the implementer of the component. The user can rely on the fact that the component has the properties described in the specification, while the implementer has the obligation to realize the component such that it will satisfy the specification. The advantages of this 'contractual approach' to system design are well-known: components may be used even before they are implemented, implementations can be changed without affecting user code, system development can be divided over teams ('subcontracting'), etc.

The notion of a component is not supported by the 'scheme language' of COLD-K which we have seen in the previous subsections. The scheme language can only be used to construct class descriptions, which do not have internal and external aspects in the above sense. By the 'external aspects' we mean everything that a *designer* has to know in order to be able to use a component in the proper way (in the implementation of some other component). If the component is given by a scheme, these external aspects will include the hidden sorts and operations of the scheme since they are vital to understanding the meaning of the scheme. So, the 'internal aspects' of a component should not be confused with the hidden parts of a class description. Hiding a sort or operation name in a class description is not meant for hiding implementation details, but rather for encapsulation (making it impossible to use the name) and abstraction (as a kind of second order existential quantification).

The notion of a component is supported by the 'design language' of COLD-K, which constitutes the top layer of the language. The design language consists of a single construct, called a *design*, describing the design of a system built from a number of *components*. The syntax of designs is as follows:

DESIGN *components* SYSTEM *schemes*

The part following the keyword DESIGN lists the components from which the system is constructed. The part following the keyword SYSTEM consists of a list of schemes describing the system in terms of its components. We shall assume (for simplicity) that the list consists of a single scheme.

We distinguish two kinds of components: those that are specified only and those that, in addition to their specification, have an implementation associated with them. These are called *specified* and *implemented* components, respectively. A specified component is described by a line of the following form:

```
COMP  x : K;
```

Here x is the name of the component and K is a scheme acting as the specification of the component. An implemented component is described by a line of the following form:

```
COMP  x : K := L;
```

Here x and K are the name and specification of the component, and L is a scheme acting as the implementation of the component. Clearly, the requirement is that L should be an implementation of K. Once defined, the name of a component may be used in subsequent components in the same way as a scheme name. Furthermore, abbreviations may be used between component definitions in the same way as in schemes (see the example in the appendix).

Just like schemes, the meaning of a design can be explained by reducing it to a normal form. In contrast with schemes, there are two different ways we can do so, corresponding with the two different views (specification and implementation) of the system described by the design. If we have a design such as:

```
DESIGN
   COMP  x₁ : K₁ ...;
   ...
   COMP  xₙ : Kₙ ...
SYSTEM S(x₁,...,xₙ)
```

we can derive the *specification* of the system by substituting the specifications $K_1, \ldots,$ K_n for the component names in $S(x_1, \ldots, x_n)$ and normalizing the scheme. We can derive the *implementation* of the system by substituting the implementations associated with the components for the component names in $S(x_1, \ldots, x_n)$ and normalizing the scheme (assuming that the implementations satisfy the corresponding specifications). If a component has no implementation associated with it, its specification (which is an obviously correct implementation) should be taken instead. This second form of normalization corresponds to what is normally called *system integration* and is what should happen before executable code can be generated for the system.

The fact that in the system integration process we take the specification of a component as its implementation if the component has no implementation associated with it is not so strange as it may seem. There are basically two reasons why a component will not have an associated implementation. The first is that the component is 'hardwired', which implies that it has been implemented in some other language than COLD-K.

In that case we may assume that the underlying language implementation knows how to link the specification code (in COLD-K) with the hardwired code. The second is that the component has not yet been implemented, in which case we cannot reasonably expect that the underlying language implementation knows how to generate executable code for it. Yet system integration still makes sense in this case since the integrated system could be used for checking or testing purposes (e.g., using some kind of 'stubs' for unimplemented components).

In the appendix of this paper we give a complete design of the class *BUFFER* discussed and described in subsections 4.4 and 5.3. In contrast with 4.4 and 5.3, we have used modularisation and parameterisation techniques where appropriate. For example, the buffer is described as a component that is parameterised over the sort of objects stored in the buffer. The system described by the design is an instantiation of this parameterised component for the natural numbers. In order to limit the size of the text, the definitions between the CLASS and END brackets have been omitted. Furthermore, the shorthand "ATTR(a, T, V, X, Y)", where a, T, V, X and Y are identifiers, has been used to denote the following scheme:

```
APPLY APPLY
  RENAME
    SORT Inst                        TO T,
    SORT Item                        TO V,
    FUNC attr   : Inst        -> Item TO a,
    PROC set_attr: Inst # Item ->      TO set_a
  IN ATTR
TO X TO Y
```

The %-sign used in the design is a token that turns the rest of a line into comment.

The example indicates that, even for small examples, designs can be quite large. This is caused, on the one hand, by the lack of syntactic sugar in COLD-K and the fact that the definitions of all 'standard components' (such as natural numbers, sequences, etc.) must be included in the design since COLD-K has no built-in data types. On the other hand, designs always *are* much larger than the systems they describe since they contain a lot more information than the plain system specification and implementation (which can be obtained by means of the two normalization procedures described above). In particular, they contain the complete information on how the system was constructed from its components, how the components were constructed from their subcomponents and exactly what the interfaces (in the semantical sense of the word) of the components are. This information is vital in the maintenance and evolution phase of the system. Due to the size of designs, one will in practice not write a complete design as a single chunk of COLD-K text. Instead, designs will be represented as the contents of some *design management system*, providing facilities for storing, retrieving and modifying designs in a component-wise manner, but this is only a matter of implementation.

References

[1] J.A. BERGSTRA, J. HEERING, P. KLINT, *Module Algebra*, CWI Report CS-R8617 (1986).

[2] L.M.G. FEIJS, H.B.M. JONKERS, C.P.J. KOYMANS, G.R. RENARDEL DE LAVALETTE, *Formal Definition of the Design Language COLD-K*, Preliminary Edition, Technical Report, ESPRIT project 432, Doc.Nr. METEOR/t7/PRLE/7 (1987).

[3] D. HAREL, *First-order Dynamic Logic*, Lecture Notes in Computer Science 68, Springer-Verlag (1979).

[4] C.B. JONES, *Systematic Software Development Using VDM*, Prentice-Hall (1986).

[5] H.B.M. JONKERS, *A Concrete Syntax for COLD-K*, Technical Report, ESPRIT project 432, Doc.Nr. METEOR/t8/PRLE/2 (1988).

[6] H.B.M. JONKERS, *Description Algebra*, this volume.

[7] D.S. SCOTT, *Identity and Existence in Intuitionistic Logic*, in: M.P. FOURMAN, C.J. MULVEY, D.S. SCOTT (Eds.), *Applications of Sheaves*, Lecture Notes in Mathematics 753, Springer Verlag, Berlin (1979), 660-696.

Appendix. Design of *BUFFER*

```
DESIGN

% Specification of instances:

LET INST_SPEC := EXPORT
                   SORT Inst,
                    PROC create: -> Inst
                 FROM
                 CLASS ... END;

% Specification of attributes:

LET ATTR_SPEC := LAMBDA X : CLASS SORT Inst    FREE END OF
                 LAMBDA Y : CLASS SORT Item    FREE END OF
                 EXPORT
                   SORT Inst,
                   SORT Item,
                   FUNC attr    : Inst          -> Item,
                    PROC set_attr: Inst # Item ->
                 FROM
                 IMPORT X INTO
                 IMPORT Y INTO
                 CLASS ... END;

% Specification of natural numbers:

LET NAT_SPEC := EXPORT
                   SORT Nat,
                   FUNC zero:       -> Nat,
                   FUNC succ: Nat -> Nat,
                   FUNC pred: Nat -> Nat,
                   PRED less: Nat # Nat
                 FROM
                 CLASS ... END;

% Specification of sequences:

LET SEQ_SPEC := LAMBDA X : CLASS SORT Item    FREE END OF
                 EXPORT
                   SORT Nat,
                   SORT Item,
                   SORT Seq,
                   FUNC empty:               -> Seq,
                   FUNC cons : Item # Seq -> Seq,
                   FUNC cat  : Seq  # Seq -> Seq,
                   FUNC len  : Seq          -> Nat
```

```
                    FROM
                    IMPORT X INTO
                    IMPORT NAT_SPEC INTO
                    CLASS ... END;
```

% Buffer specification:

```
LET BUFFER_SPEC := LAMBDA X : CLASS SORT Item   FREE END OF
                    EXPORT
                      SORT Nat,
                      FUNC zero:                  -> Nat,
                      FUNC succ: Nat              -> Nat,
                      FUNC pred: Nat              -> Nat,
                      PRED less: Nat  # Nat,
                      SORT Item,
                      SORT Buffer,
                      FUNC len : Buffer           -> Nat,
                      PROC new :                  -> Buffer,
                      PROC put : Item # Buffer -> ,
                      PROC get : Buffer           -> Item
                    FROM
                    IMPORT X INTO
                    IMPORT NAT_SPEC INTO
                    IMPORT APPLY SEQ_SPEC TO X INTO
                    CLASS ... END;
```

% Hardwired components:

```
COMP INST : INST_SPEC;
COMP ATTR : ATTR_SPEC;
COMP NAT  : NAT_SPEC;
```

% Buffer implementation:

```
LET BUFFER_IMPL := LAMBDA X : CLASS SORT Item   FREE END OF
                    EXPORT
                      SORT Nat,
                      FUNC zero:                  -> Nat,
                      FUNC succ: Nat              -> Nat,
                      FUNC pred: Nat              -> Nat,
                      PRED less: Nat  # Nat,
                      SORT Item,
                      SORT Buffer,
                      FUNC len : Buffer           -> Nat,
                      PROC new :                  -> Buffer,
                      PROC put : Item # Buffer -> ,
                      PROC get : Buffer           -> Item
                    FROM
```

```
        LET L := RENAME SORT Inst TO Link IN INST;
        LET B := RENAME SORT Inst TO Buffer IN INST;
        IMPORT X INTO
        IMPORT NAT INTO
        IMPORT L INTO
        IMPORT ATTR(item,Link,Item,L,X) INTO
        IMPORT ATTR(next,Link,Link,L,L) INTO
        IMPORT B INTO
        IMPORT ATTR(first,Buffer,Link,B,L) INTO
        IMPORT ATTR(last,Buffer,Link,B,L) INTO
        CLASS ... END;
```

% Buffer component:

```
COMP BUFFER : BUFFER_SPEC := BUFFER_IMPL
```

% System of buffers of natural numbers:

```
SYSTEM IMPORT NAT INTO
        APPLY (RENAME SORT Item TO Nat IN BUFFER) TO NAT
```

A Formal Specification of INGRES

W.E. Baats, L.M.G. Feijs, J.H.A. Gelissen*

Philips Research Laboratories Eindhoven

P.O. Box 80000, 5600 JA Eindhoven, The Netherlands

Abstract

This paper describes a case study in the application of COLD-K as a specification language. The subject of the case study is the INGRES relational data base system.

1 Introduction and Motivation

This paper describes a case study in the application of COLD-K [2] as a specification language. The subject of the case study is the INGRES relational data base system.

Query languages for relational data base systems can be classified into

- Algebraic languages, where queries are expressed by applying specialised operators to relations.
- Calculus languages, where queries describe a set of tuples by specifying a predicate the tuples must satisfy. Calculus languages at their turn can be classified into languages for *tuple relational calculus* and languages for *domain relational calculus*. In the former case the bound variables are *tuple* variables, ranging over tuples, whereas in the latter case they are *domain* variables, corresponding to components of tuples.

There exist languages which have aspects of both kinds of languages, but the query language of INGRES definitely belongs to the calculus languages (and in fact is a language for tuple relational calculus). For an introduction to the query language of INGRES we refer to [3] and [1].

The motivation for writing a formal specification of the (existing) INGRES data base system arose from the work on a prototype of a design engineering data base. Among other things, a design engineering data base should have a possibility for storing and retrieving *relations*. It follows that a relational data base system is a candidate building block for a prototype of a design engineering data base. Writing a formal specification seems a good way of obtaining an understanding of the INGRES data base system and of course such a specification can be of help during the implementation of a prototype

---

*This work has been performed within the ESPRIT project 432: METEOR

design engineering data base.

Our choice of selecting INGRES among other relational data base systems is motivated by the fact that it is widely used and that it is available (often for free) for various relevant computers, such as VAX/VMS, VAX/ULTRIX, SUN. Furthermore the fact that the query language of INGRES has already been designed, starting from a mathematical basis (see e.g. [3]), makes it feasible to write a complete formal specification of its syntax and semantics. The formal specification does not cover all features of INGRES, but focusses on what can be viewed as a kernel.

2 Overview of the Formal Description

2.1 General

The syntax of the INGRES query language (appendix A) serves as a starting point for the COLD-K specification of INGRES. The semantics of the INGRES query language has been derived from [1] and [3] and in a few cases from experiments with the system (INGRES version 7.10). The COLD-K specification of INGRES consists of the following class descriptions:

- NAME introduces names.
- FORMAT introduces so-called formats which are used to distinguish data of sort integer from data of sort character-string.
- DICTIONARY describes the possible data dictionaries, where a data dictionary describes the structure of the "contents" of a data base.
- SYNTAX describes the abstract syntax of the query language.
- IS_WF describes the well-formedness of all constructs of the query language.
- CONTENTS describes the possible relations (the "contents") of a data base.
- LEXICO is an auxiliary class description which describes the lexicographical ordering of character strings.
- SEMANTICS describes the meaning of all constructs of the query language.
- The class description INGRES describes the operations that can be performed upon a data base.

Fig 1 shows part of the import structure of the class descriptions which describe INGRES.

An arrow describes that one class description is imported by another class description. E.g. SEMANTICS is imported into INGRES. In this figure we have omitted the standard class descriptions and the class descriptions NAME and FORMAT. The formal class descriptions written in COLD-K can be found in appendix B.

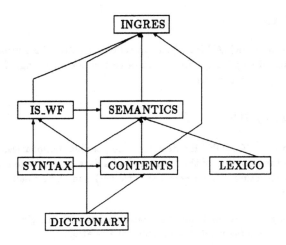

Figure 1: Import structure.

On the first pages of appendix B we give some definitions which introduce standard data types. We assume the following standard class descriptions: ITEM_SPEC, NAT_SPEC, INT_SPEC, SET_SPEC, SEQ_SPEC, MAP_SPEC, CHAR_SPEC. Due to space limitations we cannot give the actual standard class descriptions themselves. For parts of these standard class description we refer to [2] where natural numbers and sequences are discussed. In order to have an overview of the sorts, functions and predicates provided, we have explicitly added a (redundant) export operation to each of these standard class descriptions.

The formal specification makes use of the facilities offered by COLD-K for describing states and state transformations. The INGRES commands are modeled by procedures and functions. Procedures correspond to INGRES commands that modify the state of a data base. As examples of these we have the CREATE and APPEND TO commands. Functions correspond to INGRES commands that do not have any side-effect (these commands are often called *queries*). As an example of this we have the RETRIEVE command.

In the subsections below we shall discuss each class description separately.

2.2 NAME

The objective of the class description NAME is to introduce names. A name consists of a sequence of characters.

2.3 FORMAT

The class description FORMAT introduces so-called formats. These formats are used to distinguish data of sort integer from data of sort character string. There are two format constants, viz. *int* and *string*.

2.4 DICTIONARY

The class description DICTIONARY describes the possible dictionaries, where a dictionary describes the structure of the "contents" of a data base. There are procedures to modify such a structure. (*is_rel_name, is_tuple_var*) and three functions (*domains, formats, range_over*).

- The predicate *is_rel_name* holds if a relation exists with the given name.
- The function *domains* yields the domains of a relation.
- The function *formats* yields the formats of the domains of a relation.
- The predicate *is_unique* holds if all names in a sequence are unique.
- The predicates *is_domain* relate domain names to relation names.
- The function *pos* gives the 'column' position of a domain in a given relation.
- The predicate *is_tuple_var* holds for a given name if it is a tuple variable.
- The function *range_over* gives the name of the relation of a tuple variable.
- The axiom *init* says that initially there are no relations and no tuple variables.

The next functions and axioms, dealing with objects of sort *Relation_Name_List* and *Domain_Name_List*, describe the syntax and the semantics of the <relation_name_list> and the <domain_name_list> constructs as given in appendix A. We have abstract syntax functions, which have been derived from appendix A in the following manner. In appendix A we have the production rule:

        <relation_name_list> ::= relation_name
          | relation_name, <relation_name_list>

whereas in the class description DICTIONARY we have

```
SORT Relation_Name_List

FUNC relation_name: Name -> Relation_Name_List

FUNC relation_name_list: Name # Relation_Name_List -> Relation_Name_List
```

Furthermore there is a so-called *closure* clause, saying that all objects of sort *Relation_Name_List* can be constructed by finitely many applications of the abstract syntax functions. The closure clause uses an auxiliary predicate *is_gen*, which is defined inductively.

```
PRED is_gen: Relation_Name_List
IND  FORALL n: Name (is_gen(relation_name(n))) ;
     FORALL n: Name ,rnl: Relation_Name_List (
     is_gen(rnl) => is_gen(relation_name_list(n,rnl)))

AXIOM {is_gen} FORALL rnl: Relation_Name_List (is_gen(rnl))
```

The meaning functions (called *sem*, *sem_d*, *sem_f*) give the meaning of the terms that can be formed using abstract syntax functions. This meaning is either a sequence of names or a sequence of formats. The meaning functions are defined by axioms.

The subsequent procedures modify the state of the class description DICTIONARY, or, in other words, they update the dictionary of a data base.

- The procedure *range_of* corresponds to the INGRES command
  "RANGE OF tuple_variable IS relation_name", which is a kind of declaration.
- The procedure *create_d* creates the structure of a new relation. It lays down which domains are used and what formats these domains have.
- The procedure *destroy* corresponds to the INGRES command
  "DESTROY <relation_name_list>".

2.5 SYNTAX

The class description SYNTAX describes the (abstract) syntax of the arguments of the INGRES commands. As before, these operations are derived from the syntax as given in appendix A. For example if in the syntax in appendix A we have

```
<item> ::=
     Int
   | Seq_Char
```

then the corresponding abstract syntax becomes:

```
SORT Item

FUNC item: Int -> Item

FUNC item: Seq_Char -> Item
```

with closure clause

```
PRED is_gen: Item
IND  FORALL i: Int (is_gen(item(i))) ;
     FORALL s: Seq_Char (is_gen(item(s)))

AXIOM {is_gen} FORALL i: Item (is_gen(i))
```

2.6 IS_WF

The class description IS_WF describes the well-formedness of the arguments of the INGRES commands. For each sort from the class description SYNTAX there is a predicate called *is_wf*. We give one example:

```
PRED is_wf: Attribute
IND  FORALL tv: Name, dn: Name (
         is_tuple_var(tv) AND is_domain(range_over(tv),dn)
         => is_wf(attribute(tv,dn)))
```

There are functions *format* which yield the format of items, attributes and expressions. These functions are used in the definition of *is_wf* for expressions and qualifications: e.g. the assertion *format(e1) = int* AND *format(e2) = int* is a necessary condition for the well-formedness of the expression *multiplication(e1,e2)*.

For several sorts (e.g. *Target_List, Qualification, Expression, Aggre_Target_List* and *Attribute*), the *is_wf* predicates describe dynamic subsets of these sorts. This is caused by the RANGE OF and DESTROY commands, which introduce and remove tuple-variables.

2.7 CONTENTS

The class description CONTENTS describes the possible "contents" of a data base. It also provides procedures to modify the contents of a data base. The state space of this class description is spanned by one function (*relation*).

- The function *relation* yields a set of tuples. The first axiom says that the contents of the data base must be consistent with the typing as given by the data base dictionary.
- The predicate *pre_store* serves as a precondition predicate.
- The procedure *store* assigns a set of tuples to a relation name.
- The procedure *append* adds a set of tuples to a relation.

2.8 LEXICO

The class description LEXICO is an auxiliary class description. It describes the lexicographic ordering of character strings. Characters are ordered according to the ASCII character set. Before determining the ordering of strings, INGRES first "compresses" the strings by removing spaces.

2.9 SEMANTICS

In this class description the meaning of the arguments of the INGRES commands is described. The functions and predicates in this class description are defined by induction over the structure of the terms that can be constructed using the functions of the class description SYNTAX.

In order to have a compositional semantics, most meaning functions and predicates have an additional argument which can be viewed as a "table". In the formal specifications it is called *tab* or *tb*. A well-formed table consists of a mapping from tuple-variables to tuples in accordance with the relations where the tuple-variables belong to. In the example below two relations named "parts" and "supplier" are given and we shall show one table yielding tuples from these relations.

relation parts

pname	number
box	1
book	2

relation supplier

sname	number
Smith	1
Jones	2

We also give the declaration of the tuple-variables p and s (in INGRES syntax).

RANGE OF p IS parts
RANGE OF s IS supplier

For the relations "parts" and "supplier" there are four possible tables yielding tuples that are in the corresponding relations. We show one such table ($\{p \mapsto \langle box, 1 \rangle, s \mapsto \langle Jones, 2 \rangle\}$):

tab

p	box	1
s	Jones	2

The predicate *is_wf* holds for a table if it is consistent with the data base dictionary.

In the class description SEMANTICS overloading has been used quite often, i.e. different operations have the same name and can only be distinguished by the sorts of the arguments. The following functions and predicates in this class description have overloaded names:

- *sem*, which gives the semantics of a part of a query,
- *length*, which yields the number of items in the result of *sem*,
- *free*, which yields the set of (free) tuple-variables occurring in a construct.

We now turn to the so-called aggregation facilities supported by INGRES. The *get_set* function plays a role in the definition of the meaning of the queries in which one of the following keywords occur: COUNTU, ANY, SUMU, AVGU, MAX and MIN. It is possible to view such queries as the application of a set operator. Therefore the function *get_set* yields a set whereas the functions *count, any, sum, avg, max* and *min* are set operators yielding integers.

As an introduction to the definition of *get_set*, we give a somewhat simplified definition of *get_set*. The simplified definition corrresponds with the case where the *atl* and *q* arguments both are empty.

```
FUNC get_set: Attribute -> Set_Item

AXIOM
{get_set1} FORALL a: Attribute ( is_wf(a) <=> get_set(a)! ) ;
{get_set2} FORALL tv: Name, dn: Name (
            LET a: Attribute; a := attribute(tv, dn) ;
            is_wf(a) => get_set(a) =
              SOME si : Set_Item (
              FORALL i : Item (
                is_in(i, si) <=>
                  EXISTS tb: Map_Name_Seq_Item (
                  is_wf(tb) AND dom(tb) = ins(tv, empty) AND
                  sem(tb, a) = i AND
                  FORALL tv1: Name (
                   is_in(tv1, dom(tb))
                     => is_in(app(tb, tv1), relation(range_over(tv1)))
          )  )) ))
```

Let us write $tb[tv]$ for $app(tb,tv)$. It is easy to see that $get\_set(a)$ yields the set

$$\{ sem(tb,a) \mid dom(tb) = \{tv\};\ tb[tv] \in relation(range\_over(tv)) \},$$

which corresponds with our intuition that $get\_set(a)$ should yield the set of a-values that are obtained when the value of the tuple variable tv 'runs over' all tuples in its relation. On the other hand, the full definition of *get_set* as given in appendix B can be viewed as a generalisation of the definition given above.

2.10   INGRES

The class description INGRES contains the specification of the INGRES commands. The names of the functions and procedures are derived from the keywords of the corresponding INGRES commands. The results of the functions and procedures correspond to the results of the INGRES commands, except for the fact that in the COLD-K description the relations are sets of tuples whereas in INGRES there is also the possibility to view them as multisets of tuples.

A central role is played by the *retrieve* function The following example of a query will serve as an explanation of the definition of the *retrieve* function. We simplify the definition by restricting ourselves to empty qualifications. Let us first introduce some abbreviations for assertions that occur in the definition of the *retrieve* function.

$$T(tv,tab) \quad :\Leftrightarrow \quad tv \in dom(tab) \Rightarrow tab[tv] \in relation(range\_over(tv))$$

$$E(tab,u,tl) \quad :\Leftrightarrow \quad is\_wf(tab);$$
$$dom(tab) = free(tl);$$

$$\text{sem(tab,tl)} = \text{u};$$
$$\text{FORALL tv : Name}$$
$$\text{T(tv,tab)}$$

$$P(u,tl) \quad :\Leftrightarrow \quad \text{length(u)} = \text{length(tl)};$$
$$\text{EXISTS tab : Map\_Name\_Seq\_Item}$$
$$\text{E(tab,u,tl)}$$

Using these abbreviations, we have the following definition of *retrieve(tl)* for a well-formed target list *tl*:

$$\text{retrieve(tl)} = \{ \text{ u : Seq\_Item} \mid P(u,tl) \}$$

We assume that the dictionary of the data base is defined by *is_rel_name(r)*, *domains(r)* $= \langle a,b \rangle$, *is_tuple_var(t)* and *range_over(t) = r*. We assume that the contents of the data base is defined by *relation(r)* $= \{\langle 1,2 \rangle, \langle 3,4 \rangle\}$. We visualise this assumption below.

relation r

a	b
1	2
3	4

Consider the target_list *t.a*. From the assumptions we shall now prove that *retrieve(t.a)* yields $\{\langle 1 \rangle, \langle 3 \rangle\}$.

Proof. Because *t.a* is well-formed, the definition of *retrieve* as given above, applies. It is sufficient to prove that $P(u,t.a)$ holds for $u = \langle 1 \rangle$ and for $u = \langle 3 \rangle$ and that NOT $P(u,t.a)$ holds for *u* such that $u \neq \langle 1 \rangle$ and $u \neq \langle 3 \rangle$. This will be proved in three steps. In the first step we prove $P(\langle 1 \rangle, t.a)$; secondly we prove $P(\langle 3 \rangle, t.a)$ and in the third step we prove that NOT $P(u,t.a)$ holds for *u* such that $u \neq \langle 1 \rangle$ *and* $u \neq \langle 3 \rangle$.

- It is obvious that $length(\langle 1 \rangle) = length(t.a)$. We claim that $\{t \mapsto \langle 1,2 \rangle\}$ is a well-formed table for which $dom(\{t \mapsto \langle 1,2 \rangle\}) = free(t.a)$ and $sem(\{t \mapsto \langle 1,2 \rangle\}, t.a) = \langle 1 \rangle$ hold. Let *tv* be a name which is in the domain of this table, then *tv* must be equal to t. This implies that $\{t \mapsto \langle 1,2 \rangle\}[tv] \in relation(range\_over(tv))$. We conclude that for $u = \langle 1 \rangle$ there is a table such that $E(tab,u,t.a)$ holds. Therefore $P(\langle 1 \rangle, t.a)$ holds.
- Step 2 is analogous to step 1.
- Let *u* be a sequence of items such that $u \neq \langle 1 \rangle$ and $u \neq \langle 3 \rangle$. If we assume $P(u,t.a)$ then there is a table *tab* such that $E(tab,u,t.a)$ holds. However, there are only two possibilities for *tab* viz. $\{t \mapsto \langle 1,2 \rangle\}$ and $\{t \mapsto \langle 3,4 \rangle\}$. If $tab = \{t \mapsto \langle 1,2 \rangle\}$ then $u = \langle 1 \rangle$ which leads to a contradiction. Similarly $tab = \{t \mapsto \langle 3,4 \rangle\}$ leads to a contradiction.

Now it is proved that $P(\langle 1 \rangle, t.a)$, $P(\langle 3 \rangle, t.a)$ hold and that NOT $P(u,t.a)$ holds for *u* such that $u \neq \langle 1 \rangle$ *and* $u \neq \langle 3 \rangle$. Therefore *retrieve(t.a)* $= \{\langle 1 \rangle, \langle 3 \rangle\}$. $\square$

3 Conclusions

This case study can be viewed as a demonstration of the flexibility of COLD-K: first of all it is possible to describe the syntax of a (query) language by using inductive definitions. Secondly it is possible to describe the semantics of a non-trivial (query) language, using techniques from denotational semantics and finally it is possible to deal in a very natural way with systems having a "state", by using COLD-K procedures.

Some remarks of a methodological nature can be made:

- Some axioms should be viewed as invariants (e.g. the axioms *is_rel_name, is_unique* and *range_over* in DICTIONARY). Such axioms should be written *before* the pre- and postcondition style definitions of procedures are given. The preconditions then usualy follow from the requirement that the procedures should not violate the invariants.
- The construction of a modular specification is likely to proceed in a bottom-up fashion. As a typical example: it is hard to write part of SEMANTICS unless SYNTAX is defined.
- Often, reasoning about functions is easier than reasoning about procedures. It follows that (unless this turns out to be unnatural) functions are preferred over procedures. A typical example is the *retrieve* function (see class description INGRES), which is defined in a non-operational manner. In section 2.10 we actually showed some reasoning about the *retrieve* function.
- A ready-to-use collection of standard class descriptions, offering notations and definitions for numbers, characters, sets, sequences, etc. turns out to be very useful for writing large specifications.

4 Acknowledgements

The authors would like to thank H.B.M. Jonkers for the help and cooperation on the subject of this paper.

References

[1] R. Epstein, *A Tutorial On INGRES*, Memorandum No. ERL - M77 25, December 15, 1977 (Revised), Electronics Research Laboratory, College Of Engineering, University Of California, Berkeley, 94720.

[2] H.B.M. Jonkers, *Introduction to COLD-K*. this volume.

[3] J.D. Ullman, *Principles Of Database Systems*, ISBN 0-273-08476-3, Computer Science Press.

Appendix A. Syntax of INGRES commands

The following commands correspond to procedures or functions:

> RANGE OF tuple_variable IS relation_name
> CREATE relation_name (<domain_name_list>)
> DESTROY <relation_name_list>
> RETRIEVE (<target_list>) <optional_qual>
> APPEND TO relation_name (<target_list>) <optional_qual>
> RETRIEVE INTO relation_name (<target_list>) <optional_qual>

The syntax of the arguments is defined by:

> <format> ::= int
> | string
>
> <relation_name_list> ::= relation_name
> | relation_name, <relation_name_list>
>
> <domain_name_list> ::= domain_name = <format>
> | domain_name = <format>, <domain_name_list>
>
> <item> ::= Int
> | Seq_Char
>
> <attribute> ::= tuple_variable.domain_name
>
> <aggre_target_list> ::= <attribute>
> | <attribute>,<aggre_target_list>
>
> <optional_atl> ::= empty
> | BY <aggre_target_list>
>
> <expression> ::= <item>
> | <attribute>
> | COUNTU(<attribute> <optional_atl> <optional_qual>)
> | ANY(<attribute> <optional_atl> <optional_qual>)
> | SUMU(<attribute> <optional_atl> <optional_qual>)
> | AVGU(<attribute> <optional_atl> <optional_qual>)
> | MAX(<attribute> <optional_atl> <optional_qual>)
> | MIN(<attribute> <optional_atl> <optional_qual>)
> | PLUS <expression>
> | MINUS <expression>
> | <expression> ** <expression>
> | <expression> * <expression>
> | <expression> / <expression>

```
        | <expression> +  <expression>
        | <expression> -  <expression>

<qualification> ::= NOT <qualification>
        | <qualification> OR <qualification>
        | <qualification> AND <qualification>
        | (<qualification>)
        | <expression> <   <expression>
        | <expression> <= <expression>
        | <expression> >   <expression>
        | <expression> >= <expression>
        | <expression> =   <expression>
        | <expression> != <expression>

<optional_qual> ::= empty
        | WHERE <qualification>

<target> ::= domain_name = <expression>
        | <attribute>

<target_list> ::= <target>
        | <target>,<target_list>
```

Appendix B. Formal Specification

```
DESIGN

LET NAT := EXPORT SORT Nat,
                  FUNC zero:              -> Nat,
                  FUNC succ: Nat        -> Nat,
                  FUNC pred: Nat        -> Nat,
                  PRED lss : Nat # Nat,
                  PRED leq : Nat # Nat,
                  PRED gtr : Nat # Nat,
                  PRED geq : Nat # Nat
            FROM NAT_SPEC;

LET INT := EXPORT SORT Int,
                  SORT Nat,
                  FUNC zero:              -> Int,
                  FUNC succ: Int        -> Int,
                  FUNC pred: Int        -> Int,
                  PRED lss : Int # Int,
                  PRED leq : Int # Int,
                  PRED gtr : Int # Int,
                  PRED geq : Int # Int,
                  FUNC neg : Int        -> Int,
                  FUNC add : Int # Int -> Int,
                  FUNC sub : Int # Int -> Int,
                  FUNC mul : Int # Int -> Int,
                  FUNC div : Int # Int -> Int
            FROM INT_SPEC;

LET SET := EXPORT SORT Item,
                  SORT Nat,
                  SORT Set,
                  PRED is_in : Item # Set,
                  FUNC empty :              -> Set,
                  FUNC ins   : Item # Set -> Set,
                  FUNC rem   : Item # Set -> Set,
                  FUNC union : Set  # Set -> Set
            FROM SET_SPEC;

LET SEQ := EXPORT SORT Item,
                  SORT Nat,
                  SORT Seq,
                  FUNC empty:              -> Seq,
                  FUNC cons : Item # Seq -> Seq,
                  FUNC hd   : Seq        -> Item,
                  FUNC tl   : Seq        -> Seq,
                  FUNC len  : Seq        -> Nat,
                  FUNC sel  : Seq # Nat  -> Item,
                  FUNC cat  : Seq # Seq  -> Seq
            FROM SEQ_SPEC;
```

```
LET MAP := EXPORT SORT Item1,
                SORT Item2,
                SORT Set1,
                SORT Set2,
                SORT Map,
                FUNC empty:                          -> Map,
                FUNC add  : Map # Item1 # Item2 -> Map,
                FUNC app  : Map # Item1        -> Item2,
                FUNC dom  : Map               -> Set1
           FROM MAP_SPEC;

LET CHAR := EXPORT SORT Char,
                SORT Nat,
                FUNC chr: Nat -> Char,
                FUNC ord: Char -> Nat
           FROM CHAR_SPEC;

LET SEQ_CHAR := (APPLY (RENAME SORT Item TO Char,
                        SORT Seq TO Seq_Char IN SEQ)
                 TO CHAR);
```

```
LET NAME :=
IMPORT SEQ_CHAR INTO

CLASS

  SORT Name

  FUNC name: Seq_Char -> Name

  AXIOM
  {name1} FORALL s: Seq_Char, t: Seq_Char (name(s) = name(t) => s = t) ;
  {name2} FORALL n: Name (EXISTS s: Seq_Char (n = name(s)))

END;


LET FORMAT :=

CLASS

  SORT Format

  FUNC int: -> Format

  FUNC string: -> Format

  AXIOM
  {format1} NOT int = string ;
  {format2} FORALL f: Format (f = int OR f = string)

END;
```

```
LET SET_NAME := (APPLY (RENAME SORT Item TO Name,
                               SORT Set TO Set_Name IN SET)
                TO NAME);
LET SEQ_NAME := (APPLY (RENAME SORT Item TO Name,
                               SORT Seq TO Seq_Name IN SEQ)
                TO NAME);
LET SEQ_FORMAT := (APPLY (RENAME SORT Item TO Format,
                                 SORT Seq TO Seq_Format IN SEQ)
                  TO FORMAT);


LET DICTIONARY :=

IMPORT NAT INTO
IMPORT NAME INTO
IMPORT FORMAT INTO
IMPORT SET_NAME INTO
IMPORT SEQ_NAME INTO
IMPORT SEQ_FORMAT INTO

CLASS

  SORT Relation_Name_List
  SORT Domain_Name_List

  PRED is_rel_name: Name VAR

  FUNC domains: Name -> Seq_Name VAR

  FUNC formats: Name -> Seq_Format VAR

  AXIOM FORALL rn: Name (
  {is_rel_name1} is_rel_name(rn) <=> domains(rn)! ;
  {is_rel_name2} is_rel_name(rn) <=> formats(rn)! ;
  {is_rel_name3} is_rel_name(rn) => len(domains(rn)) = len(formats(rn)))

  PRED is_unique: Seq_Name
  PAR  sn: Seq_Name
  DEF  FORALL i1: Nat, i2 : Nat (
       lss(i1, len(sn)) AND lss(i2, len(sn)) AND NOT i1 = i2
        => NOT sel(sn, i1) = sel(sn, i2))

  AXIOM
  {is_unique} FORALL rn: Name (
                is_rel_name(rn) => is_unique(domains(rn)) ;
                is_rel_name(rn) => gtr(len(domains(rn)), zero))

  PRED is_domain: Name # Name
  PAR  rn: Name, n: Name
  DEF  EXISTS i: Nat (lss(i, len(domains(rn))) AND sel(domains(rn), i) = n)

  FUNC pos: Name # Name -> Nat
```

```
PAR   rn: Name, dn: Name
DEF   SOME i : Nat (lss(i, len(domains(rn)))) AND sel(domains(rn), i) = dn)


PRED is_tuple_var: Name VAR

FUNC range_over: Name -> Name VAR

AXIOM
{range_over} FORALL tv : Name (
              is_tuple_var(tv) <=> range_over(tv)! ;
              is_tuple_var(tv) => is_rel_name(range_over(tv)))


AXIOM
{init} INIT => FORALL n : Name (NOT is_rel_name(n); NOT is_tuple_var(n))

FUNC sem: Relation_Name_List -> Seq_Name

FUNC relation_name: Name -> Relation_Name_List

AXIOM
{sem1} FORALL rn: Name (sem(relation_name(rn)) = cons(rn, empty))

FUNC relation_name_list: Name # Relation_Name_List -> Relation_Name_List

AXIOM
{sem2} FORALL rn: Name, rnl: Relation_Name_List (
        sem(relation_name_list(rn,rnl)) = cons(rn, sem(rnl)))

PRED is_gen: Relation_Name_List
IND   FORALL n: Name (is_gen(relation_name(n))) ;
      FORALL n: Name ,rnl: Relation_Name_List (
       is_gen(rnl) => is_gen(relation_name_list(n,rnl)))

AXIOM
{is_gen} FORALL rnl: Relation_Name_List (is_gen(rnl))

FUNC sem_d: Domain_Name_List -> Seq_Name

FUNC sem_f: Domain_Name_List -> Seq_Format

FUNC domain_name_list: Name # Format -> Domain_Name_List

AXIOM
{sem3} FORALL dn: Name, f: Format (
        sem_d(domain_name_list(dn, f)) = cons(dn, empty) ;
        sem_f(domain_name_list(dn, f)) = cons(f, empty))

FUNC domain_name_list: Name # Format # Domain_Name_List -> Domain_Name_List

AXIOM
{sem4} FORALL dn: Name, f: Format, dnl: Domain_Name_List (
```

```
              sem_d(domain_name_list(dn, f, dnl)) = cons(dn, sem_d(dnl)) ;
              sem_f(domain_name_list(dn, f, dnl)) = cons(f, sem_f(dnl)))


PRED is_gen: Domain_Name_List
IND  FORALL dn: Name, f: Format (is_gen(domain_name_list(dn,f))) ;
     FORALL dn: Name, f: Format, dnl: Domain_Name_List (
      is_gen(dnl) => is_gen(domain_name_list(dn,f,dnl)))


AXIOM
{is_gen} FORALL dnl : Domain_Name_List (is_gen(dnl))


PROC range_of: Name # Name ->
MOD  is_tuple_var, range_over


AXIOM
{range_of1} FORALL rn: Name, tv: Name (<range_of (rn, tv)> TRUE) ;
{range_of2} FORALL rn: Name, tv: Name (is_rel_name(rn)
                => [range_of (rn, tv)] is_tuple_var(tv) AND
                                        range_over(tv) = rn) ;
{range_of3} FORALL rn: Name, tv1: Name, tv2: Name (
                is_rel_name(rn) AND NOT tv1 = tv2
                => [range_of (rn, tv1)] is_tuple_var(tv2) <=>
                    (PREV is_tuple_var(tv2)))


PROC create_d: Name # Domain_Name_List ->
MOD  is_rel_name, domains, formats


AXIOM
{create_d1} FORALL rn: Name, dnl: Domain_Name_List (
                <create_d (rn, dnl)> TRUE) ;
{create_d2} FORALL rn: Name, dnl: Domain_Name_List (
                NOT is_rel_name(rn) AND is_unique(sem_d(dnl))
                => [create_d (rn, dnl)]
                    is_rel_name(rn) AND domains(rn) = sem_d(dnl) AND
                    formats(rn) = sem_f(dnl)) ;
{create_d3} FORALL rn1: Name, rn2: Name, dnl: Domain_Name_List (
                NOT is_rel_name(rn1) AND is_unique(sem_d(dnl)) AND NOT rn1 = rn2
                => [create_d (rn1, dnl)]
                    is_rel_name(rn2)  <=> (PREV is_rel_name(rn2)) AND
                    domains(rn2) = (PREV domains(rn2)) AND
                    formats(rn2) = (PREV formats(rn2)))
```

```
PROC destroy: Relation_Name_List ->
MOD  is_tuple_var, is_rel_name

AXIOM
{destroy1} FORALL rnl: Relation_Name_List (<destroy (rnl)> TRUE) ;
{destroy2} FORALL rnl: Relation_Name_List (
            FORALL i: Nat (lss(i, len(sem(rnl)))) =>
           is_rel_name(sel(sem(rnl), i))) => (
            LET relations: Set_Name ; relations := SOME r: Set_Name (
             FORALL rn: Name (is_in(rn, r) <=>
              EXISTS i: Nat (lss(i, len(sem(rnl))) AND
                    rn = sel(sem(rnl), i)))) ;
            LET tuple_vars: Set_Name ; tuple_vars := SOME t: Set_Name (
             FORALL tv: Name (is_in(tv, t) <=>
              is_tuple_var(tv) AND is_in(range_over(tv), relations))) ;
           [destroy (rnl)] (
            FORALL rn: Name (
             is_rel_name(rn) <=> NOT is_in(rn, relations) AND
                                   (PREV is_rel_name(rn))) ;
              FORALL tv: Name (is_tuple_var(tv) <=>
               NOT is_in(tv, tuple_vars) AND
                   (PREV is_tuple_var(tv)))))))

END;
```

```
LET SYNTAX :=

IMPORT INT INTO
IMPORT CHAR INTO
IMPORT NAME INTO
IMPORT FORMAT INTO
IMPORT SEQ_CHAR INTO

CLASS

  SORT Item
  SORT Attribute
  SORT Aggre_Target_List
  SORT Optional_ATL
  SORT Expression
  SORT Qualification
  SORT Optional_Qual
  SORT Target
  SORT Target_List

{ Item }

  FUNC item: Int -> Item

  FUNC item: Seq_Char -> Item

  PRED is_gen: Item
  IND  FORALL i: Int (is_gen(item(i))) ;
       FORALL s: Seq_Char (is_gen(item(s)))

  AXIOM
  {is_gen} FORALL i: Item (is_gen(i))

{ Attribute }

  FUNC attribute: Name # Name -> Attribute

  PRED is_gen: Attribute
  IND  FORALL tv: Name, dn : Name (is_gen(attribute(tv,dn)))

  AXIOM
  {is_gen} FORALL a: Attribute (is_gen(a))

{ Aggre_Target_List }

  FUNC aggre_target_list: Attribute -> Aggre_Target_List

  FUNC aggre_target_list: Attribute # Aggre_Target_List -> Aggre_Target_List

  PRED is_gen: Aggre_Target_List
  IND  FORALL a: Attribute (is_gen(aggre_target_list(a))) ;
```

```
     FORALL a: Attribute, atl: Aggre_Target_List (
       is_gen(a); is_gen(atl) => is_gen(aggre_target_list(a,atl)))

   AXIOM
   {is_gen} FORALL atl: Aggre_Target_List (is_gen(atl))

{ Optional_ATL }

   FUNC optional_atl: -> Optional_ATL

   FUNC optional_atl: Aggre_Target_List -> Optional_ATL

   PRED is_gen: Optional_ATL
   IND  is_gen(optional_atl) ;
        FORALL atl: Aggre_Target_List (is_gen(atl) => is_gen(optional_atl(atl)))

   AXIOM
   {is_gen} FORALL atl: Optional_ATL (is_gen(atl))

{ Expression }

   FUNC expression:      Item -> Expression
   FUNC expression:      Attribute -> Expression
   FUNC countu:          Attribute # Optional_ATL # Optional_Qual -> Expression
   FUNC any:             Attribute # Optional_ATL # Optional_Qual -> Expression
   FUNC sumu:            Attribute # Optional_ATL # Optional_Qual -> Expression
   FUNC avgu:            Attribute # Optional_ATL # Optional_Qual -> Expression
   FUNC max:             Attribute # Optional_ATL # Optional_Qual -> Expression
   FUNC min:             Attribute # Optional_ATL # Optional_Qual -> Expression
   FUNC plus:            Expression -> Expression
   FUNC minus:           Expression -> Expression
   FUNC exponentiation:  Expression # Expression -> Expression
   FUNC multiplication:  Expression # Expression -> Expression
   FUNC division:        Expression # Expression -> Expression
   FUNC addition:        Expression # Expression -> Expression
   FUNC subtraction:     Expression # Expression -> Expression

   PRED is_gen: Expression
   IND  FORALL i: Item (is_gen(i) => is_gen(expression(i))) ;
        FORALL a: Attribute (is_gen(a) => is_gen(expression(a))) ;
        FORALL a: Attribute, atl: Optional_ATL, q: Optional_Qual (
         is_gen(a) AND is_gen(atl) AND is_gen(q) =>
          is_gen(countu(a,atl,q)) AND is_gen(any(a,atl,q)) AND
          is_gen(sumu(a,atl,q)) AND is_gen(avgu(a,atl,q)) AND
          is_gen(max(a,atl,q)) AND is_gen(min(a,atl,q))) ;
        FORALL e: Expression (
         is_gen(e) => is_gen(plus(e)) AND is_gen(minus(e))) ;
        FORALL e1: Expression, e2: Expression (
         is_gen(e1) AND is_gen(e2) =>
          is_gen(exponentiation(e1,e2)) AND is_gen(multiplication(e1,e2)) AND
          is_gen(division(e1,e2)) AND is_gen(addition(e1,e2)) AND
```

```
            is_gen(subtraction(e1,e2)))

AXIOM
{is_gen} FORALL e: Expression (is_gen(e))

FUNC not_qualification:   Qualification -> Qualification
FUNC or_qualification:    Qualification # Qualification -> Qualification
FUNC and_qualification:   Qualification # Qualification -> Qualification
FUNC parenthesised:       Qualification -> Qualification
FUNC less:                Expression # Expression -> Qualification
FUNC less_or_equal:       Expression # Expression -> Qualification
FUNC greater:             Expression # Expression -> Qualification
FUNC greater_or_equal:    Expression # Expression -> Qualification
FUNC equal:               Expression # Expression -> Qualification
FUNC not_equal:           Expression # Expression -> Qualification

PRED is_gen: Qualification
IND  FORALL q: Qualification (is_gen(q) => is_gen(not_qualification(q))) ;
     FORALL q1: Qualification, q2: Qualification (
      is_gen(q1) AND is_gen(q2) =>
       is_gen(or_qualification(q1,q2)) AND
       is_gen(and_qualification(q1,q2))) ;
     FORALL q: Qualification (is_gen(q) => is_gen(parenthesised(q))) ;
     FORALL e1: Expression, e2: Expression (
      is_gen(e1) AND is_gen(e2) =>
       is_gen(less(e1,e2)) AND is_gen(less_or_equal(e1,e2)) AND
       is_gen(greater(e1,e2)) AND is_gen(greater_or_equal(e1,e2)) AND
       is_gen(equal(e1,e2)) AND is_gen(not_equal(e1,e2)))

AXIOM
{is_gen} FORALL q: Qualification (is_gen(q))

{ Optional_Qual }

  FUNC optional_qual: -> Optional_Qual
  FUNC optional_qual: Qualification -> Optional_Qual

  PRED is_gen: Optional_Qual
  IND  is_gen(optional_qual) ;
       FORALL q: Qualification (is_gen(q) => is_gen(optional_qual(q)))

  AXIOM
  {is_gen} FORALL q: Optional_Qual (is_gen(q))

{ Target }

  FUNC target: Name # Expression -> Target
  FUNC target: Attribute -> Target

  PRED is_gen: Target
  IND  FORALL n: Name, e: Expression (is_gen(e) => is_gen(target(n,e))) ;
```

```
      FORALL a: Attribute (is_gen(a) => is_gen(target(a)))

  AXIOM
  {is_gen} FORALL t: Target (is_gen(t))

{ Target_List }

  FUNC target_list: Target -> Target_List
  FUNC target_list: Target # Target_List -> Target_List

  PRED is_gen: Target_List
  IND  FORALL t: Target (is_gen(t) => is_gen(target_list(t))) ;
       FORALL t: Target, tl: Target_List (
        is_gen(t) AND is_gen(tl) => is_gen(target_list(t,tl)))

  AXIOM
  {is_gen} FORALL tl: Target_List (is_gen(tl))

END;
```

```
LET IS_WF :=

IMPORT INT INTO
IMPORT CHAR INTO
IMPORT NAME INTO
IMPORT FORMAT INTO
IMPORT DICTIONARY INTO
IMPORT SYNTAX INTO
IMPORT SEQ_CHAR INTO


CLASS

{ Item }

  FUNC format: Item -> Format

  AXIOM
  {format1} FORALL i: Int (format(item(i)) = int) ;
  {format2} FORALL s: Seq_Char (format(item(s)) = string)

{ Attribute }

  PRED is_wf: Attribute
  IND  FORALL tv: Name, dn: Name (is_tuple_var(tv) AND
                                  is_domain(range_over(tv),dn) =>
       is_wf(attribute(tv,dn)))

  FUNC format: Attribute -> Format
  IND  FORALL tv: Name, dn: Name (is_tuple_var(tv) AND
                                  is_domain(range_over(tv),dn) =>
       format(attribute(tv,dn)) =
        sel(formats(range_over(tv)), pos(range_over(tv),dn)))

{ Aggre_Target_List }

  PRED is_wf: Aggre_Target_List
  IND  FORALL a: Attribute (is_wf(a) => is_wf(aggre_target_list(a))) ;
       FORALL a: Attribute, atl: Aggre_Target_List (
         is_wf(a) AND is_wf(atl) => is_wf(aggre_target_list(a,atl)))

{ Optional_ATL }

  PRED is_wf: Optional_ATL
  IND  is_wf(optional_atl) ;
       FORALL atl: Aggre_Target_List (is_wf(atl) => is_wf(optional_atl(atl)))

{ Expression }

  PRED is_wf: Expression
  IND  FORALL i: Item (is_wf(expression(i))) ;
       FORALL a: Attribute (is_wf(a) => is_wf(expression(a))) ;
```

```
    FORALL a: Attribute, atl: Optional_ATL, q: Optional_Qual (
     is_wf(a) AND  is_wf(atl) AND is_wf(q) =>
     is_wf(countu(a,atl,q)) AND is_wf(any(a,atl,q))) ;
    FORALL a: Attribute, atl: Optional_ATL, q: Optional_Qual (
     is_wf(a) AND is_wf(atl) AND is_wf(q) AND format(a) = int =>
     is_wf(sumu(a,atl,q)) AND is_wf(avgu(a,atl,q)) AND
     is_wf(max(a,atl,q)) AND is_wf(min(a,atl,q))) ;
    FORALL e: Expression (
     is_wf(e) AND format(e) = int => is_wf(plus(e)) AND is_wf(minus(e))) ;
    FORALL e1: Expression, e2: Expression (
     is_wf(e1) AND is_wf(e2) AND format(e1) = int AND format(e2) = int =>
     is_wf(exponentiation(e1,e2)) AND is_wf(multiplication(e1,e2)) AND
     is_wf(division(e1,e2)) AND is_wf(addition(e1,e2)) AND
     is_wf(subtraction(e1,e2)))

 FUNC format: Expression -> Format
 IND  FORALL i: Item (format(expression(i)) = format(i)) ;
      FORALL a: Attribute (is_wf(a) => format(expression(a)) = format(a)) ;
      FORALL a: Attribute, atl: Optional_ATL, q: Optional_Qual (
       is_wf(a) AND is_wf(atl) AND is_wf(q) =>
       format(countu(a,atl,q)) = int AND format(any(a,atl,q)) = int) ;
      FORALL a: Attribute, atl: Optional_ATL, q: Optional_Qual (
       is_wf(a) AND is_wf(atl) AND is_wf(q) AND format(a) = int =>
       format(sumu(a,atl,q)) = int AND format(avgu(a,atl,q)) = int AND
       format(max(a,atl,q)) = int AND format(min(a,atl,q)) = int) ;
      FORALL e: Expression (is_wf(e) AND format(e) = int =>
       format(plus(e)) = int AND format(minus(e)) = int) ;
      FORALL e1: Expression, e2: Expression (
       is_wf(e1) AND is_wf(e2) AND format(e1) = int AND format(e2) = int =>
       format(exponentiation(e1,e2)) = int AND
       format(multiplication(e1,e2)) = int AND
       format(division(e1,e2)) = int AND format(addition(e1,e2)) = int AND
       format(subtraction(e1,e2)) = int)


{ Qualification }

 PRED is_wf: Qualification
 IND  FORALL q: Qualification (is_wf(q) => is_wf(not_qualification(q))) ;
      FORALL q1: Qualification, q2: Qualification (
       is_wf(q1) AND is_wf(q2) =>
       is_wf(or_qualification(q1,q2)) AND is_wf(and_qualification(q1,q2))) ;
      FORALL q: Qualification (is_wf(q) => is_wf(parenthesised(q))) ;
      FORALL e1: Expression, e2: Expression (
       is_wf(e1) AND is_wf(e2) AND format(e1) = format(e2) =>
       is_wf(less(e1,e2)) AND is_wf(less_or_equal(e1,e2)) AND
       is_wf(greater(e1,e2)) AND is_wf(greater_or_equal(e1,e2)) AND
       is_wf(equal(e1,e2)) AND is_wf(not_equal(e1,e2))
      )


{ Optional_Qual }
```

```
PRED is_wf: Optional_Qual
IND  is_wf(optional_qual) ;
     FORALL q: Qualification (is_wf(q) => is_wf(optional_qual(q)))
```

{ Target }

```
PRED is_wf: Target
IND  FORALL a: Attribute (is_wf(a) => is_wf(target(a))) ;
     FORALL n: Name, e: Expression (is_wf(e) => is_wf(target(n,e)))
```

{ Target_List }

```
PRED is_wf: Target_List
IND  FORALL t: Target (is_wf(t) => is_wf(target_list(t))) ;
     FORALL t: Target, tl: Target_List (is_wf(t) AND is_wf(tl) =>
     is_wf(target_list(t,tl)))
```

END;

```
LET SEQ_ITEM := (APPLY (RENAME SORT Item TO Item,
                               SORT Seq TO Seq_Item IN SEQ)
                 TO SYNTAX);
LET SET_SEQ_ITEM := (APPLY (RENAME SORT Item TO Seq_Item,
                                   SORT Set TO Set_Seq_Item IN SET)
                    TO SEQ_ITEM);

LET CONTENTS :=

IMPORT NAT INTO
IMPORT NAME INTO
IMPORT FORMAT INTO
IMPORT DICTIONARY INTO
IMPORT SYNTAX INTO
IMPORT IS_WF INTO
IMPORT SEQ_ITEM INTO
IMPORT SET_SEQ_ITEM INTO

CLASS

  FUNC relation: Name -> Set_Seq_Item VAR

  AXIOM
  {relation1} FORALL rn: Name ( is_rel_name(rn) <=> relation(rn)! ) ;
  {relation2} FORALL rn: Name (is_rel_name(rn) =>
              FORALL t: Seq_Item (
                 is_in(t, relation(rn)) => len(domains(rn)) = len(t))) ;
  {relation3} FORALL rn: Name (is_rel_name(rn) =>
              FORALL t: Seq_Item (is_in(t, relation(rn)) =>
                FORALL i: Nat (lss(i, len(t)) => format(sel(t, i)) =
                                                 sel(formats(rn), i))))

  PRED pre_store: Name # Set_Seq_Item
  PAR  rn: Name, s: Set_Seq_Item
  DEF  is_rel_name(rn);
       FORALL t: Seq_Item (is_in(t, s) => (len(domains(rn)) = len(t);
        FORALL i: Nat (lss(i, len(t)) => format(sel(t, i)) =
                                         sel(formats(rn), i))))

  PROC store: Name # Set_Seq_Item ->
  MOD  relation

  AXIOM
  {store1} FORALL rn: Name, s: Set_Seq_Item (<store(rn, s)> TRUE) ;
  {store2} FORALL rn: Name, s: Set_Seq_Item (
           pre_store(rn, s) => [store(rn, s)] relation(rn) = s) ;
  {store3} FORALL rn1: Name, rn2: Name, s: Set_Seq_Item (
           pre_store(rn1, s) AND NOT rn1 = rn2
            => [store(rn1, s)] relation(rn2) = (PREV relation(rn2)))

  PROC append: Name # Set_Seq_Item ->
```

MOD relation

AXIOM
{append1} FORALL rn: Name, s: Set_Seq_Item (<append(rn, s)> TRUE) ;
{append2} FORALL rn: Name, s: Set_Seq_Item (
            pre_store(rn, s) => [append(rn, s)]
            relation(rn) = union((PREV relation(rn)), s)) ;
{append3} FORALL rn1: Name, rn2: Name, s: Set_Seq_Item (
            pre_store(rn1, s) AND NOT rn1 = rn2
            => [append(rn1, s)] relation(rn2) = (PREV relation(rn2)))

END;

```
LET LEXICO :=

IMPORT NAT INTO
IMPORT CHAR INTO
IMPORT SEQ_CHAR INTO

CLASS

  FUNC space: -> Char
  { space stands for the character with ordinate 32 in the ASCII table }

  FUNC compress: Seq_Char -> Seq_Char
  PAR  s: Seq_Char
  DEF  ( (len(s) = zero ? ; empty)
       | (gtr(len(s), zero) AND hd(s) = space ? ; compress(tl(s)))
       | (gtr(len(s), zero) AND NOT hd(s) = space ? ; cons(hd(s),
                                                     compress(tl(s))))
       )

  PRED less: Seq_Char # Seq_Char
  IND  FORALL s: Seq_Char, t: Seq_Char (len(s) = zero AND gtr(len(t), zero) =>
        less(s, t)) ;
       FORALL s: Seq_Char, t: Seq_Char (gtr(len(s), zero) AND
                                        gtr(len(t), zero) AND
                                        lss(ord(hd(s)), ord(hd(t))) =>
        less(s, t)) ;
       FORALL s: Seq_Char, t: Seq_Char (
        gtr(len(s), zero) AND gtr(len(t), zero) AND
        ord(hd(s)) = ord(hd(t)) AND less(tl(s), tl(t))
         => less(s, t))

  PRED equal: Seq_Char # Seq_Char
  PAR  s: Seq_Char, t: Seq_Char
  DEF  compress(s) = compress(t)

END;
```

```
LET SET_ITEM := (APPLY (RENAME SORT Item TO Item,
                               SORT Set TO Set_Item IN SET)
                 TO SYNTAX);
LET SET_TARGET_LIST := (APPLY (RENAME SORT Item TO Target_List,
                               SORT Set TO Set_Target_List IN SET)
                       TO SYNTAX);
LET MAP_NAME_SEQ_ITEM := (APPLY
                          (APPLY (RENAME SORT Map TO Map_Name_Seq_Item,
                                  SORT Set1 TO Set_Name,
                                  SORT Set2 TO Set_Seq_Item,
                                  SORT Item1 TO Name,
                                  SORT Item2 TO Seq_Item IN MAP)
                          TO NAME)
                          TO SEQ_ITEM);


LET SEMANTICS :=

IMPORT NAT INTO
IMPORT INT INTO
IMPORT CHAR INTO
IMPORT NAME INTO
IMPORT FORMAT INTO
IMPORT DICTIONARY INTO
IMPORT SYNTAX INTO
IMPORT IS_WF INTO
IMPORT CONTENTS INTO
IMPORT LEXICO INTO
IMPORT SEQ_CHAR INTO
IMPORT SEQ_NAME INTO
IMPORT SET_NAME INTO
IMPORT SEQ_ITEM INTO
IMPORT SET_ITEM INTO
IMPORT SET_TARGET_LIST INTO
IMPORT MAP_NAME_SEQ_ITEM INTO

CLASS

  PRED is_wf: Map_Name_Seq_Item
  PAR  tab: Map_Name_Seq_Item
  DEF  FORALL tv : Name (is_tuple_var(tv) AND is_in(tv, dom(tab)) =>
       len(app(tab, tv)) = len(domains(range_over(tv))))

{ Item }

  FUNC sem_i: Item -> Int
  IND  FORALL i: Int (sem_i(item(i)) = i)

  FUNC sem_s: Item -> Seq_Char
  IND  FORALL s : Seq_Char (sem_s(item(s)) = s)

{ Attribute }
```

```
FUNC free: Attribute -> Set_Name
IND  FORALL tv: Name, dn : Name (is_tuple_var(tv) AND
                              is_domain(range_over(tv),dn) =>
     free(attribute(tv,dn)) = ins(tv, empty))


FUNC sem: Map_Name_Seq_Item # Attribute -> Item
IND  FORALL tab: Map_Name_Seq_Item, tv: Name, dn: Name (
     is_wf(tab) AND is_tuple_var(tv) AND is_domain(range_over(tv),dn) AND
     is_in(tv, dom(tab)) =>
       sem(tab,attribute(tv,dn)) = sel(app(tab, tv), pos(range_over(tv),dn)))



FUNC format: Attribute -> Format
IND  FORALL tv: Name, dn: Name (is_tuple_var(tv) AND
                              is_domain(range_over(tv),dn) =>
     format(attribute(tv,dn)) =
       sel(formats(range_over(tv)), pos(range_over(tv),dn)))

FUNC domain: Attribute -> Name
IND  FORALL tv: Name, dn: Name (is_tuple_var(tv) AND
                              is_domain(range_over(tv),dn) =>
     domain(attribute(tv,dn)) = dn)


{ Aggre_Target_List }

FUNC length: Aggre_Target_List -> Nat
IND  FORALL a: Attribute (is_wf(a) =>
     length(aggre_target_list(a)) = succ(zero)) ;
     FORALL a: Attribute, atl: Aggre_Target_List (is_wf(a) AND is_wf(atl) =>
     length(aggre_target_list(a,atl)) = succ(length(atl)))

FUNC free: Aggre_Target_List -> Set_Name
IND  FORALL a: Attribute (is_wf(a) => free(aggre_target_list(a)) = free(a)) ;
     FORALL a: Attribute, atl: Aggre_Target_List (is_wf(a) AND is_wf(atl) =>
     free(aggre_target_list(a,atl)) = union(free(a), free(atl)))

FUNC sem: Map_Name_Seq_Item # Aggre_Target_List -> Seq_Item
IND  FORALL tab: Map_Name_Seq_Item, a: Attribute (is_wf(a) AND is_wf(tab) =>
     sem(tab,aggre_target_list(a)) = cons(sem(tab,a), empty)) ;
     FORALL tab: Map_Name_Seq_Item, a: Attribute, atl: Aggre_Target_List (
     is_wf(a) AND is_wf(atl) AND is_wf(tab) =>
       sem(tab,aggre_target_list(a,atl)) = cons(sem(tab,a), sem(tab,atl)))

{ Optional_ATL }

FUNC length: Optional_ATL -> Nat
IND  length(optional_atl) = zero ;
     FORALL atl: Aggre_Target_List (is_wf(atl) =>
     length(optional_atl(atl)) = length(atl))
```

```
FUNC free: Optional_ATL -> Set_Name
IND  free(optional_atl) = empty ;
     FORALL atl: Aggre_Target_List (is_wf(atl) =>
     free(optional_atl(atl)) = free(atl))


FUNC sem: Map_Name_Seq_Item # Optional_ATL -> Seq_Item
IND  FORALL tab: Map_Name_Seq_Item (sem(tab,optional_atl) = empty) ;
     FORALL tab: Map_Name_Seq_Item, atl: Aggre_Target_List (is_wf(atl) =>
     sem(tab,optional_atl(atl)) = sem(tab,atl))
```

{ Expression }

```
FUNC free: Expression -> Set_Name
IND  FORALL i: Item (free(expression(i)) = empty) ;
     FORALL a: Attribute (is_wf(a) => free(expression(a)) = free(a)) ;
     FORALL a: Attribute, atl: Optional_ATL, q: Optional_Qual (
      is_wf(a) AND is_wf(atl) AND is_wf(q) =>
      free(countu(a,atl,q)) = free(atl) AND
      free(any(a,atl,q)) = free(atl)) ;
     FORALL a: Attribute, atl: Optional_ATL, q: Optional_Qual (
      is_wf(a) AND is_wf(atl) AND is_wf(q) AND format(a) = int =>
      free(sumu(a,atl,q)) = free(atl) AND
      free(avgu(a,atl,q)) = free(atl) AND
      free(max(a,atl,q)) = free(atl) AND
      free(min(a,atl,q)) = free(atl)) ;
     FORALL e: Expression (
      is_wf(e) AND format(e) = int => free(plus(e)) = free(e) AND
                                      free(minus(e)) = free(e)) ;
     FORALL e1: Expression, e2: Expression (
      is_wf(e1) AND is_wf(e2) AND format(e1) = int AND format(e2) = int =>
      free(exponentiation(e1,e2)) = union(free(e1), free(e2)) AND
      free(multiplication(e1,e2)) = union(free(e1), free(e2)) AND
      free(division(e1,e2)) = union(free(e1), free(e2)) AND
      free(addition(e1,e2)) = union(free(e1), free(e2)) AND
      free(subtraction(e1,e2)) = union(free(e1), free(e2)))
```

{ exponentiation }

```
FUNC exp: Int # Int -> Int
PAR  a: Int, b: Int
DEF  ( (b = zero ? ; succ(zero))
     | (gtr(b, zero) ? ; mul(a, exp(a, pred(b))))
     )
```

{ set operators }

```
FUNC count: Set_Item -> Int
PAR  s: Set_Item
DEF  ( s = empty ? ; zero
     | NOT s = empty ? ; succ(count(rem((SOME i: Item (is_in(i, s))), s)))
     )
```

```
FUNC any: Set_Item -> Int
PAR  s: Set_Item
DEF  ( s = empty ? ; zero
     | NOT s = empty ? ; succ(zero)
     )

PRED intset: Set_Item
PAR  s: Set_Item
DEF  FORALL i: Item (is_in(i, s) => format(i) = int)

FUNC sum: Set_Item -> Int
IND  sum(empty) = zero ;
     FORALL i: Item, s: Set_Item (
      intset(ins(i, s)) AND NOT is_in(i, s) => sum(ins(i, s)) =
                                                 add(sum(s), sem_i(i)))

FUNC avg: Set_Item -> Int
PAR  s: Set_Item
DEF  ( s = empty ? ; zero
     | NOT s = empty ? ; div(sum(s), count(s))
     )

FUNC max: Set_Item -> Int
IND  max(empty) = zero ;
     FORALL s: Set_Item (intset(s) AND NOT s = empty =>
      is_in(item(max(s)), s) AND
       FORALL i: Item (is_in(i, s) => leq(sem_i(i), max(s))))

FUNC min: Set_Item -> Int
IND  min(empty) = zero ;
     FORALL s: Set_Item (intset(s) AND NOT s = empty =>
      is_in(item(min(s)), s) AND
       FORALL i: Item (is_in(i, s) => geq(sem_i(i), min(s))))
```

{ get_set }

```
FUNC get_set: Map_Name_Seq_Item # Attribute #
              Optional_ATL # Optional_Qual -> Set_Item

AXIOM
{get_set1} FORALL tab: Map_Name_Seq_Item, a: Attribute, atl: Optional_ATL,
               q: Optional_Qual (
             is_wf(a) AND is_wf(atl) AND is_wf(q) AND is_wf(tab) <=>
             get_set(tab, a, atl, q)! ) ;
{get_set2} FORALL tab: Map_Name_Seq_Item, atl: Optional_ATL,
               q: Optional_Qual, tv: Name, dn: Name (
             LET a: Attribute; a := attribute(tv, dn) ;
             is_wf(a) AND is_wf(atl) AND is_wf(q) AND is_wf(tab) =>
               get_set(tab, a, atl, q) = SOME si : Set_Item (
               FORALL i : Item (is_in(i, si) <=>
                 EXISTS tb: Map_Name_Seq_Item (
                 is_wf(tb) AND
                 dom(tb) = ins(tv, union(free(atl), free(q))) AND
                 sem(tb, a) = i AND sem(tb, atl) = sem(tab, atl) AND
                 sem(tb,q) AND
                 FORALL tv1: Name (is_in(tv1, dom(tb)) =>
                   is_in(app(tb, tv1), relation(range_over(tv1)))))))))

FUNC sem: Map_Name_Seq_Item # Expression -> Item
IND  FORALL tab: Map_Name_Seq_Item, i: Item (
       sem(tab,expression(i)) = i) ;
     FORALL tab: Map_Name_Seq_Item, a: Attribute (
       is_wf(tab) AND is_wf(a) => sem(tab,expression(a)) = sem(tab,a)) ;
     FORALL tab: Map_Name_Seq_Item, a: Attribute,
            atl: Optional_ATL, q: Optional_Qual (
       is_wf(tab) AND is_wf(a) AND is_wf(atl) AND is_wf(q) =>
         sem(tab,countu(a,atl,q)) = item(count(get_set(tab,a,atl,q))) AND
         sem(tab,any(a,atl,q)) = item(any(get_set(tab,a,atl,q)))) ;
     FORALL tab: Map_Name_Seq_Item, a: Attribute,
            atl: Optional_ATL, q: Optional_Qual (
       is_wf(a) AND is_wf(atl) AND is_wf(q) AND format(a) = int =>
         sem(tab,sumu(a,atl,q)) = item(sum(get_set(tab,a,atl,q))) AND
         sem(tab,avgu(a,atl,q)) = item(avg(get_set(tab,a,atl,q))) AND
         sem(tab,max(a,atl,q)) = item(max(get_set(tab,a,atl,q))) AND
         sem(tab,min(a,atl,q)) = item(min(get_set(tab,a,atl,q)))) ;
     FORALL tab: Map_Name_Seq_Item, e: Expression (
       is_wf(tab) AND is_wf(e) AND format(e) = int =>
         sem(tab,plus(e)) = sem(tab,e) AND
         sem(tab,minus(e)) = item(neg(sem_i(sem(tab,e))))) ;
     FORALL tab: Map_Name_Seq_Item, e1: Expression, e2: Expression (
       is_wf(tab) AND is_wf(e1) AND is_wf(e2) AND format(e1) = int AND
       format(e2) = int AND geq(sem_i(sem(tab,e2)), zero) =>
         sem(tab,exponentiation(e1,e2)) =
         item(exp(sem_i(sem(tab,e1)),sem_i(sem(tab,e2))))) ;
     FORALL tab: Map_Name_Seq_Item, e1: Expression, e2: Expression (
```

```
  is_wf(tab) AND is_wf(e1) AND is_wf(e2) AND
  format(e1) = int AND format(e2) = int =>
   sem(tab,multiplication(e1,e2)) =
    item(mul(sem_i(sem(tab,e1)), sem_i(sem(tab,e2))))) ;
 FORALL tab: Map_Name_Seq_Item, e1: Expression, e2: Expression (
  is_wf(tab) AND is_wf(e1) AND is_wf(e2) AND format(e1) = int AND
  format(e2) = int AND NOT sem_i(sem(tab,e2)) = zero =>
   sem(tab,division(e1,e2)) =
    item(div(sem_i(sem(tab,e1)), sem_i(sem(tab,e2))))) ;
 FORALL tab: Map_Name_Seq_Item, e1: Expression, e2: Expression (
  is_wf(tab) AND is_wf(e1) AND is_wf(e2) AND
  format(e1) = int AND format(e2) = int =>
   sem(tab,addition(e1,e2)) =
    item(add(sem_i(sem(tab,e1)), sem_i(sem(tab,e2)))) AND
   sem(tab,subtraction(e1,e2)) =
    item(sub(sem_i(sem(tab,e1)), sem_i(sem(tab,e2))))))
```

{ Qualification }

```
 FUNC free: Qualification -> Set_Name
 IND  FORALL q: Qualification (is_wf(q) =>
       free(not_qualification(q)) = free(q)) ;
      FORALL q1: Qualification, q2: Qualification (is_wf(q1) AND is_wf(q2) =>
       free(or_qualification(q1,q2)) = union(free(q1), free(q2)) AND
       free(and_qualification(q1,q2)) = union(free(q1), free(q2))) ;
      FORALL q: Qualification (is_wf(q) => free(parenthesised(q)) = free(q)) ;
      FORALL e1: Expression, e2: Expression (
       is_wf(e1) AND is_wf(e2) AND format(e1) = format(e2) =>
        free(less(e1,e2)) = union(free(e1), free(e2)) AND
        free(less_or_equal(e1,e2)) = union(free(e1), free(e2)) AND
        free(greater(e1,e2)) = union(free(e1), free(e2)) AND
        free(greater_or_equal(e1,e2)) = union(free(e1), free(e2)) AND
        free(equal(e1,e2)) = union(free(e1), free(e2)) AND
        free(not_equal(e1,e2)) = union(free(e1), free(e2)))


 PRED sem: Map_Name_Seq_Item # Qualification
 IND  FORALL tab: Map_Name_Seq_Item, q: Qualification (is_wf(q) AND
       is_wf(tab) => sem(tab,not_qualification(q)) <=> NOT sem(tab,q)) ;
      FORALL tab: Map_Name_Seq_Item, q1: Qualification, q2: Qualification (
       is_wf(q1) AND is_wf(q2) AND is_wf(tab) =>
        sem(tab,or_qualification(q1,q2)) <=> (sem(tab,q1) OR sem(tab,q2)) AND
        sem(tab,and_qualification(q1,q2)) <=> (sem(tab,q1) AND sem(tab,q2))) ;
      FORALL tab: Map_Name_Seq_Item, q: Qualification (
       is_wf(q) AND is_wf(tab) => sem(tab,parenthesised(q)) <=> sem(tab,q)) ;
      FORALL tab: Map_Name_Seq_Item, e1: Expression, e2: Expression (
       is_wf(e1) AND is_wf(e2) AND is_wf(tab) AND
       format(e1) = format(e2) AND format(e1) = int =>
        sem(tab,less(e1,e2)) <=> lss(sem_i(sem(tab,e1)),sem_i(sem(tab,e2)))) ;
      FORALL tab: Map_Name_Seq_Item, e1: Expression, e2: Expression (
       is_wf(e1) AND is_wf(e2) AND is_wf(tab) AND
       format(e1) = format(e2) AND format(e1) = string =>
```

```
  sem(tab,less(e1,e2)) <=> less(sem_s(sem(tab,e1)),sem_s(sem(tab,e2)))) ;
FORALL tab: Map_Name_Seq_Item, e1: Expression, e2: Expression (
 is_wf(e1) AND is_wf(e2) AND is_wf(tab) AND
 format(e1) = format(e2) AND format(e1) = int =>
 sem(tab,less_or_equal(e1,e2)) <=>
  leq(sem_i(sem(tab,e1)),sem_i(sem(tab,e2))));
FORALL tab: Map_Name_Seq_Item, e1: Expression, e2: Expression (
 is_wf(e1) AND is_wf(e2) AND is_wf(tab) AND
 format(e1) = format(e2) AND format(e1) = string =>
 sem(tab,less_or_equal(e1,e2)) <=>
  NOT less(sem_s(sem(tab,e2)),sem_s(sem(tab,e1)))) ;
FORALL tab: Map_Name_Seq_Item, e1: Expression, e2: Expression (
 is_wf(e1) AND is_wf(e2) AND is_wf(tab) AND
 format(e1) = format(e2) AND format(e1) = int =>
 sem(tab,greater(e1,e2)) <=>
  gtr(sem_i(sem(tab,e1)),sem_i(sem(tab,e2)))) ;
FORALL tab: Map_Name_Seq_Item, e1: Expression, e2: Expression (
 is_wf(e1) AND is_wf(e2) AND is_wf(tab) AND
 format(e1) = format(e2) AND format(e1) = string =>
 sem(tab,greater(e1,e2)) <=>
  less(sem_s(sem(tab,e2)),sem_s(sem(tab,e1)))) ;
FORALL tab: Map_Name_Seq_Item, e1: Expression, e2: Expression (
 is_wf(e1) AND is_wf(e2) AND is_wf(tab) AND
 format(e1) = format(e2) AND format(e1) = int =>
 sem(tab,greater_or_equal(e1,e2)) <=>
  geq(sem_i(sem(tab,e1)),sem_i(sem(tab,e2))) ;
FORALL tab: Map_Name_Seq_Item, e1: Expression, e2: Expression (
 is_wf(e1) AND is_wf(e2) AND is_wf(tab) AND
 format(e1) = format(e2) AND format(e1) = string =>
 sem(tab,greater_or_equal(e1,e2)) <=>
  NOT less(sem_s(sem(tab,e1)),sem_s(sem(tab,e2)))) ;
FORALL tab: Map_Name_Seq_Item, e1: Expression, e2: Expression (
 is_wf(e1) AND is_wf(e2) AND is_wf(tab) AND
 format(e1) = format(e2) AND format(e1) = int =>
 sem(tab,equal(e1,e2)) <=> sem_i(sem(tab,e1)) = sem_i(sem(tab,e2))) ;
FORALL tab: Map_Name_Seq_Item, e1: Expression, e2: Expression (
 is_wf(e1) AND is_wf(e2) AND is_wf(tab) AND
 format(e1) = format(e2) AND format(e1) = string =>
 sem(tab,equal(e1,e2)) <=>
  equal(sem_s(sem(tab,e1)),sem_s(sem(tab,e2)))) ;
FORALL tab: Map_Name_Seq_Item, e1: Expression, e2: Expression (
 is_wf(e1) AND is_wf(e2) AND is_wf(tab) AND
 format(e1) = format(e2) AND format(e1) = int =>
 sem(tab,not_equal(e1,e2)) <=>
  NOT sem_i(sem(tab,e1)) = sem_i(sem(tab,e2))) ;
FORALL tab: Map_Name_Seq_Item, e1: Expression, e2: Expression (
 is_wf(e1) AND is_wf(e2) AND is_wf(tab) AND
 format(e1) = format(e2) AND format(e1) = string =>
 sem(tab,not_equal(e1,e2)) <=>
  NOT equal(sem_s(sem(tab,e1)),sem_s(sem(tab,e2))))
```

{ Optional_Qual }

```
FUNC free: Optional_Qual -> Set_Name
IND  free(optional_qual) = empty ;
     FORALL q: Qualification (is_wf(q) => free(optional_qual(q)) = free(q))

PRED sem: Map_Name_Seq_Item # Optional_Qual
IND  FORALL tab: Map_Name_Seq_Item (sem(tab,optional_qual)) ;
     FORALL tab: Map_Name_Seq_Item, q: Qualification (
      is_wf(tab) AND is_wf(q) => sem(tab,optional_qual(q)) => sem(tab,q))
```

{ Target }

```
FUNC sem: Map_Name_Seq_Item # Target -> Item
IND  FORALL tab: Map_Name_Seq_Item, dn: Name, e: Expression (
      is_wf(e) AND is_wf(tab) => sem(tab,target(dn,e)) = sem(tab,e)) ;
     FORALL tab: Map_Name_Seq_Item, a: Attribute (
      is_wf(a) AND is_wf(tab) => sem(tab,target(a)) = sem(tab,a))

FUNC free: Target -> Set_Name
IND  FORALL dn: Name, e: Expression (is_wf(e) =>
     free(target(dn,e)) = free(e)) ;
     FORALL a: Attribute (is_wf(a) => free(target(a)) = free(a))

FUNC domain: Target -> Name
IND  FORALL dn: Name, e: Expression (is_wf(e) => domain(target(dn,e)) = dn) ;
     FORALL a: Attribute (is_wf(a) => domain(target(a)) = domain(a))

FUNC format: Target -> Format
IND  FORALL dn: Name, e: Expression (is_wf(e) =>
      format(target(dn,e)) = format(e)) ;
     FORALL a: Attribute (is_wf(a) => format(target(a)) = format(a))
```

{ Target_List }

```
FUNC sem: Map_Name_Seq_Item # Target_List -> Seq_Item
IND  FORALL tab: Map_Name_Seq_Item, t: Target (is_wf(t) AND is_wf(tab) =>
      sem(tab,target_list(t)) = cons(sem(tab,t), empty)) ;
     FORALL tab: Map_Name_Seq_Item, t: Target, tl: Target_List (
      is_wf(t) AND is_wf(tl) AND is_wf(tab) =>
      sem(tab,target_list(t,tl)) = cons(sem(tab,t), sem(tab,tl)))

FUNC length: Target_List -> Nat
IND  FORALL t: Target (is_wf(t) => length(target_list(t)) = succ(zero)) ;
     FORALL t: Target, tl: Target_List (is_wf(t) AND is_wf(tl) =>
      length(target_list(t,tl)) = succ(length(tl)))

FUNC free: Target_List -> Set_Name
IND  FORALL t: Target (is_wf(t) => free(target_list(t)) = free(t)) ;
     FORALL t: Target, tl: Target_List (is_wf(t) AND is_wf(tl) =>
      free(target_list(t,tl)) = union(free(t), free(tl)))
```

```
FUNC formats: Target_List -> Seq_Format
IND  FORALL t: Target (is_wf(t) =>
       formats(target_list(t)) = cons(format(t), empty)) ;
     FORALL t: Target, tl: Target_List (is_wf(t) AND is_wf(tl) =>
       formats(target_list(t,tl)) = cons(format(t), formats(tl)))


FUNC domains: Target_List -> Seq_Name
IND  FORALL t: Target (is_wf(t) =>
       domains(target_list(t)) = cons(domain(t), empty)) ;
     FORALL t: Target, tl: Target_List (is_wf(t) AND is_wf(tl) =>
       domains(target_list(t,tl)) = cons(domain(t), domains(tl)))


FUNC domain_name_list: Target_List -> Domain_Name_List
IND  FORALL t: Target (is_wf(t) =>
       domain_name_list(target_list(t)) =
        domain_name_list(domain(t),format(t))) ;
     FORALL t: Target, tl: Target_List (is_wf(t) AND is_wf(tl) =>
       domain_name_list(target_list(t,tl)) =
        domain_name_list(domain(t),format(t),domain_name_list(tl)))


END;
```

```
LET INGRES_SPEC :=

IMPORT NAME INTO
IMPORT FORMAT INTO
IMPORT DICTIONARY INTO
IMPORT SYNTAX INTO
IMPORT IS_WF INTO
IMPORT CONTENTS INTO
IMPORT SEMANTICS INTO
IMPORT SEQ_ITEM INTO
IMPORT MAP_NAME_SEQ_ITEM INTO
IMPORT SET_SEQ_ITEM INTO

CLASS

  PROC create: Name # Domain_Name_List ->
  PAR  rn: Name, dnl: Domain_Name_List
  DEF  NOT is_rel_name(rn) AND is_unique(sem_d(dnl)) ? ;
       create_d(rn,dnl); store(rn,empty)

  FUNC retrieve: Target_List # Optional_Qual -> Set_Seq_Item
  PAR  tl: Target_List, q: Optional_Qual
  DEF  is_wf(tl) AND is_wf(q) ? ;
       SOME ssi: Set_Seq_Item (
         FORALL u : Seq_Item (
           is_in(u, ssi) <=> len(u) = length(tl) AND
           EXISTS tab: Map_Name_Seq_Item (
             is_wf(tab) AND dom(tab) = union(free(tl), free(q)) AND
             sem(tab, tl) = u AND sem(tab, q) AND
             FORALL tv: Name (is_in(tv, dom(tab)) =>
               is_in(app(tab, tv), relation(range_over(tv)))))))

  PROC retrieve_into: Name # Target_List # Optional_Qual ->
  PAR  rn: Name, tl: Target_List, q: Optional_Qual
  DEF  is_wf(tl) AND is_wf(q) AND NOT is_rel_name(rn) AND
       is_unique(domains(tl)) ? ;
       create_d(rn,domain_name_list(tl)); store(rn,retrieve(tl,q))

  PROC append_to: Name # Target_List # Optional_Qual ->
  PAR  rn: Name, tl: Target_List, q: Optional_Qual
  DEF  is_rel_name(rn) AND is_wf(tl) AND is_wf(q) AND
       domains(rn) = domains(tl) AND formats(rn) = formats(tl) ? ;
       append(rn,retrieve(tl,q))

END ;

COMP INGRES : INGRES_SPEC
SYSTEM INGRES
```

The logic MPL$_\omega$

C.P.J. Koymans, G.R. Renardel de Lavalette[*]

Department of Philosophy, University of Utrecht
Heidelberglaan 2, 3584 CS Utrecht, The Netherlands

Abstract

MPL$_\omega$ is many-sorted partial logic with countably infinite conjunctions and disjunctions. We show in this paper that MPL$_\omega$ satisfies the interpolation property and allows the explicit definition of inductively defined predicates and functions. By these properties, MPL$_\omega$ is useful as a semantic framework for the design language COLD.

1 Introduction

MPL$_\omega$ is many-sorted partial logic with countably infinite conjunctions and disjunctions. The main reason for developing MPL$_\omega$ lies in its usefulness as a semantic framework for the design language COLD; in that respect it is the successor of MPL, defined in [3]. The relation between MPL and MPL$_\omega$ is discussed in 1.2.

MPL$_\omega$ serves as a target language for the interpretation of the design language COLD. The main properties of MPL$_\omega$ which guarantee the soundness of this interpretation are:

- inductively defined predicates and functions can be expressed explicitly in MPL$_\omega$ (see 4); this is needed to interpret repetition expressions and inductive definitions of predicates and functions;
- the presence of an interpolation theorem (3.3), needed for appropriate properties of the implementation relation and module composition.

The formal design language COLD (Common Object-oriented Language for Design) is developed at Philips Research Laboratories Eindhoven, underlying the first version of the software development method which is constructed in the ESPRIT project 432 (METEOR: An Integrated Formal Approach to Industrial Software Development).

---

[*]The research for this paper was supported by ESPRIT project METEOR (nr. 432) through Philips Research Laboratories Eindhoven.

1.1   Contents of MPL$_\omega$

In this section we compare MPL$_\omega$ with the standard language of mathematical logic: classical first-order logic with equality. MPL$_\omega$ has the following additional features:

1. *Countably infinite conjunctions.* If $A_0, A_1, A_2, \ldots$ are formulae, then we can form the formula $\bigwedge_n A_n$ with the intended meaning A_0 *and* A_1 *and* A_2 *and* .... Not in the language itself, but defined as an abbreviation we also have the infinite disjunction $\bigvee_n A_n$, denoting A_0 *or* A_1 *or* A_2 *or* .... It is to be noted that no restriction is imposed on the way the A_n are given. See also 1.2.

2. *Sorts.* A signature contains not only function and predicate symbols, but also sort symbols. Their intended meaning is: domains of objects to which the terms of that sort refer. For every sort T there is an equality predicate $=_T$.

3. *Definedness predicates.* For every sort T there is an definedness predicate $\downarrow_T$. The intended meaning of $t\downarrow_T$ (t a term of sort T) is: t refers to a defined object of type T.

4. *Partial functions.* There are no axiom schemata like $t\downarrow_S \to ft\downarrow_T$ in MPL$_\omega$: this means that the functions are (in general) not total, but partial. On the other hand, all functions and predicates are strict, i.e. $ft\downarrow_T \to t\downarrow_S$, $Pt \to t\downarrow_S$.

5. *Descriptions.* If A is a formula, then $\iota x : T(A)$ is a term of sort T with the intended meaning *the unique object x of sort T which satisfies A*. If there is no such unique x, we say that $\iota x : T(A)$ is not defined., i.e. $\neg(\iota x : T(A)\downarrow_T)$.

1.2   Relation with other systems

None of the additional ingredients of MPL$_\omega$, as listed in 1.1, is new: they all occur more or less frequently in the literature. We mention a few relevant references.

MPL$_\omega$ is related to L$_{\omega_1\omega}$, which is an instance of L$_{\alpha\beta}$ (α and β ordinals), the language with conjunctions and disjunctions of length less than α and homogeneous quantifier sequences of length less than β. These languages were introduced by Karp in [4]. Of these languages L$_{\omega_1\omega}$ has attracted most attention, and many results (completeness, cut elimination, interpolation, Scott's Isomorphism Theorem) are known: see e.g. [5].

Interesting sublanguages L$_A$ of L$_{\omega_1\omega}$ are obtained when the use of $\bigwedge$ and $\bigvee$ is restricted to those countable sets of formulae which are element of the *admissible* set A. An admissible set A can be considered as a model for the weak set theory KPU (Kripke-Platek with Urelements): this means that A is a transitive set with some closure properties (e.g. Δ_0-separation, Σ-reflection). The simplest example of such an A is V$_\omega$, the set of all hereditarily finite sets of the cumulative hierarchy. L$_A$ (A admissible and countable) inherits many of the properties of L$_{\omega_1\omega}$ (e.g. completeness, interpolation, explicit definition of inductively defined predicates), and has moreover several new ones (countable language, Barwise Compactness Theorem). For more information, see [1]. It looks promising to investigate a variant of MPL$_\omega$ based on L$_A$ instead of L$_{\omega_1\omega}$, e.g. with A based on ω_1^{CK} (the Church-Kleene ordinal, i.e. the first nonrecursive ordinal).

Logics with an existence predicate E have been studied extensively by Scott [9], [10]. He also considered descriptions in that context.

The immediate predecessor of MPL_ω is MPL, introduced in [3]. In contrast with MPL_ω, MPL lacks infinite formulae, but contains predicate variables and a minimal fixpoint operator μ which generate inductive definitions.

1.3 Outline of the rest of this paper

In section 2 we define the language, the proof system (a sequent calculus with an infinitary rule) and the semantics of MPL_ω. In section 3 we establish some properties of MPL_ω : cut elimination, elimination of descriptions, completeness and interpolation. Section 4 is about inductive definitions and their definability in MPL_ω.

2 Definition of MPL_ω

2.1 Definition of the language

2.1.1 Signature

We assume the existence of three disjoint sets SORT, FUNC and PRED of sort, function and predicate symbols, respectively. A signature Σ is a countable (possibly infinite) subset of $\text{SORT} \cup \text{FUNC} \cup \text{PRED}$.

2.1.2 Sorts

$S(\Sigma) = \Sigma \cap \text{SORT}$ is the set of sort symbols of Σ. $T, T_0, T_1, \ldots$ range over the elements of $S(\Sigma)$.

2.1.3 Functions

$F(\Sigma) = \Sigma \cap \text{FUNC}$ is the set of function symbols of Σ. $f, g, h, \ldots$ range over the elements of $F(\Sigma)$. To every $f \in F(\Sigma)$ a sequence $T_1, \ldots, T_{n+1} \in S(\Sigma)$ $(n \geq 0)$ is assigned. We call $T_1 \times \ldots \times T_n \to T_{n+1}$ the *type* of f, and write $f : T_1 \times \ldots \times T_n \to T_{n+1}$.

2.1.4 Predicates

$P(\Sigma) = \Sigma \cap \text{PRED}$ is the set of predicate symbols of Σ. $P, Q, R, \ldots$ range over the elements of $P(\Sigma)$. To every $P \in P(\Sigma)$ a sequence $T_1, \ldots, T_n \in S(\Sigma)$ $(n \geq 0)$ is assigned. We call $T_1 \times \ldots \times T_n$ the *type* of P, and write $P : T_1 \times \ldots \times T_n$.

2.1.5 Standard predicates and constants

Let Σ be a signature. The set $SP(\Sigma)$ of *standard predicate symbols of* Σ contains:

for every $T \in S(\Sigma)$ the predicate symbol $=_T : T \times T$, called *equality*;

for every $T \in S(\Sigma)$ the predicate symbol $\downarrow_T : T$, called *definedness*.

The set $SC(\Sigma)$ of *standard constant symbols* of Σ contains:

for every $T \in S(\Sigma)$ the constant symbol $\uparrow_T : T$, called *undefined*.

To enhance readability, we use $=, \downarrow, \uparrow$ without superscripts if this causes no ambiguity.

2.1.6 Variables

The language of $\mathrm{MPL}_\omega(\Sigma)$, MPL_ω with signature Σ, contains:

for every $T \in S(\Sigma)$, the variables $x, y, z, x_1, x_2, \ldots$ of sort T.

For reasons of readability, we do not use sub- or superscripts to indicate the sort of a variable. The sort of bound variables will always be clear, by our definition of the quantifiers $\forall$ and $\exists$ and the descriptor ι. When necessary, the sort of free variables will be indicated explicitly.

2.1.7 Terms and formulae

The terms and formulae of $\mathrm{MPL}_\omega(\Sigma)$ are inductively defined as follows.

1. Variables of sort T are terms of sort T, for any $T \in S(\Sigma)$.

2. If $f \in \mathrm{F}(\Sigma) \cup \mathrm{SC}(\Sigma)$, $f : T_1 \times \ldots \times T_n \to T_{n+1}$, t_i is a term of sort T_i. $(i = 1, \ldots, n)$, then $f(t_1, \ldots, t_n)$ is a term of sort T_{n+1}.

3. If A is a formula, $T \in S(\Sigma)$ and x is an variable of sort T, then $\iota x : T(A)$ is a term of sort T.

4. $\top$ and $\bot$ are formulae.

5. If $P \in \mathrm{P}(\Sigma) \cup \mathrm{SP}(\Sigma)$, $P : T_1 \times \ldots \times T_n$, t_i is a term of sort T_i $(i = 1, \ldots, n)$, then $P(t_1, \ldots, t_n)$ is a formula.

6. If A is a formula, then $\neg A$ is a formula.

7. If $\langle A_n \rangle_{n < \omega} = \langle A_0, A_1, \ldots \rangle$ are formulae, then $\bigwedge_n A_n$ is a formula.

8. If A is a formula and x a variable of sort $T \in S(\Sigma)$, then $\forall x : T(A)$ is a formula.

2.1.8 Abbreviations, conventions

We use the following abbreviations:

$$
\begin{array}{lll}
A \wedge B & := & \bigwedge_n C_n, \text{ where } C_0 = A, C_n = B \text{ if } 0 < n < \omega \\
A \vee B & := & \neg(\neg A \wedge \neg B) \\
A \to B & := & \neg A \vee B \\
A \leftrightarrow B & := & (A \to B) \wedge (B \to A) \\
\exists x : T(A) & := & \neg \forall x : T(\neg A) \\
\exists! x : T(A) & := & \exists x : T \forall y : T(A[x := y] \leftrightarrow x = y) \\
\bigvee_n A_n & := & \neg \bigwedge_n \neg A_n \\
t \downarrow_T & := & \downarrow_T (t) \\
s =_T t & := & =_T (s, t) \\
s \simeq_T t & := & (s \downarrow_T \vee t \downarrow_T) \to s =_T t \\
\underline{\forall} x : T(A) & := & \forall x : T(A) \wedge A[x := \uparrow_T] \\
\underline{\exists} x : T(A) & := & \exists x : T(A) \vee A[x := \uparrow_T]
\end{array}
$$

We drop the sort indication : T behind $\forall x, \exists y, \iota z$ etc. when it is clear from the context which sort is meant.

2.2 Definition of the proof system

2.2.1 Sequents

We write $\Gamma, \Delta, \Gamma_1, \ldots$ for arbitrary countable (possibly finite or empty) sets of formulae. For $\Gamma \cup \Delta$ we write Γ, Δ ; Γ, A stands for $\Gamma \cup \{A\}$.

A *sequent* is an expression of the form $\Gamma \vdash \Delta$, with the intended meaning: $\bigwedge \Gamma$ entails $\bigvee \Delta$.

2.2.2 Sequent calculus

The proof system of $\mathrm{MPL}_\omega(\Sigma)$ is a sequent calculus, defined as follows.

Logical axioms

(taut) $\Gamma, A \vdash \Delta, A$

($\top$) $\Gamma \vdash \Delta, \top$

($\bot$) $\Gamma, \bot \vdash \Delta$

Non-logical axioms

(AX) $\Gamma \vdash \Delta, \mathrm{AX}$

where AX is some instance of one of the following axioms:

$(T{\uparrow}\mathrm{AX})$	$\neg(\uparrow_T\downarrow)$	for every $T \in S(\Sigma)$

$(T{=}\mathrm{AX})$ $\forall x : T(x = x) \wedge \forall xyz : T(x = y \wedge x = z \rightarrow y = z)$ for every $T \in S(\Sigma)$

$(T{\downarrow}\mathrm{AX})$ $\underline{\forall} x : T \underline{\forall} y : T(x = y \rightarrow x\downarrow \wedge y\downarrow)$ for every $T \in S(\Sigma)$

$(f{=}\mathrm{AX})$ $\underline{\forall} x_1 \ldots \underline{\forall} x_n \underline{\forall} y_1 \ldots \underline{\forall} y_n(x_1 = y_1 \wedge \ldots \wedge x_n = y_n \wedge f(x_1, \ldots, x_n)\downarrow \rightarrow$
$f(x_1, \ldots, x_n) = f(y_1, \ldots, y_n))$ for every $f \in F(\Sigma)$

$(P{=}\mathrm{AX})$ $\underline{\forall} x_1 \ldots \underline{\forall} x_n \underline{\forall} y_1 \ldots \underline{\forall} y_n(x_1 = y_1 \wedge \ldots \wedge x_n = y_n \wedge P(x_1, \ldots, x_n) \rightarrow$
$P(y_1, \ldots, y_n))$ for every $P \in P(\Sigma)$

$(f{\downarrow}\mathrm{AX})$ $\underline{\forall} x_1 \ldots \underline{\forall} x_n(f(x_1, \ldots, x_n)\downarrow \rightarrow x_1\downarrow \wedge \ldots \wedge x_n\downarrow)$ for every $f \in F(\Sigma)$

$(P{\downarrow}\mathrm{AX})$ $\underline{\forall} x_1 \ldots \underline{\forall} x_n(P(x_1, \ldots, x_n) \rightarrow x_1\downarrow \wedge \ldots \wedge x_n\downarrow)$ for every $P \in P(\Sigma)$

$(\iota\mathrm{AX})$ $\forall y : T(y = \iota x : T(A) \leftrightarrow \forall x : T(A \leftrightarrow x = y))$ (y not free in A, $T \in S(\Sigma)$)

Rules

$(\neg L)$ $\dfrac{\Gamma \vdash \Delta, A}{\Gamma, \neg A \vdash \Delta}$ $(\neg R)$ $\dfrac{\Gamma, A \vdash \Delta}{\Gamma \vdash \Delta, \neg A}$

$$(\wedge L) \quad \frac{\Gamma, A_i \vdash \Delta}{\Gamma, \bigwedge_n A_n \vdash \Delta} \text{ for all } i \qquad\qquad (\wedge R) \quad \frac{\langle \Gamma \vdash \Delta, A_n \rangle_{n<\omega}}{\Gamma \vdash \Delta, \bigwedge_n A_n}$$

$$(\forall L) \quad \frac{\Gamma, A[x := t] \vdash \Delta \quad \Gamma \vdash t\!\downarrow_T, \Delta}{\Gamma, \forall x : T(A) \vdash \Delta} \qquad (\forall R) \quad \frac{\Gamma, x\!\downarrow_T \vdash \Delta, A}{\Gamma \vdash \Delta, \forall x : T(A)}$$
$$(x \text{ not free in } \Gamma, \Delta)$$

$$(\text{cut}) \quad \frac{\Gamma \vdash \Delta, A \quad \Gamma', A \vdash \Delta'}{\Gamma, \Gamma' \vdash \Delta, \Delta'}$$

2.2.3 Derivations

A *derivation* (or *proof*) is an upward growing (possibly infinite branching) tree with branches of finite length, with its nodes labeled with sequents in such a way that the labels of top nodes are axioms, and the label of any other node is obtained from the labels of its immediate successors by applying a rule.

A sequent $\Gamma \vdash \Delta$ is called *derivable* (or provable) if there exists a derivation with its downmost node labeled by $\Gamma \vdash \Delta$. Notation: $\mathrm{MPL}_\omega : \Gamma \vdash \Delta$.

We say that $\Gamma \vdash A$ is derivable, or that A is derivable from Γ, if $\Gamma \vdash \{A\}$ is derivable; if moreover Γ is empty, we call A derivable.

2.2.4 Derived rules

Without proof (which can be easily obtained), we state the following *derived rules*, i.e. rules satisfying: if the premise(s) is (are) derivable, then so is the conclusion.

$$(\wedge L') \quad \frac{\Gamma, \Gamma' \vdash \Delta}{\Gamma, \bigwedge \Gamma'' \vdash \Delta} \qquad\qquad (\text{weak}) \quad \frac{\Gamma \vdash \Delta}{\Gamma, \Gamma' \vdash \Delta, \Delta'}$$
$$(\Gamma' \subseteq \Gamma'')$$

$$(\wedge L) \quad \frac{\Gamma, A, B \vdash \Delta}{\Gamma, A \wedge B \vdash \Delta} \qquad\qquad (\wedge R) \quad \frac{\Gamma \vdash \Delta, A \quad \Gamma \vdash \Delta, B}{\Gamma \vdash \Delta, A \wedge B}$$

$$(\vee L) \quad \frac{\Gamma, A \vdash \Delta \quad \Gamma, B \vdash \Delta}{\Gamma, A \vee B \vdash \Delta} \qquad\qquad (\vee R) \quad \frac{\Gamma \vdash \Delta, A, B}{\Gamma \vdash \Delta, A \vee B}$$

$$(\to L) \quad \frac{\Gamma \vdash \Delta, A \quad \Gamma, B \vdash \Delta}{\Gamma, A \to B \vdash \Delta} \qquad\qquad (\to R) \quad \frac{\Gamma, A \vdash \Delta, B}{\Gamma \vdash \Delta, A \to B}$$

$$(\mathsf{V} L) \quad \frac{\langle \Gamma, A_n \vdash \Delta \rangle_{n<\omega}}{\Gamma, \mathsf{V}_n A_n \vdash \Delta} \qquad\qquad (\mathsf{V} R) \quad \frac{\Gamma \vdash \Delta, A_n}{\Gamma \vdash \Delta, \mathsf{V}_n A_n} \text{ for all } n$$

$$(\exists L) \quad \frac{\Gamma, x\!\downarrow_T, A \vdash \Delta}{\Gamma, \exists x : T(A) \vdash \Delta} \qquad\qquad (\exists R) \quad \frac{\Gamma \vdash \Delta, t\!\downarrow_T \quad \Gamma \vdash \Delta, A[x := t]}{\Gamma \vdash \Delta, \exists x : T(A)}$$
$$(x \text{ not free in } \Gamma, \Delta)$$

$$(\underline{\forall} L) \quad \frac{\Gamma, A[x := t] \vdash \Delta}{\Gamma, \underline{\forall} x : T(A) \vdash \Delta} \qquad\qquad (\underline{\forall} R) \quad \frac{\Gamma \vdash \Delta, A}{\Gamma \vdash \Delta, \underline{\forall} x : T(A)}$$
$$(x \text{ not free in } \Gamma, \Delta)$$

$$(\underline{\exists} L) \quad \frac{\Gamma, A \vdash \Delta}{\Gamma, \underline{\exists} x : T(A) \vdash \Delta} \qquad\qquad (\underline{\exists} R) \quad \frac{\Gamma \vdash \Delta, A[x := t]}{\Gamma \vdash \Delta, \underline{\exists} x : T(A)}$$
$$(x \text{ not free in } \Gamma, \Delta)$$

2.3 Structures for MPL$_\omega$

2.3.1 Structures

A structure **A** with signature Σ consists of:

(i) for every $T \in S(\Sigma)$ a non-empty set $T^{\mathbf{A}}$ called *domain*;
(ii) for every $f \in F(\Sigma)$, $f : T_1 \times \ldots \times T_n \to T_{n+1}$ a map $f^{\mathbf{A}} : T_1^{\mathbf{A}} \times \ldots \times T_n^{\mathbf{A}} \to T_{n+1}^{\mathbf{A}}$ (which is total);
(iii) for every $P \in P(\Sigma)$, $P : T_1 \times \ldots \times T_n$ a set $P^{\mathbf{A}} \subseteq T_1^{\mathbf{A}} \times \ldots \times T_n^{\mathbf{A}}$;
(iv) for every $T \in S(\Sigma)$ the sets $\mathrm{Eq}_T^{\mathbf{A}} \subseteq T^{\mathbf{A}} \times T^{\mathbf{A}}$ and $\mathrm{Def}_T^{\mathbf{A}} \subseteq T^{\mathbf{A}}$;
(v) for every $T \in S(\Sigma)$ the element $\uparrow_T^{\mathbf{A}} \in T^{\mathbf{A}}$.

We shall omit the superscript **A** if this causes no confusion.

2.3.2 Standard structures

The structure **A** with signature Σ is called a *standard* structure iff:

(i) for every $T \in S(\Sigma)$, $\mathrm{Eq}_T^{\mathbf{A}}$ is the actual equality on $\mathrm{Def}_T^{\mathbf{A}}$, i.e.

$$\langle d, e \rangle \in \mathrm{Eq}_T^{\mathbf{A}} \Leftrightarrow d = e \ \text{ and } \ d, e \in \mathrm{Def}_T^{\mathbf{A}};$$

(ii) for every $T \in S(\Sigma)$, $T^{\mathbf{A}} - \mathrm{Def}_T^{\mathbf{A}} = \{\uparrow_T^{\mathbf{A}}\}$;
(iii) for every $f \in F(\Sigma)$, $f^{\mathbf{A}} : T_1^{\mathbf{A}} \times \ldots \times T_n^{\mathbf{A}} \to T_{n+1}^{\mathbf{A}}$ is strict, i.e.

$$d_i = \uparrow \text{ for some } i \leq n \ \Rightarrow \ f^{\mathbf{A}}(d_1, \ldots, d_n) = \uparrow;$$

(iv) for every $P \in P(\Sigma)$, $P^{\mathbf{A}} : T_1^{\mathbf{A}} \times \ldots \times T_n^{\mathbf{A}}$ is strict, i.e.

$$d_i = \uparrow \text{ for some } i \leq n \ \Rightarrow \ \langle d_1, \ldots, d_n \rangle \notin P^{\mathbf{A}}.$$

2.3.3 Interpretation of MPL$_\omega$

First we introduce assignments, a prerequisite for the definition of the interpretation of MPL$_\omega$.

Let **A** be a structure with signature Σ: an *assignment* in **A** is a function a which maps variables of sort $T \in S(\Sigma)$ onto elements of $T^{\mathbf{A}}$. If a is such an assignment, x a variable of sort $T \in S(\Sigma)$ and $d \in T^{\mathbf{A}}$, then $a(x \to d)$ is the assignment a' which agrees with a except that $a'(x) = d$.

Now the interpretation of terms and formulae of MPL$_\omega(\Sigma)$ in some structure **A** with signature Σ, modulo the assignment a, is defined as follows. We write $t^{\mathbf{A}}[a]$ for the interpretation of a term t and $\mathbf{A} \models A[a]$ for the interpretation of a formula A, both modulo the assignment a.

$$x^{\mathbf{A}}[a] := a(x)$$
$$f(t_1, \ldots, t_n)^{\mathbf{A}}[a] := f^{\mathbf{A}}(t_1[a], \ldots, t_n[a])$$
$$\uparrow_T^{\mathbf{A}}[a] := \uparrow_T^{\mathbf{A}}$$

$\iota x : T(A)^{\mathbf{A}}[a] := $ *the unique* $d \in \mathrm{Def}_T^{\mathbf{A}}$ *such that* $\mathbf{A} \models A[a(x \to d)]$ *if this* d
exists, otherwise $\uparrow$.

not $\mathbf{A} \models \bot[a]$

$\mathbf{A} \models \top[a]$

$\mathbf{A} \models (t_1 = t_2)[a]$ *iff* $\langle t_1^{\mathbf{A}}[a], t_2^{\mathbf{A}}[a] \rangle \in \mathrm{Eq}_T^{\mathbf{A}}$

$\mathbf{A} \models (t{\downarrow}_T)[a]$ *iff* $t^{\mathbf{A}}[a] \in \mathrm{Def}_T^{\mathbf{A}}$

$\mathbf{A} \models P(t_1, \ldots, t_n)[a]$ *iff* $\langle t_1^{\mathbf{A}}[a], \ldots, t_n^{\mathbf{A}}[a] \rangle \in P^{\mathbf{A}}$

$\mathbf{A} \models \neg A[a]$ *iff not* $\mathbf{A} \models A[a]$

$\mathbf{A} \models \bigwedge_n A_n[a]$ *iff* $\mathbf{A} \models A_n[a]$ *for all* $n < \omega$

$\mathbf{A} \models \forall x : T(A)[a]$ *iff for all* $d \in \mathrm{Def}_T^{\mathbf{A}}$ $\mathbf{A} \models A[a(x \to d)]$

If the formula A of MPL_ω is closed (i.e. contains no free variables), then $\mathbf{A} \models A[a]$ does not depend on a, and we write $\mathbf{A} \models A$ (A is *valid* in $\mathbf{A}$).

$\models A$ (A is valid) means: A is valid in all structures $\mathbf{A}$ with signature Σ.

If Γ, Δ are countable sets of formulae, then $\mathbf{A} : \Gamma \models \Delta$ stands for $\mathbf{A} \models \bigwedge \Gamma \to \bigvee \Delta$, and $\Gamma \models \Delta$ for $\models \bigwedge \Gamma \to \bigvee \Delta$.

Theorem 2.3.4 (Soundness)

(i) If $\Gamma \vdash \Delta$ is derivable in $\mathrm{MPL}_\omega(\Sigma)$ *without using the non-logical axioms* and $\mathbf{A}$ is a structure with signature Σ, then $\mathbf{A} : \Gamma \models \Delta$.

(ii) If $\Gamma \vdash \Delta$ is derivable in $\mathrm{MPL}_\omega(\Sigma)$ and $\mathbf{A}$ is a *standard* structure with signature Σ, then $\mathbf{A} : \Gamma \models \Delta$.

Proof.

(i) Transfinite induction over the length of a derivation of $\Gamma \vdash \Delta$. For $(\forall L)$, the substitution property

$$\mathbf{A} \models A[x := t][a] \Leftrightarrow \mathbf{A} \models A[a(x \to t^{\mathbf{A}}[a])] \quad (x \text{ not in } t)$$

is needed, which is proved with induction over the complexity of A.

(ii) Extending the proof of (i). $\mathbf{A} \models (T{\uparrow}\mathrm{AX})$ follows from the definition of $\uparrow_T^{\mathbf{A}}$ and $\mathrm{Def}_T^{\mathbf{A}}$; $\mathbf{A} \models (T = \mathrm{AX}), (T{\downarrow}\mathrm{AX}), (f = \mathrm{AX}), (P = \mathrm{AX})$ follows from the fact that $=_T$ is interpreted by the actual equality on $T^{\mathbf{A}}$ (2.3.2 (i)); $\mathbf{A} \models (f{\downarrow}\mathrm{AX}), (P{\downarrow}\mathrm{AX})$ is a direct consequence of 2.3.2 (iii,iv); $\mathbf{A} \models (\iota\mathrm{AX})$ follows from the definition of $\iota x : T(A)^{\mathbf{A}}[a]$.

$\square$

Lemma 2.3.5 (From structures to standard structures)

Let $\mathbf{A}$ be a structure with signature Σ, satisfying

$\mathbf{A} \models$ all instances of nonlogical axioms of MPL_ω, so **A** is a model for MPL_ω. Then there is a standard structure $\mathbf{A}^*$, also with signature Σ, which is *elementary equivalent* with **A**, i.e.

$$\mathbf{A} \models A \;\Leftrightarrow\; \mathbf{A}^* \models A$$

for all *closed* formulae A of $MPL_\omega(\Sigma)$.

Proof. Define, for every sort T of Σ, the relation $\approx_T$ on $T^\mathbf{A}$ by

$$d \approx_T e \;:=\; (d,e) \in \mathrm{Eq}_T^\mathbf{A} \;\; or \;\; d, e \in T^\mathbf{A} - \mathrm{Def}_T^\mathbf{A}.$$

We write $\approx$ for $\approx_T$ if it is clear or unimportant which T is meant. By $\mathbf{A} \models (T{=}AX)$, $(T{\downarrow}AX)$, the $\approx_T$ are equivalence relations; by $\mathbf{A} \models (f{=}AX)$, $(P{=}AX)$, $(f{\downarrow}AX)$, $(P{\downarrow}AX)$, they are congruences modulo the functions and predicates in Σ, i.e.

$$d_1 \approx e_1 \wedge \ldots \wedge d_n \approx e_n \rightarrow f^\mathbf{A}(d_1,\ldots,d_n) \approx f^\mathbf{A}(e_1,\ldots,e_n),$$
$$d_1 \approx e_1 \wedge \ldots \wedge d_n \approx e_n \wedge P^\mathbf{A}(d_1,\ldots,d_n) \rightarrow P^\mathbf{A}(e_1,\ldots,e_n)$$

for all $f \in F(\Sigma)$, all $P \in P(\Sigma)$. Now define the domains T^* of $\mathbf{A}^*$ by

$$T^* := T^\mathbf{A} / \approx_T$$

(so T^* is the set of equivalence classes of $T^\mathbf{A}$ modulo $\approx_T$), and define the projection $^* : T^\mathbf{A} \rightarrow T^*$ by

$$d^* := \{e \mid e \approx d\}.$$

Since the $f \in F(\Sigma)$ and the $P \in P(\Sigma)$ preserve $\approx$, there are functions f^* and predicates P^* on the newly defined domains T^* which satisfy

$$f^*(d_1^*,\ldots,d_n^*) = (f(d_1,\ldots,d_n))^*,$$
$$\langle d_1^*,\ldots,d_n^* \rangle \in P^* \;\text{iff}\; \langle d_1,\ldots,d_n \rangle \in P.$$

Thus the structure $\mathbf{A}^*$ is obtained. One easily proves that $\mathbf{A}^*$ is a standard structure (use $\mathbf{A} \models (T{\uparrow}AX)$ to see that $T^\mathbf{A} - \mathrm{Def}_T^\mathbf{A}$ is nonempty), in which

$$(t^\mathbf{A}[a])^* = t^{\mathbf{A}^*}[^*{\circ}a],$$
$$\mathbf{A} \models A[a] \;\Leftrightarrow\; \mathbf{A}^* \models A[^*{\circ}a]$$

hold, for all terms and formulae of $MPL_\omega(\Sigma)$; from this the lemma follows. $\qquad\square$

3 Properties of MPL_ω

3.1 Cut elimination

In this section we consider some subsystems of MPL_ω and prove, for the weakest of these, that the cut rule is a *derived* rule.

3.1.1 The subsystems $MPL1_\omega$, $MPL2_\omega$ and $MPL3_\omega$

Three auxiliary subsystems of MPL_ω are introduced:

$$MPL1_\omega := MPL_\omega - (\iota AX)$$

$$MPL2_\omega := MPL1_\omega - \text{all nonlogical axioms}$$

$$MPL3_\omega := MPL2_\omega - (\text{cut})$$

The language of $MPL1\text{-}3_\omega$ is that of MPL_ω without descriptions.

We write $X : \Gamma \vdash \Delta$ for: the sequent $\Gamma \vdash \Delta$ is derivable in the system X.

Let

$NLAX :=$ the conjunction of all instances of $(T{\uparrow}AX)$, $(T{=}AX)$, $(T{\downarrow}AX)$, $(f{=}AX)$, $(f{\downarrow}AX)$, $(P{=}AX)$, $(P{\downarrow}AX)$,

so $NLAX$ is the (countable) conjunction of all instances of nonlogical axioms except (ιAX) (which has uncountably many instances, by the way).

3.1.2 Elimination of descriptions

To eliminate ι we introduce the mapping *, defined on terms and formulae. We assume that every occurrence of ι has a unique index. ε is an auxiliary mapping.

$\varepsilon(t) = T$ if ι does not occur in t

$\varepsilon(\iota x : T(A)) = A[x := y_i]^*$ if i is the index of the indicated ι.

$\varepsilon(f(t_1, \ldots, t_n)) = \varepsilon(t_1) \wedge \ldots \wedge \varepsilon(t_n)$

$t^* = t$ if ι does not occur in t

$(\iota x : T(A))^* = y_i$ if i is the index of ι

$(f(t_1, \ldots, t_n))^* = f(t_1^*, \ldots, t_n^*)$

$P(t_1, \ldots, t_n)^* = \exists! \vec{y}(\varepsilon(t_1) \wedge \ldots \wedge \varepsilon(t_n)) \wedge \exists \vec{y}(\varepsilon(t_1) \wedge \ldots \wedge \varepsilon(t_n) \wedge P(t_1^*, \ldots, t_n^*))$ where $\vec{y}$ is the (possibly empty) sequence of y_i's occurring in $\varepsilon(t_1), \ldots, \varepsilon(t_n)$

* commutes with $\neg, \wedge$ and $\forall$.

3.1.3 Some reductions

The following hold:

(1) $MPL_\omega \vdash A \leftrightarrow A^*$

(2) $MPL_\omega : \Gamma \vdash \Delta \Leftrightarrow MPL1_\omega : \Gamma^* \vdash \Delta^*$

(3) $MPL1_\omega : \Gamma \vdash \Delta \Leftrightarrow MPL2_\omega : \Gamma, NLAX \vdash \Delta$

(4) $MPL2_\omega : \Gamma \vdash \Delta \Leftrightarrow MPL3_\omega : \Gamma \vdash \Delta$

(1) and (2) are proved with induction over the complexity of A and with induction over the length of the derivation of MPL_ω: $\Gamma \vdash \Delta$, respectively. We refer to [7] where a similar proof for the finitary case is worked out in greater detail.

(3) follows directly from the definition of NLAX.

3.1.4 Cut elimination for MPL3$_\omega$

Proving (4) comes down to showing that (cut) is a derived rule in MPL3$_\omega$. As usual, this is proved with primary induction over the complexity of the cut formula and secondary induction over the size of the derivations of the premises of the cut rule. As both formula complexity and size of derivations are infinite, the induction is transfinite, but countable. For details of the inductive structure of the proof, we refer to [2] and [11], where similar proofs for related systems are worked out. Essential for the primary induction are the following transformations of derivations (the cut formulae are printed boldface), in which an application of (cut) is replaced by one or more applications of (cut) with either lower complexity of the cut formula, or the same cut formula but a shorter derivation above it.

$$
\cfrac{
  \cfrac{\begin{array}{c}\Pi\\ \Gamma, A \vdash \Delta, \neg A\end{array}}{\Gamma \vdash \Delta, \neg\mathbf{A}}
  \qquad
  \cfrac{\begin{array}{c}\Pi'\\ \Gamma', \neg A \vdash \Delta', A\end{array}}{\Gamma', \neg\mathbf{A} \vdash \Delta'}
}{\Gamma, \Gamma' \vdash \Delta, \Delta'}
\qquad \text{becomes}
$$

$$
\cfrac{
  \cfrac{
    \cfrac{\begin{array}{c}\Pi\\ \Gamma, A \vdash \Delta, \neg A\end{array}}{\Gamma \vdash \Delta, \neg\mathbf{A}}
    \qquad
    \begin{array}{c}\Pi'\\ \Gamma', \neg A \vdash \Delta', A\end{array}
  }{\Gamma, \Gamma' \vdash \Delta, \Delta', \mathbf{A}}
  \qquad
  \cfrac{
    \begin{array}{c}\Pi\\ \Gamma, A \vdash \Delta, \neg A\end{array}
    \qquad
    \cfrac{\begin{array}{c}\Pi'\\ \Gamma', \neg A \vdash \Delta', A\end{array}}{\Gamma', \neg\mathbf{A} \vdash \Delta}
  }{\Gamma, \Gamma', \mathbf{A} \vdash \Delta, \Delta'}
}{\Gamma, \Gamma' \vdash \Delta, \Delta'}
$$

If $\neg A$ does *not* occur in the right-hand side of the premise of the instance of $(\neg R)$, then the right-hand instance of (cut) with cut formula $\neg A$ is to be omitted, the conclusion being replaced by its left premise. Analogously if $\neg A$ does not occur in the left-hand side of the premise of the instance of $(\neg L)$.

$$
\cfrac{
  \cfrac{\begin{array}{c}\Pi_i\\ \langle \Gamma \vdash \Delta, \bigwedge_n A_n, A_i \rangle_{i<\omega}\end{array}}{\Gamma \vdash \Delta, \bigwedge_n A_n}
  \qquad
  \cfrac{\begin{array}{c}\Pi'\\ \Gamma', \bigwedge_n A_n, A_k \vdash \Delta'\end{array}}{\Gamma', \bigwedge_n A_n \vdash \Delta'}
}{\Gamma, \Gamma' \vdash \Delta, \Delta'}
\qquad \text{becomes}
$$

$$
\cfrac{
  \cfrac{
    \cfrac{\begin{array}{c}\Pi_k\\ \Gamma \vdash \Delta, \bigwedge_n A_n, A_k\end{array}}{}
    \qquad
    \cfrac{\begin{array}{c}\Pi'\\ \Gamma', \bigwedge_n A_n, A_k \vdash \Delta'\end{array}}{\Gamma', \bigwedge_n A_n \vdash \Delta'}
  }{\Gamma, \Gamma' \vdash \Delta, \Delta', \mathbf{A}_k}
  \qquad
  \cfrac{
    \cfrac{\begin{array}{c}\Pi_i\\ \langle \Gamma \vdash \Delta, \bigwedge_n A_n, A_i \rangle_{i<\omega}\end{array}}{\Gamma \vdash \Delta, \bigwedge_n A_n}
    \qquad
    \begin{array}{c}\Pi'\\ \Gamma', \bigwedge_n A_n, A_k \vdash \Delta'\end{array}
  }{\Gamma, \Gamma', \mathbf{A}_k \vdash \Delta, \Delta'}
}{\Gamma, \Gamma' \vdash \Delta, \Delta}
$$

Similar remarks as above apply.

$$\frac{\Pi_x}{\Gamma, x\!\downarrow_T \,\vdash\, \Delta, \forall x : T(A), A}{\Gamma \vdash \Delta, \forall x{:}T(A)} \qquad \frac{\Pi'}{\Gamma', \forall x : T(A), A[x := t] \vdash \Delta'} \qquad \frac{\Pi''}{\Gamma', \forall x : T(A) \vdash t\!\downarrow_T, \Delta'}{\Gamma', \forall x{:}T(A) \vdash \Delta'}$$

$$\Gamma, \Gamma' \vdash \Delta, \Delta'$$

becomes (in abbreviated form, dropping $\Gamma, \Gamma', \Delta, \Delta'$ and sort indications)

$$\frac{\dfrac{\Pi_x}{x\!\downarrow \,\vdash\, \forall xA, A}{\vdash \forall \mathbf{x}\mathbf{A}} \quad \Pi'' \quad \dfrac{}{\forall \mathbf{x}\mathbf{A} \vdash t\!\downarrow}}{\vdash t\!\downarrow} \quad \dfrac{\Pi_t}{t\!\downarrow \,\vdash\, \forall \mathbf{x}\mathbf{A}, At} \qquad \dfrac{\dfrac{\Pi'}{\forall xA, At \vdash} \quad \dfrac{\Pi''}{\forall xA \vdash t\!\downarrow}}{\forall \mathbf{x}\mathbf{A} \vdash} \quad \dfrac{\dfrac{\Pi_x}{x\!\downarrow \,\vdash\, \forall xA, A}{\vdash \forall \mathbf{x}\mathbf{A}} \quad \dfrac{\Pi'}{\forall xA, At \vdash}}{At \vdash}$$

$$\frac{\qquad \qquad \vdash t\!\downarrow \qquad \qquad \dfrac{\qquad}{t\!\downarrow \,\vdash\, At} \qquad \qquad \qquad \dfrac{\qquad}{At \vdash}}{\vdash}$$

Similar remarks as above can be made. □

3.2 Completeness

Structures and standard structures were defined in 2.3, and there it was also shown that the interpretation of $MPL3_\omega$ resp. MPL_ω in them is sound. Here we show the following completeness results:

(5) $MPL3_\omega(\Sigma) : \Gamma \vdash \Delta \Leftrightarrow \mathbf{A} : \Gamma \models \Delta$ for all structures $\mathbf{A}$ with signature Σ;

(6) $MPL_\omega(\Sigma) : \Gamma \vdash \Delta \Leftrightarrow \mathbf{A} : \Gamma \models \Delta$ for all standard structures $\mathbf{A}$ with signature Σ.

3.2.1 Semantic tableaux

The following proof uses semantic tableaux and is inspired by Problem 22.21 in [12], p. 210 sqq. Let some sequent $\Gamma_0 \vdash \Delta_0$ in the language of $MPL3_\omega$ with signature Σ be given. We attempt to construct a derivation for $\Gamma_0 \vdash \Delta_0$; if this fails, the construction will yield a countermodel for $\Gamma_0 \vdash \Delta_0$, i.e. a structure $\mathbf{A}$ with $\mathbf{A} \models \bigwedge \Gamma_0$ and $\mathbf{A} \models \neg(\bigvee \Delta)$.

Define

$\mathbf{T} = \mathbf{T}(\Sigma, \Gamma_0, \Delta_0) :=$ the collection of terms obtained from the functions in Σ, the free variables occurring in $\Gamma_0 \cup \Delta_0$ and ω many fresh variables of type T, for all $T \in S(\Sigma)$;

$\mathbf{S} = \mathbf{S}(\Sigma, \Gamma_0, \Delta_0) :=$ the smallest collection of formulae containing $\Gamma_0 \cup \Delta_0$ and closed under taking subformulae and under $\forall x : T(A) \in \mathbf{S} \Rightarrow A[x := t] \in \mathbf{S}$ for all terms of type T in $\mathbf{T}$.

It is clear that $\mathbf{S}$ is countable: let $\{S_0, S_1, S_2, \dots\}$ be an enumeration of $\mathbf{S}$ in which every element occurs infinitely often, so we have

$$\forall S \in \mathbf{S} \forall m < \omega \exists n > m(S = S_n).$$

We set out to construct a tree labeled with sequents, in $\leq \omega$ many steps.

Step 0: start with $\Gamma_0 \vdash \Delta_0$.

Step $n + 1$: let $\Gamma \vdash \Delta$ be any topmost sequent in the tree constructed after step n. If $\Gamma \cap \Delta \neq \emptyset$, $\top \in \Gamma$ or $\bot \in \Delta$ we do nothing; otherwise we construct a countable number (at least one) of sequents $\langle \Gamma_i' \vdash \Delta_i' \rangle_i$ as immediate predecessors of $\Gamma \vdash \Delta$. We distinguish four cases, depending on the form of S_n.

(i) S_n is prime: $\Gamma' := \Gamma, \Delta' := \Delta$.

(ii) $S_n = \neg A$: if $S_n \in \Gamma$ then put

$$\Gamma_1' := \Gamma \text{ and } \Delta_1' := \Delta \cup \{A\};$$

if $S_n \in \Delta$ then put

$$\Gamma_1' := \Gamma \cup \{A\} \text{ and } \Delta_1' := \Delta;$$

otherwise $\Gamma' := \Gamma, \Delta' := \Delta$.

(iii) $S_n = \bigwedge_m A_m$: if $S_n \in \Gamma$ then put

$$\Gamma_1' := \Gamma \cup \{A_0, \ldots, A_n\} \text{ and } \Delta_1' := \Delta;$$

if $S_n \in \Delta$ then put

$$\Gamma_i' := \Gamma \text{ and } \Delta_i' := \Delta \cup \{A_i\}, \text{ for } i < \omega;$$

otherwise $\Gamma' := \Gamma, \Delta' := \Delta$.

(iv) $S_n = \forall x : T(A)$: if $S_n \in \Gamma$ then put

$$\Gamma_i' := \Gamma \cup \{A[x := t_j] \mid j \in J_i\} \text{ and } \Delta_i' := \Delta \cup \{t_j \downarrow_T \mid j \notin J_i, j \leq n\}, \text{ for}$$
$i \leq 2^n$, where $t_1, \ldots, t_n$ are the first n terms of type T in $\mathbf{T}$, and $\{J_i \mid i \leq 2^n\}$ is an enumeration of the subsets of $\{1, \ldots, n\}$;

if $S_n \in \Delta$ then put

$$\Gamma_1' := \Gamma \cup \{y \downarrow_T\} \text{ and}$$
$$\Delta_1' := \Delta \cup \{A[x := y]\}, \text{ where } y \text{ is a fresh variable of type } T;$$

otherwise $\Gamma' := \Gamma, \Delta' := \Delta$.

Let $\Gamma \vdash \Delta$ be a sequent in the tree, with immediate predecessors $\langle \Gamma_i \vdash \Delta_i \rangle_{i \in I}$ ($I = \emptyset$ not excluded). It follows from the definition of the construction process that

$$\Gamma \vdash \Delta \text{ is derivable from } \Gamma_i \vdash \Delta_i (i \in I) \text{ without using the cut rule.}$$

So if all branches in the tree are finite, then all sequents in the tree are derivable and we see that $\Gamma_0 \vdash \Delta_0$ is derivable.

If not all branches are finite, then there is a infinite branch $\langle \Gamma_i \vdash \Delta_i \rangle_{i < \omega}$. We shall construct a structure in which all sequents $\Gamma_i \vdash \Delta_i$ are refuted. Put

$$\Gamma := \bigcup\{\Gamma_i \mid i < \omega\}, \Delta := \bigcup\{\Delta_i \mid i < \omega\},$$

then $\Gamma \cap \Delta = \emptyset$, for if $A \in \Gamma \cap \Delta$, then $A \in \Gamma_i \cap \Delta_i$ for some i, which contradicts the fact that the branch is infinite. Define the structure $\mathbf{A}$ of signature Σ by

$\mathbf{A} := \langle \mathbf{T}, f^{\mathbf{A}}, \ldots, P^{\mathbf{A}}, \ldots \rangle$, where

$f^{\mathbf{A}}(t_1, \ldots, t_n) := f(t_1, \ldots, t_n)$ for all $f \in \mathrm{F}(\Sigma)$, $t_1, \ldots, t_n \in \mathbf{T}$

$P^{\mathbf{A}}(t_1, \ldots, t_n)$ iff $P(t_1, \ldots, t_n) \in \Gamma$, for all $t_1, \ldots, t_n \in \mathbf{T}$.

We prove $\mathbf{A} \models \bigwedge \Gamma$, $\mathbf{A} \models \neg(\bigvee \Delta)$ by showing

(7) $A \in \Gamma_i \Rightarrow \mathbf{A} \models A$

(8) $A \in \Delta_i \Rightarrow \mathbf{A} \not\models A$

for all $i < \omega$, with induction over the complexity of A.

$A = P(t_1, \ldots, t_n)$: now (7), (8) follow from the definition of $\mathbf{A}$ and from $\Gamma \cap \Delta = \emptyset$.

$A = \neg B$: if $A \in \Gamma_i$ then $B \in \Delta_j$ for some j, so with induction hypothesis (8) $\mathbf{A} \not\models B$, hence $\mathbf{A} \models A$. Analogously if $A \in \Delta_i$.

$A = \bigwedge_n B_n$: if $A \in \Gamma_i$ then, by the definition of $\langle S_n \rangle_n$ and Γ', we have $\forall j \exists k (B_j \in \Gamma_k)$, so with induction hypothesis (7) $\forall j (\mathbf{A} \models B_j)$, hence $\mathbf{A} \models A$.
If $A \in \Delta_i$ then $\exists jk(B_j \in \Delta_k)$, so with induction hypothesis (8) $\mathbf{A} \not\models B_j$, hence $\mathbf{A} \not\models A$.

$A = \forall x : T(B)$: if $A \in \Gamma_i$, then we must show $\mathbf{A} \models \forall x : T(B)$, i.e. $\forall t \in \mathbf{T}(t\downarrow_T \in \Gamma \Rightarrow \mathbf{A} \models B[x := t])$. So we assume $t \in \mathbf{T}, t\downarrow_T \in \Gamma$. Then $t\downarrow_T \notin \Delta$, and by the definition of Γ' and Δ' we have $B[x := t] \in \Gamma_j$ for some j, so now $\mathbf{A} \models B[x := t]$ by induction hypothesis (7).
If $A \in \Delta_i$, then there are j, k with $y_j \downarrow_T \in \Gamma_k$ and $B[x := y_j] \in \Delta_k$, so by induction hypothesis (7) and (8) we get $\mathbf{A} \models y_j \downarrow_T$, $\mathbf{A} \not\models B[x := y_j]$, so $\mathbf{A} \not\models A$.
This completes the proof of the first completeness result (5).

3.2.2 Completeness for MPL_ω

Now we prove (6) of 3.2 by reducing it to (5). The $\Rightarrow$ part was proved in 2.3.4 (ii); for $\Leftarrow$ we argue as follows.
Assume $\mathrm{MPL}_\omega(\Sigma) : \Gamma \not\vdash \Delta$, then (by (2), (3), (4)) $\mathrm{MPL3}_\omega(\Sigma) : \Gamma^*, \mathrm{AX} \not\vdash \Delta^*$. By (5), there is a Σ-structure $\mathbf{A}$ with

$$\mathbf{A} \models \bigwedge \Gamma^*, \mathbf{A} \models \mathrm{NLAX}, \mathbf{A} \not\models \bigvee \Delta^*.$$

Now lemma 2.3.5 gives us a *standard* structure $\mathbf{A}^*$ with $\mathbf{A}^* \models \bigwedge \Gamma^*$, $\mathbf{A}^* \not\models \bigvee \Delta^*$, hence (using (1) and soundness) $\mathbf{A}^* \models \bigwedge \Gamma$, $\mathbf{A}^* \not\models \bigvee \Delta$, which completes the proof of (6).

3.3 Interpolation

Let $\mathrm{MPL}_\omega : A \vdash B$. We want to find an *interpolant* for this sequent, i.e. a formula I with:

$\mathrm{MPL}_\omega : A \vdash I$,
$\mathrm{MPL}_\omega : I \vdash B$,
$\mathrm{par}(I) \subset \mathrm{par}(A) \cap \mathrm{par}(B)$,

where par(A), the collection of parameters of A, is defined by

$$
\begin{aligned}
\text{par}(x) &:= \{x, T\} \quad (T \text{ the sort of } x) \\
\text{par}(f(t_1, \ldots, t_n)) &:= \{f, T\} \cup \text{par}(t_1) \cup \ldots \cup \text{par}(t_n) \quad (T \text{ the sort of } f(t_1, \ldots, t_n)) \\
\text{par}(\uparrow_T) &:= \{T\} \\
\text{par}(\iota x : T(A)) &:= (\text{par}(A) \cup \{T\}) - \{x\}
\end{aligned}
$$

$$
\begin{aligned}
\text{par}(\top) &:= \emptyset \\
\text{par}(\bot) &:= \emptyset \\
\text{par}(P(t_1, \ldots, t_n)) &:= \{P\} \cup \text{par}(t_1) \cup \ldots \cup \text{par}(t_n) \\
\text{par}(s = t) &:= \text{par}(s) \cup \text{par}(t) \\
\text{par}(t\downarrow) &:= \text{par}(t) \\
\text{par}(\neg A) &:= \text{par}(A) \\
\text{par}(\bigwedge_n A_n) &:= \bigcup \{\text{par}(A_n) \mid n < \omega\} \\
\text{par}(\forall x : T(A)) &:= (\text{par}(A) \cup \{T\}) - \{x\}
\end{aligned}
$$

We state some properties of par:

Lemma 3.3.1

(i) If $P \in \text{par}(A), P : T_1 \times \ldots \times T_n$, then $\{T_1, \ldots, T_n\} \subset \text{par}(A)$;

(ii) $\text{par}(T{\uparrow}\text{AX}) = \text{par}(T{=}\text{AX}) = \text{par}(T{\downarrow}\text{AX}) = \{T\}$;

(iii) if $f : T_1 \times \ldots \times T_n \to T_{n+1}$, then $\text{par}(f{=}\text{AX}) = \text{par}(f{\downarrow}\text{AX}) = \{f, T_1, \ldots, T_{n+1}\}$;

(iv) if $P : T_1 \times \ldots \times T_n$, then $\text{par}(P{=}\text{AX}) = \text{par}(P{\downarrow}\text{AX}) = \{P, T_1, \ldots, T_n\}$.

Proof. Straightforward. $\qquad\qquad\square$

3.3.2 Interpolation in MPL3$_\omega$ without function symbols

We first restrict ourselves to MPL3$_\omega(\Sigma)$ with Σ a signature *without function symbols*, so all terms (especially those in instances of $(\forall L)$) are variables, and prove:

If $F(\Sigma) = \emptyset$ and MPL3$_\omega(\Sigma)$: $A \vdash B$, then there is an interpolant for $A \vdash B$.

The corresponding theorem for the related language $L_{\omega_1\omega}$ was first proved by Lopez-Escobar in [6]. Here we give a proof-theoretical proof, in the style of Schütte's proof of the interpolation theorem for intuitionistic first-order logic [8].

Proof. In this proof, we skip MPL3$_\omega(\Sigma)$ in front of derivable sequents. Assume $F(\Sigma) = \emptyset$. The following stronger statement shall be proved:

(∗) if $\Gamma_1, \Gamma_2 \vdash \Delta_1, \Delta_2$, then there is a formula I with:

(i) $\Gamma_1 \vdash \Delta_1, I$;

(ii) $I, \Gamma_2 \vdash \Delta_2$;

(iii) $\text{par}(I) \subset \text{par}(\Gamma_1, \Delta_1) \cap \text{par}(\Gamma_2, \Delta_2)$.

From this the lemma follows: take $\Gamma_1 = \{A\}$, $\Gamma_2 = \Delta_1 = \emptyset$, $\Delta_2 = \{B\}$.

(∗) is proved with induction over the length of a derivation in MPL3$_\omega$ of $\Gamma_1, \Gamma_2 \vdash \Delta_1, \Delta_2$; such a derivation contains only logical axioms and no applications of the cut rule.

Using the shorthand notation

$$\Gamma_1 \vdash \Delta_1[I]\Gamma_2 \vdash \Delta_2 := \Gamma_1 \vdash \Delta_1, I \ \ and \ \ I, \Gamma_2 \vdash \Delta_2,$$

the method to obtain the interpolant can be rendered as follows.

(itaut1) $\Gamma_1, A \vdash \Delta_1, A[\bot]\Gamma_2 \vdash \Delta_2$

(itaut2) $\Gamma_1, A \vdash \Delta_1[A]\Gamma_2 \vdash \Delta_2, A$

(itaut3) $\Gamma_1 \vdash \Delta_1, A[\neg A]\Gamma_2, A \vdash \Delta_2$

(itaut4) $\Gamma_1 \vdash \Delta_1[\top]\Gamma_2, A \vdash \Delta_2, A$

(i$\top$1) $\quad \Gamma_1 \vdash \Delta_1, \top[\bot]\Gamma_2 \vdash \Delta_2$

(i$\top$2) $\quad \Gamma_1 \vdash \Delta_1[\top]\Gamma_2 \vdash \Delta_2, \top$

(i$\bot$1) $\quad \Gamma_1, \bot \vdash \Delta_1[\bot]\Gamma_2 \vdash \Delta_2$

(i$\bot$2) $\quad \Gamma_1 \vdash \Delta_1[\top]\Gamma_2, \bot \vdash \Delta_2$

(i$\neg$L1) $\dfrac{\Gamma_1 \vdash \Delta_1, A[I]\Gamma_2 \vdash \Delta_2}{\Gamma_1, \neg A \vdash \Delta_1[I]\Gamma_2 \vdash \Delta_2}$ $\qquad$ (i$\neg$L2) $\dfrac{\Gamma_1 \vdash \Delta_1[I]\Gamma_2 \vdash \Delta_2, A}{\Gamma_1 \vdash \Delta_1[I]\Gamma_2, \neg A \vdash \Delta_2}$

(i$\neg$R1) $\dfrac{\Gamma_1, A \vdash \Delta_1[I]\Gamma_2 \vdash \Delta_2}{\Gamma_1 \vdash \Delta_1, \neg A[I]\Gamma_2 \vdash \Delta_2}$ $\qquad$ (i$\neg$R2) $\dfrac{\Gamma_1 \vdash \Delta_1[I]\Gamma_2, A \vdash \Delta_2}{\Gamma_1 \vdash \Delta_1[I]\Gamma_2 \vdash \Delta_2, \neg A}$

(i$\wedge$L1) $\dfrac{\Gamma_1, A_i \vdash \Delta_1[I]\Gamma_2 \vdash \Delta_2}{\Gamma_1, \bigwedge_n A_n \vdash \Delta_1[I]\Gamma_2 \vdash \Delta_2}$ for all i $\quad$ (i$\wedge$L2) $\dfrac{\Gamma_1 \vdash \Delta_1[I]\Gamma_2, A_i \vdash \Delta_2}{\Gamma_1 \vdash \Delta_1[I]\Gamma_2, \bigwedge_n A_n \vdash \Delta_2}$ for all i

(i$\wedge$R1) $\dfrac{\langle \Gamma_1 \vdash \Delta_1, A_n[I_n]\Gamma_2 \vdash \Delta_2 \rangle_{n<\omega}}{\Gamma_1 \vdash \Delta_1, \bigwedge_n A_n[\bigvee_n I_n]\Gamma_2 \vdash \Delta_2}$ $\quad$ (i$\wedge$R2) $\dfrac{\langle \Gamma_1 \vdash \Delta_1[I_n]\Gamma_2 \vdash \Delta_2, A_n \rangle_{n<\omega}}{\Gamma_1 \vdash \Delta_1[\bigwedge_n I_n]\Gamma_2 \vdash \Delta_2, \bigwedge_n A_n}$

(i$\forall$L1) $\dfrac{\Gamma_2 \vdash \Delta_2[I_1]\Gamma_1 \vdash \Delta_1, y\downarrow_T \qquad \Gamma_1, A[x := y] \vdash \Delta_1[I_2]\Gamma_2 \vdash \Delta_2}{\Gamma_1, \forall x : T(A) \vdash \Delta_1[\forall y : T(I_1 \rightarrow I_2)]\Gamma_2 \vdash \Delta_2}$ $\quad$ (y not free in Γ_1, A, Δ_1)

(i$\forall$L2) $\dfrac{\Gamma_2 \vdash \Delta_2[I_1]\Gamma_1 \vdash \Delta_1, y\downarrow_T \qquad \Gamma_1, A[x := y] \vdash \Delta_1[I_2]\Gamma_2 \vdash \Delta_2}{\Gamma_1, \forall x : T(A) \vdash \Delta_1[I_1 \rightarrow I_2]\Gamma_2 \vdash \Delta_2}$ $\quad$ (y free in Γ_1, A, Δ_1)

(i$\forall$L3) $\dfrac{\Gamma_1 \vdash \Delta_1[I_1]\Gamma_2 \vdash \Delta_2, y\downarrow_T \qquad \Gamma_1 \vdash \Delta_1[I_2]\Gamma_2, A[x := y] \vdash \Delta_2}{\Gamma_1 \vdash \Delta_1[\exists y : T(I_1 \wedge I_2)]\Gamma_2, \forall x : T(A) \vdash \Delta_2}$ $\quad$ (y not free in Γ_2, A, Δ_2)

(i$\forall$L4) $\dfrac{\Gamma_1 \vdash \Delta_1[I_1]\Gamma_2 \vdash \Delta_2, y\downarrow_T \qquad \Gamma_1 \vdash \Delta_1[I_2]\Gamma_2, A[x := y] \vdash \Delta_2}{\Gamma_1 \vdash \Delta_1[I_1 \wedge I_2]\Gamma_2, \forall x : T(A) \vdash \Delta_2}$ $\quad$ (y free in Γ_2, A, Δ_2)

(i$\forall$R1) $\dfrac{\Gamma_1, x\downarrow_T \vdash \Delta_1, A[I]\Gamma_2 \vdash \Delta_2}{\Gamma_1 \vdash \Delta_1, \forall x : T(A)[I]\Gamma_2 \vdash \Delta_2}$ $\quad$ (x not free in $\Gamma_1, \Delta_1, \Gamma_2, \Delta_2$)

(i$\forall$R2) $\dfrac{\Gamma_1 \vdash \Delta_1[I]\Gamma_2, x\downarrow_T \vdash \Delta_2, A}{\Gamma_1 \vdash \Delta_1[I]\Gamma_2 \vdash \Delta_2, \forall x : T(A)}$ $\quad$ (x not free in $\Gamma_1, \Delta_1, \Gamma_2, \Delta_2$)

We explain this notation with an example.

Assume that $\Gamma_1, \Gamma_2 \vdash \Delta_1, \Delta_2$ is the conclusion of an instance of $(\forall R)$, where $\forall x : T(A)$ is formed and $y\downarrow_T, A[x := y]$ occur in the left resp. right premise. There are four possibilities:

(1) $\forall x : T(A) \in \Gamma_1$ and $y \notin \text{par}(\Gamma_1, A, \Delta_1)$;

(2) $\forall x : T(A) \in \Gamma_1$ and $y \in \text{par}(\Gamma_1, A, \Delta_1)$;

(3) $\forall x : T(A) \notin \Gamma_1$ (so $\forall x : T(A) \in \Gamma_2$) and $y \notin \text{par}(\Gamma_2, A, \Delta_2)$;

(4) $\forall x : T(A) \notin \Gamma_1$ (so $\forall x : T(A) \in \Gamma_2$) and $y \in \text{par}(\Gamma_2, A, \Delta_2)$.

By the induction hypothesis, there are interpolants I_1 and I_2 for any partition of the left resp. right premise. Now, in case (n) $(n = 1, 2, 3, 4)$, $(i\forall Ln)$ gives us the interpolant $(\forall y : T(I_1 \to I_2)$, $I_1 \to I_2$, $I_1 \wedge I_2$ or $\exists y : T(I_1 \wedge I_2)$, respectively). The condition $\text{par}(I) \subseteq \text{par}(A) \cap \text{par}(B)$ is easily checked. $\qquad\square$

3.3.3 Interpolation in MPL_ω without function symbols

We now turn to MPL_ω, but still with the restriction to signatures without function symbols. So we shall prove:

if $F(\Sigma) = \emptyset$ and $\text{MPL}_\omega(\Sigma): A \vdash B$, then there is an interpolant for $A \vdash B$.

Assume $\text{MPL}_\omega: A \vdash B$. By (1) – (4) in 3.1 we then have $\text{MPL3}_\omega: A^*, \text{NLAX} \vdash B^*$. It is not hard to see that $\text{par}(A^*) = \text{par}(A)$, $\text{par}(B^*) = \text{par}(B)$.
We need two lemmata now:

Lemma 3.3.4 Let $\text{PR} \subseteq \text{PRED}$ be a set of predicate symbols, and assume $\text{MPL3}_\omega: A \vdash B$. Then $\text{MPL3}_\omega: A[\text{PR} := \bot] \vdash B[\text{PR} := \bot]$, where $[\text{PR} := \bot]$ means: replace every formula $P(t_1, \ldots, t_n)$ with $P \in \text{PR}$ by $\bot$.

Proof. Induction over the derivation of $A \vdash B$. $\qquad\square$

Lemma 3.3.5 If $\text{MPL3}_\omega(\Sigma): A, \{(P{=}\text{AX}), (P{\downarrow}\text{AX}) \mid P \in \text{P}(\Sigma)\} \vdash B$, then $\text{MPL3}_\omega(\Sigma): A, \{(P{=}\text{AX}), (P{\downarrow}\text{AX}) \mid P \in \text{par}(A) \cup \text{par}(B)\} \vdash B$.

Proof. Apply the previous lemma with $\text{PR} := \text{P}(\Sigma) - (\text{par}(A) \cup \text{par}(B))$, observe that $(P{=}\text{AX})[P := \bot]$ and $(P{\downarrow}\text{AX})[P := \bot]$ are both derivable, and use that MPL3_ω is closed under the cut rule. $\qquad\square$

We continue the proof of 3.3.3 . Define AX_A, AX_B by

$$\text{AX}_A := \{(T{\uparrow}\text{AX}), (T{=}\text{AX}), (T{\downarrow}\text{AX}) \mid T \in \text{S}(\Sigma) \cap \text{par}(A)\}$$
$$\cup \{(P{=}\text{AX}), (P{\downarrow}\text{AX}) \mid P \in \text{P}(\Sigma) \cap \text{par}(A)\},$$
$$\text{AX}_B := \{(T{\uparrow}\text{AX}), (T{=}\text{AX}), (T{\downarrow}\text{AX}) \mid T \in \text{S}(\Sigma) - \text{par}(A)\}$$
$$\cup \{(P{=}\text{AX}), (P{\downarrow}\text{AX}) \mid P \in \text{P}(\Sigma) \cap \text{par}(B)\};$$

then

$$\text{MPL3}_\omega: A^* \wedge \bigwedge \text{AX}_A \vdash \bigwedge \text{AX}_B \to B^*;$$

$$\text{par}(\text{AX}_A) = (\text{S}(\Sigma) \cup \text{P}(\Sigma)) \cap \text{par}(A) \subseteq \text{par}(A);$$
$$\text{par}(\text{AX}_B) \subseteq [(\text{S}(\Sigma) - \text{par}(A)) \cup (\text{S}(\Sigma) \cup \text{P}(\Sigma)) \cap [\text{par}(B)]$$
$$\subseteq [(\text{S}(\Sigma) - \text{par}(A)) \cup \text{par}(B)].$$

Now let I be an interpolant for $A^* \wedge \bigwedge \text{AX}_A \vdash \bigwedge \text{AX}_B \to B^*$ in MPL3$_\omega$, i.e.:

$$\text{MPL3}_\omega: \ A^* \wedge \bigwedge \text{AX}_A \vdash I,$$
$$\text{MPL3}_\omega: \ I \vdash \bigwedge \text{AX}_B \to B^*,$$

and

$$\text{par}(I) \subseteq \text{par}(A^*, \text{AX}_A) \cap \text{par}(\text{AX}_B, B^*)$$
$$\subseteq \text{par}(A) \cap [(\text{S}(\Sigma) - \text{par}(A)) \cup \text{par}(B)]$$
$$= \text{par}(A) \cup \text{par}(B).$$

We claim that I is also an interpolant for $A \vdash B$ in MPL$_\omega$. By (1) – (4) in 3.1 and the fact that AX_A, AX_B and I, containing no descriptions, remain unchanged under *, we see that

$$\text{MPL}_\omega: \ A \vdash I, \quad \text{MPL}_\omega: \ I \vdash B;$$

this ends the proof.

3.3.6 Interpolation in MPL$_\omega$

Finally the full interpolation result is obtained:

if $\text{MPL}_\omega(\Sigma)$: $A \vdash B$, then there is an interpolant for $A \vdash B$.

We sketch the proof, which proceeds by reduction to the former result. The idea behind it is: replace the function symbols $f : T_1 \times \ldots \times T_n \to T_{n+1}$ by predicates $P_f : T_1 \times \ldots \times T_n \times T_{n+1}$, find an interpolant I and replace the occurrences of P_f in I by f. To make this more precise, we introduce the signature

$$\Sigma^p := \Sigma - \text{F}(\Sigma) \cup \{P_f \mid f \in \text{F}(\Sigma)\}$$

and the mappings

$$^p : \text{MPL}_\omega(\Sigma) \to \text{MPL}_\omega(\Sigma^p)$$
$$^f : \text{MPL}_\omega(\Sigma^p) \to \text{MPL}_\omega(\Sigma),$$

which satisfy:

$$fx =_T gy)^p = \exists z : T(P_f(x, z) \wedge P_g(y, z)),$$
$$(Q(fx))^p = \exists z : T(P_f(x, z) \wedge Qz),$$
$$(P_f(x, y, z))^f = f(x, y) = z,$$

$^f, ^p$ commute with the logical connectives.

It it easy to see that

$$\mathrm{par}(A^p) = (\mathrm{par}(A))^p,$$
$$\mathrm{par}(A^J) = (\mathrm{par}(A))^J,$$

and with induction over the length of derivations, one straightforwardly shows:

$$\mathrm{MPL}_\omega(\Sigma): \Gamma \vdash \Delta \;\Rightarrow\; \mathrm{MPL}_\omega(\Sigma^p): \Gamma^p \vdash \Delta^p,$$
$$\mathrm{MPL}_\omega(\Sigma^p): \Gamma \vdash \Delta \;\Rightarrow\; \mathrm{MPL}_\omega(\Sigma): \Gamma^J \vdash \Delta^J,$$
$$\mathrm{MPL}_\omega(\Sigma): \vdash A \leftrightarrow A^{pJ};$$

with these facts it is easy to obtain an interpolant for $\mathrm{MPL}_\omega(\Sigma): A \vdash B$, using the previous result. $\qquad\square$

4 Inductive definitions

4.1 The set-theoretic background

Let A be any set and $\Phi : P(A) \to P(A)$ a monotonic operator, that is

$$\forall X, Y \in P(A)\ (X \subseteq Y \to \Phi(X) \subseteq \Phi(Y)).$$

Then Φ has a least fixed point $\mu\Phi$, defined by

$$\mu\Phi = \bigcap\{X \mid \Phi(X) \subseteq X\}.$$
($\mu\Phi$ is a well-defined subset of A, since $\Phi(A) \subseteq A$.)

Lemma 4.1.1

  (i) $\Phi(\mu\Phi) = \mu\Phi$.

  (ii) $\forall X \in P(A)\ (\Phi(X) = X \to \mu\Phi \subseteq X)$.

Proof:
Clearly, by definition of $\mu\Phi$,

  (∗) $\forall X \in P(A)\ (\Phi(X) \subseteq X \to \mu\Phi \subseteq X)$.

Hence (ii) follows immediately.
For (i), assume $\Phi(X) \subseteq X$. Then $\mu\Phi \subseteq X$ by (∗) and $\Phi(\mu\Phi) \subseteq \Phi(X)$ by monotonicity of Φ. Hence $\Phi(\mu\Phi) \subseteq X$. We conclude $\Phi(\mu\Phi) \subseteq \mu\Phi$.
Applying Φ once more: $\Phi(\Phi(\mu\Phi)) \subseteq \Phi(\mu\Phi)$.
Again by (∗) $\mu\Phi \subseteq \Phi(\mu\Phi)$.

Altogether we proved (i). $\qquad\square$

Theorem 4.1.2 Apart from this definition of $\mu\Phi$ "from above" we have the following definition "from below".

Let

$$\Phi^\alpha = \bigcup\{\Phi(\Phi^\beta) \mid \beta < \alpha\},$$
$$\Phi^{<\alpha} = \bigcup\{\Phi^\beta \mid \beta < \alpha\}, \text{ for } \alpha \text{ an ordinal,}$$

and

$$\Phi^\infty = \bigcup\{\Phi^\alpha \mid \alpha \text{ an ordinal }\}.$$

Then:

(i) $\forall\alpha, \beta(\alpha \leq \beta \to \Phi^\alpha \subseteq \Phi^\beta)$.

(ii) $\exists\alpha(\text{card}(\alpha) \leq \text{card}(A) \wedge \forall\beta \geq \alpha(\Phi^\beta = \Phi^\infty))$.

(iii) $\mu\Phi = \Phi^\infty$.

Proof:

(i) Immediate by definition.

(ii) It suffices to prove

$$(**) \quad \exists\alpha(\text{card}(\alpha) \leq \text{card}(A) \wedge \Phi^\alpha = \Phi^{\alpha+1}).$$

For, by induction on β, we can prove
$\Phi^\alpha = \Phi^{\alpha+1} \to \forall\beta \geq \alpha(\Phi^\beta = \Phi^\alpha)$.
If $\beta \leq \alpha$ this is trivial and for $\beta > \alpha$ we have

$$\begin{aligned}
\Phi^\beta &= \bigcup\{\Phi(\Phi^\gamma)) \mid \gamma < \beta\} \\
&= \bigcup\{\Phi(\Phi^\gamma)) \mid \alpha \leq \gamma < \beta\}, \text{ using (i),} \\
&= \bigcup\{\Phi(\Phi^\alpha)) \mid \alpha \leq \gamma < \beta\}, \text{ by induction hypothesis,} \\
&= \bigcup\{\Phi^{\alpha+1} \mid \alpha \leq \gamma < \beta\}, \text{ using (i) again,} \\
&= \bigcup\{\Phi^\alpha \mid \alpha \leq \gamma < \beta\}, \text{ by assumption,} \\
&= \Phi^\alpha.
\end{aligned}$$

To prove $(**)$, assume to the contrary
$\forall\alpha(\text{card}(\alpha) \leq \text{card}(A) \to \Phi^\alpha \subseteq \Phi^{\alpha+1} \wedge \Phi^\alpha \neq \Phi^{\alpha+1})$.
Then we can construct an injection $i : \{\alpha \mid \text{card}(\alpha) \leq \text{card}(A)\} \to A$ by choosing
$i(\alpha) \in \Phi^{\alpha+1}, i(\alpha) \notin \Phi^\alpha$.
But this is impossible, since the cardinality of $\{\alpha \mid \text{card}(\alpha) \leq \text{card}(A)\}$ is the least cardinal bigger than $\text{card}(A)$.

(iii) Prove by induction that $\forall\alpha(\Phi^\alpha \subseteq \mu\Phi)$.
Hence $\Phi^\infty \subseteq \mu\Phi$.
To prove $\mu\Phi \subseteq \Phi^\infty$ it is sufficient to show $\Phi(\Phi^\infty) \subseteq \Phi^\infty$.
Choose, by (i), α such that $\Phi^\alpha = \Phi^\infty$.
Then $\Phi(\Phi^\infty) = \Phi(\Phi^\alpha) \subseteq \Phi^{\alpha+1} \subseteq \Phi^\infty$.

$\square$

Observe that

$$\Phi^0 = \emptyset,$$
$$\Phi^{\alpha+1} = \Phi(\Phi^\alpha),$$
$$\Phi^\lambda = \Phi^{<\lambda}, \text{ for limit ordinals } \lambda.$$

We call the smallest ordinal α such that $\forall \beta \geq \alpha(\Phi^\beta = \Phi^\infty)$ the *closure ordinal* of Φ.

4.2 MPL$_\omega$ with predicate variables

We extend MPL$_\omega$ with predicate variables $X, Y, Z, \ldots$ in order to be able to talk about inductive definitions inside the language. Each variable will have a type

$$X : T_1 \times \ldots \times T_n.$$

Now we extend the atomic formulae of our logic by adding the following clause:

If X has type $T_1 \times \ldots \times T_n$ and $t_1, \ldots, t_n$ are terms of type $T_1, \ldots, T_n$, then $X(t_1, \ldots, t_n)$ is a(n atomic) formula.

Note: the terms $t_1, \ldots, t_n$ may contain predicate variables again via the description operator.

Definition 4.2.1 (Positive and negative occurrences of predicate variables).

For terms t and formulae A we define the sets $[t]^+$ and $[A]^+$ of positive occurrences and the sets $[t]^-$ and $[A]^-$ of negative occurrences of predicate variables by induction: $*$ is either $+$ or $-$.

$$[x]^* = \emptyset$$
$$[f(t_1, \ldots, t_n)]^* = [t_1]^* \cup \ldots \cup [t_n]^*$$
$$[\iota x.A]^* = [A]^+ \cup [A]^-$$
$$[\top]^* = [\bot]^* = \emptyset$$
$$[P(t_1, \ldots, t_n)]^* = [t_1]^* \cup \ldots \cup [t_n]^*$$
$$[\forall x.A]^* = [A]^*$$
$$[\bigwedge_n A_n]^* = \cup\{[A_n]^* \mid n \in \omega\}$$
$$[\neg A]^+ = [A]^- \quad [\neg A]^- = [A]^+$$
$$[X(t_1, \ldots, t_n)]^+ = [t_1]^+ \cup \ldots \cup [t_n]^+ \cup \{X\}$$
$$[X(t_1, \ldots, t_n)]^- = [t_1]^- \cup \ldots \cup [t_n]^-.$$

Remark 4.2.2 A formula A with free predicate variables $X, Y, \ldots$ will be interpreted as a scheme of formulae generated by substituting arbitrary predicate-variable-free formulae $B, C, \ldots$ for $X, Y, \ldots$. The definition of the substitution of formulae for free predicate variables (notation $A[X(x_1, \ldots, x_n) := B]$) is supposed to be defined in the standard way, where the most important clause is

$$X(t_1, \ldots, t_n)[X(x_1, \ldots, x_n) := B] \equiv B[x_1, \ldots, x_n := t_1', \ldots, t_n'],$$

where $t_i' \equiv t_i[X(x_1, \ldots, x_n) := B]$ for $i = 1, \ldots, n$.

4.3 Positive formulae and inductive definitions

From now on we suppose that (unless stated otherwise) X is a specific predicate variable of type $T_1 \times \ldots \times T_n$ and $x_1, \ldots, x_n$ are specific individual variables of sorts $T_1, \ldots, T_n$.

Definition 4.3.1 An X-positive formula of MPL_ω is a formula A such that

$$[A]^- = \emptyset \text{ and } [A]^+ \subseteq \{X\}.$$

4.3.2 Abbreviation

(i) $X \subseteq Y \equiv \underline{\forall} x_1 \ldots x_n (X(x_1 \ldots x_n) \to Y(x_1 \ldots x_n))$.

(ii) $X = Y \equiv (X \subseteq Y \wedge Y \subseteq X)$.

It is obvious that, given a specific ordering of the special variables $x_1, \ldots, x_n$ of sorts $T_1, \ldots, T_n$ in A, every X-positive formula A defines a monotonic operator

$$\Phi_A : \mathcal{P}(\mathbf{A}(T_1) \times \ldots \times \mathbf{A}(T_n)) \to \mathcal{P}(\mathbf{A}(T_1) \times \ldots \times \mathbf{A}(T_n)).$$

In fact, if D is a subset of $\mathbf{A}(T_1) \times \ldots \times \mathbf{A}(T_n)$ for $i = 1, \ldots, n$, we put

$$\Phi_A(D) = \{(d_1, \ldots, d_n) \mid \mathbf{A} \models A[X \to D, \vec{x} \to \vec{d}]\}.$$

Here the $\mathbf{A}(T_i)$ are the domains of a given structure $\mathbf{A}$ for MPL_ω.
It is even the case that the formula A is derivably monotonic in the sense that

$$X \subseteq Y \vdash A(X) \subseteq A(Y).$$

The question is, whether $\mu \Phi_A$ can be *defined* by a formula in MPL_ω.

In any case, our language permits us to define a sequence of formulae $\langle A^\alpha \mid a < \omega_1 \rangle$:

$$A^\alpha(x_1, \ldots, x_n) = \bigvee \{A[X(x_1, \ldots, x_n) := A^\beta] \mid \beta < \alpha\}, \quad \text{for } \alpha < \omega_1.$$

That means that if the closure ordinal of Φ_A is a *countable* ordinal $\gamma < \omega_1$, then

$$\mu \Phi_A = \Phi_A^\gamma \text{ can be defined by } A^\gamma.$$

In other words $\Phi_A^\gamma = \{\vec{d} \mid \mathbf{A} \models A^\gamma[\vec{x} \to \vec{d}]\}$.

Example 4.3.3 In general the closure ordinal of Φ_A can become arbitrary large, e.g. let

$$A(X, x) \equiv \forall y(y \prec x \to X(y)).$$

Here $\prec$ is intended to be an arbitrary wellordering of the domain of the structure $\mathbf{A}$. In this case the closure ordinal will be the order type of $\prec$, which can get as large as one wants.

4.4 Continuous formulae and strictly positive formulae

An X-positive formula $A(X)$ is called X-*continuous* if

$$(*) \quad \{X_m \subseteq X_{m+1} \mid m \in \omega\} \vdash A(\bigvee_m X_m) \leftrightarrow \bigvee_m A(X_m).$$

Here $X_1, X_2, \ldots$ are fresh predicate variables of the same type as X and $A(\bigvee_m X_m)$ is shorthand notation for $A[X(x_1, \ldots, x_n) := \bigvee_m(X_m(x_1, \ldots, x_n))]$.

Lemma 4.4.1 If A is an X-continuous formula then the closure ordinal of Φ_A is ω.

Proof: Interpret X_m as Φ_A^m in the structure **A**.

Then $\bigvee_m X_m$ is interpreted as Φ_A^ω and assumption $(*)$ above implies that

$$\Phi_A^{\omega+1} = \Phi_A^\omega.$$

$\square$

Remark 4.4.2 It is again provably the case that the closure ordinal is ω:

  (i) $\vdash A(A^\omega) \leftrightarrow A^\omega$

  (ii) $A(X) \subseteq X \vdash A^\omega \subseteq X$.

We need an interesting class of X-continuous formulae, that is large enough to incorporate the most frequently occurring inductive definitions. A good candidate for this seems to be the class of strictly X-positive formulae, which will be defined now.

Definition 4.4.3 The class $SP(X)$ of strictly X-positive formulae is defined inductively by

  (i) If A does not contain X, then $A \in SP(X)$.

  (ii) If $X \notin t_1, \ldots, t_n$, then $X(t_1, \ldots, t_n) \in SP(X)$.

  (iii) If $A, B \in SP(X)$, then $A \wedge B \in SP(X)$.

  (iv) If $\langle A_m \rangle_{m \in \omega}$ are in $SP(X)$, then $\bigvee_m A_m \in SP(X)$.

  (v) If $A \in SP(X)$ and x is a variable of sort T, then $\exists x : T(A) \in SP(X)$.

Note that every strictly X-positive formula is in fact X-positive.

Theorem 4.4.4 Every strictly X-positive formula is X-continuous.

Proof: By induction on the structure of the strictly positive formula A we prove $(*)$ of 4.4.

  (i) If A does not contain X, then $(*)$ holds trivially.

  (ii) If $A(X) \equiv X(t_1, \ldots, t_n)$, with $X \notin t_1, \ldots, t_n$, then

$$A(\bigvee_m X_m) \equiv \bigvee_m(X_m(t_1, \ldots, t_n)) \equiv \bigvee_m A(X_m).$$

  (iii) Assume $A \equiv B \wedge C$, where B, C satisfy $(*)$.

Then (under the assumption that $X_m \subseteq X_{m+1}$ for all m):

$$A(\bigvee_m X_m) \leftrightarrow B(\bigvee_m X_m) \wedge C(\bigvee_m X_m)$$
$$\leftrightarrow \bigvee_m B(X_m) \wedge \bigvee_m C(X_m)$$
$$\leftrightarrow \bigvee_{mm'}(B(X_m) \wedge C(X_{m'}))$$
$$\leftrightarrow \bigvee_m(B(X_m) \wedge C(X_m))$$
$$\leftrightarrow \bigvee_m A(X_m).$$

In the last but one equivalence we used the monotonicity property of (strictly) positive formulae.

(iv) Assume $A \equiv \bigvee_k A_k$, where each A_k satisfies (∗).
Then under the same assumptions as in (iii):

$$A(\bigvee_m X_m) \leftrightarrow (\bigvee_k A_k)(\bigvee_m X_m)$$
$$\leftrightarrow \bigvee_k(A_k(\bigvee_m X_m))$$
$$\leftrightarrow \bigvee_k(\bigvee_m(A_k(X_m)))$$
$$\leftrightarrow \bigvee_m(\bigvee_k(A_k(X_m)))$$
$$\leftrightarrow \bigvee_m((\bigvee_k A_k)(X_m))$$
$$\leftrightarrow \bigvee_m(A(X_m)).$$

(v) Assume $A(X) \equiv \exists x(B(X,x))$, where B satisfies (∗).
Again in a similar way

$$A(\bigvee_m X_m) \leftrightarrow \exists x(B(X,x))[X := \bigvee_m X_m]$$
$$\leftrightarrow \exists x(B(\bigvee_m X_m, x))$$
$$\leftrightarrow \exists x(\bigvee_m B(X_m, x))$$
$$\leftrightarrow \bigvee_m(\exists x B(X_m, x))$$
$$\leftrightarrow \bigvee_m(A(X_m)).$$

$\square$

4.5 Horn formulae

Notation 4.5.1 We will use the notation $\bigwedge_m A_m$ for a finite conjunction of formulae A_m, where m ranges over some (finite) set of indices (which remains implicit).

In most cases an inductive definition of a predicate is given by supplying some "generating clauses", under which the predicate should be "closed". This idea can be formalised using Horn sentences.

Definition 4.5.2 An *(X-)Horn sentence* is a formula $A(X)$ of the form:

$$\bigwedge_k(\forall \vec{x}(\bigwedge_m A_{km}(X, \vec{x}) \to X(t_1(\vec{x}), \ldots, t_n(\vec{x})))),$$

where every formula $A_{km}(\vec{x})$ is of the form $X(s_1(\vec{x}), \ldots, s_n(\vec{x}))$ or does not contain X at all.
Furthermore $X \notin t_i, s_i$ for $i = 1, \ldots, n$.

Here $\vec{x}$ is shorthand for $x_1, \ldots, x_p$ and p may depend on k. (We will not make this explicit.) Similarly $\vec{t}(\vec{x})$ will abbreviate $t_1(\vec{x}), \ldots, t_n(\vec{x})$.

Remark 4.5.3 The definition implies that $A_k(X, \vec{x}) \equiv \bigwedge_m A_{km}(X, \vec{x})$ is a strictly X-positive formula. This will be the only property of A_k that will be used in this section, so that the results will hold for arbitrary strictly X-positive formulae A_k.

4.5.4 Observation

In general the terms $t_1(\vec{x}), \ldots, t_n(\vec{x})$ that are used in the definition of Horn sentences may be strict or not. In most situations in practice they will be strict, but the general theory of inductive definitions is easier if one needs not to be concerned with definedness of terms. We should only take care to use the quantifier $\underline{\forall}$ in stead of $\forall$, when needed.

Now we want to show that for every Horn sentence $A(X)$ we may define the least predicate X satisfying $A(X)$ in our theory. We accomplish this by a translation of X-Horn formulae into strictly X-positive formulae.

Definition 4.5.5 Let

$$A(X) \equiv \bigwedge_k (\forall \vec{x}(A_k(X, \vec{x}) \to X(t_1(\vec{x}), \ldots, t_n(\vec{x}))))$$

be an X-Horn sentence.
Let $\vec{y} \equiv y_1, \ldots, y_n$ be variables of sort $T_1, \ldots, T_n$.
Define $A^*(X, \vec{y}) \equiv \bigvee_k \exists \vec{x}(A_k(X, \vec{x}) \wedge \vec{y} \simeq \vec{t}(\vec{x}))$.

Lemma 4.5.6

(i) $A^*(X, \vec{y})$ is strictly X-positive.

(ii) $\vdash A(X) \leftrightarrow \underline{\forall}\vec{y}(A^*(X, \vec{y}) \to X(\vec{y}))$.

Proof:

(i) This is clear by inspection of the definition of A^*, using the remark in 4.5.3.

(ii)
$$
\begin{aligned}
A(X) &\leftrightarrow \bigwedge_k (\forall \vec{x}(A_k(X, \vec{x}) \to X(\vec{t}(\vec{x})))) \\
&\leftrightarrow \bigwedge_k (\forall \vec{x}(A_k(X, \vec{x}) \to \underline{\forall}\vec{y}(\vec{y} \simeq \vec{t}(\vec{x}) \to X(\vec{y})))) \\
&\leftrightarrow \bigwedge_k (\forall \vec{x}\underline{\forall}\vec{y}(A_k(X, \vec{x}) \wedge \vec{y} \simeq \vec{t}(\vec{x}) \to X(\vec{y}))) \\
&\leftrightarrow \underline{\forall}\vec{y}(\bigvee_k \exists \vec{x}(A_k(X, \vec{x}) \wedge \vec{y} \simeq \vec{t}(\vec{x})) \to X(\vec{y})) \\
&\leftrightarrow \underline{\forall}\vec{y}(A^*(X, \vec{y}) \to X(\vec{y}))
\end{aligned}
$$

$\square$

Now, by the methods of section 4.4, using 4.5.6 (i), we know that A^* has a least fixed point $A^{*\omega}$, satisfying

$$\vdash A^*(A^{*\omega}) \leftrightarrow A^{*\omega}$$
$$A^*(X) \subseteq X \vdash A^{*\omega} \subseteq X.$$

Then using 4.5.6 (ii) we know that $\vdash A(A^{*\omega})$ and that $A(X) \vdash A^{*\omega} \subseteq X$.

Thus $A^{*\omega}$ is the least predicate satisfying the Horn sentence ("generating clauses") $A(X)$.

Remark 4.5.7 In example 4.3.3 it seems that a Horn sentence was given that contradicts the above considerations. To solve the apparent paradox, just notice that the "Horn sentence" corresponding to the formula

$$A(X,x) \equiv \forall y(y \prec x \to X(y))$$

would be

$$B(X,x) \equiv \forall x(\forall y(y \prec x \to X(y)) \to X(x)),$$

which is clearly *not* of the right form.

One should keep in mind that one searches the *least fixed point* of A, as opposed to the least *predicate satisfying* B.

4.6 Implicit versus explicit inductive definitions

We are going to elaborate on the definition of the formula A^* in section 4.5 in order to make this translation total. An inductive definition of a mathematical object, say a set X, can be represented in two fashions:

implicitly, as the least X satisfying some presumably inductive property I of sets;
explicitly, as the least fixed point of some monotonic operator E on sets.

We illustrate this with an example: the definition of $\mathcal{N}$, the set of natural numbers. An implicit inductive definition is: the least X satisfying $I_{\mathcal{N}}(X)$, with

(1) $I_{\mathcal{N}}(X) := (0 \in X \wedge \forall x \, (x \in X \to Sx \in X));$

an explicit inductive definition reads: the least fixed point of the operator $E_{\mathcal{N}}$, defined by

(2) $E_{\mathcal{N}}(X) := \{x \mid x = 0 \vee \exists y \, (y \in X \wedge x = Sy)\}.$

Going from explicit to implicit is rather simple, put

(3) $I(X) := (E(X) \subset X),$

then one easily sees (using the monotonicity of E) that the least X satisfying $I(X)$ is equal to the least fixed point of E.

We consider the opposite direction: given I, how to obtain an E such that the least fixed point of E is equal to the least X satisfying I ? A sufficient condition is that

(4) $I(X) \leftrightarrow (E(X) \subset X),$

holds. To investigate this, we assume that I is given as a *formula* in some language, with parameter X. Let $I(X^-, X^+)$ be that formula, where X^+ is associated to the positive occurrences of X, and X^- to the negative ones. (Note that this is always possible if we first eliminate all occurrences of the description operator.) This gives us a *binary* operator $I(Y, Z)$, satisfying

(5) $I(Y, Z) \wedge Y' \subset Y \wedge Z \subset Z' \rightarrow I(Y', Z')$,

i.e. $I(Y, Z)$ is monotonic in Z and antimonotonic in Y. This follows directly from the fact that Z occurs only positively in $I(Y, Z)$ and Y only negatively. Furthermore $I(X) = I(X, X)$.

Now put

(6) $E(X) := \{x \mid \neg I(X, \{y \mid y \neq x\})\}$.

It is easily verified that E is a monotonic operator; we investigate under which conditions it satisfies (4).

The $\rightarrow$ part of (4) is easy: by (5) we have

$$I(X, X) \wedge x \notin X \rightarrow I(X, \{y \mid y \neq x\}),$$

hence (by contraposition)

$$I(X, X) \rightarrow \forall x(\neg I(X, \{y \mid y \neq x\}) \rightarrow x \in X),$$

i.e. $I(X) \rightarrow (E(X) \subset X)$, the $\rightarrow$ part of (4). The other part holds if

$$\forall x(\neg I(X, \{y \mid y \neq x\}) \rightarrow x \in X) \rightarrow I(X, X),$$

i.e., by contraposition

$$\forall x \notin X \; (I(X, \{y \mid y \neq x\})) \rightarrow I(X, X)$$

and this holds if $I(X, X)$ is $\bigcap$-*continuous* in its second argument, i.e.

$$\forall Y \in C(I(X, Y)) \rightarrow I(X, \bigcap C) \text{ for any collection } C \text{ of sets.}$$

So we conclude: (4) holds if $I(X, Y)$ is $\bigcap$-continuous in Y.

We present a syntactical criterion which entails $\bigcap$-continuity. In fact this criterion only works for formulae $I(X)$ such that $X = \bigcap \emptyset = \{x \mid x \approx x\}$ satisfies I. Since any interesting implicit inductive definition satisfies this condition, we will take it for granted.

The collection $C(X)$ of formulae is inductively defined by:

$$X(t_1, \ldots, t_n) \in C(X)$$
$$X \text{ not in } A \Rightarrow A \in C(X)$$
$$A_n \in C(X) \; (n = 0, 1, \ldots) \Rightarrow \bigwedge_n A_n \in C(X)$$
$$A \in C(X) \text{ and } X \text{ not in } B \Rightarrow A \vee B \in C(X)$$
$$A \in C(X) \Rightarrow \forall x \, A \in C(X)$$

One easily proves

(7) $A \in C(X) \Rightarrow A$ $\bigcap$-continuous in X.

Hence we have:

(8) $I \in C(X^+) \Rightarrow E$, as defined in (6), satisfies $I(X) \leftrightarrow (E(X) \subset X)$.

Finally we combine (8) with the condition upon E to guarantee its closure ordinal to be ω: it was shown in 4.4.2 that continuity w.r.t. unions of countable ascending chains was required. A sufficient syntactical condition for this is strictly positive occurrence of X, denoted by $SP(X)$. In the present setting, this leads to the collections $D^+(X), D^-(X)$ of formulae, inductively defined by:

$$X(t_1, \ldots, t_n) \in D^+(X)$$

$$X \text{ not in } A \Rightarrow A \in D^+(X) \text{ and } A \in D^-(X)$$

$$A \in D^+(X) \Rightarrow \neg A \in D^-(X)$$
$$A \in D^-(X) \Rightarrow \neg A \in D^+(X)$$

$$A \in D^+(X) \, (n = 0, 1, \ldots) \Rightarrow \bigvee_n A_n \in D^+(X)$$
$$A \in D^-(X) \, (n = 0, 1, \ldots) \Rightarrow \bigwedge_n A_n \in D^-(X)$$

$$A, B \in D^+(X) \Rightarrow A \wedge B \in D^+(X)$$
$$A, B \in D^-(X) \Rightarrow A \vee B \in D^-(X)$$

$$A \in D^+(X) \Rightarrow \exists x A \in D^+(X)$$
$$A \in D^-(X) \Rightarrow \forall x A \in D^-(X)$$

$D^+(X)$ corresponds to $SP(X)$, and we have

(9) $I(X) \in D^-(X^-) \Rightarrow E(X)$, as defined in (6), has closure ordinal ω.

Combining this with (8) and the results of 4.4 yields

$$I(X) \in C(X^+) \cap D^-(X^-) \Rightarrow \text{ the least } X \text{ satisfying } I(X) \text{ is definable in MPL}_\omega.$$

4.7 Simultaneous inductive definitions

Let $\Phi_1 : P(A) \times P(B) \to P(A)$
and $\Phi_2 : P(A) \times P(B) \to P(B)$
be monotonic mappings, that is
$\forall X, X' \in P(A), Y, Y' \in P(B) \, (X \subseteq X' \wedge Y \subseteq Y' \to \Phi_1(X, Y) \subseteq \Phi_1(X', Y'))$ and
$\forall X, X' \in P(A), Y, Y' \in P(B) \, (X \subseteq X' \wedge Y \subseteq Y' \to \Phi_2(X, Y) \subseteq \Phi_2(X', Y'))$.

Problem: To find the least simultaneous fixed point $\langle F_1, F_2 \rangle$ such that

(i) $\Phi_1(F_1, F_2) = F_1$
(ii) $\Phi_2(F_1, F_2) = F_2$
(iii) If $\Phi_1(X, Y) \subseteq X$ and $\Phi_2(X, Y) \subseteq Y$

then $F_1 \subseteq X$ and $F_2 \subseteq Y$.

We shall give three solutions to this problem. Each solution has its own (dis)advantages and all of them can be carried out inside our theory MPL_ω, as the reader easily checks.

4.7.1 Solution 1

Define $\Phi \equiv \langle \Phi_1, \Phi_2 \rangle : P(A) \times P(B) \to P(A) \times P(B)$.
Then prove the fixed point theorem as in 4.1, 4.1.1 for arbitrary complete lattices (known as Tarski's theorem). In this case the complete lattice is $(P(A) \times P(B), \leq)$, where $\leq$ is defined componentwise:

$$(X,Y) \leq (X',Y') \leftrightarrow X \subseteq X' \wedge Y \subseteq Y'.$$

Note that this lattice is not exactly of the form $(P(C), \subseteq)$ for some set C, but it is isomorphic to such a lattice, see solution 3, third attempt.

Note also that this method can be carried out straightforwardly inside MPL_ω.

4.7.2 Solution 2

In this case we will iterate the fixed point construction for one argument.
First, let $Y \in P(B)$ be fixed and consider the map

$$\Phi_1(-, Y) : P(A) \to P(A)$$

and its least fixed point $\Phi_1^\infty(Y)$.
We thus defined a map $\Phi_1^\infty : P(B) \to P(A)$.
Note that Φ_1^∞ is monotonic, for if $Y \subseteq Y'$ then

$$\Phi_1(\Phi_1^\infty(Y'), Y) \subseteq \Phi_1(\Phi_1^\infty(Y'), Y') = \Phi_1^\infty(Y'), \text{ hence}$$

$$\Phi_1^\infty(Y) \subseteq \Phi_1^\infty(Y').$$

Now consider the map

$$\Phi_2' \equiv \Phi_2(\Phi_1^\infty(-), -) : P(B) \to P(B).$$

Again Φ_2' is monotonic and we may take its least fixed point $\Phi_2'^\infty$.
Let $\langle F_1, F_2 \rangle$ be the pair $\langle \Phi_1^\infty(\Phi_2'^\infty), \Phi_2'^\infty \rangle$.
Then clearly

$$\Phi_2(F_1, F_2) = \Phi_2'(F_2) = F_2.$$

But also

$$\Phi_1(F_1, F_2) = \Phi_1(\Phi_1^\infty(\Phi_2'^\infty), \Phi_2'^\infty) = \Phi_1^\infty(\Phi_2'^\infty) = F_1.$$

Now assume $\Phi_1(X,Y) \subseteq X$ and $\Phi_2(X,Y) \subseteq Y$.
Then $\Phi_1^\infty(Y) \subseteq X$, hence

$\Phi_2'(Y) = \Phi_2(\Phi_1^\infty(Y), Y) \subseteq \Phi_2(X, Y) \subseteq Y$, therefore

$\Phi_2'^\infty \subseteq Y$, that is $F_2 \subseteq Y$.

Finally we may also conclude that

$$F_1 = \Phi_1^\infty(F_2) \subseteq \Phi_1^\infty(Y) \subseteq X.$$

4.7.3 Solution 3

We will code the complete lattice $(P(A) \times P(B), \leq)$ inside a powerset lattice $(P(C), \subseteq)$, for a suitable set C. Let us divide the possibilities in three attempts.

A) **Attempt 1.**

Let $C = A \times B$. This attempt fails, because the mapping

$$i : P(A) \times P(B) \to P(C) \text{ with } i(X, Y) = X \times Y$$

is not injective in general.
For, $\emptyset \times Y = \emptyset \times Y' = \emptyset$ for all $Y, Y' \subseteq B$.

B) **Attempt 2.**

Take some element $\Diamond \notin A \cup B$ and let $C = A^\Diamond \times B^\Diamond$, where

$$X^\Diamond = X \cup \{\Diamond\} \text{ for any set } X.$$

Define the mappings

$$i : P(A) \times P(B) \to P(C) \text{ with } i(X, Y) = X^\Diamond \times Y^\Diamond \text{ and}$$
$$\langle \pi_A, \pi_B \rangle : P(C) \to P(A) \times P(B) \text{ with}$$
$$\pi_A(Z) = \{x \in A \mid \langle x, \Diamond \rangle \in Z\} \text{ and } \pi_B(Z) = \{y \in B \mid \langle \Diamond, y \rangle \in Z\}.$$

Then $\langle \pi_A, \pi_B \rangle \circ i = \mathrm{id}_{P(A) \times P(B)}$ and the coding works as follows:
Let $\Phi_0 = i \circ \Phi \circ \langle \pi_A, \pi_B \rangle$ and consider the pair

$$\langle F_1, F_2 \rangle = \langle \pi_A(\Phi_0^\infty), \pi_B(\Phi_0^\infty) \rangle.$$

Then

$$\begin{aligned}
\langle F_1, F_2 \rangle &= \langle \pi_A, \pi_B \rangle(\Phi_0^\infty) \\
&= \langle \pi_A, \pi_B \rangle \circ \Phi_0(\Phi_0^\infty) \\
&= \Phi \circ \langle \pi_A, \pi_B \rangle(\Phi_0^\infty) \\
&= \Phi(F_1, F_2).
\end{aligned}$$

Now assume $\Phi_1(X, Y) \subseteq X$ and $\Phi_2(X, Y) \subseteq Y$, that is $\Phi(X, Y) \subseteq \langle X, Y \rangle$.
Then

$$\Phi_0 \circ i(X, Y) = i \circ \Phi \circ \langle \pi_A, \pi_B \rangle \circ i(X, Y)$$

$$= i \circ \Phi(X,Y)$$
$$\subseteq i(X,Y).$$

Hence $\Phi_0^\infty \subseteq i(X,Y)$ and by applying $\langle \pi_A, \pi_B \rangle$ to both sides we get

$$\langle F_1, F_2 \rangle \subseteq \langle X,Y \rangle.$$

This coding can be represented in MPL_ω with a little pain, but a simpler coding mechanism will be given in attempt 3.

C) **Attempt 3.**

Assume that A and B are disjoint sets (make them disjoint if they aren't). In this case it is possible to define the set $C = A \cup B$ and the mappings

$$i : P(A) \times P(B) \to P(C) \text{ with } i(X,Y) = X \cup Y \text{ and}$$
$$\langle \pi_A, \pi_B \rangle : P(C) \to P(A) \times P(B) \text{ with}$$
$$\pi_A(Z) = Z \cap A \text{ and } \pi_B(Z) = Z \cap B.$$

The same calculations as in attempt 2 also work here.

4.8 Inductively defined functions

In many situations one wants to define a function inductively by an equation like

$$f(\vec{x}) \simeq t(f, \vec{x}).$$

Speaking in terms of algorithms this means that t (an arbitrary term) specifies the algorithm to compute f with the possibility of "recursively calling" f itself.

We will rephrase the above equation as

$$f(\vec{x}) \simeq \iota y.(t(f, \vec{x}) = y),$$

or more generally as

$$f(\vec{x}) \simeq \iota y.A(f, \vec{x}, y),$$

where some further conditions on the formula A have to be specified.

To be able to write down the above equations in our formal theory one needs to introduce symbols for function variables, which can be done in a similar way as for predicate variables as in section 4.2.

We are going to translate the inductive definition of the function f into an inductive definition of a predicate F, syntactically derived from A or t. For this we fix the following notation:

f is a function variable of type $T_1 \times \ldots \times T_n \to T_{n+1}$,

F is a predicate variable of type $T_1 \times \ldots \times T_n \times T_{n+1}$,

$\vec{x} = x_1, \ldots, x_n$ are variables of types $T_1, \ldots, T_n$.

4.8.1 Translation

For every formula A we define a define a formula A' such that

(i) f does not occur in A'

(ii) A' is a strict formula (i.e. strict in the variables $\vec{x}, y$)

(iii) $\vdash A \leftrightarrow A'[F(\vec{x}, y) := (f(\vec{x}) = y)]$.

Definition.

$$
\begin{array}{llll}
\text{(i)} & (x = y)' & \equiv & x = y \\
\text{(ii)} & (g(t_1, \ldots, t_m) = y)' & \equiv & \exists y_1 \ldots y_m (g(y_1, \ldots, y_m) = y \wedge (\vec{t} = \vec{y})') \; (g \not\equiv f) \\
\text{(iii)} & (f(t_1, \ldots, t_n) = y)' & \equiv & \exists y_1 \ldots y_n (F(y_1, \ldots, y_n, y) \wedge (\vec{t} = \vec{y})') \wedge y\!\downarrow \\
\text{(iv)} & (\iota z : T(A) = y)' & \equiv & \iota z : T(A') = y \\
\text{(v)} & (s = t)' & \equiv & \exists y ((s = y)' \wedge (t = y)') \\
\text{(vi)} & (\downarrow(s))' & \equiv & \exists y ((s = y)') \\
\text{(vii)} & P(t_1, \ldots, tm)' & \equiv & \exists y_1 \ldots y_m (P(y_1, \ldots, y_m) \wedge (\vec{t} = \vec{y})') \\
\text{(viii)} & \top' & \equiv & \top \\
\text{(ix)} & \bot' & \equiv & \bot \\
\text{(x)} & (\neg A)' & \equiv & \neg A' \\
\text{(xi)} & (\bigwedge_n A_n)' & \equiv & \bigwedge_n A'_n \\
\text{(xii)} & (\forall x : T(A))' & \equiv & \forall x : T(A')
\end{array}
$$

Definition 4.8.2 We say that the formula A is *strictly f-positive* if the translated formula A' is strictly F-positive.

It is immediately clear, by inspection of the definition of the translation, that if A is of the form $(t(f, \vec{x}) = y)$ and f does not occur inside the scope of a description operator in t then A is strictly f-positive.

4.8.3 Functionality

In order to get things working we need another property of the formula A', namely the preservation property of F's functionality.

Definition.

(i) F is functional if

$$\forall \vec{x} y z (F(\vec{x}, y) \wedge F(\vec{x}, z) \rightarrow y = z).$$

(ii) A' is *functionality preserving* if

$$F \text{ is functional} \vdash \{(\vec{x}, y) \mid A'(F, \vec{x}, y)\} \text{ is functional}$$

(iii) We say that A is functionality preserving if A' is.

Remark 4.8.4 Again, if A is of the form $(t(f, \vec{x}) = y)$ then A is functionality preserving.

Now assume that the formula A is both strictly f-positive and functionality preserving. Then we can apply the methods of the previous sections to the strictly F-positive and functionality preserving formula A'. Let F^ω be the minimal fixed point of A', that is

(1) $F^\omega \leftrightarrow A'(F^\omega)$
(2) $A'(G) \subseteq G \vdash F^\omega \subseteq G$

Then define

$$f^\omega(\vec{x}) \simeq \iota y.F^\omega(\vec{x}, y).$$

We are going to show

(3) $\forall \vec{x}(f^\omega(\vec{x}) \simeq \iota y.A(f^\omega, \vec{x}, y))$
(4) $\forall \vec{x}(g(\vec{x}) \simeq \iota y.A(g, \vec{x}, y)) \wedge f^\omega(\vec{x}){\downarrow} \to g(\vec{x}) = f^\omega(\vec{x})$

Ad (3):

> We have to show $\iota y.F^\omega(\vec{x}, y) \simeq \iota y.A'[F(\vec{x}, y) := (f^\omega(\vec{x}) = y)]$.
> It is enough to show $\forall y(F^\omega(\vec{x}, y) \leftrightarrow A'[F(\vec{x}, y) := (f^\omega(\vec{x}) = y)])$.
> Because of (1) we only need $f^\omega(\vec{x}) = y \leftrightarrow F^\omega(\vec{x}, y)$.
> This is the same as $\iota y.F^\omega(\vec{x}, y) = y \leftrightarrow F^\omega(\vec{x}, y)$,
> which is correct because F^ω is functional and strict.
> Indeed, a minimal fixed point construction starts with a functional predicate (the empty set) and A' is functionality preserving by assumption.

Ad (4):

> Assume
>
> $$\forall \vec{x}(g(\vec{x}) \simeq \iota y.A(g, \vec{x}, y)) \wedge f^\omega(\vec{x}){\downarrow}.$$
>
> Let
>
> $$G(\vec{x}, y) := (g(\vec{x}) = y).$$
>
> Note that
>
> $$A'(G, \vec{x}, y) \leftrightarrow A(g, \vec{x}, y).$$
>
> We have
>
> $$\forall \vec{x}(g(\vec{x}) = y \leftrightarrow \iota y.A(g, \vec{x}, y) = y$$
> $$\leftrightarrow \iota y.A'(G, \vec{x}, y) = y$$
> $$\leftrightarrow A'(G, \vec{x}, y)).$$

In the last equivalence we used the fact that G is a functional predicate and A' preserves this functionality.
In other words

$$G \leftrightarrow A'(G).$$

By (4) we conclude

$F^\omega \subseteq G$.

So since $f^\omega(\vec{x})\downarrow$, say $f^\omega(\vec{x}) = y$, we have $F^\omega(\vec{x}, y)$, hence $G(\vec{x}, y)$, and finally $g(\vec{x}) = y = f^\omega(\vec{x})$.

Remark 4.8.5 It is possible to extend the results of this section to the situation, where a finite set of functions is defined inductively in terms of each other, using similar methods as in section 4.7.

It is even possible to mix predicates and functions in *one* simultaneous inductive definition. In this case we have a finite set of equations and equivalences as follows

$$f_1(\vec{x}) \simeq t_1(\vec{f}, \vec{X}, \vec{x})$$

$$\ldots$$

$$f_n(\vec{x}) \simeq t_n(\vec{f}, \vec{X}, \vec{x})$$

$$X_1(\vec{x}) \leftrightarrow A_1(\vec{f}, \vec{X}, \vec{x})$$

$$\ldots$$

$$X_m(\vec{x}) \leftrightarrow A_m(\vec{f}, \vec{X}, \vec{x})$$

As always we suppose that $\vec{f}, \vec{X}$ occur only positively in $t_1, \ldots, t_n$ and that $A_1, \ldots, A_m$ are strictly positive in $\vec{f}, \vec{X}$.

It then follows that we can show (inside MPL$_\omega$) that this system has a minimal fixed point $f_1^\omega, \ldots, f_n^\omega, X_1^\omega, \ldots, X_m^\omega$ with the usual properties.

References

[1] J. BARWISE, *Admissible Sets and Structures*, Springer-Verlag, Berlin (1975).

[2] S. FEFERMAN, *Lectures on Proof Theory*, in: M.H. LÖB (Ed.), *Proceedings of the Summer School in Logic, Leeds 1967*, Lecture Notes in Mathematics 70, Springer-Verlag, Berlin (1968), 1-107.

[3] H.B.M. JONKERS, C.P.J. KOYMANS, G.R. RENARDEL DE LAVALETTE, *A Semantic Framework for the COLD-Family of Languages*, Technical Report, ESPRIT project 432, Doc.Nr. METEOR/t2/PRLE/1 (1986).

[4] C. KARP, *Languages with Expressions of Infinite Length*, North-Holland, Amsterdam (1964).

[5] H.J. KEISLER, *Model Theory for Infinitary Logic*, North-Holland, Amsterdam (1971).

[6] E.G.K. LOPEZ-ESCOBAR, *An Interpolation Theorem for Denumerably Long Sentences*, Fundamenta Mathematicae 57 (1965), 253-272.

[7] G.R. RENARDEL DE LAVALETTE, *Descriptions in Mathematical Logic*, Studia Logica 43 (1984), 281-294.

[8] K. SCHÜTTE, *Der Interpolationssatz der Intuitionistischen Prädikatenlogik*, Mathematische Annalen 148 (1962), 192-200.

[9] D.S. SCOTT, *Existence and Description in Formal Logic*, in: R. SCHOENMAN (Ed.), *Bertrand Russell, Philosopher of the Century*, Allen & Unwin, London

(1967), 181-200.

[10] D.S. SCOTT, *Identity and Existence in Intuitionistic Logic*, in: M.P. FOURMAN, C.J. MULVEY, D.S. SCOTT (Eds.), *Applications of Sheaves*, Lecture Notes in Mathematics 753, Springer Verlag, Berlin (1979), 660-696.

[11] W.W. TAIT, *Normal Derivability in Classical Logic*, in: J. BARWISE (Ed.), *The Syntax and Semantics of Infinitary Languages*, Lecture Notes in Mathematics 72, Springer-Verlag, Berlin (1968), 204-236.

[12] G.TAKEUTI, *Proof Theory*, North-Holland, Amsterdam (1975).

Description Algebra

H.B.M. Jonkers*

Philips Research Laboratories
P.O. Box 80000, 5600 JA Eindhoven, The Netherlands

Abstract

Description Algebra is a many-sorted algebra, containing operators on (module) *descriptions* such as import, export, renaming and unification. The algebra incorporates a special scheme of dealing with name clashes in module composition by means of *origins* and *origin unification*. A complete definition of the algebra is given and its properties are discussed. The algebra is the basis of the modularisation constructs of the design language COLD-K, but the approach as such is independent of COLD-K.

1 Introduction

In this paper we define the algebra DA (for *Description Algebra*), which is the many-sorted algebra that has been used (in a specialized form) to give a meaning to the modularisation constructs of the design language COLD-K [3,4,5]. That is, the meaning of each (modular) 'scheme' in COLD-K is defined as a term of DA. The objects of DA are called *descriptions* and are essentially presentations (= signature + axioms) of logical theories extended with an encapsulating signature. In the case of COLD-K, these are presentations of MPL_ω theories [6], which act as the denotations of flat class descriptions. The operators of DA are defined in a syntactic way thus making the objects of DA amenable to fully formal (i.e. automated) manipulation. In other words, each object denoted by a term of DA can be computed automatically ('reduced to normal form').

The development of DA has been inspired by ASL [8] and in particular by Module Algebra [2]. An essential difference with the latter two approaches is the way name clashes in module composition are handled, which will be explained below. Description Algebra is not specific for COLD-K in any respect, and it could be used as the basis of the modularisation mechanisms of any other language. The fact that MPL_ω is used as the underlying logic of descriptions in DA is not essential either. Any other many-sorted logic could be taken instead of MPL_ω.

---

*This work has been performed in the framework of ESPRIT project 432 (METEOR).

1.1 Names

Description Algebra can be conceived of as a formal system modelling (in the engineering sense of the word) a system of real-world modules and their rules of composition. What is meant by 'real-world modules' does not really matter, but one could think of programming language or VLSI modules as represented in a computer memory or on a chip area. The important thing is that modules consist of external and internal 'parts' which have a certain 'location' in space (= the computer memory or chip area in the above examples). In a given space, a module is uniquely identified by its location.

The parts of modules are modelled by the sorts and operations of descriptions. The way we model the locations of parts is by giving *names* to parts. As in any modelling activity, we have to be very careful with such abstractions since we may lose essential information. In particular, the information we may lose in the abstraction from locations to names is that of the *identity* of module parts. Within the context of modularisation this leads to a fundamental problem in connection with names: the *name consistency problem* (discussed below). We shall argue that no good solution to this problem is possible if we stick to the traditional view of names as strings of characters (as in most algebraic specification languages).

1.2 Name consistency

The name consistency problem arises, among other things, in the following situation: We put together two descriptions D_1 and D_2 of modules M_1 and M_2 to obtain a description D of a composite module M. Certain parts of M_1 and M_2 happen to have the same names in D_1 and D_2. Do we consider these parts to be the same in D or not? A common solution to this problem is to assume that external parts with the same name are identical, while internal parts are always different (also from external parts with the same name). So in composing D from D_1 and D_2, visible names (= names of external parts) in D_1 and D_2 are allowed to clash while clashes of hidden names (= names of internal parts) with other names are avoided by automatic renamings. Such renamings are allowed since the names of internal parts do not really matter: users of the module cannot refer to them anyway.

The above solution creates two new problems. The first is that nothing withholds one to put descriptions together in which the same visible name refers to parts intended to be entirely different. In such a case we are almost certain that the composite description is a non-conservative extension of the original ones, and probably it is even inconsistent. However, if a name is just a label we have no way to tell whether two names are intended to denote the same part or not. The second problem is that the automatic renaming of hidden names leads to a duplication of hidden names which may have undesired effects. In object-based languages such as COLD-K we are dealing with a global state space where certain names represent variable parts of that state space. Such *variables* (which are similar to programming language variables) are not supposed to be duplicated when putting two class descriptions together, since this would make it impossible for two classes to share hidden variables. This problem does not occur in value-based languages such as algebraic specification languages, but there the multiplication of hidden names may still be a nuisance.

1.3 Origins and symbols

The root of the problems discussed above lies in the fact that we have lost the necessary information to determine whether two names denote the same module part or not. Therefore the solution seems quite straightforward: endow each name with an *origin* uniquely identifying the location of the module part denoted by the name. Such a combination of a name and an origin will be called a *symbol*. The use of symbols rather than names in descriptions solves the problem of name clashes in the composition of descriptions: If two symbols happen to have the same name while denoting different module parts, their origins and thereby the symbols themselves will be different, so renaming is not necessary. If two symbols happen to have the same name and the same origin they obviously denote the same module part and should be identified, so renaming is necessary neither.

Of course we want to keep the origins of names completely hidden from the user of the language. It would be very user-unfriendly if users of the language had to provide an origin with every name they write down: they should be able to work in terms of names only, which can be achieved as follows. First of all, the association of an origin with a name (i.e. the translation from name to symbol) can be done fully automatically by the language implementation (in accordance with the language definition). Secondly, we forbid references to the internal parts of a module outside the description of that module, so there is no identification problem with respect to hidden names. Finally, in order to be able to refer by means of names to the external parts of a module we require that visible symbols with the same name always have the same origin. This will be called the requirement of *origin consistency*. It implies that the origin associated with a visible name is unique and can be reconstructed automatically. As a matter of fact, origin consistency does not occur as a precondition to the operators of DA (so as to avoid partial operations). It is a requirement of a methodological nature, the satisfaction of which can be checked automatically at any time since descriptions contain the necessary information to do so.

1.4 P-Unification

The situation with respect to the origins of names is in fact a bit more subtle than suggested above. This is due to the fact that we have to distinguish between two different kinds of names in the description of a module: Those that denote parts of the module itself, called *defined names*, and those that denote parts of other modules, called *free names*. The meaning of the defined names is laid down in the description of the module, hence the origins of these names seem clear: they can be viewed as pointers to the definitions of the names. The meaning of the free names is defined elsewhere so it need not always be clear what their origin is. In particular, if a free name acts as a *parameter* in a description then we cannot know the origin of the name before it has been instantiated. To make things even worse, it may be the case that the definition of a defined name 'uses' some free name. This implies that the meaning, and thereby the origin, of such a defined name depends on the instantiation of the free name.

The way out of the above problems is, first of all, to assign *origin variables* rather than fixed origins to the free names in a description. Such origin variables can later be instantiated with real origins. Secondly, if a defined name D uses free names $F_1, \ldots, F_n$ then the origin of D should be parameterised over the origins $x_1, \ldots, x_n$ of $F_1, \ldots, F_n$. This can be achieved by viewing the origin of D as a tuple of the form $\langle c, x_1, \ldots, x_n \rangle$, where c is a fixed value uniquely identifying the definition of D. When enforcing origin consistency of a description we have to *unify* the origins of symbols with the same name (which need not be possible). This form of unification, called *P-unification* (for 'partition unification'), is slightly different from the usual notion of unification, since it amounts to finding the most general substitution simultaneously unifying all sets in a (possibly infinite) partition of an infinite set, rather than a single finite set.

1.5 Survey of the paper

The focus in this paper is on the definition of the algebra DA and its associated notions, including the necessary proofs. For examples of the use of the operators of DA in the context of COLD-K we refer to the section on modularisation and parameterisation in [5].

In Section 2 origins are introduced, together with the notions of origin substitution and bisubstitution equivalence (the fact that two origin substitutions are equal modulo origin variable renaming). The concept of P-unification of partitions of the set of origins is defined and it is shown that each P-unifiable origin partition has a most general P-unifier, which is the basis of the definition of the μ-operator of DA. The notion of a symbol is introduced as the combination of an identifier, an origin and type information. The type information is an essential part of symbols since we assume symbols to be overloaded (as in COLD-K).

In Section 3, the actual definition of the many-sorted algebra DA is given. In four separate subsections the carriers of DA and the operations on them are introduced. *Names* are defined as equivalence classes of symbols, with equality 'modulo origins' as the equivalence relation. *Signatures* are defined in the usual way as closed sets of names. *Renamings* are defined as objects representing special mappings from names to names. *Descriptions* are defined as four-tuples consisting of two signatures (defining the externally and internally visible symbols), a set of formulae (the axioms), and an origin partition indicating which origins in symbols are considered equal and which ones are not. Subsequently, the full signature and a number of properties of DA are presented. The notion of origin consistency of descriptions is defined and the relation of DA with Module Algebra is discussed.

2 Origins and symbols

2.1 Origins

We introduce the following two (disjoint) sets:

Definition 2.1.1 OCon is the countably infinite set of *origin constants*, and OVar is the countably infinite set of *origin variables*.

Origin constants and origin variables are the basic building blocks of origins. More complex origins can be built by means of tupling:

Definition 2.1.2 The set Orig of *origins* is inductively defined by:

1. $c \in \mathsf{OCon} \Rightarrow c \in \mathsf{Orig}$,
2. $x \in \mathsf{OVar} \Rightarrow x \in \mathsf{Orig}$,
3. $a_1, \ldots, a_n \in \mathsf{Orig} \Rightarrow \langle a_1, \ldots, a_n \rangle \in \mathsf{Orig}$.

The set of origin variables occurring in an origin a will be denoted $OV(a)$:

Definition 2.1.3 For origins a, the set $OV(a) \subseteq \mathsf{OVar}$ is inductively defined by:

1. $OV(c) = \emptyset$,
2. $OV(x) = \{x\}$,
3. $OV(\langle a_1, \ldots, a_n \rangle) = OV(a_1) \cup \ldots \cup OV(a_n)$.

An origin containing no origin variables represents a fixed origin. An origin a containing origin variables $x_1, \ldots, x_n$ can be viewed as a parameterised origin, which can be instantiated by substituting other origins for the $x_1, \ldots, x_n$. The typical form of a parameterised origin used in the definition of COLD-K [3] is $\langle c, x_1, \ldots, x_n \rangle$, where c is an origin constant and $x_1, \ldots, x_n$ are origin variables. Such a parameterised origin can be viewed as a function from origins to origins, where c acts as the function symbol.

In the sequel we shall be particularly concerned with origin sets and origin partitions:

Definition 2.1.4 An *origin set* is a set of origins. The set of all origin sets is denoted OSet.

Definition 2.1.5 An *origin partition* π is a partition of the set Orig of origins. The origin sets which are the elements of π are called the *blocks* of π and the set of all origin partitions is denoted OPar.

An origin partition is called finite if its blocks are finite sets and the number of non-singleton blocks is finite:

Definition 2.1.6 An origin partition π is called *finite* if each block of π is finite and $\{A \in \pi \mid card(A) \neq 1\}$ is finite.

Refinement of origin partitions is defined as usual for partitions:

Definition 2.1.7 If π_1, π_2 are origin partitions, then the fact that π_1 is a *refinement* of π_2, denoted $\pi_1 \leq \pi_2$, is defined by:

$$\pi_1 \leq \pi_2 :\Leftrightarrow \forall A \in \pi_1 \exists B \in \pi_2 (A \subseteq B).$$

A well-known property of the refinement relation on partitions is that it turns the set of all partitions into a complete lattice, hence we shall not give a detailed proof of this:

Lemma 2.1.8 $\langle \mathsf{OPar}, \leq \rangle$ is a complete lattice.

Proof. Show that an arbitrary set of partitions has an infimum by using the 1–1 correspondence of partitions and equivalence relations and the fact that the intersection of an arbitrary number of equivalence relations is again an equivalence relation. □

Notation 2.1.9 The top and bottom of the lattice $\langle \mathsf{OPar}, \leq \rangle$ are denoted $\pi_\top$ and $\pi_\perp$, respectively.

Due to Lemma 2.1.8 the following definitions of the sum and product of origin partitions are in order:

Definition 2.1.10 If P is a set of origin partitions, then the *sum* of the elements of P, denoted $\sum P$, and the *product* of the elements of P, denoted $\prod P$, are defined by:

$$\sum P := \text{the supremum of } P \text{ with respect to } \leq,$$
$$\prod P := \text{the infimum of } P \text{ with respect to } \leq.$$

Notation 2.1.11 For origin partitions π_1, π_2, we introduce the following notations:

$$\pi_1 + \pi_2 := \sum\{\pi_1, \pi_2\},$$
$$\pi_1 \cdot \pi_2 := \prod\{\pi_1, \pi_2\}.$$

The definition of OV is extended to origin sets and origin partitions by:

Definition 2.1.12 For origin sets A, the set $OV(A) \subseteq \mathsf{OVar}$ is defined by:

$$OV(A) := \bigcup_{a \in A} OV(a).$$

Definition 2.1.13 For origin partitions π, the set $OV(\pi) \subseteq \mathsf{OVar}$ is defined by:

$$OV(\pi) := \bigcup \{OV(A) \mid A \in \pi, \ card(A) \neq 1\}.$$

2.2   Origin substitutions

Origin substitutions are instantiations of origin variables:

Definition 2.2.1 An *origin substitution* is a mapping $\alpha : \mathsf{OVar} \to \mathsf{Orig}$. The set of all origin substitutions is denoted OSub.

Origin substitutions are extended to origins, origin sets and origin partitions:

Definition 2.2.2 Each origin substitution α is extended to a mapping $\alpha : \mathsf{Orig} \to \mathsf{Orig}$ by the following rules:

1. $\alpha(c) = c$,
2. $\alpha(x) = \alpha(x)$,
3. $\alpha(\langle a_1, \ldots, a_n \rangle) = \langle \alpha(a_1), \ldots, \alpha(a_n) \rangle$.

Definition 2.2.3 Each origin substitution α is extended to a mapping $\alpha : \mathsf{OSet} \to \mathsf{OSet}$ by the following rule:

$\alpha(A) = \{\alpha(a) \mid a \in A\}$.

Definition 2.2.4 Each origin substitution α is extended to a mapping $\alpha : \mathsf{OPar} \to \mathsf{OPar}$ by the following rule:

$$\alpha(\pi) := \prod\{\pi' \in \mathsf{OPar} \mid \forall A \in \pi \exists B \in \pi'(\alpha(A) \subseteq B)\}.$$

The domain of an origin substitution α consists of those origin variables that are affected by α:

Definition 2.2.5 The *domain* of an origin substitution α, denoted $dom(\alpha)$, is defined by:

$$dom(\alpha) := \{x \in \mathsf{OVar} \mid \alpha(x) \neq x\}.$$

Definition 2.2.6 The *sum* of two origin substitutions α and β with $dom(\alpha) \cap dom(\beta) = \emptyset$ is denoted $\alpha + \beta$ and defined by:

$$(\alpha + \beta)(x) := \begin{cases} \alpha(x) & \text{if } x \in dom(\alpha), \\ \beta(x) & \text{if } x \in dom(\beta), \\ x & \text{otherwise.} \end{cases}$$

2.3 Bisubstitution equivalence

We often want to consider origin substitutions identical if they have the same effect 'modulo origin variable renaming'. This is more precisely described by the bisubstitution equivalence relation introduced in this section. We first introduce a preorder on OSub which captures the fact that one origin substitution can be viewed as an instantiation of another with respect to the instantiation of the origin variables from some subset V of OVar (ignoring the variables in $\mathsf{OVar} \setminus V$).

Definition 2.3.1 For each $V \subseteq \mathsf{OVar}$ the relation $\leq_V$ on OSub is defined by:

$$\alpha \leq_V \beta :\Leftrightarrow \exists \gamma \in \mathsf{OSub} \; \forall x \in V \; (\alpha(x) = \gamma(\beta(x))).$$

We say that two origin substitutions are V-bisubstition equivalent if on V they can be viewed as instantiations of each other:

Definition 2.3.2 Two origin substitutions α and β are *V-bisubstitution equivalent*, denoted $\alpha \approx_V \beta$, if $\alpha \leq_V \beta$ and $\beta \leq_V \alpha$ ($V \subseteq \mathsf{OVar}$).

It is not difficult to see that $\approx_V$ is indeed an equivalence relation on OSub and that the extension of $\leq_V$ to equivalence classes of $\approx_V$ is a partial order:

Lemma 2.3.3 The relation $\approx_V$ on OSub is an equivalence relation ($V \subseteq \mathsf{OVar}$).

Lemma 2.3.4 The relation $\leq_V$ on OSub induces a partial order on the equivalence classes of $\approx_V$ ($V \subseteq \mathsf{OVar}$).

An equivalent formulation of V-bisubstitution equivalence is provided by the following lemma:

Lemma 2.3.5 For each $V \subseteq$ OVar, $\alpha, \beta \in$ OSub:

$$\alpha \approx_V \beta \Leftrightarrow \exists \gamma, \delta : \text{OVar} \to \text{OVar} \; \forall x \in V \; (\alpha(x) = \gamma(\beta(x)) \wedge \beta(x) = \delta(\alpha(x))).$$

Proof. $\Leftarrow$ is obvious. Let $\alpha \approx_V \beta$, then there are $\gamma, \delta \in$ OSub such that $\alpha(x) = \gamma(\beta(x))$ and $\beta(x) = \delta(\alpha(x))$ for all $x \in V$. We may assume that $\gamma(y) = y$ for all $y \in$ OVar $\setminus OV(\beta(V))$. Now let $y \in OV(\beta(V))$, then there is an $x \in V$ such that $y \in OV(\beta(x))$. Suppose that $\gamma(y) \notin$ OVar, then the fact that $\beta(x) = \delta(\gamma(\beta(x)))$ would lead to a contradiction, so $\gamma(y) \in$ OVar and $\gamma :$ OVar $\to$ OVar. Analogously we derive that $\delta :$ OVar $\to$ OVar. $\qquad\square$

One may wonder why we did not define V-bisubstitution equivalence as follows:

$$\alpha \approx'_V \beta :\Leftrightarrow \exists \text{ bijection } \gamma : \text{OVar} \to \text{OVar} \; \forall x \in V \; (\alpha(x) = \gamma(\beta(x))).$$

The reason is that $\approx'_V$ is not abstract enough, as can be seen by the following example. Let OVar $= \{x_0, x_1, \ldots\}$, $V =$ OVar, $\alpha(x_i) = x_i$, $\beta(x_i) = x_{i+1}$ $(i = 0, 1, \ldots)$, then $\alpha \approx_V \beta$ but $\alpha \not\approx'_V \beta$. If V is finite, however, $\approx_V$ and $\approx'_V$ coincide:

Lemma 2.3.6 For each $V \subseteq$ OVar, V finite, $\alpha, \beta \in$ OSub:

$$\alpha \approx_V \beta \Leftrightarrow \exists \text{ bijection } \gamma : \text{OVar} \to \text{OVar} \; \forall x \in V \; (\alpha(x) = \gamma(\beta(x))).$$

Proof. $\Leftarrow$ is obvious. Let $\alpha \approx_V \beta$, then according to Lemma 2.3.5 there are $\delta, \eta :$ OVar $\to$ OVar such that $\alpha(x) = \delta(\beta(x))$ and $\beta(x) = \eta(\alpha(x))$ for all $x \in V$. Let $W_\alpha = OV(\alpha(V))$ and $W_\beta = OV(\beta(V))$, then we have $\eta(W_\alpha) = \eta(OV(\alpha(V))) = OV(\eta(\alpha(V))) = OV(\beta(V)) = W_\beta$. Analogously we derive $\delta(W_\beta) = W_\alpha$. Since W_α and W_β are finite, this implies that the restriction δ' of δ to W_β is a bijection so we can extend δ' to a bijection $\gamma :$ OVar $\to$ OVar. For all $x \in V$ we then have $\alpha(x) = \delta(\beta(x)) = \delta'(\beta(x)) = \gamma(\beta(x))$. $\qquad\square$

We define the relations $\leq$ and $\approx$ by:

Definition 2.3.7 The relation $\leq$ on OSub is the relation $\leq_{\text{OVar}}$.

Definition 2.3.8 The relation $\approx$ on OSub is the relation $\approx_{\text{OVar}}$ and is called *bisubstitution equivalence*.

In the sequel we shall treat origin substitutions modulo bisubstitution equivalence and write $=$ for $\approx$. Only if confusion can arise the distinction between $=$ and $\approx$ will be made explicit.

2.4 P-Unification

In this section we define a notion of unification for origin partitions, called P-unification. First we define the traditional notion of unification for origin sets:

Definition 2.4.1 A *unifier* of an origin set A is an origin substitution α such that $\alpha(A)$ is a singleton. The set of all unifiers of an origin set A is denoted $\mathcal{U}(A)$.

Origin sets which can be unified are called unifiable:

Definition 2.4.2 An origin set A is *unifiable* if $\mathcal{U}(A) \neq \emptyset$.

There is a basic lemma from unification theory which, rephrased in terms of origin sets and origin substitutions, reads as follows:

Lemma 2.4.3 If A is a finite unifiable origin set, then $\mathcal{U}(A)$ has a maximum with respect to $\leq$.

For a proof of this lemma we refer to the literature on unification theory (see e.g. [7]). The following definitions introduce the notion of P-unification for origin partitions:

Definition 2.4.4 A *P-unifier* of an origin partition π is an origin substitution α such that $\alpha(A)$ is a singleton for all $A \in \pi$. The set of all P-unifiers of an origin partition π is denoted $\mathcal{U}_P(\pi)$.

Definition 2.4.5 An origin partition π is *P-unifiable* if $\mathcal{U}_P(\pi) \neq \emptyset$.

We are interested in the existence of a maximum in the set of P-unifiers of a P-unifiable origin partition π. If π is finite we can reduce P-unification in a straightforward way to normal unification and prove the following lemma:

Lemma 2.4.6 If π is a finite P-unifiable origin partition, then $\mathcal{U}_P(\pi)$ has a maximum with respect to $\leq$.

Proof. Let $\pi = \{A_0, A_1, \ldots\}$ be a finite P-unifiable origin partition with $card(A_i) = 1$ for $i \geq n$. Define the set of origins B by:

$$B := \{\langle a_0, \ldots, a_{n-1} \rangle \mid a_i \in A_i \ (i = 0, \ldots, n - 1)\},$$

then B is finite. It is easy to see that $\mathcal{U}(B) = \mathcal{U}_P(\pi)$. According to Lemma 2.4.3 $\mathcal{U}(B)$, and thereby $\mathcal{U}_P(\pi)$, has a maximum with respect to $\leq$. $\qquad\square$

Also non-finite P-unifiable origin partitions have a maximal P-unifier, but the proof of this is somewhat more complicated:

Theorem 2.4.7 If π is a P-unifiable origin partition, then $\mathcal{U}_P(\pi)$ has a maximum with respect to $\leq$.

Proof. Let π be a P-unifiable origin partition. Because Orig is countable, π is countable and hence we can choose finite origin partitions $\pi_0, \pi_1, \ldots$ such that:

1. $\pi_i \leq \pi_{i+1} \ (i = 0, 1, \ldots)$,
2. $\pi = \sum_{i=0}^{\infty} \pi_i$.

Since π is P-unifiable and $\pi_i \leq \pi$, each π_i is also P-unifiable. Lemma 2.4.6 implies that $\mathcal{U}_P(\pi_i)$ has a maximum, which will be denoted μ_i. Note that $\mu_0 \geq \mu_1 \geq \ldots$ We shall define an origin substitution μ in terms of the μ_i and show that $\mu = max(\mathcal{U}_P(\pi))$.

Let $V_0, V_1, \ldots$ be finite subsets of OVar such that:

1. $V_i \subseteq V_{i+1} \ (i = 0, 1, \ldots)$,

2. $\text{OVar} = \bigcup_{i=0}^{\infty} V_i$.

π is P-unifiable, so there is an $\alpha \in \mathcal{U}_P(\pi)$. $\pi_i \leq \pi$ implies that $\alpha \in \mathcal{U}_P(\pi_i)$ and thereby $\alpha \leq \mu_i$. From this we infer that $\alpha \leq_{V_j} \mu_i$ for all i and j. Since, for fixed j, the number of elements modulo $\approx_{V_j}$ of $\{\beta \in \text{OSub} \mid \alpha \leq_{V_j} \beta\}$ is finite and $\mu_0, \mu_1, \dots$ is a weakly decreasing sequence with lower bound α (with respect to the partial order $\leq_{V_j}$), we have that:

$$\forall j \; \exists n \; \forall i \geq n \; (\mu_i \approx_{V_j} \mu_n).$$

Hence we can choose a subsequence $\mu_0', \mu_1', \dots$ of $\mu_0, \mu_1, \dots$ and a corresponding subsequence $\pi_0', \pi_1', \dots$ of $\pi_0, \pi_1, \dots$ such that:

1. $\mu_i' = max(\mathcal{U}_P(\pi_i'))$ $(i = 0, 1, \dots)$,
2. $\mu_i' \approx_{V_j} \mu_j'$ $(i \geq j)$.

We inductively define representatives $\mu_0'', \mu_1'', \dots$ for the $\mu_0', \mu_1', \dots$ (with respect to $\approx$) such that $\mu_i''(x) = \mu_j''(x)$ for all $x \in V_j$, $i \geq j$. Define $\mu_0'' := \mu_0'$. Assume that $\mu_0'', \mu_1'', \dots, \mu_j''$ have already been defined. The fact that $\mu_j'' \approx \mu_j'$ implies that $\mu_j'' \approx_{V_j} \mu_j'$, which together with $\mu_{j+1}' \approx_{V_j} \mu_j'$ gives that $\mu_j'' \approx_{V_j} \mu_{j+1}'$. By Lemma 2.3.6 we derive from this that there is a bijection $\gamma_j : \text{OVar} \to \text{OVar}$ such that $\mu_j''(x) = \gamma_j(\mu_{j+1}'(x))$ for all $x \in V_j$. Define μ_{j+1}'' by:

$$\mu_{j+1}'' := \gamma_j \circ \mu_{j+1}'$$

then $\mu_{j+1}'' \approx \mu_{j+1}'$ because $\gamma_j : \text{OVar} \to \text{OVar}$ is a bijection. It follows from the definition of the $\mu_0'', \mu_1'', \dots$ that for all $j = 0, 1, \dots$ and $x \in V_j$ we have that $\mu_{j+1}''(x) = \gamma_j(\mu_{j+1}'(x)) = \mu_j''(x)$, which together with the fact that $V_i \subseteq V_{i+1}$ for all i implies that $\mu_i''(x) = \mu_j''(x)$ for all $x \in V_j$, $i \geq j$.

Since each $x \in \text{OVar}$ belongs to V_i if i is sufficiently large, we derive from the above that for all x, $\mu_i''(x)$ is constant for sufficiently large i.

Define μ as follows:

$$\mu(x) := \mu_i''(x) \text{ with } i \text{ sufficiently large.}$$

We have to prove two things:

1. $\mu \in \mathcal{U}_P(\pi)$: Since $OV(\pi_i')$ is finite, there is a $j \geq i$ such that $\mu(x) = \mu_j''(x)$ for all $x \in OV(\pi_i')$. Because μ_j'' unifies π_i', so does μ, hence $\mu \in \mathcal{U}_P(\pi_i')$ for all i. Suppose that μ would not unify π, then we could choose a π_i' such that $\mu \notin \mathcal{U}_P(\pi_i')$.
2. $\forall \alpha \in \mathcal{U}_P(\pi) \; (\alpha \leq \mu)$: Let $\alpha \in \mathcal{U}_P(\pi)$. Since $\mu_i'' = max(\mathcal{U}_P(\pi_i'))$ and $\alpha \in \mathcal{U}_P(\pi_i')$, we have $\alpha \leq \mu_i''$. So for each i there is $\beta_i \in \text{OSub}$ with $\alpha = \beta_i \circ \mu_i''$. For each x, $\mu_i''(x) = \mu(x)$ for i sufficiently large. Together with $\alpha(x) = \beta_i(\mu_i''(x))$ this implies that for all $y \in OV(\mu(x))$, $\beta_i(y)$ becomes constant for sufficiently large i. Define $\beta \in \text{OSub}$ by:

$$\beta(x) := \begin{cases} \beta_i(x) & \text{if } x \in OV(\mu(\text{OVar})), \; i \text{ sufficiently large,} \\ x & \text{if } x \notin OV(\mu(\text{OVar})), \end{cases}$$

then for all $x \in \text{OVar}$ and sufficiently large i:

$$\beta(\mu(x)) = \beta(\mu_i''(x)) = \beta_i(\mu_i''(x)) = \alpha(x),$$

hence $\alpha \leq \mu$.

□

As a corollary of this theorem we obtain that not only finite, but also infinite origin sets have a maximal unifier:

Corollary 2.4.8 If A is a unifiable origin set, then $\mathcal{U}(A)$ has a maximum with respect to $\leq$.

The following definition is now in order:

Definition 2.4.9 The *most general P-unifier* of a P-unifiable origin partition π is the maximum of $\mathcal{U}_P(\pi)$ and denoted μ_π.

We shall assume that $\mu_\pi(x) = x$ for all $x \in \mathrm{OVar} \setminus OV(\pi)$.

2.5 Symbols

We introduce the following set:

Definition 2.5.1 Ident is the countably infinite set of *identifiers*.

Symbols are built from identifiers, origins and types. We distinguish four different kinds of symbols: sort, object, predicate and function symbols. Correspondingly, we distinguish four different kinds of types. The types of symbols are built from the special keywords sort, obj, pred, func and sort symbols. The precise definitions are given below:

Definition 2.5.2 The sets Sort of *sort symbols*, Obj of *object symbols*, Pred of *predicate symbols* and Func of *functions symbols* are defined by:

$$\mathrm{Sort} := \{\langle i, a, \mathrm{sort}\rangle \mid i \in \mathrm{Ident},\ a \in \mathrm{Orig}\},$$
$$\mathrm{Obj} := \{\langle i, a, \langle \mathrm{obj}, T\rangle\rangle \mid i \in \mathrm{Ident},\ a \in \mathrm{Orig},\ T \in \mathrm{Sort}\},$$
$$\mathrm{Pred} := \{\langle i, a, \langle \mathrm{pred}, T_1, \ldots, T_n\rangle\rangle \mid i \in \mathrm{Ident},\ a \in \mathrm{Orig},\ T_1, \ldots, T_n \in \mathrm{Sort}\},$$
$$\mathrm{Func} := \{\langle i, a, \langle \mathrm{func}, T_1, \ldots, T_n, V\rangle\rangle \mid i \in \mathrm{Ident},\ a \in \mathrm{Orig},\ T_1, \ldots, T_n, V \in \mathrm{Sort}\}.$$

Definition 2.5.3 The set Type of *types* is the smallest set satisfying:

1. $\mathrm{sort} \in \mathrm{Type}$,
2. $T \in \mathrm{Sort} \Rightarrow \langle \mathrm{obj}, T\rangle \in \mathrm{Type}$,
3. $T_1, \ldots, T_n \in \mathrm{Sort} \Rightarrow \langle \mathrm{pred}, T_1, \ldots, T_n\rangle \in \mathrm{Type}$,
4. $T_1, \ldots, T_n, V \in \mathrm{Sort} \Rightarrow \langle \mathrm{func}, T_1, \ldots, T_n, V\rangle \in \mathrm{Type}$.

Definition 2.5.4 The set Sym of *symbols* is defined by:

$$\mathrm{Sym} := \{\langle i, a, t\rangle \mid i \in \mathrm{Ident},\ a \in \mathrm{Orig},\ t \in \mathrm{Type}\}.$$

Note that $\mathrm{Sym} = \mathrm{Sort} \cup \mathrm{Obj} \cup \mathrm{Pred} \cup \mathrm{Func}$. We introduce the following notation for the components of a symbol:

Notation 2.5.5 If $w = \langle i, a, t \rangle$ is a symbol then i, a, t will be denoted $\iota(w)$, $\omega(w)$, $\tau(w)$, respectively.

In order to avoid a frequent case analysis in definitions involving types, we introduce the following notation for types:

Notation 2.5.6 A type t in which the sorts $T_1, \ldots, T_n$ occur (in that order) will also be denoted as $t(T_1, \ldots, T_n)$.

The composite origin of a symbol is the tuple of all origins contained in the symbol:

Definition 2.5.7 For each symbol $w = \langle i, a, t(T_1, \ldots, T_n) \rangle$, the *composite origin* of w, denoted $\omega^*(w)$, is defined by:

$$\omega^*(w) := \langle a, \omega(T_1), \ldots, \omega(T_n) \rangle.$$

Note that $\omega^*(w)$ is itself an origin and that, if w is a sort, then $\omega^*(w) = \langle \omega(w) \rangle$.

The definition of OV is extended to symbols and sets of symbols in the obvious way:

Definition 2.5.8 For symbols w, the set $OV(w) \subseteq$ OVar is inductively defined by:

$$OV(\langle i, a, t(T_1, \ldots, T_n) \rangle) = OV(a) \cup OV(T_1) \cup \ldots \cup OV(T_n).$$

Definition 2.5.9 For sets of symbols W, the set $OV(W) \subseteq$ OVar is defined by:

$$OV(W) := \bigcup_{w \in W} OV(w).$$

Origin substitutions are extended to symbols:

Definition 2.5.10 Each origin substitution α is extended to a mapping $\alpha :$ Sym $\to$ Sym by the following rule:

$$\alpha(\langle i, a, t(T_1, \ldots, T_n) \rangle) = \langle i, \alpha(a), t(\alpha(T_1), \ldots, \alpha(T_n)) \rangle.$$

Origin substitutions permute with ω and ω^*:

Lemma 2.5.11 For all $w \in$ Sym, $\alpha \in$ OSub:

1. $\omega(\alpha(w)) = \alpha(\omega(w))$,
2. $\omega^*(\alpha(w)) = \alpha(\omega^*(w))$.

Proof.

1. Let $w = \langle i, a, t(T_1, \ldots, T_n) \rangle$, then $\omega(\alpha(w)) = \omega(\langle i, \alpha(a), t(\alpha(T_1), \ldots, \alpha(T_n)) \rangle) = \alpha(a) = \alpha(\omega(w))$.
2. Let $w = \langle i, a, t(T_1, \ldots, T_n) \rangle$, then $\omega^*(\alpha(w)) = \omega^*(\langle i, \alpha(a), t(\alpha(T_1), \ldots, \alpha(T_n)) \rangle) = \langle \alpha(a), \omega(\alpha(T_1)), \ldots, \omega(\alpha(T_n)) \rangle = \langle \alpha(a), \alpha(\omega(T_1)), \ldots, \alpha(\omega(T_n)) \rangle = \alpha(\langle a, \omega(T_1), \ldots, \omega(T_n) \rangle) = \alpha(\omega^*(w))$.

$\square$

We shall interpret symbols as symbols in the logic MPL_ω [6]. We choose this logic because it is the logic underlying the version of Description Algebra used in the definition of COLD-K. As indicated in the introduction, any other many-sorted logic could be chosen. The symbols are interpreted as follows:

1. each $T = \langle i, a, \text{sort} \rangle$ is a sort symbol in MPL_ω,
2. each $x = \langle i, a, \langle \text{obj}, T \rangle \rangle$ is a variable symbol $x : T$ in MPL_ω,
3. each $R = \langle i, a, \langle \text{pred}, T_1, \ldots, T_n \rangle \rangle$ is a predicate symbol $R : T_1 \times \ldots \times T_n$ in MPL_ω,
4. each $f = \langle i, a, \langle \text{func}, T_1, \ldots, T_n, V \rangle \rangle$ is a function symbol $f : T_1 \times \ldots \times T_n \to V$ in MPL_ω.

Furthermore, we shall assume that the operations defined on symbols such as origin substitution are homomorphically extended to MPL_ω formulae. The language of a symbol signature (see 3.3.1) is defined by:

Definition 2.5.12 If Σ is a symbol signature, then the *language* of Σ, denoted $\mathcal{L}(\Sigma)$, is the set of all Σ-formulae from MPL_ω.

The theory of a set of formulae is defined by:

Definition 2.5.13 If Σ is a symbol signature, $\Phi \subseteq \mathcal{L}(\Sigma)$, then the *theory* of Φ, denoted $Th(\Sigma, \Phi)$, is the set of formulae defined by:

$$Th(\Sigma, \Phi) := \{ \varphi \in \mathcal{L}(\Sigma) \mid \Phi \vdash \varphi \}.$$

3 Descriptions

In this section we introduce the notion of a description and define operations on descriptions. Together with their domains these operations constitute a many-sorted algebra, referred to as Description Algebra (DA). There are four sorts that play a role in this algebra: names, renamings, signatures and descriptions, which are introduced in that order.

3.1 Names

The fact that two symbols are the same except for the origins occurring in them is expressed by the following equivalence relation:

Definition 3.1.1 The *name equivalence* of two symbols v, w, denoted $v \equiv w$, is inductively defined by:

$$T_1 \equiv V_1, \ldots, T_n \equiv V_n \Rightarrow \langle i, a, t(T_1, \ldots, T_n) \rangle \equiv \langle i, b, t(V_1, \ldots, V_n) \rangle.$$

The notion of a name is defined by:

Definition 3.1.2 A *name* is an equivalence class of the equivalence relation $\equiv$ on **Sym**. The set of all names with representatives that are not object symbols is denoted **Nam**.

We shall use the following notation to denote names:

Notation 3.1.3 If w is a symbol, then $\overline{w}$ is the name with representative w. If W is a set of symbols, then $\overline{W}$ is the set of names $\{\overline{w} \mid w \in W\}$.

Name equivalent symbols have the same identifier, are of the same kind (sort, object, predicate or function) and the corresponding sorts in their types are name equivalent. Except for sorts, their types need not be the same, because the corresponding sorts in their types may have different origins. This is also the reason why name equivalence and equality of origins of two symbols does not imply equality of the symbols. It does so if we also require equality of the other origins occurring in the symbols:

Lemma 3.1.4 For all symbols v, w:

$$v \equiv w \wedge \omega^*(v) = \omega^*(w) \Rightarrow v = w.$$

Proof. Let $v \equiv w$, $\omega^*(v) = \omega^*(w)$, then $v = \langle i, a, t(T_1, \ldots, T_n)\rangle$, $w = \langle i, a, t(V_1, \ldots, V_n)\rangle$ with $\omega(T_i) = \omega(V_i)$ $(i = 1, \ldots, n)$. $v \equiv w$ implies $T_i \equiv V_i$, hence $\iota(T_i) = \iota(V_i)$ and $T_i = \langle \iota(T_i), \omega(T_i), \text{sort}\rangle = \langle \iota(V_i), \omega(V_i), \text{sort}\rangle = V_i$ $(i = 1, \ldots, n)$, so $v = w$. $\square$

Origin substitutions do not affect the name of a symbol:

Lemma 3.1.5 $\alpha(w) \equiv w$ for all $\alpha \in \text{OSub}$, $w \in \text{Sym}$.

Proof. Let $\alpha \in \text{OSub}$, $w \in \text{Sym}$. If $w = \langle i, a, \text{sort}\rangle$, then $\alpha(w) = \langle i, \alpha(a), \text{sort}\rangle \equiv w$. If $w = \langle i, a, t(T_1, \ldots, T_n)\rangle$, then $\alpha(w) = \langle i, \alpha(a), t(\alpha(T_1), \ldots, \alpha(T_n))\rangle$. From the definition of $\equiv$ and the fact that $\alpha(T_i) \equiv T_i$ $(i = 1, \ldots, n)$ it follows that $\alpha(w) \equiv w$. $\square$

The name equivalence relation $\equiv$ induces a partition on the set of origins of a set of symbols W. The extension of this partition to Orig by adding singletons is called the origin partition of W:

Definition 3.1.6 The *origin partition* of a set of symbols W, denoted $\pi_\omega(W)$, is the origin partition defined by:

$$\pi_\omega(W) := \prod \{\pi \in \text{OPar} \mid \forall v, w \in W \ (\overline{v} = \overline{w} \Rightarrow \exists A \in \pi \ (\omega(v), \omega(w) \in A))\}.$$

As we do with symbols, we shall interpret names as symbols of MPL_ω according to the following interpretation:

1. each $\overline{T} = \overline{\langle i, a, \text{sort}\rangle}$ is a sort symbol in MPL_ω,
2. each $\overline{x} = \overline{\langle i, a, \langle \text{obj}, T\rangle\rangle}$ is a variable symbol $\overline{x} : \overline{T}$ in MPL_ω,
3. each $\overline{R} = \overline{\langle i, a, \langle \text{pred}, T_1, \ldots, T_n\rangle\rangle}$ is a predicate symbol $\overline{R} : \overline{T}_1 \times \ldots \times \overline{T}_n$ in MPL_ω,
4. each $\overline{f} = \overline{\langle i, a, \langle \text{func}, T_1, \ldots, T_n, V\rangle\rangle}$ is a function symbol $\overline{f} : \overline{T}_1 \times \ldots \times \overline{T}_n \to \overline{V}$ in MPL_ω.

The language of a name signature (see 3.3.2) is defined by:

Definition 3.1.7 If Σ is a name signature, then the *language* of Σ, denoted $\mathcal{L}(\Sigma)$, is the set of all Σ-formulae from MPL_ω.

In order to distinguish formulae built from symbols from those built from names we shall refer to the former as symbol formulae and to the latter as name formulae. We introduce a mapping from symbol formulae to name formulae by:

Definition 3.1.8 If Σ is a symbol signature, $\varphi \in \mathcal{L}(\Sigma)$, then $\overline{\varphi} \in \mathcal{L}(\overline{\Sigma})$ is the name formula obtained by replacing all symbols w in φ by their name $\overline{w}$. If Φ is a set of symbol formulae, then $\overline{\Phi}$ is the set of name formulae $\{\overline{\varphi} \mid \varphi \in \Phi\}$.

The theory of a set of name formulae is defined by:

Definition 3.1.9 If Σ is a name signature, $\Phi \subseteq \mathcal{L}(\Sigma)$, then the *theory* of Φ, denoted $Th(\Sigma, \Phi)$, is the set of formulae defined by:

$$Th(\Sigma, \Phi) := \{\varphi \in \mathcal{L}(\Sigma) \mid \Phi \vdash \varphi\}.$$

3.2 Renamings

A renaming is a mapping from symbols to symbols such that it maps symbols of the same name to symbols of the same name, does not affect the origins of symbols and behaves homomorphically with respect to the types of symbols:

Definition 3.2.1 A *renaming* is a mapping $\rho : \text{Sym} \to \text{Sym}$ such that:

1. $v \equiv w \Rightarrow \rho(v) \equiv \rho(w)$,
2. $\omega(\rho(w)) = \omega(w)$,
3. $\tau(w) = t(T_1, \ldots, T_n) \Rightarrow \tau(\rho(w)) = t(\rho(T_1), \ldots, \rho(T_n))$.

The set of all renamings is denoted Ren.

We shall assume that renamings are extended to MPL_ω formulae in the usual homomorphic way. Renamings leave all origins in symbols unaffected and permute with origin substitutions:

Lemma 3.2.2 For all $w \in \text{Sym}$, $\alpha \in \text{OSub}$, $\rho \in \text{Ren}$:

1. $\omega^*(\rho(w)) = \omega^*(w)$,
2. $\alpha(\rho(w)) = \rho(\alpha(w))$.

Proof.

1. Let $w = \langle i, a, t(T_1, \ldots, T_n) \rangle$, then $\omega^*(\rho(w)) = \langle \omega(\rho(w)), \omega(\rho(T_1)), \ldots, \omega(\rho(T_n)) \rangle = \langle \omega(w), \omega(T_1), \ldots, \omega(T_n) \rangle = \omega^*(w)$.
2. Due to Lemma 3.1.5, $\alpha(w) \equiv w$ and $\alpha(\rho(w)) \equiv \rho(w)$. From $\alpha(w) \equiv w$ and the definition of renaming it follows that $\rho(\alpha(w)) \equiv \rho(w)$, hence $\alpha(\rho(w)) \equiv \rho(\alpha(w))$. Lemma 2.5.11 and 1 imply that $\omega^*(\alpha(\rho(w))) = \alpha(\omega^*(\rho(w))) = \alpha(\omega^*(w)) = \omega^*(\alpha(w)) = \omega^*(\rho(\alpha(w)))$. By Lemma 3.1.4 we get $\alpha(\rho(w)) = \rho(\alpha(w))$.

$\square$

We introduce two operations concerned with renamings, which will be part of the many-sorted algebra DA of descriptions. We interpret the names of these operations as formal operation symbols in DA. The first operation is the application of a renaming to a name:

Definition 3.2.3 The operation $\bullet : \mathsf{Ren} \times \mathsf{Nam} \to \mathsf{Nam}$ of *renaming* a name is defined by:

$$\rho \bullet \overline{w} := \overline{\rho(w)} \quad (\overline{w} \in \mathsf{Nam}).$$

The fact that this definition is independent of the choice of the representative w follows immediately from Definition 3.2.1.

The second operation on renamings is functional composition, which is defined in the usual way:

Definition 3.2.4 The operation $\circ : \mathsf{Ren} \times \mathsf{Ren} \to \mathsf{Ren}$ of *functional composition* of renamings is defined by:

$$(\rho_1 \circ \rho_2)(w) := \rho_1(\rho_2(w)) \quad (w \in \mathsf{Sym}).$$

It is easily verified that $\rho_1 \circ \rho_2$ is indeed a renaming.

3.3 Signatures

The notion of a signature is defined in the usual way, though we shall distinguish between two kinds of signatures:

Definition 3.3.1 A *symbol signature* is a set of symbols $\Sigma \subseteq \mathsf{Sort} \cup \mathsf{Pred} \cup \mathsf{Func}$ such that:

$$\forall w \in \Sigma(w = \langle i, a, t(T_1, \ldots, T_n)\rangle) \Rightarrow T_1, \ldots, T_n \in \Sigma).$$

Definition 3.3.2 A *name signature* is a set of names $\overline{\Sigma}$, where Σ is a symbol signature. The set of all name signatures is denoted Sig.

Often, if no confusion can arise, we shall use the word *signature* instead of symbol signature or name signature.

We shall define four operations on (name) signatures, starting with renaming:

Definition 3.3.3 The operation $\bullet : \mathsf{Ren} \times \mathsf{Sig} \to \mathsf{Sig}$ of *renaming* a signature is defined by:

$$\rho \bullet \Sigma := \rho(\Sigma).$$

It is easy to verify that $\rho \bullet \Sigma$ is indeed a signature, i.e. that Sig is closed under renaming. The same holds for the union and intersection of signatures:

Definition 3.3.4 The operation $+ : \mathsf{Sig} \times \mathsf{Sig} \to \mathsf{Sig}$ of *taking the union* of signatures is defined by:

$$\Sigma_1 + \Sigma_2 := \Sigma_1 \cup \Sigma_2.$$

Definition 3.3.5 The operation $\Box$: Sig $\times$ Sig $\to$ Sig of *taking the intersection* of signatures is defined by:

$$\Sigma_1 \Box \Sigma_2 := \Sigma_1 \cap \Sigma_2.$$

The delete operation removes a name from a signature. If that name is a sort name, it also removes all predicate and function names containing that sort name:

Definition 3.3.6 The operation Δ : Nam $\times$ Sig $\to$ Sig of *deleting* a name from a signature is defined by:

$$u \Delta \Sigma := \bigcup \{ \Sigma_1 \in \text{Sig} \mid \Sigma_1 \subseteq \Sigma \wedge u \notin \Sigma_1 \}.$$

3.4 Descriptions

A description can be viewed as an axiomatic specification of a system, consisting of four components Σ, Γ, Φ and π to be interpreted as follows. Γ is the set of all symbols used in the specification and Φ is the collection of axioms describing the behaviour of the system. The signature Σ represents that part of the system that is visible externally. The origin partition π indicates which origins in the symbols are considered equal and which ones are not.

Definition 3.4.1 A *description* is a quadruple $\langle \Sigma, \Gamma, \Phi, \pi \rangle$, where Σ and Γ are symbol signatures, $\Sigma \subseteq \Gamma$, $\Phi \subseteq \mathcal{L}(\Gamma)$ and π is an origin partition. The set of all descriptions is denoted Des.

Notation 3.4.2 If $X = \langle \Sigma, \Gamma, \Phi, \pi \rangle$ is a description, then Σ, Γ, Φ, π will be denoted Σ_X, Γ_X, Φ_X, π_X, respectively.

We extend origin substitutions to descriptions:

Definition 3.4.3 Each origin substitution α is extended to a mapping α : Des $\to$ Des by the following rule:

$$\alpha(X) = \langle \alpha(\Sigma_X), \alpha(\Gamma_X), \alpha(\Phi_X), \alpha(\pi_X) \rangle.$$

We introduce the following relation on descriptions:

Definition 3.4.4 The relation $\leq$ on Des is defined by:

$$X \leq Y :\Leftrightarrow \Sigma_X \subseteq \Sigma_Y \wedge \Gamma_X \subseteq \Gamma_Y \wedge \Phi_X \subseteq \Phi_Y \wedge \pi_X \leq \pi_Y.$$

The relation $\leq$ is a partial order with the property that:

Lemma 3.4.5 $\langle \text{Des}, \leq \rangle$ is a complete lattice.

Proof. Immediate from the facts that the powerset of a set with inclusion is a complete lattice, $\langle \text{OPar}, \leq \rangle$ is a complete lattice (Lemma 2.1.8) and the cartesian product of complete lattices is again a complete lattice. $\qquad\square$

We introduce sum and product of descriptions by:

Definition 3.4.6 If D is a set of descriptions, then the *sum* of the elements of D, denoted $\sum D$, and the *product* of the elements of D, denoted $\prod D$, are defined by:

$$\sum D := \text{the supremum of } D \text{ with respect to } \leq,$$
$$\prod D := \text{the infimum of } D \text{ with respect to } \leq.$$

We define six operations on descriptions. The first has to do with determining the visible signature of a description:

Definition 3.4.7 The operation $\Sigma : \text{Des} \to \text{Sig}$ of *taking the signature* of a description is defined by:

$$\Sigma(X) := \overline{\Sigma_X}.$$

The names of symbols in a description can be changed by means of the renaming operation:

Definition 3.4.8 The operation $\bullet : \text{Ren} \times \text{Des} \to \text{Des}$ of *renaming* a description is defined by:

$$\rho \bullet X := \langle \rho(\Sigma_X), \rho(\Gamma_X), \rho(\Phi_X), \pi_X \rangle.$$

The union of two descriptions can be taken by means of the import operation:

Definition 3.4.9 The operation $+ : \text{Des} \times \text{Des} \to \text{Des}$ of *importing* is defined by:

$$X + Y := \langle \Sigma_X \cup \Sigma_Y, \Gamma_X \cup \Gamma_Y, \Phi_X \cup \Phi_Y, \pi_X + \pi_Y \rangle$$

Note that $X + Y$ is the supremum of X and Y in the complete lattice $\langle \text{Des}, \leq \rangle$, i.e. $X + Y = \sum \{X, Y\}$.

By means of the export operation the visible signature of a description can be restricted:

Definition 3.4.10 The operation $\square : \text{Sig} \times \text{Des} \to \text{Des}$ of *exporting* is defined by:

$$\Sigma \square X := \langle \{w \in \Sigma_X \mid \overline{w} \in \Sigma\}, \Gamma_X, \Phi_X, \pi_X \rangle.$$

The unification operation has the effect of declaring the origins of symbols in the visible signature with the same name to be equal. So it amounts to enforcing 'origin consistency' of a description (see Subsection 3.6):

Definition 3.4.11 The operation $\mu : \text{Des} \to \text{Des}$ of *unifying* is defined by:

$$\mu(X) := \langle \Sigma_X, \Gamma_X, \Phi_X, \pi_X + \pi_\omega(\Sigma_X) \rangle.$$

The last operation is merely introduced as an auxiliary operation in formulating the properties of DA. It throws away all information contained in a description except the information about the equality of origins:

Definition 3.4.12 The operation $\pi : \text{Des} \to \text{Des}$ is defined by:

$$\pi(X) := \langle \emptyset, \emptyset, \emptyset, \pi_X \rangle.$$

3.5 Description Algebra

Definition 3.5.1 *Description Algebra* (DA) is the many-sorted algebra consisting of the following sorts and operations:

Sorts: Nam
  Ren
  Sig
  Des

Constants: u : Nam $(u \in \text{Nam})$
  ρ : Ren $(\rho \in \text{Ren})$
  Σ : Sig $(\Sigma \in \text{Sig})$
  X : Des $(X \in \text{Des})$

Operations: $\bullet$: Ren $\times$ Nam $\rightarrow$ Nam
  $\circ$: Ren $\times$ Ren $\rightarrow$ Ren

  $\bullet$: Ren $\times$ Sig $\rightarrow$ Sig
  $+$: Sig $\times$ Sig $\rightarrow$ Sig
  $\square$: Sig $\times$ Sig $\rightarrow$ Sig
  Δ : Nam $\times$ Sig $\rightarrow$ Sig

  Σ : Des $\rightarrow$ Sig
  $\bullet$: Ren $\times$ Des $\rightarrow$ Des
  $+$: Des $\times$ Des $\rightarrow$ Des
  $\square$: Sig $\times$ Des $\rightarrow$ Des
  μ : Des $\rightarrow$ Des
  π : Des $\rightarrow$ Des

Notice that we did not bother to define special constants for each sort. We simply took the elements of (the carriers of) each sort as constants. Notice also that all operations in the algebra are total.

The following theorem lists some of the properties of the operations of DA (in particular, the operations defined on Des):

Lemma 3.5.2 The algebra DA has the following properties:

$$\Sigma(\rho \bullet X) = \rho \bullet \Sigma(X) \tag{S1}$$
$$\Sigma(X + Y) = \Sigma(X) + \Sigma(Y) \tag{S2}$$
$$\Sigma(\Sigma_1 \square X) = \Sigma_1 \square \Sigma(X) \tag{S3}$$
$$\Sigma(\mu(X)) = \Sigma(X) \tag{S4}$$
$$\Sigma(\pi(X)) = \emptyset \tag{S5}$$

$$\rho_1 \bullet (\rho_2 \bullet X) = (\rho_1 \circ \rho_2) \bullet X \tag{R1}$$
$$\rho \bullet (X + Y) = (\rho \bullet X) + (\rho \bullet Y) \tag{R2}$$
$$\rho \bullet (\Sigma_1 \square X) = (\rho \bullet \Sigma_1) \square (\rho \bullet X) \tag{R3}$$
$$\rho \bullet \mu(X) = (\rho \bullet X) + \pi(\mu(X)) \tag{R4}$$

$$\rho \bullet \pi(X) = \pi(X) \tag{R5}$$

$$X + X = X \tag{I1}$$
$$X + Y = Y + X \tag{I2}$$
$$(X + Y) + Z = X + (Y + Z) \tag{I3}$$
$$X + \mu(X) = \mu(X) \tag{I4}$$
$$X + \pi(X) = X \tag{I5}$$
$$X + \pi(\mu(X)) = \mu(X) \tag{I6}$$

$$\Sigma(X) \square X = X \tag{E1}$$
$$\Sigma_1 \square (X + Y) = (\Sigma_1 \square X) + (\Sigma_1 \square Y) \tag{E2}$$
$$\Sigma_1 \square (\Sigma_2 \square X) = (\Sigma_1 \square \Sigma_2) \square X \tag{E3}$$
$$\Sigma_1 \square \mu(X) = \mu(\Sigma_1 \square X) + \pi(\mu(X)) \tag{E4}$$
$$\Sigma_1 \square \pi(X) = \pi(X) \tag{E5}$$

$$\mu(\rho \bullet \mu(X)) = \mu(\rho \bullet X) \tag{M1}$$
$$\mu(\mu(X) + Y) = \mu(X + Y) \tag{M2}$$
$$\mu(\Sigma_1 \square \mu(X)) = \Sigma_1 \square \mu(X) \tag{M3}$$
$$\mu(\mu(X)) = \mu(X) \tag{M4}$$
$$\mu(\pi(X)) = \pi(X) \tag{M5}$$

$$\pi(\rho \bullet X) = \pi(X) \tag{P1}$$
$$\pi(X + Y) = \pi(X) + \pi(Y) \tag{P2}$$
$$\pi(\Sigma_1 \square X) = \pi(X) \tag{P3}$$
$$\pi(\pi(X)) = \pi(X) \tag{P4}$$

Proof. Straightforward from the definitions of the operations. □

3.6 Origin consistency

The notion of a unifier of a description is defined by:

Definition 3.6.1 A *unifier* of a description X is a P-unifier of the origin partition $\pi_{\mu(X)}$. The set of all unifiers of X is denoted $\mathcal{U}_D(X)$.

A unifier α of a description X maps all symbols in the visible signature Σ_X of X with the same name to the same symbol. Descriptions which have at least one unifier are called origin consistent:

Definition 3.6.2 A description X is *origin consistent* if $\mathcal{U}_D(X) \neq \emptyset$.

From Theorem 2.4.7 we derive that an origin consistent description has a most general unifier:

Definition 3.6.3 The *most general unifier* of an origin consistent description X, denoted μ_X, is the most general unifier of the origin partition $\pi_{\mu(X)}$.

In an origin consistent description X those symbols v and w from Σ_X for which $\mu_X(v) = \mu_X(w)$ will be considered equal. This implies that in an origin consistent description X there is a unique correspondence between the names in $\Sigma(X)$ and the symbols in Σ_X. Hence we can refer to the visible symbols of X 'by name' without knowing the origins of the symbols. This allows us to attach a more abstract (i.e. origin independent) meaning to an origin consistent description. This meaning is called the theory of the description and amounts to the set of all derivable properties of the symbols in the visible signature of X.

We now define the notion of the theory of a description, which can be viewed as the meaning of a description. It is defined for all descriptions (including non-origin-consistent ones) by:

Definition 3.6.4 The *theory* of a description X, denoted $Th(X)$, is defined as follows. If X is origin consistent, then:

$$Th(X) := \overline{Th(\mu_X(\Gamma_X), \mu_X(\Phi_X)) \cap \mathcal{L}(\mu_X(\Sigma_X))}.$$

If X is not origin consistent then:

$$Th(X) := \bigcup\{ Th(Y) \mid Y \leq X, Y \text{ origin consistent}\}.$$

Notice that the theory of a description is a set of name formulae, so origins do no longer play a role there. The above definition is justified by the following lemma:

Lemma 3.6.5 If X is an origin consistent description, then:

$$Th(X) = \bigcup\{ Th(Y) \mid Y \leq X, Y \text{ origin consistent}\}.$$

Proof. Let X and Y be origin consistent descriptions with $Y \leq X$, then $\Sigma_Y \subseteq \Sigma_X$, $\Gamma_Y \subseteq \Gamma_X$, $\Phi_Y \subseteq \Phi_X$ and $\pi_Y \leq \pi_X$. It suffices to prove that $Th(Y) \subseteq Th(X)$. $\pi_{\mu(Y)} = \pi_Y + \pi_\omega(\Sigma_Y) \leq \pi_X + \pi_\omega(\Sigma_X) = \pi_{\mu(X)}$, hence μ_X is a unifier of Y and $\mu_X \leq \mu_Y$. This implies that μ_X (viewed as a symbol renaming) identifies more than μ_Y and thereby:

$$\overline{Th(\mu_X(\Gamma_X), \mu_X(\Phi_X)) \cap \mathcal{L}(\mu_X(\Sigma_X))} \supseteq \overline{Th(\mu_Y(\Gamma_Y), \mu_Y(\Phi_Y)) \cap \mathcal{L}(\mu_Y(\Sigma_Y))},$$

or, in other words, $Th(Y) \subseteq Th(X)$. $\qquad\square$

3.7 Relation with Module Algebra

In this section we shall indicate the relation between Description Algebra (DA) and Module Algebra (MA) [2], which has been a source of inspiration in the development of DA. A first technical difference between DA and MA is the fact that DA is an algebra while MA is an axiomatic *specification* of an algebra. Hence we shall discuss the relation of DA and MA by discussing which axioms of MA are satisfied by DA. A few other differences have to do with the choice of constants and operators. The symbols of the operators of MA are identical to those of the corresponding operators of DA. The only exceptions are the operators $\cap$ and . from MA which are represented by the symbols $\square$ and $\bullet$ in DA. The T operator of MA is missing in DA (and will be ignored), while DA has two operators not part of MA: the 'origin operators' μ and π. Finally, there is a difference in the fact that renamings in MA are supposed to be atomic, while in DA there are no restrictions on them. This will be solved by restricting renamings in DA to be atomic or (more generally) bijective, if necessary.

The relevant axioms of MA are listed below:

$$\Sigma(X + Y) = \Sigma(X) + \Sigma(Y) \tag{S3'}$$
$$\Sigma(\Sigma_1 \square X) = \Sigma_1 \square \Sigma(X) \tag{S4'}$$
$$\Sigma(\rho \bullet X) = \rho \bullet \Sigma(X) \tag{S5'}$$
$$\rho \bullet (X + Y) = (\rho \bullet X) + (\rho \bullet Y) \tag{R3'}$$
$$\rho \bullet (\Sigma_1 \square X) = (\rho \bullet \Sigma_1) \square (\rho \bullet X) \tag{R4'}$$
$$\rho \bullet (\rho \bullet X) = X \tag{R5'}$$
$$X + Y = Y + X \tag{C1'}$$
$$(X + Y) + Z = X + (Y + Z) \tag{C2'}$$
$$X + (\Sigma_1 \square X) = X \tag{C5'}$$
$$\Sigma(X) \square X = X \tag{E1'}$$
$$\Sigma_1 \square (\Sigma_2 \square X) = (\Sigma_1 \square \Sigma_2) \square X \tag{E2'}$$
$$\Sigma(X) \square \Sigma(Y) \subseteq \Sigma_1 \Rightarrow \Sigma_1 \square (X + Y) = (\Sigma_1 \square X) + (\Sigma_1 \square Y) \tag{E4'}$$

It follows immediately from Lemma 3.5.2 that all of these axioms are satisfied by DA, provided that we assume that ρ is atomic in (R5'). (R4') holds even for non-bijective ρ and (E4') holds unconditionally. The comparison made here is however not completely fair, because MA and DA are based on different ideas with respect to name clashes.

In MA the idea is that name clashes of visible names lead to identification of names while name clashes of hidden names are avoided by automatic renamings. In DA the idea is that names have an origin and that in a name clash, names are identified only if they have the same origin. The automatic renaming of hidden names cannot be described by means of the operators of DA, but the identification of visible names can (by means of the μ operator). A more fair comparison would therefore be to compare the operators $\bullet$, $+$ and $\square$ of MA with the operators $\bullet_\mu$, $+_\mu$ and $\square_\mu$ defined by:

$$\rho \bullet_\mu X := \mu(\rho \bullet X),$$
$$X +_\mu Y := \mu(X + Y),$$
$$\Sigma \square_\mu X := \mu(\Sigma \square X).$$

We would then also have to assume that symbols with the same name in the visible signature of a description are the same, which implies that we should replace X, Y, Z in the axioms by $\mu(X), \mu(Y), \mu(Z)$. Using Lemma 3.5.2 it is then easy to verify that the above axioms of Module Algebra also hold for the operators $\bullet_\mu$, $+_\mu$ and $\square_\mu$ (assuming that ρ is atomic in (R5')), except (R4') which holds only if ρ is bijective. Furthermore, the condition in (E4') has now become essential.

4 Conclusion

The notion of origin consistency defined in this paper is closely related to what is called the 'origin rule' in [1]. Both approaches are aimed at avoiding unintended name identifications in module composition. The main difference between the approach described here and that in [1] is the use of a more flexible origin mechanism including *origin variables, origin tupling* and *origin unification*. Among other things, this makes it possible to assign parameterised origins to names defined in a parameterised description, thus making explicit the dependency of the origins of those names on the origins of the actual parameters.

One could argue that the approach defined here is rather syntactic, in that the objects of DA are *presentations* of theories rather than theories themselves (or the sets of their models). It would of course be nice if semantical equivalence of descriptions would behave as a congruence relation with respect to the operators of DA. Unfortunately, this is not the case. In order to achieve that composition of descriptions corresponds with composition of theories (or sets of models) requirements must be put on the way we construct our systems. Two such requirements seem reasonable anyway. The first is that of origin consistency: we should take care that all descriptions we build are origin consistent. The second is that of conservativity: once a symbol has been defined in a description, other descriptions using that symbol should not impose additional (or even conflicting) constraints on that symbol. This requirement is closely related to that of hierarchy conservativity [9] in algebraic specifications. If the requirements of origin consistency and conservativity are satisfied, and the underlying logic satisfies the interpolation property (cf. [2,6]), more can be said about the extension of the operators of DA to the semantic level, but we shall not go further into this here.

Acknowledgements

The author would like to thank Loe Feijs, Karst Koymans and Gerard Renardel for their many helpful comments and suggestions.

References

[1] J.A. BERGSTRA, J. HEERING, P. KLINT, *ASF—An Algebraic Specification Formalism*, CWI Report CS-R8705 (1987).

[2] J.A. BERGSTRA, J. HEERING, P. KLINT, *Module Algebra*, CWI Report CS-R8617 (1986).

[3] L.M.G. FEIJS, H.B.M. JONKERS, C.P.J. KOYMANS, G.R. RENARDEL DE LAVALETTE, *Formal Definition of the Design Language COLD-K*, Preliminary Edition, Technical Report, ESPRIT project 432, Doc.Nr. METEOR/t7/PRLE/7 (1987).

[4] L.M.G. FEIJS, H.B.M. JONKERS, J.H. OBBINK, C.P.J. KOYMANS, G.R. RENARDEL DE LAVALETTE, P.H. RODENBURG, *A Survey of the Design Language COLD*, in: *ESPRIT '86: Results and Achievements*, Elsevier Science Publishers (1987), 631-644.

[5] H.B.M JONKERS, *An Introduction to COLD-K*, this volume.

[6] C.P.J. KOYMANS, G.R. RENARDEL DE LAVALETTE, *The Logic MPL_ω*, this volume.

[7] J.A. ROBINSON, *A Machine-Oriented Logic Based on the Resolution Principle*, Journal of the ACM 12 (1965), 23-41.

[8] M. WIRSING, *Structured Algebraic Specifications: a Kernel Language*, Habilitation thesis, Technische Universität München (1983).

[9] M. WIRSING, P. PEPPER, H. PARTSCH, W. DOSCH, M. BROY, *On Hierarchies of Abstract Data Types*, Acta Informatica 20 (1983), 1-33.

The calculus $\lambda\pi$

L.M.G. Feijs[*]

Philips Research Laboratories Eindhoven

P.O. Box 80000, 5600 JA Eindhoven, The Netherlands

Abstract

We introduce a special version of lambda calculus called $\lambda\pi$, which is defined for any algebraic system with preorder. We do not have lambda terms $\lambda x.X$, but we have terms $\lambda x \sqsubseteq R.X$, where R is a parameter restriction. The effect of the parameter restrictions is formalised by the rules of the calculus. Instead of the rule β there is a rule called π. This calculus has been used to give a meaning to the parameterisation and design constructs of COLD-K.

1 Introduction

In this paper we introduce a special version of lambda calculus called $\lambda\pi$, which is a version of lambda calculus with conditional contraction rule. This calculus has been used to give a meaning to the parameterisation constructs of COLD-K and to give a meaning to designs and components. Actually several versions of the calculus exist. We shall start with the simplest version and conclude with a version based on the description algebra DA [6] as used for COLD-K.

1.1 Lambda Abstraction

The logic MPL_ω [7] serves as a target language for the interpretation of sort definitions, function definitions, procedure definitions, axioms etc. and the algebra DA [6] offers mechanisms for structuring collections of such definitions. Since it must be possible to have highly *reusable* descriptions (i.e. modules), we want to add a *parameterisation mechanism* to this. Parameterisation is done by means of *lambda abstraction*, (as in ASL [8]). Just as in the λ-abstractions of ASL, parameter restrictions are allowed (see 1.2). The parameterisation is done in a very simple and uniform way: descriptions are parameterised over descriptions. E.g. if X is a term of DA denoting a description, then lambda abstraction is done by constructing the term $\lambda x.X$ (where we omitted the parameter restriction). If we want to instantiate this term with an argument Y, then either Y is a description or Y is a lambda term itself. We do not need so-called

---

[*]This work has been performed within the ESPRIT project 432: METEOR

"fitting morphisms", since we can always use the *renaming* operations • and ○ from DA [6].

1.2 Parameter Restrictions

Unlike in classical lambda calculus, we cannot allow arbitrary arguments to be substituted for the formal parameters of a lambda term. Therefore we shall not have lambda terms $\lambda x.X$, but we shall have terms $\lambda x \sqsubseteq R.X$, where R is a parameter restriction. There is one very natural way of expressing such a parameter restriction: we let R be a description (or a lambda term) and we require that the argument is an *implementation* of R. It thus turns out that the *implementation relation* $\sqsubseteq$ (as can be defined for DA) plays a crucial role in the parameterisation mechanism. The effect of the parameter restrictions is formalised by the rules of $\lambda\pi$ calculus. Instead of the rule (β) of classical lambda calculus we shall have a rule called (π).

1.3 Conversion

Whereas in classical lambda calculus we have the rule (β): $(\lambda x.X)Y = X[x := Y]$, in $\lambda\pi$ we have the following rule (π): $(\lambda x \sqsubseteq R.X)Y = X[x := Y]$, *provided* $Y \sqsubseteq R$. Actually, the formulation of the rule has to be somewhat more complicated, as is indicated by the following example. Consider the term $\lambda x \sqsubseteq Y.((\lambda y \sqsubseteq Y.X)x)$. It is reasonable to allow for the contraction of the subterm $((\lambda y \sqsubseteq Y.X)x)$, since it occurs within the scope of a $\lambda x \sqsubseteq Y$. As a consequence, the calculus $\lambda\pi$ must be defined by a derivation system where facts $X = Y$ are derived modulo a set of assumptions Γ. This leads to the introduction of *sequents* such as $\Gamma \vdash X = Y$. Furthermore we need sequents and rules extending the relation $\sqsubseteq$ from descriptions to arbitrary terms. It is interesting to compare this with derivation systems devised for assigning *types* to lambda terms (see e.g. [3]), the important difference being the kind of relation which is defined: in [3] it is a *typing* relation, whereas in $\lambda\pi$ it is an *ordering* $\sqsubseteq$.

2 Untyped $\lambda\pi$ calculus

2.1 General

In this section we define *untyped* $\lambda\pi$ calculus which is the simplest version of the calculus in which the terms of the calculus are untyped and in which there is only one constant. It should be noted that untyped $\lambda\pi$ calculus is *not* the version of the calculus which is used for the semantics of COLD-K but rather a simplified version of the calculus for which we can already prove the confluency property $(\Diamond)$. The proof of the $\Diamond$ property is essentially the same for both untyped and applied $\lambda\pi$ calculus.

2.2 Terms and formulae

Definition 2.2.1 Terms.

(i) All variables are terms.
(ii) The constant T is a term.
(iii) If M and N are terms, then MN is a term.
(iv) If N is a term, x a variable and M a term not containing x, then $\lambda x \sqsubseteq M.N$ is a term.

We shall identify α-congruent terms, as is usually done in classical lambda calculus; see e.g. [2] 2.1.12.

Definition 2.2.2 Formulae, sequents.

If M and N are terms, then $M \sqsubseteq N$ is a *formula*. $M = N$ abbreviates $M \sqsubseteq N$ and $N \sqsubseteq M$; we write $M \equiv N$ if M and N are identical terms.

If Γ is a finite set of formulae, then $\Gamma \vdash \varphi$ is a *sequent*. We write Γ, Δ for $\Gamma \cup \Delta$ and φ for $\{\varphi\}$; $\Gamma \vdash \varphi, \psi$ stands for $\Gamma \vdash \varphi$ *and* $\Gamma \vdash \psi$. Instead of $\emptyset \vdash \varphi$ we write $\vdash \varphi$ (and sometimes even φ *tout court*). $x \notin \Gamma$ means: the variable x does not occur free in Γ.

2.3 Rules

Definition 2.3.1 Derivation system.

(taut) $$\overline{\Gamma, \varphi \vdash \varphi}$$ (refl) $$\overline{\Gamma \vdash M \sqsubseteq M}$$

(T) $$\overline{\Gamma \vdash M \sqsubseteq T}$$ (tr) $$\frac{\Gamma \vdash M \sqsubseteq N, N \sqsubseteq P}{\Gamma \vdash M \sqsubseteq P}$$

(λI) $$\frac{\Gamma \vdash N \sqsubseteq M \qquad \Gamma, x \sqsubseteq M \vdash P \sqsubseteq Q \quad (x \notin \Gamma)}{\Gamma \vdash (\lambda x \sqsubseteq M.P) \sqsubseteq (\lambda x \sqsubseteq N.Q)}$$ (ap) $$\frac{\Gamma \vdash M \sqsubseteq N \qquad \Gamma \vdash P = Q}{\Gamma \vdash MP \sqsubseteq NQ}$$

(π) $$\frac{\Gamma \vdash P \sqsubseteq M}{\Gamma \vdash (\lambda x \sqsubseteq M.N)P = N[x := P]}$$

$\square$

Remark 2.3.2 (i) An alternative but equivalent definition of $\lambda\pi$ can be given by considering $M = N$ as a formula (not as an abbreviation) and adding the rules

$$\frac{\Gamma \vdash M \sqsubseteq N, N \sqsubseteq M}{\Gamma \vdash M = N} \qquad\qquad \frac{\Gamma \vdash M = N}{\Gamma \vdash M \sqsubseteq N, N \sqsubseteq M}$$

(ii) The rule (λI) is equivalent to the following two rules:

($\lambda I1$) $$\frac{\Gamma \vdash N \sqsubseteq M}{\Gamma \vdash (\lambda x \sqsubseteq M.P) \sqsubseteq (\lambda x \sqsubseteq N.P)}$$

($\lambda I2$) $$\frac{\Gamma, x \sqsubseteq M \vdash P \sqsubseteq Q \quad (x \notin \Gamma)}{\Gamma \vdash (\lambda x \sqsubseteq M.P) \sqsubseteq (\lambda x \sqsubseteq M.Q)}$$

(iii) We abbreviate $\lambda x \sqsubseteq T.M$ by $\lambda x.M$. The following hold:

> If $\Gamma \vdash P \sqsubseteq Q$, then $\Gamma \vdash (\lambda x.P) \sqsubseteq (\lambda x.Q)$,
> $\Gamma \vdash (\lambda x.P) \sqsubseteq (\lambda x \sqsubseteq M.P)$,
> $\Gamma \vdash (\lambda x.M)N = M[x := N]$.

2.4   Cut-rule

Lemma 2.4.1 (Weakening, Cut elimination.)

(i) If $\Gamma \vdash M \sqsubseteq N$ then $\Gamma, \Delta \vdash M \sqsubseteq N$.
(ii) If $\Gamma \vdash M \sqsubseteq N$ and $\Gamma, M \sqsubseteq N \vdash P \sqsubseteq Q$ then $\Gamma \vdash P \sqsubseteq Q$.

Proof. (i) Induction over the length of the proof of $\Gamma \vdash M \sqsubseteq N$.
(ii) Induction over the length of the proof of $\Gamma, M \sqsubseteq N \vdash P \sqsubseteq Q$. □

Lemma 2.4.2 (Substitution.)

(i) If $\Gamma \vdash M \sqsubseteq N$ then $\Gamma[x := P] \vdash M[x := P] \sqsubseteq N[x := P]$.
(ii) If $\Gamma \vdash M = N$ then $\Gamma \vdash P[x := M] = P[x := N]$.
(iii) If $\Gamma \vdash M = N$ and $\Delta \vdash P \sqsubseteq Q$ then $\Gamma, \Delta[x := M] \vdash P[x := M] \sqsubseteq Q[x := N], P[x := N] \sqsubseteq Q[x := M]$.

Proof. (i) Induction over the length of the proof of $\Gamma \vdash M \sqsubseteq N$.
(ii) Induction over the structure of P.
(iii) Assume $\Gamma \vdash M = N$ and $\Delta \vdash P \sqsubseteq Q$, then (by (ii)) $\Gamma \vdash P[x := M] = P[x := N], Q[x := M] = Q[x := N]$ and (by (i)) $\Delta[x := M] \vdash P[x := M] \sqsubseteq Q[x := M]$; now apply weakening (2.4.1(i)) and (tr). □

2.5   The diamond property ($\Diamond$)

Definition 2.5.1 We extend $\lambda \pi$ to $\lambda \pi^*$ as follows. The formulae

> $M \to N$ (M reduces in one step to N),
> $M \twoheadrightarrow N$ (M reduces to N) and
> $M \Rightarrow N$ (M reduces directly to N)

(M, N terms of $\lambda \pi$) are added to the language: they are intended as successive refinements of $M = N$ (see lemma 2.5.2). $M \Rightarrow N$ means: N is formed by contracting zero or more redexes in M (but not by contracting newly formed redexes). An example may clarify this: we have

$$((\lambda x.(\lambda y.y))M)N \to (\lambda y.y)N \to N, \quad \text{so} \quad ((\lambda x.(\lambda y.y))M)N \twoheadrightarrow N,$$

but

$$((\lambda x.(\lambda y.y))M)N \not\Rightarrow N,$$

for $(\lambda y.y)N$ is a newly formed redex.

Sequents are of the form $\Gamma \vdash \varphi$, where Γ is a finite set of formulae of $\lambda\pi$ (i.e. only $M \sqsubseteq N$ and not $M \to N$, $M \twoheadrightarrow N$, $M \Rightarrow N$) and φ is a formula of $\lambda\pi^*$. Axioms and rules are those of $\lambda\pi$ together with

$$\frac{\Gamma \vdash M \to M'}{\Gamma \vdash MN \to M'N, NM \to NM', (\lambda x \sqsubseteq M.N) \to (\lambda x \sqsubseteq M'.N)}$$

$$\frac{\Gamma \vdash P \sqsubseteq M}{\Gamma \vdash (\lambda x \sqsubseteq M.N)P \to N[x := P]} \qquad \frac{\Gamma, x \sqsubseteq M \vdash N \to N' \quad (x \notin \Gamma)}{\Gamma \vdash (\lambda x \sqsubseteq M.N) \to (\lambda x \sqsubseteq M.N')}$$

$$\frac{}{\Gamma \vdash M \twoheadrightarrow M} \qquad \frac{\Gamma \vdash M \to N}{\Gamma \vdash M \twoheadrightarrow N}$$

$$\frac{\Gamma \vdash M \twoheadrightarrow N, N \twoheadrightarrow P}{\Gamma \vdash M \twoheadrightarrow P} \qquad \frac{}{\Gamma \vdash M \Rightarrow M}$$

$$\frac{\Gamma \vdash M \Rightarrow M', N \Rightarrow N'}{\Gamma \vdash MN \Rightarrow M'N'} \qquad \frac{\Gamma \vdash M \Rightarrow M'}{\Gamma, x \sqsubseteq M \vdash N \Rightarrow N' \quad (x \notin \Gamma)}{\Gamma \vdash (\lambda x \sqsubseteq M.N) \Rightarrow (\lambda x \sqsubseteq M'.N')}$$

$$\frac{\Gamma \vdash P' \sqsubseteq M, P \Rightarrow P'}{\Gamma, x \sqsubseteq M \vdash N \Rightarrow N' \quad (x \notin \Gamma)}{\Gamma \vdash (\lambda x \sqsubseteq M.N)P \Rightarrow N'[x := P']}$$

Lemma 2.5.2 (Weakening, Cut-elimination)

(i) If $\Gamma \vdash \varphi$ then $\Gamma, \Delta \vdash \varphi$.
(ii) (Cut elimination.) If $\Gamma \vdash M \sqsubseteq N$ and $\Gamma, M \sqsubseteq N \vdash \varphi$ then $\Gamma \vdash \varphi$.

Proof. As 2.4.1. □

Lemma 2.5.3

(i) $\Gamma \vdash M \to N$ implies $\Gamma \vdash M \Rightarrow N$;
(ii) $\Gamma \vdash M \Rightarrow N$ implies $\Gamma \vdash M \twoheadrightarrow N$;
(iii) $\Gamma \vdash M \twoheadrightarrow N$ implies $\Gamma \vdash M = N$.

Proof. (i) Inspection of the rules for $\to$.
(ii) Induction over the length of the proof of $\Gamma \vdash M \Rightarrow N$.
(iii) Replace all $\to$, $\twoheadrightarrow$ in the proof of $\Gamma \vdash M \twoheadrightarrow N$ by $=$. □

Lemma 2.5.4 If $\Gamma \vdash M \Rightarrow M'$ and $\Delta \vdash N \Rightarrow N'$, then $\Gamma[x := N], \Delta \vdash M[x := N] \Rightarrow M'[x := N']$.

Proof. Induction on the length of the derivation of $\Gamma \vdash M \Rightarrow M'$. We assume $\Delta \vdash N \Rightarrow N'$.

- *Case 1.* $M \equiv M'$. Now $\Delta \vdash M[x := N] \Rightarrow M[x := N']$ follows with induction over the structure of M, using $N \Rightarrow N'$.

- *Case 2.* $M \equiv PQ$, $M' \equiv P'Q'$, $\Gamma \vdash P \Rightarrow P', Q \Rightarrow Q'$. Apply the induction hypothesis.

- *Case 3.* $M \equiv \lambda y \sqsubseteq P.Q$, $M' \equiv \lambda y \sqsubseteq P'.Q'$, $\Gamma \vdash P \Rightarrow P'$, $\Gamma, y \sqsubseteq P \vdash Q \Rightarrow Q'$. Idem.

- *Case 4.* $M \equiv (\lambda y \sqsubseteq P.Q)R$, $M' \equiv Q'[y := R']$, $\Gamma \vdash R' \sqsubseteq P, R \Rightarrow R'$, $\Gamma, y \sqsubseteq P \vdash Q \Rightarrow Q'$. By lemma 2.5.3 ($\Rightarrow$ implies $=$) we have $\Delta \vdash N = N'$, so with lemma 2.4.2(iii) we get $\Gamma[x := N], \Delta \vdash R'[x := N'] \sqsubseteq P[x := N]$. Now apply the induction hypothesis.

$\square$

Lemma 2.5.5 (i) If $\Gamma \vdash \lambda x \sqsubseteq M.N \Rightarrow P$, then $P \equiv \lambda x \sqsubseteq M'.N'$ with $\Gamma \vdash M \Rightarrow M'$, $\Gamma, x \sqsubseteq M \vdash N \Rightarrow N'$.
(ii) If $\Gamma \vdash MN \Rightarrow P$, then

- $P \equiv M'N'$ with $\Gamma \vdash M \Rightarrow M', N \Rightarrow N'$, or

- $M \equiv \lambda x \sqsubseteq Q.R$, $P \equiv R'[x := N']$ with $\Gamma \vdash N' \sqsubseteq Q, N \Rightarrow N', \Gamma, x \sqsubseteq Q \vdash R \Rightarrow R'$.

Proof. Easy, with induction on the length of the derivation of $\Gamma \vdash \lambda x \sqsubseteq M.N \Rightarrow P$, resp. $\Gamma \vdash MN \Rightarrow P$. $\square$

Lemma 2.5.6 $\Rightarrow$ has the Diamond property, i.e. if $\Gamma \vdash M \Rightarrow M_1, M \Rightarrow M_2$, then there is an M_3 with $\Gamma \vdash M_1 \Rightarrow M_3, M_2 \Rightarrow M_3$.

Proof. Induction over the length of the proof of $\Gamma \vdash M \Rightarrow M_1$.

- $M \equiv M_1$. Take $M_3 \equiv M_2$.
- $M \equiv AB$, $M_1 \equiv A_1 B_1$, $\Gamma \vdash A \Rightarrow A_1, B \Rightarrow B_1$. By lemma 2.5.5(ii): either (a) $M_2 \equiv A_2 B_2$ with $\Gamma \vdash A \Rightarrow A_2, B \Rightarrow B_2$ or (b) $A \equiv \lambda x \sqsubseteq P.Q, M_2 \equiv Q_2[x := B_2]$ with $\Gamma \vdash B_2 \sqsubseteq P, B \Rightarrow B_2$, $\Gamma, x \sqsubseteq P \vdash Q \Rightarrow Q_2$. If (a), then the induction hypothesis gives us A_3, B_3 with $\Gamma \vdash A_1 \Rightarrow A_3, A_2 \Rightarrow A_3, B_1 \Rightarrow B_3, B_2 \Rightarrow B_3$, so take $M_3 \equiv A_3 B_3$; For (b) we argue as follows. By lemma 2.5.5(i): $A_1 \equiv \lambda x \sqsubseteq P_1.Q_1$, $\Gamma \vdash P \Rightarrow P_1$, $\Gamma, x \sqsubseteq P \vdash Q \Rightarrow Q_1$. The induction hypothesis gives us B_3, Q_3 with $\Gamma \vdash B_1 \Rightarrow B_3, B_2 \Rightarrow B_3$, $\Gamma, x \sqsubseteq P \vdash Q_1 \Rightarrow Q_3, Q_2 \Rightarrow Q_3$. Put $M_3 \equiv Q_3[x := B_3]$. By lemma 2.5.3 ($\Rightarrow$ implies $=$) and lemma 2.5.2(ii) (cut elimination) we get $\Gamma, x \sqsubseteq P_1 \vdash Q_1 \Rightarrow Q_3$, hence $\Gamma \vdash (\lambda x \sqsubseteq P_1.Q_1)B_1 \Rightarrow Q_3[x := B_3]$, i.e. $\Gamma \vdash M_1 \Rightarrow M_3$, and by lemma 2.5.4 we have $\Gamma, B_2 \sqsubseteq P \vdash Q_2[x := B_2] \Rightarrow Q_3[x := B_3]$, i.e. $\Gamma, B_2 \sqsubseteq P \vdash M_2 \Rightarrow M_3$, so (by $\Gamma \vdash B_2 \sqsubseteq P$ and cut elimination) $\Gamma \vdash M_2 \Rightarrow M_3$.

- $M \equiv \lambda x \sqsubseteq A.B$, $M_1 \equiv \lambda x \sqsubseteq A_1.B_1$. $\Gamma \vdash A \Rightarrow A_1$, $\Gamma, x \sqsubseteq A \vdash B \Rightarrow B_1$. By lemma 2.5.5(i): $M_2 \equiv \lambda x \sqsubseteq A_2.B_2$ with $\Gamma \vdash A \Rightarrow A_2$ and $\Gamma, x \sqsubseteq A \vdash B \Rightarrow B_2$. The induction hypothesis gives us A_3, B_3 with $\Gamma \vdash A_1 \Rightarrow A_3, A_2 \Rightarrow A_3$ and $\Gamma, x \sqsubseteq A \vdash B_1 \Rightarrow B_3, B_2 \Rightarrow B_3$. By lemma 2.5.3 and cut elimination we get $\Gamma, x \sqsubseteq A_1 \vdash B_1 \Rightarrow B_3$ and $\Gamma, x \sqsubseteq A_2 \vdash B_2 \Rightarrow B_3$. Now $M := \lambda x \sqsubseteq A_3.B_3$ satisfies $\Gamma \vdash M_1 \Rightarrow M_3, M_2 \Rightarrow M_3$.

- $M \equiv (\lambda x \sqsubseteq A.B)C, M_1 \equiv B_1[x := C_1], \Gamma \vdash C_1 \sqsubseteq A, C \Rightarrow C_1, \Gamma, x \sqsubseteq A \vdash B \Rightarrow B_1$. By lemma 2.5.5(ii): either (c) $M_2 \equiv (\lambda x \sqsubseteq A_2.B_2)C_2$ with $\Gamma \vdash A \Rightarrow A_2, C \Rightarrow C_2$ and $\Gamma, x \sqsubseteq A \vdash B \Rightarrow B_2$ or (d) $M_2 \equiv B_2[x := C_2]$ with $\Gamma \vdash C_2 \sqsubseteq A, C \Rightarrow C_2$ and $\Gamma, x \sqsubseteq A \vdash B \Rightarrow B_2$. (c) is treated as (b) under (2), for (d) we argue as follows. The induction hypothesis gives us B_3, C_3 with $\Gamma \vdash C_1 \Rightarrow C_3, C_2 \Rightarrow C_3$, and $\Gamma, x \sqsubseteq A \vdash B_1 \Rightarrow B_3, B_2 \Rightarrow B_3$ and by lemma 2.5.4 we have $\Gamma, C_1 \sqsubseteq A \vdash B_1[x := C_1] \Rightarrow B_3[x := C_3]$ and $\Gamma, C_2 \sqsubseteq A \vdash B_2[x := C_2] \Rightarrow B_3[x := C_3]$. Now (by $\Gamma \vdash C_1 \sqsubseteq A, C_2 \sqsubseteq A$ and cut elimination) $M_3 := B_3[x := C_3]$ satisfies $\Gamma \vdash M_1 \Rightarrow M_3, M_2 \Rightarrow M_3$.

$\square$

Theorem 2.5.7 ($\Diamond$). $\twoheadrightarrow$ has the Diamond property, i.e. if $\Gamma \vdash M \twoheadrightarrow M_1, M \twoheadrightarrow M_2$ then there is an M_3 with $\Gamma \vdash M_1 \twoheadrightarrow M_3, M_2 \twoheadrightarrow M_3$.

Proof. Assume $\Gamma \vdash M \twoheadrightarrow M_1, M \twoheadrightarrow M_2$. Then there are $M \equiv P_0, \ldots, P_m \equiv M_1$, $M \equiv Q_0, \ldots, Q_n \equiv M_2$, with

$$\Gamma \vdash P_0 \rightarrow P_1 \rightarrow \ldots \rightarrow P_m, Q_0 \rightarrow Q_1 \rightarrow \ldots \rightarrow Q_n.$$

By applying lemma 2.5.3(i) $m + n$ times and lemma 2.5.6 $m.n$ times, we find an M_3 which satisfies, by lemma 2.5.3(ii), $\Gamma \vdash M_1 \twoheadrightarrow M_3, M_2 \twoheadrightarrow M_3$. $\square$

3 Applied $\lambda\pi$ calculus

3.1 Algebraic systems with preorder

We consider an algebraic system with preorder $\mathcal{A}$ as follows:

$$\mathcal{A} = \langle A, R, \{F_j \mid j \in J\}, \{C_i \mid i \in I\}\rangle$$

(J, I index sets) where A is a set (called the *domain* of $\mathcal{A}$), R is a preorder, each F_j is a function and each C_i is an element (a *constant*) of A. We assume that the arity of each F_j is given as a natural number a_j. Later we shall instantiate this calculus by taking the algebra of description descriptions with the implementation relation for $\mathcal{A}$.

Of course we also allow for many-sorted algebraic systems with preorder. However we require that there is one *domain of interest* (A) on which the preorder R is defined. In such a case we shall say that there are *secondary domains* and we shall deal with such secondary domains somewhat informally.

3.2 Terms and formulae

We want to put a version of lambda calculus "on top" of $\mathcal{A}$.

Definition 3.2.1 ($\Lambda[\mathcal{A}]$)

(i) The set of *Curry type symbols* is inductively defined by

1. 0 is a Curry type symbol,
2. if σ, τ are Curry type symbols, then also is $(\sigma \to \tau)$.

We write $(\sigma_1, \ldots, \sigma_n \to \tau)$ for $(\sigma_1 \to \ldots \to \sigma_n \to \tau)$, where parentheses are associated to the right. Note every $\sigma \neq 0$ is of the form $(\sigma_1, \ldots, \sigma_n \to 0)$.

(ii) We assume infinitely many variables of each Curry type. These are denoted by $x_0, x_1, \ldots$. (The Curry type superscript τ in x_i^τ is used with variables only when necessary to avoid ambiguity.) The *alphabet* to be used for constructing the set of lambda terms consists of the following symbols:

1. *Function symbols:* f_j (one for each F_j),
2. *Constant symbols:* c_i (one for each C_i),
3. *Variables:* $x_0^\tau, x_1^\tau, x_2^\tau, \ldots$ (countably many for each Curry type symbol τ),
4. *Auxiliary symbols:* . , (,), $\lambda, \sqsubseteq$.

(iii) The set of *lambda terms* for $\mathcal{A}$, denoted as $\Lambda[\mathcal{A}]$ and the *Curry type* of each lambda term are inductively defined by

1. $x_i^\tau \in \Lambda[\mathcal{A}]$ $(i \in \mathcal{N})$ with type τ,
2. $c_i \in \Lambda[\mathcal{A}]$ $(i \in I)$ with type 0 ,
3. if $P_1, \ldots, P_{a_j} \in \Lambda[\mathcal{A}]$ with types 0, then $f_j(P_1, \ldots, P_{a_j}) \in \Lambda[\mathcal{A}]$ with type 0,
4. if $P, Q \in \Lambda[\mathcal{A}]$ and P is of type $(\sigma \to \tau)$ and Q is of type σ, then $(PQ) \in \Lambda[\mathcal{A}]$ with type τ,
5. if $P, Q \in \Lambda[\mathcal{A}]$ where P is of type σ, Q is of type τ and x_i^σ does not occur in P, then $(\lambda x_i^\sigma \sqsubseteq P.Q) \in \Lambda[\mathcal{A}]$ with type $(\sigma \to \tau)$.

As typical elements of $\Lambda[\mathcal{A}]$ we shall use $A, B, P, Q, R, S, Z, \Delta$ and their indexed versions. We shall sometimes be somewhat sloppy in the distinction between actual variables $(x_0, x_1, \ldots)$ and the typical elements of the set of variables $(x, y, z$ and their indexed versions). The purpose of the Curry types is to exclude terms such as $(\lambda x \sqsubseteq P.xx)$. We shall identify α-congruent terms, as is usually done in classical lambda calculus; see e.g. [2] 2.1.12.

If the algebraic system with preorder $\mathcal{A}$ is many-sorted with domains $A_1, \ldots, A_n$, we need in fact a set of terms for each domain. In this case we shall have sets of terms $\Lambda_{A_1}[\mathcal{A}], \ldots, \Lambda_{A_n}[\mathcal{A}]$.

The algebraic system $\mathcal{A}$ has a preorder R (typically an *implementation relation*). We write $\mathcal{A} \models P \sqsubseteq Q$ if the elements denoted by P and Q are in R. Now we want to extend this relation $\sqsubseteq$, or more precisely, we want to compare also lambda terms. We shall adopt a rather syntactic point of view and we shall define a notion of *derivability* for so-called sequents, based on a set of rules, which will be given in a Gentzen-style formulation. We shall simultaneously define derivability for sequents of the form $\Gamma \vdash P = Q$ and of the form $\Gamma \vdash P \sqsubseteq Q$. In this way we shall obtain a calculus to which we shall refer as (applied) $\lambda\pi$ calculus.

Before we can give the actual rules, we need, by way of preparation, a number of definitions.

Definition 3.2.2 (*FV*, Substitution)

(i) For $P \in \Lambda[\mathcal{A}]$, $FV(P)$ denotes the set of *free variables* of P which is defined as usual.

(ii) We define substitutions $[x_i := P]$ where x_i and P have the same Curry type. We assume that renaming of bound variables automatically takes place if this is needed to avoid clashes of variables. We use $\equiv$ to denote syntactical equality. *Substitution* is inductively defined by

    1. $x_i[x_i := P] \equiv P$,
       $x_i[x_j := P] \equiv x_i \ (i \neq j)$,
    2. $c_i[x_j := P] \equiv c_i$,
    3. $f_j(P_1, \ldots, P_{a_j})[x_i := P] \equiv f_j(P_1[x_i := P], \ldots, P_{a_j}[x_i := P])$,
    4. $(Q_1 Q_2)[x_i := P] \equiv ((Q_1[x_i := P])(Q_2[x_i := P]))$,
    5. $(\lambda x_i \sqsubseteq Q_1.Q_2)[x_i := P] \equiv (\lambda x_i \sqsubseteq Q_1.Q_2)$,
       $(\lambda x_i \sqsubseteq Q_1.Q_2)[x_j := P] \equiv (\lambda x_i \sqsubseteq Q_1[x_j := P].Q_2[x_j := P]) \ (i \neq j)$.

Definition 3.2.3 ($\mathcal{A} \models$) (i) The set of *formulae* is defined as the set of formulae in the language of $\mathcal{A}$ which have been constructed from atomic formulae, the constant true, conjunction and implication. A formula is *closed* if no variables occur in it.

(ii) We assume that *truth* in $\mathcal{A}$ is defined as usual where $\sqsubseteq$ corresponds to R and $=$ corresponds to real equality. Formulae which are not closed, are interpreted as implicitly universally quantified. We denote truth in $\mathcal{A}$ as $\mathcal{A} \models \varphi$.

(iii) The set of *atomic flat-term* formulae for $\mathcal{A}$ is defined as the set of formulae $P_1 = P_2$ and $P_1 \sqsubseteq P_2$ for $P_1, P_2 \in \Lambda[\mathcal{A}]$ where in both cases we require that P_1, P_2 have Curry type 0 and do not contain the symbol λ.

Definition 3.2.4 (Context) (i) An *assumption* is an equality or an inequality between two lambda terms where these lambda terms must have equal Curry types: If $P, Q \in \Lambda[\mathcal{A}]$ where both P and Q are of Curry type σ, then $[P \sqsubseteq Q]$ is an assumption (viz. an *inequality*), and $[P = Q]$ is an assumption (viz. an *equality*).

(ii) A *context* is a finite set set of assumptions, e.g. $\{[P_1 \sqsubseteq Q_1], \ldots, [P_n \sqsubseteq Q_n]\}$. We shall use Γ to denote a context.

Notation 3.2.5 We assume that (in formulae) $\top, \wedge$ and $\rightarrow$ correspond to the constant true, conjunction and implication.

    (i) $\bigwedge\{[\varphi_1], \ldots, [\varphi_n]\}$ abbreviates $\varphi_1 \wedge \ldots \wedge \varphi_n$ ($1 \leq n$) and $\bigwedge \emptyset$ abbreviates $\top$.
    (ii) We shall write $\Gamma, [\varphi]$ for $\Gamma \cup \{[\varphi]\}$ and we shall write $[\varphi]$ for $\{[\varphi]\}$.
    (iii) $x \in \Gamma$ means that x occurs freely in Γ.

3.3 Rules

Definition 3.3.1 (Sequents). A *sequent* is a pair (Γ, φ), written as $\Gamma \vdash \varphi$, where Γ is a context and where φ is either of the form $P \sqsubseteq Q$ or of the form $P = Q$, $(P, Q \in \Lambda[\mathcal{A}]$ and of equal Curry type). We shall write $\vdash \psi$ for $\emptyset \vdash \psi$.

Definition 3.3.2 (Rule ($\models$)) For each atomic flat-term formula φ such that $A \models \bigwedge \Gamma \to \varphi$ (where Γ contains only atomic flat-term formulae) we have $\Gamma \cup \Gamma' \vdash \varphi$. This is denoted by the following rule:

$$(\models) \quad \frac{A \models \bigwedge \Gamma \to \varphi}{\Gamma \cup \Gamma' \vdash \varphi}$$

The rule ($\models$) allows us to import context dependent facts (such as monotonicity of functions) into the calculus. Note that if a function F_j of A is monotonic, we can express this fact as $A \models \bigwedge\{[x_1 \sqsubseteq y_1], \ldots, [x_n \sqsubseteq y_n]\} \to f_j(x_1, \ldots, x_n) \sqsubseteq f_j(y_1, \ldots, y_n)$. Therefore, for the general case we need not include a rule which expresses monotonicity. In fact a rule expressing monotonicity for *all* lambda terms would not even be acceptable.

The following rule expresses that the assumptions in a context can be derived in that context.

Definition 3.3.3 (Rule context)

$$(\text{context}) \; \frac{}{\Gamma, \varphi \vdash \varphi}$$

Although they may be redundant, reflexivity and transitivity have been added as rules. Furthermore abstraction is monotonic with respect to $\sqsubseteq$ in the second argument and it is antimonotonic with respect to $\sqsubseteq$ in its first argument (!). Application is monotonic in its first argument.

Definition 3.3.4 (Rules refl. trans. λI_1, λI_2, λI_3, appl.)

$$(\text{refl.}) \; \frac{}{\Gamma \vdash P \sqsubseteq P} \qquad\qquad (\text{trans.}) \; \frac{\Gamma \vdash P_1 \sqsubseteq P_2, P_2 \sqsubseteq P_3}{\Gamma \vdash P_1 \sqsubseteq P_3}$$

$$(\lambda I_1) \; \frac{\Gamma, [x \sqsubseteq P] \vdash Q_1 \sqsubseteq Q_2 \quad (x \notin \Gamma)}{\Gamma \vdash (\lambda x \sqsubseteq P.Q_1) \sqsubseteq (\lambda x \sqsubseteq P.Q_2)} \quad (\lambda I_2) \; \frac{\Gamma \vdash P_1 \sqsubseteq P_2}{\Gamma \vdash (\lambda x \sqsubseteq P_2.Q) \sqsubseteq (\lambda x \sqsubseteq P_1.Q)}$$

$$(\text{appl.}) \; \frac{\Gamma \vdash P_1 \sqsubseteq P_2}{\Gamma \vdash (P_1 Q) \sqsubseteq (P_2 Q)} \qquad\qquad (\lambda I_3) \; \frac{\Gamma, [x \sqsubseteq P] \vdash Q_1 = Q_2 \quad (x \notin \Gamma)}{\Gamma \vdash (\lambda x \sqsubseteq P.Q_1) = (\lambda x \sqsubseteq P.Q_2)}$$

We also have the rule (π) which resembles the well-known rule (β) of classical lambda calculus, but which is *partial*, by which we mean that contraction is conditional.

Definition 3.3.5 (Rule π)

$$(\pi) \quad \frac{\Gamma \vdash P_2 \sqsubseteq P_1}{\Gamma \vdash (\lambda x \sqsubseteq P_1.Q)P_2 = Q[x := P_2]}$$

Finally we have a general substitution rule and a reflexivity rule for $=$.

Definition 3.3.6 (Rules subst., refl$_=$)

$$\text{(subst.)} \quad \frac{\Gamma \vdash \varphi(P)}{\Gamma \vdash P = Q} \qquad \qquad \text{(refl}_=) \quad \frac{}{\Gamma \vdash P = P}$$

We shall briefly discuss the intuition behind the rules (λI_1), (λI_2) and (π). Each lambda term $(\lambda x \sqsubseteq P.Q)$ can be viewed as the denotation of a function having a restriction concerning its argument. Therefore it is reasonable that the evaluation of an application term cannot take place unless the argument provably meets this restriction (rule π). The rules (λI_1) and (λI_2) describe the conditions under which one function can be viewed as the implementation of another function. First of all, two functions with the same argument restriction are in the implementation relation if for every acceptable argument their results are in the implementation relation (rule λI_1). Secondly, if two functions have equal function bodies but the restriction of one function is weaker than the restriction of the other function, then the function with the *weakest* restriction implements the other function (rule λI_2). The fact that in the rules $(\lambda I_1, \lambda I_3)$ an assumption $[x \sqsubseteq P]$ is discharged is motivated as follows: by the condition in the rule (π) we know that whatever is going to be substituted for x will meet the restriction $x \sqsubseteq P$ and therefore it is reasonable that the assumption $[x \sqsubseteq P]$ can be used when comparing the function bodies Q_1 and Q_2.

Definition 3.3.7 $(\lambda \pi)$ *Derivability* for sequents is defined inductively by:

1. If $\Gamma \vdash \varphi$ is the conclusion of a rule from $(\models,$ context, refl., refl.$_=)$, then $\Gamma \vdash \varphi$ is derivable.

2. If $\Gamma \vdash \varphi$ is the conclusion of a rule from (trans., λI_1, λI_2, λI_3, appl., π, subst.) and all premises of this rule are derivable, then $\Gamma \vdash \varphi$ is derivable.

In general we write $\Gamma \vdash \varphi$ if $\Gamma \vdash \varphi$ is derivable.

3.4 The model $\mathcal{A}^+$ of $\lambda \pi$.

There are several reasons why we want to have a model for applied $\lambda \pi$ calculus. First of all, if we have a non-trivial model, then we know that the calculus is consistent in the sense that not every equality is derivable. Secondly by constructing a model, we can make our intuition that a lambda term $\lambda x \sqsubseteq P.Q$ denotes a function more precise. The model $\mathcal{A}^+$ which we shall construct below is obtained as an extension of the underlying algebraic system with preorder $\mathcal{A}$. Lambda terms are interpreted as functions. The model contains elements $*_r$ which correspond to the terms which cannot be contracted because of the condition in the rule (π).

Notation 3.4.1 If z is a function $z : X \to A$ then $z[x \to a]$ denotes the function which everywhere equals z but for the argument x for which it results a; formally $z[x \to a](y) = z(y)$ for $y \neq x$ and $z(x) = a$.

First we define the function domains and we define the ordering of functions.

Definition 3.4.2 $(A_\tau, \sqsubseteq_\tau)$. Consider A as before. Let τ be a Curry type symbol. We define $A_\tau, \sqsubseteq_\tau$ by induction on the structure of τ.

1. $A_0 := A \cup \{*_0\}$,
   $a \sqsubseteq_0 b :\Leftrightarrow aRb$ or $b = *_0$.

2. $A_{\sigma \to \tau} := A_\sigma \to A_\tau$,
   $f \sqsubseteq_{\sigma \to \tau} g :\Leftrightarrow \forall x \in A_\sigma (f(x) \sqsubseteq_\tau g(x))$.

We shall write $*_{\sigma \to \tau}$ for $\lambda\!\!\lambda\, a \in A_\sigma.*_\tau$. If no confusion arises we omit the subscripts for $*$, $\sqsubseteq$. Note that $*_{\sigma \to \tau}$ is the maximum element of $A_{\sigma \to \tau}$.

Definition 3.4.3 $(A^+$, assignment). Consider A as before. Typ denotes the set of Curry type symbols.

(i) The model A^+ is defined as
   $\langle \{A_\tau \mid \tau \in Typ\}, \{\sqsubseteq_\tau \mid \tau \in Typ\}, \{\sim_\tau \mid \tau \in Typ\}, \{F_j \mid j \in J\}, \{C_i \mid i \in I\}\rangle$.

(ii) An *assignment* z is a map variables $\to \bigcup\{A_\tau \mid \tau \in Typ\}$ such that $z(x^\tau) \in A_\tau$.

Definition 3.4.4 (Interpretation) Consider A as before. The *interpretation* of terms under an assignment z is defined by induction over the structure of terms.

1. $x_i \langle z \rangle = z(x_i)$,
2. $c_i \langle z \rangle = C_i$,
3. $f_j(P_1, \ldots, P_n)\langle z \rangle = F_j(P_1\langle z \rangle, \ldots, P_n \langle z \rangle)$ if $P_1\langle z \rangle \neq *, \ldots, P_n\langle z \rangle \neq *$, $*$ otherwise,
4. $(PQ)\langle z \rangle = P\langle z \rangle(Q\langle z \rangle)$
5. $(\lambda x^\sigma \sqsubseteq P.Q)\langle z \rangle = \lambda\!\!\lambda\, a \in A_\sigma.$ if $a \sqsubseteq P\langle z \rangle$ then $Q\langle z[x^\sigma \to a]\rangle$ else $*$.

Definition 3.4.5 $(A^+ \models \varphi)$. Consider A as before.

(i) $A^+ \models (P = Q)\langle z \rangle :\Leftrightarrow P\langle z \rangle = Q\langle z \rangle$.
(ii) $A^+ \models (P \sqsubseteq Q)\langle z \rangle :\Leftrightarrow P\langle z \rangle \sqsubseteq Q\langle z \rangle$.
(iii) $A^+ \models (\varphi \land \psi)\langle z \rangle :\Leftrightarrow A^+ \models \varphi\langle z \rangle$ and $A^+ \models \psi\langle z \rangle$.
(iv) $A^+ \models (\varphi \to \psi)\langle z \rangle :\Leftrightarrow A^+ \models \varphi\langle z \rangle \Rightarrow A^+ \models \psi\langle z \rangle$.
(v) $A^+ \models \varphi :\Leftrightarrow$ for all z $A^+ \models \varphi\langle z \rangle$.

Lemma 3.4.6 For atomic φ in the language of A we have

$$A \models \varphi \Leftrightarrow A^+ \models \varphi.$$

Proof. Immediate from the definitions of $A \models \varphi$ and $A^+ \models \varphi$. $\square$

3.5 Soundness of A^+

Lemma 3.5.1 $R[x := P]\langle z \rangle = R\langle z[x \to P\langle z \rangle]\rangle$.

Proof. By induction over the structure of R.

- (i) $R \equiv x$. Then $R[x := P]\langle z \rangle = P\langle z \rangle$ and $R\langle z[x \to P\langle z \rangle]\rangle = x\langle z[x \to P\langle z \rangle]\rangle = P\langle z \rangle$

(ii) $R \equiv y \not\equiv x$. Then $R[x := P]\langle z \rangle = z(y)$ and $R\langle z[x \to P\langle z \rangle] \rangle = y\langle z[x \to \ldots] \rangle = z(y)$.

- $R \equiv c_i$: trivial.
- $R \equiv f_j(P_1, \ldots, P_n)$. Then $R[x := P]\langle z \rangle = f_j(P_1[x := P], \ldots, P_n[x := P])\langle z \rangle = f_j(P_1[x := P]\langle z \rangle, \ldots, P_n[x := P]\langle z \rangle) = $ (using i.h.) $f_j(P_1\langle z[x \to P\langle z \rangle] \rangle, \ldots, P_n\langle z[x \to P\langle z \rangle] \rangle) = f_j(P_1, \ldots P_n)\langle z[x \to P\langle z \rangle] \rangle = R\langle z[x \to P\langle z \rangle] \rangle$.
- $R \equiv (P_1 P_2)$. Then $R[x := P]\langle z \rangle = P_1[x := P]\langle z \rangle (P_2[x := P]\langle z \rangle)$ which we write as $f(a)$. Similarly we write $R\langle z[x \to P\langle z \rangle] \rangle$ as $g(b)$. By i.h. we have $f = g$ and $a = b$. therefore $f(a) = g(b)$.
- $R \equiv \lambda y \sqsubseteq Q_1 . Q_2$.

  (i) If $x \equiv y$ then $R[x := P]\langle z \rangle = R\langle z \rangle$ and $R\langle z[x \to P\langle z \rangle] \rangle = \lambda\!\!\lambda \, a$. if $a \sqsubseteq Q_1\langle z[x \to P\langle z \rangle] \rangle$ then $Q_2\langle z[x \to P\langle z \rangle][y \to a] \rangle$ else $*$ which is in fact the function $R\langle z \rangle$, because $x \equiv y$ does not occur in Q_1 and the modification $[x \to P\langle z \rangle]$ is always undone by the modification $[y \to a]$.

  (ii) If $x \not\equiv y$ then define $f := R[x := P]\langle z \rangle = \lambda\!\!\lambda \, a$. if $a \sqsubseteq Q_1[x := P]\langle z \rangle$ then $Q_2[x := P]\langle z[y \to a] \rangle$ else $*$, and define $g := R\langle z[x \to P\langle z \rangle] \rangle = \lambda\!\!\lambda \, a$. if $a \sqsubseteq Q_1\langle z[x \to P\langle z \rangle] \rangle$ then $Q_2\langle z[x \to P\langle z \rangle][y \to a] \rangle$ else $*$. Now consider an arbitrary argument, c say and prove (using i.h.) that $f(c) = g(c)$. $\qquad\square$

Lemma 3.5.2 (Substitution) Let z be an assignment. Assume $P\langle z \rangle = Q\langle z \rangle$.

(i) $R[x := P]\langle z \rangle = R[x := Q]\langle z \rangle$.
(ii) If $R_1[x := P]\langle z \rangle = R_2[x := P]\langle z \rangle$, then $R_1[x := Q]\langle z \rangle = R_2[x := Q]\langle z \rangle$.
(iii) If $R_1[x := P]\langle z \rangle \sqsubseteq R_2[x := P]\langle z \rangle$, then $R_1[x := Q]\langle z \rangle \sqsubseteq R_2[x := Q]\langle z \rangle$.

Proof. (i) We have $R\langle z[x \to P\langle z \rangle] \rangle = R\langle z[x \to Q\langle z \rangle] \rangle$ and hence by lemma 3.5.1 we obtain $R[x := P]\langle z \rangle = R[x := Q]\langle z \rangle$.
(ii) Write $R[x := P]$ as $R(P)$ etc. By (i) we have $R_1(Q)\langle z \rangle = R_1(P)\langle z \rangle$ and by assumption $R_1(P)\langle z \rangle = R_2(P)\langle z \rangle$ so by (i) again $R_2(P)\langle z \rangle = R_2(Q)\langle z \rangle$.
(iii) By (i) we have $R_1(Q)\langle z \rangle = R_1(P)\langle z \rangle$, and by assumption $R_1(P)\langle z \rangle \sqsubseteq R_2(P)\langle z \rangle$ so by (i) again $R_2(P)\langle z \rangle = R_2(Q)\langle z \rangle$. $\qquad\square$

Theorem 3.5.3 (Soundness).

$$\Gamma \vdash \varphi \;\Rightarrow\; \mathcal{A}^+ \models \bigwedge \Gamma \to \varphi.$$

Proof. The proof is by induction on the length of the derivation of $\Gamma \vdash \varphi$.

- $(\models)$. $\Gamma \vdash \varphi$ because for some $\Gamma' \subseteq \Gamma$ we have $\mathcal{A} \models \bigwedge \Gamma' \to \varphi$. By lemma 3.4.6 we have $\mathcal{A}^+ \models \bigwedge \Gamma' \to \varphi$ and hence $\mathcal{A}^+ \models \bigwedge \Gamma \to \varphi$.
- (context). $\Gamma, \varphi \vdash \varphi$. We must show that $\mathcal{A}^+ \models (\bigwedge \Gamma \wedge \varphi)\langle z \rangle$ implies $\mathcal{A}^+ \models \varphi\langle z \rangle$ which is obvious.

- (refl.). $\Gamma \vdash P \sqsubseteq P$ We must show that $\mathcal{A}^+ \models \bigwedge \Gamma$ implies $\mathcal{A}^+ \models P \sqsubseteq P$ which follows from the fact that $\sqsubseteq$ is a partial order.

- (trans.). As refl.

- (λI_1). $\Gamma \vdash (\lambda x \sqsubseteq P.Q_1) \sqsubseteq (\lambda x \sqsubseteq P.Q_2)$. We have $\mathcal{A}^+ \models \bigwedge \Gamma \wedge x \sqsubseteq P \to Q_1 \sqsubseteq Q_2$ (i.h.). Take an arbitrary z and assume $\mathcal{A}^+ \models \bigwedge \Gamma \langle z \rangle$.
  Define $f := (\lambda x \sqsubseteq P.Q_1)\langle z \rangle$ and $g := (\lambda x \sqsubseteq P.Q_2)\langle z \rangle$. For $a \sqsubseteq P\langle z \rangle$ we shall show $f(a) \sqsubseteq g(a)$. Since $x \notin \Gamma$ we have $\mathcal{A}^+ \models \bigwedge \Gamma \langle z[x \to a] \rangle$. ¿From i.h. $Q_1\langle z[x \to a] \rangle \sqsubseteq Q_2\langle z[x \to a] \rangle$, i.e. $f(a) \sqsubseteq g(a)$. This shows $\mathcal{A}^+ \models \bigwedge \Gamma \langle z \rangle \Rightarrow f \sqsubseteq g$.

- (λI_2). $\Gamma \vdash (\lambda x \sqsubseteq P_2.Q) \sqsubseteq (\lambda x \sqsubseteq P_1.Q)$. We have $\mathcal{A}^+ \models \bigwedge \Gamma \to P_1 \sqsubseteq P_2$ (i.h.). Take an arbitrary z and assume $\mathcal{A}^+ \models \bigwedge \Gamma \langle z \rangle$.
  Define $f := (\lambda x \sqsubseteq P_2.Q)\langle z \rangle$ and $g := (\lambda x \sqsubseteq P_1.Q)\langle z \rangle$. We show for arbitrary a that $f(a) \sqsubseteq g(a)$.
  If $a \not\sqsubseteq P_1\langle z \rangle$ and $a \not\sqsubseteq P_2\langle z \rangle$ then $f(a) = g(a) = *$.
  If $a \sqsubseteq P_2\langle z \rangle$ but $a \not\sqsubseteq P_1\langle z \rangle$ then $f(a) \sqsubseteq g(a) = *$.
  If $a \sqsubseteq P_1\langle z \rangle \sqsubseteq P_2\langle z \rangle$ then $f(a) = g(a)$.
  This shows $\mathcal{A}^+ \models \bigwedge \Gamma \langle z \rangle \Rightarrow f \sqsubseteq g$ so $\mathcal{A}^+ \models \bigwedge \Gamma \to (\lambda x \sqsubseteq P_2.Q) \sqsubseteq (\lambda x \sqsubseteq P_1.Q)$.

- (λI_3). As (λI_1).

- (appl.). $\Gamma \vdash (P_1 Q) \sqsubseteq (P_2 Q)$. Take an arbitrary z. Assume $\mathcal{A}^+ \models \bigwedge \Gamma \langle z \rangle$.
  We have $\mathcal{A}^+ \models \bigwedge \Gamma \to P_1 \sqsubseteq P_2$ (i.h.). Define $a := Q\langle z \rangle$, $f := P_1\langle z \rangle$ and $g := P_2\langle z \rangle$. We have $f \sqsubseteq g$ (by i.h.). We must show $f(a) \sqsubseteq g(a)$. This follows directly from the definition of $\sqsubseteq$.

- (π). $\Gamma \vdash (\lambda x \sqsubseteq P_1.Q)P_2 = Q[x := P_2]$. We have $\mathcal{A}^+ \models \bigwedge \Gamma \to P_2 \sqsubseteq P_1$ (i.h.). Take an arbitrary z. Assume $\mathcal{A}^+ \models \bigwedge \Gamma \langle z \rangle$.
  $(\lambda x \sqsubseteq P_1.Q)P_2\langle z \rangle = (\lambda a.$ if $a \sqsubseteq P_1\langle z \rangle$ then $Q\langle z[x \to a] \rangle$ else $*)(P_2\langle z \rangle) =$ (i.h.) $Q\langle z[x \to P_2\langle z \rangle] \rangle = Q[x := P_2]\langle z \rangle$ where we used lemma 3.5.1.

- (subst.). $\Gamma \vdash R_1(Q) = R_2(Q)$ where we assume that φ is an equality. We have $\mathcal{A}^+ \models \bigwedge \Gamma \to R_1(P) = R_2(P)$ and $\mathcal{A}^+ \models \bigwedge \Gamma \to P = Q$ (i.h.). Take an arbitrary z and assume $\mathcal{A}^+ \models \bigwedge \Gamma \langle z \rangle$. ¿From (i.h.) $R_1(P)\langle z \rangle = R_2(P)\langle z \rangle$ and $P\langle z \rangle = Q\langle z \rangle$ so by the substitution lemma (ii) we get $(R_1(Q)\langle z \rangle = R_2(Q)\langle z \rangle$, i.e. $\mathcal{A}^+ \models (R_1(Q) = R_2(Q))\langle z \rangle$. If φ contains the symbol $\sqsubseteq$ instead of $=$, we proceed in a similar way, using the substitution lemma (iii).

- (refl$_=$). Use that $=$ is equality on A_r. □

3.6 Cut-rule

First we shall list a number of lemmas that can be viewed as derived rules.

Lemma 3.6.1 (Weakening) If $\Gamma \vdash \varphi$, then $\Gamma, \psi \vdash \varphi$.

Proof. The proof is by induction over the length of the derivation of $\Gamma \vdash \varphi$.

- If $\Gamma \vdash \varphi$ because $\mathcal{A}^+ \models \bigwedge \Gamma \to \varphi$ then we assume $\mathcal{A}^+ \models \bigwedge \Gamma \wedge \psi$. Hence $\mathcal{A}^+ \models \bigwedge \Gamma$ and therefore $\mathcal{A}^+ \models \varphi$. This shows $\mathcal{A}^+ \models \bigwedge \Gamma \wedge \psi \to \varphi$ so by $(\models)$ $\Gamma, \psi \vdash \varphi$.
- If $\varphi \in \Gamma$, then $\Gamma \vdash \varphi$.
- If $\varphi \equiv (\lambda x \sqsubseteq R.S_1) \sqsubseteq (\lambda x \sqsubseteq R.S_2)$ and $\Gamma, \psi \vdash \varphi$ by rule (λI_1), then we know

$$\Gamma, \psi, [x \sqsubseteq R] \vdash S_1 \sqsubseteq S_2$$

and $x \notin (\Gamma, \psi)$ so certainly $x \notin \Gamma$. By i.h. $\Gamma, \psi, [x \sqsubseteq R] \vdash S_1 \sqsubseteq S_2$ so by rule (λI_1) we have

$$\Gamma, \psi \vdash (\lambda x \sqsubseteq R.S_1) \sqsubseteq (\lambda x \sqsubseteq R.S_2).$$

- Other rules: analogously. □

Lemma 3.6.2 If $\Gamma \vdash \varphi$, then $\Gamma[x := P] \vdash \varphi[x := P]$.

Proof. The proof is by induction over the length of the derivation of $\Gamma \vdash \varphi$.

- If $\mathcal{A} \models \varphi$, then we distinguish two cases. If $x \notin FV(\varphi)$, then we are done immediately. If $x \in FV(\varphi)$, then φ is implicitly universally quantified, so we know $\Gamma \vdash \forall_x \varphi$. Hence $\Gamma \vdash \varphi[x := P]$.
- If $\varphi \equiv f_j(P_1, \ldots, P_n) \sqsubseteq f_j(Q_1, \ldots, Q_n)$ because $\Gamma \vdash P_1 \sqsubseteq Q_1, \ldots, \Gamma \vdash P_n \sqsubseteq Q_n$ by rule (F_j), we have (i.h.) $\Gamma[x := M] \vdash P_1[\ ] \sqsubseteq Q_1[\ ], \ldots, \Gamma[x := M] \vdash P_n[\ ] \sqsubseteq Q_n[\ ]$. Apply rule (F_j).
- If $\varphi \equiv (P \sqsubseteq P)$, apply rule (refl.).
- If $\varphi \equiv (P_1 \sqsubseteq P_3)$ because $\Gamma \vdash P_1 \sqsubseteq P_2$ and $\Gamma \vdash P_2 \sqsubseteq P_3$ by rule (trans.), then by (i.h.) $\Gamma[\ ] \vdash P_1[\ ] \sqsubseteq P_2[\ ]$ and $\Gamma[\ ] \vdash P_2[\ ] \sqsubseteq P_3[\ ]$. Apply rule (trans.).
- If $\Gamma \vdash \varphi$ is $\Gamma \vdash (\lambda y \sqsubseteq P.Q_1) \sqsubseteq (\lambda y \sqsubseteq P.Q_2)$ because $\Gamma, [y \sqsubseteq P] \vdash Q_1 \sqsubseteq Q_2$ by rule (λI_1), then we distinguish two cases. If $x \equiv y$ then $x \notin \Gamma$, $x \notin FV(\varphi)$ so $\Gamma[\ ] \equiv \Gamma$ and $\varphi[\ ] \equiv \varphi$. If $x \not\equiv y$ then by (i.h.) $\Gamma[y \sqsubseteq P][\ ] \vdash Q_1[\ ] \sqsubseteq Q_2[\ ]$, so $\Gamma[\ ][y \sqsubseteq P[\ ]] \vdash Q_1[\ ] \sqsubseteq Q_2[\ ]$. Now apply rule (λI_1) again.
- Other rules: analogously. □

Theorem 3.6.3 (Cut-rule) If $\Gamma \vdash \varphi$, and $\Gamma, \varphi \vdash \psi$, then $\Gamma \vdash \psi$.

Proof. The proof is by induction over the length of the derivation of $\Gamma, \varphi \vdash \psi$. We assume $\Gamma \vdash \varphi$.

- If $\Gamma, \varphi \vdash \psi$ because $\mathcal{A} \models \bigwedge \Gamma \wedge \varphi \rightarrow \psi$ then by soundness from $\Gamma \vdash \varphi$ we obtain $\mathcal{A}^+ \models \bigwedge \Gamma \rightarrow \varphi$. Assume $\mathcal{A}^+ \models \bigwedge \Gamma$ then $\mathcal{A}^+ \models \varphi$. Therefore $\mathcal{A}^+ \models \bigwedge \Gamma \wedge \varphi$ and hence $\mathcal{A}^+ \models \psi$. This shows $\mathcal{A}^+ \models \bigwedge \Gamma \rightarrow \psi$ so $\mathcal{A} \models \bigwedge \Gamma \rightarrow \psi$ and by applying rule ($\models$) again we get $\Gamma \vdash \psi$.
- If $\psi \in \Gamma$, then $\Gamma \vdash \psi$. If $\psi \equiv \varphi$ then $\Gamma \vdash \varphi$.
- If $\psi \equiv (\lambda x \sqsubseteq R.S_1) \sqsubseteq (\lambda x \sqsubseteq R.S_2)$ and $\Gamma, \varphi \vdash \psi$ by rule (λI_1), then we know

$$\Gamma, \varphi, [x \sqsubseteq R] \vdash S_1 \sqsubseteq S_2$$

and $x \notin (\Gamma, \varphi)$ so certainly $x \notin \Gamma$. By i.h. $\Gamma, [x \sqsubseteq R] \vdash S_1 \sqsubseteq S_2$ so by rule (λI_1) we have

$$\Gamma \vdash (\lambda x \sqsubseteq R.S_1) \sqsubseteq (\lambda x \sqsubseteq R.S_2).$$

- If $\psi \equiv \psi(Q)$ and $\Gamma, \varphi \vdash \psi(Q)$ by rule (subst.), then we know $\Gamma, \varphi \vdash \psi(P)$ and $\Gamma, \varphi \vdash P = Q$ for some p. By i.h. $\Gamma \vdash \psi(P)$ and $\Gamma \vdash P = Q$ so by rule (subst.) again we have $\Gamma \vdash \psi(Q)$.
- Other rules: analogously. □

Lemma 3.6.4 If $\Gamma \vdash P = Q$, then $\Gamma \vdash R[x := P] = R[x := Q]$.

Proof. We want to use the rule (subst.) and we take $\varphi(P) = (R[x := P] = R[x := P])$ which we denote as $\varphi(P) = (R(P) = R(P))$. Clearly $\Gamma \vdash \varphi(P)$. Now consider the second occurrence of P and apply rule (subst.). We obtain $\Gamma \vdash \varphi(Q)$, i.e. $\Gamma \vdash R(P) = R(Q)$. □

Lemma 3.6.5 (Generalised cut-rule). If $\Gamma \vdash \varphi_1, \ldots, \Gamma \vdash \varphi_n$ and $\Gamma, \varphi_1, \ldots, \varphi_n \vdash \psi$ then $\Gamma \vdash \psi$.

Proof. By iterated application of the cut-rule. □

3.7 Reduction

The following definition can be viewed as a reformulation of part of [2] 3.1.5 for the $\lambda \pi$ calculus.

Definition 3.7.1 $(\to, \twoheadrightarrow)$. Let Γ be a context.

(i) The relation $\to$ is defined inductively by:

1. $\Gamma \vdash R \sqsubseteq A \Rightarrow \Gamma \vdash (\lambda x \sqsubseteq A.B)R \to B[x := R]$,
2. $\Gamma \vdash M \to N \Rightarrow \Gamma \vdash f_j(\ldots, M, \ldots) \to f_j(\ldots, N, \ldots)$,
3. $\Gamma \vdash M \to N \Rightarrow \Gamma \vdash ZM \to ZN$,
4. $\Gamma \vdash M \to N \Rightarrow \Gamma \vdash MZ \to NZ$,
5. $\Gamma \vdash P \to Q \Rightarrow \Gamma \vdash (\lambda x \sqsubseteq P.M) \to (\lambda x \sqsubseteq Q.M)$,
6. $\Gamma, [x \sqsubseteq P] \vdash M \to N, x \notin \Gamma \Rightarrow \Gamma \vdash (\lambda x \sqsubseteq P.M) \to (\lambda x \sqsubseteq P.N)$.

(ii) The relation $\twoheadrightarrow$ is defined inductively by:

1. $\Gamma \vdash M \to N \Rightarrow \Gamma \vdash M \twoheadrightarrow N$,
2. $\Gamma \vdash M \twoheadrightarrow M$,
3. $\Gamma \vdash M \twoheadrightarrow N, \Gamma \vdash N \twoheadrightarrow L \Rightarrow \Gamma \vdash M \twoheadrightarrow L$.

Lemma 3.7.2

(i) $\Gamma \vdash M \to N \Rightarrow \Gamma \vdash M = N$,

(ii) $\Gamma \vdash M \twoheadrightarrow N \Rightarrow \Gamma \vdash M = N$.

Proof.

(i) By induction over the definition of $\to$,

(ii) By induction over the definition of $\twoheadrightarrow$. □

In classical lambda calculus every term $(\lambda x.Q)R$ can be contracted and therefore such a term is called a *redex*. In the $\lambda \pi$ calculus it is *not* the case that every term $(\lambda x \sqsubseteq P.Q)R$ can be contracted. It follows that for the $\lambda \pi$ calculus some care is needed in using the word *redex*. We reserve the word *redex* for those terms which can be contracted (in a given context). We also introduce the term *candidate-redex*. The following should be contrasted with [2] 3.1.8.

Definition 3.7.3 (Candidate-redex, redex, fully reducible, reduction path).

(i) A *candidate-redex* is a term $(\lambda x \sqsubseteq P.Q)R$.

(ii) A candidate-redex $M \equiv (\lambda x \sqsubseteq P.Q)R$ can be *contracted* (is a *redex*) in context Γ if $\Gamma \vdash R \sqsubseteq P$. In this case $Q[x := R]$ is called a *contractum* of M.

(iii) A term M is *fully reducible* in context Γ if $\Gamma \vdash M \twoheadrightarrow N$ for some N not containing any candidate-redex.

(iv) A *reduction path* is a sequence $\Gamma \vdash M_0 \to M_1 \to M_2 \to \ldots$.

3.8 The diamond property ($\Diamond$)

The diamond property also holds for applied $\lambda\pi$ calculus.

Theorem 3.8.1 ($\Diamond$). $\twoheadrightarrow$ has the Diamond property, i.e. if $\Gamma \vdash M \twoheadrightarrow M_1, M \twoheadrightarrow M_2$ then there is an M_3 with $\Gamma \vdash M_1 \twoheadrightarrow M_3, M_2 \twoheadrightarrow M_3$.

Proof. As theorem 2.5.7. $\qquad\qquad\square$

3.9 The strong normalisation property (SN)

We consider applied $\lambda\pi$ calculus, i.e. the typed version of the calculus. We write Λ_σ to denote the set of terms from $\Lambda[\mathcal{A}]$ with type σ. We write Λ_σ^0 to denote the closed terms from Λ_σ. We write $\mathrm{SN}(M)$ if M strongly normalises by which we mean that it does not have an infinite reduction path.

Definition 3.9.1 ($\lambda\beta$). We define $\lambda\beta$ as the calculus with terms from $\Lambda[\mathcal{A}]$ and with all rules of $\lambda\pi$ but for the rule (π) which has been replaced by the rule (β):

(β)
$$\overline{\Gamma \vdash (\lambda x \sqsubseteq P_1.Q)P_2 = Q[x := P_2]}$$

We shall prove strong normalisation (SN) for $\lambda\beta$, using the "computability" argument as given in [2] A2. Then SN for $\lambda\pi$ follows easily from SN for $\lambda\beta$.

Definition 3.9.2 Define the following classes of terms:

$$C_0 = \{M \in \Lambda_0^0 \mid \mathrm{SN}(M)\},$$
$$C_{\sigma\to\tau} = \{M \in \Lambda_{\sigma\to\tau}^0 \mid \forall N \in C_\sigma(MN \in C_\tau)\}.$$

Lemma 3.9.3 (i) $M \in C_\sigma \Rightarrow \mathrm{SN}(M)$,
(ii) $\lambda x^{\sigma_1}\ldots x^{\sigma_n}.c \in C_\sigma$ if $\sigma = \sigma_1 \to \ldots \to \sigma_n \to 0$, where c is an arbitrary closed flat term in the language of $\mathcal{A}$.

Proof. The proof is by simultaneous induction on σ.

Basis. Obviously $M \in C_0 \Rightarrow \mathrm{SN}(M)$ and $c \in C_0$.

Induction step. We consider the type $\sigma \to \tau = \sigma \to \tau_1 \to \ldots \to \tau_m \to 0$ and we assume (i) and (ii) for $\sigma, \tau_1, \ldots, \tau_m$ (i.h.). We must prove (i) $M \in C_{\sigma \to \tau} \Rightarrow \mathrm{SN}(M)$ and (ii) $\lambda x^\sigma x^{\tau_1} \ldots x^{\tau_m}.c \in C_{\sigma \to \tau}$.

(i) Let $M \in C_{\sigma \to \tau}$, so $\forall N \in C_\sigma (MN \in C_\tau)$. We have $\sigma = \sigma_1 \to \ldots \to \sigma_n \to 0$ for some $\sigma_1, \ldots, \sigma_n$. Hence $M(\lambda x^{\sigma_1} \ldots x^{\sigma_n}.c) \in C_\tau$ and by i.h. has no infinite reduction. So certainly M has not, i.e. $\mathrm{SN}(M)$.

(ii) $\lambda x^\sigma x^{\tau_1} \ldots x^{\tau_m}.c \in C_{\sigma \to \tau}$ if
for $N \in C_\sigma$, $(\lambda x^\sigma x^{\tau_1} \ldots x^{\tau_m}.c)N \in C_\tau$ if
for $P_1 \in C_{\tau_1}, \ldots, P_m \in C_{\tau_m}$, $(\lambda x^\sigma x^{\tau_1} \ldots x^{\tau_m}.c)NP_1 \ldots P_m \in C_0$ which holds since one can do at most $m + 1$ reductions + finitely many ones in N and $P_1, \ldots, P_m$. In the last step we used the induction hypothesis which gives us $\mathrm{SN}(N)$, and $\mathrm{SN}(P_1), \ldots, \mathrm{SN}(P_m)$. $\qquad \square$

Definition 3.9.4 Define the following classes of terms:

$$C = \bigcup \{ C_\sigma \mid \sigma \text{ is a type } \},$$
$$C_\sigma^* = \{ M \in \Lambda_\sigma \mid M[\vec{x} := \vec{P}] \in C \text{ for } \vec{P} \subseteq C \}.$$

where $\vec{P} \subseteq C$ denotes an arbitrary sequence of terms in C and where $\vec{x}$ should always contain all free variables of M.

The intuition behind C_σ^* is the set of terms M in Λ_σ such that every instance of M with elements in C is in C.

Lemma 3.9.5 (Preservation properties).

(i) $M \in C \land M \twoheadrightarrow M' \Rightarrow M' \in C$,
(ii) $M \in C_\sigma^* \land M \twoheadrightarrow M' \Rightarrow M' \in C_\sigma^*$,
(iii) $M \in C^* \land \vec{P} \subseteq C \Rightarrow M' :\equiv M[\vec{x} := \vec{P}] \in C^*$.

Proof. (i) The proof is by induction on the type of M. If $M \in C_0$, i.e. $\mathrm{SN}(M)$ then $\mathrm{SN}(M')$ for if not, then $M \twoheadrightarrow M' \to \ldots$, contradiction. If $M \in C_{\sigma \to \tau}$, then for arbitrary $N \in C_\sigma$ we have $MN \in C_\tau$ so by i.h. $M'N \in C_\tau$. This shows $M' \in C$.

(ii) Assume $M \in C_\sigma^*$ and $M \twoheadrightarrow M'$. It follows that $M[\vec{x} := \vec{P}] \twoheadrightarrow M'[\vec{x} := \vec{P}]$. This can be proved by induction on the derivation of $\twoheadrightarrow$, cf. [2] 3.1.14. Let $\vec{P} \subseteq C$, then we know $M[\vec{x} := \vec{P}] \in C$ and by (i), $M'[\vec{x} := \vec{P}] \in C$. This shows $M' \in C_\sigma^*$.

(iii) Let $\vec{y}$ contain the free variables of M'. We must show that for $\vec{Q} \subseteq C$ we have $M'[\vec{y} := \vec{Q}] \in C$, i.e. $M[\vec{x} := \vec{P}][\vec{y} := \vec{Q}] \in C$, i.e. $M[\vec{x}, \vec{y} := \vec{P}, \vec{Q}] \in C$, which holds because $M \in C^*$. $\qquad \square$

Lemma 3.9.6 $M \in \Lambda_\sigma \Rightarrow M \in C_\sigma^*$.

Proof. The proof is by induction on M.

Case 1. $M \equiv x$. Now $x[x := P] \in C$.

Case 2. $M \equiv c_i$. Trivial.

Case 3. $M \equiv f_j(M_1, \ldots, M_{a_j})$. Use i.h. and the fact that each M_i is of type 0.

Case 4. $M \equiv AB$ with $A \in \Lambda_{\sigma \to \tau}$, $B \in \Lambda_\sigma$. Let $\vec{P} \subseteq C$. By i.h. $A \in C^*_{\sigma \to \tau}$ and $B \in C^*_\sigma$, i.e. $A[\vec{x} := \vec{P}] \in C_{\sigma \to \tau}$ and $B[\vec{x} := \vec{P}] \in C_\sigma$. $M[\vec{x} := \vec{P}] \equiv A[\vec{x} := \vec{P}]B[\vec{x} := \vec{P}]$ which is in C_τ and hence is in C.

Case 5. $M \equiv \lambda y \sqsubseteq A.B$ with $A \in \Lambda_\sigma, B \in \Lambda_\tau$. Let $\vec{P} \subseteq C$. By i.h. $A \in C^*_\sigma$, $B \in C^*_\tau$. We may assume $y \notin \vec{x}$. $A' := A[\vec{x} := \vec{P}]$, $B' := B[\vec{x} := \vec{P}]$ so by 3.9.5 (iii) $A' \in C^*$ and $B' \in C^*$. Let $\tau = \tau_1 \to \ldots \to \tau_n \to 0$.

$M \in C^*$ if

$\lambda y \sqsubseteq A'.B' \in C_{\sigma \to \tau}$ if

for $S \in C_\sigma$, $(\lambda y \sqsubseteq A'.B')S \in C_\tau$ if

for $T_1 \in C_{\tau_1}, \ldots, T_n \in C_{\tau_n}$, $\mathrm{SN}((\lambda y \sqsubseteq A'.B')ST_1 \ldots T_n)$ which holds, for if not, then three possibilities arise, each leading to a contradiction.

Either (a) A' or B' have an infinite reduction. But $B' \in C^*$ so $B'[y := Q] \in C$ (where $Q \in C$ arbitrary) and therefore by lemma 3.9.3(i) $\mathrm{SN}(B'[y := Q])$ so certainly $\mathrm{SN}(B')$. Also $\mathrm{SN}(A')$. Contradiction.

or (b) S or $T_1 \ldots T_n$ have an infinite reduction which contradicts $S \in C$, $T_1 \in C$, ..., $T_n \in C$ and lemma 3.9.3(i).

or (c) $(\lambda y \sqsubseteq A'.B')ST_1 \ldots T_n \twoheadrightarrow (\lambda y \sqsubseteq A''.B'')S'T_1' \ldots T_n') \to B''[y := S']T_1' \ldots T_n' \to \ldots$. But by lemma 3.9.5 (i) $S' \in C$, $T_1' \ldots T_n' \in C$ and by lemma 3.9.5 (ii) $B'' \in C^*$. Therefore by the definition of C^* we have $B''[y := S'] \in C$. From the definition of C we have $B''[y := S']T_1' \ldots T_n' \in C_0$, i.e. $\mathrm{SN}(B''[\ldots]T_1' \ldots T_n')$. Contradiction. $\square$

Theorem 3.9.7 (SN). In $\lambda\pi$ every term strongly normalises.

Proof. By lemma 3.9.3(i) and lemma 3.9.6 we have that in $\lambda\beta$ every term strongly normalises. It follows that in $\lambda\pi$ every term strongly normalises, for suppose that M has an infinite reduction in $\lambda\pi$, then so it has in $\lambda\beta$ which cannot be the case. $\square$

Remark 3.9.8 An alternative proof of SN for $\lambda\pi$ calculus can be given by using a technique due to Plotkin (who actually considered lambda-typed lambda calculus). Let $\Lambda[\mathcal{A}]$ denote the set of terms of $\lambda\pi$ calculus and let Λ denote the set of terms of classical typed lambda calculus. Define a mapping $\overline{} : \Lambda[\mathcal{A}] \to \Lambda$ as follows:

$\overline{x^\tau} :\equiv x^\tau$,

$\overline{c_i} :\equiv c_i$,

$\overline{f_j(P_1, \ldots, P_{a_j})} :\equiv f_j(\overline{P_1}, \ldots, \overline{P_{a_j}})$,

$\overline{(MN)} :\equiv (\overline{M}\ \overline{N})$,

$\overline{(\lambda x^\sigma \sqsubseteq M.N)} :\equiv ((\lambda y^\sigma.\lambda x^\sigma.\overline{N})\overline{M})$ $\qquad\qquad (y^\sigma$ fresh$)$.

By induction on the structure of M it can be shown that $\overline{M[x := N]} \equiv \overline{M}[x := \overline{N}]$. Using this, one shows by induction on the derivation of $\Gamma \vdash M \to N$ that

$$\Gamma \vdash M \to N \;\Rightarrow\; \overline{M} \xrightarrow{\neq} \overline{N}.$$

Now if a term $M \in \Lambda[\mathcal{A}]$ has an infinite reduction path, then so does $\overline{M}$, which cannot be the case by SN for classical typed lambda calculus.

4 Description Calculus

4.1 General

In this section we shall define two applied $\lambda\pi$ calculi, viz. *description calculus* and *signature calculus*. As a next step we shall briefly sketch some generalisations of the operations $+$, $\square$ and $\bullet$ from DA [6]. For a complete treatment of these generalisations we refer to [5].

4.2 Description Calculus

Description calculus is the applied $\lambda\pi$ calculus obtained by defining the underlying algebraic system with preorder as the algebra of descriptions DA together with the implementation relation. For the formal details of this implementation relation we refer to [5].

Definition 4.2.1 Let Des denote the set of descriptions as defined in [6] and let $\Sigma, \bullet, +, \square$ be the operations on these descriptions. Let $\sqsubseteq$ denote the implementation relation on descriptions. $\mathcal{D}$ is defined as

$$\langle \mathrm{Des}, \sqsubseteq, \{\Sigma, \bullet, +, \square\}, \mathrm{Des} \rangle$$

where it is understood that we have secondary domains for names, renamings and signatures as introduced in [6]. If the implementation relation is reflexive and transitive, then $\mathcal{D}$ is an algebraic system with preorder in the sense of section 3.1. Note that the operations that do not apply to the domain of interest (Des) have not been made explicit.

Definition 4.2.2 $(\mathcal{D} \models)$. The language of $\mathcal{D}$ contains the following symbols:

(i) Function symbols $\Sigma, \bullet, +, \square$ which are interpreted as the operations on descriptions $\Sigma, \bullet, +, \square$.

(ii) The elements of Des as constant symbols with the obvious interpretation,

(iii) $\sqsubseteq$ which is interpreted as the implementation relation $\sqsubseteq$,

(iv) $=$ which is interpreted as equality on Des.

Definition 4.2.3 *Description calculus* is the calculus as defined in section 3.2 where $\mathcal{D}$ is given by the definitions 4.2.1 and 4.2.2.

Remark 4.2.4 Note that definition 3.4.3 automatically gives us a model $\mathcal{D}^+$ for description calculus. One easiliy verifies that lambda terms (description terms) of Curry type $0 \to 0$ are interpreted as functions from descriptions to descriptions.

4.3 Signature Calculus

Signature calculus is the applied $\lambda\pi$ calculus obtained by defining the underlying algebraic system with preorder as the algebra of signatures [6] with the (reversed) inclusion relation (which can be viewed as a simplified version of the implementation relation).

Definition 4.3.1 S is defined as

$$\langle \text{Sig}, \supseteq, \{\bullet, +, \Box, \Delta\}, \text{Sig} \rangle$$

where it is understood that we have secondary domains for renamings and for names. Note that S is an algebraic system with preorder. Note also that the operations that do not apply to the domain of interest (Sig) have not been made explicit.

Definition 4.3.2 $(S \models)$. The language of S contains the function symbols $\bullet, +, \Box$, Δ and the elements of Sig as constant symbols with the obvious interpretation. $\sqsubseteq$ is interpreted as $\supseteq$ and $=$ as equality.

Definition 4.3.3 *Signature calculus* is the calculus as defined in section 3.2 where the algebraic system with preorder is S as given by the definitions 4.3.1 and and 4.3.2. The terms of signature calculus are called *signature terms*.

4.4 Generalised Description Calculus

It is possible to generalise $\bullet$, $+$ and $\Box$ to terms of non-0 Curry types. In this way it becomes possible to apply the renaming, import and export operations also to *parameterised descriptions*. This turns out to be very convenient in practical applications. In particular the possibility to apply a renaming to a parameterised description is indispensable. The reader can find many examples of this in [1].

5 Conclusions

In this paper we have presented the calculus $\lambda\pi$ and shown that it has the important properties $\Diamond$ and SN. This calculus has been used for giving a meaning to the parameterisation and design constructs of COLD-K. This has been done by taking for the algebraic system A a version of the description algebra DA [6] based on MPL_ω[7]. For the formal details we refer to [5]. The paper [4] provides a lot of intuition and examples for the theory presented in this paper. Also in [4] it is explained how $\lambda\pi$ calculus is used for giving a meaning to components and designs.

6 Acknowledgements

The work reported in this paper has been performed in cooperation with H.B.M. Jonkers, C.P.J. Koymans and G.R. Renardel de Lavalette.

References

[1] W.E. BAATS, L.M.G. FEIJS, J.H.A. Gelissen. *A Formal Specification of IN-GRES*, this volume.

[2] H. BARENDREGT. *The Lambda Calculus, its Syntax and Semantics*, (Revised Edition), North-Holland, Amsterdam, (1984).

[3] H. BARENDREGT, M. COPPO, M. DEZANI-CIANCAGLINI. *A Filter Lambda Model and the Completeness of Type Assignment*, Journal of Symbolic Logic, 48 (1983), 931-940.

[4] L.M.G. Feijs. *A Formalisation of Design Structures*. Proceedings of CompEuro 88, Brussels, April 1988. Computer Society IEEE.

[5] L.M.G. Feijs, H.B.M. Jonkers, C.P.J. Koymans, G.R. Renardel de Lavalette. *Formal definition of the design language COLD-K, Preliminary edition*. ESPRIT document METEOR/t7/PRLE/7.

[6] H.B.M. Jonkers. *Description Algebra*, this volume.

[7] C.P.J. Koymans, G.R. Renardel de Lavalette. *The Logic MPL$_\omega$*. this volume.

[8] M. WIRSING. *Structured Algebraic Specifications: a Kernel Language*, Habilitation thesis, Technische Universität München (1983).

Algebraic ADT Specifications of an Extended Relational Algebra and
their Conversion into a Working Prototype 419

L. Lavazza, S. Crespi-Reghizzi

The RAP System
as a Tool for Testing COLD Specifications

Heinrich Hussmann
Alfons Geser

Universität Passau
Fakultät für Mathematik und Informatik
Postfach 2540
D-8390 Passau

EUNet: hussmann@unipas.uucp

Abstract:

This paper describes the practical use of the RAP system, a rapid prototyping system for algebraic specifications combining term rewriting and resolution techniques. After a sketch of the general aims of RAP, the behaviour of the system is described from the user's point of view, illustrated by detailed examples of moderate size. All examples are presented in COLD-K syntax.

1. Rapid Prototyping for Algebraic Specifications

In this chapter the general aims of the RAP system are explained. The relationship to software engineering and programming concepts is discussed.

1.1. Software Development by Formal Methods

Nowadays' attempts to improve the software development process aim at the following points:
- reliability of the final product
- exact fulfilment of the users' requirements
- modularity of the product as well as of the development process
- ease of modification and maintenance
- reusability of development work.

It is a widely accepted thesis that all these aims can be achieved by using a formal approach ([Bauer, Wössner 82]). For this purpose, a homogeneous formal framework ("single linguistic framework", cf. [Jonkers, Koymans, Renardel 85]) is needed which
- allows powerful notations to express the users' requirements simply
- allows operational notations to describe concrete implementations
- has a sound mathematical basis usable for verification of development steps
- supports modular specification and development.

We believe that hierarchical algebraic specifications ([Wirsing et al. 83]) constitute a formalism which meets these requirements. They comprise specification styles on different levels of abstraction:
- very compact abstract specifications (using e.g. full first order logic)
- rather abstract but already operational specifications (using Horn clause logic and term rewriting, cf. [Padawitz 88])
- concrete implementations (using specifications of machine models).

Furthermore, stepwise correct transformations of specifications can be formulated and formally verified which lead from more abstract to more concrete levels.

In this paper we address the second level, i. e. Horn clause logic. This specification style turns out to be abstract enough to describe abstract data types in a natural way, and operational enough to admit powerful interpreters.

The specification language adressed above is a subset of the COLD-K language. In order to keep with METEOR's single lingustic framework, we use the language COLD-K ([Feijs, Jonkers, Koymans, Renardel 87]) for the presentation of examples.

1.2. Rapid Prototyping and Specification Testing

One of the recently much discussed concepts in software engineering is "Prototyping" ([Budde et al. 84]). Prototyping means the construction of a simplified predecessor ("prototype") of the final product during an early phase of the software development process, in order to compare the informal requirements of the customer with the actual behaviour of the intended software product. There is an increasing number of software engineering scientists which do no longer see a contradiction between formal specification and rapid prototyping, but consider specifications as very high level prototypes ([Berry, Wing 85]). An interesting research direction in this field is the investigation of tools for the systematic construction of prototypes out of formal specifications. Prototypes produced this way may be fairly inefficient compared to hand-made ones, but they are built up automatically and hence quickly - an important factor of economy - and they ensure correctness w.r.t. the specification. RAP ([Hussmann 85/87]) is an experimental tool for prototyping algebraic specifications.

Usually, prototypes serve for testing against expected properties of the intended product. Unfortunately, tests do not guarantee correctness: If the specification and the requirements differ, this will be detected eventually, but if they are equal, this cannot be proved. Program testing cannot give full safety but confidence and insight in the product and its behaviour, and this is all we can gain at this stage. For specification testing, as done in RAP, the same holds. Therefore, it is important to do a *systematic* test with the specification. The RAP system offers facilities for this, since it is able to answer more complex questions about a specification than just evaluation of specified functions.

1.3. Questions to an Interpreter for Algebraic Specifications

In [Spec 85], a requirement definition for an interpreter for algebraic specifications is given by a list of questions an interpreter should be able to answer. The following list is a subset of the questions proposed there. Assume that an algebraic specification defines a set of function symbols, a set of terms built from these function symbols and the input-output behaviour of the function symbols.
1. Given fixed arguments, what is the value of a specified function?
2. Given a term built from the specified functions, what is its value?
3. Given a value for a specified function, which arguments have to be supplied to the function to obtain it?
4. Given two terms built from the specified functions, are their values equivalent?
5. Given a proposition formulated by the specified functions and free variables, are there substitutions of terms for the variables, such that the proposition holds in the specified theory?

To some extent, all these questions can be answered by the RAP system. The RAP interpreter is able to solve systems of equations over the given specification, i.e. it looks for substitutions which fulfil a system of equations containing free variables. This allows an adequate treatment of question 5 above. The other questions (1-4) turn out to be special cases of question 5. An example for a treatment of the five questions by RAP can be found in chapter 3.

1.4. Algebraic Programming

It is an interesting observation that there is no sharp edge between very high level programming languages and specifications of a certain style, since these specifications have an operational behaviour as well. So, a new class of programming languages arises; they use algebraic specifications as their main construct. Apart from the software engineering concepts involved, the RAP system is an interpreter for a such a language. We use the term "Algebraic Programming" to stress the similarity to logic programming as well as the differences to the usual PROLOG implementations. RAP is a functional logic programming language. Similar to SLOG ([Fribourg 84]), it uses oriented equational clauses based on a functional language (this way better reflecting the particular role of equality than PROLOG). In difference to usual approaches to logic programming, RAP provides complete evaluation strategies which simulate exactly the abstract mathematical semantics (and are independent of details like e.g. the order of formulae). Moreover, RAP contains a number of built-in criteria to detect properties of the specifications which may speed up the performance of the interpreter without loss of completeness.

2. The RAP System from the User's Point of View

This chapter contains an introduction to the practical use of algebraic specifications. A well-known example for a specification is presented. A number of useful shorthand notations within COLD-K is introduced. The user interface of the system and the possibilities for observation and control of the internal actions of the interpreter are illustrated using this example.

2.1. SEQ - An Example for an Algebraic Specification

The following text is an algebraic specification of sequences of natural numbers, formulated in a slightly enriched version of COLD-K.

```
LET SEQ :=

IMPORT NAT INTO

IMPORT BOOL INTO

  CLASS

  SORT Seq
  FUNC empty: Seq
  FUNC append:  Nat # Seq -> Seq
  FUNC first:  Seq -> Nat
  FUNC rest:  Seq -> Seq
  FUNC conc:  Seq # Seq -> Seq
  FUNC isempty:  Seq -> Bool
  FUNC length:  Seq -> Nat
  CONS (Seq, empty, append)

AXIOM
```

```
FORALL   s: Seq, s1: Seq, s2: Seq,
         n: Nat, n1: Nat, n2: Nat

( {1} first(append(n,s)) = n;
  {2} rest(append(n,s)) = s;
  {3} conc(empty,s1) = s1;
  {4} conc(append(n,s1),s2) = append(n,conc(s1,s2));
  {5} isempty(empty) = true;
  {6} isempty(append(n,s)) = false;
  {7} length(empty) = 0;
  {8} length(append(n,s)) = succ(length(s))  )
```

END

SEQ has the following intended (informal) meaning: Seq is the sort of sequences of natural numbers, empty creates an empty sequence, append adds an element to a sequence, first delivers the first element of a sequence, rest removes it, isempty asks whether a sequence is empty, length computes the number of entries of a sequence, and conc yields the concatenation of two sequences.

SEQ is written as a COLD class definition where only a restricted part of COLD (corresponding to algebraic specifications) is used. In order to improve the readability of the text, some shorthand notations (language extensions) have been used. The next section gives an overview of this variant of the COLD-K language.

2.2. A Sublanguage of COLD for Algebraic Specifications

The COLD sublanguage supported by RAP consists of "static" (i.e. state-independent) class schemes without use of parameterization. In terms of [Jonkers 88] (pp. 13-15), RAP admits only
- schemes consisting of import, export and a definition set (class)
- definitions of sorts, functions and axioms (no predicates, no procedures).

The sort and function definitions are restricted to the (default) case of an empty dependency set. The axioms are restricted to assertions of a "positive conditional" shape which are interpreted as conditional rewrite rules. The general form of the axioms is

$$t1 = t1' \text{ \textbf{AND} } \ldots \text{ \textbf{AND} } tn = tn' \implies tl = tr$$

(where ti, ti', tl and tr are terms built from the signature and variables of the current type and from the visible part of the signature of its primitive types). In this scheme, $n \geq 0$ is assumed, in the example SEQ all axioms are unconditional ($n = 0$). The variables occurring within the axioms are universally quantified, which can be expressed by a single quantification, as in the example above.

From the semantical point of view, it should be noted that RAP implicitly assumes all functions to be *total* (in order to apply standard term rewriting techniques). As the rewrite rules are applied in one direction only, completeness is lost, unless the set of rules is *confluent* (i.e. has the Church-Rosser property). This has, however, to be ensured by the user, and is not checked within RAP. More detailed material about this topic can be found in [Hussmann 85].

2.3. Useful Shorthand Notations for Algebraic Specifications within COLD

The example given above does not strictly follow the concrete COLD-K syntax. There are two notations used which can be easily translated into the standard COLD-K language, but improve the readability of the text.

RAP uses a simpler notation for EXPORT parts. In standard COLD-K, the whole signature has to be written down, which is repeated immediately below in the class body. To avoid this clumsy notation, we just assume that a missing EXPORT statement means to export the whole signature of the class body. In addition, a special statement for "Hiding" sort and function symbols has been introduced, which is not needed for the examples SEQ.

The CONS declaration of a function symbol is an abbreviation for a generation principle. CONS stands for *constructor*, i.e. for a function symbol which is used for generating data values. For instance, if the following signature is given:

```
SORT s
FUNC c1 : s
FUNC c2 : s # t -> s
FUNC c3 : s # s # s -> s
```

the statement

```
CONS (s, c1, c2, c3)
```

means a shorthand for the following COLD-K text using an auxiliary predicate symbol:

```
PRED isconstr : s

IND FORALL x1: s, x2: s, x3: s, y: t

  ( isconstr(c1);
    isconstr(x1) => isconstr(c2(x1,y));
    (isconstr(x1) AND isconstr(x2) AND isconstr(x3))
       => isconstr(c3(x1,x2,x3)) )

AXIOM FORALL x: s ( isconstr(x) ).
```

The predicate isconstr(x) holds iff x (of sort s) can be reached by a constructor term of sort s. Such a term may contain arbitrary terms of other sorts, but the generation principle can be applied for these sorts, too. So the axioms together ensure that every object can be reached by a ground constructor term.

The keyword IND in the predicate definition leads to a restriction to the least predicate fulfilling the formula given as the predicate body. So a structural induction principle on constructor terms becomes available.

RAP does not use the structural induction principle, but it makes use of the fact that for every term there is an equivalent constructor term. (The set of computed solutions for a given system of equations is restricted to constructor solutions.)

2.4. A First Look to the RAP System

The RAP system has been developed at the University of Passau in 1985. A revised version of RAP is currently in use at about 30 research institutions throughout Europe.

RAP is written in a fairly portable PASCAL dialect. It has been ported up to now to the operating systems VAX/VMS, UNIX 4.2 BSD, ULTRIX and VM/CMS. The examples in this paper have been performed by RAP 2.1 on a SUN 3/160 workstation with 4 Mb RAM running UNIX 4.2 BSD. The standard versions of RAP use a particular specification syntax described in [Hussmann 85/87]. For a better integration into the METEOR framework, a version of RAP has been built which uses the sublanguage of COLD-K indicated above. In addition, there exists an automatic tool for translating RAP's standard syntax into COLD notation. The examples within this paper have been written and run using the COLD version of RAP 2.1.

The user interface of RAP consists just of a specification parser and a command interpreter (on SUN systems there is a window/mouse-based interface to the command interpreter available). The latest version of RAP contains also an interactive editor but only for part of the language the so-called tasks (i.e. questions which are asked to the interpreter). The specification text has to be prepared by a standard text editor.

Let us assume that a file contains the type specification above and we ask the query formulated in the equation below:

$$conc(u, append(2, empty)) = append(1, append(2, empty))$$

Such a question is called a *task* in RAP terminology. A task consists of a list of equations which may contain open variables (called *unknowns*) like u in the task above. For these variables the system will try to find correct substitutions. Note that here equations are neither rewrite rules nor axioms, and that these equations may not have premises.

The example task above asks for a substitution of the sequence variable u such that the concatenation of u with the sequence append(2,empty) yields the sequence append(1,append(2,empty)) . Obviously, we expect that the variable u is characterized to be append(1,empty) .

The following text is a listing of a dialogue with the RAP system working on this example. User input is printed boldface. Let the input file for the example be called "seqfile":

UNIX %**rap seqfile**

COLD/RAP System based on version 2.1-5 SUN/UNIX

Reading standard type declarations.

STEP 1: Syntax check

Reading type SEQ.

No syntax errors detected.

STEP 2: Property check

noetherian SEQ -- by criteria
complete SEQ except first, rest -- by criteria

STEP 3: Interactive interpreter

Preprocessing the axioms.

RAP>**task t1**

RAP/EDIT>**create**

Please start with the left hand side of the new equation.

Use `?` for help, `-` to delete last entry and `@` to abort this equation!

Goal No 1:

```
?left side?  =  *
```

```
>> conc(u,
```

```
### `u` was declared as a variable of sort Seq !
```

```
Goal No 1:
```

```
conc(u,?Seq?)  =  *
```

Now the task is composed in an interactive, syntax-guided way. Details are skipped here. The result of the editing process is:

```
   Equations of task T1:
```

```
Nr. 1: conc(u,append(2,empty)) = append(1,append(2,empty))
```

```
RAP/EDIT>exit
```

```
Task T1 generated.
```

```
RAP>run t1
```

```
*** Solution found ***
```

```
[u = append(1,empty)]
```

```
CPU time: 0.12 secs
```

```
More solutions?  yes
```

```
No more solutions found.
```

```
Total CPU time: 0.22 secs
```

```
RAP>exit
```

When RAP starts up, it does some initialization work, essentially reading the defining text of standard types (NAT, BOOL etc.). Then three subsequent steps of analysis are performed.

Step 1 consists in reading the input file and checking the syntax and context conditions of the specification language.

Step 2 applies a number of criteria to the specifications read in order to detect interesting properties of the types, which are used by RAP to improve the efficiency of the interpreter:
- termination property of the term rewriting system (**noetherian**)
- completeness of functional definitions by case analysis over constructors (**complete**).

The messages issued by RAP show that the criteria have been applied successfully to SEQ with a minor exception: The function symbols first and rest are not defined by complete case analysis.

Step three is performed interactively. The prompt "RAP>" means that RAP is ready to process commands. The most important commands are
TASK - generate a new task within the system
RUN - execute a task.

The command TASK leads into an editing mode (indicated by the prompt RAP/EDIT>) where the equations for a new task can be entered incrementally.

There are many other commands for inspection of the system status, for retrieving results of earlier executions, for adjustment of system parameters etc. On-line help (in English) is available via the command HELP. A number of system parameters allow to control the behaviour of the system (search strategies, redex selection, garbage collection, for instance). A complete description of the user interface to RAP is given in the RAP user's manual ([Hussmann 85/87]).

3. Simple Experiments Using RAP

This chapter contains the results of a number of simple RAP experiments based on the example SEQ above.

3.1. Typical Tasks

We present four additional tasks below, each of them representing a typical kind of task. The first one is a task which is unsatisfiable: If a sequence remains non-empty after 3 rest-operations, it cannot have the length 2.

```
length(u) = 2,
isempty(rest(rest(rest(u)))) = false
```

When executing this task, the system correctly responds:

```
No solutions found.
```

```
Total CPU time: 0.23 secs
```

A second task has several solutions:

```
conc(x,y) = append(10,append(20,empty))
```

It asks the question: How can a sequence of length 2 be composed from two other sequences by concatenation?

```
*** Solution found ***
```

```
[x = empty,
 y = append(10,append(20,empty))]
```

```
CPU time: 0.07 secs
```

More solutions? **yes**

```
*** Solution found ***
```

```
[x = append(10,empty),
 y = append(20,empty)]
```

```
CPU time: 0.13 secs
```

More solutions? **yes**

```
*** Solution found ***
```

```
[x = append(10,append(20,empty)),
 y = empty]
```

```
CPU time: 0.20 secs
```

```
More solutions? yes
```

```
No more solutions found.
```

```
Total CPU time: 0.25 secs
```

The next task has an infinite number of solutions.

```
    length(x) = length(y)
```

If the user did not stop the system on this task, it would proceed enumerating solutions infinitely. In order to cope with such situations the user is asked everytime a solution is found whether continuation is desired.

The *<number>-terms occurring in the solutions below denote "new" free variables generated by the system. Any term can be substituted for them to obtain a more special correct solution.

```
*** Solution found ***
```

```
[x = *1,
 y = *1]
```

```
CPU time: 0.05 secs
```

```
More solutions? yes
```

```
*** Solution found ***
```

```
[x = append(*2,empty),
 y = append(*8,empty)]
```

```
CPU time: 0.37 secs
```

```
More solutions? yes
```

```
*** Solution found ***
```

```
[x = append(*2,append(*6,empty)),
 y = append(*14,append(*18,empty))]
```

```
CPU time: 0.85 secs
```

```
More solutions? yes
```

```
*** Solution found ***
```

```
[x = append(*2,append(*6,append(*10,empty))),
 y = append(*20,append(*26,append(*32,empty)))]
```

```
CPU time: 1.70 secs
```

```
More solutions? no
```

```
Total CPU time: 1.74 secs
```

Note that the solution

```
[x = empty,
 y = empty]
```

is not shown by the system, since it is a special case of the first solution.

A fourth example shows an·unsatisfactory property of the RAP interpreter (which is known from interpreters at all). The system sometimes does not terminate.

```
mult(length(x),length(y)) = 4,
length(x) = length(y)
```

Fortunately, non-termination takes place after all solutions have been found:

```
*** Solution found ***
```

```
[x = append(*2,append(*12,empty)),
 y = append(*32,append(*42,empty))]
```

```
CPU time: 1.28 secs
```

```
More solutions? yes
```

```
- - - non-termination - - -
```

3.2. The Semantical Unification Algorithm Used by RAP

The algorithm used by the system is an optimized variant of the so-called *conditional narrowing* algorithm ([Hussmann 85]). Below a sketch of the conditional narrowing algorithm is given.

We call a system of equations together with a substitution a *goal*. The very first goal is given by the equation system supplied in the user's task; its substitution is empty. There are basically two ways to proceed from a given goal G:

Unification Step:

> If there is a substitution for the variables which leads to a syntactical identity of the left and right hand sides of each equation in G, a most general substitution with this property is computed (unification) and applied to the substitution part of G. The resulting substitution is displayed as a solution.

Narrowing Step:

> If there is a substitution for the variables which allows the application of a (conditional) rewrite rule to an equation of G, a most general substitution with this property is computed. A new goal is generated which is composed as follows:
> * the computed substitution is applied to the goal and the rewrite rule
> * the conclusion of the rewrite rule is applied to the goal
> * the premises of the rewrite rule are added to the new goal.

The narrowing step is a combination of rewriting with *resolution* techniques. The RAP system looks for all possible derivations which start from a given task (resp. its goals) and, after a sequence of narrowing steps, lead to a unification step. In addition, the intermediate goals are simplified (rewriting to normal form, expansion of auxiliary variables, decomposition into a simpler goal) and useless goals are discarded (unsatisfiability, subsumption - i.e. special case of another goal).

Note that a considerable gain in power is achieved by this combination of resolution (logic programming) and rewriting (functional programming). In difference to PROLOG, the simplification of intermediate goals allows to treat function symbols appropriate: Function symbols have a functional semantics (usually simulated in PROLOG by "modes", i.e. input/output positions of predicates) and they are applied in a "trap-door" manner, i.e. without preparing a backtracking point. Moreover, the simplification is applied to the whole goal, so even the last equation of the goal may turn out to be unsatisfiable and lead to a failure. This is the main reason why a number of RAP tasks terminate while their PROLOG counterparts do not.

To ensure the termination of rewriting to normal form, only a subset of the rules is chosen for normalization which has been proven to be noetherian in step 2. This feature is very useful in practice, nevertheless theoretical considerations showed that this strategy may lead to a loss of completeness in special cases. Completeness is preserved if the whole set of rules is noetherian. (Work on this field is still in progress.)

3.3. Observing Internal Steps of the Algorithm

Since the algorithm used by RAP has exponential complexity and does not always terminate, facilities for observing the internal steps of the algorithm are important. The RAP system offers two possibilities for this purpose: the TRACE and DEBUG options of the RUN command. The TRACE option creates a listing file of all internal steps, the DEBUG option allows interactive observation of the algorithm during a terminal session.

If the DEBUG option is used, trace information appears on the screen. After a certain amount of computation (controlled by a system parameter) the system is stopped and input from the user is expected: Empty input causes the system to proceed by one step. A command language is available to obtain information about the status of the execution (inspection of subgoals, of the proof tree structure, of the applied rules, etc.). RAP also keeps book of all results achieved in a session and allows to inspect them interactively or to write them onto a file.

3.4. Search Strategies

The conditional narrowing algorithm consists of an inspection of all derivation sequences composed from narrowing and unification steps. The set of possible sequences can be considered as a (generally infinite) tree (*proof tree*). So, the question arises in which order the nodes of this tree are visited. Both *depth-first* and *breadth-first* strategies can be chosen in RAP. The examples above have been performed breadth-first, because depth-first in general is not fair. Consider the following type/task combination (enumeration of ordered sequences) which is also used in [Bouge et al. 85] as an example for test set generation out of algebraic specifications. The function symbol le means here the built-in "less or equal"-function on natural numbers.

```
LET ISSORTED :=

IMPORT SEQ INTO

IMPORT NAT INTO

IMPORT BOOL INTO

  CLASS

  FUNC issorted: Seq -> Bool
```

AXIOM

   FORALL x, y: Nat, s: Seq

   ({1} issorted(empty) = true;
     {2} issorted(append(x,empty)) = true;
     {3} le(x,y) = true =>
        issorted(append(x,append(y,s))) =
                         issorted(append(y,s));
     {4} le(x,y) = false =>
        issorted(append(x,append(y,s))) = false)

   END

If the RAP system executes this task with the default breadth-first strategy, it starts to enumerate the following solutions:

```
Task ISS1 , Run number 1

/DEPTHLIMIT = INFINITE   /SEARCH = BF (breadth-first)

[x = empty]
[x = append(*1,empty)]
[x = append(*3,append(*3,empty))]
[x = append(0,append(*3,empty))]
[x = append(1,append(succ(*13),empty))]
[x = append(*17,append(*17,append(*17,empty)))]

CPU time: 1.22 secs
```

Using the depth-first search the enumeration starts as follows

```
Task ISS1 , Run number 2

/DEPTHLIMIT = INFINITE   /SEARCH = DF (depth-first)

[x = empty]
[x = append(*1,empty)]
[x = append(*3,append(*3,empty))]
[x = append(*9,append(*9,append(*9,empty)))]
[x = append(*15,append(*15,append(*15,append(*15,empty))))]
[x = append(*21,append(*21,append(*21,append(*21,
                                     append(*21,empty)))))]

CPU time: 0.67 secs
```

The reason why the depth-first strategy delivers a correct but very special set of solutions is that it follows a leftmost and infinite way down the proof tree while the breadth-first strategy exhausts the whole tree in a safe manner. The result of the breadth-first strategy is complete in the sense that in an infinite enumeration every solution will occur eventually.

RAP allows to experiment freely with different ways to handle the fairness problem. For instance, there is a option (/DEPTHLIMIT) to restrict the search process to a finite initial part of the proof tree. Use of this option leads to a completeness for "small" solutions even when combined with depth-first strategy:

```
Task ISS1 , Run number 4

/DEPTHLIMIT = 6    /SEARCH = DF (depth-first)

[x = empty]
[x = append(*1,empty)]
[x = append(*3,append(*3,empty))]
[x = append(*9,append(*9,append(*9,empty)))]
[x = append(0,append(0,append(*9,empty)))]
[x = append(1,append(1,append(succ(*44),empty)))]

CPU time: 1.17 secs
```

Other strategies can be easiliy implemented. As an example, a heuristic "smallest-first" strategy has beenn added which chooses the goal with smallest number of symbols to be executed next. As a most flexible alternative to these predefined strategies, RAP allows interactive search control if a task is run in DEBUG mode. In this mode, at every step the user may judge under the subgoals available in the current computation state and select the most promising one as the continuation point.

4. Summary

4.1. Further Experimentation

A lot of other experiments have been performed with the RAP system, some of them are documented in an extended version of this paper ([Geser, Hussmann 85/88]). Experiments with RAP have been conducted on examples of non-trivial size and difficulty, e. g. a microprocessor containing about 260 axioms ([Geser 86/88]). Experiments with a specification of a programming language including higher-order and communication features are described in [Padawitz 87]. For a simple applicative programming language a compiler to an abstract stack machine has been specified within RAP ([Hussmann, Rank 88]). There is an increasing number of experiments using RAP at other universities. For instance, an example concerning code generation is given in [Berghammer et al. 87]. The largest specification processed by RAP up to now is a specification of the INGRES database system ([Gelissen 88]) with about 470 axioms.

Almost every specification submitted to RAP turned out to contain (usually trivial) bugs. So the system in its present form is a good tool for debugging specifications. For this purpose it is extremely important to make the interpreter transparent for the user. The DEBUG mode of RAP is a first step in this direction, but more advanced interface techniques will be necessary to manage the large amount of information produced during the execution of a task. Experiments with the window/mouse surface of the SUN workstation showed that pointing devices and graphic displays do not solve these problems completely, a need for better structured output still remains. The best solution would be a technique for viewing terms, goals etc. at different levels of abstraction, hiding as much unimportant details as possible.

4.2. Applicability

We believe that interpreters for algebraic specifications (like RAP) will play an important role in software development environments based on formal methods. It looks most promising that three powerful techniques, namely logic programming, symbolic evaluation and hierarchical algebraic specifications fit together consistently in one tool.

Moreover, the deductive framework used in RAP (conditional narrowing) seems to be an interesting alternative to logic programming languages. The concepts of many-sorted terms and hierarchical structuring are very useful, in particular for large programs.

RAP is an experimental system, i.e. the implementation gave more emphasis to a simple structure of the system than to efficiency. It is clear that the performance of the present system does not allow to use it for the construction of prototypes in industrial applications, but this is the price we paid for the flexibility, completeness and safety of the algorithm. Nevertheless, we achieved an essential improvement in efficiency of the current system version compared with the first versions (by a factor of 10, sometimes much higher). Much faster implementations can be imagined using a structure similar to Warren's PROLOG machine. Due to the exponential complexity, there will always be examples which cannot be run effectively. For studying a new specification, however, usually typical examples of moderate size suffice. It seems quite realistic to treat such examples by RAP-like systems in the near future.

RAP is a rapid prototyping tool for the specification developer rather than the customer. To get prototypes to be presented to a customer, further tools have to be added, for example a "specification compiler" producing efficient code and library packages for user interface, data management etc. For experimental purposes, a compiler to PASCAL code for a sublanguage of RAP is currently being integrated into the system (cf. [Geser, Hussmann, Mueck 88]).

References:

[Bauer, Wössner 82] F. L. Bauer, H. Wössner, Algorithmic language and program development. Springer 1982.

[Berghammer, et al. 87] R. Berghammer, H. Ehler, H. Zierer, Towards an algebraic specification of code generation. Report No. TUM-I8707 Technische Universität München.

[Berry, Wing 85] D. M. Berry, J. M. Wing, Specifying and prototyping: some thoughts on why they are successful. Proc. TAPSOFT 85 Conf., Vol. 2, LNCS 186, Springer 1985, pp. 117-128.

[Bouge et al. 85] L. Bouge, N. Choquet, L. Fribourg, M. C. Gaudel, Test sets generation from algebraic specifications using logic programming. Proc. TAPSOFT 85 Conf., LNCS 186, Springer 1986, pp. 262-275.

[Budde et al. 85] R. Budde, K. Kuhlenkamp, L. Matthiassen, H. Züllinghoven (Eds.), Approaches to prototyping. Springer 1984.

[Feijs, Jonkers, Koymans, Renardel 87] L. M. G. Feijs, H. B. M. Jonkers, C. P. J. Koymans, G. R. Renardel de Lavalette, Formal definition of the design language COLD-K. Report ESPRIT METEOR Task 7, 1987.

[Fribourg 84] L. Fribourg, Oriented equational clauses as a programming language. Report 84002 Laboratoires de Marcoussis, 1984. Short version in: Proc. 11th ICALP Conf., LNCS 172, Springer 1984, pp. 162-173

[Gelissen 88] J. H. A. Gelissen, Rapid prototyping of COLD specifications using RAP. Report ESPRIT METEOR Task 8, 1988.

[Geser 86/88] A. Geser, An algebraic specification of the INTEL 8085 microprocessor: A case study. Report MIP-8608 Universität Passau, 1986. Revised version contained within this volume.

[Geser, Hussmann 85/88] A. Geser, H. Hussmann, Rapid prototyping for algebraic specifications - Examples for the use of the RAP system. Report MIP-8517 Universität Passau, 1985. Second, revised edition to appear.

[Geser, Hussmann 86] A. Geser, H. Hussmann, Experiences with the RAP system - a specification interpreter combining term rewriting and resolution. Proc. ESOP 86 Conf., LNCS 213, Springer 1986, pp. 339-350.

[Geser, Hussmann, Mueck 88] A. Geser, H. Hussmann, A. Mueck, A compiler for a class of conditional term rewriting systems. In: Conditional Term Rewriting Systems, LNCS 308, Springer 1988, pp. 84-90.

[Huet, Hullot 80] G. Huet, J.-M. Hullot, Proofs by induction in equational theories with constructors. Journal of Computer and System Sciences 25, 239-266 (1982)

[Hussmann 85] H. Hussmann, Unification in conditional-equational theories. Report Universität Passau MIP-8502, 1985. Short version in: Proc. EUROCAL 85 Conf., LNCS 204, Springer 1985, pp. 543-553.

[Hussmann 85/87] H. Hussmann, Rapid prototyping for algebraic specifications - RAP system user's manual. Report Universität Passau MIP-8504, 1985. Second, completely revised edition, 1987.

[Hussmann, Rank 88] H. Hussmann, C. Rank, Specification and Prototyping of a Compiler for a Small Applicative Language. Contained within this volume.

[Jonkers 88] H. B. M. Jonkers, A concrete syntax for COLD-K. Report ESPRIT METEOR Task 8, 1988.

[Jonkers, Koymans, Renardel 85] H. B. M. Jonkers, C. P. J. Koymans, G. R. Renardel de Lavalette, A semantic framework for the COLD family of languages. Report Philips Research Laboratories Eindhoven, 1985.

[Padawitz 87] P. Padawitz, ECDS-A rewrite rule based interpreter for a programming language with abstraction and communication, Report Universität Passau MIP-8703, 1987.

[Padawitz 88] P. Padawitz, Computing in Horn clause theories. EATCS Monographs in Computer Science Vol. 16, Springer 1988.

[Spec 85] Hansi A. Spec, Possible and impossible questions to an interpreter for algebraic specifications [in German]. Report No. 4/85 Universität Bremen, 1985.

[Rety et al. 85] P. Rety, C. Kirchner, H. Kirchner, P. Lescanne, NARROWER: a new algorithm for unification and its application to logic programming. In Proc. RTA 85 Conf., LNCS 202, Springer 1985, pp. 141-155.

[Wirsing et al. 83] M. Wirsing, P. Pepper, H. Partsch, W. Dosch, M. Broy, On hierarchies of abstract data types. Acta Informatica 20, 1-33 (1983).

A Specification of the intel[1] 8085 Microprocessor: A Case Study

Alfons Geser,
Universität Passau, Fakultät für Mathematik und Informatik, Postfach 2540, D-8390 Passau

Abstract

As an instance for a large specification, an algebraic specification of the intel 8085 microprocessor is given. The specification is based on the concepts of hierarchical abstract types and conditional equations. With the help of the specification interpreter RAP, the specification is validated against some of its informal requirements. In the design of large software systems, a number of informal specification properties have to be considered such as style, readability, and structuredness of a specification. These properties are talked about using a couple of small examples.

1 Introduction

Among the various languages that allow specification and verification, abstract data types (in the following also called abstract types or just types for short) have both a proper theoretical foundation and a small notational framework. For algebraic specifications, there is a clean model semantics, and notions for abstract implementation, modularization and hiding exist (see e.g. [Wirsing 85]). The type language essentially consists of functions specified by equations.

Abstract types are particularly easy to use - as long as the specification remains sufficiently small. However, with large specifications, as they are typical in practice, complexity problems come up. If the specification language itself is already fairly complicated, then there is no chance to master these problems at all. Only by a careful decomposition of the specification into rather small parts which can be understood and treated separately (as far as possible), and by abstraction of superfluous detail, it seems possible to get good results.

Still, many computer scientists believe that the verification, even the formal specification of "real programs" (i.e. programs of practical size) is unfeasible. We have to perform case studies which can tell us whether this is true, and if so, what the precise reasons are. The case studies must have a "nontrivial" size, i.e. the modularization of the specification must be essential for an adequate treatment. On the other hand, they should not be too large, in order not to consume too much manpower. This is certainly a tradeoff.

In order to illustrate the power of algebraic methods, a hardware device, viz. the 8 bit microprocessor device 8085A, is specified and parts of the specification are validated. The main reasons for this choice are the moderate but "industrial" size of the specification, the widespread familiarity of computer science people with the device, and a handbook about the device that uses various informal and semi-formal description styles.

The paper is arranged as follows: In section 2, the specification method and the specification interpreter are described in a brief, informal way. The next section goes into the central concepts of the specification. In section 4 finally, the results obtained from the specification interpretation are shown for a collection of examples. The paper is concerned only about some critical points of the specification; for the whole specification text, the reader is referred to the appendix.

---

[1] *intel* is a registered trademark of intel Corporation, Santa Clara, CA.

Comment on the Revised Version

This paper is a revised version of the report [Geser 86]. Apart from documentation and presentation, the main changes are:

- it is tuned to the recent COLD/RAP 2.0 version, for which a new syntax similar to COLD-K has been defined,
- a few bugs could be removed,
- the proper instruction cycle has been specified,
- a couple of new tasks were added.

Several parts are still imprecise compared with the handbooks ([intel 79], [intel 83]), or missing. These parts (e.g. the SIM instruction) are indicated by fixes. It appeared straightforward, but boring to correct them completely. For the questions treated in this paper, this made no difference.

2 The Specification Interpreter

2.1 The Specification Languages RAP and COLD

In the following, we assume familiarity of the reader with the notions of abstract data type and conditional rewriting. As is the custom in this volume, the COLD-K specification language (for short called COLD in the sequel) serves to express the type part of the specification. We assume familiarity with COLD; the interested reader may consult [Jonkers 88] for an informal overview. COLD is a specification language that is built upon a powerful logic kernel, including many-sorted partial first-order functions and predicates. Equality and definedness are built-in predicates. The axioms are formulae in the first-order predicate calculus.

The algebraic specifications treated in this paper were originally formulated in the RAP specification language ([Hußmann 85a]). The RAP system is a *specification interpreter*. It is based upon the notions of hierarchical abstract types ([Wirsing et al. 83]) and conditional rewrite calculus (for a survey on conditional rewriting see e.g. [Padawitz 88]). The RAP system can be used not only for syntax (and context) checks of the specification but also for solving equation systems ("tasks") built up with function symbols and variables taken from a given collection of types.

RAP and COLD came with different aims, and the languages were therefore not coherently designed. Recently, [Hußmann, Geser 88] undertook first steps to bring RAP and COLD together (). As an outcome, an automatic RAP-to-COLD converter has been implemented which has among others been used to produce the type specification text in appendix A.

Let us briefly sketch the relevant deviations of RAP wrt. COLD. For another such comparison from the COLD point of view, see [Gelissen 88].

- In RAP, there are no imperative features such as procedures or states. All these things must be modelled explicitly, when necessary. In COLD terms, RAP types are *static immutable classes*.
- all RAP functions are total.
- RAP contains the notion of *constructor function*. Constructors are to build up objects of a certain sort. COLD does not distinguish between constructors and other functions, but allows to specify that all objects of a given sort are representable by certain terms, which usually are precisely the ground constructor terms. In order to keep the presentation simple, this possibility has not been taken, but the constructor functions have been marked with the comment {CONS} instead. For a more precise treatment cf. [Hußmann, Geser 88].
- RAP laws (axioms) are *universally quantified conditional equations*, of the form
  all $(x_1 : T_1, ..., x_m : T_m)$ (NAME) $l_1 = r_1$ & ... & $l_n = r_n \Rightarrow l \rightarrow r$
  which is to say:

If the equations $l_i = r_i$ (the premises) are satisfied, then $l = r$ (the conclusion) shall be satisfied as well, in particular, l may be replaced by r.

NAME is an optional axiom identifier. In COLD, the above axiom would be written

  forall $(x_1 : T_1, ..., x_m : T_m)$ {NAME} $l_1 = r_1$ *AND* ... *AND* $l_n = r_n \Rightarrow l = r$

When the set of premises is empty, the whole axiom shrinks to $l = r$.

- In RAP, the equations are *oriented* left to right, and are therefore also called *rules*. Accordingly, the axiom system must be confluent, in order to be consistent with model semantics. The rule system is assumed to be confluent, although currently no check is made.

- Because RAP is itself a prototype, more elaborate features are missing. The only built-in types are BOOL (truth values), NAT (natural numbers), and ID (identifiers). In RAP, like in COLD, higher order functions and tupling are missing; unlike in COLD, also parameterized types, renaming, partial functions, etc. are missing in RAP.

- "Tasks" in RAP have not yet their counterpart in COLD, and are therefore kept written in RAP syntax. A COLD-like syntax is in preparation.

2.2 The Narrowing Algorithm

In order to perform a session with RAP, the user first supplies a collection of hierarchical types. Afterwards, the user may formulate queries to the interpreter. A query, in the RAP language called a *task*, specifies the solutions of a system of equations wrt. a given set of axioms. The terms that occur there may use visible function symbols, the unknown variables, and existentially quantified auxiliary variables. The allowed function symbols and the axiom set are determined by the list of types following the keyword *basedon*, just as in type specifications. An instance of a task is

```
task EQ1
 basedon BOOL, BIT, BIT_EQ
 unknown x: Bit

goals
 equal_Bit(x,0) = false
endoftask
```

If we apply a substitution to both sides of each equation in the task body, and we can, for each equation we get, rewrite both sides towards a common term, then this substitution is called a *computed solution* of the given task. Obviously, [x = I] is the only solution of the task example above, since equal_Bit(I,0) rewrites to false using rule E2.

RAP evaluates a system of equations by the *conditional narrowing algorithm*, described in detail in [Hußmann 85a], together with correctness and completeness proofs. [Hußmann, Geser 88] gives a brief sketch of the narrowing algorithm.

3 The Specification Design

3.1 What is Modelled

The device we are going to model is (in essence) the microprocessor 8085 as it is described in [intel 79] and [intel 83]. The specification given here is to cover the machine instructions and their observable effect. There are a lot of details which are also (even more) interesting to model, but for lack of time were not included. For instance the interrupt mechanism, wait states, and memory refresh have been dropped.

3.2 Basic Data Structures

When we speak about a microprocessor, we always begin with bits and bytes. Bits have been defined already in the previous section. A byte is an 8-tuple of bits, which we can form by a constructor function

```
FUNC{CONS} make_Byte: (Bit,Bit,Bit,Bit,Bit,Bit,Bit,Bit) -> Byte
```

and we can select e.g. the first bit of a byte by the selector function

```
FUNC sel_Bit_0: Byte -> Bit,
AXIOM FORALL x0: Bit, x1: Bit, x2: Bit, x3: Bit, x4: Bit, x5: Bit, x6: Bit, x7: Bit
( {SEL_0} sel_Bit_0(make_Byte(x0,x1,x2,x3,x4,x5,x6,x7)) = x0 )
```

Machine words are formed likewise as pairs of bytes. Such instances of product types will still occur later.

The elementary data structures given so far are now enriched by some often needed auxiliary operations. This includes operations like a full-adder for bytes or the computation of the flags. Let us just consider the 8-bit full-adder in detail. We first specify the two outputs of the 1-bit full-adder, viz. the sum and the carry output. Unfortunately, multiple-valued (here: two-valued) functions exist neither in RAP nor in COLD. Nevertheless, let us for the moment use an enriched specification language – a COLD extension that also allows multiple-valued functions (i.e. functions that return a tuple as their result). All the specifications are listed in the appendix, in ordinary COLD syntax.

There are two ways to specify a 1-bit-adder: By its truth table,

```
LET BIT_EXT :=
IMPORT BIT INTO
  CLASS
    FUNC add_Bit:  Bit # Bit # Bit -> Bit # Bit
                                      {sum} {carry}

AXIOM
   ( add_Bit(0,0,0) = (0,0);    add_Bit(0,0,I) = (I,0);
     add_Bit(0,I,0) = (I,0);    add_Bit(0,I,I) = (0,I);
     add_Bit(I,0,0) = (I,0);    add_Bit(I,0,I) = (0,I);
     add_Bit(I,I,0) = (0,I);    add_Bit(I,I,I) = (I,I) )
END;
```

and by majority and minority:

```
LET BIT_EXT :=
IMPORT BIT INTO
  CLASS
    FUNC add_Bit:  Bit # Bit # Bit -> Bit # Bit
                                      {sum} {carry}

AXIOM
  FORALL  x: Bit, y: Bit
   ( add_Bit(x,x,y) = (y,x);
     add_Bit(x,y,x) = (y,x);
     add_Bit(y,x,x) = (y,x) )
END;
```

It can be shown easily by case analysis that these two variants of BIT_EXT are equivalent, i.e. they have the same class of term generated models. We will come back to this point in the next section.

Before the 8-bit addition is defined, the bits within a byte need to be assigned their weight. Usually, within a byte more significant bits are followed by less significant ones. The converse holds for bytes within a word. For reasons of uniformity, throughout the specification less significant items precede more significant ones. This applies for the bits within a byte, too, although it might be unfamiliar in this special case. In informal text, we keep the usual notation (juxtaposition, and more significant bits to the left).

The 8-bit full-adder has three outputs of relevance, viz. the sum, the intermediate ('auxiliary') carry, and the overall carry. In order to use the power of multiple-valued functions, we should use a (fairly restricted form of) conditional rewriting:

```
LET ADD_BYTE :=
{8-bit-addition}

IMPORT BIT INTO
IMPORT BYTE INTO
IMPORT BIT_EXT INTO
 CLASS
  FUNC add_Byte:  Byte # Byte # Bit -> Byte # Bit # Bit

AXIOM
 FORALL  x0: Bit, x1: Bit, x2: Bit, x3: Bit, x4: Bit, x5: Bit, x6: Bit, x7: Bit,
         y0: Bit, y1: Bit, y2: Bit, y3: Bit, y4: Bit, y5: Bit, y6: Bit, y7: Bit,
         z0: Bit, z1: Bit, z2: Bit, z3: Bit, z4: Bit, z5: Bit, z6: Bit, z7: Bit,
         z8: Bit,
         w0: Bit, w1: Bit, w2: Bit, w3: Bit, w4: Bit, w5: Bit, w6: Bit, w7: Bit
 ( {ADD_BYTE}
 (w0,z1) = add_Bit(x0,y0,z0)  AND  (w1,z2) = add_Bit(x1,y1,z1)  AND
 (w2,z3) = add_Bit(x2,y2,z2)  AND  (w3,z4) = add_Bit(x3,y3,z3)  AND
 (w4,z5) = add_Bit(x4,y4,z4)  AND  (w5,z6) = add_Bit(x5,y5,z5)  AND
 (w6,z7) = add_Bit(x6,y6,z6)  AND  (w7,z8) = add_Bit(x7,y7,z7)  =>
add_Byte(make_Byte(x0,x1,x2,x3,x4,x5,x6,x7),
         make_Byte(y0,y1,y2,y3,y4,y5,y6,y7),z0) =
 (make_Byte(w0,w1,w2,w3,w4,w5,w6,w7),z4,z8)
END;
```

It is much more messy to do all that without multiple-valued functions. There are two ways to make it (e.g. for add_Bit):

- two functions sum: Bit # Bit # Bit -> Bit, and carry: Bit # Bit # Bit -> Bit are specified instead. This means some overhead by axiom duplication.
- a product type is used to express tupling explicitly. If we are given a parameterized specification PROD(T1,T2) of cartesian product of the parameter types T1 and T2, then me might specify

```
    LET BIT_PAIR :=
    RENAME
     Prod -> Bit_Pair,
     make_Prod -> make_Bit_Pair,
     sel_1 -> sel_sum,
     sel_2 -> sel_carry
    IN
     APPLY PROD TO
      ADD BIT TO BIT;
```

In RAP we have not even parameterized types, so we must still expand the parameter instantiation (note that we use COLD syntax, all the same):

```
    LET BIT_PAIR:=
    IMPORT BIT INTO
     CLASS
      SORT Bit_Pair
      FUNC{CONS} make_Bit_Pair:  Bit # Bit -> Bit_Pair
      FUNC sel_sum:  Bit_Pair -> Bit
      FUNC sel_carry:  Bit_Pair -> Bit

     AXIOM
      FORALL  x: Bit, y: Bit
```

```
( {SUM} sel_sum(make_make_Bit_Pair(x,y)) = x;
  {CARRY} sel_carry(make_Bit_Pair(x,y)) = y )
END;
```

In the final specification, the first one of these two techniques is used for add_Bit (because there it gives still a short text), and the second one e.g. for add_Byte.

3.3 The State Concept

A state is specified by the tuple of those values that might have influence on the instructions eventually. Our state model for the 8085 includes

- the word (or, double) registers BC, DE, and HL,
- the processor status word (PSW),
- the stack pointer (SP), and the instruction pointer (PC, 'program counter'),
- the interrupt mask,
- the flipflops for halt, interrupt enable, and the 7.5 interrupt edge.

The operations on states are selection (read) and update (selective alteration, write) of values for either a word register, the interrupt mask, or a state flipflop. The access is done via the names PSW, BC, DE, HL, SP, PC, for the double registers, and via the names halt, inte, and rst7_5, for the state flipflops (for the interrupt mask, we need no proper name). For example, let u be some processor state, then the term sel_Dreg(u,PC) denotes the contents of the instruction pointer, given state u, and alt_Flipflop(u,inte,O) means the state that u changes into, after the interrupt enable flipflop is reset to O.

A register is half of a double register (of course). There are registers A (higher part of PSW), B, C, D, E, H, L (higher and lower part of BC, DE, HL, resp.). A is also called the accumulator register. In the 8085 machine language, there is also a register M; it is not a true register, but a hidden memory access, and is consequently not modelled as a register here. Register access is a special case of double register access, and can as such be defined hierarchically on top of STATE. The same holds for the flags. A flag is one of the bits of the lower part of the PSW double register. There are flags Cy ('carry', bit 0), P ('parity', bit 2), Ac ('auxiliary carry', bit 4), Z ('zero', bit 6), and S ('sign', bit 7). The bits 1, 3, and 5 are not used as flags. The specification texts for STATE, REG, and FLAG are listed in the appendix.

3.4 Communication Streams

A microprocessor acts as a communicating agent. It communicates with its environment – memory, I/O devices, and so on – via three channels: The address bus, the data bus, and the control bus. Buses are bi-directional (two-way) channels, i.e. values can be sent and received from the same agent on the same bus. The microprocessor may perform output to each bus, but input from data and control buses only. As mentioned earlier, we ignore furthergoing structure. Addresses which are transmitted on the address bus are actually words, and data on the data bus are bytes. The device multiplexes address and data bus, in order to save connection pins – a fact that we need not mirror in the specification. The control bus carries all the information about timing and readiness of address and data bus, and the current communication mode. All this forms a rather technical protocol. Since we are not interested in the precise signalling behaviour, we represent the control information abstractly. We put the data-ready signal for the data bus together with the bus value, so as to form an action "data d is ready on the data bus", and likewise for the address-ready signal and the address bus. Besides this, we distinguish five possible modes: opcode fetch, memory read, memory write, and input and output on an I/O-device. In the actual device, there is an additional 'idle' mode. As it adds nothing but time tags (a typical real-time information), it is not adopted here. To summarize, there are communication actions of the following kind:

```
LET ACTION :=
IMPORT BYTE INTO
IMPORT WORD INTO
 CLASS
  SORT Action
  FUNC{CONS} opcode:  -> Action
  FUNC{CONS} read:  -> Action
  FUNC{CONS} write:  -> Action
  FUNC{CONS} in:  -> Action
  FUNC{CONS} out:  -> Action
   {Control actions}
  FUNC{CONS} data:  Byte -> Action
   {Data ready on the data bus}
  FUNC{CONS} address:  Word -> Action
   {Address ready on the addtess bus}
END;
```

Informal explanations like of this kind are however misleading because events like "datum d2 is read from address a2" need not really happen. In fact, the processor and its environment just agree to pretend. The processor might actually read d2 from a memory at address a2, but it might as well be the case that there is no memory at all, and the environment delivers just some arbitrary datum d2.

Now it happens that communication is done in packages, where a package consists of the mode token, an address word, and a data byte (in this order). Therefore, for reasons of compactness and adequacy of the term representation, we better model composite communication actions:

```
LET ACTION :=
IMPORT BYTE INTO
IMPORT WORD INTO
 CLASS
  SORT Action
  FUNC{CONS} opcode:  Byte # Word -> Action
  FUNC{CONS} read:  Byte # Word -> Action
  FUNC{CONS} write:  Byte # Word -> Action
  FUNC{CONS} in:  Byte # Word -> Action
  FUNC{CONS} out:  Byte # Word -> Action
END;
```

In a composite action like read(d,a), read is output on the control bus, then a is output on the address bus, then d is input on the data bus. In write(d,a), write is output on the control bus, then d is output on the address bus, and a is output on the data bus. Observe that input and output may happen within one composite action, and input and output are represented in the same way. Consequently, we must also use a communication concept where input and output are symmetric. Such a concept is present e.g. in Hoare's TCSP ([Hoare 83]). We just need to consider TCSP without hiding and nondeterministic choice. In TCSP, each process may, or may not, perform some action and thereby change itself to another process. Two processes may be put in parallel in which case each common action must be performed synchronously by both processes. In this paper, the two processes in question are the microprocessor and its environment. A microprocessor is represented by its state. All actions we defined above are common to the processor and the environment. Below is a strongly simplified example that gives an impression about a specification of microprocessor and memory in a TCSP-like notation. The symbol [] denotes the binary choice operator; it is also used for comprehensive choice ("the choice of all p where x is of sort T", in the form [] x: T (p)). Let us assume that the processor is in a state where it wants to read a datum from the memory at address w, and the memory is prepared to correctly perform read and write operations:

    pro = [] d: Byte (read(w,d) -> change(pro,d)),

```
mem = ([] a: Word, d: Byte  (write(a,d) -> update(mem,a,d)))  []
        ([] a: Word  (read(a,get(mem,a)) -> mem)),
```

pro stands for the processor (initial state), and mem for the memory (initial state). pro || mem denotes their parallel composition. Now, according to the laws of TCSP, pro || mem may be rewritten into

```
pro || mem = read(w,get(mem,w)) -> (change(pro,get(mem,w)) || mem)
```

In informal words, the processor and the memory agree upon a read action with address w fixed (because the processor insists in that), and the data get(mem,w) (as the memory matches its a to w demanded by the processor, and the processor in turn matches its d to get(mem,w)). This sounds very much like term rewriting and unification, and in fact, it can be modelled by these techniques.

TCSP admits to view a process in two ways: As an action generating, or as an action accepting device. The former needs nondeterministic term rewriting, and the latter does not. Since we want to stay in the classical term rewriting framework, our communication model must take the microprocessor as an action accepting (i.e. consuming) device, and guards must be disjoint. I.e., we propose the processor an action, and if it accepts, it transits to a certain successor state. Which actions are accepted, and which successor states are taken, is specified by rewrite rules. More precisely, each alternative of the choice operator is translated into a rewrite rule, and the comprehensive choice becomes an universally quantified variable.

In order to demonstrate how read and write operations are specified, we give a simplified example. The processor fetch(u,a,r) is prepared to read any datum d at address a, and if such an action is given, the internal state u of the processor changes such that register r is assigned the value d. fetch(u,a,r) corresponds to the pro specification in TCSP above. Likewise, the processor store(u,a,r) is prepared to write d at a, and in case of success it leaves its internal state unchanged. In TCSP-like notation, this would be specified by

```
fetch(u,a,r) = [] b: Byte  (read(a,b) -> alt_Dreg(u,r,b)),
store(u,a,r) = write(a,sel_Reg(u,r)) -> u
```

Now assume we wish to specify the processes fetch'(u,act,a,r) and store'(u,act,a,r) according to our method, to meet the behaviour of their TCSP correspondents fetch(u,a,r) and store(u,a,r), resp.. Here is the specification:

```
LET FS :=
IMPORT BYTE INTO
IMPORT WORD INTO
IMPORT STATE INTO
IMPORT REG INTO
IMPORT ACTION INTO
 CLASS
  FUNC fetch':  State # Action # Word # Reg -> State
  FUNC store':  State # Action # Word # Reg -> State

AXIOM
  FORALL a: Word, b: Byte, r: Reg, u: State
  ( {1} fetch'(u,read(a,b),a,r) = alt_Reg(u,r,b);
    {2} sel_Reg(u,r) = b => store'(u,write(a,b),a,r) = u )
END;
```

Streams (i.e. finite or infinite sequences) of actions are now formed by a type STREAM, which is hierarchically based on the type ACTION:

```
LET STREAM :=
IMPORT ACTION INTO
 CLASS
  SORT Stream
  FUNC{CONS} empty:  -> Stream
  FUNC{CONS} prefix:  Action # Stream -> Stream
```

END;

Streams of actions can as well be defined at once:

```
LET STREAM :=
IMPORT BYTE INTO
IMPORT WORD INTO
  CLASS
   SORT Stream
   FUNC{CONS} empty:  -> Stream
   FUNC{CONS} opcode:  Word # Byte # Stream -> Stream
   FUNC{CONS} read:  Word # Byte # Stream -> Stream
   FUNC{CONS} write:  Word # Byte # Stream -> Stream
   FUNC{CONS} in:  Word # Byte # Stream -> Stream
   FUNC{CONS} out:  Word # Byte # Stream -> Stream
  END;
```

Let us consider an example illustrating the possible action and stream representations: In terms of the atomic action specification,

```
prefix(opcode,prefix(address(a1),prefix(data(d1),
prefix(read,prefix(address(a2),prefix(data(d2),
prefix(write,prefix(address(make_Word(d1,d2)),prefix(data(d3),s)))))))))
```

is a well-formed object of sort Stream. Its representation in the composite specification would look like

```
prefix(opcode(a1,d1),prefix(read(a2,d2),prefix(write(make_Word(d1,d2),d3),s)))
```

and in the shortened form,

```
opcode(a1,d1,read(a2,d2,write(make_Word(d1,d2),d3,s)))
```

Our example above reads with streams as follows:

```
LET FS :=
IMPORT BYTE INTO
IMPORT WORD INTO
IMPORT STATE INTO
IMPORT REG INTO
IMPORT STREAM INTO
IMPORT PROCESS INTO
  CLASS
   FUNC fetch:  Process # Word # Reg -> Process
   FUNC store:  Process # Word # Reg -> Process
  AXIOM
   FORALL  a: Word, b: Byte, r: Reg, u: State, s: Stream
   ( {1} fetch(make_Process(u,read(a,b,s)),a,r) = make_Process(alt_Reg(u,r,b),s);
     {2} sel_Reg(u,r) = b =>
       store(make_Process(u,write(a,b,s)),a,r) = make_Process(u,s) )
  END;
```

The stream, assigned to a processor, can be imagined as a "predicted" future behaviour of the processor. The processor accepts the first "predicted" action that comes in the stream, if, and only if, a corresponding rewrite rule applies. Then the rule application removes the event from the stream and causes a state change. Refusal means that no such rule is applicable, in which case execution has reached a dead end.

The constant empty in the STREAM specification is somewhat strange since it will occur in no axiom. So the processor cannot really work with an empty stream. empty can be seen as a "broken", "diverging" or "deadlock" stream, as a stream that blocks the device from further communication. Nevertheless empty has been included so as to have the signature of STREAM sensible, a fact that ensures the existence of an initial model ([Wirsing 85]). An adequate treatment of infinite objects is however not possible within the classical abstract type framework. One rather needs continuous abstract types ([Wirsing 86]).

3.5 About the Instructions

Now all the needed prerequisites are established to enter in a formalization of the execution of instructions according to their informal descriptions in the handbook. For abbreviation, pairs of state and stream are put together, and are called processes (not to be confused with the TCSP process notion). There are many instructions, and most of them can be specified in a straightforward way. Let us just develop one of them, the conditional jump, in detail. What we still need are essentially specifications for: A conditional, an argument fetch operation, and the (unconditional) jump.

A conditional for processes is specified easily by case analysis:

```
FUNC cond:  Process # Flag # Bit # Process -> Process
AXIOM
FORALL  p1: Process, p2: Process, f: Flag, x: Bit

( {BRANCH} sel_Flag(sel_State(p1),f) = x  =>  cond(p1,f,x,p2) = p2;
  {STRAIGHT} sel_Flag(sel_State(p1),f) = not_Bit(x)  =>  cond(p1,f,x,p2) = p1 )
```

The condition is satisfied if the given flag contains the given value, in the current state of the process p1. If the condition is satisfied, the result of cond(p1,f,x,p2) is p2, i.e. branching takes place, otherwise the result is p1, i.e. nothing happens.

Fetching the argument (or equivalently, the parameter) of an instruction means to read a byte, word, resp., at the address which is currently contained in the PC double register. Whether a byte or a word is fetched, is dependent on the instruction opcode. We give here only the specification text for the byte fetch (the whole text is anyway documented in the appendix). It is the function (in 'extended' COLD)

```
FUNC fetch_Byte: Process -> Process # Byte
   ...
{FETCH_BYTE} w = sel_Dreg(u,PC) =>
fetch_Byte(make_Process(u,read(w,b,s))) =
     make_Process_Byte_pair(make_Process(incr_Dreg(u,PC),s),b)
```

that delivers the process (remember, this is pair of state and stream) after it fetched a byte, and the fetched byte itself. The jump that takes place if the condition is satisfied, is specified thus:

```
{JMP} fetch_Word(p) = (make_Process(u,s),w) =>
     jump(p) = make_Process(alt_Dreg(u,PC,w),s)
```

Informally, jump(p) fetches (i.e. reads at the address contained in PC) a word w, and changes the PC contents into w. Even if the condition of a conditional jump is not satisfied, the first byte of the parameter is fetched (this is a peculiarity that must be modelled). That superfluous step is made by the function

```
FUNC drop_Byte: Process -> Process
   ...
{DROP_BYTE} fetch_Byte(p) = make_Process_Byte_pair(p1,b) =>
drop_Byte(p) = incr_Dreg(p1,PC) )
```

That is almost all we need to specify the conditional jump execution. The type EXECUTION (which we will see back later) takes the rest; it contains the axiom

```
{JMP_COND} execute(p,make_Byte(0,I,0,x1,x2,x3,I,I)) =
           cond(drop_Byte(p),decode_Flag(x2,x3),x1,jump(p))
```

and this axiom cares for all conditional jump instructions, in the handbook referred to as jnz ('jump if not zero'), jnc ('jump if not carry'), jpo ('jump if parity odd'), jp ('jump if positive'), jz ('jump if zero'), jc ('jump if carry'), jpe ('jump if parity even'), and jm ('jump if minus'). These instructions have common opcode $IIx_3x_2x_1OIO$ where the pair x_3x_2 of bits encodes the flag, decoded by the function

```
FUNC decode_Flag: Bit # Bit -> Flag
```

that is specified by case analysis according to a table given in the handbook. The bit x_3 encodes at which value of the resp. flag the jump should take place.

3.6 The Instruction Cycle

The specification hierarchy is completed by the instruction cycle specification:

```
LET RUN :=
{run a process}

IMPORT BIT INTO
IMPORT BYTE INTO
IMPORT WORD INTO
IMPORT STATE INTO
IMPORT STREAM INTO
IMPORT PROCESS INTO
IMPORT INCR_DECR_DREG INTO
IMPORT EXECUTION INTO
  CLASS
   FUNC step:  Process -> Process
   FUNC run:  Process -> Process

AXIOM
 FORALL  b: Byte, w: Word, u: State, s: Stream, p: Process
  ( {ONESTEP} sel_Dreg(u,PC) = w =>
step(make_Process(u,opcode(w,b,s))) =
     execute(incr_Dreg(make_Process(u,s),PC),b);
    {HALT}  sel_Flipflop(sel_State(p),halt) = I => run(p) = p;
    {LOOP}  sel_Flipflop(sel_State(p),halt) = O => run(p) = run(step(p)) )
END;
```

The cycle is formed by steps, which repeat until the halt flipflop is set to I. Note that the cycle may loop forever, which means that it features a nonterminating rewrite system caused by the rule LOOP. A step is formed by an opcode fetch, followed by the execution of the opcode. The type EXECUTION has the instruction executions branch dependent on the opcode pattern. It may therefore be seen as the instruction decoder specification. The parameter fetch, and the execution is done by a call to a specific function which can be specified separately elsewhere. The large number (48) of cases to be distinguished makes the abstract type EXECUTION large, unfortunately, but this is a consequence of the instruction complexity - not of bad specification structuring.

4 Results of Experimentation

In this section, the results of some sessions with the specification interpreter RAP are summarized and commented. The task specification texts are given in appendix B. The following results were obtained at a SUN-3/160 computer with 4MB RAM, using the UNIX 4.2 bsd operating system, and the RAP version 2.0. The cpu times are given in seconds. An asterisk followed by a number denotes a new variable created by the system.

4.1 Experimentation with ADD_BYTE

We begin our validation with experiments on the full-adder ADD_BYTE, and the type BIT_EXT. As claimed in the previous section, we have two 'ground equivalent' specification variants. In other words: The abstract meaning of the two specifications (viz. the class of term generated models) is the same. But, as we are going to show now, the interpreter distinguishes them.

The validation is done with two matching problems: The first one, OSPEC, specifies a byte b that yields no carry when added to the byte which contains I bits only. The second one, DOUB, specifies the quotient and remainder by 2 of $OIOIOIIO$. The RAP system terminates with each combination of type and task. The performance is summarized next, like it has been output by the RAP 'show summary' command:

```
Task OSPEC , Run number 1
Solutions:
[b = make_Byte(0,0,0,0,0,0,0,0)]
CPU time: 39.78 secs

Task DOUB , Run number 1
Solutions:
[x = 0,
 d = make_Byte(I,I,0,I,0,I,0,0)]
[x = 0,
 d = make_Byte(I,I,0,I,0,I,0,I)]
CPU time: 3.55 secs
```

That was the output produced with the first variant, and this is output by the second one:

```
Task OSPEC , Run number 1
Solutions:
[b = make_Byte(0,0,0,0,0,0,0,0)]
CPU time: 2.90 secs

Task DOUB , Run number 1
Solutions:
[x = 0,
 d = make_Byte(I,I,0,I,0,I,0,*24)]
CPU time: 0.45 secs
```

Obviously, the two variants 'perform' quite differently. This is, on the one hand, due to the absence of case analysis and induction in the interpreter – and the proof for equivalence of the solutions of DOUB needs a case analysis. On the other hand, the two tasks are better suited to the second variant, since they draw use of the more general form of the axioms. This explains why OSPEC takes much more time with the first variant.

4.2 Instruction Evaluations

The specification is mainly designed for the evaluation of machine instructions. So the evaluation of machine instructions is probably the most interesting validation step. In the following we describe some tasks informally, to mirror their intended meaning, and then show the results of the resp. RAP sessions: For abbreviation, the special constant triv_State of type State is predefined which contains O bits only. The denotation of the task EVAL_ADC can then be translated like this:

> "Yield the Byte b, which is defined to be the contents of the A register, in the State after having executed the code $IOOOIOOO$ (the code for adc B). The initial State is given by triv_State, but with the PSW double register changed to IIIIIIII $OIOOIIII$, and the BC double register changed to $OOOOOOOO$ $IIOIIOIO$."

Its evaluation in RAP gives rise to the following output:

```
Task EVAL_ADC , Run number 2
Solutions:
[b = make_Byte(0,I,0,I,I,0,I,I)]
CPU time: 2.87 secs
```

We could have used the depth-first strategy as well, getting the same result, because the whole search tree is exhausted. Basically the same holds for all other instruction evaluations; we do not consider them here due to lack of space.

4.3 Matching

A term to be evaluated needs not to be ground. The interpreter can evaluate terms with variables, too. This can be used to drop unnecessary details from task descriptions. This is an advantage RAP shares with logic programming languages over usual (functional and imperative) programming languages. When too few information is given to the interpreter, i.e. there are variables at an occurrence where a non-variable term is required, the interpreter is forced to make assumptions about the terms the variable stands for. For this, rewriting alone is no longer sufficient; the interpreter has to use narrowing-like techniques. Now the proof tree complexity becomes exponential compared to the term rewrite effort, and termination becomes rather rare.

In the next example, the machine instruction sbb B ('subtract register B from accumulator with borrow') is performed, where the initial state of the execution is not given explicitly, but by a description. We find the following informal specification in the assembler language handbook [intel 79], page 3-57:

> "Assume that register B contains 2, the accumulator contains 4, and the carry flag is set to 1. The instruction SBB B operates as follows:
>
> $$(\ldots) \text{ Accumulator} = (\ldots) \ 00000001 = 1\text{H}$$
>
> $(\ldots)$ The flag settings resulting from the SBB B instruction are as follows:
>
> | | | |
> |---|---|---|
> | Carry | = | 0 |
> | Sign | = | 0 |
> | Zero | = | 0 |
> | Parity | = | 0 |
> | Aux. Carry | = | 1 " |

It is used there as an illustration, after the sbb instruction has been explained in general. A good system should support exercising examples like this. We may type in the formal RAP counterpart in a straightforward way, cf. the appendix. RAP terminates with the answer

```
Task EXEC_SBB , Run number 1
Solutions:
[Accu = make_Byte(I,0,0,0,0,0,0,0),
 Carry = 0,
 Sign = 0,
 Zero = 0,
 Parity = 0,
 AuxCarry = I]
CPU time: 4.32 secs
```

4.4 Simple Direct Proofs

To a certain extent, also direct proofs can be performed with RAP. This is demonstrated nicely with the property of the xchg instruction that the instruction sequence 'xchg; xchg' leaves a process completely unchanged (if we neglect opcode fetches). We would now like to have a response like [x1 = *1, x2 = *1], the actual answer however is:

```
Task XCHG2 , Run number 1
Solutions:
[x1 = make_Process(make_State(*9,*10,*11,*12,*13,*14,*15,*16,*17,*18),*6),
 x2 = make_Process(make_State(*9,*10,*11,*12,*13,*14,*15,*16,*17,*18),*6)]
CPU time: 0.43 secs
```

The solution mirrors the fact that for execution of the *xchg* instruction, the process x1 must obey a certain form (it must contain double registers, for example), though another form is impossible. We need a (trivial) case analysis to get the result we intuitively expect. As this effect is quite usual, some support for automated case analysis is desirable. In a professional system, the user should not be confused with such "raw" output.

We may even do a little bit more than "just" perform proofs. RAP can (help) answer questions like

"What will ral do different to adc A ?"

A prover could only find out *whether* ral and adc A are different. Formulated in the RAP task language the question may read like MATCH_RAL_ADC in appendix B. The test in RAP gave the answer

```
Task MATCH_RAL_ADC , Run number 2
Solutions:
[p = make_Process(make_State(
     make_Word(make_Byte(*188,*188,*190,*190,*192,*192,*194,*195),
               make_Byte(I,*342,*194,*343,*190,*344,0,*194)),
                         *34,*35,*36,*37,*38,*39,*40,*41,*42),*13)]
[p = make_Process(make_State(
     make_Word(make_Byte(*188,*188,*190,*190,*192,*193,*192,*195),
               make_Byte(I,*342,*193,*343,*190,*344,0,*192)),
                         *34,*35,*36,*37,*38,*39,*40,*41,*42),*13)]
CPU time: 9.78 secs
```

The enumeration for the solutions has been stopped since there were too many cases to consider. The first two solutions show already that the claim is satisfiable, but probably not valid in general. The special form of the contents of A register (first 'make_Byte'-expression) and of the flags (second 'make_Byte'-expession) come from the fact that the instructions treat some flags differently. An experienced user might now use the RAP 'debug mode' to retrieve more detail about it.

4.5 Instruction Synthesis

A particularly difficult problem class for an interpreter is to synthesize some instructions that fulfil a certain input-output relation, not to speak about instruction sequences. For instance, we can look for all machine instructions that change the carry flag from I to O while leaving the A register unchanged. This is in a straightforward way expressed by a task denotation SYNT_CLEAR. Although the task looks rather small, the search space is enormous. E.g. the start goal generates 47 sons ... . With a timelimit of approximately one hour of cpu time, RAP gets the solutions

```
task SYNT_CLEAR , Run number 1
Solutions:
[i = make_Byte(I,I,I,I,I,I,0,0)]
[i = make_Byte(I,0,0,0,I,I,I,I)]
[i = make_Byte(I,I,I,0,0,0,0,0)]
[i = make_Byte(I,I,I,I,0,0,0,0)]
[i = make_Byte(I,0,0,I,0,I,0,0)]
[i = make_Byte(I,I,I,0,0,0,0,I)]
```

```
CPU time: 3001.37 secs
```

Thanks to the leftmost-innermost redex selection strategy, RAP still finds six interesting solutions: cmc, pop PSW, rlc, rrc, dad H, add A. Even with much more time at its disposal, RAP will not find much more than these solutions automatically. As one reason for this, let us just mention that certain subproblems occur repeatedly, maybe often. For instance, the problem TRIAL occurs sometimes during the execution of SYNT_CLEAR. Although that task does not contribute solutions, it consumes resources (time and space):

```
Task TRIAL , Run number 1
No solutions found.
CPU time: 210.57 secs
```

5 Conclusion

Large specifications play an important role in specification research. They have to show that specifications are feasible not only for small, "academic" examples, but also for software products of industrial size. In this paper an attempt was made to give such a specification. Among those specifications which can be compared to this one, there are to mention among others:

- specifications of interpreters and compilers ([Bergstra et al. 85], [Berghammer et al. 86], [Padawitz 87], [Hußmann, Rank 88]),
- a specification of the CIP-S program transformation system (e.g. [CIP 87]),
- specifications of data base management systems ([Lavazza, Crespi-Reghizzi 87], [Gelissen 88])

The main difficulty in the design of the specification has been the specification complexity – as was to be expected. The specification has therefore been structured carefully in two aspects:

- by means of orthogonal identifier naming (e.g. 'make_Byte', where make means the only constructor, and Byte denotes the sort that is constructed), and
- by extensive use of hierarchical types, which constitutes the source of modularity in algebraic specifications. The specification contains 36 (!) such modules.

Unfortunately, parameterized types were not available in RAP; they would have alleviated much work. The same can be said about multiple-valued functions.

Abstract data types can really not be called a hardware description language (see e.g. [Iverson 63], [Sint 80]), since the latter are designed and used for specific hardware description support. So it is a remarkable fact that algebraic specifications do their job rather nicely here. The hidden entities in a device like state and communication streams must however be made explicit. This looks pretty unfamiliar, but once the concepts are established they can be used in a straightforward way. COLD is certainly more comfortable in this point of view since it supports imperative features like procedures and states, too.

During the sessions, a lot of bugs in the specification could be eliminated. Most of them were quite trivial, they were syntax or typing errors. Some nontrivial bugs however came up at runtime, during the execution of small tasks for test purposes.

The specification interpreter had usually no problems to solve equation systems on top of the microprocessor specification. This is a bit surprising, because of the large amount of data around. For instance, about 260 laws have to be considered, and the terms can easily grow over a couple of screens. All the same, many tasks terminate already after a few seconds with a most general solution. Sometimes however, even if nice properties hold for the specification, the interpreter is likely to fail. This is when the proof tree complexity becomes exponential. Even simple-looking goals can by exponential growth become non-manageable. This fact is demonstrated by the SYNT_CLEAR task. It shows also that the difference between "toy" and "large scale" examples is by no means apparent from their specification text size.

Well, that does not mean the end for specification interpreters. Certainly, narrowing techniques will not answer difficult theoretical questions (that would be 'artificial intelligence'). But narrowing succeeds with carefully chosen, small (of complexity) examples. Among others, EXEC_SBB is an example for a realistic use of narrowing-like systems at present.

User interaction may play an important role in the design. Maybe the first work even cannot be supported by machine at all. With the answers for a couple of basic questions – more and more within the algebraic framework – specifications may be designed that allow a transition to a more efficient, "machine oriented", treatment. At the end of such a development, there might be a compiler for a specification sublanguage that produces (really) efficient machine code. Work in this field is currently done ([Kaplan 87], [Geser et al. 87]).

By a thorough experimentation with a formal specification, the programmer gains confidence in the specification and so in the intended final program. Following this philosophy, the specifier may not begin with an "efficient" specification style. This is a trivial, but nevertheless often forgotten rule. To some extent, a specification interpreter leads the specifier to a more executable specification style as originally wanted. It is to the specifiers as well as to the tool designers to help avoid it. For instance, for the BIT_EXT type, I chose the second variant in the final specification. I must admit that this choice (and other choices) was not only "beauty-driven". Let us say, it was a compromise.

Acknowledgements

I would like to thank S. Crespi-Reghizzi for his hints about hardware description languages, C. Jones and M. Wirsing for fruitful discussions on algebraic specifications, and H. Hussmann for continuously improving the RAP system and carefully reading several drafts of the paper. Special thanks to "bug detector" J. Mulder who pointed out a serious bug in the first version of the specification. The work reported here has been carried out within, and sponsored by the ESPRIT project 432, METEOR.

References

The following abbreviations are used:
LNCS = Lecture Notes in Computer Science
MET = METEOR working paper

[Berghammer et al. 86] R. Berghammer, H. Ehler, H. Zierer: *Towards an algebraic specification of code generation*. Report TUM-I8707, Technische Universität München, June 1987.

[Bergstra et al. 85] J. A. Bergstra, J. Heering, P. Klint: *Algebraic Definition of a Simple Programming Language*. Report CS-R8504, CWI, Amsterdam, Feb. 1985.

[Broy 84] M. Broy: *Specification and Top Down Design of Distributed Systems*. Report MIP-8401, Universität Passau, Dec. 1984, MET.

[Broy 88] M. Broy: *An Example for the Design of Distributed Systems in a Formal Setting: The Lift Problem*. Report MIP-8802, Universität Passau, Feb. 1988

[CIP 87] A. Horsch, B. Möller, H. Partsch, O. Paukner, P. Pepper: *The Munich Project CIP, Vol. II: The Program Transformation System CIP-S, Part I: Formal Specification*. LNCS 292, 1987.

[Feijs et al. 88] L. M. G. Feijs, H. B. M. Jonkers, C. P. J. Koymans, G. R. Renardel de Lavalette: *Formal Definition of the Design Language COLD-K*. Technical Report, Philips Research Labs., Eindhoven, 1988, MET.

[Gelissen 88]   J. H. A. Gelissen: *Rapid Prototyping of COLD Specifications using RAP*. Technical Report, Philips Research Labs., Eindhoven, April 1988, MET.

[Geser 86]   A. Geser: *A Specification of the intel 8085 Microprocessor: A Case Study*. Report MIP-8608, Universität Passau, May 1986, MET.

[Geser, Hußmann 85] A. Geser, H. Hußmann: *Rapid Prototyping for Algebraic Specifications — Examples for the Use of the RAP System*. Report MIP-8517, Universität Passau, Dec. 1985, MET. Updated version to appear.

[Geser, Hußmann 86] A. Geser, H. Hußmann: *Experiences with the RAP system — A Specification Interpreter combining Term Rewriting and Resolution*. In: Proc. ESOP 86 Conf., March 1986, LNCS 213, also as MET.

[Geser et al. 87] A. Geser, H. Hußmann: *A Compiler for a Class of Conditional Rewrite Systems*. In: Proc. 1st Workshop on Conditional Rewriting, June 1987, LNCS 308, pp. 84-90.

[Hoare 83]   C. A. R. Hoare: *Notes on Communicating Sequential Processes*. Technical Monograph PRG-33, Oxford, Aug. 1983.

[Huet, Oppen 80] G. Huet, D. C. Oppen: *Equations and Rewrite Rules - A Survey*. In: R. V. Book (ed.): *Formal Language Theory - Perspectives and Open Problems*. Academic Press, 1980.

[Hullot 80]   J. M. Hullot: *Canonical Forms and Unification*. Proc. 5th CADE Conf., LNCS 87, pp. 318-334, 1980.

[Hußmann 85a] H. Hußmann: *Unification in Conditional-Equational Theories*. Report MIP-8502, Universität Passau, Passau 1985. Short version also in: Proc. EUROCAL 85 Conf., Vol. 2, LNCS 204, pp. 543-553, April 1985.

[Hußmann 85b] H. Hußmann: *Rapid Prototyping for Algebraic Specifications — RAP System User's Manual (Second Edition)*. Report MIP-8504, Universität Passau, Feb. 1987.

[Hußmann, Geser 88] H. Hußmann, A. Geser: *The RAP system as a tool for testing COLD specifications*. In this volume.

[Hußmann, Rank 88] H. Hußmann, C. Rank: *Specification and Prototyping of a Compiler for a Small Applicative Language*. In this volume.

[intel 79]   Intel Corporation: *8080/8085 Assembly Language Programming*. Santa Clara, 1979.

[intel 83]   Intel Corporation: *The MCS-80/85 Family User's Manual*. Santa Clara, 1983.

[Iverson 63]   K. E. Iverson: *Programming in Systems Design*. IBM Systems Journal, Vol. 2, June 1963, pp. 117-128.

[Jonkers 88]   H. B. M. Jonkers: *An Introduction to COLD-K*. Technical Report, Philips Research Labs., Eindhoven, July 1988.

[Kaplan 87]   S. Kaplan: *A Compiler for Conditional Term Rewriting Systems*. Proc. RTA 87 Conf., LNCS 256, pp. 25-41, May 1987.

[Lavazza, Crespi-Reghizzi 87] L. Lavazza, S. Crespi-Reghizzi: *Algebraic ADT Specifications of an Extended Relational Algebra and their Conversion into a Working Prototype*. To appear as MET.

[Padawitz 87] P. Padawitz: *ECDS - A Rewrite Rule Based Interpreter for a Programming Language with Abstraction and Communication.* Report MIP-8703, Universität Passau, Feb. 1987, MET.

[Padawitz 88] P. Padawitz: *Computing in Horn Clause Theories.* EATCS Monographs in Theoretical Computer Science Vol. 16, 1988.

[Sint 80] H. J. Sint: *A Survey of High Level Microprogramming Languages.* Proc. 13th Annual Workshop on Microprogramming, 1980.

[Wirsing et al. 83] M. Wirsing, P. Pepper, H. Partsch, W. Dosch, M. Broy: *On Hierarchies of Abstract Data Types.* Acta Informatica 20, pp. 1-33, 1983.

[Wirsing 85] M. Wirsing: *Structured Algebraic Specifications: A Kernel Language.* Habilitation Thesis, Technische Universitaet Muenchen, 1983. also as: Report MIP-8511, Universitaet Passau, 1985, MET. also in Theoretical Computer Science.

[Wirsing 86] A. Tarlezki, M. Wirsing: *Continuous Abstract Types.* In: Proc. MFCS 86, LNCS 233, 1986, MET.

Index

Appendix A. Specification of the 8085A Instruction Execution

A.1 Basic Data Structures

```
DESIGN

 LET BOOL :=
  CLASS
   SORT Bool
   FUNC{CONS} true:  -> Bool
   FUNC{CONS} false:  -> Bool
   FUNC not:  Bool -> Bool
   FUNC and:  Bool # Bool -> Bool
   FUNC or:  Bool # Bool -> Bool
   FUNC impl:  Bool # Bool -> Bool
   FUNC equiv:  Bool # Bool -> Bool

 AXIOM
  FORALL  x: Bool
   ( {1}   not(true) = false;
     {2}   not(false) = true;
     {3}   and(true,x) = x;
     {4}   and(x,true) = x;
     {5}   and(false,x) = false;
     {6}   and(x,false) = false;
     {7}   or(false,x) = x;
     {8}   or(x,false) = x;
     {9}   or(true,x) = true;
     {10}  or(x,true) = true;
     {11}  impl(x,x) = true;
     {12}  impl(true,false) = false;
     {13}  impl(false,x) = true;
     {14}  impl(x,true) = true;
     {15}  equiv(x,x) = true;
     {16}  equiv(true,x) = x;
     {17}  equiv(x,true) = x )
  END;



 LET BIT :=
  CLASS
   SORT Bit
   FUNC{CONS} O:  -> Bit
   FUNC{CONS} I:  -> Bit
{the bits zero and one. }
   FUNC not_Bit:  Bit -> Bit

 AXIOM
  FORALL  x: Bit
   ( {NOT_INV} not_Bit(not_Bit(x)) = x;
{can be inferred from the following rules by case analysis}
     {NOT_O}   not_Bit(O) = I;
     {NOT_I}   not_Bit(I) = O )
  END;
```

```
LET BYTE :=
{A byte is a 8-tuple of bits. Note the unusual order of the bits within the byte:
The least significant bit is the first one. }

  IMPORT BIT INTO
   CLASS
    SORT Byte
    FUNC{CONS} make_Byte:  Bit # Bit # Bit # Bit # Bit # Bit # Bit # Bit -> Byte
    FUNC sel_Bit_0:  Byte -> Bit
    FUNC sel_Bit_1:  Byte -> Bit
    FUNC sel_Bit_2:  Byte -> Bit
    FUNC sel_Bit_3:  Byte -> Bit
    FUNC sel_Bit_4:  Byte -> Bit
    FUNC sel_Bit_5:  Byte -> Bit
    FUNC sel_Bit_6:  Byte -> Bit
    FUNC sel_Bit_7:  Byte -> Bit

   AXIOM
    FORALL  x0: Bit, x1: Bit, x2: Bit, x3: Bit, x4: Bit, x5: Bit, x6: Bit, x7: Bit
     ( {1} sel_Bit_0(make_Byte(x0,x1,x2,x3,x4,x5,x6,x7)) = x0;
       {2} sel_Bit_1(make_Byte(x0,x1,x2,x3,x4,x5,x6,x7)) = x1;
       {3} sel_Bit_2(make_Byte(x0,x1,x2,x3,x4,x5,x6,x7)) = x2;
       {4} sel_Bit_3(make_Byte(x0,x1,x2,x3,x4,x5,x6,x7)) = x3;
       {5} sel_Bit_4(make_Byte(x0,x1,x2,x3,x4,x5,x6,x7)) = x4;
       {6} sel_Bit_5(make_Byte(x0,x1,x2,x3,x4,x5,x6,x7)) = x5;
       {7} sel_Bit_6(make_Byte(x0,x1,x2,x3,x4,x5,x6,x7)) = x6;
       {8} sel_Bit_7(make_Byte(x0,x1,x2,x3,x4,x5,x6,x7)) = x7 )
    END;



LET WORD :=
{A word is a pair of bytes where the least significant one comes first.}

  IMPORT BYTE INTO
   CLASS
    SORT Word
    FUNC{CONS} make_Word:  Byte # Byte -> Word
    FUNC lower_Byte:  Word -> Byte
    FUNC higher_Byte:  Word -> Byte

   AXIOM
    FORALL  b1: Byte, b2: Byte
     ( {LOWER}  lower_Byte(make_Word(b1,b2)) = b1;
       {HIGHER} higher_Byte(make_Word(b1,b2)) = b2 )
    END;
```

```
LET STATE :=
{the processor state, i.e. the values of the double registers, the interrupt mask byte,
and of the state flipflops. Also selection and alteration access on these via their
names.}

  IMPORT BIT INTO
  IMPORT BYTE INTO
  IMPORT WORD INTO
   CLASS
    SORT State
    SORT Dreg
    SORT Flipflop
    FUNC{CONS} make_State:  Word # Word # Word # Word # Word # Word #
                            {PSW}  {BC}   {DE}   {HL}   {SP}   {PC}
                            Byte  #  Bit  #  Bit  #  Bit   -> State
                            {int_mask} {inte}  {halt}  {rst7_5}
    FUNC{CONS} PSW:  -> Dreg
    FUNC{CONS} BC:   -> Dreg
    FUNC{CONS} DE:   -> Dreg
    FUNC{CONS} HL:   -> Dreg
    FUNC{CONS} SP:   -> Dreg
    FUNC{CONS} PC:   -> Dreg
{the double (i.e. 16-bit) registers}
    FUNC{CONS} inte:  -> Flipflop
    FUNC{CONS} halt:  -> Flipflop
    FUNC{CONS} rst7_5:  -> Flipflop
{the state flipflops interrupt-enable, halt, restart-7.5-edge}
    FUNC sel_Dreg:  State # Dreg -> Word
{selection of the value of a Dreg.}
    FUNC alt_Dreg:  State # Dreg # Word -> State
{selective alteration of a Dreg.}
    FUNC sel_int_mask:  State -> Byte
{select the interrupt mask}
    FUNC alt_int_mask:  State # Byte -> State
{alter the interrupt mask}
    FUNC sel_Flipflop:  State # Flipflop -> Bit
    FUNC alt_Flipflop:  State # Flipflop # Bit -> State

  AXIOM
    FORALL y1: Bit, y2: Bit, y3: Bit, y: Bit, b1: Byte, b: Byte,
           w1: Word, w2: Word, w3: Word, w4: Word, w5: Word, w6: Word, w: Word,
           u: State
{Double registers}
    ( {SEL_PSW}    sel_Dreg(make_State(w1,w2,w3,w4,w5,w6,b,y1,y2,y3),PSW) = w1;
      {SEL_BC}     sel_Dreg(make_State(w1,w2,w3,w4,w5,w6,b,y1,y2,y3),BC) = w2;
      {SEL_DE}     sel_Dreg(make_State(w1,w2,w3,w4,w5,w6,b,y1,y2,y3),DE) = w3;
      {SEL_HL}     sel_Dreg(make_State(w1,w2,w3,w4,w5,w6,b,y1,y2,y3),HL) = w4;
      {SEL_SP}     sel_Dreg(make_State(w1,w2,w3,w4,w5,w6,b,y1,y2,y3),SP) = w5;
      {SEL_PC}     sel_Dreg(make_State(w1,w2,w3,w4,w5,w6,b,y1,y2,y3),PC) = w6;
      {ALT_PSW}    alt_Dreg(make_State(w1,w2,w3,w4,w5,w6,b,y1,y2,y3),PSW,w) =
                     make_State(w,w2,w3,w4,w5,w6,b,y1,y2,y3);
      {ALT_BC}     alt_Dreg(make_State(w1,w2,w3,w4,w5,w6,b,y1,y2,y3),BC,w) =
                     make_State(w1,w,w3,w4,w5,w6,b,y1,y2,y3);
      {ALT_DE}     alt_Dreg(make_State(w1,w2,w3,w4,w5,w6,b,y1,y2,y3),DE,w) =
                     make_State(w1,w2,w,w4,w5,w6,b,y1,y2,y3);
      {ALT_HL}     alt_Dreg(make_State(w1,w2,w3,w4,w5,w6,b,y1,y2,y3),HL,w) =
```

```
                    make_State(w1,w2,w3,w,w5,w6,b,y1,y2,y3);
    {ALT_SP}        alt_Dreg(make_State(w1,w2,w3,w4,w5,w6,b,y1,y2,y3),SP,w) =
                    make_State(w1,w2,w3,w4,w,w6,b,y1,y2,y3);
    {ALT_PC}        alt_Dreg(make_State(w1,w2,w3,w4,w5,w6,b,y1,y2,y3),PC,w) =
                    make_State(w1,w2,w3,w4,w5,w,b,y1,y2,y3);
{Interrupt mask}
    {SEL_IM}        sel_int_mask(make_State(w1,w2,w3,w4,w5,w6,b,y1,y2,y3)) = b;
    {ALT_IM}        alt_int_mask(make_State(w1,w2,w3,w4,w5,w6,b,y1,y2,y3),b1) =
                    make_State(w1,w2,w3,w4,w5,w6,b1,y1,y2,y3);
{bug: still not quite correct wrt. the informal description since
    sel(alt(*)) is not precisely the identity on Byte. }
{State flipflops}
    {SEL_INTE}      sel_Flipflop(make_State(w1,w2,w3,w4,w5,w6,b,y1,y2,y3),inte) =
                    y1;
    {SEL_HALT}      sel_Flipflop(make_State(w1,w2,w3,w4,w5,w6,b,y1,y2,y3),halt) =
                    y2;
    {SEL_RST}       sel_Flipflop(make_State(w1,w2,w3,w4,w5,w6,b,y1,y2,y3),
                            rst7_5) = y3;
    {ALT_INTE}      alt_Flipflop(make_State(w1,w2,w3,w4,w5,w6,b,y1,y2,y3),inte,
                            y) = make_State(w1,w2,w3,w4,w5,w6,b,y,y2,y3);
    {ALT_HALT}      alt_Flipflop(make_State(w1,w2,w3,w4,w5,w6,b,y1,y2,y3),halt,
                            y) = make_State(w1,w2,w3,w4,w5,w6,b,y1,y,y3);
    {ALT_RST}       alt_Flipflop(make_State(w1,w2,w3,w4,w5,w6,b,y1,y2,y3),
                            rst7_5,y) =
                    make_State(w1,w2,w3,w4,w5,w6,b,y1,y2,y) )
    END;
```

```
LET REG :=
{the 8-bit register names, and their access in a state}

IMPORT BIT INTO
IMPORT BYTE INTO
IMPORT WORD INTO
IMPORT STATE INTO
 CLASS
  SORT Reg
  FUNC{CONS} A:  -> Reg
  FUNC{CONS} B:  -> Reg
  FUNC{CONS} C:  -> Reg
  FUNC{CONS} D:  -> Reg
  FUNC{CONS} E:  -> Reg
  FUNC{CONS} H:  -> Reg
  FUNC{CONS} L:  -> Reg
  FUNC sel_Reg:  State # Reg -> Byte
{selection of the value of a register}
  FUNC alt_Reg:  State # Reg # Byte -> State
{selective alteration}

AXIOM
 FORALL  b: Byte, u: State
  ( {SEL_A}      sel_Reg(u,A) = higher_Byte(sel_Dreg(u,PSW));
    {SEL_B}      sel_Reg(u,B) = higher_Byte(sel_Dreg(u,BC));
    {SEL_C}      sel_Reg(u,C) = lower_Byte(sel_Dreg(u,BC));
    {SEL_D}      sel_Reg(u,D) = higher_Byte(sel_Dreg(u,DE));
    {SEL_E}      sel_Reg(u,E) = lower_Byte(sel_Dreg(u,DE));
    {SEL_H}      sel_Reg(u,H) = higher_Byte(sel_Dreg(u,HL));
    {SEL_L}      sel_Reg(u,L) = lower_Byte(sel_Dreg(u,HL));
    {ALT_A}      alt_Reg(u,A,b) =
                  alt_Dreg(u,PSW,make_Word(lower_Byte(sel_Dreg(u,PSW)),b));
    {ALT_B}      alt_Reg(u,B,b) =
                  alt_Dreg(u,BC,make_Word(lower_Byte(sel_Dreg(u,BC)),b));
    {ALT_C}      alt_Reg(u,C,b) =
                  alt_Dreg(u,BC,make_Word(b,higher_Byte(sel_Dreg(u,BC))));
    {ALT_D}      alt_Reg(u,D,b) =
                  alt_Dreg(u,DE,make_Word(lower_Byte(sel_Dreg(u,DE)),b));
    {ALT_E}      alt_Reg(u,E,b) =
                  alt_Dreg(u,DE,make_Word(b,higher_Byte(sel_Dreg(u,DE))));
    {ALT_H}      alt_Reg(u,H,b) =
                  alt_Dreg(u,HL,make_Word(lower_Byte(sel_Dreg(u,HL)),b));
    {ALT_L}      alt_Reg(u,L,b) =
                  alt_Dreg(u,HL,make_Word(b,higher_Byte(sel_Dreg(u,HL)))) )
END;
```

```
LET FLAG :=
{the flag names carry, parity, auxiliary carry, zero, sign, and the access to the flags
in a state}

IMPORT BIT INTO
IMPORT BYTE INTO
IMPORT WORD INTO
IMPORT STATE INTO
 CLASS
  SORT Flag
  FUNC{CONS} Cy:  -> Flag
  FUNC{CONS} P:  -> Flag
  FUNC{CONS} Ac:  -> Flag
  FUNC{CONS} Z:  -> Flag
  FUNC{CONS} S:  -> Flag
  FUNC sel_Flag:  State # Flag -> Bit
{selection of a flag value}
  FUNC alt_Cy:  State # Bit -> State
{alteration of the carry-Flag value}

AXIOM
 FORALL  x1: Bit, x2: Bit, x3: Bit, x4: Bit, x5: Bit, x6: Bit, x7: Bit,
          x8: Bit, x: Bit, y1: Bit, y2: Bit, y3: Bit, a: Byte, b: Byte,
          w1: Word, w2: Word, w3: Word, w4: Word, w5: Word, u: State
  ( {SEL_S}  sel_Flag(u,S) = sel_Bit_7(lower_Byte(sel_Dreg(u,PSW)));
    {SEL_Z}  sel_Flag(u,Z) = sel_Bit_6(lower_Byte(sel_Dreg(u,PSW)));
    {SEL_AC} sel_Flag(u,Ac) = sel_Bit_4(lower_Byte(sel_Dreg(u,PSW)));
    {SEL_P}  sel_Flag(u,P) = sel_Bit_2(lower_Byte(sel_Dreg(u,PSW)));
    {SEL_CY} sel_Flag(u,Cy) = sel_Bit_0(lower_Byte(sel_Dreg(u,PSW)));
    {ALT_CY} alt_Cy(
            make_State(make_Word(make_Byte(x1,x2,x3,x4,x5,x6,x7,x8),a),w1,w2,
                      w3,w4,w5,b,y1,y2,y3),x) =
make_State(make_Word(make_Byte(x,x2,x3,x4,x5,x6,x7,x8),a),w1,w2,w3,w4,w5,b,y1,
          y2,y3) )
END;
```

```
LET STREAM :=
{The communication streams}

 IMPORT BYTE INTO
 IMPORT WORD INTO
  CLASS
   SORT Stream
   FUNC{CONS} empty:  -> Stream
   FUNC{CONS} opcode:  Word # Byte # Stream -> Stream
   FUNC{CONS} read:  Word # Byte # Stream -> Stream
   FUNC{CONS} write:  Word # Byte # Stream -> Stream
   FUNC{CONS} in:  Word # Byte # Stream -> Stream
   FUNC{CONS} out:  Word # Byte # Stream -> Stream
{Note: There is no law for empty. So, the objects of sort Stream can be seen as partial
objects that approximate potentially infinite streams, by taking the variable
occurrence as the "unknown", "arbitrary", or "undefined" stream.}
 END;




LET PROCESS :=
{A process is formed by a state together with a stream.}

 IMPORT STATE INTO
 IMPORT STREAM INTO
  CLASS
   SORT Process
   FUNC{CONS} make_Process:  State # Stream -> Process
   FUNC sel_State:  Process -> State
   FUNC sel_Stream:  Process -> Stream

 AXIOM
  FORALL  u: State, s: Stream
   ( {STATE}  sel_State(make_Process(u,s)) = u;
     {STREAM} sel_Stream(make_Process(u,s)) = s )
 END;
```

```
LET TRIV_STATE :=
IMPORT BIT INTO
IMPORT BYTE INTO
IMPORT WORD INTO
IMPORT STATE INTO
 CLASS
  FUNC triv_State:  -> State
{the 0 State, for easy denotation of State expressions}

 AXIOM
   ( {TRIV} triv_State =
make_State(make_Word(make_Byte(0,0,0,0,0,0,0,0),make_Byte(0,0,0,0,0,0,0,0)),
           make_Word(make_Byte(0,0,0,0,0,0,0,0),make_Byte(0,0,0,0,0,0,0,0)),
           make_Word(make_Byte(0,0,0,0,0,0,0,0),make_Byte(0,0,0,0,0,0,0,0)),
           make_Word(make_Byte(0,0,0,0,0,0,0,0),make_Byte(0,0,0,0,0,0,0,0)),
           make_Word(make_Byte(0,0,0,0,0,0,0,0),make_Byte(0,0,0,0,0,0,0,0)),
           make_Word(make_Byte(0,0,0,0,0,0,0,0),make_Byte(0,0,0,0,0,0,0,0)),
           make_Byte(0,0,0,0,0,0,0,0),0,0,0) )
END;
```

A.2 Derived Basic Operations

```
LET BIT_EXT :=
{the arithmetic/logic fundamental operations on bits}

 IMPORT BIT INTO
  CLASS
   FUNC and_Bit:  Bit # Bit -> Bit
   FUNC or_Bit:  Bit # Bit -> Bit
   FUNC exor_Bit: Bit # Bit -> Bit
{the "logical" operations}
   FUNC sum:  Bit # Bit # Bit -> Bit
   FUNC carry: Bit # Bit # Bit -> Bit
{sum and carry form the resp. outputs of a one-bit full adder}

 AXIOM
  FORALL  x: Bit, y: Bit
   ( {AND_0}        and_Bit(0,x) = 0;
     {AND_I}        and_Bit(I,x) = x;
     {OR_I}         or_Bit(I,x) = I;
     {OR_0}         or_Bit(0,x) = x;
     {EXOR_0}       exor_Bit(0,x) = x;
     {EXOR_I}       exor_Bit(I,x) = not_Bit(x);
     {SUM_1}        sum(x,y,y) = x;
     {SUM_2}        sum(y,x,y) = x;
     {SUM_3}        sum(y,y,x) = x;
     {CARRY_1}      carry(x,x,y) = x;
     {CARRY_2}      carry(x,y,x) = x;
     {CARRY_3}      carry(y,x,x) = x )
  END;


 LET BYTE_EXT :=
{auxiliary constants and operations on bytes}

 IMPORT BIT INTO
 IMPORT BYTE INTO
  CLASS
   FUNC 0_Byte:  -> Byte
   FUNC I_Byte:  -> Byte
{constant zero, one byte, resp.}
   FUNC not_Byte: Byte -> Byte
{bitwise complement of a byte}

 AXIOM
  FORALL  x0: Bit, x1: Bit, x2: Bit, x3: Bit, x4: Bit, x5: Bit, x6: Bit,
          x7: Bit
   ( {0_BYTE_DEF}  0_Byte = make_Byte(0,0,0,0,0,0,0,0);
     {I_BYTE_DEF}  I_Byte = make_Byte(I,I,I,I,I,I,I,I);
     {NOT_BYTE_DEF} not_Byte(make_Byte(x0,x1,x2,x3,x4,x5,x6,x7)) =
make_Byte(not_Bit(x0),not_Bit(x1),not_Bit(x2),not_Bit(x3),not_Bit(x4),
          not_Bit(x5),not_Bit(x6),not_Bit(x7)) )
  END;
```

```
LET RESULT :=
{This type is used to form a tuple out of the adder outputs.}

 IMPORT BIT INTO
 IMPORT BYTE INTO
  CLASS
   SORT Result
   FUNC{CONS} make_Result:  Byte # Bit # Bit -> Result
   FUNC byte:  Result -> Byte
   FUNC aux:  Result -> Bit
   FUNC cy:  Result -> Bit

 AXIOM
  FORALL  b: Byte, x1: Bit, x2: Bit
   ( {BYTE} byte(make_Result(b,x1,x2)) = b;
     {AUX}  aux(make_Result(b,x1,x2)) = x1;
     {CY}   cy(make_Result(b,x1,x2)) = x2 )
END;




LET ADD_BYTE :=
{8-bit-addition}

 IMPORT BIT INTO
 IMPORT BYTE INTO
 IMPORT BIT_EXT INTO
 IMPORT RESULT INTO
  CLASS
   FUNC add_Byte:  Byte # Byte # Bit -> Result

 AXIOM
  FORALL  x0: Bit, x1: Bit, x2: Bit, x3: Bit, x4: Bit, x5: Bit, x6: Bit, x7: Bit,
          y0: Bit, y1: Bit, y2: Bit, y3: Bit, y4: Bit, y5: Bit, y6: Bit, y7: Bit,
          z0: Bit, z1: Bit, z2: Bit, z3: Bit, z4: Bit, z5: Bit, z6: Bit, z7: Bit
   ( {ADD_BYTE} z1 = carry(x0,y0,z0) AND z2 = carry(x1,y1,z1) AND
                z3 = carry(x2,y2,z2) AND z4 = carry(x3,y3,z3) AND
                z5 = carry(x4,y4,z4) AND z6 = carry(x5,y5,z5) AND
                z7 = carry(x6,y6,z6) =>
add_Byte(make_Byte(x0,x1,x2,x3,x4,x5,x6,x7),
         make_Byte(y0,y1,y2,y3,y4,y5,y6,y7),z0) =
make_Result(
             make_Byte(sum(x0,y0,z0),sum(x1,y1,z1),sum(x2,y2,z2),sum(x3,y3,z3),
                       sum(x4,y4,z4),sum(x5,y5,z5),sum(x6,y6,z6),sum(x7,y7,z7)),
             z4,carry(x7,y7,z7)) )
END;
```

```
LET WORD_ARITH :=
IMPORT BIT INTO
IMPORT BYTE INTO
IMPORT WORD INTO
IMPORT BYTE_EXT INTO
IMPORT ADD_BYTE INTO
IMPORT RESULT INTO
 CLASS
  FUNC incr_Word:  Word -> Word
  FUNC decr_Word:  Word -> Word

AXIOM
 FORALL  b1: Byte, b2: Byte, r1: Result, r2: Result
  ( {INCR_WORD} r1 = add_Byte(b1,0_Byte,I) AND
                 r2 = add_Byte(b2,0_Byte,cy(r1)) =>
                 incr_Word(make_Word(b1,b2)) = make_Word(byte(r1),byte(r2));
     {DECR_WORD} r1 = add_Byte(b1,I_Byte,0) AND
                 r2 = add_Byte(b2,I_Byte,cy(r1)) =>
                 decr_Word(make_Word(b1,b2)) = make_Word(byte(r1),byte(r2)) )
END;
```

```
LET SET_FLAGS :=
{explains how the flags are set after an operation}

 IMPORT BIT INTO
 IMPORT BYTE INTO
 IMPORT WORD INTO
 IMPORT STATE INTO
 IMPORT REG INTO
 IMPORT FLAG INTO
 IMPORT BIT_EXT INTO
 IMPORT RESULT INTO
 EXPORT set_Flags_and_A FROM
  CLASS
   FUNC test_Z: Byte -> Bit
   FUNC test_P: Byte -> Bit
{tests for Z, P flag resp.}
   FUNC set_Flags_and_A: State # Result # Byte -> State
{gives the new state, changing the flags and the A register}

 AXIOM
  FORALL  x0: Bit, x1: Bit, x2: Bit, x3: Bit, x4: Bit, x5: Bit, x6: Bit, x7: Bit,
         fill1: Bit, fill2: Bit, fill3: Bit, a: Byte, c: Byte, u: State
    ( {TEST_Z_1}        test_Z(make_Byte(x0,x1,x2,x3,x4,x5,x6,I)) = 0;
      {TEST_Z_2}        test_Z(make_Byte(x0,x1,x2,x3,x4,x5,I,x7)) = 0;
      {TEST_Z_3}        test_Z(make_Byte(x0,x1,x2,x3,x4,I,x6,x7)) = 0;
      {TEST_Z_4}        test_Z(make_Byte(x0,x1,x2,x3,I,x5,x6,x7)) = 0;
      {TEST_Z_5}        test_Z(make_Byte(x0,x1,x2,I,x4,x5,x6,x7)) = 0;
      {TEST_Z_6}        test_Z(make_Byte(x0,x1,I,x3,x4,x5,x6,x7)) = 0;
      {TEST_Z_7}        test_Z(make_Byte(x0,I,x2,x3,x4,x5,x6,x7)) = 0;
      {TEST_Z_8}        test_Z(make_Byte(I,x1,x2,x3,x4,x5,x6,x7)) = 0;
      {TEST_Z_SUCCESS} test_Z(make_Byte(0,0,0,0,0,0,0,0)) = I;
      {TEST_P}          test_P(make_Byte(x0,x1,x2,x3,x4,x5,x6,x7)) =
                        sum(x7,x6,sum(x5,x4,sum(x3,x2,sum(x1,x0,I)))));
{the modulo-2 sum of the bits of the given byte, plus one}
      {SET_FLAGS}       set_Flags_and_A(u,make_Result(c,x0,x1),a) =
 alt_Dreg(u,PSW,
                     make_Word(
                     make_Byte(x1,fill1,test_P(c),fill2,x0,fill3,test_Z(c),
                         sel_Bit_7(c)),a)) )
END;
{Note: The bits fill1, fill2, fill3 are arbitrary fillers. They are an instance for the
use of new variables at the right hand side of a rewrite rule, here used to introduce
unspecified (i.e. nondeterministic) items. The rule is not Church-Rosser,and can so
lead to incomplete solution sets.}


LET ALU :=
{the 'arithmetic/logic unit' of the processor}

 IMPORT BIT INTO
 IMPORT BYTE INTO
 IMPORT STATE INTO
 IMPORT REG INTO
 IMPORT FLAG INTO
 IMPORT BIT_EXT INTO
 IMPORT BYTE_EXT INTO
```

```
IMPORT RESULT INTO
IMPORT SET_FLAGS INTO
IMPORT ADD_BYTE INTO
 CLASS
  FUNC alu:  State # Bit # Bit # Bit # Byte -> State
{perform an arithmetic/logic operation, given 3 bits of the opcode, and the 2nd operand}

 AXIOM
  FORALL  x0: Bit, x1: Bit, x2: Bit, x3: Bit, x4: Bit, x5: Bit, x6: Bit, x7: Bit,
          y0: Bit, y1: Bit, y2: Bit, y3: Bit, y4: Bit, y5: Bit, y6: Bit, y7: Bit,
          z: Bit, a: Byte, b: Byte, c: Byte, u: State, r: Result
   ( {ADD}              r = add_Byte(sel_Reg(u,A),b,0) =>
                           alu(u,0,0,0,b) = set_Flags_and_A(u,r,byte(r));
     {ADD_WITH_CY}       r = add_Byte(sel_Reg(u,A),b,sel_Flag(u,Cy)) =>
                           alu(u,I,0,0,b) = set_Flags_and_A(u,r,byte(r));
     {SUB}
make_Result(a,y0,y1) = add_Byte(sel_Reg(u,A),not_Byte(b),I) =>
alu(u,0,I,0,b) = set_Flags_and_A(u,make_Result(a,y0,not_Bit(y1)),a);
     {SUB_WITH_BORROW}
make_Result(a,y0,y1) =
add_Byte(sel_Reg(u,A),not_Byte(b),not_Bit(sel_Flag(u,Cy))) =>
alu(u,I,I,0,b) = set_Flags_and_A(u,make_Result(a,y0,not_Bit(y1)),a);
     {AND}              a = sel_Reg(u,A) AND
c =
make_Byte(and_Bit(sel_Bit_0(a),y0),and_Bit(sel_Bit_1(a),y1),
         and_Bit(sel_Bit_2(a),y2),and_Bit(sel_Bit_3(a),y3),
         and_Bit(sel_Bit_4(a),y4),and_Bit(sel_Bit_5(a),y5),
         and_Bit(sel_Bit_6(a),y6),and_Bit(sel_Bit_7(a),y7)) =>
alu(u,0,0,I,make_Byte(y0,y1,y2,y3,y4,y5,y6,y7)) =
                       set_Flags_and_A(u,make_Result(c,0,0),c);
     {EXOR}             a = sel_Reg(u,A) AND
c =
make_Byte(exor_Bit(sel_Bit_0(a),y0),exor_Bit(sel_Bit_1(a),y1),
         exor_Bit(sel_Bit_2(a),y2),exor_Bit(sel_Bit_3(a),y3),
         exor_Bit(sel_Bit_4(a),y4),exor_Bit(sel_Bit_5(a),y5),
         exor_Bit(sel_Bit_6(a),y6),exor_Bit(sel_Bit_7(a),y7)) =>
alu(u,I,0,I,make_Byte(y0,y1,y2,y3,y4,y5,y6,y7)) =
                       set_Flags_and_A(u,make_Result(c,0,0),c);
     {OR}               a = sel_Reg(u,A) AND
c =
make_Byte(or_Bit(sel_Bit_0(a),y0),or_Bit(sel_Bit_1(a),y1),
         or_Bit(sel_Bit_2(a),y2),or_Bit(sel_Bit_3(a),y3),
         or_Bit(sel_Bit_4(a),y4),or_Bit(sel_Bit_5(a),y5),
         or_Bit(sel_Bit_6(a),y6),or_Bit(sel_Bit_7(a),y7)) =>
alu(u,0,I,I,make_Byte(y0,y1,y2,y3,y4,y5,y6,y7)) =>
                       set_Flags_and_A(u,make_Result(c,0,0),c);
     {COMPARE}
make_Result(a,y0,y1) = add_Byte(sel_Reg(u,A),not_Byte(b),I) =>
alu(u,I,I,I,b) =
set_Flags_and_A(u,make_Result(a,y0,not_Bit(y1)),sel_Reg(u,A)) )
END;
```

```
LET COND :=
{conditional execution}

 IMPORT BIT INTO
 IMPORT STATE INTO
 IMPORT FLAG INTO
 IMPORT PROCESS INTO
  CLASS
   FUNC cond:  Process # Flag # Bit # Process -> Process

 AXIOM
  FORALL  p1: Process, p2: Process, f: Flag, x: Bit
   ( {BRANCH}   sel_Flag(sel_State(p1),f) = x => cond(p1,f,x,p2) = p2;
     {STRAIGHT} sel_Flag(sel_State(p1),f) = not_Bit(x) =>
                  cond(p1,f,x,p2) = p1 )
 END;



 LET INCR_DECR_DREG :=
{increment and decrement functions for double registers}

 IMPORT STATE INTO
 IMPORT STREAM INTO
 IMPORT PROCESS INTO
 IMPORT WORD_ARITH INTO
  CLASS
   FUNC incr_Dreg:  Process # Dreg -> Process
{inx}
   FUNC decr_Dreg:  Process # Dreg -> Process
{dcx}

 AXIOM
  FORALL  d: Dreg, u: State, s: Stream
   ( {INX} incr_Dreg(make_Process(u,s),d) =
           make_Process(alt_Dreg(u,d,incr_Word(sel_Dreg(u,d))),s);
     {DCX} decr_Dreg(make_Process(u,s),d) =
           make_Process(alt_Dreg(u,d,decr_Word(sel_Dreg(u,d))),s) )
 END;
```

```
LET FETCH_ARGS :=
{Get a byte, word, resp., and update PC accordingly.}

IMPORT BYTE INTO
IMPORT WORD INTO
IMPORT STATE INTO
IMPORT STREAM INTO
IMPORT PROCESS INTO
IMPORT WORD_ARITH INTO
IMPORT INCR_DECR_DREG INTO
 CLASS
  SORT Process_Byte_pair
  SORT Process_Word_pair
  FUNC{CONS} make_Process_Byte_pair:  Process # Byte -> Process_Byte_pair
  FUNC{CONS} make_Process_Word_pair:  Process # Word -> Process_Word_pair
  FUNC fetch_Byte:  Process -> Process_Byte_pair
  FUNC fetch_Word:  Process -> Process_Word_pair
  FUNC drop_Byte:  Process -> Process
{dummy fetch, needed for the jump instructions. A byte is fetched, and PC is incremented
twice. }

AXIOM
 FORALL  b: Byte, b1: Byte, b2: Byte, w: Word, w1: Word, w2: Word, u: State,
         s: Stream, p: Process, p1: Process
  ( {FETCH_BYTE} w = sel_Dreg(u,PC) =>
fetch_Byte(make_Process(u,read(w,b,s))) =
make_Process_Byte_pair(make_Process(alt_Dreg(u,PC,incr_Word(w)),s),b);
    {FETCH_WORD} w1 = sel_Dreg(u,PC) AND w2 = incr_Word(w1) =>
fetch_Word(make_Process(u,read(w1,b1,read(w2,b2,s)))) =
make_Process_Word_pair(make_Process(alt_Dreg(u,PC,incr_Word(w2)),s),
                 make_Word(b1,b2));
    {DROP_BYTE} fetch_Byte(p) = make_Process_Byte_pair(p1,b) =>
                 drop_Byte(p) = incr_Dreg(p1,PC) )
END;
```

A.3 The Machine Instructions in Detail

```
LET LOAD_STORE :=
{machine instructions for memory load to and store from A register and HL double
register}

IMPORT BIT INTO
IMPORT BYTE INTO
IMPORT WORD INTO
IMPORT STATE INTO
IMPORT REG INTO
IMPORT STREAM INTO
IMPORT PROCESS INTO
IMPORT WORD_ARITH INTO
IMPORT FETCH_ARGS INTO
  CLASS
  FUNC store_A_by_Dreg:  Process # Dreg -> Process
{stax}
  FUNC load_A_by_Dreg:  Process # Dreg -> Process
{ldax}
  FUNC store_A_direct:  Process -> Process
{sta}
  FUNC load_A_direct:  Process -> Process
{lda}
  FUNC store_HL_direct:  Process -> Process
{shld}
  FUNC load_HL_direct:  Process -> Process
{lhld}

AXIOM
  FORALL  b: Byte, b1: Byte, b2: Byte, w: Word, w1: Word, w2: Word, d: Dreg,
          u: State, s: Stream, p0: Process, p1: Process
  ( {STAX}  w = sel_Dreg(u,d) AND sel_Reg(u,A) = b =>
store_A_by_Dreg(make_Process(u,write(w,b,s)),d) = make_Process(u,s);
    {SHLD}   fetch_Word(p0) = make_Process_Word_pair(p1,w1) AND
             p1 = make_Process(u,write(w1,b1,write(incr_Word(w1),b2,s))) AND
             sel_Dreg(u,HL) = make_Word(b1,b2) =>
             store_HL_direct(p0) = make_Process(u,s);
    {STA}    fetch_Word(p0) = make_Process_Word_pair(p1,w) AND
             p1 = make_Process(u,write(w,b,s)) AND sel_Reg(u,A) = b =>
             store_A_direct(p0) = make_Process(u,s);
    {LDAX}   sel_Dreg(u,d) = w =>
load_A_by_Dreg(make_Process(u,read(w,b,s)),d) =
             make_Process(alt_Reg(u,A,b),s);
    {LHLD}   fetch_Word(p0) = make_Process_Word_pair(p1,w1) AND
             p1 = make_Process(u,read(w1,b1,read(incr_Word(w1),b2,s))) =>
load_HL_direct(p0) = make_Process(alt_Dreg(u,HL,make_Word(b1,b2)),s);
    {LDA}    fetch_Word(p0) = make_Process_Word_pair(p1,w) AND
             p1 = make_Process(u,read(w,b,s)) =>
             load_A_direct(p0) = make_Process(alt_Reg(u,A,b),s) )

END;
```

```
      LET DAA :=
      {the 'decimal adjust accumulator' specification}

      IMPORT BOOL INTO
      IMPORT BIT INTO
      IMPORT BYTE INTO
      IMPORT STATE INTO
      IMPORT REG INTO
      IMPORT FLAG INTO
      IMPORT STREAM INTO
      IMPORT PROCESS INTO
      IMPORT RESULT INTO
      IMPORT SET_FLAGS INTO
      IMPORT ADD_BYTE INTO
      EXPORT decimal_adjust FROM
       CLASS
         FUNC need_adjust:  Bit # Bit # Bit # Bit # Bit -> Bool
      {yields true, if the 4-bit number is greater than 9, or if the 5th bit is set to I,
      else false. }
         FUNC adjust_lower:  Result -> Result
         FUNC adjust_higher:  Result -> Result
      {decimal adjust lower and higher four bits of the given byte according to the settings
      of the carry and auxiliary carry flags. }
         FUNC decimal_adjust:  Process -> Process
      {daa}

      AXIOM
        FORALL  x0: Bit, x1: Bit, x2: Bit, x3: Bit, x4: Bit, x5: Bit, x6: Bit, x7: Bit,
                y1: Bit, y2: Bit, b: Byte, r: Result, u: State, s: Stream
        ( {LT_7}        need_adjust(x0,x1,x2,0,0) = false;
          {LE_9}        need_adjust(x0,0,0,I,0) = false;
          {BIT}         need_adjust(x0,x1,x2,x3,I) = true;
          {GE_C}        need_adjust(x0,x1,I,I,x4) = true;
          {GT_9}        need_adjust(x0,I,x2,I,x4) = true;
          {LOWER_1}     r = make_Result(make_Byte(x0,x1,x2,x3,x4,x5,x6,x7),y1,y2) AND
                        need_adjust(x0,x1,x2,x3,y1) = false =>
                        adjust_lower(r) = r;
          {LOWER_2}     b = make_Byte(x0,x1,x2,x3,x4,x5,x6,x7) AND
                        need_adjust(x0,x1,x2,x3,y1) = true =>
      adjust_lower(make_Result(b,y1,y2)) = add_Byte(b,make_Byte(0,I,I,0,0,0,0,0),0);
          {HIGHER_1}    r = make_Result(make_Byte(x0,x1,x2,x3,x4,x5,x6,x7),y1,y2) AND
                        need_adjust(x4,x5,x6,x7,y2) = false =>
                        adjust_higher(r) = r;
          {HIGHER_2}    b = make_Byte(x0,x1,x2,x3,x4,x5,x6,x7) AND
                        need_adjust(x4,x5,x6,x7,y2) = true AND
                        r = add_Byte(b,make_Byte(0,0,0,0,0,I,I,0),0) =>
      adjust_higher(make_Result(b,y1,y2)) = make_Result(byte(r),y1,cy(r));
          {DAA}
      r = adjust_higher(adjust_lower(
                        make_Result(sel_Reg(u,A),sel_Flag(u,Ac),sel_Flag(u,Cy)))) =>
      decimal_adjust(make_Process(u,s)) =
                        make_Process(set_Flags_and_A(u,r,byte(r)),s) )
      END;
```

```
LET A_OP :=
{special machine instructions concerning the A register}

 IMPORT BYTE INTO
 IMPORT WORD INTO
 IMPORT STATE INTO
 IMPORT REG INTO
 IMPORT STREAM INTO
 IMPORT PROCESS INTO
 IMPORT BYTE_EXT INTO
  CLASS
   FUNC compl_A:  Process -> Process
{cma}
   FUNC in_A:  Process -> Process
{in}
   FUNC out_A:  Process -> Process
{out}

 AXIOM
  FORALL  b: Byte, c: Byte, w: Word, u: State, s: Stream
   ( {CMA} compl_A(make_Process(u,s)) =
             make_Process(alt_Reg(u,A,not_Byte(sel_Reg(u,A))),s);
     {IN}  sel_Dreg(u,PC) = w =>
in_A(make_Process(u,read(w,b,in(make_Word(b,b),c,s)))) =
             make_Process(alt_Reg(u,A,c),s);
     {OUT} sel_Reg(u,A) = c AND sel_Dreg(u,PC) = w =>
out_A(make_Process(u,read(w,b,out(make_Word(b,b),c,s)))) = make_Process(u,s) )
 END;



 LET CY_OP :=
 IMPORT BIT INTO
 IMPORT STATE INTO
 IMPORT FLAG INTO
 IMPORT STREAM INTO
 IMPORT PROCESS INTO
  CLASS
   FUNC set_Cy:  Process -> Process
{stc}
   FUNC compl_Cy:  Process -> Process
{cmc}

 AXIOM
  FORALL  u: State, s: Stream
   ( {STC} set_Cy(make_Process(u,s)) = make_Process(alt_Cy(u,I),s);
     {CMC} compl_Cy(make_Process(u,s)) =
            make_Process(alt_Cy(u,not_Bit(sel_Flag(u,Cy))),s) )
 END;
```

```
LET MOVE :=
{the large class of 'move' instructions; the instructions are divided into those
concerning the 'M register' and those which do not, because of their different
behaviour w.r.t. the memory and because of the fact that the opcode of 'mov M M'
is occupied by the halt instruction. So, a fine case analysis is needed.}

IMPORT BYTE INTO
IMPORT WORD INTO
IMPORT STATE INTO
IMPORT REG INTO
IMPORT STREAM INTO
IMPORT PROCESS INTO
IMPORT FETCH_ARGS INTO
 CLASS
  FUNC move_imm:  Process # Reg -> Process
  FUNC move_from_M:  Process # Reg -> Process
  FUNC move_to_M:  Process # Reg -> Process
  FUNC move:  Process # Reg # Reg -> Process
  FUNC move_to_M_imm:  Process -> Process

AXIOM
 FORALL  b: Byte, w: Word, w1: Word, r: Reg, q: Reg, u: State, s: Stream, p: Process
 ( {MVI_WITHOUT_M}
fetch_Byte(p) = make_Process_Byte_pair(make_Process(u,s),b) =>
                    move_imm(p,r) = make_Process(alt_Reg(u,r,b),s);
    {MVI_TO_M}
fetch_Byte(p) = make_Process_Byte_pair(make_Process(u,write(w,b,s)),b) AND
                    w = sel_Dreg(u,HL) =>
                    move_to_M_imm(p) = make_Process(u,s);
    {MOV_WITHOUT_M}  move(make_Process(u,s),r,q) =
                    make_Process(alt_Reg(u,r,sel_Reg(u,q)),s);
    {MOV_FROM_M}     w = sel_Dreg(u,HL) =>
move_from_M(make_Process(u,read(w,b,s)),r) = make_Process(alt_Reg(u,r,b),s);
    {MOV_TO_M}       w = sel_Dreg(u,HL) AND sel_Reg(u,r) = b =>
move_to_M(make_Process(u,write(w,b,s)),r) = make_Process(u,s) )
END;
```

```
  LET LXI :=
{the machine instruction 'lxi'}

 IMPORT BYTE INTO
 IMPORT WORD INTO
 IMPORT STATE INTO
 IMPORT STREAM INTO
 IMPORT PROCESS INTO
 IMPORT WORD_ARITH INTO
 IMPORT FETCH_ARGS INTO
  CLASS
   FUNC load_Dreg_imm:  Process # Dreg -> Process
{lxi}

 AXIOM
  FORALL  w: Word, d: Dreg, u: State, s: Stream, p: Process
   ( {LXI} fetch_Word(p) = make_Process_Word_pair(make_Process(u,s),w) =>
           load_Dreg_imm(p,d) = make_Process(alt_Dreg(u,d,w),s) )
  END;



  LET DAD :=
{the machine instruction 'dad'}

 IMPORT BIT INTO
 IMPORT BYTE INTO
 IMPORT WORD INTO
 IMPORT STATE INTO
 IMPORT FLAG INTO
 IMPORT STREAM INTO
 IMPORT PROCESS INTO
 IMPORT RESULT INTO
 IMPORT ADD_BYTE INTO
  CLASS
   FUNC add_Dreg_to_HL:  Process # Dreg -> Process
{dad}

 AXIOM
  FORALL  x1: Bit, x2: Bit, y1: Bit, y2: Bit, b1: Byte, b2: Byte, c1: Byte,
          c2: Byte, d: Dreg, u: State, s: Stream, r1: Result, r2: Result
   ( {DAD} sel_Dreg(u,d) = make_Word(b1,b2) AND
           sel_Dreg(u,HL) = make_Word(c1,c2) AND add_Byte(b1,c1,0) = r1 AND
           add_Byte(b2,c2,cy(r1)) = r2 =>
 add_Dreg_to_HL(make_Process(u,s),d) =
 make_Process(alt_Dreg(alt_Cy(u,cy(r2)),HL,make_Word(byte(r1),byte(r2))),s) )
  END;
```

```
LET INCR_DECR_REG :=
{increment and decrement instructions for registers; for the different treatment of the
'M register' w.r.t. the memory, a case analysis is needed.}

IMPORT BIT INTO
IMPORT BYTE INTO
IMPORT WORD INTO
IMPORT STATE INTO
IMPORT REG INTO
IMPORT FLAG INTO
IMPORT STREAM INTO
IMPORT PROCESS INTO
IMPORT BYTE_EXT INTO
IMPORT RESULT INTO
IMPORT SET_FLAGS INTO
IMPORT ADD_BYTE INTO
 CLASS
  FUNC incr_Reg:  Process # Reg -> Process
  FUNC decr_Reg:  Process # Reg -> Process
  FUNC incr_M:  Process -> Process
  FUNC decr_M:  Process -> Process

AXIOM
 FORALL x: Bit, y: Bit, b: Byte, c: Byte, w: Word, r: Reg, u: State, s: Stream,
        res: Result
  ( {INR_WITHOUT_M} make_Result(b,x,y) = add_Byte(sel_Reg(u,r),O_Byte,I) =>
incr_Reg(make_Process(u,s),r) =
make_Process(
                    set_Flags_and_A(alt_Reg(u,r,b),
                                    make_Result(b,x,sel_Flag(u,Cy)),
                                    sel_Reg(u,A)),s);
    {DCR_WITHOUT_M} make_Result(b,x,y) = add_Byte(sel_Reg(u,r),I_Byte,O) =>
decr_Reg(make_Process(u,s),r) =
make_Process(
                    set_Flags_and_A(alt_Reg(u,r,b),
                                    make_Result(b,x,sel_Flag(u,Cy)),
                                    sel_Reg(u,A)),s);
    {INR_M}          w = sel_Dreg(u,HL) AND
                     make_Result(c,x,y) = add_Byte(b,O_Byte,I) =>
incr_M(make_Process(u,read(w,b,write(w,c,s)))) =
make_Process(set_Flags_and_A(u,make_Result(c,x,sel_Flag(u,Cy)),sel_Reg(u,A)),
            s);
    {DCR_M}          w = sel_Dreg(u,HL) AND res = add_Byte(b,I_Byte,O) AND
                     c = byte(res) =>
decr_M(make_Process(u,read(w,b,write(w,c,s)))) =
make_Process(set_Flags_and_A(u,make_Result(c,x,sel_Flag(u,Cy)),sel_Reg(u,A)),
            s) )
END;
```

```
LET SHIFT :=
{the class of shift instructions}

IMPORT BIT INTO
IMPORT BYTE INTO
IMPORT STATE INTO
IMPORT REG INTO
IMPORT FLAG INTO
IMPORT STREAM INTO
IMPORT PROCESS INTO
EXPORT rotate FROM
  CLASS
   FUNC shift_right:  Byte # Bit -> Byte
   FUNC shift_left:   Byte # Bit -> Byte
{shift a byte by one position to the right, left resp., insert thereby a new bit into
the void position}
   FUNC rotate:  Process # Bit # Bit -> Process
{rotate the A register contents according to 2 bits of the opcode}

AXIOM
  FORALL  x0: Bit, x1: Bit, x2: Bit, x3: Bit, x4: Bit, x5: Bit, x6: Bit,
          x7: Bit, x: Bit, a: Byte, u: State, s: Stream
   ( {1}      shift_left(make_Byte(x0,x1,x2,x3,x4,x5,x6,x7),x) =
               make_Byte(x,x0,x1,x2,x3,x4,x5,x6);
     {2}      shift_right(make_Byte(x0,x1,x2,x3,x4,x5,x6,x7),x) =
               make_Byte(x1,x2,x3,x4,x5,x6,x7,x);
    {RLC}    a = sel_Reg(u,A) AND x7 = sel_Bit_7(a) =>
rotate(make_Process(u,s),0,0) =
               make_Process(alt_Cy(alt_Reg(u,A,shift_left(a,x7)),x7),s);
    {RRC}    a = sel_Reg(u,A) AND x0 = sel_Bit_0(a) =>
rotate(make_Process(u,s),I,0) =
               make_Process(alt_Cy(alt_Reg(u,A,shift_right(a,x0)),x0),s);
    {RAL}    a = sel_Reg(u,A) =>
rotate(make_Process(u,s),0,I) =
make_Process(alt_Cy(alt_Reg(u,A,shift_left(a,sel_Flag(u,Cy))),sel_Bit_7(a)),s);
    {RAR}    a = sel_Reg(u,A) =>
rotate(make_Process(u,s),I,I) =
make_Process(alt_Cy(alt_Reg(u,A,shift_right(a,sel_Flag(u,Cy))),sel_Bit_0(a)),
               s) )
END;
```

```
LET ARITH_LOG :=
{the arithmetic/logic machine instructions}

IMPORT BIT INTO
IMPORT BYTE INTO
IMPORT WORD INTO
IMPORT STATE INTO
IMPORT REG INTO
IMPORT STREAM INTO
IMPORT PROCESS INTO
IMPORT FETCH_ARGS INTO
IMPORT ALU INTO
 CLASS
  FUNC arith_log_imm:  Process # Bit # Bit # Bit -> Process
{2nd operand is immediate}
  FUNC arith_log:  Process # Bit # Bit # Bit # Reg -> Process
{2nd operand is a register}

AXIOM
 FORALL  x1: Bit, x2: Bit, x3: Bit, b: Byte, r: Reg, u: State, s: Stream, p: Process
  ( {IMM} fetch_Byte(p) = make_Process_Byte_pair(make_Process(u,s),b) =>
          arith_log_imm(p,x1,x2,x3) = make_Process(alu(u,x1,x2,x3,b),s);
{adi, aci, sui, sbi, ani, xri, ori, cpi}
    {REG} arith_log(make_Process(u,s),x1,x2,x3,r) =
          make_Process(alu(u,x1,x2,x3,sel_Reg(u,r)),s) )
{add, adc, sub, sbb, ana, xra, ora, cmp}

 END;
```

```
LET STACK_OP :=
{the machine instructions that operate on the stack, except the call, which is specified
in JUMP later.}

IMPORT BYTE INTO
IMPORT WORD INTO
IMPORT STATE INTO
IMPORT STREAM INTO
IMPORT PROCESS INTO
IMPORT WORD_ARITH INTO
 CLASS
  FUNC push:  Process # Dreg -> Process
  FUNC pop:  Process # Dreg -> Process
  FUNC exch_ST_with_HL:  Process -> Process

AXIOM
 FORALL  b1: Byte, b2: Byte, w: Word, w1: Word, w2: Word, d: Dreg, u: State, s: Stream
  ( {PUSH} w2 = decr_Word(sel_Dreg(u,SP)) AND w1 = decr_Word(w2) AND
           sel_Dreg(u,d) = w =>
push(make_Process(u,write(w1,lower_Byte(w),write(w2,higher_Byte(w),s))),d) =
          make_Process(alt_Dreg(u,SP,w1),s);
    {POP} w1 = sel_Dreg(u,SP) AND w2 = incr_Word(w1) =>
pop(make_Process(u,read(w1,b1,read(w2,b2,s))),d) =
make_Process(alt_Dreg(alt_Dreg(u,d,make_Word(b1,b2)),SP,incr_Word(w2)),s);
    {XTHL} w1 = sel_Dreg(u,SP) AND w2 = incr_Word(w1) AND
           sel_Dreg(u,HL) = w =>
```

```
exch_ST_with_HL(
        make_Process(u,
        read(w1,b1,
        read(w2,b2,write(w1,lower_Byte(w),write(w2,higher_Byte(w),s)))))) =
         make_Process(alt_Dreg(u,HL,make_Word(b1,b2)),s) )
END;



LET JUMP :=
{the class of (conditional and unconditional) jump instructions}

IMPORT BIT INTO
IMPORT BYTE INTO
IMPORT WORD INTO
IMPORT STATE INTO
IMPORT STREAM INTO
IMPORT PROCESS INTO
IMPORT BYTE_EXT INTO
IMPORT WORD_ARITH INTO
IMPORT FETCH_ARGS INTO
IMPORT STACK_OP INTO
 CLASS
  FUNC jump:  Process -> Process
  FUNC call:  Process -> Process
  FUNC restart:  Process # Bit # Bit # Bit # Bit -> Process

AXIOM
  FORALL  x0: Bit, x1: Bit, x2: Bit, x3: Bit, w: Word, u: State, s: Stream,
          p: Process, p1: Process
  ( {JMP}  fetch_Word(p) = make_Process_Word_pair(make_Process(u,s),w) =>
              jump(p) = make_Process(alt_Dreg(u,PC,w),s);
    {CALL} fetch_Word(p) = make_Process_Word_pair(p1,w) AND
           push(p1,PC) = make_Process(u,s) =>
              call(p) = make_Process(alt_Dreg(u,PC,w),s);
{Note: 1st step: address fetched, 2nd step: PC pushed. This order must be followed,
because it affects the order of read and write operations. Hence it is observable.}
    {RST}  push(p,PC) = make_Process(u,s) =>
  restart(p,x0,x1,x2,x3) =
  make_Process(alt_Dreg(u,PC,make_Word(make_Byte(0,0,x0,x1,x2,x3,0,0),0_Byte)),s) )
{x0 is set to 0 for the restart instruction, and to I for the interrupts 5.5, 6.5, 7.5,
and trap}
 END;
```

```
LET HL_OP :=
{special machine instructions concerning the HL double register, except 'xthl' (in
STACK_OP), and 'dad' (in DAD)}

IMPORT STATE INTO
IMPORT STREAM INTO
IMPORT PROCESS INTO
 CLASS
  FUNC exch_DE_with_HL:  Process -> Process
{xchg}
  FUNC set_Dreg_from_HL:  Process # Dreg -> Process

AXIOM
 FORALL  d: Dreg, u: State, s: Stream
  ( {XCHG}       exch_DE_with_HL(make_Process(u,s)) =
make_Process(alt_Dreg(alt_Dreg(u,DE,sel_Dreg(u,HL)),HL,sel_Dreg(u,DE)),s);
    {PCHL_SPHL} set_Dreg_from_HL(make_Process(u,s),d) =
                 make_Process(alt_Dreg(u,d,sel_Dreg(u,HL)),s) )
END;




LET INTERRUPT :=
{the halt instruction, the interrupt enable/disable, and the interrupt mask read/send}

IMPORT BIT INTO
IMPORT STATE INTO
IMPORT REG INTO
IMPORT STREAM INTO
IMPORT PROCESS INTO
 CLASS
  FUNC stop:  Process -> Process
{hlt}
  FUNC send_int_mask:  Process -> Process
{sim}
  FUNC receive_int_mask:  Process -> Process
{rim}
  FUNC interrupt:  Process # Bit -> Process
{change the interrupt enable bit}

AXIOM
 FORALL  x: Bit, u: State, s: Stream
  ( {HLT}   stop(make_Process(u,s)) = make_Process(alt_Flipflop(u,halt,I),s);
    {DI_EI} interrupt(make_Process(u,s),x) =
            make_Process(alt_Flipflop(u,inte,x),s);
    {SIM}   send_int_mask(make_Process(u,s)) =
            make_Process(alt_int_mask(u,sel_Reg(u,A)),s);
{Bug: Behaviour not precisely modelled}
    {RIM}   receive_int_mask(make_Process(u,s)) =
            make_Process(alt_Reg(u,A,sel_int_mask(u)),s) )
{Bug: Behaviour not precisely modelled}

END;
```

A.4   Instruction Execution

```
LET DECODE :=
{to obtain the Reg, Dreg, Flag, resp. from their code.}

IMPORT BIT INTO
IMPORT STATE INTO
IMPORT REG INTO
IMPORT FLAG INTO
 CLASS
  FUNC decode_Dreg:  Bit # Bit -> Dreg
  FUNC decode_Reg:   Bit # Bit # Bit -> Reg
  FUNC decode_Flag:  Bit # Bit -> Flag

AXIOM
  ( {BC}          decode_Dreg(0,0) = BC;
   {DE}           decode_Dreg(I,0) = DE;
   {HL}           decode_Dreg(0,I) = HL;
   {SP}           decode_Dreg(I,I) = SP;
   {B}            decode_Reg(0,0,0) = B;
   {C}            decode_Reg(I,0,0) = C;
   {D}            decode_Reg(0,I,0) = D;
   {E}            decode_Reg(I,I,0) = E;
   {H}            decode_Reg(0,0,I) = H;
   {L}            decode_Reg(I,0,I) = L;
   {A}            decode_Reg(I,I,I) = A;
   {CY}           decode_Flag(0,0) = Cy;
   {Z}            decode_Flag(I,0) = Z;
   {P}            decode_Flag(0,I) = P;
   {S}            decode_Flag(I,I) = S )
END;
```

```
LET M_TEST :=
{a test for the 'M register' that respects its prominent role within the instruction
execution.}

IMPORT BOOL INTO
IMPORT BIT INTO
 CLASS
  FUNC equal_to_M:  Bit # Bit # Bit -> Bool

AXIOM
 FORALL  x1: Bit, x2: Bit, x3: Bit
  ( {M}        equal_to_M(0,I,I) = true;
   {NOT_M_1} equal_to_M(I,x2,x3) = false;
   {NOT_M_2} equal_to_M(x1,0,x3) = false;
   {NOT_M_3} equal_to_M(x1,x2,0) = false )
END;
```

LET EXECUTION :=
{The function execute takes a process and a byte of instruction code and delivers the
process that comes up after the instruction execution. Note that the size of this type
specification is inherently determined by the case analysis over the instruction codes.
To keep it reasonably small, each right hand side of a rewrite rule were made a call to
a function that is defined elsewhere. So the burden of the specification is spread among
various primitive types.}

```
IMPORT BOOL INTO
IMPORT BIT INTO
IMPORT BYTE INTO
IMPORT STATE INTO
IMPORT PROCESS INTO
IMPORT INTERRUPT INTO
IMPORT FETCH_ARGS INTO
IMPORT COND INTO
IMPORT SHIFT INTO
IMPORT LOAD_STORE INTO
IMPORT INCR_DECR_REG INTO
IMPORT INCR_DECR_DREG INTO
IMPORT DAD INTO
IMPORT DAA INTO
IMPORT A_OP INTO
IMPORT CY_OP INTO
IMPORT LXI INTO
IMPORT MOVE INTO
IMPORT ARITH_LOG INTO
IMPORT STACK_OP INTO
IMPORT JUMP INTO
IMPORT HL_OP INTO
IMPORT DECODE INTO
IMPORT M_TEST INTO
 CLASS
  FUNC execute: Process # Byte -> Process

AXIOM
 FORALL p: Process, x1: Bit, x2: Bit, x3: Bit, y1: Bit, y2: Bit, y3: Bit
 ( {NOP}        execute(p,make_Byte(0,0,0,0,0,0,0,0)) = p;
   {RIM}        execute(p,make_Byte(0,0,0,0,0,I,0,0)) =
                receive_int_mask(p);
   {SIM}        execute(p,make_Byte(0,0,0,0,I,I,0,0)) = send_int_mask(p);
   {LXI}        execute(p,make_Byte(I,0,0,0,x1,x2,0,0)) =
                load_Dreg_imm(p,decode_Dreg(x1,x2));
   {STAX}       execute(p,make_Byte(0,I,0,0,x1,0,0,0)) =
                store_A_by_Dreg(p,decode_Dreg(x1,0));
   {SHLD}       execute(p,make_Byte(0,I,0,0,0,I,0,0)) =
                store_HL_direct(p);
   {STA}        execute(p,make_Byte(0,I,0,0,I,I,0,0)) = store_A_direct(p);
   {INX}        execute(p,make_Byte(I,I,0,0,y1,y2,0,0)) =
                incr_Dreg(p,decode_Dreg(y1,y2));
   {DCX}        execute(p,make_Byte(I,I,0,I,y1,y2,0,0)) =
                decr_Dreg(p,decode_Dreg(y1,y2));
   {INR}        execute(p,make_Byte(0,0,I,y1,y2,y3,0,0)) =
                incr_Reg(p,decode_Reg(y1,y2,y3));
   {DCR}        execute(p,make_Byte(I,0,I,y1,y2,y3,0,0)) =
                decr_Reg(p,decode_Reg(y1,y2,y3));
```

```
    {MVI_TO_M}       execute(p,make_Byte(0,I,I,0,I,I,0,0)) = move_to_M_imm(p);
    {MVI_WITHOUT_M} equal_to_M(x1,x2,x3) = false =>
  execute(p,make_Byte(0,I,I,x1,x2,x3,0,0)) = move_imm(p,decode_Reg(x1,x2,x3));
    {ROTATE}         execute(p,make_Byte(I,I,I,x1,x2,0,0,0)) = rotate(p,x1,x2);
{ral, rar, rlc, rrc}
    {DAA}            execute(p,make_Byte(I,I,I,0,0,I,0,0)) = decimal_adjust(p);
    {STC}            execute(p,make_Byte(I,I,I,0,I,I,0,0)) = set_Cy(p);
    {DAD}            execute(p,make_Byte(I,0,0,I,x1,x2,0,0)) =
                       add_Dreg_to_HL(p,decode_Dreg(x1,x2));
    {LDAX}           execute(p,make_Byte(0,I,0,I,x1,0,0,0)) =
                       load_A_by_Dreg(p,decode_Dreg(x1,0));
    {LHLD}           execute(p,make_Byte(0,I,0,I,0,I,0,0)) = load_HL_direct(p);
    {LDA}            execute(p,make_Byte(0,I,0,I,I,I,0,0)) = load_A_direct(p);
    {CMA}            execute(p,make_Byte(I,I,I,I,0,I,0,0)) = compl_A(p);
    {CMC}            execute(p,make_Byte(I,I,I,I,I,I,0,0)) = compl_Cy(p);
    {MOV_WITHOUT_M} equal_to_M(y1,y2,y3) = false AND
                       equal_to_M(x1,x2,x3) = false =>
  execute(p,make_Byte(y1,y2,y3,x1,x2,x3,I,0)) =
                       move(p,decode_Reg(x1,x2,x3),decode_Reg(y1,y2,y3));
    {MOV_FROM_M}     equal_to_M(x1,x2,x3) = false =>
  execute(p,make_Byte(0,I,I,x1,x2,x3,I,0)) =
                       move_from_M(p,decode_Reg(x1,x2,x3));
    {MOV_TO_M}       equal_to_M(y1,y2,y3) = false =>
  execute(p,make_Byte(y1,y2,y3,0,I,I,I,0)) = move_to_M(p,decode_Reg(y1,y2,y3));
    {HLT}            execute(p,make_Byte(0,I,I,0,I,I,I,0)) = stop(p);
    {ALU}            execute(p,make_Byte(x1,x2,x3,y1,y2,y3,0,I)) =
                       arith_log(p,y1,y2,y3,decode_Reg(x1,x2,x3));
{add, adc, sub, sbb, ana, xra, ora, cmp}
    {RET_COND}       execute(p,make_Byte(0,0,0,x1,x2,x3,I,I)) =
                       cond(p,decode_Flag(x2,x3),x1,pop(p,PC));
{rnz, rnc, rpo, rp, rz, rc, rpe, rm}
    {POP_PSW}        execute(p,make_Byte(I,0,0,0,I,I,I,I)) = pop(p,PSW);
    {POP_1}          execute(p,make_Byte(I,0,0,0,x1,0,I,I)) =
                       pop(p,decode_Dreg(x1,0));
    {POP_2}          execute(p,make_Byte(I,0,0,0,0,x2,I,I)) =
                       pop(p,decode_Dreg(0,x2));
    {JMP_COND}       execute(p,make_Byte(0,I,0,x1,x2,x3,I,I)) =
                       cond(drop_Byte(p),decode_Flag(x2,x3),x1,jump(p));
{jnz, jnc, jpo, jp, jz, jc, jpe, jm}
{1st step: 1st Byte fetched, 2nd step: test on condition}
    {JMP}            execute(p,make_Byte(I,I,0,0,0,0,I,I)) = jump(p);
    {OUT}            execute(p,make_Byte(I,I,0,0,I,0,I,I)) = out_A(p);
    {XTHL}           execute(p,make_Byte(I,I,0,0,0,I,I,I)) =
                       exch_ST_with_HL(p);
    {DI_EI}          execute(p,make_Byte(I,I,0,x1,I,I,I,I)) = interrupt(p,x1);
    {CALL_COND}      execute(p,make_Byte(0,0,I,x1,x2,x3,I,I)) =
                       cond(drop_Byte(p),decode_Flag(x2,x3),x1,call(p));
{cnz, cnc, cpo, cp, cz, cc, cpe, cm}
{see also the conditional jumps}
    {PUSH_PSW}       execute(p,make_Byte(I,0,I,0,I,I,I,I)) = push(p,PSW);
    {PUSH_1}         execute(p,make_Byte(I,0,I,0,x1,0,I,I)) =
                       push(p,decode_Dreg(x1,0));
    {PUSH_2}         execute(p,make_Byte(I,0,I,0,0,x2,I,I)) =
                       push(p,decode_Dreg(0,x2));
    {ALU_IMM}        execute(p,make_Byte(0,I,I,x1,x2,x3,I,I)) =
                       arith_log_imm(p,x1,x2,x3);
```

```
{adi, aci, sui, sbi, ani, xri, ori, cpi}
     {RST}          execute(p,make_Byte(I,I,I,x1,x2,x3,I,I)) =
                       restart(p,0,x1,x2,x3);
     {RET}          execute(p,make_Byte(I,0,0,I,0,0,I,I)) = pop(p,PC);
     {PCHL}         execute(p,make_Byte(I,0,0,I,0,I,I,I)) =
                       set_Dreg_from_HL(p,PC);
     {SPHL}         execute(p,make_Byte(I,0,0,I,I,I,I,I)) =
                       set_Dreg_from_HL(p,SP);
     {IN}           execute(p,make_Byte(I,I,0,I,I,0,I,I)) = in_A(p);
     {XCHG}         execute(p,make_Byte(I,I,0,I,0,I,I,I)) =
                       exch_DE_with_HL(p);
     {CALL}         execute(p,make_Byte(I,0,I,I,0,0,I,I)) = call(p) )
END;


LET RUN :=
{run a process}

IMPORT BIT INTO
IMPORT BYTE INTO
IMPORT WORD INTO
IMPORT STATE INTO
IMPORT STREAM INTO
IMPORT PROCESS INTO
IMPORT INCR_DECR_DREG INTO
IMPORT EXECUTION INTO
 CLASS
  FUNC step:  Process -> Process
  FUNC run:  Process -> Process

AXIOM
 FORALL b: Byte, w: Word, u: State, s: Stream, p: Process
  ( {ONESTEP} sel_Dreg(u,PC) = w =>
step(make_Process(u,opcode(w,b,s))) =
                execute(incr_Dreg(make_Process(u,s),PC),b);
     {HALT}    sel_Flipflop(sel_State(p),halt) = I => run(p) = p;
     {LOOP}    sel_Flipflop(sel_State(p),halt) = 0 => run(p) = run(step(p)) )
END

SYSTEM NONE
```

Appendix B. Task specifications

B.1 Instruction Evaluations

```
task EVAL_ADC
basedon BIT, BYTE, WORD, STATE, REG, TRIV_STATE, STREAM, PROCESS,
        BYTE_EXT, EXECUTION
unknown b: Byte

goals exist (w: Word, u: State, s: Stream)
   u = alt_Dreg(alt_Dreg(triv_State,PSW,
                         make_Word(make_Byte(I,I,I,I,0,0,I,0),I_Byte)),
                BC,make_Word(0_Byte,make_Byte(0,I,0,I,I,0,I,I))),
   b = sel_Reg(sel_State(execute(make_Process(u,s),
                                 make_Byte(0,0,0,I,0,0,0,I))),A)
   {adc B}
endoftask


task EVAL_LXI
basedon BIT, BYTE, WORD, STATE, TRIV_STATE, STREAM, PROCESS,
        BYTE_EXT, WORD_ARITH, EXECUTION
unknown w1: Word

goals exist (w: Word, u: State, s, s0: Stream)
   u = alt_Dreg(alt_Dreg(triv_State,PSW,
                         make_Word(make_Byte(I,I,I,I,0,0,I,0),I_Byte)),
                BC,make_Word(make_Byte(0,I,0,I,I,0,I,I),0_Byte)),
   s = read(w,make_Byte(0,0,I,I,0,0,I,I),
            read(incr_Word(w),make_Byte(0,0,0,I,I,I,I,I),s0)),
   w1 = sel_Dreg(sel_State(execute(make_Process(u,s),
                                   make_Byte(I,0,0,0,0,0,0,0))),BC)
   {lxi B}
endoftask


task EVAL_PUSH
basedon BIT, BYTE, WORD, STATE, TRIV_STATE, STREAM, PROCESS,
        WORD_ARITH, EXECUTION
unknown p: Process

goals exist (b1, b2: Byte, w, w1: Word, u: State, s, s0: Stream)
   w = make_Word(make_Byte(0,0,0,I,I,0,0,0),make_Byte(I,I,0,I,0,I,0,0)),
   u = alt_Dreg(alt_Dreg(triv_State,DE,
                         make_Word(make_Byte(0,0,I,I,0,0,I,I),
                                   make_Byte(0,0,0,I,I,I,I,I))),
                SP,w1),
   s = write(w,b1,write(incr_Word(w),b2,s0)),
   p = execute(make_Process(u,s),make_Byte(I,0,I,0,I,0,I,I))
   {push D}
endoftask
```

```
task EVAL_POP
basedon BIT, BYTE, WORD, STATE, TRIV_STATE, STREAM, PROCESS,
        WORD_ARITH, EXECUTION
unknown psw: Word

goals exist(b1, b2: Byte, w: Word, u: State, s, s0: Stream)

  w = make_Word(make_Byte(0,0,0,I,I,0,0,0),make_Byte(I,I,0,I,0,I,0,0)),
  u = alt_Dreg(alt_Dreg(triv_State,PSW,
                        make_Word(make_Byte(0,0,I,I,0,0,I,I),
                                  make_Byte(0,0,0,I,I,I,I,I))),
               SP,w),
  s = read(w,make_Byte(0,0,I,I,0,0,I,I),
           read(incr_Word(w),make_Byte(0,I,0,I,0,I,0,I),s0)),
  psw = sel_Dreg(sel_State(execute(make_Process(u,s),
                                   make_Byte(I,0,0,0,I,I,I,I))),PSW)

  {pop PSW}
endoftask


task EVAL_RET
basedon BIT, BYTE, WORD, STATE, TRIV_STATE, STREAM, PROCESS,
        WORD_ARITH, EXECUTION
unknown pc, sp: Word

goals exist (w: Word, u, u1: State, s, s0: Stream)
  w = make_Word(make_Byte(0,0,0,I,I,0,0,0),make_Byte(I,I,0,I,0,I,0,0)),
  u = alt_Dreg(triv_State,SP,w),
  s = read(w,make_Byte(0,0,I,I,0,0,I,I),
           read(incr_Word(w),make_Byte(0,I,0,I,0,I,0,I),s0)),
  u1 = sel_State(execute(make_Process(u,s),make_Byte(I,0,0,I,0,0,I,I))),
  {ret}
  pc = sel_Dreg(u1,PC),
  sp = sel_Dreg(u1,SP)
endoftask
```

```
task STEP_CMA
{runs a cma instruction}

basedon BIT, BYTE, WORD, STATE, STREAM, PROCESS, TRIV_STATE, RUN
unknown p: Process

goals exist (w: Word, s: Stream)
  p = step(make_Process(triv_State,opcode(w,make_Byte(I,I,I,I,0,I,0,0),s)))
  {cma}
endoftask


task STEP_CALL
{runs a call instruction and gives its protocol}

basedon BIT, BYTE, WORD, STATE, STREAM, PROCESS, TRIV_STATE, RUN
unknown s: Stream, p: Process

goals exist (w: Word)
  p = step(make_Process(triv_State,opcode(w,make_Byte(I,0,I,I,0,0,I,I),s)))
  {call ...}
endoftask


task PROG2
{a small program run}

basedon BIT, BYTE, WORD, STATE, STREAM, PROCESS, TRIV_STATE, RUN
unknown psw: Word

goals exist (w1, w2, w3, w4, w5, w6, w7, w8: Word, s1, s2: Stream)
  s1 = opcode(w1,make_Byte(I,0,0,0,0,I,0,0) {lxi h ...},
         read(w2,make_Byte(0,0,0,0,I,I,I,I),
         read(w3,make_Byte(I,I,I,I,0,0,0,0),
       opcode(w4,make_Byte(0,I,I,I,I,I,I,0) {mov A M},
         read(w5,make_Byte(I,I,I,I,I,I,I,0),
       opcode(w6,make_Byte(0,0,I,I,I,I,0,0) {inr A},
       opcode(w7,make_Byte(I,I,I,0,I,I,0,0) {stc},
       opcode(w8,make_Byte(0,I,I,0,I,I,I,0) {hlt},
             s2)))))))),
  psw = sel_Dreg(sel_State(run(make_Process(triv_State,s1))),PSW)
endoftask
```

B.2 Matching

```
task EXEC_XRI
basedon BIT, BYTE, WORD, STATE, REG, STREAM, PROCESS, EXECUTION
unknown p: Process

goals exist (w: Word, u: State, s: Stream)
  sel_Reg(u,A) = make_Byte(I,I,I,I,O,O,I,O),
  p = execute(make_Process(u,read(w,make_Byte(O,I,O,I,I,O,I,I),s)),
              make_Byte(O,I,I,I,O,I,I,I))
  {xri D}
endoftask


task EXEC_SBB
{schematic, implicit evaluation of 'sbb B'. The informal definition is
 drawn from [intel 79], page 3-57. }

basedon BIT, BYTE, STATE, REG, FLAG, STREAM, PROCESS, EXECUTION
unknown Accu: Byte, Carry, Sign, Zero, Parity, AuxCarry: Bit

goals exist (u1, u2: State, s1, s2: Stream)
  sel_Reg(u1,A) = make_Byte(O,O,I,O,O,O,O,O),
  sel_Reg(u1,B) = make_Byte(O,I,O,O,O,O,O,O),
  sel_Flag(u1,Cy) = I,
  make_Process(u2,s2) =
  execute(make_Process(u1,s1),make_Byte(O,O,O,I,I,O,O,I)), {sbb B}
  Accu = sel_Reg(u2,A),
  Carry = sel_Flag(u2,Cy),
  Sign = sel_Flag(u2,S),
  Zero = sel_Flag(u2,Z),
  Parity = sel_Flag(u2,P),
  AuxCarry = sel_Flag(u2,Ac)
endoftask


task TRIAL
{searching for all pairs of bytes where after addition, Cy is reset, and one
 of the arguments is left unchanged.}

basedon BIT, BYTE, RESULT, ADD_BYTE
unknown b1, b2: Byte

goals exist (x: Bit)
  add_Byte(b1,b2,I) = make_Result(b1,x,O)
endoftask


task ADD0
basedon BIT, BYTE, BYTE_EXT, RESULT, ADD_BYTE
unknown b1: Byte

goals exist (x: Bit)
  add_Byte(b1,I_Byte,I) = make_Result(b1,x,O)
endoftask
```

```
task OSPEC
basedon BIT, BYTE, RESULT, ADD_BYTE
unknown b: Byte

goals
  cy(add_Byte(b,make_Byte(I,I,I,I,I,I,I,I),0)) = 0
endoftask


task DOUB
basedon BIT, BYTE, RESULT, ADD_BYTE
unknown x: Bit, d: Byte

goals
  make_Byte(O,I,I,O,I,O,I,O) = byte(add_Byte(d,d,x))
endoftask
```

B.3   Simple Direct Proofs

```
task XCHG2
{direct proof that 'xchg' is of degree 2}

basedon BIT, BYTE, WORD, PROCESS, EXECUTION
unknown x1, x2: Process

goals exist (i: Byte)
  i = make_Byte(I,I,0,I,0,I,I,I), {xchg}
  x2 = execute(execute(x1,i),i)
endoftask


task RAR9
{direct proof that 'rar' is of degree 9}

basedon BIT, BYTE, WORD, PROCESS, EXECUTION
unknown p1, p2: Process

goals exist (i: Byte)
  i = make_Byte(I,I,I,I,I,0,0,0), {rar}
  p2 = execute(execute(execute(execute(execute(execute(execute(
        execute(execute(p1,i),i),i),i),i),i),i),i),i)
endoftask


task MATCH_RAL_ADC
{comparison between 'ral' and 'adc A'}

basedon BIT, BYTE, PROCESS, EXECUTION
unknown p: Process

goals
  execute(p,make_Byte(I,I,I,0,I,0,0,0)) = {ral}
  execute(p,make_Byte(I,I,I,I,0,0,0,I)) {adc A}
endoftask


task MOVCC
{direct proof that 'mov C C' is equivalent to 'nop'}

basedon BIT, BYTE, PROCESS, BYTE_EXT, EXECUTION
unknown p1, p2: Process

goals
  execute(p2,0_Byte) =  {nop}
  execute(p1,make_Byte(I,0,0,I,0,0,I,0))  {mov C C}
endoftask
```

B.4 Instruction Synthesis

```
task SYNT_CLEAR
{searching for all codes of instruction that clear Cy and leave A unchanged}

basedon BIT, BYTE, STATE, REG, FLAG, STREAM, PROCESS, EXECUTION
unknown i: Byte

goals exist (u1, u2: State, s1, s2: Stream)
  execute(make_Process(u1,s1),i) = make_Process(u2,s2),
  sel_Reg(u2,A) = sel_Reg(u1,A),
  sel_Flag(u2,Cy) = 0,
  sel_Flag(u1,Cy) = I
endoftask


task SEARCH
{searching for all states where 'adc E' clears Cy and leaves A unchanged}

basedon BIT, BYTE, STATE, REG, FLAG, STREAM, PROCESS, DECODE, EXECUTION
unknown u1: State

goals exist (x1, x2, x3: Bit; u2: State, s1, s2: Stream)
  execute(make_Process(u1,s1),make_Byte(I,I,0,I,0,0,0,I) {adc E}) =
make_Process(u2,s2),
  sel_Reg(u2,A) = sel_Reg(u1,A),
  sel_Flag(u2,Cy) = 0,
  sel_Flag(u1,Cy) = I
endoftask


task SYNT_MINUS
{searching for all codes of instruction that set S without changing A}

basedon BIT, BYTE, STATE, REG, FLAG, STREAM, PROCESS, EXECUTION
unknown i: Byte

goals exist (u1, u2: State, s1, s2: Stream)
  sel_Flag(u2,S) = I,
  sel_Flag(u1,S) = 0,
  sel_Reg(u2,A) = sel_Reg(u1,A),
  execute(make_Process(u1,s1),i) = make_Process(u2,s2)
endoftask
```

Specification and Prototyping of a Compiler for a Small Applicative Language

Heinrich Hussmann
Christian Rank
Universität Passau
Postfach 2540
D-8390 Passau

Abstract

A compiler for a simple applicative language into stack-oriented
target code is specified within the RAP/COLD specification language. Some experiments with the RAP tool are summarized.
Using this example, different approaches to an implementation
of this algebraic specification are compared: interpretation of the
specification by RAP, automatic compilation into PASCAL code
and hand-written C code.

1. Introduction

This article summarizes an experiment in algebraic programming. As a non-trivial example for an
algebraic specification, the compilation of a simple applicative programming language (called AS)
with recursive functions into stack-machine code (called KMS) has been treated. This comprises
the specification of

- an interpreter for the language
- an interpreter for the stack machine
- a compiler from AS to KMS.

The specification has been carried out in a modular (hierarchical) way, according to
[Wirsing et al. 83]. The specification is written in the RAP sublanguage of COLD (see [Huss-
mann, Geser 88]). The RAP system ([Hussmann 85/87]) has been used for some experiments on
the specification.

The most natural specification for the language interpreter is to give explicitly recursive definitions
of the interpreter functions. For the compiler, the simplest specification could be, in a rather
implicit style:

$\forall$ p: program, d: data: interpret_KMS(compile(p),d) = interpret_AS(p,d)

could be considered. For this approach, the question of consistency arises: It has to be shown
that there is a hierarchical model satisfying the axiom. In this paper. we go around this difficulty
by giving a constructive specification of the compiler, i.e. we describe all details of the generated
code explicitly, by recursive definitions. The equation above has to be proven as a theorem relying
on the detailed specification. (This verification proof is subject of ongoing work.)

For the explicit specifications, we can use not only the RAP interpreter ([Hussmann 85/87])
but also an experimental compiler from RAP/COLD specifications into PASCAL ([Geser, Huss-

mann, Mueck 88]). The efficiency of the PASCAL code produced by this tool has been compared with the RAP interpreter and with "custom-made" hand-written code (in C).

This article is structured as follows: The second section gives a definition of the source language AS by an algebraic specification of an interpreter. The definition of the target language KMS is surveyed in the third section. Section 4 contains a description of the compiler from AS to KMS, explaining in detail how the translation of recursive procedures is performed. The last section concerns the comparison of different ways to obtain a prototype implementation of the given algebraic specifications.

The whole experiment was carried out by Christian Rank, under the supervision of Heinrich Hussmann and Martin Wirsing. A more detailed version of this paper is available as a technical report ([Rank 88]).

To obtain a better readability of the specfications presented in this paper, we use a slightly more flexible notation than strict RAP/COLD syntax. For terms, a mixfix (display) style is used, and particularly functions with arity > 1 are expressed by special abbreviating operator symbols. Moreover, these symbols can be overloaded, i. e. distinct functions with different functionalities are displayed with the same operator symbol. This applies in particular for two symbols: ε denotes an empty list (of parameters, definitions, expressions or values), _o_ the concatenation of two arbitrary lists of the same type. The operands of o can be single list elements, too; they are implicitly converted into lists of one element. Occasionally, enumerations in angle brackets are used for the notation of lists.

2. The Semantics of AS – an Interpreter for AS

2.1. Informal Description

AS (from German "Applikative Sprache", [Broy 86]) is a simple applicative language. It comprises the declaration of (recursive) functions and the evaluation of expressions built up of basic arithmetic operations, if-then-else constructs and function applications. The evaluation of an expression always yields an integer result.

As an example for the syntax of AS we consider the program for calculating the factorial function from a given input value:

```
input M
functions G(X) =
   if X=0 then 1
          else X*G(X-1)
   fi
output G(M)
end
```

When an AS program is run, every input identifier is assigned a value from a list of values to be supplied. The list of input values must be as long as the list of input parameters. Evaluation of expressions is done by using the ususal call-by-value semantics.

The context conditions of AS are as follows:
– The global identifiers (input- and function identifiers) must be unique, i. e. they must not be declared twice. In particular, an input identifier must not occur as a function identifier and vice versa. Likewise, the formal parameter lists of any function must be unique.

- A function call <ident>(<exp_list>) requires a declaration of a function <ident>; its function-ality must correspond to the length of the <exp_list> (i. e. the number of actual parameters).
- All identifiers occurring in expressions which are not followed by a parenthesized <exp_list> (and therefore being no function calls) must be visible during evaluation, i. e. they must be input parameters or – within a function body – formal parameters of this function. These identifiers are called variable identifiers.

The values of the expressions occurring in the output list are entered into a list of output values (which is the output of the interpreter).

Scanning and parsing of AS programs are not treated here. The specified interpreter takes the AS program in abstract syntax as input.

2.2. Abstract Syntax of AS

Below, the abstract syntax for AS is given in a BNF-like notation. It is quite obvious how this description of the syntax can be translated into a RAP/COLD specification: Every nontermi-nal symbol corresponds to a sort in the corresponding algebraic specification, every syntax rule corresponds to a constructor operation.

```
<Prog>       ::=   program(<Par_list>,<Def_list>,<Exp_list>)
<Par_list>   ::=   emptypar | appendpar(<Ident>,<Par_list>)
<Def_list>   ::=   emptydef | appenddef(<Def>,<Def_list>)
<Exp_list>   ::=   emptyexp | appendexp(<Exp>,<Exp_list>)
<Val_list>   ::=   emptyval | appendval(<Int>,<Val_list>)
<Def>        ::=   funct(<Ident>,<Par_list>,<Exp>)
<Exp>        ::=   const(<Int>) | var(<Ident>) | neg(<Exp>) |
                   [plusop | minusop | multop | divop](<Exp>,<Exp>) |
                   if(<Exp>,[EQ | LT | LE],<Exp>,<Exp>,<Exp>) |
                   appl(<Ident>,<Exp_list>)
<Ident>      ::=   F | G | M | N | X | Y
<Int>        ::=   int([plus | minus],<Nat>)
<Nat>        ::=   zero | succ(<Nat>)
```

Within the RAP/COLD specification (omitted here) we use the same operation and sort names as in this syntax.

2.3. Context Checking and Identifier Management

To implement the interpreter (and later on the compiler), we need two more abstract data types, for the context check, and for the management of the values for identifiers ("environment"). Both types are only sketched here.

For the purpose of context checking we define the type CONTEXT, which comprises four global functions (visible outside the type) and some auxiliary functions: The global functions are
    allunique: Prog $\rightarrow$ Bool
which checks the uniqueness of global identifiers and formal parameters,
    unique: Par_list $\rightarrow$ Bool
which checks the uniqueness of an arbitrary list of identifiers,
    matchlist: Par_list # Val_list $\rightarrow$ Bool
which tests if the length of a parameter list agrees with the length of the value list, and
    aritycheck: Def_list # Exp_list $\rightarrow$ Bool

which checks both if a function used in a call is declared and the declaration has the same arity as the call.

The management of identifiers is done with the type ENVIRONMENT, which defines the sort Env (short for environment). An environment can be constructed in the usual way from a constructor
    emptyenv: → Env
for the empty environment (in the text displayed by ε) and a constructor
    upd: Env # Ident # Int → Env
for appending a new entry to an environment, displayed here by
    <Env>[<Ident>←<Int>].
The access to a certain identifier in the environment takes place by using the function
    val: Env # Ident → Int
(symbolically <Env>[<Ident>]). The function
    isentry: Env # Ident → Bool
checks whether a certain identifier is already present in the environment. It is used to implement the static binding of identifiers. To assign the actual parameters to the formal ones in a function call, we need the function
    updlist: Env # Par_list # Val_list → Env,
which works as follows:
    updlist(e,ε,ε) = e
    updlist(e,x o p,n o v) = updlist(e[x←n],p,v)
Note that this function is only defined for parameter and value lists of equal length.

2.4. The Type AS_INTERPRETER

We define the semantics of AS by specifying an interpreter for it. In general an interpreter is a function
    〚 〛: Prg # Input → Output
with Prg being the set of permitted programs, Input the set of input values, Output the set of output values. In practice, the set of permitted programs contains erroneous programs, too. For AS, we restrict the error handling to a minimum: if the program is incorrect or the interpretation detects errors, this can be noted only in the fact that the RAP system does not find a solution. On the specification level this means just underspecification: an arbitrary result is allowed for the error cases. (A more comfortable error handling by introduction of special error elements would lead to a much more complex specification.)

The interpreter itself is rather straightforward, its functions and axioms are listed in figure 1. The auxiliary function
    lookup: Ident # Def_list → Def
used there is assumed to search for a definition in a definition list.

2.5. Example

Here is a short example to show that the AS interpreter works. We interpret the factorial program, shown here in concrete AS syntax:
    program =
    input M
    functions G(X) = if X=0 then 1 else X * G(X-1) fi
    output M, G(M)
    end

This program was executed symbolically by RAP using the specification of the interpreter above.

Functions:

    interpret: Prog # Val_list → Val_list,

    evalexplist: Explist # Def_list # Env # Env → Val_list,

    evalexp: Exp # Def_list # Env # Env → Int,

    evalfun: Def # Def_list # Val_list # Env # Env → Int

Axioms:

    allunique(program(in,d,out)) ∧ matchlist(in,v) ⇒

        interpret(program(in,d,out),v) = evalexplist(out,d,updlist(ε,in,v),ε)

    evalexplist(ε,d,b,l) = ε

    evalexplist(e ∘ el,d,b,l) = evalexp(e,d,b,l) ∘ evalexplist(el,d,b,l)

    evalexp(const(n),d,b,l) = n

    isentry(l,x) ⇒ evalexp(var(x),d,b,l) = l[x]

    ¬isentry(l,x) ⇒ evalexp(var(x),d,b,l) = b[x]

    evalexp(neg(e),d,b,l) = −evalexp(e,d,b,l)

    evalexp(plusop(e1,e2),d,b,l) = evalexp(e1,d,b,l) + evalexp(e2,d,b,l)

    {and similarly for minusop, multop, divop}

    evalexp(e1,d,b,l) = evalexp(e2,d,b,l) ⇒

        evalexp(if(e1,EQ,e2,e3,e4),d,b,l) = evalexp(e3,d,b,l)

    evalexp(e1,d,b,l) ≠ evalexp(e2,d,b,l) ⇒

        evalexp(if(e1,EQ,e2,e3,e4),d,b,l) = evalexp(e4,d,b,l)

    {and similarly for LE and LT}

    evalexp(appl(x,el),d,b,l) = evalfun(lookup(x,d),d,evalexplist(el,d,b,l),b,l)

    matchlist(p,v) ⇒ evalfun(funct(x,p,e),d,v,b,l) = evalexp(e,d,b,updlist(ε,p,v))

Fig. 1: The functions and axioms for the AS interpreter

The capability of the RAP system to solve systems of equations by conditional narrowing ([Hussmann 85]) was used to formulate a rather general task: The required input was specified as a list consisting of one element, a RAP "unknown" variable x for a natural number. The output was assigned to the RAP "unknown" v (for a list of integers), so the task altogether looks like:

    v = interpret($program$,$< +x>$)

A sample run of this task should yield a value table of the factorial function. We get

x	v	CPU time[1]
−0	<−0, +1>	6.73 sec.
+0	<+0, +1>	7.58 sec.
+1	<+1, +1>	13.45 sec.
+2	<+2, +2>	20.80 sec.
+3	<+3, +6>	28.92 sec.
+4	<+4, +24>	46.00 sec.
+5	<+5, +120>	315.12 sec.

...

Note that the execution time increases largely with the size of the input variable. Moreover, the input value 0 yields two solutions. This is not surprising, since integers were constructed as the cartesian product of a sign and a natural number, so the integer 0 has two representations.

---

[1] when executed on a SUN 3/160 with 4 Mb RAM

2.6. An Experiment in Program Synthesis

An even more interesting alternative to simple evaluation of given programs is suggested by the features of RAP: Equation systems can be used to generate programs from given input and output values. Such tasks for "program synthesis" are known as very complicated. For theoretical reasons, one cannot expect to synthesize recursive function definitions. Nevertheless, is is recommendable to do some experiments with program synthesis.

Pretty naively, we start with the following task:

   interpret($p,<+1>$) = $<+2>$,

with p being the program wanted. This task was executed with RAP search strategy "smallest first".

After a few seconds the trivial programs appear:

   input x **functions** ε **output** +2 **end**
   input x **functions** ε **output** –(–2) **end**

After more than 800 CPU seconds the generated programs start to make use of the input parameter:

   $p =$ **input** F **functions** ε **output** 1+F **end**

Close to reaching the time limit of 3000 CPU seconds, solutions like

   $p =$ **input** F **functions** ε **output** F+F **end**

are found.

We can get more interesting solutions if we specialize the task in a certain way: We specify certain parts of the wanted program and ask the RAP system to compute the rest. We choose as an example

   $p =$ **input** i **functions** G(X) = **if** X it $n1$ **then** $n2$ **else** $n3$ **fi** **output** G(M), G(2) **end**
   interpret($p,<+1>$) = $<+1, +2>$

where i is a variable for identifiers, it is a variable for the type of condition (=, <, ≤) and $n1$, $n2$, $n3$ are variables for integer numbers. This task yields all four possible solutions and even terminates after about 400 CPU seconds:

   if X=+1 **then** +1 **else** +2 **fi**
   if X≤+1 **then** +1 **else** +2 **fi**
   if X<+2 **then** +1 **else** +2 **fi**
   if X=+2 **then** +2 **else** +1 **fi**

3. KMS – a Machine Oriented Language

To implement an AS compiler, we must define a suitable target language first. Here we choose the stack machine language (KMS from German "Kellermaschinensprache") introduced in [Broy 86], which has a relatively simple instruction set.

3.1. Structure of the Stack Machine

The stack machine (a zero address machine) comprises a code area (memory for instructions) and a stack. The code area consists of 2^{n1} memory cells, numbered from 1 upwards (= addresses of the cells). The code area contains an executable KMS program starting at address 1, where every cell up to the end of the program contains one KMS instruction[2]. There is an instruction counter

---

[2] The concrete representation of KMS instructions is not discussed here; they are denoted by english keywords.

which points to the instruction to be performed next. Program execution is sequential by default, i. e. instruction by instruction, unless a jump instruction is encountered. All KMS instructions have no explicitly specified operands (that is the reason for the name "zero address machine"). The operands have to be supplied via the stack, and the results are pushed on the stack, too.

The stack contains 2^{n2} cells, each of them able to store an integer value. The cells are numbered from 1 upwards. The management of the stack is done with the help of a pointer which contains the address of the element at the top of the stack. The stack grows starting at address 1 to the higher addresses. There is no KMS instruction for explicit manipulation of the stack pointer. The usual concept of stacks is extended in the way that there is a random access to cells located beyond the stack pointer.

The execution of a KMS program starts with an empty stack at address 1 of the instruction memory and stops when a special termination instruction is encountered.

3.2. The KMS Instruction Set

This section describes the KMS instruction set. We use the following format:

in_1 in_2 ... in_m **instruction** out_1 out_2 ... out_n

instruction gives the name of an instruction whic needs m arguments. To the left of the instruction name the names of the m elements on top of the stack are listed (if there are no such elements, this is indicated by a minus sign). The element in_m is the top element of the stack. Likewise, to the right of the instruction name the state of the stack top after execution of the instruction is listed. If the elements left of the instruction name do not occur on the right hand side this means that the input elements were popped off the stack. If the stack does not contain the required number of elements before instruction execution, an error occurs.

Below follows the table of the KMS instructions:

op **MINUS** −op	Inverts the top element of the stack.
op_2 op_1 **ADD|MULT|DIV** op_2+op_1	Replaces the two top elements by their sum resp. product resp integer quotient.
target op_2 op_1 **IF=|IF<=|IF<** −	If $op_2 =\|\leq\|< op_1$, program execution continues at address **target**. In this case, **target** must be a valid address. In the other case nothing happens. Anyway, the three top elements are popped off the stack.
target **GOTO** −	Program execution continues at address **target**.
item **FREE** −	Deletes (i. e. pops) the top element.
− **<intnum>** <intnum>	Pushes <intnum> onto the stack.
− **COUNT** dp	The depth of the stack valid prior to instruction execution (i. e. the value of the stack pointer) + 1 is pushed onto the stack.
data adrs **STORE** data	The integer data is stored at stack address adrs. The address must be less than the current value of the stack pointer.

adrs **LOAD** data	The top element of the stack (containing adrs) is replaced by the contents **data** of the stack cell at **adrs**. The address must be less than or equal to the current value of the stack pointer. (Like STORE, this instruction extends the stack machine concept by random access.)
data **PRINT** data	The top element data is written to output.
– **READ** item	An integer is read from input and pushed onto the stack.
⊢ **STOP** ⊢	Termination of KMS program execution. The stack must be empty before this instruction is encountered. (This fact is denoted by the symbol ⊢).

An interpreter for KMS has been defined in RAP, analoguously to the AS interpreter. We skip the details here.

3.3. An Example

The following KMS program reads an input value n, iteratively calculates the factorial of this value and prints the result. The input value is stored in stack cell 1, it is used simultaneously as a loop counter. The intermediate result is located on top of the stack at the beginning of the loop.

```
 1:      READ    % reads input value N (in stack cell 1)
 2:      1       % default value for result
 3:      21      % jump address for termination
 4:      1
 5:      LOAD    % N
 6:      0
 7:      IF=     % N = 0 ? yes -> jump to address 21
 8:      1
 9:      LOAD    % N
10:      MULT    % multiply with intermediate result
11:      1
12:      LOAD    % N := N - 1
13:      1
14:      MINUS
15:      ADD
16:      1
17:      STORE
18:      FREE    % remove N from stack
19:      3
20:      GOTO    % back to beginning of loop
21:      PRINT   % print final result
22:      FREE    % and remove it from the stack
23:      FREE    % remove counter N from stack
24:      STOP
```

If this program is interpreted with the specified KMS interpreter on the RAP system, we obtain the following computation times (in CPU seconds) depending on the input value n:

n	result	time
0	1	4.07
1	1	11.13
2	2	18.12
3	6	25.70
4	24	33.27

```
5   120   40.00
6   720   47.35
```

Corresponding to the iterative character of this factorial program, execution time increases linear with the input value: The termination case needs about 4 seconds, and every loop pass needs additional 7 seconds.

4. Compiling AS Programs to KMS

4.1. The Strategy

For a better understanding of the specification of the AS compiler, we introduce its concepts by words. The strategy of compiling was essentially taken from [Broy 86]. Motivation (and a complete understanding) of the concepts introduced in this section partially will not be clear before the description of the compiler specification in a later section.

Due to the relative simplicity of AS, translation can essentially be syntax directed. However, one must remember the location of variables by means of an environment. The translation does not directly deliver a KMS program, but an object of a special intermediate language which contains all KMS instructions and some additional instructions. The intermediate language is described briefly in the next section.

The main problem in compilation is the organization of identifiers and the evaluation of expressions with the help of the stack. We use the stack in the following way: The stack cells 1 and 2 are reserved for special management purposes. The next cells contain the values of the input parameters, thus, address 3 contains the value of the first input parameter, address 4 contains the value of the second input parameter, and so on up to address $n+2$ which contains the value of the n-th input parameter. Therefore, input parameters can be accessed via these addresses. The first $n+2$ stack cells are allocated until end of program and must be released on termination. Stack cells from addresses $n+3$ upwards are used for evaluation of expressions. Evaluation follows the principle that the result of evaluation is placed on top of the stack (see figure 2).

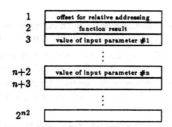

Fig. 2: The stack organization of the stack machine

During compilation, two environments are carried along, which contain pairs of an identifier and its stack address. The global environment contains the input parameters with the absolute stack addresses of their values .

The local environment is used for the formal parameters of functions. The relative addresses of the parameters are entered into the local environment, where the addresses are relative to a certain offset located in stack cell 1. The need for relative addressing arises out of the fact that a function can be called several times, so the parameter values passed via the stack could be located at different addresses (which are not fixed at compile time). The actual parameter values are placed on the stack successively, the value of the last parameter coming first.

When compiling an AS program, we must generate several pieces of code:

- Code to reserve stack cells 1 and 2,
- Code to read in the input values,
- Code for evaluation and output of the output expressions,
- Code for termination of the program (that includes "tidying up" of the stack) and
- Code for the evaluation of the defined functions.

These separate pieces are put together to a program in the same order as listed above (that yields the output of the compiler). Although the function definitions are not the last entity in the concrete syntax of AS they are compiled last, because the code for a function definition must be realized as subroutine. So the code for evaluation of the defined functions yields a sequence of subroutines to be appended to the main program (consisting of the other code segments).

4.2. The Intermediate Language and its Compilation into KMS

To recognize the reason for inserting an intermediate language into compilation process from AS to KMS, we must have a look at the code generation for the evaluation of expressions.

One problem is that the evaluation of function calls requires a jump to the program segment which does the calculation of the corresponding functions. However, the starting address of this program segment is not known when the code for the function call is generated. This problem is solved by adding an instruction to mark a certain program location and another instruction to refer to this marked location. During compilation of the function call, one can use the reference instruction instead of the (unknown) absolute address of the function. The code for the function definition starts with a mark instruction. A similar problem arises from the compilation of if-then-else constructs.

The intermediate language is almost a copy of the KMS language, but enriched by three additional instructions. These instructions are (indicated in concrete syntax here):

<Ident>:   Marks the following instruction with the identifier <Ident>. An object program must not contain more than one such instruction with the same <Ident>.

PUSH <Ident>   The absolute address of the program location marked with <Ident> is pushed onto the stack. Use of this instruction implies that the program contains a <Ident>: instruction.

BRANCH <Nat> The sum of the absolute address of this instruction and the natural number spcified is incremented by 1 and pushed onto the stack. In connection with GOTO this instruction realizes a jump relatively to the current instruction.

A compiler from the intermediate language into KMS (called the linker below) can be easily defined. The linking process started by
    link: Obj_list → KMS_Prog
is divided into two parts: First, the absolute addresses of the marks defined by the <Ident>:-instructions are collected. In the second pass, the object program is translated into KMS instruction by instruction.

4.3. Compiling AS into the Intermediate Language

Now we come to our main problem which is the compilation of AS into the intermediate language.

The compiler is described by the function

compile: Prog → Obj_list,

for which we have to check some context conditions of AS (uniqueness of global identifiers, formal parameters and correct use of arities) prior to execution:

allunique(program(p,dl,el)) AND aritycheck(dl,el) ⇒
    compile(program(p,dl,el)) =
    gen_init ∘ gen_input(p) ∘ compileh(p,dl,el,setup_global_env(p))

So the function compile essentially consists of calls to auxiliary functions like

gen_init: → Obj_list

which generates code for reserving the first two stack cells,

gen_input: Par_list → Obj_list

which generates code for reading the input parameters (which consists of a number of READ instructions corresponding to the length of the parameter list in the argument), and

compileh: Par_list # Def_list # Exp_list # Env → Obj_list

which takes the remaining tasks. The last argument of compileh consists of the global environment which is generated by

setup_global_env: Par_list → Env

in the way described in section 4.1.

Like compile, compileh essentially does the delegation of tasks to further auxiliary functions:

compileh(p,dl,el,genv) = gen_output(el,genv,ε) ∘ gen_cleanup(p) ∘ gen_exit ∘
    STOP ∘ gen_def(dl,genv)

So the structure of the generated programs is shown completely: The code for evaluating the output expressions generated by

gen_output: Exp_list # Env # Env → Obj_list

is followed by code for "tidying up" the stack.

The function

gen_cleanup: Par_list → Obj_list

generates a number of FREE instructions according to the length of the parameter list specified in the argument. This is used to remove the input parameters located on the stack. Finally,

gen_exit: → Obj_list

generates two more FREE instructions to free up the reserved stack cells 1 and 2.

Compilation of the function definitions is done by

gen_def: Def_list # Env → Obj_list.

If we assume a function

gen_exp: Exp # Env # Env → Obj_list

(which is explained later), the specification of gen_output is easy. The value of an evaluated expression is on top of the stack, so this element is printed and removed:

gen_output(ε,genv,lenv) = ε
gen_output(e ∘ el,genv,lenv) =
    gen_exp(e,genv,lenv) ∘ PRINT ∘ FREE ∘ gen_output(el,genv,lenv)

The most important function is gen_exp. The arguments of gen_exp are the expression to be evaluated, the global and the local environment. To specify gen_exp, we have to distinguish between the different possibilities for constructing an expression. As stated in section 4.1, the value of an expression should be placed on top of the stack after execution of the corresponding code for evaluating this expression. No further changes to the stack should be visible at this point. We show the principles of gen_exp here only for the most interesting kind of expression: for the call of a (recursive) function.

As explained in section 4.1, the code for evaluating the function is located in a subroutine-like segment. The return from a subroutine is realized by a GOTO. Therefore, the return address must be pushed onto the stack by the calling program before the subroutine is called. Then the subroutine is provided with the actual parameter values via the stack. The top element of the stack contains the return address when the function is called.

Besides that, the offset for relative addressing located in stack cell 1 must be set correctly. During evaluation of the called function, parameters are addressed in the following way: The absolute address of the j-th parameter is the contents of stack cell 1 minus the parameter number j. So the offset is set to the address containing the return address, (because the next address from there contains the value of the first parameter).

To allow recursive function calls, the old offset must be saved on the stack before updating it. The old offset has to be restored after return to the calling program. Likewise, the parameter values are removed from stack by the calling program after return.

The function result calculated by execution of the function code cannot be placed on top of the stack, because the top of the stack must contain the return address when finishing the subroutine. Therefore we use stack cell 2 for returning the result. The calling program moves the result from stack cell 2 to the top of the stack.

Now we have divided the code for a function call into the following segments:
[1] saving of the old offset on the stack
[2] evaluating the parameter list (in reverse order), the values of the parameters are located sequentially on top of the stack
[3] setting the new offset
[4] generating the return address
[5] calling of the function by jumping to the corresponding code
[6] removing the parameter values from the stack
[7] restoring the old offset
[8] moving the function result to the top of the stack

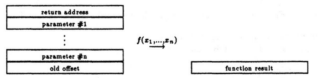

Fig. 3: The stack before ([5]) and after ([8]) a function call

These code segments can be generated by using two auxiliary functions (in the following axioms, the boxed numbers denote the code segments to which the code belongs):

gen_exp(appl(id,el),genv,lenv) =
    [1] 1 o LOAD o
    [2] gen_explist(el,genv,lenv) o
    [3] COUNT o 1 o STORE o FREE o

> 4 BRANCH 2 ∘
> 5 PUSH id ∘ GOTO ∘
> 6 – 8 gen_appl_clean(lenexp(el))

gen_appl_clean(n+1) =
> 6 FREE ∘ gen_appl_clean(n)
gen_appl_clean(0) =
> 7 1 ∘ STORE ∘ FREE ∘
> 8 2 ∘ LOAD

Please note that gen_explist must generate code for evaluating the *last* expression *first* and therefore has to be specified as follows:
gen_explist(ε,genv,lenv) = ε
gen_explist(e ∘ el,genv,lenv) = gen_explist(el,genv,lenv) ∘ gen_exp(e,genv,lenv)

Since the code for the function definitions generaed by gen_def is essentially a sequence of independent subroutines, we just concatenate the code segments generated for every function definition:
gen_def(ε,genv) = ε
gen_def(d ∘ dl,genv) = gen_funct(d,genv) ∘ gen_def(dl,genv)

Here we have a function
gen_funct: Def # Env → Obj_list
generating the code for one function definition. The second argument of this function is the global environment (like the second argument of gen_def).

The code generated for function evaluation is mainly the code generated by gen_exp for evaluation of the function body (with a local environment containing the relative addresses of the formal parameters). The remaining thing is to take care for instructions which realize the technique of subroutines: The result of evaluation is located on top of the stack; it must be copied to stack cell 2 and removed from the stack top. A final GOTO instruction does the return to the calling program:
gen_funct(funct(id,p,e),genv) =
    id: ∘ gen_exp(e,genv,setup_env(p,1)) ∘ 2 ∘ STORE ∘ FREE ∘ GOTO
Please note that the instruction generated first marks the beginning of the code, so the generation of the call address in the calling program can be done by using the BRANCH instruction.

4.4. Examples

In the following, we give some examples for the compilation of AS programs. The purpose of these examples is to give an impression of the execution times for the specification. The four programs shown in figure 4 were compiled into intermediate language and then into KMS in separate passes.

Compiling (i. e. translating into intermediate language) and linking (i. e. translating intermediate language into KMS) needed the following execution times when the compiler was interpreted by the RAP system[3]:

Program	Compile	Link
1	26.12	6.30
2	244.60	71.32
3	63.82	22.53
4	280.57	77.73

---

[3] in CPU seconds on a SUN 3/160 with 4 Mb RAM

```
Program 1:                          Program 2: (gcd)
input M, N                          input N, M
functions ε                         functions F(N,M) =
output M*M, M*N, 2-M/N+1               if N=M then N
end                                         else if N<M then F(N,M-N)
                                                    else F(N-M,M)
                                              fi
                                    fi
                                    output F(N,M)
                                    end


Program 3: (factorial)              Program 4: (Ackermann)
input M                             input M, N
functions G(X) =                    functions X(M,N) =
  if X=0 then 1                       if M=0 then N+1
        else X*G(X-1)                       else if N=0 then X(M-1,1)
  fi                                              else X(M-1,X(M,N-1))
output G(M)                                 fi
end                                 fi
                                    output X(M,N)
                                    end
```

Fig. 4: The test programs for the AS compiler

5. Concrete Implementation of the AS Compiler

5.1. General Remarks

In the latter section, the introduced examples showed that the specification of the AS compiler is not suitable for practical use, due to the high execution times on the RAP system. To generate a more usable prototype from an algebraic specification, we have to implement the specification "concretely". Concrete implementation means here the generation of a program which is (efficiently) executable on a real von-Neumann computer. This can be done by hand (using a classical programming language), but there are also automatic tools for this step which apply well for the explicit specification style chosen here.

5.2. CASPER – a Compiler from RAP to PASCAL

CASPER, a compiler for algebraic specifications in the RAP system, was designed at the University of Passau in summer 1987 as an exercise in programming methodology. It translates RAP specifications (and tasks), which fulfill certain requirements, into PASCAL programs (cf. [Geser, Hussmann, Mueck 88]). The PASCAL program generated from a specification is only able to transform ground terms constructed from function symbols into their normal form by evaluation of the functions; CASPER is unable to solve arbitrary equational systems.

Fortunately, the specifications for AS, KMS and the compiler met the requirements of CASPER (after some slight modifications). This is possible only because these "specifications" are algebraic programs: They are very similar to a program in an abstract functional language (like ML).

The specification of the AS compiler was translated by CASPER together with the test programs from section 4.4. The following table shows the execution times of the PASCAL code compared with the times from section 4.4.

Program	RAP Compile	RAP Link	PASCAL Compile&Link
1	26.12	6.30	0.05
2	244.60	71.32	0.16
3	63.82	22.53	0.08
4	280.57	77.73	0.17

Roughly speaking, run time increases by the factor 1000. But note that this comparison is not very fair, since the RAP system is mainly designed for the more complex tasks of solving equation systems, not for pure evaluation of terms. However, the translation of the specification into PASCAL yields a great gain in execution time.

This can also be seen when we execute a compiled and linked program (using the KMS interpreter). On the level of algebraic specification, the RAP system sometimes does not yield results at all (this is caused by the limited virtual memory of the used computer). However, with the KMS interpreter translated by CASPER, acceptable results can be obtained.

We have considered this second experiment not under the aspect of execution time gain when going from RAP to PASCAL, rather than under the aspect of efficiency of a PASCAL program generated by CASPER. We executed the KMS code for the Ackermann function introduced in section 4.4
a) with the KMS interpreter $K1$ generated by CASPER and
b) with a KMS interpreter $K2$, written in C, which was written manually.
The results (in CPU seconds) are summarized in figure 5.

$x \backslash y$	0	1	2	3	4	5
0	0.03	0.03	0.03	0.03	0.03	0.03
	0.03	0.03	0.03	0.03	0.03	0.03
1	0.08	0.13	0.27	0.33	0.45	0.55
	0.05	0.05	0.05	0.05	0.05	0.08
2	0.22	0.62	1.35	2.20	3.68	5.55
	0.05	0.09	0.12	0.15	0.16	0.23
3	0.65	6.00	43.22	—	—	—
	0.08	0.22	0.87	3.88	14.92	65.55
4	6.23	—	—	—	—	—
	0.22	—	—	—	—	—

Fig. 5: Execution times of the Ackermann function for different values

There are two values indicated for each execution of $ackermann(x,y)$. The upper value is the time consumed by $K1$, the lower value is the time consumed by $K2$. A "—" means that the execution could not be performed in a reasonable time by the computer system (SUN 3/160 with 4 MByte RAM and 16 MByte swap space).

Compared with direct interpretation of the specification, the execution times of $K1$ are much better: When trying to execute the Ackermann program with the KMS interpreter in RAP, results are yielded only for $x=0$ and y arbitrary (needs about 140 CPU seconds) or for $x=1$ and $y=0$ (350 CPU seconds). For small values of x and y, the CASPER-generated code is even comparable with the performance of the hand-written stack machine.

Thus, generation of prototypes in PASCAL using CASPER is efficient if one needs an executable program promptly. Of course, this program is not to be considered as a final product, but is still faster than execution with RAP. In the case of the Ackermann function, the prototype is still inefficient for larger values of x and y.

The PASCAL program generated by CASPER for the Ackermann function does not yield results for comperatively small arguments due to lack of memory. The reason for this is that the memory allocated (with NEW) is not disposed when a term is no longer needed. If this would be done, programs with very deep recursion could be executed properly, too.

6. Summary

We have presented a non-trivial example for the application of algebraic programming. It turned out that in the case of compiler construction an abstract program is a very natural way of specification. Using automatic tools, such an executable specification can be translated into machine code which has acceptable performance for small examples. This means, the algebraic specification is a prototype of the intended compiler.

The main experience from this experiment was that the use of the clear and simple RAP/COLD specification language led to a rather clear and well-structured design of the compiler. An even more important advantage is that the calculus of conditional equations and structural induction is available for the verification of the AS compiler with respect to the AS interpreter. Ongoing work focuses on this verification task (and on the question how the verification can be computer-assisted in a useful way).

References

[Broy 86]   M. Broy: Lecture notes to the course "Informatik III" at the University of Passau in winter term 1986/87.

[Geser, Hussmann, Mueck 88]   A. Geser, H. Hussmann, A. Mueck: A compiler for a class of conditional term rewriting systems. In: Conditional Term Rewriting, LNCS 308, pp. 84-90, Springer 1988.

[Hussmann 85]   H. Hussmann: Unification in conditional-equational theories. In: Proc. EUROCAL 85, LNCS 204, pp. 543-555, Springer 1985.

[Hussmann 85/87]   H. Hussmann: RAP-system user's manual (second edition). Technical Report MIP-8504, University of Passau, 1985. Second, revised edition 1987.

[Hussmann, Geser 88]   H. Hussmann, A. Geser: The RAP system as a tool for testing COLD specifications. Contained in this volume.

[Rank 88]   C. Rank: Specification and prototyping of a compiler for a small applicative language. Technical Report MIP-8823, University of Passau, 1988

[Wirsing et al. 83]   M. Wirsing, P. Pepper, H. Partsch, W. Dosch, M. Broy: On hierarchies of abstract data types. Acta Informatica 20, pp. 1-33, 1983.

Algebraic ADT specifications of an extended relational algebra and their conversion into a working prototype

L. Lavazza (†), S. Crespi-Reghizzi (‡)

(†) TXT SpA
Via Guastalla 2 - 20122 Milano   Tel. 02-5456761

(‡) Dipartimento di Elettronica - Politecnico di Milano
P.za L. da Vinci 32 - 20133 Milano Tel. 02-23993518

Abstract

In this paper an algebraic specification of an extended (i.e. non first normal form) relational algebra is reported. Such specification has been written in RAP and in COLD and has been executed using RAP. In order to improve efficiency specifications were translated to Prolog.

1. Introduction

The core of relational data-base theory is the algebra of relations. In this context a relation is a subset of a Cartesian product of some elementary domains. Algebraic operators are the set operations, projection, selection and product; other operators - notably join - are derived from the previous ones. This algebra, due to Codd, provides a convenient but limited way to manipulate data.

In the course of time, extensions have been proposed in various directions. We report here the ALGRES programming language, a comprehensive proposal for expressing relations and relational algorithms [Ceri88]. The chief features are:

- relations can be (finitely) nested, i.e. an attribute of a relation can itself be a relation; nesting and unnesting operations are introduced.
- tuples of a relation can be updated and extended by new attributes.
- a fixpoint operator is introduced, in order to achieve computational completeness [Chandra81].

Other features are omitted from this presentation, in particular the possibility to deal with ordered sets and sets with replications in addition to traditional sets.

ALGRES is considerably more complex than Codd's algebra, and we had to consider alternative approaches to its formal specification and to the implementation of an interpreter. The Abstract Data Type (ADT) technique was selected, while in parallel another effort [Ceri86a] provided a formal (but not executable) defintion of ALGRES using syntax-directed translations.

Other formal definitions of extended relational algebras have appeared recently [Schek85], but they are based on a more or less rigorous mathematical style which is not amenable to execution and formal derivation of properties; none of these proposals considers the transitive closure.

A piece of work that bears similarity to ours is [Wong86], an algebraic ADT specification of Codd's algebra using Hope.

An important benefit of the ADT algebraic specifications is that they are executable, in principle, and can be turned into a working prototype. The experience of specifying a complex system like ALGRES using the formalism of COLD is reported here. We also describe a systematic conversion from the COLD notation to Prolog clauses, in order to obtain a reasonably efficient prototype of Algres interpreter.

2. The language ALGRES

To convey an idea of ALGRES we first present a relational algorithm for transforming a nondeterministic finite-state automaton (NDFSA) into a deterministic one (DFSA).

An automaton is described by a triple $M = (Q,S,d)$, where Q denotes the set of states, S is the input alphabet and d is the transition function $Q \times S \rightarrow Q$.

The Algres definition of an automaton M is reported below. Note that sets are represented by curly brackets, while tuples are enclosed in parentheses.

M is a set of arcs, each arc has three components: the present state, the input symbol and a set of next states.

```
DEF M { arc ( present_state: integer,
              input: char,
              next_states { ( state: integer ) } ) }
```

The equivalent DFSA $M' = (Q',S,d')$ is defined as follows:

1. be Q' included or equal to the powerset of Q.

2.   for any q' in Q' and for any a in S it is d'(q',a) = p', where
      p'= { p | p in d(q,a) and q in q' }

The ALGRES program that transforms non-deterministic automata into deterministic ones is described below.

A1 < - make_structure [present_states { present_state: integer }] M;
A2 < - rename [new_states = next_states] A1;

Notice that operators are prefix and carry on a specific part (enclosed by square brackets).
A1 and A2 are auxiliary relations: the first is obtained from M transforming (through the make_structure operation) the attribute present_state into a (singleton) set present_states, the latter has the same instance as A1, but the name of the third attribute is new_states instead of next_states.

R < - closure [A2]
   (make_structure [next_states { (state) }]
    delete_structure [next_states { (state) }]
    project   [new_states, input, next_states]
    join   [intersect new_states, present_states /= empty]
               project [new_states] A2,
               A1
)

The effect of the operation delete_structure followed by operation make_structure is to perform the union of all the "next_states" belonging to tuples having equal "present_states" and "input". Delete_structure and make_structure are the usual unnest and nest operations, respectively (see also [Dadam86]). The closure computes the union of A2 and the result of the expression in parentheses, and replaces A2 with the latter result until a fixpoint is reached.

It is obvious that the transformation from NDFSA to DFSA could not be formulated using Codd's algebra because the number of iterations cannot be fixed ahead.

3. The specification

In this section we give an outline of the formal specification of ALGRES written in COLD. The complete specification text is shown in the appendix.
At this stage, the specification is partial, since it does not cover errors. Work in this direction is in progress.

COLD is a design language, i.e. a language for recording a software product in intermediate stages of its design, including the specification and implementation stages. It embeds algebraic specification techniques into an object oriented framework. More details about COLD can be found in [Feijs86], [Feijs87], [Jonkers86].

RAP is a specification interpreter that features both (context-sensitive) syntax checking and solving systems of equations by conditional narrowing. The main features of the RAP specification language are sketched below. More details about RAP can be found in [Wirsing84], [Geser 85], [Hussmann 85a] and [Hussmann 85b].

Specifications are composed of a signature (declaring sorts and functions together with the function arities) and a collection of conditional equational axioms (also called equational horn clauses). Axioms (laws) have the following syntax:
[tl = ul & ... & tn = un = >] tl -> tr,
where the optional premises part (precondition) is a conjunction of equations ti = ui, and the left and right hand side (tl and tr, respectively) of the conclusion are terms. We

assume terms to be built in the usual way from functions and variables.

Please note that even though symbols could be overloaded in COLD, we have preferred to use unique names in order to improve legibility.

3.1. Constructors of relations

Extended relations are sets of tuples; tuples are ordered sequences of attributes. An attribute is an element having one of the following types: integer, boolean, identifier (i.e. character or string), tuple, relation. For this reason, attributes, tuples, and relations must be introduced within a single type specification, as already stated.

In order to build such relations the following constructors have been introduced:

att_Int:	Nat -> Att	att_Bool:	Bool -> Att
att_Id:	Id -> Att	att_Rel:	Relation -> Att
att_Tup:	Tuple -> Att	empty_Tup:	-> Tuple
append_Tup:	Att # Tuple -> Tuple	empty_Rel:	-> Relation
insert:	:Relation # Tuple -> Relation		

Variables used in the specification are declared as follows:

n,n1,m:Nat	b,b1:Bool	d,d1:Id
a,a1:Att	T,T1,t,t1:Tuple	R,R1:Relation
l:Pos_list	ai,a1:Att_Id	
o,o1,o2:Ops	p,p1,P,P1,P2,exp:Expression	spc,sp1,sp2:Specifier
il:Nat_list	pth:Att_path	

3.2. Comparison functions

Some functions have been defined in order to test equality and containment:

- "eq_Att","eq_Tup" and "eq_Rel" test for equality two attributes, tuples or relations, respectively;
- "in" tests the presence of a tuple in a relation;
- "cont" tests if a relation is contained in another one.

Function "eq_Att" calls the equality function that applies to the attribute's type:

eq_Att(att_Int(n),att_Int(n1)) = equal_Int(n,n1);
eq_Att(att_Bool(b),att_Bool(b1)) = equiv(b,b1);
eq_Att(att_Tup(t),att_Tup(t1)) = eq_Tup(t,t1);
eq_Att(att_Rel(R),att_Rel(R1)) = eq_Rel(R,R1);
eq_Att(att_Id(d),att_Id(d1)) = equal_Id(d,d1);

Function "eq_Tup" is similar to any sequence comparison, while definition of "eq_Rel", "in" and "cont" are similar to the usual definitions of set equality and subset_of.

3.3. Utility functions defined on attributes and tuples

In this section we describe some utility functions, defined on attributes and tuples, that are used quite often in the definition of complex functions: the defining axioms of such utility functions are trivial and have been omitted.

- kind_Att: returns the type of the given attribute;
- tup_from_Att: given an attribute of type tuple, returns the value of the attribute (i.e. the tuple);
- rel_from_Att: given an attribute of type relation, returns the value of the attribute (i.e. the relation).

- conc_Tup: concatenates two tuples;
- nth: given a tuple and a position, returns the attribute in the given position;
- chng: given a tuple, a position and an attribute value, replaces the attribute in the given position with the given value;
- tleft: given a tuple and a position, returns the tuple made of attributes placed at the left of the given position;
- tright: given a tuple and a position, returns the tuple made of attributes placed at the right of the given position.

3.4. Set operations

The usual set operations (union, difference, intersection, cartesian product) are defined on extended relations. Again, such functions are defined by the same axioms as the corresponding set operations, so axioms are not reported here.
Some utility functions have also been defined on relations:

remove   removes a tuple from a relation,

union_nc   union of two disjoint relations,

add_Tup   given a tuple and a relation inserts the tuple into the relation only if it is not already present.

3.5. Classical relational operations

In this section we present the extended version of Codd's algebraic operators, i.e. projection and selection. Join is defined, as usual, in terms of selection and product. Join axioms have been omitted.

3.5.1. Projection

The extended projection operation is similar to the corresponding classical operation, except that the attributes on which the projection is performed do not directly belong, in general, to the same tuple.
As a consequence, the parameter of an extended projection is not a list of attributes, but a tree of attribute positions; for example the list < 2,3.1.4,3.1.5> corresponds to the following tree:

```
     root
     / \
    2   3
        |
        1
       / \
      4   5
```

Such trees are build with the following constructors:

```
empty_plist  : -> Pos_list
append_plist :Att_Id # Pos_list -> Pos_list
all_att      :Nat -> Att_Id
list_att     :Nat # Pos_list -> Att_Id
```

The tree in the example above is written as follows:

append_plist(all_att(2),
   append_plist(list_att(3,append_plist(
         list_att(1,append_plist(all_att(4),
              append_plist(all_att(5),empty_plist))),
        empty_plist)),
      empty_plist))

Extended projection is defined by the following axioms:

project(R,empty_plist) = empty_Rel;
project(empty_Rel,l) = empty_Rel;
project(insert($\overline{R}$,T),l) = add_Tup(project(R,l),proj_Tup(T,l));

proj_Tup(empty_Tup,l) = empty_Tup;
proj_Tup(T,empty_plist) = empty_Tup;
proj_Tup(append_Tup(a,T),append_plist(ai,l)) =
  append_Tup(cx_Att(append_Tup(a,T),ai), proj_Tup(append_Tup(a,T),l));

cx_Att(t,all_att(n)) = nth(t,n);
kind_Att(nth(t,n)) = tup_k = > cx_Att(t,list_att(n,l)) =
       att_Tup(proj_Tup(tup_from_Att(nth(t,n)),l));
kind_Att(nth(t,n)) = rel_k = > cx_Att(t,list_att(n,l)) =
       att_Rel(project(rel_from_Att(nth(t,n)),l));

function cx_Att needs some explanation: if the attribute list consists simply of an attribute position n, it extracts from the given tuple t the n-th attribute; otherwise it calls the appropriate project function (either project or proj_Tup) passing the n-th attribute as a parameter.

3.5.2. Selection

Extended selection is much more complex than Codd's selection, because of two reasons: first, the predicate can refer to an arbitrarily nested relation belonging to the operand and the selection predicate can consist of any relational operation.
Our selection has three parameters:

- the first is an identifier of the relation R on which selection is performed;
- the second is called a path and identifies an attribute of type relation of the operand. Such object can be nested at any level in the operand and it is the relation on which the selection predicate is evaluated;
- the third parameter is a predicate that can only contain references to attributes directly belonging to tuples of the relation indicated by second parameter.

Paths are lists of natural numbers built using the following constructors:

empty_path : -> Att_path,
app_path : Nat # Att_path -> Att_path

Example: it is given a relation R:
Def R { (a1: Nat,
      a2: { (a21: { (a211: Id) },
          a22: Bool,
          a23: (a231: Nat,
               a232: { (a2311: Id) })))) }

and we want to select tuples such that the intersection of attributes a21 and a232 is not empty: path is app_path(2,empty_path), indicating that the predicate is expressed on the second attribute of relation R, i.e. on a2.

Expressions (and predicates) are defined by the following constructors:

```
emptyilst  : -> Nat_list
app_i      :Nat # Nat_list -> Nat_list
eq,df,be,bl,ab,ae,lan,lnt,lor,lxr
ad,su,mu,di,pj,sl,un,dr,cp,jn,it,af: Ops
pp         :Nat_list -> Expression
li         :Nat -> Expression
lb         :Bool -> Expression
ld         :Id -> Expression
lu         :Tuple -> Expression
lr         :Relation -> Expression
op2        :Ops # Expression # Expression # Specifier -> Expression
op1        :Ops # Expression # Specifier -> Expression
empty_spec : -> Specifier
pspec      :Att_path # Expression -> Specifier
aspec      :Expression # Ops -> Specifier
lspec      :Pos_list -> Specifier
```

For the previous example, predicate is

```
op2(df,
   op2(it,
      pp(app_i(1,emptyilst)),
      pp(app_i(3,app_i(2,emptyilst)))),
      empty_spec),
   lr(empty_rel),
   empty_spec)
```

where df is the code of difference, it is the code for intersection, pp(X) indicates the attribute in position X and lr is a literal (i.e. a constant).

Function eval_Tup, defines the evaluation of a given Expression over a Tuple. Such function is omitted here for semplicity.

Selection definition is based on function eval_Tup and sl_sel, the classical relational selection:

```
sl_sel(empty_Rel,p) = empty_Rel;
eval_Tup(t,p) = true = > sl_sel(insert(R,t),p) = insert(sl_sel(R,p),t);
eval_Tup(t,p) = false = > sl_sel(insert(R,t),p) = sl_sel(R,p);
```

When selection is performed directly on the operand (i.e. the path is empty), it is equivalent to sl_sel:

```
select(empty_Rel,pth,p) = empty_Rel;
select(insert(R,T),empty_path,p) = sl_sel(insert(R,T),p);
```

Otherwise, the path has to be followed, and the selection performed on the attribute identified:

select(insert(R,T),app_path(n,empty_path),p) =
  add_Tup(select(R,app_path(n,empty_path),p),
      chng(T,n,att_Rel(sl_sel(rel_from_Att(nth(T,n)),p)))));
select(insert(R,T),app_path(n,app_path(n1,pth)),p) =
  add_Tup(select(R,app_path(n,app_path(n1,empty_path)),p),
      chng(T,n,sel2(nth(T,n),n1,pth,p)));

sel2(att_Rel(R),n1,pth,p) -> att_Rel(select(R,app_path(n1,pth),p));
sel2(att_Tup(t),n,app_path(n1,pth),p) =
  att_Tup(chng(t, n, sel2(nth(t,n),n1,pth,p)));
sel2(att_Tup(t),n,empty_path,p) =
  att_Tup(chng(t, n, att_Rel(sl_sel(rel_from_Att(nth(t,n)),p)))));

3.6. Nesting and unnesting functions

In this section we introduce two functions, "delete_structure" and "make_structure", whose purpose is to delete or create complex structures internal to other complex structures.

3.6.1. Delete structure (unnesting)

In this section the unnesting function "delete_structure" is presented.
"delete_structure" applies to an attribute of type set belonging to a tuple which directly belongs to a set. The effect of the function is to delete the structure while preserving the values. In order to do so the structure of the enclosing tuple is modified: the set attribute is replaced by the attributes of its tuple, and each tuple of the deleted set produces a new tuple of the enclosing set.

For example, consider relation R defined below:
Def R { (a: Nat,
        b: Nat,
        c: { (c1: Nat,
            c2: Nat) },
        d: Nat) }

R < - { (1,2,{(11,12),(13,14)},4),
      (7,8,{(21,22)},10),
      (1,2,{(13,14)},4)}
The result of delete_structure applied to attribute 'c' of R is:
{(1,2,11,12,4),(1,2,13,14,4),(7,8,21,22,10)}

"delete_structure" is defined by the following axioms:

delete_structure(empty_Rel,pth) -> empty_Rel;
delete_structure(insert(R,t),app_path(n,empty_path)) =
    union(delete_structure(R,app_path(n,empty_path)),
        multiply(tleft(t,n),tright(t,n),rel_from_Att(nth(t,n))));
delete_structure(insert(R,t),app_path(n,app_path(n1,pth))) =
    add_Tup(delete_structure(R,app_path(n,app_path(n1,pth))),
        chng(t,n,del_k(nth(t,n),n1,pth)));

del_k(att_Tup(t),n,empty_path) = att_Rel(ds_Tup(t,n));
del_k(att_Tup(t),n,app_path(n1,pth)) =
    att_Tup(chng(t,n,del_k(nth(t,n),n1,pth)));
del_k(att_Rel(R),n,pth) = att_Rel(delete_structure(R,app_path(n,pth)));

multiply(t1,t,empty_Rel) = empty_Rel;
multiply(t1,t,insert(R,T)) = insert(multiply(t1,t,R),
        conc_Tup(conc_Tup(t1,T),t));

3.6.2. Create structure (nesting)

The nesting function "make_structure" applies to a set A of attributes of a tuple T directly belonging to a set and replaces such attributes with one attribute defined as a set of tuples comprehending the attributes of A.

Let A' be the attributes of T not belonging to A: all the tuples having equal values of attributes in A' (a subset T' of T) contribute in the result to a single tuple having attributes belonging to A' and a new attribute which is the projection on A of T'.

Example:
Def R { (a, b, c, d, e: Nat) }

R < - { (1,2,3,4,5), (1,2,6,4,9), (1,2,1,4,10), (1,2,2,3,3) }

S < - make_structure [s: { (c, e) }] R

S = { (1,2,{(3,5),(6,9),(1,10)},4),
   (1,2,{(2,3)},3) }

The axioms defining the "make_structure" are the following:

make_structure(empty_Rel,pth,l) = empty_Rel;
make_structure(insert(R,t),empty_path,l) = mk_stru(insert(R,t),l);
make_structure(insert(R,t),app_path(n,pth),l) =
   add_Tup(make_structure(R,app_path(n,pth),l),
     chng(t,n,make_k(nth(t,n),pth,l)));

make_k(att_Rel(R),pth,l) = att_Rel(make_structure(R,pth,l));
make_k(att_Tup(t),empty_path,l) = att_Tup(mk_Tup(t,l));
make_k(att_Tup(t),app_path(n,pth),l) =
    att_Tup(chng(t,n,make_k(nth(t,n),pth,l)));

mk_stru(empty_Rel,l) = empty_Rel;
mk_stru(insert(R,t),l) = mk_build(mk_stru(R,l),mk_Tup(t,l));

mk_build(empty_Rel,t) = insert(empty_Rel,t);
not(eq_Rel(R,empty_Rel)) = > mk_build(R,t) =
  union_nc(diff(R,common(R,t)),merge(insert(common(R,t),t)));

common(empty_Rel,t) = empty_Rel;
eq_rest(t,t1) = > common(insert(R,t),t1) = insert(common(R,t1),t);
not(eq_rest(t,t1)) = > common(insert(R,t),t1) = common(R,t1);

eq_rest(append_Tup(a,T),append_Tup(a1,T1)) = eq_Tup(T,T1);

merge(insert(empty_Rel,t)) = insert(empty_Rel,append_Tup(a,t));
merge(insert(insert(R,append_Tup(a,t)),append_Tup(a1,t))) =
  merge(insert(R,
    append_Tup(att_Rel(union(rel_from_Att(a),
        rel_from_Att(a1))),t))));

mk_Tup(t,l) = append_Tup(att_Rel(insert(empty_Rel,in_atts(t,l))),
        out_atts(t,l));

in_atts(t,empty_plist) = empty_Tup;
in_atts(t,append_plist(all_att(n),l)) =
        append_Tup(nth(t,n),in_atts(tright(t,n),dim_by(l,n)));

out_atts(t,empty_plist) = t;
out_atts(t,append_plist(all_att(n),l)) =
        conc_Tup(tleft(t,n),out_atts(tright(t,n),dim_by(l,n)));

3.7. Tuple functions

Tuple functions are operators that take an expression as parameter and apply it to each tuple of the operand; the result is an attribute that is either added to each tuple (tuple extension) or is used to replace an existing attribute (tuple update). Since the definition of tuple extensions is an obvious simplification of the tuple update, it is not reported here.

Function "tuple_update" is defined below with the following meaning of parameters:

1. operand relation;
2. attribute identifier: indicates the relation to which tuple update is applied (if empty indicates the operand itself);
3. position of the attribute to be updated;
4. expression to be applied to tuples to produce the new value.

tuple_update(empty_Rel,pth,n,p) = empty_Rel;
tuple_update(insert(R,t),empty_path,n,p) = tt_upd(insert(R,t),n,p);
tuple_update(insert(R,t),app_path(n,empty_path),m,p) =
        add_Tup(tuple_update(R,app_path(n,empty_path),m,p),
            chng(t,n,tpupd3(nth(t,n),m,p)));
tuple_update(insert(R,t),app_path(n,app_path(n1,pth)),m,p) =
        add_Tup(tuple_update(R,app_path(n,app_path(n1,pth)),m,p),
            chng(t,n,tpupd2(nth(t,n),n1,pth,m,p)));

tpupd2(att_Rel(R),n,pth,m,p) =
        att_Rel(tuple_update(R,app_path(n,pth),m,p));
tpupd2(att_Tup(t),n,app_path(n1,pth),m,p) =
        att_Tup(chng(t,n,tpupd2(nth(t,n),n1,pth,m,p)));
tpupd2(att_Tup(t),n,empty_path,m,p) =
        att_Tup(chng(t,n,tpupd3(nth(t,n),m,p)));
tpupd3(att_Rel(R),m,p) = att_Rel(tt_upd(R,m,p));
tpupd3(att_Tup(t),m,p) = att_Tup(chng(t,m,eval_expr(t,p)));

tt_upd(empty_Rel,m,p) = empty_Rel;
tt_upd(insert(R,t),m,p) = add_tup(tt_upd(R,m,p),
                    chng(t,m,eval_expr(t,p)));

3.8. Aggregate functions

An aggregate function is used to perform operations such as summation; it takes as parameters the operand, an attribute identifier and an operation: the given operation is

applied to the attribute in each tuple of the operand.
Aggregate function is defined by the following axioms:

aggr_fun(R,p,o) = att_pr(aggr_pr(R,p,o));

aggr_pr(insert(empty_Rel,t),p,o) = red_ilst(p,t);
aggr_pr(insert(insert(R,t1),t),p,o) =
    eval_op2(o,aggr_pr(insert(R,t1),p,o),red_ilst(p,t),emp_spec);

Function att_pr transforms a predicate into an attribute. Aggregate function actually returns an attribute and hence has to be used in an enclosing expression, it is not a standalone function.
Red_ilst extracts from tuple t the value in the position indicated by p.
Eval_op2 evaluates a binary operation.

3.9. Closure

In this section the closure operation is introduced [Ceri86b].
The CLOSURE is a unary operator having the following syntax:

> CLOSURE [Expression] Operand

The CLOSURE is applied to an object of type set, called the Argument of the CLOSURE, which appears as operand of the expression in the specification part. The CLOSURE operation consists of an iterative evaluation of the expression: at each iteration, the expression is evaluated over the Argument and the result is united to the current Argument, yielding next Argument value. The iteration terminates when the Argument remains identical for two consecutive iterations; the result of the CLOSURE is then the last value of the Argument.

Obviously, the correctness of the CLOSURE requires that the Expression's result be type-compatible with the Argument. Since we deal with finite ALGRES objects, the CLOSURE terminates in a finite number of iterations.

To understand the meaning of this operator, consider that if the Expression is monotone (with respect to set inclusion) in its Argument, then the CLOSURE operation evaluates the unique minimal fixpoint of the algebraic equation:

> X = Expression (X) U Argument

The axioms are:
closure(exp,R) = cl_loop(exp,R,empty_Rel);

or(eq_Rel(R,R1),cont(R1,R)) = > cl_loop(exp,R,R1) = R1;
not(or(eq_Rel(R,R1),cont(R1,R))) = > cl_loop(exp,R,R1) =
    cl_loop(exp, compute(exp,union(R,R1)), union(R,R1));

compute(exp,R) =
    rel_from_Att(eval_expr(append_Tup(att_Rel(R),empty_Tup),exp));

4. Translating algebraic specifications into Prolog

In this section we present a straightforward algorithm to translate COLD clauses into Prolog.
We have used a RAP version of Algres specification, in order to execute sample ALgres programs. Unfortunately, we have found that RAP execution of algebraic specifications of the size of ours is excessively slow. In order to experiment with a prototype, we have systematically converted COLD specifications into Prolog programs.

However, RAP is more powerful than Prolog, so only specifications whose depth-first and breadth-first executions are equivalent are considered. Even so the Prolog interpreter can only be used to execute Algres programs, and not to solve general equations of the extended relational algebra , such as union(X,Y)= Y.

4.1. The translation algorithm

A RAP rule has the following form:
[precondition] = > lt(p1,..pm) -> rt(q1,..,qn),

The following utilities are used in the main translation procedure:

function is_const(X:term) return BOOLEAN;
     - - true iff term X is constant
function is_function_parameter(P:term, I:INTEGER) return BOOLEAN;
     - - true iff the I-th parameter of P if a function
function get_parameter(P:term, I:INTEGER) return term;
     - - gets the I-th parameter of P
procedure new_var(out X:variable); — produces a new variable name X;
procedure substitute(I:INTEGER, X:variable, P:in out term);
     - - replaces the I-th parameter of P with the variable X
procedure add_parameter(X:variable, P:in out term);
     - - appends variable X to the parameter list of P

The translation algorithm is reported below. (String concatenation is written "+ ").
function translate(rap_clause:clause) return clause;
begin
  if rap_clause.precondition /= "" — there is a precondition
   then prolog_precondition:= ":-" + transl_prec(rap_clause.precondition);
   else prolog_precondition:= "";
  end if;
  if is_const(rap_clause.rt)
   then add_parameter(rap_clause.rt,rap_clause.lt);
     return(rap_clause.lt + prolog_precondition + ".");
   else new_var(X);
     add_parameter(X,rap_clause.lt);
     add_parameter(X,rap_clause.rt);
     move_function_outward(rap_clause.rt);
     return(rap_clause.lt + prolog_precondition + rap_clause.rt + ".");
  end if;
end;

procedure move_function_outward applies to a term and recursively replaces each complex argument with a new variable matching the result of a new goal corresponding to the complex term. It is defined as follows:

```
procedure move_function_outward(in out P:term);
T,V: term; X:variable;
begin
  V := empty_term;
  for I in 1..number_of_arguments(P)
  loop
    if is_function_parameter(P,I)
    then new_var(X);
        T:= get_parameter(P,I);
        substitute(I,X,P);
        add_parameter(X,T);
        move_function_outward(T);
        V:= V + "," + T;
    end if;
  end loop;
  P:= P+ V;
end;
```

RAP's preconditions are conjunctions of equality tests:
< precondition> ::= t1= t1' & t2= t2' & ... & tn= tn'
Here we consider only cases such that ti' are constants.
The translation consists in the generation of a Prolog term, new_prec, corresponding to the precondition:

```
function transl_prec(rap_prec:precondition)return list_of_goals;
begin
  new_prec:= "";
  for I in 1..number_of_tests(rap_prec)
  loop add_parameter(I,rap_prec(I).left,rap_prec(I).right);
      move_function_outward(rap_prec(I).left);
      new_prec:= new_prec + rap_prec(I).left + ",";
  end loop;
  return(new_prec);
end;
```

4.2. Optimizations

Some optimizations are possible:

1. variables that occur only once in a rule can be replaced by the '_' Prolog variable;

2. often preconditions are computed twice or more, e.g. in the translation of the difference,

```
diff(insert(R,T),R1,RES):- in(R1,T,true), diff(R,R1,RES).
diff(insert(R,T),R1,insert(RT,T)):- in(R1,T,false),
                                     diff(R,R1,RT).
```

$in(R1,T,B)$ is computed $(cardinality(R)+ N)$ times, where N is the number of tuples belonging to R and not to $R1$ (i.e. the cardinality of the result).
This number can be reduced to $(cardinality(R))$ if the original axioms are translated in the following way:

```
diff(insert(R,T),R1,RES):- in(R1,T,B),
                    diff_bool(R,R1,T,B,RES).
diff_bool(R,R1,_,true,RES):- diff(R,R1,RES).
diff_bool(R,R1,T,false,insert(RT,T)):- diff(R,R1,RT).
```

5. Acknowledgments

We would like to thank Alfons Geser of Universitaet Passau for his useful comments and suggestions. The Algres Project is mainly supported by the EEC-Esprit Project 432 "Meteor". We also acknowledge partial support of CNR, MPI 40% and Rank Xerox University Grant Program.

6. Conclusion

We have presented the language Algres extending the data-structures and operations of Codd's relational algebra [Ceri88]. Algres has been rigorously developed using algebraic interpretable specifications, which have been subsequently converted into Prolog for efficiency reasons.

Algebraic specifications were executed using RAP interpreter, in order to formally prove properties of the system, but RAP proved too slow on examples of almost realistic dimensions.

The conversion from algebraic specifications to Prolog clauses is straightforward and can presumably be further optimized. Prolog interpretation allows relatively fast execution of Algres programs.

The extended relational language Algres is a complex system whose implementation with traditional software development techniques requires a large effort. In comparison, we have estimated a ratio of about 1 to 10 between a COLD-Prolog effort and the one of a traditional implementation in C.

Several extensions to relational algebra similar to Algres have been recently proposed, but none of these rely on executable formal definitions. As future work we intend to improve the man-machine interface of the COLD-Prolog interpreter, to make it more easily usable: this will allow efficiency comparison between the formally derived and the engineered interpreters.

REFERENCES

[Abiteboul86] S. Abiteboul and N. Bidoit "Non First Normal Form Relations to Represent Hierarchically Organized Data", Proc. 3rd ACM SIGMOD-SIGACT Symp. on Principles of Database Systems (PODS), March 1984, and Journal of Computer and System Sciences, 33, 1986.

[Ceri86a]
S. Ceri, S. Crespi-Reghizzi "Formal definition of ALGRES: algebra for extended relations", Dipt. Elettronica, Politecnico di Milano, 1986.

[Ceri86b]
S. Ceri, G. Gottlob, L. Lavazza "Translation and optimization of logic queries: the algebraic approach" Very Large Data Bases - Kyoto 1986

[Ceri87]
S. Ceri, L. Tanca "Optimization of Systems of Algebraic Equations for Evaluating DATALOG Queries", Proc. Very Large Data Bases, August 1987.

[Ceri88]
S. Ceri, S. Crespi-Reghizzi, L. Lamperti, L. Lavazza, R. Zicari "Algres: a system for specification and prototyping of complex databases" Submitted to IEEE Software

[Ceri88b]
S. Ceri, G. Gottlob, L. Tanca {"Relational Databases and Logic Programming"}, Surveys in Computer Science, Springer-Verlag (to appear).

[Chandra81]
Chandra A. "Programming Primitives for Database Languages" ACM POPL 1981.

[Dadam86]
P. Dadam et al. "A DBMS Prototype to Support Extended NF2 Relations: An Integrated View on Flat Tables and Hierarchies", Proc. ACM SIGMOD, May 1986.

[Feijs86]
Feijs L.M.G., Jonkers H.B.M., Obbink J.H., Koymans C.P.J., Renardel de Lavalette G.R., Rodenburg P.H. "A survey of the design language COLD", Meteor Deliverable

[Feijs87]
Feijs L.M.G., Jonkers H.B.M., Koymans C.P.J., Renardel de Lavalette G.R. "Formal definition of the design language COLD-K", Meteor Deliverable

[Fisher83]
P.C. Fisher and S.J.Thomas "Operators for Non-First-Normal-Form Relations", Proc. IEEE COMPSAC, 1983.

[Geser85]
Geser A., Hussmann H. "Rapid Prototyping for Algebraic Specifications - Examples for the Use of the RAP System" Report Universitaet Passau, MIP-8517, Passau, Dec. 1985.

[Geser86]
Geser A. "A Specification of the intel 8085 Microprocessor: A Case Study" Report Universitaet Passau, MIP-8608, Passau, May 1986.

[Hussmann85a]
Hussmann H. "Unification in Conditional-Equational Theories" Report Universitaet Passau, MIP-8502, Passau, Jan. 1985.

[Hussmann85b]
Hussmann H. "Rapid Prototyping for Algebraic Specifications - RAP System User's Manual (Second Edition)" Report Universitaet Passau, MIP-8504, Passau, Feb. 1987.

[Jonkers86]
Jonkers H.B.M. "Informal description of the design language COLD-K", Meteor Deliverable

[Schek86]
Schek H. Scholl M. "The relational model with relation-valued attributes" Inform. Systems vol.11 n.2 1986

[Wirsing84]
Wirsing M. "Structured Algebraic Specifications: A Kernel Language", Habilitation Thesis, Techn. Univ. Munchen, 1983, to apper in TCS, also Univ. Passau, Tech Rep. MIP-8511.

[Wong86]
Wong E. and Samson W.B. "The specification of a relational database (PRECI) as an abstract data type and its realisation in HOPE", Comp. Jour.,29, 1986.

Appendix - The complete COLD Specification

DESIGN

LET NAT_LIST :=

IMPORT NAT INTO

 CLASS

  SORT Nat_list

  FUNC{CONS} emptyilst: -> Nat_list
  FUNC{CONS} app_i: Nat # Nat_list -> Nat_list

END;

LET ATT_KIND :=

 CLASS

  SORT Att_kind

  FUNC{CONS} int_k: -> Att_kind
  FUNC{CONS} bool_k: -> Att_kind
  FUNC{CONS} tup_k: -> Att_kind
  FUNC{CONS} rel_k: -> Att_kind
  FUNC{CONS} id_k: -> Att_kind

END;

LET POS_LIST :=

IMPORT BOOL INTO
IMPORT NAT INTO

 CLASS

  SORT Pos_list
  SORT Att_Id
  SORT Att_path

  FUNC{CONS} empty_plist: -> Pos_list
  FUNC{CONS} append_plist: Att_Id # Pos_list -> Pos_list
  FUNC{CONS} all_att: Nat -> Att_Id
  FUNC{CONS} list_att: Nat # Pos_list -> Att_Id
  FUNC{CONS} empty_path: -> Att_path
  FUNC{CONS} app_path: Nat # Att_path -> Att_path

  FUNC dim_by: Pos_list # Nat -> Pos_list

AXIOM
FORALL n: Nat, m: Nat, l: Pos_list

({1} dim_by(empty_plist,n) = empty_plist;
  {2} dim_by(append_plist(all_att(m),l),n) =
          append_plist(all_att(sub(m,n)),dim_by(l,n)))

END;

LET OPERATIONS :=

CLASS

SORT Ops

    FUNC{CONS} eq: -> Ops   { equal }
    FUNC{CONS} df: -> Ops   { unequal }
    FUNC{CONS} be: -> Ops   { below or equal }
    FUNC{CONS} bl: -> Ops   { below }
    FUNC{CONS} ab: -> Ops   { above }
    FUNC{CONS} ae: -> Ops   { above or equal }
    FUNC{CONS} lan: -> Ops   { and }
    FUNC{CONS} lnt: -> Ops   { not }
    FUNC{CONS} lor: -> Ops   { or }
    FUNC{CONS} lxr: -> Ops   { exclusive or }
    FUNC{CONS} ad: -> Ops   { addition }
    FUNC{CONS} su: -> Ops   { subtraction }
    FUNC{CONS} mu: -> Ops   { multiplication }
    FUNC{CONS} di: -> Ops   { division }
    FUNC{CONS} pj: -> Ops   { projection }
    FUNC{CONS} sl: -> Ops   { selection }
    FUNC{CONS} un: -> Ops   { union }
    FUNC{CONS} dr: -> Ops   { set difference }
    FUNC{CONS} cp: -> Ops   { cartesian product }
    FUNC{CONS} jn: -> Ops   { join }
    FUNC{CONS} it: -> Ops   { intersection }
    FUNC{CONS} af: -> Ops   { aggregate function }

END;

LET RELATION :=

IMPORT BOOL INTO
IMPORT NAT INTO
IMPORT ID INTO
IMPORT POS_LIST INTO
IMPORT OPERATIONS INTO
IMPORT NAT_LIST INTO
IMPORT ATT_KIND INTO

CLASS

SORT Att
SORT Tuple
SORT Relation
SORT Expression
SORT Specifier

FUNC{CONS} att_Int: Nat -> Att
FUNC{CONS} att_Bool: Bool -> Att
FUNC{CONS} att_Id: Id -> Att
FUNC{CONS} att_Rel: Relation -> Att
FUNC{CONS} att_Tup: Tuple -> Att
FUNC{CONS} empty_Tup: -> Tuple
FUNC{CONS} append_Tup: Att # Tuple -> Tuple
FUNC{CONS} empty_Rel: -> Relation
FUNC{CONS} insert: Relation # Tuple -> Relation
FUNC{CONS} pp: Nat_list -> Expression
FUNC{CONS} li: Nat -> Expression
FUNC{CONS} lb: Bool -> Expression
FUNC{CONS} ld: Id -> Expression
FUNC{CONS} lu: Tuple -> Expression
FUNC{CONS} lr: Relation -> Expression
FUNC{CONS} op2: Ops # Expression # Expression # Specifier -> Expression
FUNC{CONS} op1: Ops # Expression # Specifier -> Expression
FUNC{CONS} emp_spec: -> Specifier
FUNC{CONS} pspec: Att_path # Expression -> Specifier
FUNC{CONS} aspec: Expression # Ops -> Specifier
FUNC{CONS} lspec: Pos_list -> Specifier

FUNC eq_Att: Att # Att -> Bool
FUNC eq_Tup: Tuple # Tuple -> Bool
FUNC conc_Tup: Tuple # Tuple -> Tuple
FUNC nth: Tuple # Nat -> Att
FUNC tup_from_Att: Att -> Tuple
FUNC kind_Att: Att -> Att_kind
FUNC chng: Tuple # Nat # Att -> Tuple
FUNC tleft: Tuple # Nat -> Tuple
FUNC tright: Tuple # Nat -> Tuple
FUNC proj_Tup: Tuple # Pos_list -> Tuple
FUNC cx_Att: Tuple # Att_Id -> Att
FUNC union: Relation # Relation -> Relation
FUNC diff: Relation # Relation -> Relation
FUNC intersec: Relation # Relation -> Relation
FUNC union_nc: Relation # Relation -> Relation
FUNC cart_prod: Relation # Relation -> Relation
FUNC project: Relation # Pos_list -> Relation
FUNC remove: Relation # Tuple -> Relation
FUNC in: Relation # Tuple -> Bool
FUNC eq_Rel: Relation # Relation -> Bool
FUNC cont: Relation # Relation -> Bool
FUNC tup_prod: Tuple # Relation -> Relation
FUNC rel_from_Att: Att -> Relation
FUNC add_Tup: Relation # Tuple -> Relation

FUNC sl_sel: Relation # Expression -> Relation
FUNC select: Relation # Att_path # Expression -> Relation
FUNC sel2: Att # Nat # Att_path # Expression -> Att
FUNC join: Relation # Relation # Att_path # Expression -> Relation
FUNC pjoin: Relation # Relation # Att_path # Expression # Pos_list
       -> Relation
FUNC eval_Tup: Tuple # Expression -> Bool
FUNC reduc: Expression # Tuple -> Expression
FUNC eval_Bool: Expression -> Bool
FUNC is_lt: Expression -> Bool
FUNC eval_pr: Expression -> Expression
FUNC eval_op1: Ops # Expression # Specifier -> Expression
FUNC eval_op2: Ops # Expression # Expression # Specifier -> Expression
FUNC red_ilst: Expression # Tuple -> Expression
FUNC val: Att -> Expression
FUNC eval_expr: Tuple # Expression -> Att
FUNC att_pr: Expression -> Att
FUNC multiply: Tuple # Tuple # Relation -> Relation
FUNC del_stru: Relation # Att_path -> Relation
FUNC del_k: Att # Nat # Att_path -> Att
FUNC ds_Tup: Tuple # Nat -> Relation
FUNC make_stru: Relation # Att_path # Pos_list -> Relation
FUNC make_k: Att # Att_path # Pos_list -> Att
FUNC mk_stru: Relation # Pos_list -> Relation
FUNC mk_build: Relation # Tuple -> Relation
FUNC common: Relation # Tuple -> Relation
FUNC eq_rest: Tuple # Tuple -> Bool
FUNC merge: Relation -> Relation
FUNC mk_Tup: Tuple # Pos_list -> Tuple
FUNC splim: Tuple # Pos_list -> Tuple
FUNC splin: Tuple # Pos_list -> Tuple
FUNC tt_ext: Relation # Expression -> Relation
FUNC tup_ext: Relation # Att_path # Expression -> Relation
FUNC tpext2: Att # Nat # Att_path # Expression -> Att
FUNC tpext3: Att # Expression -> Att
FUNC tup_upd: Relation # Att_path # Nat # Expression -> Relation
FUNC tpupd2: Att # Nat # Att_path # Nat # Expression -> Att
FUNC tpupd3: Att # Nat # Expression -> Att
FUNC tt_upd: Relation # Nat # Expression -> Relation
FUNC aggr_pr: Relation # Expression # Ops -> Expression
FUNC aggr_fun: Relation # Expression # Ops -> Att
FUNC closure: Expression # Relation -> Relation
FUNC compute: Expression # Relation -> Relation
FUNC cl_loop: Expression # Relation # Relation -> Relation

AXIOM
FORALL n: Nat, n1: Nat, m: Nat, b: Bool, b1: Bool, T: Tuple, T1: Tuple,
     t: Tuple, t1: Tuple, a: Att, a1: Att, d: Id, d1: Id, R: Relation,
     R1: Relation, l: Pos_list, ai: Att_Id, al: Att_Id, o: Ops, o1: Ops,
     o2: Ops, p: Expression, pl: Expression, P: Expression,
     P1: Expression, P2: Expression, exp: Expression, spc: Specifier,
     sp1: Specifier, sp2: Specifier, il: Nat_list, pth: Att_path

({1} eq_Att(att_Int(n),att_Int(n1)) = equal_Nat(n,n1);
{2} eq_Att(att_Id(d),att_Id(d1)) = equal_Id(d,d1);
{3} eq_Att(att_Bool(b),att_Bool(b1)) = equiv(b,b1);
{4} eq_Att(att_Tup(t),att_Tup(t1)) = eq_Tup(t,t1);
{5} eq_Att(att_Rel(R),att_Rel(R1)) = eq_Rel(R,R1);

{6} eq_Tup(empty_Tup,empty_Tup) = true;
{7} eq_Tup(empty_Tup,append_Tup(a,T)) = false;
{8} eq_Tup(append_Tup(a,T),empty_Tup) = false;
{9} eq_Tup(append_Tup(a,T),append_Tup(a1,T1)) =
      and(eq_Att(a,a1),eq_Tup(T,T1));

{10} conc_Tup(empty_Tup,T) = T;
{11} conc_Tup(append_Tup(a,T),T1) = append_Tup(a,conc_Tup(T,T1));

{12} nth(append_Tup(a,T),succ(zero)) = a;
{13} gt(n,succ(zero)) = true = >
          nth(append_Tup(a,T),n) = nth(T,pred(n));

{14} tup_from_Att(att_Tup(T)) = T;

{15} chng(empty_Tup,n,a) = empty_Tup;
{16} chng(append_Tup(a,T),succ(zero),a1) = append_Tup(a1,T);
{17} gt(n,succ(zero)) = true = > chng(append_Tup(a,T),n,a1) =
                        append_Tup(a,chng(T,pred(n),a1));
{18} tleft(T,succ(zero)) = empty_Tup;
{19} gt(n,succ(zero)) = true = > tleft(append_Tup(a,T),n) =
                        append_Tup(a,tleft(T,pred(n)));
{20} tright(append_Tup(a,T),succ(zero)) = T;
{21} gt(n,succ(zero)) = true = > tright(append_Tup(a,T),n) =
                        tright(T,pred(n));

{22} kind_Att(att_Tup(t)) = tup_k;
{23} kind_Att(att_Rel(R)) = rel_k;
{24} kind_Att(att_Int(n)) = int_k;
{25} kind_Att(att_Id(d)) = id_k;
{26} kind_Att(att_Bool(b)) = bool_k;

{27} rel_from_Att(att_Rel(R)) = R;

{28} in(empty_Rel,T) = false;
{29} in(insert(R,T),T1) = or(eq_Tup(T,T1),in(R,T1));

{30} remove(empty_Rel,T) = empty_Rel;
{31} not(eq_Tup(T,T1)) = true = > remove(insert(R,T),T1) =
                        insert(remove(R,T1),T);
{32} eq_Tup(T,T1) = true = > remove(insert(R,T),T1) = R;

{33} in(R,T) = true = > add_Tup(R,T) = R;
{34} not(in(R,T)) = true = > add_Tup(R,T) = insert(R,T);

{35} eq_Rel(empty_Rel,empty_Rel) = true;
{36} eq_Rel(insert(R,T),empty_Rel) = false;
{37} eq_Rel(empty_Rel,insert(R,T)) = false;

{38} eq_Rel(insert(R,T),R1) = and(in(R1,T),eq_Rel(R,remove(R1,T)));

{39} cont(R,empty_Rel) = true;
{40} cont(R,insert(R1,T)) = and(in(R,T),cont(R,R1));

{41} union(R,empty_Rel) = R;
{42} union(R,insert(R1,T)) = add_Tup(union(R,R1),T);

{43} union_nc(R,empty_Rel) = R;
{44} union_nc(R,insert(R1,T)) = insert(union_nc(R,R1),T);

{45} diff(empty_Rel,R) = empty_Rel;
{46} in(R1,T) = true = > diff(insert(R,T),R1) = diff(R,R1);
{47} not(in(R1,T)) = true = > diff(insert(R,T),R1) = insert(diff(R,R1),T);
{48} intersec(empty_Rel,R) = empty_Rel;
{49} in(R1,T) = true = > intersec(insert(R,T),R1) =
                  insert(intersec(R,R1),T);
{50} in(R1,T) = false = > intersec(insert(R,T),R1) = intersec(R,R1);

{51} tup_prod(T,empty_Rel) = empty_Rel;
{52} tup_prod(T, insert(R,T1)) = insert(tup_prod(T,R),conc_Tup(T,T1));

{53} cart_prod(empty_Rel,R) = empty_Rel;
{54} cart_prod(insert(R,T),R1) = union_nc(cart_prod(R,R1),tup_prod(T,R1));

{55} cx_Att(T,all_att(n)) = nth(T,n);
{56} kind_Att(nth(t,n)) = tup_k = > cx_Att(T,list_att(n,l)) =
                  att_Tup(proj_Tup(tup_from_Att(nth(t,n)),l));
{57} kind_Att(nth(t,n)) = rel_k = > cx_Att(t,list_att(n,l)) =
                  att_Rel(project(rel_from_Att(nth(t,n)),l));

{58} proj_Tup(empty_Tup,l) = empty_Tup;
{59} proj_Tup(T, empty_plist) = empty_Tup;
{60} proj_Tup(append_Tup(a, T), append_plist(ai,l)) =
    append_Tup(cx_Att(append_Tup(a,T),ai),proj_Tup(append_Tup(a,T),l));

{61} project(R, empty_plist) = empty_Rel;
{62} project(empty_Rel,l) = empty_Rel;
{63} project(insert(R,T), l) = add_Tup(project(R,l),proj_Tup(T,l));

{64} eval_Tup(T, p) = eval_Bool(reduc(p,T));

{65} is_lt(pp(il)) = false;
{66} is_lt(lb(b)) = true;
{67} is_lt(li(n)) = true;
{68} is_lt(ld(d)) = true;
{69} is_lt(lu(t)) = true;
{70} is_lt(lr(R)) = true;
{71} is_lt(op1(o,P,spc)) = is_lt(P);
{72} is_lt(op2(o,P1,P2,spc)) = and(is_lt(P1),is_lt(P2));

{73} red_ilst(pp(app_i(n,emptyilst)),t) = val(nth(t,n));
{74} red_ilst(pp(app_i(n,il)),t) = red_ilst(pp(il),tup_from_Att(nth(t,n)));

{75} is_lt(P) = true = > reduc(P,T) = P;
{76} reduc(pp(il),T) = red_ilst(pp(il),T);
{77} reduc(op1(o,P,spc),T) = op1(o,reduc(P,T),spc);
{78} reduc(op2(o,P1,P2,spc),T) = op2(o,reduc(P1,T),reduc(P2,T),spc);

{79} val(att_Int(n)) = li(n);
{80} val(att_Bool(b)) = lb(b);
{81} val(att_Id(d)) = ld(d);
{82} val(att_Tup(t)) = lu(t);
{83} val(att_Rel(R)) = lr(R);

{84} att_pr(li(n)) = att_Int(n);
{85} att_pr(lb(b)) = att_Bool(b);
{86} att_pr(ld(d)) = att_Id(d);
{87} att_pr(lu(t)) = att_Tup(t);
{88} att_pr(lr(R)) = att_Rel(R);

{89} sl_sel(empty_Rel,p) = empty_Rel;
{90} eval_Tup(t,p) = true = > sl_sel(insert(R,t),p) = insert(sl_sel(R,p),t);
{91} not(eval_Tup(t,p)) = true = > sl_sel(insert(R,t),p) = sl_sel(R,p);

{92} select(empty_Rel,pth,p) = empty_Rel;
{93} select(insert(R,T),empty_path,p) = sl_sel(insert(R,T),p);
{94} select(insert(R,T),app_path(n,empty_path),p) =
    add_Tup(select(R,app_path(n,empty_path),p),
        chng(T,n,att_Rel(sl_sel(rel_from_Att(nth(T,n)),p))));
{95} select(insert(R,T),app_path(n,app_path(n1,pth)),p) =
    add_Tup(select(R,app_path(n,app_path(n1,empty_path)),p),
        chng(T,n,sel2(nth(T,n),n1,pth,p)));
{96} sel2(att_Rel(R),n1,pth,p) = att_Rel(select(R,app_path(n1,pth),p));
{97} sel2(att_Tup(t),n,app_path(n1,pth),p) =
    att_Tup(chng(t,n,sel2(nth(t,n),n1,pth,p)));
{98} sel2(att_Tup(t),n,empty_path,p) =
    att_Tup(chng(t,n,att_Rel(sl_sel(rel_from_Att(nth(t,n)),p))));

{99} join(empty_Rel,R,pth,p) = empty_Rel;
{100} join(insert(R,T),R1,pth,p) =
    union_nc(join(R,R1,pth,p),select(tup_prod(T,R1),pth,p));

{101} pjoin(empty_Rel,R,pth,p,l) = empty_Rel;
{102} pjoin(insert(R,T),R1,pth,p,l) =
    union_nc(pjoin(R,R1,pth,p,l),project(select(tup_prod(T,R1),pth,p),l));
{103} eval_Bool(lb(b)) = b;
{104} eval_Bool(op2(o,P,P1,spc)) = eval_Bool(eval_pr(op2(o,P,P1,spc)));
{105} eval_Bool(op1(o,P,spc)) = eval_Bool(eval_pr(op1(o,P,spc)));

{106} eval_pr(lb(b)) = lb(b);
{107} eval_pr(li(n)) = li(n);
{108} eval_pr(ld(d)) = ld(d);
{109} eval_pr(lu(t)) = lu(t);
{110} eval_pr(lr(R)) = lr(R);
{111} eval_pr(op2(o,lb(b),lb(b1),spc)) = eval_op2(o,lb(b),lb(b1),spc);
{112} eval_pr(op2(o,li(n),li(n1),spc)) = eval_op2(o,li(n),li(n1),spc);
{113} eval_pr(op2(o,ld(d),ld(d1),spc)) = eval_op2(o,ld(d),ld(d1),spc);

{114} eval_pr(op2(o,lu(T),lu(T1),spc)) = eval_op2(o,lu(T),lu(T1),spc);
{115} eval_pr(op2(o,lr(R),lr(R1),spc)) = eval_op2(o,lr(R),lr(R1),spc);
{116} eval_pr(op2(o,op1(o1,P,sp1),P1,spc)) =
        eval_pr(op2(o,eval_pr(op1(o1,P,sp1)),P1,spc));
{117} eval_pr(op2(o,op2(o2,P,P1,sp2),P2,spc)) =
        eval_pr(op2(o,eval_pr(op2(o2,P,P1,sp2)),P2,spc));
{118} eval_pr(op2(o,P1,op1(o1,P,sp1),spc)) =
        eval_pr(op2(o,P1,eval_pr(op1(o1,P,sp1)),spc));
{119} eval_pr(op2(o,P2,op2(o2,P,P1,sp2),spc)) =
        eval_pr(op2(o,P2,eval_pr(op2(o2,P,P1,sp2)),spc));
{120} eval_pr(op1(o,lb(b),spc)) = eval_op1(o,lb(b),spc);
{121} eval_pr(op1(o,li(n),spc)) = eval_op1(o,li(n),spc);
{122} eval_pr(op1(o,ld(d),spc)) = eval_op1(o,ld(d),spc);
{123} eval_pr(op1(o,lu(T),spc)) = eval_op1(o,lu(T),spc);
{124} eval_pr(op1(o,lr(R),spc)) = eval_op1(o,lr(R),spc);
{125} eval_pr(op1(o,op1(o1,P,sp1),spc)) =
        eval_pr(op1(o,eval_pr(op1(o1,P,sp1)),spc));
{126} eval_pr(op1(o,op2(o2,P,P1,sp2),spc)) =
        eval_pr(op1(o,eval_pr(op2(o2,P,P1,sp2)),spc));

{127} eval_op2(lan,lb(b),lb(b1),spc) = lb(and(b,b1));
{128} eval_op2(lor,lb(b),lb(b1),spc) = lb(or(b,b1));
{129} eval_op2(eq,lb(b),lb(b1),spc) = lb(equiv(b,b1));
{130} eval_op2(lxr,lb(b),lb(b1),spc) =
             lb(or(and(b,not(b1)),and(not(b),b1)));
{131} eval_op1(lnt,lb(b),spc) = lb(not(b));
{132} eval_op2(ad,li(n),li(n1),spc) = li(add(n,n1));
{133} eval_op2(su,li(n),li(n1),spc) = li(sub(n,n1));
{134} eval_op2(mu,li(n),li(n1),spc) = li(mult(n,n1));
{135} eval_op2(di,li(n),li(n1),spc) = li(div(n,n1));
{136} eval_op2(eq,li(n),li(n1),spc) = lb(equal_Nat(n,n1));
{137} eval_op2(df,li(n),li(n1),spc) = lb(not(equal_Nat(n,n1)));
{138} eval_op2(ae,li(n),li(n1),spc) = lb(ge(n,n1));
{139} eval_op2(ab,li(n),li(n1),spc) = lb(gt(n,n1));
{140} eval_op2(be,li(n),li(n1),spc) = lb(le(n,n1));
{141} eval_op2(bl,li(n),li(n1),spc) = lb(lt(n,n1));
{142} eval_op2(un,lr(R),lr(R1),spc) = lr(union(R,R1));
{143} eval_op2(it,lr(R),lr(R1),spc) = lr(intersec(R,R1));
{144} eval_op2(dr,lr(R),lr(R1),spc) = lr(diff(R,R1));
{145} eval_op2(cp,lr(R),lr(R1),spc) = lr(cart_prod(R,R1));
{146} eval_op2(eq,lr(R),lr(R1),spc) = lb(eq_Rel(R,R1));
{147} eval_op2(df,lr(R),lr(R1),spc) = lb(not(eq_Rel(R,R1)));
{148} eval_op2(eq,lu(T),lu(T1),spc) = lb(eq_Tup(T,T1));
{149} eval_op2(df,lu(T),lu(T1),spc) = lb(not(eq_Tup(T,T1)));
{150} eval_op2(eq,ld(d),ld(d1),spc) = lb(equal_Id(d,d1));
{151} eval_op2(df,ld(d),ld(d1),spc) = lb(not(equal_Id(d,d1)));
{152} eval_op2(jn,lr(R),lr(R1),pspec(pth,p)) = lr(join(R,R1,pth,p));
{153} eval_op1(sl,lr(R),pspec(pth,p)) = lr(select(R,pth,p));
{154} eval_op1(pj,lr(R),lspec(l)) = lr(project(R,l));
{155} eval_op1(af,lr(R),aspec(p,o)) = aggr_pr(R,p,o);

{156} multiply(t1,t,empty_Rel) = empty_Rel;
{157} multiply(t1,t,insert(R,T)) =
        insert(multiply(t1,t,R),conc_Tup(conc_Tup(t1,T),t));

{158} del_stru(empty_Rel,pth) = empty_Rel;
{159} del_stru(insert(R,t),app_path(n,empty_path)) =
         union(ds_Tup(t,n),del_stru(R,app_path(n,empty_path)));
{160} del_stru(insert(R,t),app_path(n,app_path(n1,pth))) =
         add_Tup(del_stru(R,app_path(n,app_path(n1,pth))),
            chng(t,n,del_k(nth(t,n),n1,pth)));
{161} ds_Tup(t,n) = multiply(tleft(t,n),tright(t,n),
            rel_from_Att(nth(t,n)));
{162} del_k(att_Tup(t),n,empty_path) = att_Rel(ds_Tup(t,n));
{163} del_k(att_Tup(t),n,app_path(n1,pth)) =
         att_Tup(chng(t,n,del_k(nth(t,n),n1,pth)));
{164} del_k(att_Rel(R),n,pth) = att_Rel(del_stru(R,app_path(n,pth)));

{165} make_stru(empty_Rel,pth,l) = empty_Rel;
{166} make_stru(insert(R,t),empty_path,l) = mk_stru(insert(R,t),l);
{167} make_stru(insert(R,t),app_path(n,pth),l) =
         add_Tup(make_stru(R,app_path(n,pth),l),
            chng(t,n,make_k(nth(t,n),pth,l)));
{168} make_k(att_Rel(R),pth,l) = att_Rel(make_stru(R,pth,l));
{169} make_k(att_Tup(t),empty_path,l) = att_Tup(mk_Tup(t,l));
{170} make_k(att_Tup(t),app_path(n,pth),l) =
         att_Tup(chng(t,n,make_k(nth(t,n),pth,l)));
{171} mk_stru(empty_Rel,l) = empty_Rel;
{172} mk_stru(insert(R,t),l) = mk_build(mk_stru(R,l),mk_Tup(t,l));
{173} mk_build(empty_Rel,t) = insert(empty_Rel,t);
{174} not(eq_Rel(R,empty_Rel)) = true = > mk_build(R,t) =
         union_nc(diff(R,common(R,t)),merge(insert(common(R,t),t)));
{175} common(empty_Rel,t) = empty_Rel;
{176} eq_rest(t,t1) = true = > common(insert(R,t),t1) =
            insert(common(R,t1),t);
{177} not(eq_rest(t,t1)) = true = > common(insert(R,t),t1) = common(R,t1);
{178} eq_rest(append_Tup(a,T),append_Tup(a1,T1)) = eq_Tup(T,T1);
{179} merge(insert(empty_Rel,t)) = insert(empty_Rel,append_Tup(a,t));
{180} merge(insert(insert(R,append_Tup(a,t)),append_Tup(a1,t))) =
      merge(insert(R,append_Tup(att_Rel(union(rel_from_Att(a),
                              rel_from_Att(a1))),t)));
{181} mk_Tup(t,l) = append_Tup(att_Rel(insert(empty_Rel,splim(t,l))),
            splin(t,l));
{182} splim(t,empty_plist) = empty_Tup;
{183} splim(t,append_plist(all_att(n),l)) =
         append_Tup(nth(t,n),splim(tright(t,n),dim_by(l,n)));
{184} splin(t,empty_plist) = t;
{185} splin(t,append_plist(all_att(n),l)) =
         conc_Tup(tleft(t,n),splin(tright(t,n),dim_by(l,n)));

{186} eval_expr(t,p) = att_pr(eval_pr(reduc(p,t)));

{187} tt_ext(empty_Rel,p) = empty_Rel;
{188} tt_ext(insert(R,t),p) = insert(tt_ext(R,p),
                        append_Tup(eval_expr(t,p),t));

{189} tup_ext(empty_Rel,pth,p) = empty_Rel;
{190} tup_ext(insert(R,t),empty_path,p) = tt_ext(insert(R,t),p);
{191} tup_ext(insert(R,t),app_path(n,empty_path),p) =

```
        insert( tup_ext( R,app_path(n,empty_path),p),
               chng(t,n,tpext3(nth(t,n),p)));
{192} tup_ext( insert( R,t),app_path(n,app_path(n1,pth)),p) =
        insert( tup_ext( R,app_path(n,app_path(n1,pth)),p),
               chng(t,n,tpext2(nth(t,n),n1,pth,p)));

{193} tpext2(att_Rel(R),n,pth,p) = att_Rel( tup_ext(R,app_path(n,pth),p));
{194} tpext2(att_Tup(t),n,app_path(n1,pth),p) =
        att_Tup(chng(t,n,tpext2(nth(t,n),n1,pth,p)));
{195} tpext2(att_Tup(t),n,empty_path,p) =
        att_Tup(chng(t,n,tpext3(nth(t,n),p)));
{196} tpext3(att_Rel(R),p) = att_Rel( tt_ext(R,p));
{197} tpext3(att_Tup(t),p) = att_Tup(append_Tup(eval_expr(t,p),t));

{198} tup_upd(empty_Rel,pth,n,p) = empty_Rel;
{199} tup_upd(insert(R,t),empty_path,n,p) = tt_upd(insert(R,t),n,p);
{200} tup_upd(insert(R,t),app_path(n,empty_path),m,p) =
        add_Tup( tup_upd(R,app_path(n,empty_path),m,p),
               chng(t,n,tpupd3(nth(t,n),m,p)));
{201} tup_upd(insert(R,t),app_path(n,app_path(n1,pth)),m,p) =
        add_Tup( tup_upd(R,app_path(n,app_path(n1,pth)),m,p),
               chng(t,n,tpupd2(nth(t,n),n1,pth,m,p)));

{202} tpupd2(att_Rel(R),n,pth,m,p) =
        att_Rel( tup_upd(R,app_path(n,pth),m,p));
{203} tpupd2(att_Tup(t),n,app_path(n1,pth),m,p) =
        att_Tup(chng(t,n,tpupd2(nth(t,n),n1,pth,m,p)));
{204} tpupd2(att_Tup(t),n,empty_path,m,p) =
        att_Tup(chng(t,n,tpupd3(nth(t,n),m,p)));
{205} tpupd3(att_Rel(R),m,p) = att_Rel(tt_upd(R,m,p));
{206} tpupd3(att_Tup(t),m,p) = att_Tup(chng(t,m,eval_expr(t,p)));

{207} tt_upd(empty_Rel,m,p) = empty_Rel;
{208} tt_upd(insert(R,t),m,p) = insert(tt_upd(R,m,p),
                               chng(t,m,eval_expr(t,p)));

{209} aggr_fun(R,p,o) = att_pr(aggr_pr(R,p,o));
{210} aggr_pr( insert( empty_Rel,t),p,o) = red_ilst(p,t);
{211} aggr_pr( insert( insert(R,t1),t),p,o) =
        eval_op2(o,aggr_pr( insert(R,t1),p,o),red_ilst(p,t),emp_spec);

{212} closure(exp,R) = cl_loop(exp,R,empty_Rel);
{213} or(eq_Rel(R,R1),cont(R1,R)) = true => cl_loop(exp,R,R1) = R1;
{214} not( or(eq_Rel(R,R1),cont(R1,R))) = true => cl_loop(exp,R,R1) =
        cl_loop(exp,compute(exp,union(R,R1)),union(R,R1));
{215} compute(exp,R) =
        rel_from_Att(eval_expr(append_Tup(att_Rel(R),empty_Tup),exp))
)

END
```

An Algebraic Specification of Process Algebra, Including Two Examples

ACP$_\tau$

A Universal Axiom System for Process Specification

J.A. Bergstra

University of Amsterdam, Department of Computer Science
P.O. Box 19268, 1000 GG Amsterdam
State University of Utrecht, Department of Philosophy
P.O. Box 8810, 3508 TA Utrecht

J.W. Klop

Centre for Mathematics and Computer Science
P.O. Box 4079, 1009 AB Amsterdam
Free University, Department of Mathematics and Computer Science
De Boelelaan 1081, 1081 HV Amsterdam

Starting with Basic Process Algebra (BPA), an axiom system for alternative composition (+) and sequential composition (·) of processes, we give a presentation in several intermediate stages leading to ACP$_\tau$, Algebra of Communicating Proccesses with abstraction. At each successive stage an example is given showing that the specification power is increased. Also some graph models for the respective axiom systems are informally presented. We conclude with the Finite Specification Theorem for ACP$_\tau$, stating that each finitely branching, effectively presented process (as an element of the graph model) can be specified in ACP$_\tau$ by means of a finite system of guarded recursion equations.

Key Words & Phrases: communicating processes, process algebra, bisimulation semantics, graph models, recursive specifications.
1985 Mathematical Subject Classification: 68Q10, 68Q55, 68Q45, 68N15.
1982 CR Categories: F.1.2, F.3.2, F.4.3, D.3.3.

Note: This paper is reprinted with kind permission of the CWI Newsletter and the Centre for Mathematics and Computer Science from Issue no. 15 of the CWI Newsletter (June 1987).

0. INTRODUCTION

Following R. Milner's development of his widely known Calculus of Communicating Systems, there have been in the last decade several approaches to *process algebra*, i.e. the algebraic treatment of communicating processes. In this paper we give a short and informal presentation of some developments in process algebra which started five years ago at the Centre for Mathematics and Computer Science, and since two years in cooperation with the University of Amsterdam and the State University of Utrecht . Most of the present paper can be found in the more complete survey [6], where the subjects of specification and verification of processes are treated in so-called bisimulation semantics. Here, we adopt a further restriction by concentrating on the specification issue.

We start with a very simple axiom system for processes called Basic Process Algebra, in which no communication facilities are present. This system is interesting not only because it is a nucleus for all process axiom systems that are devised and analyzed in the 'Algebra of Communicating Processes', but also because it provides a link with the classical and successful theory of formal languages, in particular where regular languages and context-free languages are concerned. In Section 2 we explain this link.

Next, we introduce more and more operators, leading first to the axiom system ACP (Algebra of Communicating Processes) where communication between processes is possible, and finally to ACP_τ (Algebra of Communicating Processes with abstraction). Examples are given showing that the successive extensions yield more and more specification power; and a culmination point is the Finite Specification Theorem for ACP_τ, stating that every finitely branching, effectively presented process can be specified in ACP_τ by a finite system of recursion equations. Of course, an algebraic system for processes is only really interesting and useful if also sufficient facilities for process *verification* are present. These require an extension with some infinitary proof rules which will not be discussed here (for these, see the full version of this paper [6]). We refer also to the same paper for a more extensive list of references than the one below.

1. BASIC PROCESS ALGEBRA

The kernel of all axiom systems for processes that we will consider, is Basic Process Algebra. Not only is for that reason an analysis of BPA and its models worth-while, but also because it presents a new angle on some old questions in the theory of formal languages, in particular about context-free languages and deterministic push-down automata. First let us explain what is meant by 'processes'.

The processes that we will consider are capable of performing atomic steps or *actions* $a, b, c, \ldots$, with the idealization that these actions are events without positive duration in time; it takes only one moment to execute an action. The actions are combined into composite processes by the operations $+$ and $\cdot$, with the interpretation that $(a + b) \cdot c$ is the process that first chooses between executing a or b and, second, performs the action c after which it is finished. At this stage it does not matter how the choice is made. These operations, *alternative composition* and *sequential composition* (or just sum and product), are the basic constructors of processes. Since time has a direction, multiplication is not commutative; but addition is, and in fact it is stipulated that the options (summands) possible at some stage of the process form a *set*. Formally, we will require that processes $x, y, z, \ldots$ satisfy the following axioms (where the product sign is suppressed):

$$
\begin{array}{|c|}
\hline
\text{BPA} \\
\hline
x + y = y + x \\
(x + y) + z = x + (y + z) \\
x + x = x \\
(x + y)z = xz + yz \\
(xy)z = x(yz) \\
\hline
\end{array}
$$

TABLE 1

In the Introduction we used the term 'process algebra' in the generic sense of denoting the area of algebraic approaches to concurrency, but we will also adopt the following technical meaning for it: any model of these axioms will be a *process algebra*. The simplest process algebra is the *term model* of BPA, whose elements are BPA-expressions (built from the atoms $a, b, c, \ldots$ by means of the basic constructors) modulo the equality generated by the axioms. The term model itself (let us call it **T**) is not very exciting: it contains only finite processes. In order to specify also infinite processes, we introduce *recursion variables* $X, Y, Z, \ldots$. Using these, one can specify the process $aaaaaa \cdots$ (performing infinitely many consecutive a-steps) by the recursion equation $X = aX$; indeed, by 'unwinding' we have $X = aX = aaX = aaaX = \cdots$. In general, we will admit simultaneous recursion, i.e. systems of recursion equations. A nontrivial example is the following specification of the process behaviour of a Stack with data 0,1:

STACK
$X = 0{\downarrow} YX + 1{\downarrow} ZX$
$Y = 0{\uparrow} + 0{\downarrow} YY + 1{\downarrow} ZY$
$Z = 1{\uparrow} + 0{\downarrow} YZ + 1{\downarrow} ZZ$

TABLE 2

Here $0{\downarrow}$ and $0{\uparrow}$ are the actions 'push 0' and 'pop 0', respectively; likewise for 1. Now Stack is specified by the first recursion variable, X. Indeed, according to the first equation the process X is capable of performing either the action $0{\downarrow}$, after which the process is transformed into YX, or $1{\downarrow}$, after which the process is transformed into ZX. In the first case we have, using the second equation, $YX = (0{\uparrow} + 0{\downarrow} YY + 1{\downarrow} ZY)X = 0{\uparrow} \cdot X + 0{\downarrow} YYX + 1{\downarrow} ZYX$. This means that the process YX has three options; after performing the first one ($0{\uparrow}$) it behaves like the original X. Continuing in this manner we find a transition diagram or *process graph* as in Figure 1.

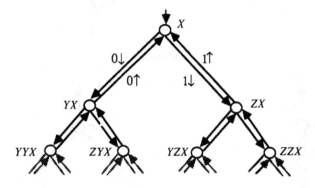

FIGURE 1. Stack

It is not hard to imagine how such a process graph (a rooted, directed, connected, labeled graph) can be associated with a system of recursion equations; we will not give a formal definition here. Actually, one can use such process graphs and build various models *(graph models)* for BPA from them; this will be discussed now.

2. GRAPH MODELS FOR BPA

Let $\mathbf{G}$ be the set of all at most countably branching process graphs $g, h, \ldots$ over the action alphabet $A = \{a, b, c, \ldots\}$. (I.e. a node in such a graph may have at most countably many one-step successors.) On $\mathbf{G}$ we define operations $+$ and $\cdot$ as follows: $g \cdot h$ is the result of appending (the root of) h at each termination node of g, and $g + h$ is the result of identifying the roots of g and h. (To be more precise, we first have to unwind g and h a little bit so as to make their roots 'acyclic', otherwise the sum would not have the intended interpretation of making an irreversible choice.) Letting $\mathbf{a}$ be the graph consisting of a single arrow with label a, we now have a structure $\mathcal{G} = \mathbf{G}(+, \cdot, \mathbf{a}, \mathbf{b}, \mathbf{c}, \ldots)$ which corresponds to the signature of BPA. But it is not a model of BPA. For instance the law $x + x = x$ does not hold in $\mathcal{G}$, since $\mathbf{a} + \mathbf{a}$ is not the same as $\mathbf{a}$; the former is a graph with two arrows and the latter has one arrow.

Here we need the fundamental notion of D. PARK (see [13]), called *bisimulation equivalence* or *bisimilarity*. Two graphs *g* and *h* are bisimilar if there is a matching between their nodes (i.e. a binary relation with domain the set of nodes of *g*, and codomain the set of nodes of *h*) such that (1) the roots are matched; (2) if nodes *s,t* in *g,h* respectively are matched and an a-step is possible from *s* to some *s'* then in *h* an a-step is possible from *t* to some *t'* such that *s'* and *t'* again *are matched* ; (3) likewise with the roles of *g,h* reversed. A matching satisfying (1-3) is a bisimulation. An example is given in Figure 2, where (part of) the matching is explicitly displayed; another example is given in Figure 3 where the matching is between each pair of nodes on the same horizontal level.

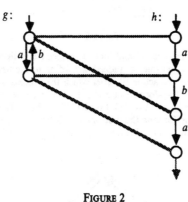

FIGURE 2

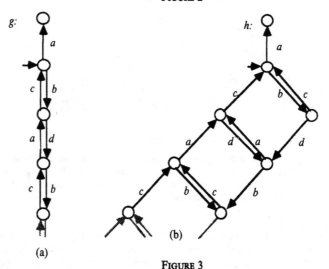

(a)   (b)

FIGURE 3

We use the notation $g \leftrightarrow h$ to express that *g* and *h* are bisimilar. Now one proves that $\leftrightarrow$ is not only an equivalence on **G**, but even a congruence on $\mathcal{G}$. Thus the quotient $\mathbf{G} = \mathcal{G}/\leftrightarrow$ is well-defined, and it is a model of BPA. (**G** has constants $a = \mathbf{a}/\leftrightarrow$ etc., and operations $+,\cdot$ defined by $g + h = (\mathbf{g} + \mathbf{h})/\leftrightarrow$ for $g = \mathbf{g}/\leftrightarrow$ and $h = \mathbf{h}/\leftrightarrow$; likewise for $\cdot$. (For typographical reasons we will not distinguish between the syntactic $+,\cdot$ and the semantic $+,\cdot$ in our notation.)

Even more, **G** is a very nice model of BPA: all systems of recursion equations in the syntax of BPA have a solution in G, and systems of *guarded* recursion equations like in Table 1 have moreover a *unique* solution. 'Guarded' means that in the right-hand sides of the recursion equations no recursion variable can be accessed without passing an atomic action. (E.g. $X = a + X$ is not a guarded equation; it has many solutions: $a+b$, $a+c$, ...)

Some submodels (all satisfying the axioms of BPA) of G are of interest: G_{fb}, built from *finitely branching* process graphs; R, built from finite (but possibly cycle-containing) graphs; and F, built from finite and acyclic graphs. Also G_{fb} has the property of providing unique solutions for systems of guarded recursion equations. Without the condition of guardedness, there need not be solutions. E.g. the equation

$$X = Xa + a$$

cannot be solved in G_{fb}. In the model R of regular processes one can always find unique solutions for guarded recursion equations provided they are *linear*, that is, the expressions (terms) in the equations may only be built by sum and a restricted form of product called *prefix multiplication* $a \cdot s$ ('a' an atom, s a general expression) which excludes products of recursion variables as in Table 1. For a complete proof system for regular processes, see [11].

EXAMPLE

$$\{X = aX + bY, Y = cX + dY\}$$

is a linear system;

$$\{X = aXX + bY, Y = cX + dYXY\}$$

is not.

The model R contains the *finite-state* processes; hence the notation R for 'regular' as in formal language theory. Finally, F contains only finite processes and is in fact isomorphic to the term model T.

Some systems of recursion equations should be taken as equivalent. Clearly, $X = aX$ and $X = aaX$ specify the same process in G. Less clearly, the two systems

$$E_1 = \{X = a + bYX, \ Y = c + dXY\}$$

$$E_2 = \{X = a + bU, \ U = cX + dZX, \ Y = c + dZ, \ Z = aY + bUY\}$$

are equivalent in this sense: E_1 specifies the process graph in Figure 3a above, and E_2 specifies the graph in Figure 3b. Moreover, as we already saw, these two graphs are bisimilar. So E_1 and E_2 denote the same process in G. So the question arises: *Is equivalence of recursion equations over BPA, relative to the graph model G, decidable?* At the moment this question is wide open. There is an interesting connection here with *context-free languages*, as follows.

A guarded system of recursion equations over BPA corresponds in an obvious way (for details see [2]) to a context-free grammar (CFG) in Greibach Normal Form, and vice versa. Hence each context-free language (CFL) can be obtained as the set of finite traces of a process in G denoted by a system of guarded recursion equations. (A finite trace is the word obtained by following a path from the root to a termination node.) In fact, to generate a CFL it is sufficient to look at certain restricted systems of recursion equations called 'normed'. A system is normed if in every state (of the corresponding process) there is a possibility to terminate. E.g. $X = aX$ is not normed, but $X = b + aX$ is. There is a simple syntactical check to determine whether a system is normed or not. Clearly, the property 'normed' also pertains to process graphs. In [2] it is proved that the equivalence problem stated above is solvable for such normed systems. This is rather surprising in view of the well-known fact that the equality problem for CFLs is unsolvable. The point is that the process semantics in G of a CFG bears much more information than the trace set semantics, which is an abstraction from the process semantics.

The link with deterministic context-free languages resides in the following observation from

[2]:

THEOREM 2.1. *Let $g,h \in G$ be two normed and deterministic process graphs. Then $g \leftrightarrow h$ iff g and h have the same sets of finite traces.*

Here a graph is 'deterministic' if two arrows leaving the same node always have different label. The CFL (i.e. the set of finite traces) determined by a normed and deterministic graph, corresponding to a system of guarded recursion equations in BPA, is known as a *simple* CFL; the simple CFLs form a proper subclass of the deterministic CFLs.

Summarizing, we can state that BPA and its graph model obtained via the concept of bisimulation provide a new angle on some problems in the theory of formal languages, concerned with context-free languages. Here we think especially of *deterministic* context-free languages (DCFLs), obtained by deterministic push-down automata, with the well-known open problem whether the equality problem for DCFLs is solvable. Thus, even in the absence of the many operators for parallellism, abstraction etc. which are still to be introduced below, we have in BPA and its models an interesting theory with potential implications for the DCFL problem.

3. DEADLOCK

After the excursion to semantics in the preceding section we return to the development of more syntax for processes. A vital element in the present set-up of process algebra is the process δ, signifying 'deadlock'. The process ab performs its two steps and then terminates, succesfully; but the process $ab\delta$ *deadlocks* after the a- and b-action: it wants to do a proper (i.e. non-δ) action but it cannot. So δ is the acknowledgement of stagnation. With this in mind, the axioms to which δ is subject, may be clear:

DEADLOCK
$\delta + x = x$
$\delta \cdot x = \delta$

TABLE 3

The axiom system of BPA (Table 1) together with the present axioms for δ is called BPA$_\delta$. We are now in a position to motivate the absence in BPA of the 'other' distributive law: $z(x+y) = zx + zy$. For, suppose it would be added. Then $ab = a(b+\delta) = ab + a\delta$. This means that a process with deadlock possibility is equal to one without, conflicting with our intention to model also deadlock behaviour of processes.

The essential role of the new process δ will only be fully appreciated after the introduction of communication, below.

4. THE MERGE OPERATOR

If x,y are processes, their parallel composition' $x \| y$ is the process that first chooses whether to do a step in x or in y, and proceeds as the parallel composition of the remainders of x,y. In other words, the steps of x,y are interleaved or merged. Using an auxiliary operator $\mathbb{L}$ (with the interpretation that $x \mathbb{L} y$ is like $x \| y$ but with the commitment of choosing the initial step from x) the operation $\|$ can be succinctly defined by the axioms:

FREE MERGE
$x\|y=x\mathbin{\rule[0.3ex]{1.2ex}{0.4pt}\!\!\rule[0ex]{0.4pt}{1.4ex}}y+y\mathbin{\rule[0.3ex]{1.2ex}{0.4pt}\!\!\rule[0ex]{0.4pt}{1.4ex}}x$
$ax\mathbin{\rule[0.3ex]{1.2ex}{0.4pt}\!\!\rule[0ex]{0.4pt}{1.4ex}}y=a(x\|y)$
$a\mathbin{\rule[0.3ex]{1.2ex}{0.4pt}\!\!\rule[0ex]{0.4pt}{1.4ex}}y=ay$
$(x+y)\mathbin{\rule[0.3ex]{1.2ex}{0.4pt}\!\!\rule[0ex]{0.4pt}{1.4ex}}z=x\mathbin{\rule[0.3ex]{1.2ex}{0.4pt}\!\!\rule[0ex]{0.4pt}{1.4ex}}z+y\mathbin{\rule[0.3ex]{1.2ex}{0.4pt}\!\!\rule[0ex]{0.4pt}{1.4ex}}z$

TABLE 4

The system of nine axioms consisting of BPA and the four axioms for merge will be called PA. Moreover, if the axioms for δ are added, the result will be PA$_\delta$. The operators $\|$ and $\mathbin{\rule[0.3ex]{1.2ex}{0.4pt}\!\!\rule[0ex]{0.4pt}{1.4ex}}$ will also be called *merge* and *left-merge* respectively.

The merge operator corresponds to what in the theory of formal languages is called *shuffle*. The shuffle of the words ab and cd is the set of words $\{abcd, acbd, cabd, acdb, cadb, cdab\}$. Merging the processes ab and cd yields the process

$$ab\|cd=ab\mathbin{\rule[0.3ex]{1.2ex}{0.4pt}\!\!\rule[0ex]{0.4pt}{1.4ex}}cd+cd\mathbin{\rule[0.3ex]{1.2ex}{0.4pt}\!\!\rule[0ex]{0.4pt}{1.4ex}}ab=a(b\|cd)+c(d\|ab)$$
$$=a(b\mathbin{\rule[0.3ex]{1.2ex}{0.4pt}\!\!\rule[0ex]{0.4pt}{1.4ex}}cd+cd\mathbin{\rule[0.3ex]{1.2ex}{0.4pt}\!\!\rule[0ex]{0.4pt}{1.4ex}}b)+c(d\mathbin{\rule[0.3ex]{1.2ex}{0.4pt}\!\!\rule[0ex]{0.4pt}{1.4ex}}ab+ab\mathbin{\rule[0.3ex]{1.2ex}{0.4pt}\!\!\rule[0ex]{0.4pt}{1.4ex}}d)$$
$$=a(bcd+c(d\|b))+c(dab+a(b\|d))$$
$$=a(bcd+c(db+bd))+c(dab+a(bd+db)),$$

a process having as trace set the shuffle above.

An example of a process recursively defined in PA, is $X=a(b\|X)$. It turns out that this process can already be defined in BPA, by the system of recursion equations

$$\{X=aYX, Y=b+aYY\}.$$

To see that both ways of defining X yield the same process, one may 'unwind' according to the given equations:

$$X=a(b\|X)=a(b\mathbin{\rule[0.3ex]{1.2ex}{0.4pt}\!\!\rule[0ex]{0.4pt}{1.4ex}}X+X\mathbin{\rule[0.3ex]{1.2ex}{0.4pt}\!\!\rule[0ex]{0.4pt}{1.4ex}}b)=a(bX+a(b\|X)\mathbin{\rule[0.3ex]{1.2ex}{0.4pt}\!\!\rule[0ex]{0.4pt}{1.4ex}}b)$$
$$=a(bX+a((b\|X)\|b))$$
$$=a(bX+a\ldots),$$

while on the other hand

$$X=aYX=a(b+aYY)X=a(bX+aYYX)=a(bX+a\ldots).$$

So at least up to level 2 the processes are equal. By further unwinding they can be proved equal up to each finite level.

Yet there are processes definable in PA but not in BPA. An example (from [4]) of such a process is given by the recursion equation

$$X=0{\downarrow}\cdot(0{\uparrow}\|X)+1{\downarrow}\cdot(1{\uparrow}\|X)$$

describing the process behaviour of a Bag (or multiset), in which arbitrarily many instances of the data 0,1 can be inserted (the actions $0{\downarrow},1{\downarrow}$ respectively) or retrieved ($0{\uparrow},1{\uparrow}$), with the restriction that no more 0's and 1's can taken from the Bag than were put in first. The difference with a Stack or a Queue is that all order between incoming and outgoing 0's and 1's is lost. The process graph corresponding to the process Bag is as in Figure 4.

We conclude this section on PA by mentioning the following fact (see [4]), which is useful for establishing non-definability results:

THEOREM 4.1. *Every process which is recursively defined in PA and has an infinite trace, has an eventually periodic trace.*

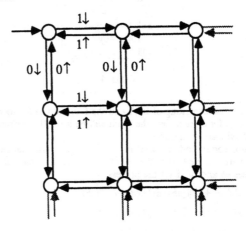

FIGURE 4. Bag

5. COMMUNICATION

So far, the parallel composition or merge ($\|$) did not involve communication in the process $x\|y$: one could say that x and y are 'freely' merged or interleaved. However, some actions in one process may need an action in another process for an actual execution, like the act of shaking hands requires simultaneous acts of two persons. In fact, 'handshaking' is the paradigm for the type of communication which we will introduce now. If $A=\{a,b,c,\ldots,\delta\}$ is the action alphabet, let us adopt a binary communication function $|:A\times A\to A$ satisfying the axioms in Table 5.

COMMUNICATION FUNCTION
$a\,|\,b=b\,|\,a$
$(a\,|\,b)\,|\,c=a\,|\,(b\,|\,c)$
$\delta\,|\,a=\delta$

TABLE 5

Here a,b vary over A, including δ. We can now specify *merge with communication* ; we use the same notation $\|$ as for the 'free' merge in Section 4 since in fact 'free' merge is an instance of merge with communication by choosing the communication function trivial, i.e. $a\,|\,b=\delta$ for all $a,b\in A$. There are now two auxiliary operators, allowing a finite axiomatisation: left-merge ($\|\!\lfloor$) as before and $|$ *(communication merge* or simply 'bar'), which is an extension of the communication function in Table 5 to all processes, not only the atoms. The axioms for $\|$ and its auxiliary operators are given in Table 6.

MERGE WITH COMMUNICATION
$x\|y=x\mathbin{\rule[-.3ex]{.8ex}{1.2ex}}y+y\mathbin{\rule[-.3ex]{.8ex}{1.2ex}}x+x\,|\,y$
$ax\mathbin{\rule[-.3ex]{.8ex}{1.2ex}}y=a(x\|y)$
$a\mathbin{\rule[-.3ex]{.8ex}{1.2ex}}y=ay$
$(x+y)\mathbin{\rule[-.3ex]{.8ex}{1.2ex}}z=x\mathbin{\rule[-.3ex]{.8ex}{1.2ex}}z+y\mathbin{\rule[-.3ex]{.8ex}{1.2ex}}z$
$ax\,|\,b=(a\,|\,b)x$
$a\,|\,bx=(a\,|\,b)x$
$ax\,|\,by=(a\,|\,b)(x\|y)$
$(x+y)\,|\,z=x\,|\,z+y\,|\,z$
$x\,|\,(y+z)=x\,|\,y+x\,|\,z$

TABLE 6

We also need the so-called *encapsulation* operators ∂_H (for every $H\subseteq A$) for removing unsuccessful attempts at communication:

ENCAPSULATION
$\partial_H(a)=a$ if $a\notin H$
$\partial_H(a)=\delta$ if $a\in H$
$\partial_H(x+y)=\partial_H(x)+\partial_H(y)$
$\partial_H(xy)=\partial_H(x)\cdot\partial_H(y)$

TABLE 7

These axioms express that ∂_H 'kills' all atoms mentioned in H, by replacing them with δ. The axioms for BPA, DEADLOCK together with the present ones in Tables 5-7 constitute the axiom system ACP (Algebra of Communicating Processes). Typically, a system of communicating processes $x_1,\ldots,x_n$ is now represented in ACP by the expression $\partial_H(x_1\|\cdots\|x_n)$. Prefixing the encapsulation operator says that the system $x_1,\ldots,x_n$ is to be perceived as a separate unit with respect to the communication actions mentioned in H; no communications between actions in H with an environment are expected or intended.

A useful theorem to break down such expressions is the *Expansion Theorem* (first formulated by Milner, for the case of CCS; see [12]) which holds under the assumption of the *handshaking axiom* $x\,|\,y\,|\,z=\delta$. This axiom says that all communications are binary. (In fact we have to require associativity of '$\|$' first - see Table 8.)

THEOREM 5.1 (EXPANSION THEOREM).

$$x_1\|\cdots\|x_k=\sum_i x_i\mathbin{\rule[-.3ex]{.8ex}{1.2ex}}X_k^i+\sum_{i\neq j}(x_i\,|\,x_j)\mathbin{\rule[-.3ex]{.8ex}{1.2ex}}X_k^{ij}$$

Here X_k^i denotes the merge of $x_1,\ldots,x_k$ except x_i, and X_k^{ij} denotes the same merge except x_i,x_j ($k\geqslant3$). For instance, for $k=3$:

$$x\|y\|z=x\mathbin{\rule[-.3ex]{.8ex}{1.2ex}}(y\|z)+y\mathbin{\rule[-.3ex]{.8ex}{1.2ex}}(x\|x)+z\mathbin{\rule[-.3ex]{.8ex}{1.2ex}}(x\|y)+(y\,|\,z)\mathbin{\rule[-.3ex]{.8ex}{1.2ex}}x+(z\,|\,x)\mathbin{\rule[-.3ex]{.8ex}{1.2ex}}y+(x\,|\,y)\mathbin{\rule[-.3ex]{.8ex}{1.2ex}}z.$$

In order to prove the Expansion Theorem, one first proves by simultaneous induction on term complexity that for all closed ACP-terms (i.e. ACP-terms without free variables) the following *axioms of standard concurrency* hold:

AXIOMS OF STANDARD CONCURRENCY
$(x \parallel y) \parallel z = x \parallel (y \parallel z)$
$(x \mid y) \parallel z = x \mid (y \parallel z)$
$x \mid y = y \mid x$
$x \parallel y = y \parallel x$
$x \mid (y \mid z) = (x \mid y) \mid z$
$x \parallel (y \parallel z) = (x \parallel y) \parallel z$

TABLE 8

As in Section 2 one can construct graph models $\mathbf{G}, \mathbf{G}_{fb}, \mathbf{R}, \mathbf{F}$ for ACP; in these models the axioms in Table 8 are valid. We will discuss the construction of these models in Section 7. (It is however also possible to construct 'non-standard' models of ACP in which these axioms do not hold. We will not be interested in such pathological models.)

The defining power of ACP is strictly greater than that of PA. The following is an example (from [4]) of a process U, recursively defined in ACP, but not definable in PA: let the alphabet be $\{a, b, c, d, \delta\}$ and let the communication function be given by $c \mid c = a$, $d \mid d = b$, and all other communications equal to δ. Let $H = \{c, d\}$. Now we recursively define the process U as in Table 9:

$U = \partial_H(dcY \parallel Z)$
$X = cXc + d$
$Y = dXY$
$Z = dXcZ$

TABLE 9

Then, we claim, $U = ba(ba^2)^2(ba^3)^2(ba^4)^2 \cdots$. Indeed, using the axioms in ACP and putting

$$U_n = \partial_H(dc^n Y \parallel Z)$$

for $n \geqslant 1$, a straightforward computation shows that

$$U_n = ba^n ba^{n+1} U_{n+1}.$$

By Theorem 4.1, U is not definable in PA, since the one infinite trace of U is not eventually periodic.

We will often adopt a special format for the communication function, called *read-write communication*. Let a finite set D of *data* d and a set $\{1, \ldots, p\}$ of *ports* be given. Then the alphabet consists of *read* actions $ri(d)$ and *write* actions $wi(d)$, for $i = 1, \ldots, p$ and $d \in D$. The interpretation is: read datum d at port i, write datum d at port i respectively. Furthermore, the alphabet contains actions $ci(d)$ for $i = 1, \ldots, p$ and $d \in D$, with interpretation: *communicate d at i*. These actions will be called *transactions*. The only non-trivial communications (i.e. not resulting in δ) are: $wi(d) \mid ri(d) = ci(d)$. Instead of $wi(d)$ we will also use the notation $si(d)$ (send d along i). Note that read-write communication satisfies the handshaking axiom: all communications are binary.

EXAMPLE 5.1.

Using the present read-write communication format we can write the recursion equation for a Bag B_{12} (cf. Section 4) which reads data $d \in D$ at port 1 and writes them at port 2 as follows:

$$B_{12} = \sum_{d \in D} r1(d)(w2(d) \parallel B_{12}).$$

6. ABSTRACTION

A fundamental issue in the design and specification of hierarchical (or modularized) systems of communicating processes is *abstraction*. Without having an abstraction mechanism enabling us to abstract from the inner workings of modules to be composed to larger systems, specification of all but very small systems would be virtually impossible. We will now extend the axiom system ACP, obtained thus far, with such an abstraction mechanism.

Consider two Bags B_{12}, B_{23} (cf. Example 5.1) with action alphabets $\{r1(d), s2(d) | d \in D\}$ and $\{r2(d), s3(d) | d \in D\}$, respectively. That is, B_{12} is a bag-like channel reading data d at port 1, sending them to port 2; B_{23} reads data at 2 and sends them to 3. (That the channels are bags means that, unlike the case of a queue, the order of incoming data is lost in the transmission.) Suppose the bags are connected at port 2; so we adopt communications $s2(d) | r2(d) = c2(d)$ where $c2(d)$ is the transaction of d at 2.

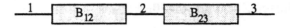

FIGURE 5. Transparent Bag B_{13}

The composite system $\mathbf{B}_{13} = \partial_H(B_{12} \| B_{23})$ where $H = \{s2(d), r2(d) | d \in D\}$, should, intuitively, be again a Bag between ports 1,3. However, from some (rather involved) calculations we learn that

$$\mathbf{B}_{13} = \sum_{d \in D} r1(d) \cdot (c2(d) \cdot s3(d)) \| \mathbf{B}_{13}).$$

So $\mathbf{B}_{13}$ is a 'transparent' Bag: the passage of d through 2 is visible as the transaction event $c2(d)$. (Note that this terminology conflicts with the usual one in the area of computer networks, where a network is called transparent if the internal structure is *not* visible.)

How can we *abstract* from such internal events, if we are only interested in the external behaviour at 1,3? The first step to obtain such an abstraction is to remove the distinctive identity of the actions to be abstracted, that is, to rename them all into one designated action which we call, after Milner, τ: the *silent* action. This renaming is realised by the *abstraction operator* τ_I, parameterized by a set of actions $I \subseteq A$ and subject to the following axioms:

ABSTRACTION
$\tau_I(\tau) = \tau$
$\tau_I(a) = a$ if $a \notin I$
$\tau_I(a) = \tau$ if $a \in I$
$\tau_I(x + y) = \tau_I(x) + \tau_I(y)$
$\tau_I(xy) = \tau_I(x) \cdot \tau_I(y)$

TABLE 10

The second step is to attempt to devise axioms for the silent step τ by means of which τ can be removed from expressions, as e.g. in the equation $a\tau b = ab$. However, it is not possible to remove *all* τ's in an expression if one is interested in a faithful description of deadlock behaviour of processes (at least in bisimulation semantics, the framework adopted in this paper). For, consider the process (expression) $a + \tau\delta$; this process can deadlock, namely if it chooses to perform the silent action. Now, if one would propose naively the equations $\tau x = x\tau = x$, then $a + \tau\delta = a + \delta = a$, and the latter process has no deadlock possibility. It turns out that one of the proposed equations, $x\tau = x$, can be safely adopted, but the other one is wrong. Fortunately, R. Milner has devised some simple axioms which give a complete description of the properties of the silent step (complete with respect to a certain semantical notion of process equivalence called $\tau\tau\delta$-bisimulation, which does respect deadlock behaviour; this notion is discussed below), as follows.

SILENT STEP
$x\tau = x$
$\tau x = \tau x + x$
$a(\tau x + y) = a(\tau x + y) + ax$

TABLE 11

To return to our example of the 'transparent' Bag $\mathbf{B}_{13}$, after abstraction of the set of transactions $I = \{c\,2(d)\,|\,d \in D\}$ the result is indeed an 'ordinary' Bag:

$$\tau_I(\mathbf{B}_{13}) = \tau_I(\sum_{d \in D} r\,1(d)(c\,2(d)\cdot s\,3(d)\|\mathbf{B}_{13})) \tag{*}$$

$$= \sum_{d \in D} r\,1(d)(\tau \cdot s\,3(d)\|\tau_I(\mathbf{B}_{13})) = \sum_{d \in D} (r\,1(d)\cdot\tau \cdot s\,3(d))\|\!\underline{}\,\tau_I(\mathbf{B}_{13})$$

$$= \sum_{d \in D} (r\,1(d)\cdot s\,3(d))\|\!\underline{}\,\tau_I(\mathbf{B}_{13}) = \sum_{d \in D} r\,1(d)(s\,3(d)\|\tau_I(\mathbf{B}_{13}))$$

from which it follows that $\tau_I(\mathbf{B}_{13}) = B_{13}$ (**), the Bag defined by

$$B_{13} = \sum_{d \in D} r\,1(d)(s\,3(d)\|B_{13}).$$

Here we were able to eliminate all silent actions, but this will not always be the case. For instance, 'chaining' two Stacks instead of Bags as in Figure 5 yields a process with 'essential' τ-steps. Likewise for a Bag followed by a Stack. (Here 'essential' means: non-removable in bisimulation semantics.) In fact, the computation above is not as straightforward as was suggested: to justify the equations marked with (*) and (**) we need additional proof principles. As to (**), this equation is justified by the *Recursive Specification Principle* (RSP) stating that a *guarded system of recursion equations in which no abstraction operator τ_I appears, has a unique solution.* We will not discuss the justification of equation (*) here. The justification of a principle like RSP is that it is valid in all 'sensible' models of our axioms; however note that for formal computations one has to postulate such a principle explicitly.

Combining all the axioms presented above in Tables 1,3,4,5,6,7,10,11 and a few axioms specifying the interaction between τ and communication merge |, we have arrived at the system ACP$_\tau$, *Algebra of Communicating Processes with abstraction* (see Table 12).

Actually, in spite of our restriction to specification of processes as stated in the Introduction, the last computation concerned a very simple process *verification*, showing that the combined system has the desired external behaviour of a Bag. Abstraction, realized in ACP$_\tau$ by the abstraction operator and the silent process τ, clearly is of crucial importance for process verification. But also for process specification abstraction is important. Let $f : \mathbb{N} \to \{a,b\}$ be a sequence of symbols a,b, and let p_f be the proces $f(0)\cdot f(1)\cdot f(2)\ldots$, that is, the unique solution of the infinite system of recursion equations $\{X_n = f(n)\cdot X_{n+1}\,|\,n \geqslant 0\}$. Now we have:

THEOREM 6.1. *There is a computable function f such that process p_f is not definable by a finite system of recursion equations in ACP$_\tau$ without abstraction operator.*

On the other hand, according to the Finite Specification Theorem 8.1, every process p_f with computable f *is* definable by a finite system of recursion equations in full ACP$_\tau$.

ACP_τ			
$x+y=y+x$	A1	$x\tau=x$	T1
$x+(y+z)=(x+y)+z$	A2	$\tau x+x=\tau x$	T2
$x+x=x$	A3	$a(\tau x+y)=a(\tau x+y)+ax$	T3
$(x+y)z=xz+yz$	A4		
$(xy)z=x(yz)$	A5		
$x+\delta=x$	A6		
$\delta x=\delta$	A7		
$a\mid b=b\mid a$	C1		
$(a\mid b)\mid c=a\mid(b\mid c)$	C2		
$\delta\mid a=\delta$	C3		
$x\parallel y=x\mathbin{\|\!\lfloor} y+y\mathbin{\|\!\lfloor} x+x\mid y$	CM1		
$a\mathbin{\|\!\lfloor} x=ax$	CM2	$\tau\mathbin{\|\!\lfloor} x=\tau x$	TM1
$ax\mathbin{\|\!\lfloor} y=a(x\parallel y)$	CM3	$\tau x\mathbin{\|\!\lfloor} y=\tau(x\parallel y)$	TM2
$(x+y)\mathbin{\|\!\lfloor} z=x\mathbin{\|\!\lfloor} z+y\mathbin{\|\!\lfloor} z$	CM4	$\tau\mid x=\delta$	TC1
$ax\mid b=(a\mid b)x$	CM5	$x\mid\tau=\delta$	TC2
$a\mid bx=(a\mid b)x$	CM6	$\tau x\mid y=x\mid y$	TC3
$ax\mid by=(a\mid b)(x\parallel y)$	CM7	$x\mid\tau y=x\mid y$	TC4
$(x+y)\mid z=x\mid z+y\mid z$	CM8		
$x\mid(y+z)=x\mid y+x\mid z$	CM9	$\partial_H(\tau)=\tau$	DT
		$\tau_I(\tau)=\tau$	TI1
$\partial_H(a)=a$ if $a\notin H$	D1	$\tau_I(a)=a$ if $a\notin I$	TI2
$\partial_H(a)=\delta$ if $a\in H$	D2	$\tau_I(a)=\tau$ if $a\in I$	TI3
$\partial_H(x+y)=\partial_H(x)+\partial_H(y)$	D3	$\tau_I(x+y)=\tau_I(x)+\tau_I(y)$	TI4
$\partial_H(xy)=\partial_H(x)\cdot\partial_H(y)$	D4	$\tau_I(xy)=\tau(x)\cdot\tau_I(y)$	TI5

TABLE 12

7. GRAPH MODELS FOR ACP_τ

We will now construct graph models for ACP_τ, in analogy with the construction of these models for BPA in Section 2. Again we start with a domain of at most countably branching process graphs **G**, the only difference being that arrows may now also bear label τ and δ. (By abuse of language we use the same notation **G**.) Next, we define on **G** in addition to $+,\cdot$ operations $\parallel,\mathbin{\|\!\lfloor},\mid,\boldsymbol{\tau_I},\boldsymbol{\partial_H}$ corresponding to the syntactic operations $\parallel,\mathbin{\|\!\lfloor},\mid,\tau_I,\partial_H$. We will only discuss the definition of the first operation $\parallel$. Let **ab** and **cd** be two process graphs as in Figure 6, and suppose there are communications $a\mid d=f$ and $b\mid c=k$, all other communications being trivial (i.e. resulting in δ). Then **ab**$\parallel$**cd** is the process graph indicated in Figure 6, a cartesian product with diagonal edges for the successful communications.

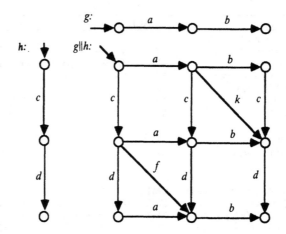

FIGURE 6

We now have a structure $\vartheta = G(+,\cdot,\|,\mathbb{L},|,\tau_I,\partial_H,\tau,\delta,a,b,c,\ldots)$, which is not yet a model of ACP$_\tau$ but becomes so after dividing out the congruence $r\tau\delta$-*bisimilarity* (notation: $\underset{r\tau\delta}{\leftrightarrow}$), a generalization of the 'ordinary' bisimilarity $\leftrightarrow$ of Section 2. Here we say that $g \underset{r\tau\delta}{\leftrightarrow} h$ if there is a relation between the nodes of g and the nodes of h such that (1) the roots are related; (2) a non-root node is only related to non-root nodes; (3) if nodes s,t in g,h respectively are related and there is in g an a-step from s to some s', then there is in g a path $\tau\tau\cdots\tau a\tau\tau\cdots\tau$ (i.e. zero or more τ-steps followed by an a-step followed by zero or more τ-steps) from t to some t' such that s' and t' are again related; (4) as (3) with the roles of g,h interchanged. (See for an example of such a $r\tau\delta$-bisimulation Figure 7.) Again, this equivalence is a congruence on ϑ and putting $G = \vartheta / \underset{r\tau\delta}{\leftrightarrow}$ we have a model for ACP$_\tau$, in which all systems of guarded recursion equations have a solution, and even a unique solution if abstraction operators are absent from the system.

As before in Section 2, G has submodels R,F (regular and finite processes, respectively). Remarkably, as observed in [1], there is no model G_{fb} based on all finitely branching graphs now. (For ACP such a model does exist.) The reason is that there is no structure ϑ_{fb}, since G_{fb} is not closed under the operations $\|,\mathbb{L},|,\tau_I$. The auxiliary operator $|$ is the culprit here.

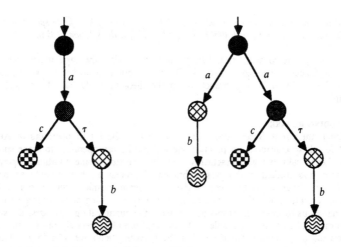

FIGURE 7. Example of $r\tau\delta$-bisimulation: nodes of the same colour are
related

8. THE FINITE SPECIFICATION THEOREM

ACP$_\tau$ is a powerful specification mechanism; in a sense it is a universal specification mechanism: *every finitely branching, computable process in the graph model* **G** *can be finitely specified* in ACP$_\tau$. (We use the word 'specification' for 'system of recursion equations'.) We have to be more precise about the notion of 'computable process'. First, an intuitive explanation: suppose a finitely branching process graph $g \in$ **G** is 'actually' given; the labels may include τ, and there may be even infinite τ-traces. That g is 'actually' given means that the process graph g must be 'computable': g can be described by some coding of the nodes in natural numbers and recursive functions giving in-degree, out-degree, edge-labels, etc. This notion of a computable process graph is rather obvious, and we will not give details of the definition here.

Now even if the computable graph g is an infinite process graph, it can trivially be specified by an infinite computable specification, as follows. First rename all τ-edges in g to t-edges, for a 'fresh' atom t. Call the resulting process graph: g_t. Next assign to each node s of g_t a recursion variable X_s and write down the recursion equation for X_s according to the outgoing edges of node s. Let X_{s_0} be the variable corresponding to the root s_0 of g_t. As g is computable, g_t is computable and the resulting 'direct' specification

$$E = \{X_s = T_s(\mathbf{X}) | s \in \text{NODES}(g_t)\}$$

is evidently also computable (i.e.: the nodes can be numbered as s_n $(n \geqslant 0)$, and after coding the sequence e_n of codes of equations $E_n : X_{s_n} = T_{s_n}(\mathbf{X})$ is a computable sequence). Now the infinite specification which uniquely determines g, is simply: $\{Y = \tau_{\{t\}}(X_{s_0})\} \cup E$. In fact all specifications below will have the form $\{X = \tau_I(X_0),\ X_n = T_n(\mathbf{X}) | n \geqslant 0\}$ where the guarded expressions $T_n(X)$ $(= T_n(X_{i_1}, \ldots, X_{i_k}))$ contain no abstraction operators τ_J. They may contain all other process operators. We will say that such specifications have *restricted abstraction*.

However, we want more than a computable infinite specification with restricted abstraction: to describe process graph g we would like to find a *finite* specification with restricted abstraction for g. Indeed this is possible:

THEOREM 8.1 (FINITE SPECIFICATION THEOREM). *Let the finitely branching and computable process graph g determine* **g** *in the graph model* **G** *of* ACP$_\tau$. *Then there is a finite specification with restricted abstraction E in* ACP$_\tau$ *such that* $[E] = g$. *Here* $[E]$ *is the solution of E in* **G**.

The proof in [1] is by constructing a Turing machine in ACP$_\tau$; the 'tape' is obtained by glueing together two Stacks as defined in Table 2. There does not seem to be an essential difficulty in removing the condition 'finitely branching' in the theorem, in favour of 'at most countably branching'.

9. CONCLUDING REMARKS

Even though the Finite Specification Theorem declares the set of operators of ACP$_\tau$ to be sufficient for all specifications, in practice one will need more operators to make specifications not only theoretically but also practically possible. Therefore some additional operators have been defined and studied in the present branch of process algebra, notably an operator by means of which different priorities can be given to different atomic actions, and a state operator taking into account information from a suitable state space. Using priorities imposed on atomic actions enables us to model interrupts in a system of communicating processes; the state operator has turned out to be indispensable in the construction of process algebra semantics for some object-oriented programming languages. For these developments we refer to [6]. Lately, some thorough studies have been made about extending ACP$_\tau$ with some new constants: ϵ for the empty process and η for an alternative to the silent step τ ([16,3]). The typical equation here is $\tau = \eta + \epsilon$.

A substantial amount of effort has been invested in extending ACP$_\tau$ to a suitable framework also for process verification, which was barely discussed in the present paper. Process verifications have been realized now for several non-trivial protocols ([14,9]), and recently also for some systolic algorithms ([10,15]) for tasks like palindrome recognition, matrix-vector multiplication. Some positive experience was also obtained using process algebra for the specification and verification of a simple production control system for a configuration of workcells.

Finally we mention that bisimulation semantics, as adopted in the present paper, is by no means the only process semantics. It is possible to identify many processes which are different in bisimulation semantics while still retaining an adequate description of relevant aspects such as deadlock behaviour, leading for instance to readiness semantics or failure semantics, embodying different views on processes. For a study in this area we refer to [7]. For an investigation of models of ACP$_\tau$ based on Petri Nets, see [8].

REFERENCES

1. J.C.M. BAETEN, J.A. BERGSTRA, J.W. KLOP (1987). On the consistency of Koomen's Fair Abstraction Rule. *TCS 51 (1/2)*, 129-176.
2. J.C.M. BAETEN, J.A. BERGSTRA, J.W. KLOP (1987). Decidability of bisimulation equivalence for processes generating context-free languages. J.W. DE BAKKER, A.J. NIJMAN, P.C. TRELEAVEN (eds.). *Proceedings of the PARLE Conference, Eindhoven 1987, Vol. II,* Springer LNCS 259, 94-113.
3. J.C.M. BAETEN, R.J. VAN GLABBEEK (1987). *Abstraction and Empty Process in Process Algebra,* CWI Report CS-R8721, Centre for Mathematics and Computer Science, Amsterdam.
4. J.A. BERGSTRA, J.W. KLOP (1984). The algebra of recursively defined processes and the algebra of regular processes. J. PAREDAENS (ed.). *Proc. 11th ICALP,* Antwerpen 1984, Springer LNCS 172, 82-95.
5. J.A. BERGSTRA, J.W. KLOP (1986). Algebra of communicating processes. J.W. DE BAKKER, M. HAZEWINKEL, J.K. LENSTRA (eds.). *CWI Monograph I, Proceedings of the CWI Symposium Mathematics and Computer Science,* North-Holland, Amsterdam, 89-138.
6. J.A. BERGSTRA, J.W. KLOP (1986). Process algebra: specification and verification in bisimulation semantics. M. HAZEWINKEL, J.K. LENSTRA, L.G.L.T. MEERTENS (eds.). *CWI Monograph 4, Proceedings of the CWI Symposium Mathematics and Computer Science II,*

North-Holland, Amsterdam, 61-94.

7. J.A. BERGSTRA, J.W. KLOP, E.-R. OLDEROG (1987). Failures without chaos: a new process semantics for fair abstraction. M. WIRSING (ed.). *Proceedings IFIP Conference on Formal Description of Programming Concepts, Gl. Avernaes 1986,* North-Holland, Amsterdam, 77-103.

8. R.J. VAN GLABBEEK, F.W. VAANDRAGER (1987). Petri net models for algebraic theories of concurrency. J.W. DE BAKKER, A.J. NIJMAN, P.C. TRELEAVEN (eds.). *Proc. PARLE Conference, Eindhoven 1987, Vol. II,* Springer LNCS 259, 224-242.

9. C.P.J. KOYMANS, J.C. MULDER (1986). *A Modular Approach to Protocol Verification using Process Algebra,* Logic Group Preprint Series Nr.6, Dept. of Philosophy, State University of Utrecht.

10. L. KOSSEN, W.P.WEIJLAND (1987). *Correctness Proofs for Systolic Algorithms: Palindromes and Sorting,* Report FVI 87-04, Computer Science Department, University of Amsterdam.

11. S. MAUW (1987). *A Constructive Version of the Approximation Induction Principle,* Report FVI 87-09, Computer Science Department, University of Amsterdam.

12. R. MILNER (1980). *A Calculus of Communicating Systems,* Springer LNCS 92.

13. D. PARK (1981). Concurrency and automata on infinite sequences. *Proc. 5th GI Conference,* Springer LNCS 104.

14. F.W. VAANDRAGER (1986). *Verification of Two Communication Protocols by Means of Process Algebra,* CWI Report CS-R8608, Centre for Mathematics and Computer Science, Amsterdam.

15. W.P.WEIJLAND (1987). *A Systolic Algorithm for Matrix-Vector Multiplication,* Report FVI 87-08, Computer Science Department, University of Amsterdam.

16. J.L.M. VRANCKEN (1986). *The Algebra of Communicating Processes with Empty Process,* Report FVI 86-01, Computer Science Department, University of Amsterdam.

Modular Specifications in Process Algebra

With Curious Queues

(extended abstract)

Rob van Glabbeek and Frits Vaandrager

Centre for Mathematics and Computer Science
P.O. Box 4079, 1009 AB Amsterdam, The Netherlands

In recent years a wide variety of process algebras has been proposed in the literature. Often these process algebras are closely related: they can be viewed as homomorphic images, submodels or restrictions of each other. The aim of this paper is to show how the semantical reality, consisting of a large number of closely related process algebras, can be reflected, and even used, on the level of algebraic specifications and in process verifications. This is done by means of the notion of a module. The simplest modules are building blocks of operators and axioms, each block describing a feature of concurrency in a certain semantical setting. These modules can then be combined by means of a union operator $+$, an export operator $\square$, allowing to forget some operators in a module, an operator H, changing semantics by taking homomorphic images, and an operator S which takes subalgebras. These operators enable us to combine modules in a subtle way, when the direct combination would be inconsistent. We show how auxiliary process algebra operators can be hidden when this is needed. Moreover it is demonstrated how new process combinators can be defined in terms of the more elementary ones in a clean way. As an illustration of our approach, a methodology is presented that can be used to specify FIFO-queues, and that facilitates verification of concurrent systems containing these queues.

Key Words & Phrases: process algebra, concurrency, modular algebraic specifications, export operator, union of modules, homomorphism operator, subalgebra operator, FIFO-queues, chaining operator, communication protocols.

1985 Mathematical Subject Classification: 68Q10, 68Q55, 68Q60.

1980 Mathematical Subject Classification: 68B10, 68C01, 68D25, 68F20.

1982 CR Categories: C.2.2, D.1.3, D.2.1, D.2.2, F.1.1, F.1.2, F.3.2.

Note: The research of the authors was supported by ESPRIT project no. 432, An Integrated Formal Approach to Industrial Software Development (METEOR). The research of the second author was also supported by RACE project no. 1046, Specification and Programming Environment for Communication Software (SPECS). A full version of this paper appeared as [23].

INTRODUCTION

During the last decade, a lot of research has been done on *process algebra*: the branch of theoretical computer science concerned with the modelling of concurrent systems as elements of an algebra. Besides the Calculus of Communicating Systems (CCS) of MILNER [31, 32], several related formalisms have been developed, such as the theory of Communicating Sequential Processes (CSP) of HOARE [17, 25], the MEIJE calculus of AUSTRY & BOUDOL [2] and the Algebra of Communicating Processes (ACP) of BERGSTRA & KLOP [11-14].

When work on process algebra started, many people hoped that it would be possible to come up, eventually, with the 'ultimate' process algebra, leading to a 'Church thesis' for concurrent computation. This process algebra, one imagined, should contain only a few fundamental operators and it should be suited to model all concurrent computational processes. Moreover there should be a calculus for this model making it possible to prove the identity of processes algebraically, thus proving correctness of implementations with respect to specifications. As far as we know, the ultimate process algebra has not yet been found, but we will not exclude that it will be discovered in the near future.

Two things however, have become clear in the meantime: (1) it is doubtful whether algebraic system verification, as envisaged in [31], will be possible in this model, and (2) even if the ultimate process algebra exists, this certainly does not mean that all other process algebras are no longer interesting. We elaborate on this below.

A central idea in process algebra is that two processes which cannot be distinguished by observation should preferably be identified: the process semantics should be fully abstract with respect to some notion of testing (see [20, 31]). This means that the choice of a suitable process algebra may depend on the tools an environment has to distinguish between certain processes. In different applications the tools of the environment may be different, and therefore different applications may require different process algebras. A large number of process semantics are not fully abstract with respect to any (reasonable) notion of testing (bisimulation semantics and partial order semantics, for instance). Still these semantics can be very interesting because they have simple definitions or correspond to some strong operational intuition. Our hypothetical ultimate process algebra will make very few identifications, because it should be resistant against all forms of testing. Therefore not many algebraic laws will be valid in this model and algebraic system verification will presumably not be possible (specification and implementation correspond to different processes in the model).

Another factor which plays a role has to do with the operators of process algebras. For theoretical purposes it is in general desirable to work with a single, small set of fundamental operators. We doubt however that such a unique optimal and minimal collection exists. What is optimal depends on the type of result one likes to prove. This becomes even more clear if we look towards practical applications. One could say that the main message of sections 4 and 5 of this paper is that chaining operators (which are not considered to be fundamental theoretically) are extremely useful for the specification of various types of queues and for the verification of properties of concurrent systems containing these queues. Some operators in process algebra can be used for a wide range of applications, but we agree with JIFENG & HOARE [26] that we may have to accept that each application will require derivation of specialised laws (and operators) to control its complexity.

Many people are embarrassed by the multitude of process algebras occurring in the literature. They should be aware of the fact that there are close relationships between the various process algebras: often one process algebra can be viewed as a homomorphic image, subalgebra or restriction of another one. The aim of this paper is to show how the semantical reality, consisting of a large number of closely related process algebras, can be reflected, and even used, on the level of algebraic specifications and in process verifications.

This paper is about process algebras, their mutual relationships, and strategies to prove that a formula is valid in a process algebra. Still, we do not present any particular process algebra in this paper. We only define classes of models of process modules. One reason for doing this is that a detailed description of particular process algebras would make this paper too long. Another reason is that there is often no clear argument for selecting a particular process algebra. In such situations we are interested in assertions saying that a formula is valid in all algebras satisfying a certain theory. A number of times we need results stating that some formulas *cannot* be proven from a certain module. A standard way to prove this is to give a model of the module where the formulas are not true. For this reason we will often refer to particular process algebras which have been described elsewhere in the literature.

The discussion of this paper takes place in the setting of ACP. We think however that the results can be carried over to CCS, CSP, MEIJE, or any other process algebra formalism.

Modularisation.
The creation of an algebraic framework suitable to deal with realistic applications, gives rise to the construction of building blocks, or modules, of operators and axioms, each block describing a feature of concurrency in a certain semantical setting. These modules can then be combined by means of a module combinator +. We give some examples:

i) A kernel module, that expresses some basic features of concurrent processes, is the module ACP. For a lot of applications however, ACP does not provide enough operators. Often the use of *renaming operators* makes specifications shorter and more comprehensible. These renaming operators can be defined in a separate module RN. Now the module ACP+RN combines the specification and verification power of modules ACP and RN.

ii) The axioms of module ACP correspond to the semantical notion of bisimulation. For some applications bisimulation semantics does not make enough identifications. In these cases one would like to deal with processes on the level of, for example, failure semantics. Now one can define a module F, corresponding to the identifications made in failure semantics on top of the identifications of bisimulation semantics. The module ACP+F then corresponds to the failure model.

Once a number of modules have been defined, they can be combined in a lot of ways. Some combinations are interesting (for example the module ACP+RN+F), for other combinations no interesting applications exist (the module RN+F). Didactical aspects aside, a major advantage of the modular approach is that results which have been proved from a module M, can also be proved from a module M+N. This means that process verifications become *reusable*.

It turns out that certain pairs of modules are incompatible in a very strong sense: with the combination of two modules strange and counter-intuitive identities can be derived. In BAETEN, BERGSTRA & KLOP [6], for example, it is shown that the combination of failure semantics and the priority operator is inconsistent in the sense that an identity can be derived which says that a process that can do a b-action after it has done an a-action, equals a process that cannot do this. Another example can be found in BERGSTRA, KLOP & OLDEROG [15], where it is pointed out that the combination of failure semantics and Koomen's Fair Abstraction Rule (KFAR) is inconsistent.

In the first section of this paper we present, beside the combinator +, some other operators on modules. We discuss an export operator $\Box$, allowing to forget some operators in a module, an operator H, changing semantics by taking homomorphic images, and an operator S which takes subalgebras. These operators enable us to combine modules in a subtle way, when the direct combination would be inconsistent. In section 2 we describe all the basic process modules used in the rest of the paper. Section 3 contains two examples of applications of the new module operators in process algebra:

1. The axiom system ACP contains auxiliary operators $\mathbin{\parallel}$ and $\mid$ (left-merge and communication-merge) which drastically simplify computations and have some desirable 'metamathematical' consequences (finite axiomatisability[1]; greater suitability for term

---

1. Recently, Faron Moller from Edinburgh showed that the merge operator cannot be finitely axiomatised without auxiliary operators.

rewriting analysis). These auxiliary operators can be defined in a large class of process algebras. However, it turns out that in a setting with the silent step τ the left-merge cannot be added consistently to all algebras (for instance not to the usual variants of failure semantics). Now one may think that this result means that someone who is doing failure semantics with τ's cannot profit from the nice properties of the left-merge. However, we will show in this paper that use of the module approach makes it possible to do failure semantics with τ's but still benefit from the left-merge in verifications. The idea is that verifications take place on two levels: the level of bisimulation semantics where the left-merge can be used, and a level of for instance failure semantics, where no left-merge is present. The failure model can be obtained from the bisimulation model by removing the auxiliary operators and taking a homomorphic image. Now we use the observation that certain formulas (the 'positive' ones without auxiliary operators) are preserved under this procedure. A consequence of this application is that even if bisimulation semantics is not considered to be an appropriate process semantics (since it is not fully abstract with respect to any reasonable notion of testing), it still can be useful as an expedient for proving formulas in failure semantics.

2. As already pointed out above, one would like to have, from a theoretical point of view, as few operators or combinators as possible. On the other hand, when dealing with applications, it is often very rewarding to introduce new operators. This paradox can be resolved if the new operators are definable in terms of the more elementary ones. In that case the new operators can be considered as notations which are useful, but do not complicate the underlying theory. A problem with defining operators in terms of other operators is that often auxiliary atomic actions are needed in the definition. These auxiliary actions can then not be used in any other place, because that would disturb the intended semantics of the operator. In the laws that can be derived for the defined operator, the auxiliary actions occur prominently. These 'side effects' are often quite unpleasant. One may think that side effects are unavoidable and that someone who really does not like them should define new operators directly in the algebras (even though this is in conflict with the desire to have as few operators as possible). However, we will show that the module approach can be used to solve also this problem: with the restriction operator we remove the auxiliary actions from the signature and then we apply the subalgebra operator in order to 'move' to algebras where the auxiliary actions are not present at all.

The concept of hiding auxiliary operators in a module in some formal way is quite familiar in the literature (see BERGSTRA, HEERING & KLINT [9] for example), but the use of module operators H and S, and their application in combining modules that would be incompatible otherwise, is, as far as we know, new. The H and S operations are in spirit related to the **abstract** operation of SANNELLA & WIRSING [38] and SANNELLA & TARLECKI [37], which also extends the model class of a module.

In previous papers on ACP, the underlying logic used in process verifications was not made explicit. The reason for this was that a long definition of the logic would distract the reader's attention from the more essential parts of the paper. It was felt that filling in the details of the logic would not be too difficult and that moreover different options were equivalent. In this paper we generalise the classical notion of a formal proof of a formula from a theory to the notion of a formal proof of a formula from a module. The definition of this last notion is parametrised by the underlying logic. What is provable from a module really depends on the logic that is used, and this makes it necessary to consider in more detail the issue of logics. In an appendix we present three alternatives: (1) Equational logic. This logic is suited for dealing with finite processes, but not strong enough for handling infinite processes; (2) Infinitary conditional equational logic. This is the logic used in the process verifications of this paper; (3) First order logic with equality.

Our investigations into the precise nature of the calculi used in process algebra, led us to alternative formulations of some of the proof principles in ACP which fit better in our formal setup. We present a reformulation of the Recursive Specification Principle (RSP) and also an alphabet operator which returns a process instead of a set of actions.

Queues.
As an illustration of the techniques developed in sections 1 to 3, we present in section 4 an algebraic treatment of FIFO-queues. FIFO-queues play an important role in the description of languages with asynchronous message passing, the modelling of communication channels occurring in computer networks and the implementation of languages with synchronous communication. We show how the chaining operator can be used to give short specifications of various (faulty) queues and simple proofs of numerous identities, for example of the fact that the chaining of a queue with unbounded capacity and a one datum buffer is again a queue.

We give an example of an identity that holds intuitively (there is no experiment that distinguishes between the two processes) but is not valid in bisimulation semantics. We use the machinery developed in section 1-3 to extend the axiom system in a neat way (avoiding inconsistencies) so that we can prove the processes identical.

A protocol verification.
The usefulness of the proof technique for queues is illustrated in section 5, where we sketch a modular verification of a concurrent alternating bit protocol. The complete verification, which is presented in [23], takes 4 pages (or 5 if the proof of the standard facts about the queues is included) and is thereby considerably shorter than the proof of similar protocols in papers by KOYMANS & MULDER [27] and LARSEN & MILNER [28] (15 and 11 pages respectively). The verification shows that the protocol is correct if the channels behave as faulty FIFO-queues with unbounded capacity. However, a minor change in the proof is enough to show that the protocol also works if the channels behave as n-buffers, faulty n-buffers, etc. In our view the basic merit of our way of dealing with queues is that it becomes possible to use inductive arguments when dealing with the length of queues in protocol systems.

§1 MODULE LOGIC
In this paper, as in many other papers about process algebra, we use formal calculi to prove statements about concurrent systems. In this section we answer the following questions:
- Which kind of calculi do we use?
- What do we understand by a proof?
In the next sections we will apply this general setup to the setting of concurrent systems.

1.1. Statements about concurrent systems. In many theories of concurrency it is common practice to represent processes - the behaviours of concurrent systems - as elements in an *algebra*. This is a mathematical domain, on which some operators and predicates are defined. Algebras, which are suitable for the representation of processes are called *process algebras*. Thus a statement about the behaviour of concurrent systems can be regarded as a statement about the elements of a certain process algebra. Such a statement can be represented by a formula in a suitable language which is interpreted in this process algebra. Sometimes we consider several process algebras at the same time and want to formulate a statement about concurrent processes without choosing one of these algebras. In this case we represent the statement by a formula in a suitable language which has an interpretation in all these process algebras. Hence we are interested in assertions of the form: 'Formula ϕ holds in the process algebra $\mathcal{C}$, notation $\mathcal{C} \vDash \phi$, or 'Formula ϕ holds in the class of process algebras $\mathcal{C}$, notation $\mathcal{C} \vDash \phi$. Now we can formulate the goal that is pursued in the present section: to propose a method for proving assertions $\mathcal{C} \vDash \phi$, or $\mathcal{C} \vDash \phi$.

1.2. Proving formulas from theories. Classical logic gave us the notion of a formal proof of a formula ϕ from a theory T. Here a theory is a set of formulas. We write $T \vdash \phi$ if such a proof exists. The use of this notion is revealed by the following soundness theorem: *If $T \vdash \phi$ then ϕ holds in all algebras satisfying T.* Here an algebra $\mathcal{C}$ satisfies T, notation $\mathcal{C} \vDash T$, if all formulas of T hold in this algebra. Thus if we want to prove $\mathcal{C} \vDash \phi$ it suffices to prove $T \vdash \phi$ and $\mathcal{C} \vDash T$ for a suitable theory T. Likewise, if we want to prove $\mathcal{C} \vDash \phi$, with $\mathcal{C}$ a class of algebras, it suffices to prove $T \vdash \phi$ and $\mathcal{C} \vDash T$.

At first sight the method of proving $\mathcal{C} \vDash \phi$ by means of a formal proof of ϕ out of T seems very inefficient. Instead of verifying $\mathcal{C} \vDash \phi$, one has to verify $\mathcal{C} \vDash \psi$ for all $\psi \in T$, and moreover the formal proof has to be constructed. However, there are two circumstances in which this method *is* efficient, and in most applications both of them apply. First of all it might be the case that ϕ is more complicated than the formulas of T and that a direct verification of $\mathcal{C} \vDash \phi$ is much more work than the formal proof and all verifications $\mathcal{C} \vDash \psi$ together. Secondly, it might occur that a single theory T with $\mathcal{C} \vDash T$ is used to prove many formulas ϕ, so that many verifications $\mathcal{C} \vDash \phi$ are balanced against many formal proofs of ϕ out of T and a single set of verifications $\mathcal{C} \vDash \psi$. Especially when constructing formal proofs is considered easier then making verifications $\mathcal{C} \vDash \phi$, this reusability argument is very powerful. It also indicates that for a given algebra $\mathcal{C}$ we want to find a theory T from which most interesting formulas ϕ with $\mathcal{C} \vDash \phi$ can be proved.

Often there are reasons for representing processes in an algebra that satisfies a particular theory T, but there is no clear argument for selecting one of these algebras. In this situation we are interested in assertions $\mathcal{C} \vDash \phi$ with $\mathcal{C}$ the class of all algebras satisfying T. Of course assertions of this type can be conveniently proved by means of a formal proof of ϕ from T.

1.3. Proving formulas from modules. In process algebra we often want to modify the process algebra currently used to represent processes. Such a modification might be as simple as the addition of another operator, needed for the proper modelling of yet another feature of concurrency, but it can also be a more involved modification, such as factoring out a congruence, in order to identify processes that should not be distinguished in a certain application. It is our explicit concern to organise proofs of statements about concurrent systems in such a way that, whenever possible, our results carry over to modifications of the process algebra for which they were proved.

Now suppose $\mathcal{C}$ is a process algebra satisfying the theory T and a statement $\mathcal{C} \vDash \phi$ has been proved by means of a formal proof of ϕ out of T. Furthermore suppose that $\mathcal{B}$ is obtained from $\mathcal{C}$ by factoring out a congruence relation on $\mathcal{C}$ (so $\mathcal{B}$ is a *homomorphic image* of $\mathcal{C}$) and for a certain application $\mathcal{B}$ is considered to be a more suitable model of concurrency than $\mathcal{C}$. Then in general $\mathcal{B} \vDash \phi$ cannot be concluded, but if ϕ belongs to a certain class of formulas (the *positive* ones) it can. So if ϕ is positive we can use the following theorem: 'If $\mathcal{C} \vDash T$, $T \vdash \phi$, ϕ is positive, and $\mathcal{B}$ is a homomorphic image of $\mathcal{C}$, then $\mathcal{B} \vDash \phi$'. This saves us the trouble of finding another theory U, verifying that $\mathcal{B} \vDash U$ and proving $U \vdash \phi$ for many formulas ϕ that have been proved from T already. Another way of formulating the same idea is to introduce a module $H(T)$. We postulate that one may derive '$H(T) \vdash \phi$' from '$T \vdash \phi$' and 'ϕ is positive', and $H(T) \vdash \phi$ implies that ϕ holds in all homomorphic images of algebras satisfying T.

Thus we propose a generalisation of the notion of a formal proof. Instead of theories we use the more general notion of *modules*. Like a theory a module characterises a class $\mathcal{C}$ of algebras, but besides the class of all algebras satisfying a given set of formulas, $\mathcal{C}$ can for instance also be the class of homomorphic images or subalgebras of a class of algebras specified earlier. Now a proof in the framework of module algebra is a sequence or tree of assertions $M \vdash \phi$ such that in each step either the formula ϕ is manipulated, as in classical proofs, or the module M is manipulated. Of course we will establish a soundness theorem as before, and then an assertion $\mathcal{C} \vDash \phi$ can be proved by means of a module M with $\mathcal{C} \vDash M$ and a formal proof of ϕ out of M. We will now turn to the formal definitions.

1.4. Signatures. Let NAMES be a given set of names.

A *sort declaration* is an expression $\mathbf{S}{:}S$ with $S \in$ NAMES.

A *function declaration* is an expression $\mathbf{F}{:}f{:}S_1 \times \cdots \times S_n {\rightarrow} S$ with $f, S_1, \cdots, S_n, S \in$ NAMES.

A *predicate declaration* is an expression $\mathbf{R}{:}p \subseteq S_1 \times \cdots \times S_n$ with $p, S_1, \cdots, S_n \in$ NAMES.

A *signature* σ is a set of sort, function and predicate declarations, satisfying:

$$\mathbf{F}_\sigma{:}f{:}S_1 \times \cdots \times S_n {\rightarrow} S \;\Rightarrow\; \mathbf{S}_\sigma{:}S_i \;(i=1,\cdots,n) \wedge \mathbf{S}_\sigma{:}S$$

$$\mathbf{R}_\sigma{:}p \subseteq S_1 \times \cdots \times S_n \;\Rightarrow\; \mathbf{S}_\sigma{:}S_i \;(i=1,\cdots,n)$$

Here $\mathbf{S}_\sigma{:}S$ is an abbreviation for $(\mathbf{S}{:}S) \in \sigma$ and likewise for $\mathbf{F}_\sigma$ and $\mathbf{R}_\sigma$. A function declaration $\mathbf{F}{:}f{:}{\rightarrow}S$ of arity 0 is sometimes called a *constant declaration* and written as $\mathbf{F}{:}f \in S$.

1.5. σ-Algebras. Let σ be a signature. A *σ-algebra* $\mathcal{A}$ is a function on σ that maps

$\mathbf{S}_\sigma{:}S$ to a set $S^{\mathcal{A}}$

$\mathbf{F}_\sigma{:}f{:}S_1 \times \cdots \times S_n {\rightarrow} S$ to a function $f^{\mathcal{A}}_{S_1 \times \cdots \times S_n \rightarrow S}{:}S_1^{\mathcal{A}} \times \cdots \times S_n^{\mathcal{A}} {\rightarrow} S^{\mathcal{A}}$ and

$\mathbf{R}_\sigma{:}p \subseteq S_1 \times \cdots \times S_n$ to a predicate $p^{\mathcal{A}}_{S_1 \times \cdots \times S_n} \subseteq S_1^{\mathcal{A}} \times \cdots \times S_n^{\mathcal{A}}$.

Let $\mathcal{A}$ and $\mathcal{B}$ be σ-algebras.

$\mathcal{B}$ is a *subalgebra* of $\mathcal{A}$ if $S^{\mathcal{B}} \subseteq S^{\mathcal{A}}$ for all $\mathbf{S}_\sigma{:}S$, if moreover $f^{\mathcal{A}}_{S_1 \times \cdots \times S_n \rightarrow S}$ restricted to $S_1^{\mathcal{B}} \times \cdots \times S_n^{\mathcal{B}} {\rightarrow} S^{\mathcal{B}}$ is just $f^{\mathcal{B}}_{S_1 \times \cdots \times S_n \rightarrow S}$ for all $\mathbf{F}_\sigma{:}f{:}S_1 \times \cdots \times S_n {\rightarrow} S$, and if $p^{\mathcal{A}}_{S_1 \times \cdots \times S_n}$ restricted to $S_1^{\mathcal{B}} \times \cdots \times S_n^{\mathcal{B}}$ is just $p^{\mathcal{B}}_{S_1 \times \cdots \times S_n}$ for all $\mathbf{R}_\sigma{:}p \subseteq S_1 \times \cdots \times S_n$.

A *homomorphism* $h{:}\mathcal{A}{\rightarrow}\mathcal{B}$ consists of mappings $h_S{:}S^{\mathcal{A}}{\rightarrow}S^{\mathcal{B}}$ for all $\mathbf{S}_\sigma{:}S$, such that

$$h_S(f^{\mathcal{A}}_{S_1 \times \cdots \times S_n \rightarrow S}(x_1, \cdots, x_n)) = f^{\mathcal{B}}_{S_1 \times \cdots \times S_n \rightarrow S}(h_{S_1}(x_1), \cdots, h_{S_n}(x_n))$$

for all $\mathbf{F}_\sigma{:}f{:}S_1 \times \cdots \times S_n {\rightarrow} S$ and all $x_i \in S_i^{\mathcal{A}}(i=1,\cdots,n)$

$$p^{\mathcal{A}}_{S_1 \times \cdots \times S_n}(x_1, \cdots, x_n) \Leftrightarrow p^{\mathcal{B}}_{S_1 \times \cdots \times S_n}(h_{S_1}(x_1), \cdots, h_{S_n}(x_n))$$

for all $\mathbf{R}_\sigma{:}p \subseteq S_1 \times \cdots \times S_n$ and all $x_i \in S_i^{\mathcal{A}}(i=1,\cdots,n)$

$\mathcal{B}$ is a *homomorphic image* of $\mathcal{A}$ if there exists a surjective homomorphism $h{:}\mathcal{A}{\rightarrow}\mathcal{B}$.

Let $\mathcal{A}$ be a σ-algebra. The *restriction* $\rho \square \mathcal{A}$ of $\mathcal{A}$ to the signature ρ is the $\rho \cap \sigma$-algebra $\mathcal{B}$, defined by

$$S^{\mathcal{B}} = S^{\mathcal{A}} \text{ for all } \mathbf{S}_{\rho \cap \sigma}{:}S$$

$$f^{\mathcal{B}}_{S_1 \times \cdots \times S_n \rightarrow S} = f^{\mathcal{A}}_{S_1 \times \cdots \times S_n \rightarrow S} \text{ for all } \mathbf{F}_{\rho \cap \sigma}{:}f{:}S_1 \times \cdots \times S_n {\rightarrow} S$$

$$p^{\mathcal{B}}_{S_1 \times \cdots \times S_n} = p^{\mathcal{A}}_{S_1 \times \cdots \times S_n} \text{ for all } \mathbf{R}_{\rho \cap \sigma}{:}p \subseteq S_1 \times \cdots \times S_n$$

1.6. Logics. A *logic* $\mathcal{L}$ is a complex of prescriptions, defining for any signature σ

a set $F^{\mathcal{L}}_\sigma$ of *formulas* over σ such that $F^{\mathcal{L}}_\sigma \cap F^{\mathcal{L}}_\rho = F^{\mathcal{L}}_{\sigma \cap \rho}$,

a binary relation $\vdash^{\mathcal{L}}_\sigma$ on σ-algebras $\times F^{\mathcal{L}}_\sigma$ such that for all ρ-algebras $\mathcal{A}$ and $\phi \in F^{\mathcal{L}}_{\sigma \cap \rho}$:

$$\sigma \square \mathcal{A} \vdash^{\mathcal{L}}_{\sigma \cap \rho} \phi \;\Leftrightarrow\; \mathcal{A} \vdash^{\mathcal{L}}_\rho \phi$$

and a set $I^{\mathcal{L}}_\sigma$ of *inference rules* $\dfrac{H}{\phi}$ with $H \subseteq F^{\mathcal{L}}_\sigma$ and $\phi \in F^{\mathcal{L}}_\sigma$.

If $\mathcal{A} \vdash^{\mathcal{L}}_\sigma \phi$ we say that the σ-algebra $\mathcal{A}$ *satisfies* the formula ϕ, or that ϕ *holds* in $\mathcal{A}$. A *theory* over σ is a set of formulas over σ. If T is a theory over σ and $\mathcal{A} \vdash^{\mathcal{L}}_\sigma \phi$ for all $\phi \in T$ we say that $\mathcal{A}$ satisfies T, notation $\mathcal{A} \vdash^{\mathcal{L}}_\sigma T$. We also say that $\mathcal{A}$ is a *model* of T.

A logic $\mathcal{L}$ is *sound* if $\dfrac{H}{\phi} \in I^{\mathcal{L}}_\sigma$ implies $\mathcal{A} \vdash^{\mathcal{L}}_\sigma H \;\Rightarrow\; \mathcal{A} \vdash^{\mathcal{L}}_\sigma \phi$ for any σ-algebra $\mathcal{A}$.

A formula $\phi \in F_\sigma^\mathcal{L}$ is *preserved under subalgebras* if $\mathcal{A} \vdash_\sigma^\mathcal{L} \phi$ implies $\mathcal{B} \vdash_\sigma^\mathcal{L} \phi$, for any subalgebra $\mathcal{B}$ of $\mathcal{A}$.

A formula $\phi \in F_\sigma^\mathcal{L}$ is *preserved under homomorphisms* if $\mathcal{A} \vdash_\sigma^\mathcal{L} \phi$ implies $\mathcal{B} \vdash_\sigma^\mathcal{L} \phi$, for any homomorphic image $\mathcal{B}$ of $\mathcal{A}$.

Without doubt, the definition of a 'logic' as presented above is too general for most applications. However, it is suited for our purposes and anyone can substitute his/her favourite (and more restricted) definition whenever he/she likes.

In the process algebra verifications of this paper we will use infinitary conditional equational logic. The definition of this logic can be found in the appendix. For comparison, the definitions of equational logic and first order logic with equality are included too.

1.7. Classical logic.
DERIVABILITY. A *σ-proof* of a formula $\phi \in F_\sigma^\mathcal{L}$ from a theory $T \subseteq F_\sigma^\mathcal{L}$ using the logic $\mathcal{L}$, is a well-founded, upwardly branching tree of which the nodes are labelled by σ-formulas, such that
·   the root is labelled by ϕ
·   and if ψ is the label of a node q and H is the set of labels of the nodes directly above q then
    -   either $\psi \in T$ and $H = \varnothing$,
    -   or $\dfrac{H}{\psi} \in I_\sigma^\mathcal{L}$.

If a σ-proof of ϕ from T using $\mathcal{L}$ exists, we say that ϕ is *σ-provable* from T by means of $\mathcal{L}$, notation $T \vdash_\sigma^\mathcal{L} \phi$.

TRUTH. Let $\mathcal{C}$ be a class of σ-algebras and $\phi \in F_\sigma^\mathcal{L}$. Then ϕ is said to be *true* in $\mathcal{C}$, notation $\mathcal{C} \vDash_\sigma^\mathcal{L} \phi$, if ϕ holds in all σ-algebras $\mathcal{A} \in \mathcal{C}$. Let $Alg(\sigma, T)$ be the class of all σ-algebras satisfying T.

SOUNDNESS THEOREM: *If $\mathcal{L}$ is sound then* $T \vdash_\sigma^\mathcal{L} \phi$ *implies* $Alg(\sigma, T) \vDash_\sigma^\mathcal{L} \phi$.
PROOF: Straightforward with induction. $\square$

If no confusion is likely to result, the sub- and superscripts of $\vDash$ and $\vdash$ may be dropped without further warning.

1.8. Module logic. The set $\mathfrak{M}$ of modules is defined inductively as follows:
-   If σ is a signature and T a theory over σ, then $(\sigma, T) \in \mathfrak{M}$,
-   If M and $N \in \mathfrak{M}$ then $M + N \in \mathfrak{M}$,
-   If σ is a signature and $M \in \mathfrak{M}$ then $\sigma \square M \in \mathfrak{M}$,
-   If $M \in \mathfrak{M}$ then $H(M) \in \mathfrak{M}$,
-   If $M \in \mathfrak{M}$ then $S(M) \in \mathfrak{M}$.

Here $+$ is the composition operator, allowing to organise specifications in a modular way, and $\square$ is the export operator, restricting the visible signature of a module, thereby hiding auxiliary items. These operators occur in some form or other frequently in the literature on software engineering. Our notation is taken from BERGSTRA, HEERING & KLINT [9] in which also additional references can be found. The homomorphism operator H and the subalgebra operator S are, as far as we know, new in the context of algebraic specifications. Of course they are well known in model theory, see for instance MONK [33].

The *visible signature* $\Sigma(M)$ of a module M is defined inductively by:
-   $\Sigma(\sigma, T) = \sigma$,
-   $\Sigma(M + N) = \Sigma(M) \cup \Sigma(N)$,
-   $\Sigma(\sigma \square M) = \sigma \cap \Sigma(M)$,
-   $\Sigma(H(M)) = \Sigma(M)$,
-   $\Sigma(S(M)) = \Sigma(M)$.

TRUTH. The class $Alg(M)$ of models of a module M is defined inductively by:
- $\mathcal{C}$ is a model of (σ, T) if it is a σ-algebra, satisfying T;
- $\mathcal{C}$ is a model of $M + N$ if it is a $\Sigma(M+N)$-algebra, such that $\Sigma(M)\square\mathcal{C}$ is a model of M and $\Sigma(N)\square\mathcal{C}$ is a model of N;
- $\mathcal{C}$ is a model of $\sigma\square M$ if it is the restriction of a model $\mathcal{B}$ of M to the signature σ;
- $\mathcal{C}$ is a model of $H(M)$ if it is a homomorphic image of a model $\mathcal{B}$ of M;
- $\mathcal{C}$ is a model of $S(M)$ if it is a subalgebra of a model $\mathcal{B}$ of M.

Note that $Alg(M)$ is a generalisation of $Alg(\sigma, T)$ as defined earlier. All the elements of $Alg(M)$ are $\Sigma(M)$-algebras. A $\Sigma(M)$-algebra $\mathcal{C}\in Alg(M)$ is said to *satisfy* M. A formula $\phi\in F^{\mathcal{L}}_{\Sigma(M)}$ is *satisfied* by a module M, notation $M \vDash^{\mathcal{L}} \phi$, if $Alg(M) \vDash_{\Sigma(M)} \phi$, thus if ϕ holds in all $\Sigma(M)$-algebras satisfying M.

DERIVABILITY. A *proof* of a formula $\phi\in F^{\mathcal{L}}_{\Sigma(M)}$ from a module M using the logic $\mathcal{L}$, is a well-founded, upwardly branching tree of which the nodes are labelled by assertions $N \vdash \psi$, such that
·   the root is labelled by $M \vdash \phi$
·   and if $N \vdash \psi$ is the label of a node q and H is the set of labels of the nodes directly above q then $\dfrac{H}{N \vdash \psi}$ is one of the inference rules of table 1.

$$
\begin{array}{ll}
(\sigma, T) \vdash \phi & \text{if } \phi\in T \\[2mm]
\dfrac{M \vdash \phi_j \ (j\in J)}{M \vdash \phi} & \text{whenever } \dfrac{\phi_j \ (j\in J)}{\phi} \in I^{\mathcal{L}}_{\Sigma(M)} \\[4mm]
\dfrac{M \vdash \phi}{M + N \vdash \phi} \qquad \dfrac{N \vdash \phi}{M + N \vdash \phi} & \\[4mm]
\dfrac{M \vdash \phi}{\sigma\square M \vdash \phi} & \text{if } \phi\in F^{\mathcal{L}}_{\sigma} \\[4mm]
\dfrac{M \vdash \phi}{H(M) \vdash \phi} & \text{if } \phi \text{ is } positive \\[4mm]
\dfrac{M \vdash \phi}{S(M) \vdash \phi} & \text{if } \phi \text{ is } universal
\end{array}
$$

TABLE 1.

Here *positive* and *universal* are syntactic criteria, to be defined for each logic $\mathcal{L}$ separately, ensuring that a formula is preserved under homomorphisms and subalgebras respectively. We write $N \vdash \psi$ for $\dfrac{\varnothing}{N \vdash \psi}$, and omit braces in the conditions of inference rules. If a proof of ϕ from M using $\mathcal{L}$ exists, we say that ϕ is *provable* from M by means of $\mathcal{L}$, notation $M \vdash^{\mathcal{L}} \phi$.

LEMMA: *If* $M \vdash^{\mathcal{L}} \phi$ *then* $\phi\in F^{\mathcal{L}}_{\Sigma(M)}$.
PROOF: With induction. The only nontrivial cases are the rules for $+$ and $\square$. These follow from $F^{\mathcal{L}}_{\sigma} \subseteq F^{\mathcal{L}}_{\sigma\cup\rho}$ and $F^{\mathcal{L}}_{\sigma} \cap F^{\mathcal{L}}_{\rho} \subseteq F^{\mathcal{L}}_{\sigma\cap\rho}$ respectively. $\square$

SOUNDNESS THEOREM: *If* $\mathcal{L}$ *is sound then* $M \vdash^{\mathcal{L}} \phi$ *implies* $M \vDash^{\mathcal{L}} \phi$.
PROOF: With induction. Again the only nontrivial cases are the rules for $+$ and $\square$. These follow since for all ρ-algebras $\mathcal{C}$ and $\phi\in F^{\mathcal{L}}_{\sigma\cap\rho}$: $\sigma\square\mathcal{C} \vDash \phi \Rightarrow \mathcal{C} \vDash \phi$ and $\sigma\square\mathcal{C} \vDash \phi \Leftarrow \mathcal{C} \vDash \phi$

respectively. □

§2 PROCESS ALGEBRA

This is not an introductory paper on process algebra. We only give a listing of the process modules used in the rest of the paper. For an introduction to the ACP formalism we refer the reader to [11-14].

2.1. ACP$_\tau$. In this paper a central role will be played by the module ACP$_\tau$, the Algebra of Communicating Processes with abstraction. ACP$_\tau$ has two parameters. The first parameter is a finite set A of atomic actions. For each atomic action $a \in A$ there is a constant a in the language, representing the process, starting with an a-step and terminating after some time. Furthermore we have a special constant δ, denoting deadlock, the acknowledgement of a process that it cannot do anything anymore. We write $A_\delta = A \cup \{\delta\}$. The second parameter of ACP$_\tau$ is a binary communication function $\gamma : A_\delta \times A_\delta \to A_\delta$, which is commutative, associative and has δ as zero element:

$$\gamma(a,b) = \gamma(b,a) \quad \gamma(a,\gamma(b,c)) = \gamma(\gamma(a,b),c) \quad \gamma(a,\delta) = \delta$$

If $\gamma(a,b) = c \neq \delta$ this means that actions a and b can synchronise. The synchronous performance of a and b is then regarded as a performance of the communication action c. Formally we should add the parameters to the name of a module: ACP$_\tau(A,\gamma)$. However, in order to keep notation simple, we will always omit the parameters if this can be done without causing confusion.

In table 2 we give the signature of module ACP$_\tau$.

Σ (ACP$_\tau$):	**S** (sort):	P		the set of processes
	F (functions):	$+$:	$P \times P \to P$	alternative composition (sum)
		$\cdot$:	$P \times P \to P$	sequential composition (product)
		$\parallel$:	$P \times P \to P$	parallel composition (merge)
		$\mathbb{L}$:	$P \times P \to P$	left-merge
		$\mid$:	$P \times P \to P$	communication-merge
		∂_H:	$P \to P$	encapsulation, for any $H \subseteq A$
		τ_I:	$P \to P$	abstraction, for any $I \subseteq A$
		a	$\in P$	for any atomic action $a \in A$
		δ	$\in P$	deadlock
		τ	$\in P$	silent action

TABLE 2.

Table 3 contains the theory of the module ACP$_\tau$. In this paper we present ACP$_\tau$ as a monolithic module. In [13, 14] however, it has been shown that ACP$_\tau$ can be viewed as the sum of a large number of sub-modules which are interesting in their own right. The module consisting of axioms A1-5 only is called BPA (from Basic Process Algebra). If we add axioms A6-7 we obtain BPA$_\delta$, and BPA$_\delta$ plus axioms T1-3 gives BPA$_{\tau\delta}$. The module ACP consists of the axioms A1-7, CF, CM1-9 and D1-4, i.e. the left column of table 3. All axioms in table 3 are in fact axiom schemes in a, b, H and I. Here a and b range over A_δ (unless further restrictions are made in the table) and $H, I \subseteq A$. In a product $x \cdot y$ we will often omit the $\cdot$. We take $\cdot$ to be more binding than other operations and $+$ to be less binding than other operations. In case we are dealing with an associative operator, we also leave out parentheses.

ACP_τ

$x+y = y+x$	A1	$x\tau = x$	T1
$x+(y+z) = (x+y)+z$	A2	$\tau x+x = \tau x$	T2
$x+x = x$	A3	$a(\tau x+y) = a(\tau x+y)+ax$	T3
$(x+y)z = xz+yz$	A4		
$(xy)z = x(yz)$	A5		
$x+\delta = x$	A6		
$\delta x = \delta$	A7		
$a\mid b = \gamma(a,b)$	CF		
$x\Vert y = x\lfloor\!\lfloor y +y\lfloor\!\lfloor x +x\mid y$	CM1		
$a\lfloor\!\lfloor x = ax$	CM2	$\tau\lfloor\!\lfloor x = \tau x$	TM1
$(ax)\lfloor\!\lfloor y = a(x\Vert y)$	CM3	$(\tau x)\lfloor\!\lfloor y = \tau(x\Vert y)$	TM2
$(x+y)\lfloor\!\lfloor z = x\lfloor\!\lfloor z +y\lfloor\!\lfloor z$	CM4	$\tau\mid x = \delta$	TC1
$(ax)\mid b = (a\mid b)x$	CM5	$x\mid \tau = \delta$	TC2
$a\mid(bx) = (a\mid b)x$	CM6	$(\tau x)\mid y = x\mid y$	TC3
$(ax)\mid(by) = (a\mid b)(x\Vert y)$	CM7	$x\mid(\tau y) = x\mid y$	TC4
$(x+y)\mid z = x\mid z +y\mid z$	CM8		
$x\mid(y+z) = x\mid y +x\mid z$	CM9		
		$\partial_H(\tau) = \tau$	DT
		$\tau_I(\tau) = \tau$	TI1
$\partial_H(a) = a$ if $a\notin H$	D1	$\tau_I(a) = a$ if $a\notin I$	TI2
$\partial_H(a) = \delta$ if $a\in H$	D2	$\tau_I(a) = \tau$ if $a\in I$	TI3
$\partial_H(x+y) = \partial_H(x)+\partial_H(y)$	D3	$\tau_I(x+y) = \tau_I(x)+\tau_I(y)$	TI4
$\partial_H(xy) = \partial_H(x)\cdot\partial_H(y)$	D4	$\tau_I(xy) = \tau_I(x)\cdot\tau_I(y)$	TI5

TABLE 3.

2.1.1. Note. Let $n>0$. Let $D = \{d_1, \ldots, d_n\}$ be a finite set. Let $x_{d_1}, \ldots, x_{d_n}$ be processes. We will use the notation $\sum_{d\in D} x_d$ for the sum $x_{d_1} + \cdots + x_{d_n}$. $\sum_{d\in\emptyset} x_d = \delta$ by definition.

2.1.2. Summand inclusion. In process verifications the summand inclusion predicate $\subseteq$ turns out to be a useful notation. It is defined by: $x\subseteq y \Leftrightarrow x+y=y$. From the ACP_τ-axioms A1, A2 and A3 respectively it follows that $\subseteq$ is antisymmetrical, transitive and reflexive, and hence a partial order.

The following proposition will play an important role in sections 4 and 5.

2.1.3. PROPOSITION: ACP_τ $\vdash \tau x\Vert y = \tau(x\Vert y)$.
PROOF: $\tau x\Vert y \supseteq \tau x\lfloor\!\lfloor y = \tau(x\Vert y) = \tau x\lfloor\!\lfloor y = \tau\tau x\lfloor\!\lfloor y = \tau(\tau x\Vert y) \supseteq \tau x\Vert y$. Now use the fact that $\subseteq$ is a partial order. □

2.1.4. Monotony. Most of the operators of ACP_τ are monotonous with respect to the summand inclusion ordering. Using essentially the distributivity of the operators over $+$, one can show that if $x\subseteq y$, ACP_τ proves:
-   $x+z\subseteq y+z$,
-   $x\cdot z\subseteq y\cdot z$,
-   $x\lfloor\!\lfloor z\subseteq y\lfloor\!\lfloor z$,
-   $x\mid z\subseteq y\mid z$,

- $\partial_H(x) \subseteq \partial_H(y)$,
- $\tau_I(x) \subseteq \tau_I(y)$.

Due to branching time, in general $z \cdot x \not\subseteq z \cdot y$, $x \| z \not\subseteq y \| z$ and $z \Lfloor x \not\subseteq z \Lfloor y$. However, we do have monotony of the merge for the case were x is of the form $\tau x'$. If $\tau x' \subseteq y$, then $ACP_\tau \vdash \tau x' \| z \subseteq y \| z$:

$$\tau x' \| z \overset{2.1.3}{=} \tau(x' \| z) = \tau x' \Lfloor z \subseteq y \Lfloor z \subseteq y \| z.$$

2.2. Standard Concurrency. Often we add to the module ACP_τ the following module SC of Standard Concurrency $(a \in A_\delta)$, which is parametrised by A. A proof that these axioms hold for all closed recursion-free terms can be found in [12].

SC		
$(x \Lfloor y) \Lfloor z = x \Lfloor (y \| z)$	SC1
$(x \| ay) \Lfloor z = x \| (ay \Lfloor z)$	SC2
$x \| y = y \| x$	SC3
$x \| y = y \| x$	SC4
$x \| (y \| z) = (x \| y) \| z$	SC5
$x \| (y \| z) = (x \| y) \| z$	SC6

TABLE 4.

2.3. Renamings. Let $A_{\tau\delta} = A_\delta \cup \{\tau\}$. For every function $f : A_{\tau\delta} \to A_{\tau\delta}$ with the property that $f(\delta) = \delta$ and $f(\tau) = \tau$, we define an operator $\rho_f : P \to P$. Axioms for ρ_f are given in table 5 (Here $a \in A_{\tau\delta}$ and id is the identity). Module RN is parametrised by A.

RN		
$\rho_f(a) = f(a)$	RN1
$\rho_f(x + y) = \rho_f(x) + \rho_f(y)$	RN2
$\rho_f(xy) = \rho_f(x) \cdot \rho_f(y)$	RN3
$\rho_{id}(x) = x$	RN4
$\rho_f \circ \rho_g(x) = \rho_{f \circ g}(x)$	RN5

TABLE 5.

For $t \in A_{\tau\delta}$ and $H \subseteq A$ we define mappings $r_{t,H} : A_{\tau\delta} \to A_{\tau\delta}$ as follows:

$$r_{t,H}(a) = \begin{cases} t & \text{if } a \in H \\ a & \text{otherwise} \end{cases}$$

In the following we will implicitly identify the operators ∂_H and $\rho_{r_{\delta,H}}$, and also the operators τ_I and $\rho_{r_{\tau,I}}$: encapsulation is just renaming of actions into δ, and abstraction is renaming of actions into the silent step τ.

2.4. Chaining operators. A basic situation we will encounter is one in which processes input and output values in a domain D. Often we want to 'chain' two processes in such a way that the output of the first one becomes the input of the second. In order to describe this, we define *chaining* operators $\ggg$ and $\gg$. In the process $x \ggg y$ the output of process x serves as input of process y. Operator $\gg$ is identical to operator $\ggg$, but hides in addition the communications that take place at the internal communication port. The reason for introducing two operators is a technical one: the operator $\gg$ (in which we are interested most) often leads to *unguarded recursion* (cf. sections 2.8.1 and 2.12.1). We will define the chaining operators in terms of the operators of $ACP_r + RN$. In this way we obtain a simple, finite axiomatisation of the operators. The operator $\gg$ occurs (in a different notation) already in HOARE [24] and MILNER [31]. In the context of ACP the operators $\ggg$ and $\gg$ were introduced in VAANDRAGER [40].

Let for $d \in D$, $\downarrow d$ be the action of reading d, and $\uparrow d$ be the action of sending d. Furthermore let $ch(D)$ be the following set

$$ch(D) = \{\uparrow d, \downarrow d, s(d), r(d), c(d) \mid d \in D\}$$

Here $r(d)$, $s(d)$ and $c(d)$ $(d \in D)$ are auxiliary actions which play a role in the definition of the chaining operators. The module for the chaining operators is parametrised by an action alphabet A satisfying $ch(D) \subseteq A$. The module should occur in a context with a module $ACP_r(A, \gamma)$ where $range(\gamma) \cap \{\downarrow d, \uparrow d, s(d), r(d) \mid d \in D\} = \varnothing$ and communication on $ch(D)$ is defined by

$$\gamma(s(d), r(d)) = c(d)$$

(all other communications give δ). The renaming functions $\uparrow s$ and $\downarrow r$ are defined by

$$\uparrow s(\uparrow d) = s(d) \quad \text{and} \quad \downarrow r(\downarrow d) = r(d) \quad (d \in D)$$

and $\uparrow s(a) = \downarrow r(a) = a$ for every other $a \in A_{r\delta}$. Now the 'concrete' chaining of processes x and y, notation $x \ggg y$, is defined by means of the axiom $(H = \{s(d), r(d) \mid d \in D\})$:

$$\boxed{x \ggg y = \partial_H(\rho_{\uparrow s}(x) \| \rho_{\downarrow r}(y)) \quad \text{CH1}}$$

The 'abstract' chaining of processes x and y, notation $x \gg y$, is defined by means of the axiom $(I = \{c(d) \mid d \in D\})$:

$$\boxed{x \gg y = \tau_I(x \ggg y) \quad \text{CH2}}$$

The module CH^+ consists of axioms CH1 and CH2, and is parametrised by A. The '+' in CH^+ refers to the auxiliary actions in the module, which will be removed in section 3.

2.5. Recursion. A *recursive specification* E is a set of equations $\{x = t_x \mid x \in V_E\}$ with V_E a set of variables and t_x a process expression for $x \in V_E$. Only the variables of V_E may appear in t_x. A solution of E is an interpretation of the variables of V_E as processes (in a certain domain), such that the equations of E are satisfied.

Recursive specifications are used to define (or specify) infinite processes. For each recursive specification E and $x \in V_E$, the module REC introduces a constant $<x|E>$, denoting the x-component of a solution of E.

In most applications the variables $X \in V_E$ in a recursive specification E will be chosen fresh, so that there is no need to repeat E in each occurrence of $<X|E>$. Therefore the convention will be adopted that once a recursive specification has been declared, $<X|E>$ can be abbreviated by X. If this is done, X is called a *formal variable*. Formal variables are denoted by capital letters. So after the declaration $X = aX$, a statement $X = aaX$ should be interpreted as an abbreviation of $<X|X = aX> = aa <X|X = aX>$.

Let $E = \{x = t_x \mid x \in V_E\}$ be a recursive specification, and t a process expression. Then $<t|E>$ denotes the term t in which each free occurrence of $x \in V_E$ is replaced by $<x|E>$. In a recursive language we have for each E as above and $x \in V_E$ an axiom

$$\boxed{<x|E> = <t_x|E> \quad \text{REC}}$$

If the above convention is used, these formulas seem to be just the equations of E. The module REC is parametrised by the signature in which the recursive equations are written. In the presence of module REC each system of recursion equations over this signature has a solution.

2.6. Projection. The operator $\pi_n : P \to P$ $(n \in \mathbb{N})$ *stops* processes after they have performed n atomic actions, with the understanding that τ-steps are transparent. The axioms for π_n are given in table 6. Module PR is parametrised by A.

$$
\text{PR} \quad \boxed{
\begin{array}{ll}
\pi_n(\tau) = \tau & \text{PR1} \\
\pi_0(ax) = \delta & \text{PR2} \\
\pi_{n+1}(ax) = a \cdot \pi_n(x) & \text{PR3} \\
\pi_n(\tau x) = \tau \cdot \pi_n(x) & \text{PR4} \\
\pi_n(x+y) = \pi_n(x) + \pi_n(y) & \text{PR5}
\end{array}
}
$$

TABLE 6.

In this paper, as in other papers on process algebra, we have an infinite collection of unary projection operators. Another option, which we do not pursue here, but which might be more fruitful if one is interested in finitary process algebra proofs, is to introduce a single binary projection operator $\mathbf{F} : \pi : \mathbb{N} \times P \to P$.

2.7. Boundedness. The predicate $B_n \subseteq P$ $(n \in \mathbb{N})$ states that the nondeterminism displayed by a process before its nth atomic step is bounded. If for all $n \in \mathbb{N}$: $B_n(x)$, we say x is bounded. Axioms for B_n are in table 7 $(a \in A_\delta)$. Module B is parametrised by A.

$$
\text{B} \quad \boxed{
\begin{array}{cc}
B_0(x) & \text{B1} \\[4pt]
B_n(\tau) & \text{B2} \\[4pt]
\dfrac{B_n(x)}{B_n(\tau x)} & \text{B3} \\[8pt]
\dfrac{B_n(x)}{B_{n+1}(ax)} & \text{B4} \\[8pt]
\dfrac{B_n(x), \ B_n(y)}{B_n(x+y)} & \text{B5}
\end{array}
}
$$

TABLE 7.

Boundedness predicates were introduced in [22].

2.8. Approximation Induction Principle. AIP⁻ is a proof rule which is vital if we want to prove things about infinite processes. The rule expresses the idea that if two processes are equal to any depth, and one of them is bounded then they are equal.

$$
(\text{AIP}^-) \quad \boxed{\dfrac{\forall n \in \mathbb{N} \quad \pi_n(x) = \pi_n(y), \ B_n(x)}{x = y}}
$$

The *" − "* in AIP⁻, distinguishes the rule from a variant without predicates B_n.

2.8.1. DEFINITION. Let t be an open ACP$_\tau$-term without abstraction operators. An occurrence of a variable X in t is *guarded* if t has a subterm of the form $a \cdot M$, with $a \in A_\delta$, and this X occurs in M. Otherwise, the occurrence is *unguarded*.

Let $E = \{x = t_x \mid x \in V_E\}$ be a recursive specification in which all t_x are ACP$_\tau$-terms without abstraction operators. For $X, Y \in V_E$ we define:

$$X \xrightarrow{u} Y \Leftrightarrow Y \text{ occurs unguarded in } t_X$$

We call E *guarded* if relation $\xrightarrow{u}$ is well-founded (i.e. there is no infinite sequence $X \xrightarrow{u} Y \xrightarrow{u} Z \xrightarrow{u} \cdots$).

2.8.2. THEOREM *(Recursive Specification Principle* (RSP)*)*:
ACP$_\tau$ + REC + PR + B + AIP$^-$ ⊢

$$(\text{RSP}) \quad \frac{E}{x = <x|E>} \quad E \text{ guarded}$$

In plain English the RSP rule says that every guarded recursive specification has at most one solution.

Example. Let $E = \{X=(a+b)\cdot X\}$ and $F = \{Y=a\cdot(a+b)\cdot Y+b\cdot Y\}$ be two recursive specifications. Since

$$<X|E> = (a+b)\cdot<X|E> = a\cdot<X|E>+b\cdot<X|E> =$$

$$=a\cdot(a+b)\cdot<X|E>+b\cdot<X|E>,$$

the constant $<X|E>$ satisfies the equation of F. Because the specification F is guarded, RSP now gives that $<X|E> = <Y|F>$.

2.9. Koomen's Fair Abstraction Rule (KFAR). In the verification of communication protocols we often use the following rule, called Koomen's Fair Abstraction Rule ($I \subseteq A$). Module KFAR is parametrised by A.

$$(\text{KFAR}) \quad \frac{x=ix+y \quad (i \in I)}{\tau_I(x)=\tau\cdot\tau_I(y)}$$

Fair abstraction here means that $\tau_I(x)$ will eventually exit the hidden i-cycle. Below we will formulate a generalisation of KFAR, the Cluster Fair Abstraction Rule (CFAR), which can be derived from KFAR.

2.9.1. DEFINITION: Let $E = \{X=t_X \mid X \in V_E\}$ be a recursive specification, and let $I \subseteq A$. A subset C of V_E is called a *cluster (of I)* in E iff for all $X \in C$:

$$t_X = \sum_{k=1}^{m} i_k \cdot X_k + \sum_{l=1}^{n} Y_l$$

(For $m \geq 0$, $i_1, \ldots, i_m \in I \cup \{\tau\}$, $X_1, \ldots, X_m \in C$, $n \geq 0$ and $Y_1, \ldots, Y_n \in V_E - C$). Variables $X \in C$ are called *cluster variables*. For $X \in C$ and $Y \in V_E$ we say that

$$X \leadsto Y \Leftrightarrow Y \text{ occurs in } t_X$$

We define

$$e(C) = \{Y \in V_E - C \mid \exists X \in C : X \leadsto Y\}$$

Variables in $e(C)$ are called *exits*. $\leadsto^*$ is the transitive and reflexive closure of $\leadsto$. Cluster C is *conservative* iff every exit can be reached from every cluster variable via a path in the cluster:

$$\forall X \in C \, \forall Y \in e(C) : X \leadsto^* Y$$

Example. In the transition diagram of figure 1, the sets {1,2,3}, {4,5,6,7}, {8} and {1,2,3,4,5,6,7,8} are examples of conservative clusters. Cluster {1,2,3,4,5,6,7} is not conservative since exit Z cannot be reached from cluster variables 4, 5, 6 and 7.

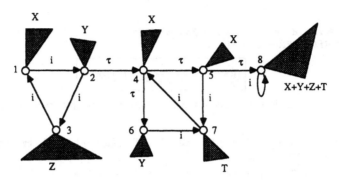

FIGURE 1.

2.9.2. DEFINITION: The *Cluster Fair Abstraction Rule (CFAR)* reads as follows:

(CFAR) Let E be a guarded recursive specification; let $I \subseteq A$ with $|I| \geqslant 2$; let C be a finite conservative cluster of I in E; and let $X, X' \in C$ with $X \leadsto X'$. Then: $\tau_I(X) = \tau \cdot \displaystyle\sum_{Y \in e(C)} \tau_I(Y)$

2.9.3. THEOREM: $\text{ACP}_\tau + \text{RN} + \text{REC} + \text{RSP} + \text{KFAR} \vdash \text{CFAR}.$
PROOF: See [39]. □

2.10. Alphabets. Intuitively the alphabet of a process is the set of atomic actions which it can perform. This idea is formalised in [4], where an operator $\alpha : P \to 2^A$ is introduced, with axioms such as:

$$\alpha(\delta) = \varnothing$$
$$\alpha(ax) = \{a\} \cup \alpha(x)$$
$$\alpha(x + y) = \alpha(x) \cup \alpha(y)$$

In this approach the question arises what axioms should be adopted for the set-operators $\cup$, $\cap$, etc. One option, which is implicitly adopted in previous papers on process algebra, is to take the equalities which are true in set theory. This collection is unstructured and too large for our purposes. Therefore we propose a different, more algebraic solution. We view the alphabet of a process as a *process*; the alphabet operator α goes from sort P to sort P. Process $\alpha(x)$ is the alternative composition of the actions which can be performed by x. In this way we represent a set of actions by a process. A set B of actions is represented by the process expression $B =_{def} \sum_{b \in B} b$. So the empty set is represented by δ, a singleton-set $\{a\}$ by the expression a, and a set $\{a,b\}$ by expression $a + b$. Set union corresponds to alternative composition. The process algebra axioms A1-3 and A6 correspond to similar axioms for the set union operator. The notation $\subseteq$ for summand inclusion between processes (section 2.1.2), fits with the notation for the subset predicate on sets.

The following axioms in table 8 define the alphabet of finite processes ($a \in A$). Module AB is parametrised by A.

AB	$\alpha(\delta) = \delta$	AB1
	$\alpha(ax) = a + \alpha(x)$	AB2
	$\alpha(x+y) = \alpha(x) + \alpha(y)$	AB3
	$\alpha(\tau) = \delta$	AB4
	$\alpha(\tau x) = \alpha(x)$	AB5

TABLE 8.

In order to compute the alphabet of infinite processes, we introduce an additional module **AA** which is parametrised by A.

AA	$\alpha(x) \subseteq A$	AA1
	$\alpha(x \| y) = \alpha(x) + \alpha(y) + \alpha(x) \mid \alpha(y)$	AA2
	$\alpha \circ \rho_f(x) \subseteq \rho_f \circ \partial_H \circ \alpha(x)$ (where $H = \{a \in A \mid f(a) = \tau\}$)	AA3
	$\dfrac{\forall n \in \mathbf{N} \quad \alpha(\pi_n(x)) \subseteq y}{\alpha(x) \subseteq y}$	AA4

TABLE 9.

It is not hard to see that the axioms of AA hold for all closed recursion-free terms.

Example. (from [4]). Let $p = <X \mid \{X = aX\}>$, and define $q = \tau_{\{a\}}(p)$, $r = q \cdot b$ (with $b \neq a$). What is the alphabet of r? We derive:

$$\alpha(r) = \alpha(qb) = \alpha(\tau_{\{a\}}(p) \cdot b) = \alpha(\tau_{\{a\}}(p) \cdot \tau_{\{a\}}(b)) =$$
$$\overset{AA3}{=} \alpha(\tau_{\{a\}}(pb)) \subseteq \tau_{\{a\}} \circ \partial_{\{a\}} \circ \alpha(pb) \overset{RN5}{=} \partial_{\{a\}} \circ \alpha(pb).$$

Since

$$\alpha(pb) = \alpha(apb) \overset{AB2}{=} a + \alpha(pb),$$

we have that $a \subseteq \alpha(pb)$. On the other hand we derive for $n \in \mathbf{N}$:

$$\alpha(\pi_n(pb)) = \alpha(a^n \cdot \delta) \subseteq a$$

and therefore, by application of axiom AA4, $\alpha(pb) \subseteq a$. Consequently $\alpha(pb) = a$ and

$$\alpha(r) = \partial_{\{a\}} \circ \alpha(pb) = \partial_{\{a\}}(a) = \delta.$$

Information about alphabets must be available if we want to apply the following rules. These rules, which are a generalisation of the conditional axioms of [4], occur in a slightly different form also in [40]. Rules like these are an important tool in system verifications based on process algebra. Module RR is parametrised by A and γ. Observe that axioms AA1 and RR1 together imply axiom RN4 of table 5. Axiom RR2, which describes the interaction between renaming and parallel composition, looks complicated, but that is only because it is so general. The axioms RR are derivable for closed recursion-free terms.

$$RR \quad \boxed{\begin{array}{l} \dfrac{\alpha(x) \subseteq B}{\rho_f(x) = x} \forall b \in B : f(b) = b \hfill \text{RR1} \\[3mm] \dfrac{\alpha(x) \subseteq B, \ \alpha(y) \subseteq C}{\rho_f(x \| y) = \rho_f(x \| \rho_f(y))} \forall c \in C : f(c) = f^2(c) \wedge (\forall b \in B : f \circ \gamma(b,c) = f \circ \gamma(b, f(c))) \hfill \text{RR2} \end{array}}$$

TABLE 10.

2.11. ACP♯. The combination of all modules presented thus far, except for KFAR, will be called ACP♯ (the system ACP♯ as presented here slightly differs from a system with the same name occurring in [13]). The module is defined by:

$$\text{ACP}♯ = \text{ACP}_r + \text{SC} + \text{RN} + \text{CH}^+ + \text{REC} + \text{PR} + \text{B} + \text{AIP}^- + \text{AB} + \text{AA} + \text{RR}$$

Bisimulation semantics, as described in for instance [5], gives a model for the module ACP♯ + KFAR. Work of BERGSTRA, KLOP & OLDEROG [15] showed that in a large number of interesting models KFAR is not valid. Therefore we have chosen not to include KFAR in the 'standard' module ACP♯.

2.12. Generalised Recursive Specification Principle. For many applications the RSP is too restrictive. Therefore we will present below a more general version of this rule, called RSP$^+$.

2.12.1. DEFINITION: Let $\mathscr{P}$ be the set of closed expressions in the signature of ACP♯. A process expression $p \in \mathscr{P}$ is called *guardedly specifiable* if there exists a guarded recursive specification F with $Y \in V_F$ such that

$$\text{ACP}♯ \vdash p = <Y|F>.$$

We have the following theorem:

2.12.2. THEOREM *(Generalised Recursive Specification Principle* (RSP$^+$)*):* ACP♯ ⊢

$$(\text{RSP}^+) \quad \boxed{\dfrac{E}{x = <x|E>} \ <x|E> \text{ guardedly specifiable}}$$

2.12.3. Remarks. In the definition of the notion 'guardedly specifiable', it is essential that the identity $p = <Y|F>$ is *provable*. If we would only require that $p = <Y|F>$, then the corresponding version of RSP$^+$ would not be provable from ACP♯, since this rule would then not be valid in the action relation model of [22]. In this model we have the identity $<X|\{X=X\}> = \delta.$[1] Hence $<X|\{X=X\}> = <Y|\{Y=\delta\}> = \delta$. Since the specification $\{Y=\delta\}$ is guarded, this would mean that expression $<X|\{X=X\}>$ is guardedly specifiable. But then RSP$^+$ gives that for arbitrary x: $x = <X|\{X=X\}> = \delta$. This is clearly false.

We conjecture that an expression p is guardedly specifiable iff it is provably bounded, i.e. for all $n \in \mathbb{N}$: ACP♯ ⊢ $B_n(x)$.

---

1. Strictly speaking, this is not correct. In [22], a recursion construct $<X|E>$ is viewed as a kind of variable which ranges over the X-components of the solutions of E. Since any process X satisfies $X=X$, the identity $<X|\{X=X\}> = \delta$ does not hold under this interpretation. However, if one interprets the construct $<X|E>$ as a constant in the model of [22], then the most natural choice is to relate to $<X|E>$ the bisimulation equivalence class of the term $<X|E>$. Under this interpretation $<X|\{X=X\}> = \delta$.

§3 APPLICATIONS OF THE MODULE APPROACH IN PROCESS ALGEBRA

3.1. The auxiliary status of the left-merge.

3.1.1. Semantics. Sometimes it happens that our 'customers' complain that they do not succeed in proving the identity of two processes in ACP‡, whose behaviour is considered 'intuitively the same'. Often, this is because there are many intuitions possible, and ACP‡ happens not to represent the particular intuitions of these customers. Therefore we have defined some auxiliary modules that should bridge the gaps between intuitions.

In general a user of process algebra wants that his system proves $p = q$ (here p and q are closed process expressions in the signature of ACP‡), whenever p and q have the same interesting properties. So it depends on what properties are interesting for a particular user, whether his system should be designed to prove the equality of p and q or not. For this reason the semantical branch of process algebra research generated a variety of process algebras in which different identification strategies were pursued. In *bisimulation semantics* we find algebras that distinguish between any two processes that differ in the precise timing of internal choices; in *trace semantics* only processes are distinguished which can perform different sequences of actions; and, somewhere in between, the algebras of *failure semantics* identify processes if they have the same traces (can perform the same sequences of actions) and have the same deadlock behaviour in any context. A lot of these process algebras can be organised as homomorphic images of each other, as indicated in figure 2.

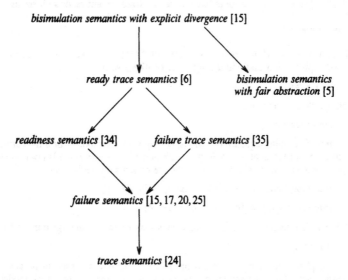

FIGURE 2. *The linear time - branching time spectrum*

If two process expressions p and q represent the same process in bisimulation semantics with explicit divergence, they have many properties in common; if they only represent the same process in trace semantics, this only guarantees that they share some of these properties; and, descending from bisimulation semantics with explicit divergence to trace semantics, less and less distinctions are made. Now a user should state exactly in which properties of processes he is interested. Suppose he is only interested in traces and deadlock behaviour, then we can tell him that for his purposes failure semantics suffices. This means that if processes p and q are proven equal in failure semantics, this guarantees that they have the same relevant properties. If they are only identified in trace semantics (somewhere in the lattice below failure semantics) such a conclusion cannot be drawn, but if they are identified in a semantics finer than failure semantics (such as bisimulation semantics with explicit divergence), then they certainly have the same interesting properties, and probably some uninteresting ones as well. Hence a proof in bisimulation semantics with explicit divergence is just as good as one in failure semantics (or even better).

This is the reason that we do our proofs mostly in bisimulation semantics: the entire module ACP⁴ is sound with respect to bisimulation semantics with explicit divergence. However, if two processes are different in bisimulation semantics, we will never succeed in proving them equal from ACP⁴. In such a case we might add some axioms to the system, that represent the extra identifications made in a less discriminating semantics. If we find a proof from this enriched module, it can be used by anyone satisfied with the properties of this coarser semantics.

It is in the light of the above considerations that one should judge the appearance of the following module T4:

$$\text{T4} \quad \boxed{\tau(\tau x + y) = \tau x + y}$$

The law of this module does not hold in bisimulation semantics, but it does hold in all other semantics of figure 2. Thus any identity derived from ACP⁴ + T4 holds in ready trace semantics and hence also in the courser ones like failure and trace semantics, or so it seems ....

3.1.2. An inconsistency.

3.1.2.1. DEFINITION: Let M be a process module with $\Sigma(M) \supseteq \Sigma(\text{BPA}_{\tau\delta})$. We call M *consistent* if for all closed expressions x and y in the signature of $\text{BPA}_{\tau\delta}$ with

$$M \vdash x = y,$$

the sets of complete traces agree:

$$trace(x) = trace(y).$$

A *complete trace* is a finite sequence of actions, ending with a symbol $\sqrt{}$ or δ indicating successful resp. unsuccessful termination. A formal definition of the set $trace(x)$ is given in [15]. Here we only give some examples, which should make the notion sufficiently clear:

$$trace(abc + ad\delta + a(\tau bc + d)) = \{abc\sqrt{}, ad\delta, ad\sqrt{}\}$$
$$trace(\tau) = \{\sqrt{}\} \neq \{\delta, \sqrt{}\} = trace(\tau + \tau\delta)$$

A model $\mathcal{C}$ of M is *consistent* if for all closed expressions x and y in the signature of $\text{BPA}_{\tau\delta}$ with

$$\mathcal{C} \vDash x = y,$$

the sets of complete traces agree. The module ACP⁴ + KFAR is consistent because bisimulation semantics with fair abstraction, as described in [5], gives a consistent model for this module. However, KFAR is not valid in any of the other semantics of figure 2.

3.1.2.2. PROPOSITION: $\text{ACP}_\tau + \text{T4} \vdash \tau(ac + ca) + bc = \tau(\tau(ac + ca) + bc + c(\tau a + b))$.
PROOF:

$$\tau(\tau a + b)\lfloor c = (\tau a + b)\lfloor c = \tau(a\|c) + bc = \tau(ac + ca) + bc$$
$$\tau(\tau a + b)\lfloor c = \tau((\tau a + b)\|c) = \tau(\tau(ac + ca) + bc + c(\tau a + b)) \quad \square$$

Proposition 3.1.2.2 shows that module $\text{ACP}_\tau + \text{T4}$ is not consistent. This sudden inconsistency must be the result of a serious misunderstanding. And indeed, what's wrong is the use of ACP_τ

in the less discriminating models (say in failure semantics). It happens that, in a setting with τ, failure equivalence (or ready trace equivalence for that matter) is not a congruence for the left-merge $\parallel\!\!\!\!\_$, and this causes all the trouble.

3.1.3. Solution. In applications we do not use the operators $\parallel\!\!\!\!\_$ and $|$ directly. In specifications we use the merge operator $\parallel$, and $\parallel\!\!\!\!\_$ and $|$ are only auxiliary operators, needed to give a complete axiomatisation of the merge.

Let sacp_τ be the signature obtained from $\Sigma(\text{ACP}_\tau)$ by stripping the left-merge and communication-merge:

$$\text{sacp}_\tau = \Sigma(\text{ACP}_\tau) - \{\mathbf{F}:\parallel\!\!\!\!\_ : P\times P\rightarrow P,\ \mathbf{F}:|:P\times P\rightarrow P\}$$

Failure equivalence as in [15], etc. are congruences for the operators of sacp_τ. However, the operators $\parallel\!\!\!\!\_$ and $|$ in ACP_τ are needed to axiomatise the $\parallel$-operator, and without them even the most elementary equations cannot be derived. Our solution to this problem is based on the following idea. Suppose we want to prove an equation $p=q$ in the signature sacp_τ that holds in ready trace semantics (and hence in failure semantics) but not in bisimulation semantics. Then we first prove an intermediate result from ACP_τ: one or more equations holding in bisimulation semantics (with explicit divergence) and in which no $\parallel\!\!\!\!\_$ and $|$ appear. This intermediate result is preserved after mapping the bisimulation model homomorphically on the ready trace or failure model, and can be combined consistently with the axiom T4. Thus the proof of $p=q$ can be completed. In our language of modules we can describe this as follows. The module

$$SACP_\tau = H(\text{sacp}_\tau\,\square(\text{ACP}_\tau+SC))$$

does not contain the operators $\parallel\!\!\!\!\_$ and $|$ in its visible signature and since failure semantics can be obtained as a homomorphic image of bisimulation semantics, considering that $\text{ACP}_\tau+SC$ is sound w.r.t. bisimulation semantics and that the operators of sacp_τ carry over to failure semantics, we conclude that this module is sound w.r.t. failure semantics. Hence it can be combined consistently with T4, and $SACP_\tau$ is a suitable framework for proving statements in failure semantics.

We would like to stress that the use of the H-operator is essential here. The H-operator makes that from module $SACP_\tau$ only *positive* formulas are provable. The following example shows what goes wrong if we also allow non-positive formulas. From the proof of proposition 3.1.2.2 it follows that:

$$\text{sacp}_\tau\,\square(\text{ACP}_\tau+SC)\vdash \frac{\tau(\tau x+y)=\tau x+y}{c(\tau a+b)\subseteq\tau(ac+ca)+bc}$$

Consequently we can prove an inconsistency if we add law T4:

$$\text{sacp}_\tau\,\square(\text{ACP}_\tau+SC)+\,<\tau(\tau x+y)=\tau x+y>\,\vdash c(\tau a+b)\subseteq\tau(ac+ca)+bc$$

So although the formulas provable from module $\text{sacp}_\tau\,\square(\text{ACP}_\tau+SC)$ contain no left-merge, some of them (which are non-positive) cannot be combined consistently with the laws of ready trace semantics and failure semantics.

3.2. Definition of the chaining operator. ACP_τ is a universal specification formalism in the sense that in bisimulation semantics every finitely branching, effectively presented process can be specified in ACP_τ by a finite system of recursion equations (see [5, 14]). Still it often turns out that adding new operators to the theory facilitates specification and verification of concurrent systems. In general, adding new operators and laws can have far reaching consequences for the underlying mathematical theory. Often however, new operators are *definable* in terms of others operators and the axioms are *derivable* from the other axioms. In that case the new operators can be considered as notations which are useful, but do not complicate the underlying theory in any way. Examples of definable operators are the projection operators, the process creation operator of [8] and the state operators of [3].

Just like the left-merge and the communication-merge are needed in order to axiomatise the parallel composition operator, new atomic actions are often needed if we want to define a new operator in terms of more elementary operators. As an example we mention the actions $s(d)$ and $r(d)$ which we need in the definition of the chaining operators. These auxiliary atoms will never be used in process specifications. Unfortunately they have the unpleasant property that they occur in some important algebraic laws for the new operators. One of the properties of the chaining operators we use most is that they are associative under some very weak assumptions. In the model of bisimulation semantics, the following law is valid (here $H = \{s(d), r(d) | d \in D\}$):

$$\frac{\partial_H(x)=x, \partial_H(y)=y, \partial_H(z)=z}{(x \ggg y) \ggg z = x \ggg (y \ggg z)} \text{ CC}$$

We do not have general associativity in the model. Counterexample:

$$(r(d) \ggg (s(d)+s(e))) \ggg r(e) = c(d) \cdot \delta$$
$$r(d) \ggg ((s(d)+s(e)) \ggg r(e)) = c(e) \cdot \delta$$

It would be much nicer if we somehow could 'hide' the auxiliary atoms, and, for the $\ggg$-operator, have associativity in general. In this section we will see how this can be accomplished by means of the module approach.

3.2.1. The associativity of the chaining operators. Although the rule CC holds in the model of bisimulation semantics, we have not been able to prove it algebraically from module ACP$^{\sharp}_\tau$. However, we can prove algebraically a weaker version of rule CC if we make some additional assumptions about the alphabet. We assume that besides actions $ch(D)$, the alphabet A contains actions:

$$\overline{H} = \{\overline{s}(d), \overline{r}(d) | d \in D\} \text{ en } \underline{H} = \{\underline{s}(d), \underline{r}(d) | d \in D\}$$

One may think about these actions as special fresh atoms which are added to A only in order to prove the associativity of the chaining operators.[1] Let $H = \{r(d), s(d) | d \in D\}$ and let $\hat{H} = H \cup \overline{H} \cup \underline{H}$. We assume that actions from $\hat{H}$ do not synchronise with the other actions in the alphabet, and that $range(\gamma) \cap \hat{H} = \varnothing$. On $\hat{H}$ communication is given by $(d \in D)$:

$$\gamma(\overline{s}(d), \overline{r}(d)) = \gamma(\overline{s}(d), r(d)) = \gamma(s(d), \overline{r}(d)) = \gamma(s(d), r(d)) =$$
$$= \gamma(\underline{s}(d), \underline{r}(d)) = \gamma(s(d), r(d)) = \gamma(s(d), \underline{r}(d)) = c(d)$$

We define for $v, w \in \{\uparrow, \downarrow, s, r, \overline{s}, \overline{r}, \underline{s}, \underline{r}\}$ the renaming function vw:

$$vw(a) = \begin{cases} w(d) & \text{if } a = v(d) \text{ for some } d \in D \\ a & \text{otherwise} \end{cases}$$

3.2.1.1. Lemma: $SACP_\tau + RN + CH^+ + AB + AA + RR \vdash$

$$\frac{\partial_{\hat{H}}(x)=x, \ \partial_{\hat{H}}(y)=y, \ \partial_{\hat{H}}(z)=z}{\partial_{\overline{H}}(\rho_{\uparrow\overline{s}}(x) \| \rho_{\downarrow\overline{r}}(y)) = x \ggg y = \partial_H(\rho_{\uparrow s}(x) \| \rho_{\downarrow r}(y))}$$

Proof: The proof of the first equality in this lemma has been spelled out in Van Glabbeek & Vaandrager [23], the full version of this paper. In this proof it is essential that

---

[1]. The *Fresh Atom Principle (FAP)* says that we can use new (or 'fresh') atomic actions in proofs. In [7], it is shown that FAP holds in bisimulation semantics. We have not included FAP in the theoretical framework of this paper. Therefore, if we need certain 'fresh' atoms in a proof, we have to assume that they were in the alphabet right from the beginning.

$$\gamma(\overline{s}(d), \overline{r}(d)) = \gamma(\overline{s}(d), r(d)) = \gamma(s(d), \overline{r}(d)) = \gamma(s(d), r(d)) = c(d)$$

The second equality then follows by symmetry. $\square$

3.2.1.2. THEOREM: $SACP_\tau + RN + CH^+ + AB + AA + RR \vdash$

$$\frac{\partial_{\hat{H}}(x)=x, \ \partial_{\hat{H}}(y)=y, \ \partial_{\hat{H}}(z)=z}{x \ggg (y \ggg z) = (x \ggg y) \ggg z}$$

PROOF: This is essentially theorem 1.12.2 of [40]. A sketch of the proof is given in [23]. There $x \ggg (y \ggg z)$ is written as $\partial_{\overline{H}}(\rho_{\uparrow\overline{s}}(x) \| \rho_{\downarrow\overline{r}} \circ \partial_{H}(\rho_{\uparrow s}(y) \| \rho_{\downarrow r'}(z)))$, using lemma 3.2.1.1. Now a crucial element in the proof is the observation that there is no communication possible between elements of $\overline{H}$ and H. This is the reason that the sets $\overline{H}$ and $\underline{H}$ had to be introduced both. $\square$

3.2.1.3. THEOREM: $SACP_\tau + RN + CH^+ + AB + AA + RR \vdash$

$$\frac{\partial_{\hat{H}}(x)=x, \ \partial_{\hat{H}}(y)=y, \ \partial_{\hat{H}}(z)=z}{x \gg (y \gg z) = (x \gg y) \gg z}$$

PROOF: See [23]. $\square$

3.2.2. Removing auxiliary atoms. We will now apply the module approach to remove completely the auxiliary atoms which where used in the definition of the chaining operators and in the proofs of their associativity. Below we will employ the notation:

$$\sigma \Delta M \equiv (\Sigma(M) - \sigma) \square M.$$

Consider the module:

$$CH^- = (\{\mathbf{F} : a \in P \mid a \in \hat{H}\} \cup \{\mathbf{F} : \rho_f : P \to P \mid f : A_{\tau\delta} \to A_{\tau\delta}\})$$
$$\Delta(SACP_\tau + RN + CH^+ + AB + AA + RR).$$

This module cannot be used to prove any formula containing atoms in $\hat{H}$. But unfortunately module CH^- still does not prove the general associativity of the chaining operators:

$$CH^- \ \forall \ x \ggg (y \ggg z) = (x \ggg y) \ggg z$$

The reason is that the auxiliary atoms, although removed from the language, are still present in the models of module CH^-. Thus the counterexample $(r(d) \ggg (s(d) + s(e))) \ggg r(e)$ still works in the models. Let $A^- = A - \hat{H}$. We are interested in consistent models which only contain actions of A^-. The module $CH^- + <\alpha(x) \subseteq A^->$ does not denote such models: all consistent models of CH^- contain the process A with $\alpha(A) = A \not\subseteq A^-$. Adding the law $\alpha(x) \subseteq A^-$ therefore throws away all consistent models. The right class of models can be denoted with the help of operator S. We consider the module

$$CH = S(CH^-) + <\alpha(x) \subseteq A^->.$$

Some models of module CH^- have consistent submodels which do not contain auxiliary atoms. In these models the law $\alpha(x) \subseteq A^-$ holds. Thus module CH has consistent models.

From theorems 3.2.1.2 and 3.2.1.3, together with axiom RR1, it follows that:

$$CH^- \ \vdash \ \frac{\alpha(x) \subseteq A^-, \ \alpha(y) \subseteq A^-, \ \alpha(z) \subseteq A^-}{(x \ggg y) \ggg z = x \ggg (y \ggg z)}$$

$$CH^- \ \vdash \ \frac{\alpha(x) \subseteq A^-, \ \alpha(y) \subseteq A^-, \ \alpha(z) \subseteq A^-}{(x \gg y) \gg z = x \gg (y \gg z)}$$

From this we can easily see that module CH proves the general associativity of the chaining operators:

$$CH \vdash x \ggg (y \ggg z) = (x \ggg y) \ggg x \text{ and}$$

$$CH \vdash x \gg (y \gg z) = (x \gg y) \gg x.$$

3.2.3. The following laws can be easily proven from module CH (here $d, e \in D$):

$$\uparrow d \cdot x \gg (\sum_{e \in D} \downarrow e \cdot y^e) = \tau(x \gg y^d) \qquad\qquad\qquad L1$$

$$\uparrow d \cdot x \gg \uparrow e \cdot y = \uparrow e \cdot (\uparrow d \cdot x \gg y) \qquad\qquad\qquad L2$$

$$(\sum_{d \in D} \downarrow d \cdot x^d) \gg (\sum_{e \in D} \downarrow e \cdot y^e) = \sum_{d \in D} \downarrow d \cdot (x^d \gg (\sum_{e \in D} \downarrow e \cdot y^e)) \qquad\qquad L3$$

$$(\sum_{d \in D} \downarrow d \cdot x^d) \gg \uparrow e \cdot y = \sum_{d \in D} \downarrow d \cdot (x^d \gg \uparrow e \cdot y) + \uparrow e \cdot ((\sum_{d \in D} \downarrow d \cdot x^d) \gg y) \qquad L4$$

The laws are equally valid when the operator $\gg$ is replaced by $\ggg$, except for law L1 where in addition the τ has to be replaced by $c(d)$.

3.3. SACP⁴. Module SACP⁴ is an 'improved' version of module ACP⁴. It is defined by:

$$SACP^4 = SACP_\tau + RN + CH + REC + PR + B + AIP^- + AB + AA + RR.$$

If modules in the above equation have an alphabet as parameter, this is A^-, and if they are parametrised by a communication function this is the restriction γ^- of γ to $(A^- \cup \{\delta\}) \times (A^- \cup \{\delta\})$. All proofs in the rest of this paper, unless stated otherwise, are proofs from the module SACP⁴. The rules RSP, RSP⁺ and CFAR can still be used in a setting with module SACP⁴. We have SACP⁴ ⊢ RSP, SACP⁴ ⊢ RSP⁺ and SACP⁴ + KFAR ⊢ CFAR.

§4 Queues

In the specification of concurrent systems FIFO queues with unbounded capacity often play an important role. We give some examples:

- The semantical description of languages with asynchronous message passing such as CHILL (see [19]),
- The modelling of communication channels occurring in computer networks (see Larsen & Milner [28] and Vaandrager [39]),
- The implementation of languages with many-to-one synchronous communication, such as POOL (see America [1] and Vaandrager [40]).

Consequently the questions how queues can be specified, and how one can prove properties of systems containing queues, are important. For a nice sample of queue-specifications we refer to the solutions of the first problem of the STL/SERC workshop [21]. Some other references are Broy [18], Hoare [25] and Pratt [36].

4.1. Also in the setting of ACP a lot of attention has been paid to the specification of queues. Below we give an infinite specification of the process behaviour of a queue. Here D is a finite set of data, D^* is the set of finite sequences σ of elements from D, the empty sequence is ϵ. Sequence $\sigma \star \sigma'$ is the concatenation of sequences σ and σ'. The sequence, only consisting of $d \in D$ is denoted by d as well.

$$\boxed{\begin{aligned} QUEUE &= Q_\epsilon = \sum_{d \in D} \downarrow d \cdot Q_d \\ Q_{\sigma \star d} &= \sum_{e \in D} \downarrow e \cdot Q_{e \star \sigma \star d} + \uparrow d \cdot Q_\sigma \end{aligned}}$$

Note that this infinite specification uses only the signature of BPA_δ (see section 2.1). We have the following fact:

4.1.1. THEOREM: *Using read/send communication, the process QUEUE cannot be specified in ACP by finitely many recursion equations.*
PROOF: See BAETEN & BERGSTRA [3] and BERGSTRA & TIURYN [16]. □

It turns out that if one allows an arbitrary communication function, or extends the signature with an (almost) arbitrary additional operator, the process *QUEUE can* be specified by finitely many recursion equations. For some nice examples we refer to BERGSTRA & KLOP [13].

4.2. Definition of the queue by means of chaining. A problem we had with all ACP-specifications of the queue is that they are difficult to deal with in process verifications. For example, let *BUF*1 be a buffer with capacity one:

$$
\begin{aligned}
BUF1 &= \sum_{d \in D} \downarrow d \cdot BUF1^d \\
BUF1^d &= \uparrow d \cdot BUF1
\end{aligned}
$$

In process verifications we need propositions like $QUEUE \gg BUF1 = QUEUE$ (in section 5 we present a protocol verification where a similar fact is actually used). However, the proof of this fact starting from the infinite specification is rather complicated. Now the following specification of a queue by means of the (abstract) chaining operator allows for a simple proof of the proposition and numerous other useful identities involving queues. This specification is also described by HOARE [25] (p. 158).

$$
Q = \sum_{d \in D} \downarrow d \cdot (Q \gg BUF1^d)
$$

The first thing we have to prove is that the process described above really is a queue.

4.2.1. THEOREM: $Q = QUEUE$.
PROOF: Define for every $n \in \mathbb{N}$ and $\sigma = d_1, \ldots, d_m \in D^*$ processes D_σ^n as follows:

$$
D_\sigma^n = Q \gg BUF1 \cdots _{n \text{ times}} \gg BUF1^{d_1} \cdots \gg BUF1^{d_m}
$$

So by definition $D_\epsilon^0 = Q$. Using the laws of section 3.2.3, we derive the following recursion equations:

$$
\begin{aligned}
D_\epsilon^0 &= \sum_{d \in D} \downarrow d \cdot D_d^0 \\
D_{\sigma * d}^n &= \sum_{e \in D} \downarrow e \cdot D_{e * \sigma * d}^n + \uparrow d \cdot D_\sigma^{n+1}
\end{aligned}
$$

In this derivation, which has been worked out in [23], we use the equation

$$
BUF1^d \gg BUF1 = \tau \cdot (BUF1 \gg BUF1^d)
$$

which is an instance of law L1 of section 3.2.3. Furthermore we use that $a(p \gg \tau q) = a(p \gg q)$, which follows from proposition 2.1.3 and T1. Define the process Q_ϵ^0 by:

$$
\begin{aligned}
Q_\epsilon^0 &= \sum_{d \in D} \downarrow d \cdot Q_d^0 \\
Q_{\sigma * d}^n &= \sum_{e \in D} \downarrow e \cdot Q_{e * \sigma * d}^n + \uparrow d \cdot Q_\sigma^{n+1}
\end{aligned}
$$

The specification of process Q_ϵ^0 is clearly guarded. Applying RSP gives us on the one hand that $QUEUE = Q_\epsilon^0$, and on the other hand that $Q = D_\epsilon^0 = Q_\epsilon^0$. Consequently $QUEUE = Q$. □

The proof above shows the 'view of a queue' that lies behind the specification of Q. During execution there is a long chain of 1-datum buffers passing messages from 'the left to the right'. After the input of a new datum on the left, a new buffer is created, containing the new datum and placed at the leftmost position in the chain. Because no buffer is ever removed from the system, the number of empty buffers increases after every output of a datum.

4.2.2. LEMMA: $Q \gg BUF1 = Q$.
PROOF:

$$Q \gg BUF1 = \sum_{d \in D} \downarrow d \cdot ((Q \gg BUF1^d) \gg BUF1) =$$

$$= \sum_{d \in D} \downarrow d \cdot (Q \gg (BUF1^d \gg BUF1)) =$$

$$= \sum_{d \in D} \downarrow d \cdot (Q \gg \tau \cdot (BUF1 \gg BUF1^d)) =$$

$$\overset{2.1.3}{=} \sum_{d \in D} \downarrow d \cdot (Q \gg (BUF1 \gg BUF1^d)) =$$

$$= \sum_{d \in D} \downarrow d \cdot ((Q \gg BUF1) \gg BUF1^d)$$

Now apply RSP$^+$ (from the proof of theorem 4.2.1 it follows that Q is guardedly specifiable). □

By means of an inductive argument we can easily prove the following corollary of lemma 4.2.2.

4.2.3. COROLLARY: *Let for $\sigma \in D^*$, Q^σ be a queue with content σ:*

$$\boxed{\begin{aligned} Q^\epsilon &= Q \\ Q^{\sigma \cdot d} &= Q^\sigma \gg BUF1^d \end{aligned}}$$

Then: $\tau \cdot (Q^\sigma \gg BUF1) = \tau \cdot Q^\sigma$.

4.2.4. PROPOSITION: $Q \gg Q = Q$.
PROOF: Like the proof of proposition 4.2.2. A new ingredient is the identity

$$BUF1^d \gg Q = BUF1 \gg (Q \gg BUF1^d)$$

which is again an instance of L1. Details can be found in [23]. □

4.2.5. COROLLARY: *Let $\sigma, \rho \in D^*$. Then:* $\tau(Q^\sigma \gg Q^\rho) = \tau Q^{\sigma \cdot \rho}$.

4.2.6. Remark. It will be clear that the implementation which is suggested by the specification of process Q is not very efficient: at each time the number of empty storage elements equals the number of data that have left the queue. But we can do it even more inefficiently: the following queue doubles the number of empty storage elements each time a datum is written.

$$\boxed{\overline{Q} = \sum_{d \in D} \downarrow d \cdot (\overline{Q} \gg \uparrow d \cdot \overline{Q})}$$

A standard proof gives that $\overline{Q} = QUEUE$. From the point of view of process algebra this specification is very efficient. It is the shortest specification of a FIFO-queue known to the authors, except for a 5-character specification of PRATT [36]: $\downarrow \uparrow \times D^*$. A problem with Pratt's specification is that a neat axiomatisation of the orthocurrence operator $\times$ is not available. Our Q-specification has the disadvantage that it does not allow for simple proofs of identities like

$$\overline{Q} \gg \overline{Q} = \overline{Q}.$$

4.3. Bags. In [10] a bag over data domain D is defined by:

$$BAG = \sum_{d \in D} \downarrow d \cdot (\uparrow d \| BAG)$$

In our full paper ([23]) it has been proved that $Q \gg BAG = BAG$. However, the identity $BAG \gg Q = BAG$ does not hold. The intuitive argument for this is as follows: if a bag contains an apple and an orange, and the environment wants an apple, then it can just take this apple from the bag. In the case where a system, consisting of the chaining of a bag and a queue, contains an apple and an orange, it can occur that the first element in the queue is an orange. In this situation the environment *has* to take the orange first. The argument that processes $Q \gg BAG$ and BAG are different, because in the first process the environment is not able to pick an apple that is still in the queue, does not hold. In ACP_τ we abstract from the real-time behaviour of concurrent systems. If the environment waits long enough then the apple will be in the bag.

4.4. A queue that can lose data. In the specification of communication protocols, we often encounter transmission channels that can make errors: they can lose, damage or duplicate data. All process algebra specifications of these channels we have seen thus far were lengthy and often incomprehensible. Consequently it was difficult to prove properties of systems containing these queues. Now, interestingly, the same idea that was used to specify the normal queue by means of the chaining operator, can also be used to specify the various faulty queues. One just has to replace the process $BUF1$ in the definition by a process that behaves like a buffer but can lose, damage or duplicate data.

First we describe a queue FQ that can lose every datum contained in it at every moment, without any possibilities for the environment to prevent this from happening. The basic component of this queue is the following Faulty Buffer with capacity one:

$$FBUF1 = \sum_{d \in D} \downarrow d \cdot FBUF1^d$$

$$FBUF1^d = (\uparrow d + \tau) \cdot FBUF1$$

If the faulty buffer contains a datum, then this can get lost at any moment through the occurrence of a τ-action. In the equation for $FBUF1^d$ there is no τ-action before the $\uparrow d$-action because this would make it possible for the buffer to reach a state where datum d could not get lost.

We use the above specification in the definition of the faulty queue FQ:

$$FQ = \sum_{d \in D} \downarrow d \cdot (FQ \gg FBUF1^d)$$

The idea behind this specification of the faulty queue is illustrated in figure 3.

FIGURE 3. *The faulty queue*

4.4.1. LEMMA: $FBUF1^d \gg FBUF1 = \tau \cdot (FBUF1 \gg FBUF1^d)$.
PROOF:

$$FBUF1^d \gg FBUF1 = \tau \cdot (FBUF1 \gg FBUF1^d) + \tau \cdot (FBUF1 \gg FBUF1) =$$
$$= \tau \cdot (FBUF1 \gg FBUF1^d)$$

In the last step we use that: $\tau \cdot (FBUF1 \gg FBUF1) \subseteq FBUF1 \gg FBUF1^d \subseteq \tau \cdot (FBUF1 \gg FBUF1^d)$.
$\square$

Compare the simple definition of FQ with the following $BPA_{\tau\delta}$-specification of the same process.

4.4.2. Let $\sigma, \rho \in D^*$. We write $\sigma \rightarrow \rho$ if ρ can be obtained from σ by deleting one datum. Let $R(\sigma) = \{\rho \mid \sigma \rightarrow \rho\}$ be the finite set of residues of σ after one deletion. Now $FQUEUE$ is the following process.

$$FQUEUE = FQ_\epsilon = \sum_{d \in D} \downarrow d \cdot FQ_d$$

$$FQ_{\sigma*d} = \sum_{e \in D} \downarrow e \cdot FQ_{e*\sigma*d} + \uparrow d \cdot FQ_\sigma + \sum_{\rho \in R(\sigma*d)} \tau \cdot FQ_\rho$$

4.4.3. THEOREM: $FQ = FQUEUE$.
PROOF: Analogously to the proof of theorem 4.2.1. Use lemma 4.4.1 instead of the corresponding equation for $BUF1$. $\square$

Analogous versions of the identities we derived for the normal queue can be derived for the faulty queue in the same way.

4.4.4. PROPOSITION:
i) $FQ \gg FBUF1 = FQ$,
ii) Let for $\sigma \in D^*$, FQ^σ be a faulty queue with content σ:

$$FQ^\epsilon = FQ$$

$$FQ^{\sigma * d} = FQ^\sigma \gg FBUF 1^d$$

Then: $\tau \cdot (FQ^\sigma \gg FBUF 1) = \tau \cdot FQ^\sigma$,

iii) $Q \gg FQ = FQ \gg FQ = FQ$,

iv) Let $\sigma, \rho \in D^*$. Then: $\tau \cdot (FQ^\sigma \gg FQ^\rho) = \tau \cdot FQ^{\sigma * \rho}$.

PROOF: Exactly as in section 4.2. Use lemma 4.4.1 instead of the corresponding equation for $BUF 1$ and in the proof of $FQ \gg FQ = FQ$ use

$$FBUF 1^d \gg FQ = \tau (FBUF 1 \gg (FQ \gg FBUF 1^d))$$

instead of the corresponding equation for $BUF 1^d \gg Q$. This identity can be proved in the same way as lemma 4.4.1. □

4.5. An identity that does nót hold. In this subsection we will discuss the identity

$$FQ = Q \gg FBUF 1.$$

'Intuitively' the processes FQ and $Q \gg FBUF 1$ are equal since both behave like a FIFO-queue that can lose data. Furthermore, with both processes the environment cannot prevent in any way that a datum gets lost. Unlike the situation with the processes $BAG \gg Q$ and BAG which we discussed in section 4.3, we can think of no 'experiment' that distinguishes between the two processes. Still the identity cannot be proved with the axioms presented thus far.

4.5.1. THEOREM: *If parameter D of operator $\gg$ contains more than one element, then $SACP^\ddagger \not\vdash FQ = Q \gg FBUF 1$.*
PROOF: We show that the identity is not valid in the model of process graphs modulo bisimulation congruence as presented in BAETEN, BERGSTRA & KLOP [5]. Suppose that there exists a bisimulation between processes FQ and $Q \gg FBUF 1$. Suppose that process FQ reads successively two different data, starting from the initial state. Because of the bisimulation it must be possible for the process $Q \gg FBUF 1$ to read the same data in such a way that the resulting state is bisimilar to the state process FQ has reached. Now process FQ executes a τ-step and forgets the second datum. We claim that process $Q \gg FBUF 1$ is not capable to perform a corresponding sequence of zero or more τ-step. This is because there are only two possibilities:
1) $Q \gg FBUF 1$ forgets the second datum. But this means that also the first datum is forgotten. In the resulting state $Q \gg FBUF 1$ cannot output any datum (before reading one), whereas process FQ can do this.
2) $Q \gg FBUF 1$ does not forget the second datum. In the resulting state $Q \gg FBUF 1$ can output this datum. Process FQ cannot do that. □
The argument is illustrated in figure 4.

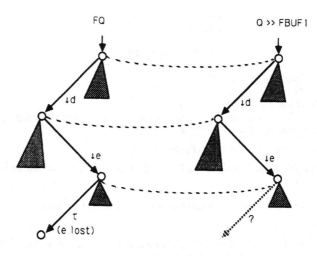

FIGURE 4.

The next theorem shows that, if we add law T4, the two faulty queues can be proven equivalent.

4.5.2. THEOREM: $SACP\sharp + T4 \vdash FQ = Q \gg FBUF1$.

PROOF: The rather complicated proof of this theorem can be found in [23]. □

4.6. The faulty and damaging queue. In the specification of certain link layer protocols we have to deal with a communication channel that behaves like a FIFO-queue with unbounded capacity (this is of course a simplifying assumption), but has some additional properties: (1) a datum can be damaged at every moment it is in the queue; the environment cannot prevent this event, and (2) a datum can be lost at every moment it is in the queue. We give a process algebra specification of this process in two steps. First we specify the Faulty and Damaging Buffer with capacity one (FDBUF1). We assume that the domain of data D contains a special element er, representing a damaged datum.

$$FDBUF1 = \sum_{d \in D} \downarrow d \cdot FDBUF1^d$$

$$FDBUF1^d = \uparrow d \cdot FDBUF1 + \tau \cdot (\uparrow er + \tau) \cdot FDBUF1$$

With the help of this process we can now easily define the Faulty and Damaging Queue (FDQ):

$$FDQ = \sum_{d \in D} \downarrow d \cdot (FDQ \gg FDBUF1^d)$$

4.6.1. LEMMA: $FDBUF1^d \gg FDBUF1 = \tau \cdot (FDBUF1 \gg FDBUF1^d)$.

PROOF: By means of T2, as in lemma 4.4.1, but more complicated. See [23]. □

Once we have lemma 4.6.1, it is standard to prove that process FDQ is guardedly specifiable. It is moreover easy to derive an analogous version of proposition 4.4.4 for FDQ.

4.6.2. Remark. One might ask if there is not a τ too many in the specification of process *FDBUF*1. Why not specify the faulty and damaging buffer simply as follows?

$$FDB\,1 = \sum_{d\in D}\downarrow\cdot FDB\,1^d$$

$$FDB\,1^d = (\uparrow d + \uparrow er + \tau)\cdot FDB\,1$$

A first observation we make is that if $D\neq\{er\}$:

$$\text{SACP}^{\ddagger} \;\nvdash\; FDBUF1 = FDB\,1$$

This is because the two processes are different in bisimulation semantics. Process *FDBUF*1 can input a datum d different from er, and then get into a state where either an output action $\uparrow er$ will be performed or no output action at all. This means that it is possible that a datum is first damaged and then lost. Process *FDB*1 does not have such a state.

For similar reasons we also have the following fact:

$$\text{SACP}^{\ddagger} \;\nvdash\; FDB\,1^d \gg FDB\,1 = \tau\cdot(FDB\,1\gg FDB\,1^d)$$

This means that if we work with a queue defined with the help of *FDB*1, our standard technique to prove facts about queues is not applicable. Note that processes *FDB*1 and *FDBUF*1 are trivially equal if we work in a setting where the law T4 ($\tau(\tau x + y)=\tau x + y$) is valid.

4.7. The faulty and stuttering queue. This section is about a very curious queue: a FIFO-queue that can lose or duplicate any element contained in it at every moment. An infinite specification of this process can be found in LARSEN & MILNER [28]. The basic component we use in the specification of the Faulty and Stuttering Queue is a Faulty and Stuttering Buffer with capacity 1:

$$FSBUF1 = \sum_{d\in D}\downarrow d\cdot FSBUF1^d$$

$$FSBUF1^d = \uparrow d\cdot FSBUF1^d + \tau\cdot FSBUF1$$

$$FSQ = \sum_{d\in D}\downarrow d\cdot(FSQ\gg FSBUF1^d)$$

When we place two faulty and stuttering buffers in a chain, then we have the possibility of an infinite number of internal actions (the first buffer stutters and the second one loses all its input). This implies that, in the specification of the faulty and stuttering queue, we have to guard against unguarded recursion. We need a fairness assumption if we want to exclude the possibility of infinite stuttering. This explains the presence of KFAR in the following lemma.

4.7.1. LEMMA: $\text{SACP}^{\ddagger} + \text{KFAR} \vdash FSBUF1^d\gg FSBUF1 = \tau\cdot(FSBUF1\gg FSBUF1^d)$.
PROOF: See [23]. This proof is rather involved. $\square$

From lemma 4.7.1 all the rest follows: process *FSQ* is guardedly specifiable and we can derive an analogous version of proposition 4.4.4.

§5 A PROTOCOL VERIFICATION

In this section we present the specification and verification of a variant of the Alternating Bit Protocol, resembling the ones discussed in KOYMANS & MULDER [27] and LARSEN & MILNER [28]. The aim of this exercise is to illustrate the usefulness of the proof technique developed in the previous section. The architecture of the *Concurrent Alternating Bit Protocol (CABP)* is as follows:

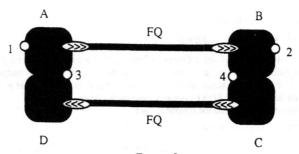

FIGURE 5.

Elements of a finite set of data are to be transmitted by the CABP from port 1 to port 2. Verification of the CABP amounts to a proof that (1) the protocol will eventually send at port 2 all and only data it has read at port 1, and (2) the protocol will send the data at port 2 in the same order as it has read them at port 1.

In the CABP sender and receiver send frames continuously. Since sender and receiver will have a different clock in general, the number of data that can be in the channels at a certain moment is in principle unlimited. In this section we assume that the channels behave like the process *FQ* as described in section 4.4: a FIFO-queue with unbounded capacity that can either lose frames or pass them on correctly.

In the protocol, the sender consists of two components A and D, whereas the receiver consists of components B and C. One might propose to collapse A and D into a sender process, and B plus C into a receiver process. The resulting processes would be more complicated and in the correctness proof we would have to decompose them again.

5.1. Specification. Let D be a finite set of data which have to be sent by the CABP from port 1 to port 2. Let $B = \{0,1\}$. $\mathcal{D} = (D \times B) \cup B$ is the set of data which occur as parameter in the actions of the chaining operators. The set of ports is $\mathbf{P} = \{1,2,3,4\}$, the set of data that can be communicated at these ports is $\mathbf{D} = D \cup \{next\}$. Alphabet A and communication function γ are now defined by the standard scheme for the chaining operators, augmented with actions $ri(d)$, $si(d)$ and $ci(d)$, for which we have communications $\gamma(ri(d), si(d)) = ci(d)$ ($i \in \mathbf{P}$ and $d \in \mathbf{D}$).

We now give the specifications of processes A, B, C and D. Here b ranges over $B = \{0,1\}$ and d over D (the overloading of names B and D should cause no confusion). The specifications are standard and need no further comment.

$$A = A^0$$

$$A^b = \sum_{d \in D} r\,1(d) \cdot A^{db}$$

$$A^{db} = \uparrow db \cdot A^{db} + r\,3(next) \cdot A^{1-b}$$

$$D = D^0$$

$$D^b = \downarrow(1-b) \cdot D^b + \downarrow b \cdot s\,3(next) \cdot D^{1-b}$$

$$B = B^0$$

$$B^b = \sum_{d \in D} \downarrow(d, 1-b) \cdot B^b + \sum_{d \in D} \downarrow db \cdot B^{db}$$

$$B^{db} = s\,2(d) \cdot s\,4(next) \cdot B^{1-b}$$

$$C = C^1 \qquad \text{(not } C^0!)$$

$$C^b = \uparrow b \cdot C^b + r\,4(next) \cdot C^{1-b}$$

Let H and I be the following sets of actions:

$$H = \{r\,3(next), s\,3(next), r\,4(next), s\,4(next)\}$$

$$I = \{c\,3(next), c\,4(next)\}$$

The Concurrent Alternating Bit Protocol is defined by:

$$CABP = \tau_I \circ \partial_H((A \gg FQ \gg B) \| (C \gg FQ \gg D))$$

5.2. Verification. If we do not abstract from the internal actions of the protocol, then the number of states is infinite. This means that a straightforward calculation of the state graph is not possible. A strategy which is often applied in cases like this is that one substitutes a buffer with capacity 1 for the communication channels. As a result the system is finite and can be verified automatically. Next a buffer with capacity 2 is substituted, followed by another automatic verification, etc.. The verification for the case of buffers with capacity 155 takes 23 hours CPU time. Thereafter it is decided that 'the protocol is correct'.

Of course it is not so difficult to specify a protocol that is correct for buffers with capacity less or equal than 155, but fails when the capacity is 156. The conclusion that the protocol is correct for arbitrary buffer size because it works in the cases where the buffer size is less than 156, is therefore influenced by other observations. It is for example intuitively not very plausible that the CABP works for buffer size 155, but not for buffer size 156, because the specification is so short and the only numbers which occur in it are 0 and 1.

Because intuitions can be wrong people look for formal techniques which tell in which situations induction over certain protocol parameters is allowed.

The basic merit of the results of section 4 is that they make it possible to use inductive arguments when dealing with the length of queues in protocol systems. In the verification below we show that the protocol is correct if the channels behave as faulty FIFO-queues with unbounded capacity. However, a minor change in the proof is enough to show that the protocol also works if the channels behave as n-buffers, faulty n-buffers, perfect queues, faulty and stuttering queues, etc.

The following two lemmas will be used to show that, after abstraction, the number of states of the protocol is finite. The first lemma says that if, at the head of the queue, there is a datum that will be thrown away by the receiver because it is of the wrong type, this datum can be thrown away immediately.

5.2.1. LEMMA:
i) $FBUF1^{db} \gg B^{1-b} = \tau \cdot (FBUF1 \gg B^{1-b})$;
ii) $FBUF1^{db} \gg s\,4(next) \cdot B^{1-b} = \tau \cdot (FBUF1 \gg s\,4(next) \cdot B^{1-b})$;
iii) $FBUF1^{db} \gg B^{db} = \tau \cdot (FBUF1 \gg B^{db})$.

PROOF: Straightforward with summand inclusion and T2. See [23]. $\square$

The next lemma says that if two frames, of a type that the receiver is willing to accept, are at the head of the queue, one of these can be deleted without changing the process (modulo an initial τ).

5.2.2. LEMMA: $FBUF1^{db} \gg FBUF1^{db} \gg B^b = \tau \cdot (FBUF1 \gg FBUF1^{db} \gg B^b)$.
PROOF: Likewise; see [23]. $\square$

5.2.3. We can now derive a transition diagram for process $A \ggg FQ \gg B$. In the derivation we use lemmas 5.2.1 and 5.2.2 to keep the diagram finite. Furthermore we stop the derivation at those places where an action is performed that corresponds to the acknowledgement of a frame that has not yet arrived. In [23] the derivation is carried out in detail. The result of the calculations is presented in lemma 5.2.4, which is pictured in figure 6. The grey arcs correspond to places where we stopped the derivation.

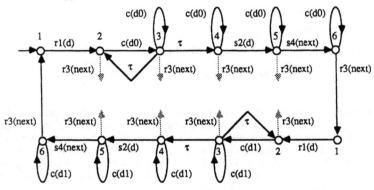

FIGURE 6. Transition diagram of process $A \ggg FQ \gg B$

5.2.4. LEMMA: $A \ggg FQ \gg B$ satisfies the following system of recursion equations.

$X = X_1^0$	
$X_1^0 = \sum_{d \in D} r1(d) \cdot X_2^{0b}$	
$X_2^{\phi} = c(db) \cdot X_3^{\phi} + Y_2^0$	$Y_2^0 = r3(next) \cdot (A^{1-b} \ggg FQ \gg B^b)$
$X_3^{\phi} = \tau \cdot X_2^{\phi} + c(db) \cdot X_3^{\phi} + \tau \cdot X_4^{\phi} + Y_3^{\phi}$	$Y_3^{\phi} = r3(next) \cdot (A^{1-b} \ggg FQ \gg FBUF1^{db} \gg B^b)$
$X_4^{\phi} = c(db) \cdot X_4^{\phi} + s2(d) \cdot X_5^{\phi} + Y_4^{\phi}$	$Y_4^{\phi} = r3(next) \cdot (A^{1-b} \ggg FQ \gg B^{db})$
$X_5^{\phi} = c(db) \cdot X_5^{\phi} + s4(next) \cdot X_6^{\phi} + Y_5^{\phi}$	$Y_5^{\phi} = r3(next) \cdot (A^{1-b} \ggg FQ \gg s4(next) \cdot B^{1-b})$
$X_6^{\phi} = r3(next) \cdot X_1^{1-b} + c(db) \cdot X_6^{\phi}$	

Using CFAR immediately gives the next lemma.

5.2.5. LEMMA: Let U be specified by:

499

$U = U_1^b$	
$U_1^b = \sum_{d \in D} r1(d) \cdot U_2^{db}$	
$U_2^{db} = \tau \cdot U_4^{db} + V_2^b + V_3^{db}$	$V_2^b = r3(next) \cdot (A^{1-b} \gg FQ \gg B^b)$
	$V_3^{db} = r3(next) \cdot (A^{1-b} \gg FQ \gg FBUF1^{db} \gg B^b)$
$U_4^{db} = s2(d) \cdot U_5^{db} + V_4^{db}$	$V_4^{db} = r3(next) \cdot (A^{1-b} \gg FQ \gg B^{db})$
$U_5^{db} = s4(next) \cdot U_6^{db} + V_5^{db}$	$V_5^{db} = r3(next) \cdot (A^{1-b} \gg FQ \gg s4(next) \cdot B^{1-b})$
$U_6^{db} = r3(next) \cdot U_1^{1-b}$	

Then: $SACP_\tau^\sharp + KFAR \vdash U = A \gg FQ \gg B$.

In the same way we can derive similar lemmas for 'the other side' of the protocol.

5.2.6. LEMMA:
i) $FBUF1^b \gg D^{1-b} = \tau \cdot (FBUF1 \gg D^{1-b})$;
ii) $FBUF1^b \gg s3(next) \cdot D^{1-b} = \tau \cdot (FBUF1 \gg s3(next) \cdot D^{1-b})$;
iii) $FBUF1^b \gg FBUF1^b \gg D^b = \tau \cdot (FBUF1 \gg FBUF1^b \gg D^b)$.

5.2.7. LEMMA: *Let W be specified by:*

$W = W_1^b$	
$W_1^b = \tau \cdot r4(next) \cdot W_2^{1-b}$	$Z_1^b = r4(next) \cdot (C^{1-b} \gg FQ \gg D^b)$
$W_2^b = \tau \cdot W_3^b + Z_1^b + Z_2^b$	$Z_2^b = r4(next) \cdot (C^{1-b} \gg FQ \gg FBUF1^b \gg D^b)$
$W_3^b = s3(next) \cdot W_1^b + Z_3^b$	$Z_3^b = r4(next) \cdot (C^{1-b} \gg FQ \gg s3(next) \cdot D^{1-b})$

Then: $SACP_\tau^\sharp + KFAR \vdash C \gg FQ \gg D = W$.

The fact that CABP is a correct protocol is asserted by

5.2.8. THEOREM: $SACP_\tau^\sharp + KFAR \vdash CABP = \tau \cdot (\sum_{d \in D} r1(d) \cdot s2(d)) \cdot CABP$.

PROOF: Lemmas 5.2.5 and 5.2.7 together give that we can write $CABP$ as:

$$CABP = \tau_I \circ \partial_H(U \| W)$$

A straightforward expansion gives:

$$\tau_I \circ \partial_H(U \| W) = \tau \cdot (\sum_{d \in D} r1(d) \cdot s2(d)) \cdot (\sum_{e \in D} r1(e) \cdot s2(e)) \cdot \tau_I \circ \partial_H(U \| W)$$

The variables V and Z vanish in the expansion, due to the fact that they only occur in situations where a receiver component sends a premature acknowledgement. An application of RSP concludes the proof of the theorem. $\square$

5.2.9. Remark. A serious problem that has to be faced in the context of algebraic protocol verification is the fairness issue. In the verifications of this paper we used KFAR to deal with fairness. KFAR is the algebraic equivalent of the statement: 'if anything can go well infinitely often, it will go well infinitely often'. In most applications a more subtle treatment of fairness is desirable. Moreover KFAR is incompatible with lots of semantics between bisimulation and trace semantics. In [15] it is proved that failure semantics is inconsistent with the rule KFAR. In the same paper a restricted version KFAR⁻ of KFAR is presented which *is* consistent with the axioms of failure semantics, but this version is not powerful enough to allow for a verification of the CABP. The argument for this is simple: KFAR⁻ allows for the fair abstraction of *unstable divergence*. This means that a process will never stay forever in a conservative cluster of internal τ-steps if it can be exited by another internal τ-step. Since in the CABP component C can always perform an internal step, and since the protocol is finite state (after suitable abstraction), there must be a conservative cluster of internal steps which can only be exited by performing an observable action. Thus the CABP contains stable divergence.

§6 Conclusions and open problems

In this paper we presented a language making it possible to give modular specifications of process algebras. The language contains operations $+$ and $\Box$, which are standard in the theory of structured algebraic specifications, and moreover two new operators H and S. Two applications have been presented of the new operators: we showed how the left-merge operator can be hidden if this is needed and we described how the chaining operator can be defined in a clean way in terms of more elementary operators. It is clear that there are much more applications of our approach. Numerous other process combinators can be defined in terms of more elementary operators in the same way as we did with the chaining operators. Maybe also other model theoretic operations can be used in a process algebra setting (cartesian products?).

Strictly speaking we have not introduced a 'module algebra' as in [9]: we do not interpret module expressions in an algebra. However, this can be done without any problem. An interesting topic of research is to look for axioms to manipulate module expressions. Due to the presence of the operators H and S, an elimination theorem for module expressions as in [9] will probably not be achievable.

An important open problem for us is the question whether the proof system of table 1 is complete for first order logic.

In this paper the modules are parametrised by a set of actions. These actions themselves do not have any structure. The most natural way to look towards actions like $s\,1(d_0)$ however, is to see them as actions parametrised by data. We would like to include the notion of a parametrised action in our framework but it turns out that this is not trivial. Related work in this area has been done by MAUW [29] and MAUW & VELTINK [30].

In order to prove the associativity of the chaining operators, we needed auxiliary actions $\bar{s}(d)$, $\bar{r}(d)$, etc. Also in other situations it often turns out to be useful to introduce auxiliary actions in verifications. At present we have to introduce these actions right at the beginning of a specification. This is embarrassing for a reader who does not know about the future use of these actions in the verification. But of course also the authors don't like to rewrite their specification all the time when they work on the verification. Therefore we would like to have a proof principle saying that it is allowed to use 'fresh' atomic actions in proofs. We think that it is possible to add a 'Fresh Atom Principle' (FAP) to our formal setting, but some work still has to be done.

In our view section 4 convincingly shows that chaining operators are useful in dealing with FIFO-queues. We think that in general it will be often the case that a new application requires new operators and laws.

In section 4.5 we presented a simple example of a realistic situation where bisimulation semantics does not work: a FIFO-queue which can loose data at every place is different from a

FIFO-queue which can only loose data at the end. Adding the law T4, which holds in ready trace semantics (and hence in failure semantics), made it possible to prove the two queues equal.

For the correctness of protocols which involve faulty queues one normally needs some fairness assumption. Koomen's Fair Abstraction Rule (KFAR) often forms an adequate, although not optimal, way to model fairness. An interesting open problem is therefore the question whether the module SACP$\frac{\tau}{\delta}$ + T4 + KFAR is consistent (conjecture: yes).

The verification of the Concurrent Alternating Bit Protocol as presented in the full version of this report takes 4 pages (or 5 if the proofs of the standard facts about the queues are included). Our proof is considerably shorter than the proof of similar protocols in [27] and [28] (15 and 11 pages respectively). But maybe this comparison is not altogether fair because the proofs in these papers were meant as an illustration of new modular proof techniques. Our proof shows that the axioms of bisimulation semantics with fair abstraction are sufficient for the modular verification of simple protocols like this. The axioms of bisimulation semantics will turn out to be not sufficient for more substantial modular verifications because bisimulation semantics is not fully abstract. We could give a shorter and simpler proof of the protocol by using the notion of redundancy in context of [41]: the grey arcs in figure 6 all correspond to summands which are redundant in the context in which they occur. Additional proof techniques will certainly be needed for the modular verification of more complex protocols.

ACKNOWLEDGEMENTS
Our thanks to Jan Bergstra for his help in the development of the H-operator and to Kees Middelburg for helpful comments on an earlier version.

APPENDIX: LOGICS
In this appendix equational, conditional equational and first order logic are defined. Since all these logics share the concepts of variables and terms, these will be treated first.

1. Variables and terms. Let σ be a signature. A σ-*variable* is an expression x_S with $x \in$ NAMES and $\mathbf{S}_\sigma : S$. A *valuation* of the σ-variables in a σ-algebra $\mathcal{C}$ is a function ξ that takes every σ-variable x_S into an element of $S^{\mathcal{C}}$.

For any $\mathbf{S}_\sigma : S$ the set T_S^σ of σ-*terms* of sort S is defined inductively by:
- $x_S \in T_S^\sigma$ for any σ-variable x_S.
- If $\mathbf{F}_\sigma : f : S_1 \times \cdots \times S_n \to S$ and $t_i \in T_{S_i}^\sigma$ for $i = 1, ..., n$ then $f_{S_1 \times \cdots \times S_n \to S}(t_1, \cdots, t_n) \in T_S^\sigma$.

The ξ-*evaluation* $[\![t]\!]^\xi \in S^{\mathcal{C}}$ of a σ-term $t \in T_S^\sigma$ in a σ-algebra $\mathcal{C}$ (with ξ a valuation) is defined by:
- $[\![x_S]\!]^\xi = \xi(x_S) \in S^{\mathcal{C}}$.
- $[\![f_{S_1 \times \cdots \times S_n \to S}(t_1, \cdots, t_n)]\!]^\xi = f_{S_1 \times \cdots \times S_n \to S}^{\mathcal{C}}([\![t_1]\!]^\xi, \cdots, [\![t_n]\!]^\xi)$.

2. Equational logic. The set F_σ^{eql} of *equations* or *equational formulas* over σ is defined by:
- If $t_i \in T_S^\sigma$ for $i = 1,2$ and certain $\mathbf{S}_\sigma : S$ then $(t_1 = t_2) \in F_\sigma^{eql}$.

An equation $(t_1 = t_2) \in F_\sigma^{eql}$ is ξ-*true* in a σ-algebra $\mathcal{C}$, notation $\mathcal{C}, \xi \vDash_\sigma^{eql} t_1 = t_2$, if $[\![t_1]\!]^\xi = [\![t_2]\!]^\xi$. Such an equation $\phi \in F_\sigma^{eql}$ is *true* in $\mathcal{C}$, notation $\mathcal{C} \vDash_\sigma^{eql} \phi$, if $\mathcal{C}, \xi \vDash_\sigma^{eql} \phi$ for all valuations ξ.

An inference system I_σ^{eql} for equational logic is displayed in table 11 below. There t, u and v are terms over σ and x is a variable. Furthermore $t[u/x]$ is the result of substituting u for all occurrences of x in t. Of course u and x should be of the same sort. Finally an inference rule $\frac{H}{\phi}$ with $H = \varnothing$ is called an *axiom* and denoted simply by ϕ.

$$\begin{array}{c|c|c|c|c} t=t & \dfrac{u=v}{v=u} & \dfrac{t=u,\ u=v}{t=v} & \dfrac{u=v}{t[u/x]=t[v/x]} & \dfrac{u=v}{u[t/x]=v[t/x]} \end{array}$$

TABLE 11.

3. Conditional equational logic.

3. *Conditional equational logic.* The set F_σ^{at} of *atomic formulas* over σ is defined by:
- If $t_i \in T_S^\sigma$ for $i=1,2$ and certain $\mathbf{S}_\sigma:S$ then $(t_1=t_2) \in F_\sigma^{at}$.
- If $\mathbf{R}_\sigma:p \subseteq S_1 \times \cdots \times S_n$ and $t_i \in T_{S_i}^\sigma$ for $i=1,...,n$ then $p_{S_1 \times \cdots \times S_n}(t_1, \cdots, t_n) \in F_\sigma^{at}$.

The set F_σ^{ceql} of *conditional equational formulas* over σ is defined by:
- If $C \subseteq F_\sigma^{at}$ and $\alpha \in F_\sigma^{at}$ then $(C \Rightarrow \alpha) \in F_\sigma^{ceql}$.

The ξ-*truth* of formulas $\phi \in F_\sigma^{at} \cup F_\sigma^{ceql}$ in a σ-algebra $\mathcal{C}$ is defined by:
- $\mathcal{C},\xi \vDash_\sigma^{ceql} t_1=t_2$ if $[\![t_1]\!]^\xi = [\![t_2]\!]^\xi$.
- $\mathcal{C},\xi \vDash_\sigma^{ceql} p_{S_1 \times \cdots \times S_n}(t_1, \cdots, t_n)$ if $p_{S_1 \times \cdots \times S_n}^\xi ([\![t_1]\!]^\xi, \cdots, [\![t_n]\!]^\xi)$.
- $\mathcal{C},\xi \vDash_\sigma^{ceql} C \Rightarrow \alpha$ if $\mathcal{C},\xi \nvDash_\sigma^{ceql} \beta$ for some $\beta \in C$ or $\mathcal{C},\xi \vDash_\sigma^{ceql} \alpha$.

ϕ is *true* in $\mathcal{C}$, notation $\mathcal{C} \vDash_\sigma^{ceql} \phi$, if $\mathcal{C},\xi \vDash_\sigma^{ceql} \phi$ for all valuations ξ.

An inference system I_σ^{ceql} for conditional equational logic is displayed in table 12 below. There α and α_i are atomic formulas, C is a set of atomic formulas, ϕ is a conditional equational formula, t_i, t, u and v are terms over σ and x_i and x are variables. Furthermore $\alpha[u/x]$ is the result of substituting u for all occurrences of x in α. Of course u and x should be of the same sort. Likewise $\phi[t_i/x_i\ (i \in I)]$ is the result of simultaneous substitution for $i \in I$ of t_i for all occurrences of x_i in ϕ. An inference rule $\dfrac{\varnothing}{\phi}$ is again denoted by ϕ and a conditional equational formula $\varnothing \Rightarrow \alpha$ by α.

$$\begin{array}{c|c|c|c} C \Rightarrow \alpha \quad \text{if } \alpha \in C & & \dfrac{C \Rightarrow \alpha_i\ (i \in I),\ \{\alpha_i \,|\, i \in I\} \Rightarrow \alpha}{C \Rightarrow \alpha} & \dfrac{\phi}{\phi[t_i/x_i\ (i \in I)]} \\ \hline t=t & \{u=v\} \Rightarrow (v=u) & \{t=u,\ u=v\} \Rightarrow (t=u) & \{u=v,\ \alpha[u/x]\} \Rightarrow (\alpha[v/x]) \end{array}$$

TABLE 12.

The logic described above is *infinitary conditional equational logic*. *Finitary conditional equational logic* is obtained by the extra requirement that in conditional equational formulas $C \Rightarrow \alpha$ the set of conditions C should be finite. In that case the inference rule

$$\dfrac{\phi}{\phi[t_i/x_i\ (i \in I)]} \quad \text{can be replaced by} \quad \dfrac{\phi}{\phi[t/x]}.$$

Furthermore *(in)finitary conditional logic* is obtained by omitting all reference to the equality predicate $=$.

4. First order logic.

4. *First order logic.* The set F_σ^{foleq} of *first order formulas with equality* over σ is defined by:
- If $t_i \in T_S^\sigma$ for $i=1,2$ and certain $\mathbf{S}_\sigma:S$ then $(t_1=t_2) \in F_\sigma^{foleq}$.
- If $\mathbf{R}_\sigma:p \subseteq S_1 \times \cdots \times S_n$ and $t_i \in T_{S_i}^\sigma$ for $i=1,...,n$ then $p_{S_1 \times \cdots \times S_n}(t_1, \cdots, t_n) \in F_\sigma^{foleq}$.
- If $\phi \in F_\sigma^{foleq}$ then $\neg \phi \in F_\sigma^{foleq}$.
- If ϕ and $\psi \in F_\sigma^{foleq}$ then $(\phi \rightarrow \psi) \in F_\sigma^{foleq}$.
- If ϕ and $\psi \in F_\sigma^{foleq}$ then $(\phi \wedge \psi) \in F_\sigma^{foleq}$.
- If ϕ and $\psi \in F_\sigma^{foleq}$ then $(\phi \vee \psi) \in F_\sigma^{foleq}$.
- If ϕ and $\psi \in F_\sigma^{foleq}$ then $(\phi \leftrightarrow \psi) \in F_\sigma^{foleq}$.
- If x_S is a σ-variable and $\phi \in F_\sigma^{foleq}$ then $\forall x_S(\phi) \in F_\sigma^{foleq}$.
- If x_S is a σ-variable and $\phi \in F_\sigma^{foleq}$ then $\exists x_S(\phi) \in F_\sigma^{foleq}$.

The ξ-*truth* of a formula $\phi \in F_\sigma^{foleq}$ in a σ-algebra $\mathcal{C}$ is defined inductively by:

- $\mathcal{C}, \xi \vDash_\sigma^{foleq} t_1 = t_2$ if $[\![t_1]\!]^\xi = [\![t_2]\!]^\xi$.
- $\mathcal{C}, \xi \vDash_\sigma^{foleq} p_{S_1 \times \cdots \times S_n}(t_1, \cdots, t_n)$ if $p_{S_1 \times \cdots \times S_n}^\mathcal{C}([\![t_1]\!]^\xi, \cdots, [\![t_n]\!]^\xi)$.
- $\mathcal{C}, \xi \vDash_\sigma^{foleq} \neg\phi$ if $\mathcal{C}, \xi \nvDash_\sigma^{foleq} \phi$.
- $\mathcal{C}, \xi \vDash_\sigma^{foleq} \phi \to \psi$ if $\mathcal{C}, \xi \nvDash_\sigma^{foleq} \phi$ or $\mathcal{C}, \xi \vDash_\sigma^{foleq} \psi$.
- $\mathcal{C}, \xi \vDash_\sigma^{foleq} \phi \wedge \psi$ if $\mathcal{C}, \xi \vDash_\sigma^{foleq} \phi$ and $\mathcal{C}, \xi \vDash_\sigma^{foleq} \psi$.
- $\mathcal{C}, \xi \vDash_\sigma^{foleq} \phi \vee \psi$ if $\mathcal{C}, \xi \vDash_\sigma^{foleq} \phi$ or $\mathcal{C}, \xi \vDash_\sigma^{foleq} \psi$.
- $\mathcal{C}, \xi \vDash_\sigma^{foleq} \phi \leftrightarrow \psi$ if $\mathcal{C}, \xi \vDash_\sigma^{foleq} \phi$ if and only if $\mathcal{C}, \xi \vDash_\sigma^{foleq} \psi$.
- $\mathcal{C}, \xi \vDash_\sigma^{foleq} \forall x_S(\phi)$ if $\mathcal{C}, \xi' \vDash_\sigma^{foleq} \phi$ for all valuations ξ' with $\xi'(y_{S'}) = \xi(y_{S'})$ for all variables $y_{S'} \neq x_S$.
- $\mathcal{C}, \xi \vDash_\sigma^{foleq} \exists x_S(\phi)$ if $\mathcal{C}, \xi' \vDash_\sigma^{foleq} \phi$ for some valuation ξ' with $\xi'(y_{S'}) = \xi(y_{S'})$ for all variables $y_{S'} \neq x_S$.

ϕ is *true* is $\mathcal{C}$, notation $\mathcal{C} \vDash_\sigma^{foleq}$, if $\mathcal{C}, \xi \vDash_\sigma^{foleq} \phi$ for all valuations ξ.

An inference system I_σ^{foleq} for first order logic with equality is displayed in table 13 below. There ϕ, ψ and ρ are elements of F_σ^{foleq}, α is an atomic formula (constructed by means of the first two clauses in the definition of F_σ^{foleq} only), t, u and v are terms over σ and x is a variable. An occurrence of a variable x in a formula ϕ is *bound* if it occurs in a subformula $\forall x(\psi)$ or $\exists x(\psi)$ of ϕ. Otherwise it is *free*. $\phi[t/x]$ denotes the result of substituting u for all free occurrences of x in t. Of course u and x should be of the same sort. Now t *is free for x in ϕ* if all free occurrences of variables in t remain free in $\phi[t/x]$. As before an inference rule $\dfrac{H}{\phi}$ with $H = \varnothing$ is called an *axiom* and denoted simply by ϕ.

$\dfrac{\phi,\ \phi \to \psi}{\psi}$ *modus ponens*		$\dfrac{\phi}{\forall x(\phi)}$ *generalisation*
$\phi \to (\psi \to \phi)$		
$\{\phi \to (\psi \to \rho)\} \to \{(\phi \to \psi) \to (\phi \to \rho)\}$		$\Big\}$ *deduction axioms*
$\{\forall x(\phi \to \psi)\} \to \{\phi \to \forall x(\psi)\}$, if x does not occur free in ϕ		
$(\neg\phi \to \phi) \to \phi$		*axiom of the excluded middle*
$\neg\phi \to (\phi \to \psi)$		*axiom of contradiction*
$\forall x(\phi) \to \phi[t/x]$, if t is free for x in ϕ		*axiom of specialisation*
$(\phi \wedge \psi) \to \phi$	$\phi \to (\phi \vee \psi)$	$(\phi \leftrightarrow \psi) \to \{(\phi \to \psi) \wedge (\psi \to \phi)\}$
$(\phi \wedge \psi) \to \psi$	$\psi \to (\phi \vee \psi)$	$\{(\phi \to \psi) \wedge (\psi \to \phi)\} \to (\phi \leftrightarrow \psi)$
$\phi \to \{\psi \to (\phi \wedge \psi)\}$	$(\phi \vee \psi) \to (\neg\phi \to \psi)$	$\exists x(\phi) \leftrightarrow \neg\forall x(\neg\phi)$
$t = t$ $(u = v) \to (v = u)$	$\{(t = u) \wedge (u = v)\} \to (t = v)$	$(u = v) \to (\alpha[u/x] \leftrightarrow \alpha[v/x])$

TABLE 13.

First order logic is obtained from first order logic with equality by omitting all reference to $=$. It is also possible to present first order logic without the connectives $\wedge$, $\vee$ and $\leftrightarrow$ and the quantifier $\exists$, and introduce them as notational abbreviations. In that case the third block of table 13 can be omitted.

5. Expressiveness. One can translate an equation $\alpha \in F_\sigma^{eql}$ by a (finitary) conditional equational formula $\varnothing \Rightarrow \alpha \in F_\sigma^{ceql}$ and a finitary conditional equational formula $\{\alpha_1, \cdots, \alpha_n\} \Rightarrow \alpha \in F_\sigma^{fceql}$ into a first order formula $(\alpha_1 \wedge \cdots \wedge \alpha_n) \to \alpha \in F_\sigma^{foleq}$. Using this translation we have $F_\sigma^{eql} \subset F_\sigma^{fceql} \subset F_\sigma^{foleq}$ and furthermore $\mathcal{C} \vDash_\sigma^{eql} \phi \Leftrightarrow \mathcal{C} \vDash_\sigma^{ceql} \phi$ for $\phi \in F_\sigma^{eql}$ and $\mathcal{C} \vDash_\sigma^{ceql} \phi \Leftrightarrow \mathcal{C} \vDash_\sigma^{foleq} \phi$ for $\phi \in F_\sigma^{fceql}$. This means that first order logic with equality is more expressive then equational logic and finitary conditional equational logic is somewhere in between. However first order logic with equality and infinitary conditional equational logic are incomparable.

6. *Completeness.* For all logics mentioned above the following completeness result is known to hold: $Alg(\sigma,T) \vDash_\sigma^\mathcal{L} \phi \Rightarrow T \vdash_\sigma^\mathcal{L} \phi$. The reverse direction also holds, since all these logics are obviously sound. As a corollary we have

$$T \vdash_\sigma^{eql} \phi \Leftrightarrow T \vdash_\sigma^{ceql} \phi \quad \text{for } \phi \in F_\sigma^{eql} \text{ and}$$

$$T \vdash_\sigma^{ceql} \phi \Leftrightarrow T \vdash_\sigma^{foleq} \phi \quad \text{for } \phi \in F_\sigma^{fceql}.$$

For this reason in a lot of process algebra papers it is not made explicit which logic is used in verifications: the space needed for stating this could be saved, since the resulting notion of provability would be the same anyway. However, the situation changes when formulas are proved from modules. Equational logic and conditional equational logic are not complete anymore and for first order logic with equality this is still an open problem (for us). Here a logic $\mathcal{L}$ is complete if $M \vDash^\mathcal{L} \phi \Rightarrow M \vdash^\mathcal{L} \phi$. It is easily shown that

$$M \vdash^{eql} \phi \Rightarrow M \vdash^{ceql} \phi \quad \text{for } \phi \in F_{\Sigma(M)}^{eql} \text{ and}$$

$$M \vdash^{ceql} \phi \Rightarrow M \vdash^{foleq} \phi \quad \text{for } \phi \in F_{\Sigma(M)}^{fceql},$$

but the reverse directions do not hold. Thus we should state exactly in which logic our results are proved.

7. *Notation.* This paper employs infinitary conditional equational logic. However, no proof trees are constructed; proofs are given in a slightly informal way, that allows a straightforward translation into formal proofs by the reader. Furthermore all type information given in the subscripts of variables, function and predicate symbols is omitted, since confusion about the correct types is almost impossible. Outside section 1 and this appendix inference rules $\dfrac{H}{\phi}$ do not occur, but all conditional equational formulas $C \Rightarrow \alpha$ are written $\dfrac{C}{\alpha}$, as is usual. However, the suggested similarity between inference rules and conditional equational formulas is misleading: $\dfrac{H}{\phi}$ holds in an algebra $\mathcal{C}$ if $(\mathcal{C},\xi \vDash \psi$ for all $\psi \in H$ and all valuations $\xi)$ implies $(\mathcal{C},\xi \vDash \phi$ for all valuations $\xi)$, while $\dfrac{C}{\alpha}$ holds in $\mathcal{C}$ if for all valuations ξ: $(\mathcal{C},\xi \vDash \beta$ for all $\beta \in C$ implies $\mathcal{C},\xi \vDash \alpha)$.

8. *Positive and universal formulas.* In equational logic all formulas are both positive and universal. In conditional equational logic all formulas are universal and the positive formulas are the atomic ones. In first order logic with equality the positive formulas are the ones without the connectives $\neg$ and $\rightarrow$ and the universal ones are the formulas without quantifiers. Model theory (see for instance [33]) teaches us that a formula ϕ is preserved under homomorphisms (respectively subalgebras) iff there is a positive (respectively universal) formula ψ with $\vdash^{foleq} \psi \leftrightarrow \phi$.

REFERENCES

[1] P. AMERICA (1985): *Definition of the programming language POOL-T*. ESPRIT project 415, Doc. Nr. 91, Philips Research Laboratories, Eindhoven.

[2] D. AUSTRY & G. BOUDOL (1984): *Algèbre de processus et synchronisations*. Theoretical Computer Science 30(1), pp. 91-131.

[3] J.C.M. BAETEN & J.A. BERGSTRA (1987): *Global Renaming Operators in Concrete Process Algebra (revised version)*. Report P8709, Programming Research Group, University of Amsterdam, to appear in I&C.

[4] J.C.M. BAETEN, J.A. BERGSTRA & J.W. KLOP (1987): *Conditional Axioms and α/β Calculus in Process Algebra*. In: Formal Description of Programming Concepts - III, Proceedings of

the third IFIP WG 2.2 working conference, Ebberup 1986 (M. Wirsing, ed.), North-Holland, Amsterdam, pp. 53-75.

[5] J.C.M. BAETEN, J.A. BERGSTRA & J.W. KLOP (1987): *On the Consistency of Koomen's Fair Abstraction Rule.* Theoretical Computer Science 51(1/2), pp. 129-176.

[6] J.C.M. BAETEN, J.A. BERGSTRA & J.W. KLOP (1987): *Ready trace semantics for concrete process algebra with priority operator.* The Computer Journal 30(6), pp. 498-506.

[7] J.C.M. BAETEN & R.J. VAN GLABBEEK (1987): *Merge and termination in process algebra.* In: Proceedings 7th Conference on Foundations of Software Technology & Theoretical Computer Science, Pune, India (K.V. Nori, ed.), LNCS 287, Springer-Verlag, pp. 153-172.

[8] J.A. BERGSTRA (1985): *A Process Creation Mechanism in Process Algebra.* Logic Group Preprint Series Nr. 2, CIF, State University of Utrecht, to appear in: Applications of Process Algebra, (J.C.M. Baeten, ed.), CWI Monograph, North-Holland, 1988.

[9] J.A. BERGSTRA, J. HEERING & P. KLINT (1986): *Module Algebra.* Report CS-R8617, Centrum voor Wiskunde en Informatica, Amsterdam, to appear in: Journal of the ACM.

[10] J.A. BERGSTRA & J.W. KLOP (1984): *The algebra of recursively defined processes and the algebra of regular processes.* In: Proceedings 11th ICALP, Antwerpen (J. Paredaens, ed.), LNCS 172, Springer-Verlag, pp. 82-95.

[11] J.A. BERGSTRA & J.W. KLOP (1984): *Process algebra for synchronous communication.* I&C 60(1/3), pp. 109-137.

[12] J.A. BERGSTRA & J.W. KLOP (1985): *Algebra of communicating processes with abstraction.* Theoretical Computer Science 37(1), pp. 77-121.

[13] J.A. BERGSTRA & J.W. KLOP (1986): *Process Algebra: Specification and Verification in Bisimulation Semantics.* In: Mathematics and Computer Science II, CWI Monograph 4 (M. Hazewinkel, J.K. Lenstra & L.G.L.T. Meertens, eds.), North-Holland, Amsterdam, pp. 61-94.

[14] J.A. BERGSTRA & J.W. KLOP: ACP_τ: *A Universal Axiom System for Process Specification.* This volume.

[15] J.A. BERGSTRA, J.W. KLOP & E.-R. OLDEROG (1987): *Failures without chaos: a new process semantics for fair abstraction.* In: Formal Description of Programming Concepts - III, Proceedings of the third IFIP WG 2.2 working conference, Ebberup 1986 (M. Wirsing, ed.), North-Holland, Amsterdam, pp. 77-103.

[16] J.A. BERGSTRA & J. TIURYN (1987): *Process Algebra Semantics for Queues.* Fund. Inf. X, pp. 213-224, also appeared as: MC Report IW 241, Amsterdam 1983.

[17] S.D. BROOKES & A.W. ROSCOE (1985): *An improved failures model for communicating processes.* In: Seminar on Concurrency (S.D. Brookes, A.W. Roscoe & G. Winskel, eds.), LNCS 197, Springer-Verlag, pp. 281-305.

[18] M. BROY (1987): *Views of Queues.* Report MIP-8704, Fakultät für Mathematik und Informatik, Universität Passau.

[19] CHILL (1980): *Recommendation Z.200 (CHILL Language Definition).* CCITT Study Group XI.

[20] R. DE NICOLA & M. HENNESSY (1984): *Testing equivalences for processes.* Theoretical Computer Science 34, pp. 83-134.

[21] T. DENVIR, W. HARWOOD, M. JACKSON & M. RAY (1985): *The Analysis of Concurrent Systems, Proceedings of a Tutorial and Workshop, Cambridge University 1983*, LNCS 207, Springer-Verlag.

[22] R.J. VAN GLABBEEK (1987): *Bounded Nondeterminism and the Approximation Induction Principle in Process Algebra.* In: Proceedings STACS 87 (F.J. Brandenburg, G. Vidal-Naquet & M. Wirsing, eds.), LNCS 247, Springer-Verlag, pp. 336-347.

[23] R.J. VAN GLABBEEK & F.W. VAANDRAGER (1988): *Modular Specifications in Process Algebra - With Curious Queues.* Report CS-R8821, Centrum voor Wiskunde en Informatica, Amsterdam.

[24] C.A.R. HOARE (1980): *Communicating sequential processes.* In: On the construction of

programs - an advanced course (R.M. McKeag & A.M. Macnaghten, eds.), Cambridge University Press, pp. 229-254.

[25] C.A.R. HOARE (1985): *Communicating Sequential Processes*, Prentice-Hall International.

[26] HE JIFENG & C.A.R. HOARE (1987): *Algebraic specification and proof of a distributed recovery algorithm.* Distributed Computing 2(1), pp. 1-12.

[27] C.P.J. KOYMANS & J.C. MULDER (1986): *A Modular Approach to Protocol Verification using Process Algebra.* Logic Group Preprint Series Nr. 6, CIF, State University of Utrecht, to appear in: Applications of Process Algebra, (J.C.M. Baeten, ed.), CWI Monograph, North-Holland, 1988.

[28] K.G. LARSEN & R. MILNER (1987): *A Complete Protocol Verification Using Relativized Bisimulation.* In: Proceedings 14th ICALP, Karlsruhe (Th. Ottmann, ed.), LNCS 267, Springer-Verlag, pp. 126-135.

[29] S. MAUW (1987): *An algebraic specification of process algebra, including two examples.* This volume.

[30] S. MAUW & G.J. VELTINK (1988): *A Process Specification Formalism.* Report P8814, Programming Research Group, University of Amsterdam.

[31] R. MILNER (1980): *A Calculus of Communicating Systems*, LNCS 92, Springer-Verlag.

[32] R. MILNER (1985): *Lectures on a Calculus for Communicating Systems.* In: Seminar on Concurrency (S.D. Brookes, A.W. Roscoe & G. Winskel, eds.), LNCS 197, Springer-Verlag, pp. 197-220.

[33] J.D. MONK (1976): *Mathematical Logic*, Springer-Verlag.

[34] E.-R. OLDEROG & C.A.R. HOARE (1986): *Specification-Oriented Semantics for Communicating Processes.* Acta Informatica 23, pp. 9-66.

[35] I.C.C. PHILLIPS (1987): *Refusal Testing.* Theoretical Computer Science 50, pp. 241-284.

[36] V.R. PRATT (1986): *Modelling Concurrency with Partial Orders.* International Journal of Parallel Programming 15(1), pp. 33-71.

[37] D.T. SANNELLA & A. TARLECKI (1988): *Toward Formal Development of Programs from Algebraic Specifications: Implementations Revisited.* Acta Informatica 25, pp. 233-281.

[38] D.T. SANNELLA & M. WIRSING (1983): *A kernel language for algebraic specification and implementation (extended abstract).* In: Proc. Intl. Conf. on Foundations of Computation Theory, Borgholm (M. Karpinski, ed.), LNCS 158, pp. 413-427, long version: Report CSR-131-83, Dept. of Computer Science, Univ. of Edinburgh, 1983.

[39] F.W. VAANDRAGER (1986): *Verification of Two Communication Protocols by Means of Process Algebra.* Report CS-R8608, Centrum voor Wiskunde en Informatica, Amsterdam.

[40] F.W. VAANDRAGER (1986): *Process algebra semantics of POOL.* Report CS-R8629, Centrum voor Wiskunde en Informatica, Amsterdam, to appear in: Applications of Process Algebra, (J.C.M. Baeten, ed.), CWI Monograph, North-Holland, 1988.

[41] F.W. VAANDRAGER (1988): *Some Observations on Redundancy in a Context.* Report CS-R8812, Centrum voor Wiskunde en Informatica, Amsterdam, to appear in: Applications of Process Algebra, (J.C.M. Baeten, ed.), CWI Monograph, North-Holland, 1988.

An Algebraic Specification of Process Algebra, including two examples

S. Mauw
Programming Research Group, University of Amsterdam,
P.O. Box 41882, 1009 DB Amsterdam, The Netherlands.

Abstract A study is made of the possibilities to describe process algebra as an algebraic specification. Two examples from the field of the specification of communication protocols are discussed to analyse the adequacy of this approach in practical situations.
Note: This work was sponsored in part by ESPRIT contract nr. 432, Meteor.

1. Introduction

Both process algebra and algebraic specifications can be viewed as specification formalisms. Process algebra can be used to specify the behaviour of (concurrent) processes, while algebraic specifications can be used to specify abstract data types. It is an interesting question whether the combination of the two forms a more powerful tool for specification then each of them separately.
Process algebra is one of the theories developed in the last decade to describe concurrency (see e.g. [8]). Some alternative theories are CCS [19], CSP [17] and Petri-nets [20]. An important and growing topic of interest in the field of process algebra is the development of applications to significant and practical cases. These cases include e.g. the specification and verification of communication protocols and CAM-architectures, or the specification of programming languages. When applying process algebra new features are developed and added to process algebra, in order to make specification and verification easier. So process algebra can be considered as a dynamic and modular theory.
Because the growth of specifications in practical cases leads to an increasing chance of being imprecise and making errors, software tools for the development of specifications and proofs are needed. This paper is meant to be a first step from the stage of manual specification in process algebra towards Computer Integrated Specification. This step is done by using algebraic specifications as a method to describe process algebra. When using algebraic specifications a specification is forced to be precise. The specification is written in a subset of the COLD language (see [15] and [18]). It was translated by hand from the ASF-language, which is described in [6] and [7]. Some features from ASF are added to COLD, in order to make the translation as simple as possible. The subset of COLD which is used is roughly equal to the complete ASF-language. ASF offers the possibility to define abstract data types, consisting of sorts, elements of these sorts and functions on these elements. The intended meaning of a function or a constant is given by a set of algebraic equations. As a semantics of algebraic specifications we will use the Initial Algebra semantics (see e.g. [14]). The question whether algebraic specification methods, with initial algebra semantics, are flexible and expressive enough to describe process algebra is discussed in this paper.
The combination of algebraic specifications with a concurrency theory is not a new

approach. The ISO specification language LOTOS [12] is a combination of ACT ONE and CCS. In LOTOS the concurrency theory is part of the language, while in this paper process algebra is described by means of the specification language.

This paper contains the following sections: After a brief description of the specification language, the basic modules BOOLEANS, SEQUENCES, SETS and SUMMATION are defined. Some alternative specifications of Sets are considered, and after that, the notion of an implicit definition is introduced. In the chapter about process algebra some building blocks of the theory are described, followed by their algebraic specification. At the end of this chapter some problematic notions are considered. The section about the protocols contains the description of the PAR and the OBSW protocol. Each protocol is specified by defining the appropriate set of atoms, providing the definition of the "parameters" and specifying all extra processes. In the final section various observations about the specification of process algebra are made.

I would like to express my thanks to Jos Baeten, Jan Bergstra, Wiet Bouma, Paul Klint, Pum Walters and Freek Wiedijk for their useful comments.

2. The Specification Language

The specifications are written in an enhanced subset of the COLD language (see [15] and [18]). The COLD constructs dealing with algebraic specification and modularization are all used. New features from ASF are listed below.

- We assume existance of a polymorphic function "if", with three arguments. The first is of sort BOOL, and the other two have the same unspecified type. The intended meaning of a term starting with the "if" is obvious: if the BOOL equals true, then the term equals its second argument; if the term equals false then it equals its third argument.
- We adopt the poosibility to use infix and prefix operator-symbols. They of course can be viewed as shorthand for normal functional notation, but are needed because process algebra expression would be hard to read without them.
- All functions are considered to be total, so all terms are defined.

The intended semantics of the specification is the initial algebra semantics.

More about algebraic specifications, specification languages and initial algebra semantics can be found in [13, 14, 16].

3. Basic Modules

3.1. Booleans
The module Booleans describes the sort BOOL, with values true and false, and some boolean functions.

```
LET Booleans :=
CLASS
   SORT BOOL
   FUNC true  :                  -> BOOL
   FUNC false :                  -> BOOL
   FUNC _|_   : BOOL # BOOL  -> BOOL      %or
   FUNC _&_   : BOOL # BOOL  -> BOOL      %and
   FUNC not   : BOOL             -> BOOL
   FUNC eq    : BOOL # BOOL  -> BOOL
AXIOM
   FORALL b:BOOL, b1:BOOL, b2:BOOL (
{Bo1}   true  | b        = true;
{Bo2}   false | b        = b;
```

```
{Bo3}    true & b        = b;
{Bo4}    false & b       = false;
{Bo5}    not(true)       = false;
{Bo6}    not(false)      = true;
{Bo7}    eq(b1,b2)       = (b1 & b2) | (not(b1) & not(b2)) )
END;
```

3.2. Sequences

In the specification of the OBSW-protocol a communication-channel is described which acts as a FIFO-queue. This can be modeled by indexing the process-variable with the sequence of items that is contained in the queue. The module sequences has a parameter for the sequenced items. The constant eps denotes the empty sequence, seq transforms an item into a one-item sequence and _+_ concatenates two sequences.

```
LET Items :=
CLASS
    SORT ITEM FREE
END;
LET Sequences :=
LAMBDA Items_Parameter: Items OF
    IMPORT Items_Parameter INTO
CLASS
    SORT SEQ
    FUNC eps :              -> SEQ
    FUNC seq : ITEM         -> SEQ
    FUNC _+_ : SEQ # SEQ -> SEQ
AXIOM
    FORALL q:SEQ, q1:SEQ, q2:SEQ, q3:SEQ (
{Sq1}    eps + q      = q;
{Sq2}    q + eps      = q;
{Sq3}    (q1+q2)+q3 = q1+(q2+q3) )
END;
```

3.3. Sets

A notion which is frequently used in specifications is the notion of a set. Examples are the set of data-items, which can be read in, and the set of atoms to be encapsulated. The easiest way to form a set is just summing up all its elements. The constructor functions ∅ (the empty set) and insert (add an element to a set) can easily be specified. With these constructors, other set-operators can be specified using recursion. This approach has been used in e.g. [12]. The next specification is derived from the LOTOS standard library of data types (see section A.5.2 of [12]). The specification is rewritten in COLD. Functions that are of no interest are omitted, while some other functions are renamed. Note again that all functions are total.

```
LET Items :=
    IMPORT Booleans INTO
CLASS
    SORT ITEM FREE
    FUNC eq : ITEM # ITEM -> BOOL
END;
LET sets :=
LAMBDA Items_Parameter: Items OF
    IMPORT Items_Parameter INTO
CLASS
    SORT SET
```

```
    FUNC null-set:                 -> SET
    FUNC is-in    : SET # ITEM -> BOOL
    FUNC delete   : SET # ITEM -> SET
    FUNC insert   : SET # ITEM -> SET
    FUNC union    : SET # SET  -> SET
    FUNC inters   : SET # SET  -> SET
    FUNC diff     : SET # SET  -> SET
    FUNC incl     : SET # SET  -> BOOL
    FUNC eq       : SET # SET  -> BOOL
AXIOM
    FORALL s:SET, s1:SET, s2:SET, s3:SET, i:ITEM, j:ITEM (
        insert(insert(s, i), i)       = insert(s, i);
        insert(insert(s, i), j)       = insert(insert(s, j), i);
        is-in(s, i) = false =>
           delete(insert(s, i), i)    = s;
        is-in(s, i) = false =>
           delete(s, i)               = s;
        union(null-set, s)            = s;
        union(insert(s1, i), s2)      = insert(union(s1, s2), i);
        inters(null-set, s)           = null-set;
        inters(s1, s2)                = inters(s2, s1);
        is-in(s2, i) = true =>
           inters(insert(s1, i), s2) = insert(inters(s1, s2), i);
        is-in(s2, i) = false =>
           inters(insert(s1, i), s2) = inters(s1, s2);
        diff(s, null-set)             = s;
        diff(s1, s2)                  = diff(s1, inters(s1, s2));
        diff(s1, insert(s2, i))       = diff(delete(s1,i), delete(s2, i));
        is-in(null-set, i)            = false;
        is-in(insert(s, j), i)        = eq(i, j) | is-in(s, i)
        diff(s2, s1) = null-set =>
           incl(s1, s2)               = true;
        diff(s2, s1) = insert(s3, i) =>
           incl(s1, s2)               = false;
        eq(s1, s2)                    = incl(s1, s2) & incl(s2, s1) )
END;
```

It is easy to verify that all elements of the initial algebra can be written in the form:

$$\text{insert}(\text{insert}(\dots \text{insert}(\emptyset, x_1), \dots, x_{n-1}), x_n) \qquad [n \geq 0]$$

Moreover, this specification forces every instance of a set to be specified using the $\emptyset$ and insert constructor. Of course union and other operators may be used, but all elements of a set are eventually summed up one by one. This introduces difficulties when specifying large sets, or sets over sorts which are imported as a parameter. For example consider the set of all Data-elements, where the elements of the sort Data are not individually known. It is not possible to specify this set using an expression with repeated inserts, nor is there an alternative.

So the need for a stronger mechanism for constructing sets is apparent. Suppose the parameter ITEM is bound to the sort Data. If we consider the set

$$T = \{x \in \text{Data} \mid x = d_0 \vee x = d_1\}$$

then it should be equal to the set

```
S = insert(insert(∅,d₀),d₁)).
```

A specification in which the first form is supported should not only involve the Zermelo-Fraenkel axioms, but also a specification of first-order logic, including the notions of variables, formulas, etc. This would take several pages of specifications.

Another way to specify the set T is as follows:

```
is-in(T, x) = eq(x,d₀) | eq(x,d1)
```
$$\text{(where } x \text{ is a variable of sort Data.)}$$

Now the initial algebra of Sets contains an extra element T, which is not equal to the element S. The set T is defined implicitly, giving the value of some special function (is-in) on T. To find an equation which forces S and T to be equal, the notion of an implicit definition is investigated.

Given some existing specification, a new constant is said to be <u>specified implicitly</u> if instead of giving its intended meaning, only some characterizing properties of the constant are given. Some examples can clarify this definition.

Consider the sort N with successor (s) and zero (0). Without any equations the initial algebra of this signature equals $\mathbb{N}$, the nonnegative integers. Suppose a constant one is defined with equation

```
s(one) = s(s(0))
```

Now the *intended meaning* of one is the term s (0), but in the initial algebra it is a new element, unequal to s (0). To force these two elements to be equal the next equation should be included:

```
s(x)=s(y) => x=y
```

This equation justifies all implicit definitions of the form s (constant)=some_term. In general the equation

```
f(x)=f(y) => x=y
```

for some function f (or a composition of functions), makes implicit definitions of the form

```
f(constant) = some_term
```

possible. Notice that the function f has to be an injection and that the righthand term has to be in the range of f (relative to the initial algebra without the implicitly defined constant). Consider e.g. an extension of the previous specification with the predecessor-function, which is not injective:

```
p(0) = 0
p(s(x)) = x.
```

Now adding

```
p(x)=p(y) => x=y
```

results in p (s (0))=0=p (0), so s (0)=0. The predecessor function can not be specified implicitly.

Now return to sets. An implicit definition of a set looks like:

```
is-in(T, i) = eq(i,d₀) | eq(i,d1)
```

Notice that in contrast to the previous example a variable i is needed, so the equation to add would look like:

$$\forall_i [\ (i \in X) = (i \in Y) \ ] \Rightarrow X=Y.$$

Adding this equation to the specification is not possible if we want to use initial algebra semantics. This is because in general a specification with universal quantification has no initial algebra. Now there are two approaches to simulate this equation. The first one is by decrementing the range of the variable x to the class of closed terms. An initial algebra still can be defined, but COLD doesn't support this kind of expressions.

The second one is to recursively check the condition $(i \in X) = (i \in Y)$ for all elements in the sort, and conclude x=y if this succeeds. This is only possible if the sort is finite and some mechanism for summing up all elements is provided. A possible way is to indicate the first element and define for all elements a next element, yielding a kind of linked list. Define the predicate last so that it indicates if its argument is the last in the list. Now the equation can be simulated by:

```
eq(X,Y)     = eq2(X, Y, firstItem)
eq2(X,Y,i) = if( last(i),
                    (i∈X)⇔(i∈Y),
                 if( (i∈X)⇔(i∈Y),
                     eq2(X,Y,next(i)),
                     false))
eq(X,Y) = true => X = Y
```

When these equations are added, the sets T and S are equal. This is easily checked by looking at the definition of eq(T,S).

So an equation of the form

$$\forall_i [\ f(i,X) = f(i,Y) \ ] \Rightarrow X=Y$$

in general justifies implicit definitions like

```
f(i,const) = some_term(i).
```

Again the function f has to meet some injectivity criterion

$$\forall_{X \neq Y} \ \exists_i \quad f(i,X) \neq f(i,Y)$$

and some_term(i) has to be an element of the "range" of f

$$\exists_X \ \forall_i \quad f(i,X) = some\_term(i).$$

This technique can be used when dealing with datatypes, whose elements can be defined in more then one way. When unifying these different ways, a user can choose the one which is the most appropriate for his purpose. So e.g. in working with matrices, the definition of the unity could be written as

```
U = mat(row(1,0,0,0),
        row(0,1,0,0),
        row(0,0,1,0),
        row(0,0,0,1))
```

or, using an implicit definition:

```
elt(U,i,j) = if(eq(i,j), 1, 0).
```

Now a simulation of the following equation has to be added:

$$\forall_{i,j}[\ elt(X,i,j) = elt(Y,i,j)\ ] => X=Y.$$

For sets the resulting specification looks like the following. Notice that the parameter Items must contain a firstItem and an enumerating function, called next. The last element of Items is determined as the unique element which is invariant under the next-function. Notice also that the definition of the various set operators is much more close to their mathematical definition then it would be when using a recursive definition, as used in the previous example from the LOTOS document.

```
LET Items :=
    IMPORT Booleans INTO
CLASS
    SORT ITEM FREE
    FUNC eq        : ITEM # ITEM -> BOOL
    FUNC firstItem :              -> ITEM
    FUNC next      : ITEM         -> ITEM
END;
LET sets :=
    LAMBDA Items_Parameter: Items OF
IMPORT Items_Parameter INTO
CLASS
    SORT SET
    FUNC null-set :              -> SET
    FUNC is-in    : SET # ITEM -> BOOL
    FUNC delete   : SET # ITEM -> SET
    FUNC insert   : SET # ITEM -> SET
    FUNC union    : SET # SET  -> SET
    FUNC inters   : SET # SET  -> SET
    FUNC eq       : SET # SET  -> BOOL
    FUNC eq2 : SET # SET # ITEM -> BOOL
AXIOM
    FORALL s:SET, s1:SET, s2:SET, i:ITEM, j:ITEM (
{S1}    is-in(null-set, j)       = false;
{S2}    is-in(delete(s, i), j)   = is-in(s, j) & not(eq(i, j));
{S3}    is-in(insert(s, i), j)   = is-in(s, j) | eq(i, j);
{S4}    is-in(union(s1, s2), i)  = is-in(s1, i) | is-in(s2, i);
{S5}    is-in(inters(s1, s2), i) = is-in(s1, i) & is-in(s2, i);
{S6}    eq(s1, s2)               = eq2(s1, s2, firstItem);
{S7}    eq2(s1, s2, i)           = if(eq(next(i),i),
                                      eq(is-in(s1,i), is-in(s2,i)),
                                      if(eq(is-in(s1,i), is-in(s2,i)),
```

```
                                          eq2(s1,s2,next(i)),
                                          false));
{S8}     eq(s1,s2)=true => s1=s2 )
END;
```

It is worth mentioning that in contrast to the specification without implicit definitions, this specification only works for sets over a finite domain. In the infinite case, the universal quantifier would range over an infinite domain, resulting in infinitely many conditions that have to be satisfied. Such a quantification can not be simulated, as the next example will show. Suppose the set A, with infinite domain D, is defined as:

```
        (i∈A) = false.
```

Then a proof that in the initial algebra A equals the empty set, uses finitely many instances of this equation. Because D is infinite one can find some element d0 which is not encountered in these finite equations. Now define the set B as:

```
        (i∈B) = if(i=d0, true, false).
```

Now the same proof can be used to prove that B also equals the empty set.

3.4. Summation

In process algebra summation over an indexed set of processes is frequently used, e.g. when reading in data, or defining the state-operator. Summation always takes place over a finite index set. If the index set is empty, the summation yields deadlock (i(i(delta))), which is the neutral element for summation. The parameter Items is inherited from the imported sort Sets, and provides the sort ITEM with the known first/next structure as the sort of indexes. To define the operation of indexing a process, a kind of function space is required. A new sort (FuncsToP) consisting of functions from elements of the index-set to processes has to be defined. The most natural definition would look like:

```
   SORT        FuncsToP : ITEM -> process.
```

Unfortunately this construction is not allowed. To solve this problem a new, initially empty sort FuncsToP has to be introduced, together with an application function from FuncsToP # ITEM to processes. If one wishes to construct some summation, a constant of sort FuncsToP has to be introduced, and for all elements of sort ITEM, the application of the function on this element must be specified. For examples of the use of Sum, see the module SumsOverData.

Notice that the definition of the function Sum resembles the definition of the function eq in the module Sets. Addition of processes and the special process i(i(delta)) are provided by the imported module Base.

```
LET Sum :=                    %Summation of indexed processes
LAMBDA Items_Parameter2: Items OF
   IMPORT APPLY Sets TO Items_Parameter2 INTO
   IMPORT Base INTO
   EXPORT
      SORT FuncsToP,                    %Functions from ITEMs to processes
      FUNC Sum : SET # FuncsToP  -> process,      %summation
      FUNC app : FuncsToP # ITEM -> process       %application
   FROM
```

```
CLASS
    SORT FuncsToP                    %Functions from ITEMs to processes
    FUNC Sum : SET # FuncsToP  -> process         %summation
    FUNC app : FuncsToP # ITEM -> process         %application
    FUNC Sum2 : SET # FuncsToP # ITEM -> process
AXIOM
    FORALL set:SET, it:ITEM, f:FuncsToP (
{Su1}   Sum(set,f)        = Sum2(set,f,firstItem);
{Su2}   Sum2(set,f,it) = if(eq(next(it),it),
                            if(is-in(set,it), app(f,it), i(i(delta))),
                            if(is-in(set,it),
                               app(f,it) + Sum2(set,f,next(it)),
                               Sum2(set,f,next(it)))) )
END;
```

4. Process Algebra

In this section some topics in process algebra will briefly be introduced and, if possible, an algebraic specification will be given. Process algebra is the study of processes, as described in e.g. [8, 11]. A process can be viewed as a list of (possible) activities that some actor (a computer e.g.) can perform. Each action is thought to be an indivisible unit, called atom.

4.1. Base

Let a finite set of atomic actions be given. Every atom is a process (injection i), and new processes can be created by application of the choice-operator (_+_) and the sequencing-operator (_·_).

```
LET Base :=        %Definition of the basic operations
    IMPORT Atoms INTO
CLASS
    SORT process
    FUNC i   : Atoms                -> process %embed Atoms in process
    FUNC _._ : process # process -> process
    FUNC _+_ : process # process -> process
END;
```

4.2. BPA

The axiom system BPA (Basic Process Algebra) provides some mathematical laws for processes.

$$
\begin{array}{ll}
A1 & x+y = y+x \\
A2 & x+(y+z) = (x+y)+z \\
A3 & x+x = x \\
A4 & (x+y)z = xz+yz \\
A5 & (xy)z = x(yz)
\end{array}
$$

```
LET BPA :=              %Axioms for the system BPA
    IMPORT Atoms INTO
    IMPORT Base INTO
CLASS
AXIOM
    FORALL x:process, y:process, z:process (
{A1}    x+y = y+x;
{A2}    (x+y)+z = x+(y+z);
{A3}    x+x = x;
```

```
{A4}    (x+y).z = (x.z) + (y.z);
{A5}    (x.y).z = x.(y.z) )
END;
```

4.3. Delta

A new Atom `delta` can be introduced to denote the machine that is in a deadlock, unable to do anything at all. Equation A6 states that deadlock will be avoided if there are some alternatives left. Equation A7 shows that after a deadlock has occurred, nothing more can happen. The system BPA_δ can be obtained by importing both the modules `BPA` and `Delta`.

$$A6 \qquad x+\delta = x$$

$$A7 \qquad \delta x = \delta$$

In the section about the definition of the atoms the function `delta` will be declared. The atom δ will be denoted by `i(delta)`, so the process δ will be denoted by `i(i(delta))`.

```
LET Delta :=               %Axioms for dead-lock
    IMPORT Base INTO
CLASS
AXIOM
    FORALL x:process (
{A6}    x+i(i(delta)) = x;
{A7}    i(i(delta)).x = i(i(delta)) )
END;
```

4.4. Encapsulation

With the encapsulation operator it is possible to control what atoms can be performed by a process. If the machine that the process is running on, lacks the possibility to do certain actions, this can be expressed using the encapsulation operator. It takes as its input a process and a set of atoms that should be encapsulated. Each atom from this set will be substituted by `delta`, so the process is forced to make an alternative choice if possible. The imported module `encapsset` can contain various sets of atoms. An example will be given in the sequel.

$$D1 \qquad \partial_H(a) = a \quad \text{if } a \notin H$$

$$D2 \qquad \partial_H(a) = \delta \quad \text{if } a \in H$$

$$D3 \qquad \partial_H(x+y) = \partial_H(x) + \partial_H(y)$$

$$D4 \qquad \partial_H(xy) = \partial_H(x) \cdot \partial_H(y)$$

```
LET Encaps :=               %Axioms for the encapsulation-operator
    IMPORT Booleans INTO
    IMPORT Atoms INTO
    IMPORT Base INTO
    IMPORT Delta INTO
    IMPORT encapsset INTO
CLASS
    FUNC d : SetsAtoms # process -> process
AXION
    FORALL a:Atoms, x:process, y:process, H:SetsAtoms (
{D1-2}  d(H,i(a)) = if(is-in(H,a), i(i(delta)), i(a));
```

```
{D3}     d(H,x+y) = d(H,x) + d(H,y);
{D4}     d(H,x.y) = d(H,x) . d(H,y) )
END;
```

4.5. ACP

Two processes can run simultaneously. The new process created is called the merge of these processes, which is denoted by the operator ‖. This operator is defined in terms of the leftmerge (⫇, in the specification denoted by \\) and the communication-operator (|). The first action of the leftmerge is the first atom of its left operand. Then the merge of the rest follows. Two processes can communicate if their first actions have the possibility to communicate. The communication of two atoms results in a new atom. For every application the resulting atom has to be defined seperately. This must be done in the module Commerge, where a communication-function between atoms must be defined. In the first equation (CM0) of the module Comm, this function is extended to processes.

$$\text{CM1} \quad x \| y = x ⫇ y + y ⫇ x + x | y$$

$$\text{CM2} \quad a ⫇ x = ax$$

$$\text{CM3} \quad ax ⫇ y = a(x \| y)$$

$$\text{CM4} \quad (x+y) ⫇ z = x ⫇ z + y ⫇ z$$

$$\text{CM5} \quad (ax) | b = (a|b)x$$

$$\text{CM6} \quad a | (bx) = (a|b)x$$

$$\text{CM7} \quad (ax) | (by) = (a|b)(x \| y)$$

$$\text{CM8} \quad (x+y) | z = x | z + y | z$$

$$\text{CM9} \quad x | (y+z) = x | y + x | z$$

$$\text{C1} \quad a | b = b | a$$

$$\text{C2} \quad (a|b) | c = a | (b|c)$$

$$\text{C3} \quad \delta | a = \delta$$

```
LET Comm :=        %Communication axioms (used in ACP)
    IMPORT Atoms INTO
    IMPORT Base INTO
    IMPORT Delta INTO
    IMPORT Commerge INTO
CLASS
    FUNC _||_ : process # process -> process %merge
    FUNC _\\_ : process # process -> process %leftmerge
    FUNC _|_  : process # process -> process %Communication merge on processes
AXIOM
    FORALL a:Atoms, b:Atoms, d:Atoms, x:process, y:process, z:process (
{CM0}   i(a)|i(b) = i(a|b);        %identify overloaded _|_
{CM1}   x||y = (x\\y) + (y\\x) + (x|y);
{CM2}   i(a)\\x = i(a).x;
{CM3}   (i(a).x)\\y = i(a).(x||y);
{CM4}   (x+y)\\z = (x\\z) + (y\\z);
{CM5}   (i(a).x)|i(b) = (i(a)|i(b)).x;
{CM6}   i(a)|(i(b).x) = (i(a)|i(b)).x;
{CM7}   (i(a).x)|(i(b).y) = (i(a)|i(b)).(x||y);
```

```
{CM8}    (x+y)|z = (x|z) + (y|z);
{CM9}    x|(y+z) = (x|y) + (x|z);
{C1}     i(a)|i(b) = i(b)|i(a);
{C2}     (i(a)|i(b))|i(d) = i(a)|(i(b)|i(d));
{C3}     i(i(delta))|i(a) = i(i(delta)) )
END;
```

The system ACP (Algebra of communicating processes, see e.g. [11]) is constructed from BPA, Delta, Encapsulation and Communication.

```
LET ACP :=              %Axioms for the system ACP
    IMPORT BPA INTO
    IMPORT Delta INTO
    IMPORT Encaps INTO
        Comm
END;
```

4.6. ACP$_\tau$

The special process tau denotes the silent step (see e.g. [9, 19]). It can be used to model internal actions. Tau is not an atom.

$$T1 \quad x\tau = x$$

$$T2 \quad \tau x + x = \tau x$$

$$T3 \quad a(\tau x + y) = a(\tau x + y) + ax$$

```
LET Tau :=              %Axioms for the silent step
    IMPORT Atoms INTO
    IMPORT Base INTO
CLASS
    FUNC tau : -> process
AXIOM
    FORALL a:Atoms, x:process, y:process (
{T1}    x.tau = x;
{T2}    (tau.x) + x = tau.x;
{T3}    i(a).((tau.x)+y) = (i(a).((tau.x)+y)) + (i(a).x) )
END;
```

If one is only interested in some external actions of a process, the internal actions must be hidden. The abstraction-operator has as a parameter a set of atoms that are declared to be invisible. All these atoms are changed into tau.
A module abstrset must be provided to indicate what sets of atoms can be abstracted from.

$$TI1 \quad \tau_I(\tau) = \tau$$

$$TI2 \quad \tau_I(a) = a \quad \text{if } a \notin I$$

$$TI3 \quad \tau_I(a) = \tau \quad \text{if } a \in I$$

$$TI4 \quad \tau_I(x+y)) = \tau_I(x) + \tau_I(y)$$

$$TI5 \quad \tau_I(xy)) = \tau_I(x) \cdot \tau_I(y)$$

```
LET Abstr :=              %Axioms for the abstraction-operator
```

```
    IMPORT SetsAtoms INTO
    IMPORT Tau INTO
    IMPORT abstrset INTO
CLASS
    FUNC abstr : SetsAtoms # process -> process
AXIOM
    FORALL a:Atoms, x:process, y:process, I:SetsAtoms (
{TI1}    abstr(I,tau) = tau;
{TI2-3}  abstr(I,i(a)) = if(is-in(I,a), tau, i(a));
{TI4}    abstr(I,x+y) = abstr(I,x) + abstr(I,y);
{TI5}    abstr(I,x.y) = abstr(I,x) . abstr(I,y) )
END;
```

The system ACP$_\tau$ (see e.g. [9]) combines ACP with abstraction.

$$\text{TM1} \quad \tau \mathbin{\llfloor} x = \tau x$$

$$\text{TM2} \quad (\tau x) \mathbin{\llfloor} y = \tau(x \| y)$$

$$\text{TC1} \quad \tau | x = \delta$$

$$\text{TC2} \quad x | \tau = \delta$$

$$\text{TC3} \quad (\tau x) | y = x | y$$

$$\text{TC4} \quad x | (\tau y) = x | y$$

$$\text{DT} \quad \partial_H(\tau) = \tau$$

```
LET ACP-Tau :=                    %Axioms for the system ACP-Tau
    IMPORT ACP INTO
    IMPORT Tau INTO
    IMPORT Abstr INTO
CLASS
AXIOM
    FORALL x:process, y:process, H:SetsAtoms (
{TM1}    tau\\x = tau.x;
{TM2}    (tau.x)\\y = tau.(x||y);
{TC1}    tau|x = i(i(delta));
{TC2}    x|tau = i(i(delta));
{TC3}    (tau.x)|y = x|y;
{TC4}    x|(tau.y) = x|y;
{DT}     d(H,tau) = tau )
END;
```

4.7. Standard Concurrency

In ACP$_\tau$ often some extra laws are assumed. These laws are called Standard Concurrency (see [9]).

$$\text{SC1} \quad (x \mathbin{\llfloor} y) \mathbin{\llfloor} z = x \mathbin{\llfloor} (y \| z)$$

$$\text{SC2} \quad (x | ay) \mathbin{\llfloor} z = x | (ay \mathbin{\llfloor} z)$$

$$\text{SC3} \quad x | y = y | x$$

$$\text{SC4} \quad x \| y = y \| x$$

$$\text{SC5} \quad x | (y | z) = (x | y) | z$$

```
        SC6    x‖(y‖z)  =  (x‖y)‖z

LET SC :=                    %standard concurrency for ACP-Tau
    IMPORT Atoms INTO
    IMPORT ACP-Tau INTO
CLASS
AXIOM
    FORALL x:process, y:process, z:process, a:Atoms (
{SC1}    (x\\y)\\z = x\\(y||z);
{SC2}    (x|((i(a).y))\\z = x|((i(a).y)\\z);
{SC3}    x|y = y|x;
{SC4}    x||y = y||x;
{SC5}    x|(y|z) = (x|y)|z;
{SC6}    x||(y||z) = (x||y)||z )
END;
```

4.8. ACP_θ

Instead of adding the silent step to ACP, forming ACP_τ, it is also possible to add priorities, forming the system ACP_θ (see e.g. [4]). Relative to a given partial order on the atoms, the operator theta determines which actions should be enabled or disabled. The smallest atoms in this partial order ($<$) have the lowest priority. The following equations define a partial order on the atoms, requiring that deadlock has the lowest priority of all atoms.

1. $\neg(a<a)$
2. $a<b \Rightarrow \neg(b<a)$
3. $a<b \wedge b<c \Rightarrow a<c$
4. $\delta<a$ (if $a\neq\delta$)

These laws are not included in the algebraic specification. When defining some specific partial order, one just has to meet these requirements.

Now, introducing one auxiliary operator ($\lhd$, in the specification denoted by \$), the priority operator can be defined. This $\lhd$ operator deadlocks if its lefthand-side has lower priority then its righthand-side, else yields its lefthand-side. Now the priority operator can easily be defined.

P1 $a\lhd b = a$ if $\neg(a<b)$

P2 $a\lhd b = \delta$ if $a<b$

P3 $x\lhd yz = x\lhd y$

P4 $x\lhd(y+z) = (x\lhd y)\lhd z$

P5 $xy\lhd z = (x\lhd z)y$

P6 $(x+y)\lhd z = x\lhd z+y\lhd z$

TH1 $\theta(a) = a$

TH2 $\theta(xy) = \theta(x)\cdot\theta(y)$

TH3 $\theta(x+y) = \theta(x)\lhd y + \theta(y)\lhd x$

```
LET Theta :=
   IMPORT Base INTO
   IMPORT PO INTO
   IMPORT Booleans INTO
CLASS
   FUNC theta : process              -> process
   FUNC _$_   : process # process -> process
AXIOM
   FORALL a:Atoms, b:Atoms, x:process, y:process, z:process (
{P1-2}  i(a)$i(b) = if(sm(a,b), i(i(delta)), i(a));
{P3}    x $ (y.z) = x $ y;
{P4}    x $ (y+z) = (x$y)$z;
{P5}    (x.y) $ z = (x$z).y;
{P6}    (x+y) $ z = (x$z) + (y$z);
{TH1}   theta(i(a)) = i(a);
{TH2}   theta(x.y) = theta(x).theta(y);
{TH3}   theta(x+y) = (theta(x)$y) + (theta(y)$x) )
END;


LET ACP-Theta :=
   IMPORT ACP INTO
         Theta
END;
```

4.9. State-Operator

The state operator (see e.g. [22]) can very well be used to describe a system with some kind of memory. This operator is indexed by an object. To each object a state has been assigned, which can change depending on the atomic action that is being performed. The effect of every action on an arbitrary state of an arbitrary object is defined by the effect-function. When encountering an atom in a certain state, the action-function determines which actions possibly can be executed. So this function yields a set of atoms. The resulting action that is actually chosen influences the outcome of the effect-function. The following equations define the state-operator, supposing that the set of Objects, the set of States and two functions are given which satisfy:

$$\text{action}: A \times \text{Objects} \times \text{States} \rightarrow \text{Pow}(A_\tau)$$

$$\text{effect}: A \times A_\tau \times \text{Objects} \times \text{States} \rightarrow \text{States}$$

L1 $\quad \Lambda^m_\sigma(\delta) = \delta$

L2 $\quad \Lambda^m_\sigma(\tau) = \tau$

L3 $\quad \Lambda^m_\sigma(\tau x) = \tau \cdot \Lambda^m_\sigma(x)$

L4 $\quad \Lambda^m_\sigma(ax) = \sum_{b \in \text{action}(a,m,\sigma)} b \cdot \Lambda^m_{\text{effect}(a,b,m,\sigma)}(x)$

L5 $\quad \Lambda^m_\sigma(x+y) = \Lambda^m_\sigma(x) + \Lambda^m_\sigma(y)$

The imported modules Objects, States and ACTION-EFFECT can be viewed as parameters, determined by the application. Because summation is needed over the set of all atoms enriched with the process τ, a new (finite) sort Atoms-Tau is introduced. In this sort the atom pre-tau is defined, which, when considered as a process, should equal the process tau. See the definition of the atoms for the OBSW-protocol for more information about the structure of Atoms-Tau.

```
LET Atoms-Tau :=
   IMPORT Booleans INTO
   IMPORT Tau INTO
CLASS
   SORT Atoms-Tau
   FUNC j        : Atoms      -> Atoms-Tau
   FUNC pre-tau :             -> Atoms-Tau
   FUNC i        : Atoms-Tau -> process

   FUNC eq                : Atoms-Tau # Atoms-Tau -> BOOL
   FUNC firstAT  :                                -> Atoms-Tau
   FUNC next     : Atoms-Tau                      -> Atoms-Tau
   FUNC penultimateAT :                           -> Atoms-Tau
AXIOM
   FORALL a:Atoms, x:Atoms-Tau, y:Atoms-Tau (
{AT1}    i(j(a))   = i(a);           %identify identical processes
{AT2}    i(pre-tau) = tau;

{ATf}    firstAT = pre-tau;
{ATn1}   next(pre-tau) = j(firstAtom);
{ATn2}   next(j(a)) = j(next(a));
{ATp}    penultimateAT = j(penultimateAtom);

{ATeq1} eq(penultimateAT, next(penultimateAT)) = false;
{ATeq2} eq(next(penultimateAT), penultimateAT) = false;
{ATeq3} eq(x, y) = false         when eq(next(x), next(y)) = false;
{ATeq4} eq(x, x) = true )
END;


LET SumsOverAtoms-Tau :=
RENAME
   SORT SET         -> SetsOfAtoms-Tau,
   FUNC null-set    -> AtomsT-null-set,
   FUNC FuncsToP    -> FuncsAtoms-TauToP
IN
APPLY
   RENAME
      SORT ITEM       -> Atoms-Tau,
      FUNC eq         -> eq,
      FUNC firstItem -> firstAT,
      FUNC next       -> next
   IN Sum
TO
   IMPORT Atoms-Tau INTO
CLASS
   FUNC tau-set : -> SetsOfAtoms-Tau
AXIOM
   FORALL d:Data
{SuAT1} tau-set = insert(AtomsT-null-set, pre-tau)
END;


LET lambda :=              %Axioms for the extended state-operator
   IMPORT Objects INTO
   IMPORT States INTO
   IMPORT ACTION-EFFECT INTO
   IMPORT SumsOverAtoms-Tau INTO
CLASS
```

```
      FUNC lambda : Objects # States # process -> process    %state operator
      FUNC FL     : Atoms # Objects # States # process -> FuncsAtoms-TauToP
   AXIOM
      FORALL a:Atoms, at:Atoms-Tau, x:process, y:process, m :Objects, st:States(
   {LA0}    app(FL(a, m, st, x), at)  = i(at).lambda(m, EFFECT(a, at, m, st), x);
   {LA1}    lambda(m,st,i(i(delta)))  = i(i(delta));
   {LA2}    lambda(m,st,tau)          = tau;
   {LA3}    lambda(m,st,tau.x)        = tau.lambda(m,st,x);
   {LA4}    lambda(m,st,i(a).x)       = Sum(ACTION(a, m, st), FL(a, m, st, x));
   {LA5}    lambda(m,st,x+y)          = lambda(m,st,x) + lambda(m,st,y) )
   END;
```

4.10. Some Problems

In this section some topics in process algebra are elaborated, which (seem to) have no algebraically specifiable counterpart. This implies that too few identifications are made, so the initial algebra of the resulting specification is too large.

The first kind of problems arises from the fact that all previously encountered notions worked on all processes. In the following notions the way in which a process is defined is taken into account. So some extra information is needed to identify a process, for example whether it is the solution of some guarded recursive equation. A new sort, the sort of guarded equations, has to be introduced and some way to form a process from an equation. An equation should be an object, instead of being an expression in the specification language. About such an object we must be able to determine if it is guarded, and if it contains abstraction. It is obvious that this approach leads to a counterintuitive specification. It violates the elegant thought that an axiom of process algebra can easily be represented by an algebraic equation.

The Recursive Specification Principle (RSP) is a rule that uses the way in which a process is defined (see e.g. [3]). It states that two processes that are both solutions of the same guarded recursive equation without abstraction, are equal. The notation $E(x,-)$ indicates that x is a solution of equation E.

$$\text{RSP} \quad \frac{E(x,-) \; E(y,-)}{x=y} \qquad \text{(E guarded, no abstraction)}$$

The only way to model this equation as an algebraic specification is to define some mechanism that deals with the notion of a guarded equation.

The Recursive Definition Principle (RDP) states that all guarded recursive equations without abstraction have a solution.

$$\text{RDP} \quad \frac{E \text{ guarded, no abstraction}}{\exists x \; E(x,-)}$$

The approach, of defining a process by introducing a new constant and giving some equation over this constant, satisfies this principle. In the initial algebra every recursively defined process exists as a (new) constant.

Using the Approximation Induction Principle (AIP) it is possible to identify two processes, if their projections are equal. The projection of a process is a simple notion that can be specified easily.

$$\text{AIP} \quad \frac{\forall_{n\geq1}\ \pi_n(x) = \pi_n(y) \quad E(x,-)}{x=y} \qquad \text{(E guarded, no abstraction)}$$

This equation not only uses guardedness, it also has an infinite number of premises. This is not algebraically expressible. An attempt has been made to reduce the number of premises, obtaining a constructive form of AIP.

Often a set of Conditional Axioms (CA) is used to verify equalities in process algebra (see e.g. [2]). These axioms all depend on the alphabet function, which determines all atoms "present" in a process. On finite processes it is defined by:

1. $\alpha(\delta) = \emptyset$
2. $\alpha(\tau) = \emptyset$
3. $\alpha(\tau x) = \alpha(x)$
4. $\alpha(ax) = \{a\} \cup \alpha(x) \qquad (a \in A)$
5. $\alpha(x+y) = \alpha(x) \cup \alpha(y)$

On infinite processes it is defined by:

6. $$\frac{E(x,-)}{\alpha(x) = \bigcup_{n=1}^{\infty} \alpha(\pi_n(x))} \qquad \text{(E guarded, no abstraction)}$$

7. $$\frac{E(x,-)}{\alpha(\tau_I(x)) = \alpha(x) - I} \qquad \text{(E guarded, no abstraction)}$$

The problem arises from the infinite union, which can not be modelled using an algebraic specification. Though the resulting set is finite, in general the alphabet of a process is undecidable. In [2] some results about alphabets are gathered.

If the alphabet function is presumed to exist, the Conditional Axioms can easily be specified. They look like:

$$\text{CA1} \quad \frac{\alpha(x)\mid(\alpha(y)\cap H)\subseteq H}{\partial_H(x\|y) = \partial_H(x\|\partial_H(y))} \qquad\qquad \text{CA2} \quad \frac{\alpha(x)\mid(\alpha(y)\cap I)=\emptyset}{\tau_I(x\|y) = \tau_I(x\|\tau_I(y))}$$

$$\text{CA3} \quad \frac{\alpha(x)\cap H=\emptyset}{\partial_H(x)=x} \qquad\qquad\qquad\quad \text{CA4} \quad \frac{\alpha(x)\cap I=\emptyset}{\tau_I(x)=x}$$

CA5 $\qquad$ $H=H_1\cup H_2$ $\qquad$ CA6 $\qquad$ $I=I_1\cup I_2$

$$\frac{}{\partial_H(x)=\partial_{H_1}\circ\partial_{H_2}(x)} \qquad\qquad \frac{}{\tau_I(x)=\tau_{I_1}\circ\tau_{I_2}(x)}$$

CA7 $\qquad$ $H\cap I=\emptyset$

$$\frac{}{\tau_I\circ\partial_H(x)=\partial_H\circ\tau_I(x)}$$

Because it uses guardedness, the Cluster Fair Abstraction Rule (CFAR, see [22]) is not easily transformed to an algebraic specification. This will be stated without going into detail. Another function on processes, which is defined using an infinite union is the trace function.

This section will end by indicating how to solve some of these problems.
As mentioned some problems can be solved by introducing a new sort equation, with predicates guarded, no_abstraction and has_solution(x). This approach would be less natural than the one used. Instead of transforming an equation in process algebra into an equation in COLD, it introduces the higher level objects "equation" and "variable".
Another possibility is adding all needed instances of some problematic laws by hand. This would be the same as rewriting (parts of) a known proof in the specification. All identifications that are not generated by the specified features should be added. This method seems not to add extra value to the specification. On the other hand it can serve as a check on type-correctness of the proof.
One way to solve these problems within the field of process algebra is to find more constructive counterparts of the mentioned laws. If this is not possible, due to e.g. undecidability, maybe some restricted form could be obtained, which only holds for simple (regular) processes.

5. The PAR-Protocol

5.1. Global Description
As an example of the use of the algebraic specification of process algebra two specifications of communication protocols are transferred to COLD. These specifications, and also their verifications, can be found in [22]. The first protocol, Positive Acknowledgement with Retransmission, as described in [21], consists of four components: a Sender (S), a Data transmission channel (K), a Receiver (R) and an Acknowledgement transmission channel (L).

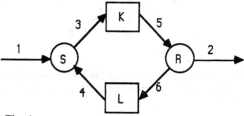

Fig. 1

The intended behaviour is that every data-element offered at port 1 eventually arrives, in the right order, at port 2, using the two unreliable channels K and L.

5.2. Atoms

Before specifying the process PAR, first the construction of the Atoms and auxiliary sorts must be given (See Fig. 2) The first sort is the sort of Ports. It consists of the elements p1, ... , p6. At every port an interaction between the two connected processes takes place. Therefore the sort Interaction-Types contains send (s), receive (r) and communicate (c).

The different types of data that can be transmitted over the channels are gathered in the sort D. It embeds the sorts Data and DB. The sort Data contains all data-elements that can arrive at port p1, and should be transmitted to port p2. This sort of elementary Data items should be provided by the environment and can be viewed as a "parameter" of the specified protocol.

Over the ports p3 and p5 *frames* (of sort DB) are communicated. These frames consist of a data-element and a boolean, which can be seen as an indicator for retransmission. At ports p4 and p6, acknowledgements (ac) are communicated. To describe a mutilated message, a checksum-error (ce) can be communicated at ports p4 and p5. This completes the description of all "interaction atoms", which together form sort D. There are some other atomic actions, all gathered in the sort Events: the internal actions i and j, the time-out action (tio) and the deadlock (delta). Now all atoms are either an event (i(i), i(j), i(tio), i(delta)) or have the form do(int_type, port, d). All atoms can be viewed as processes, using the injection function i, which was defined in the module Base. The expression i(i(i)) is correct and denotes the internal process i . The function-symbol i is overloaded.

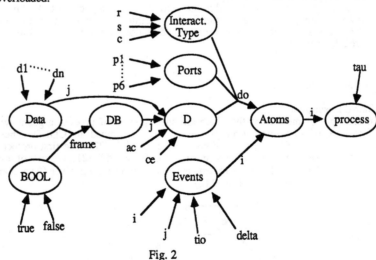

Fig. 2

Notice that for a proper definition of equality on the Atoms, as indicated in the section about sets, all auxiliary sorts are provided with the same first/next/penultimate structure.

```
LET Data :=          %Definition of the set of data to be transmitted
   IMPORT Booleans INTO
CLASS
   SORT Data
   FUNC d1 : -> Data              %three sample data-elements
   FUNC d2 : -> Data
   FUNC d3 : -> Data

   FUNC eq               : Data # Data -> BOOL
   FUNC firstDatum       :             -> Data
   FUNC next             : Data        -> Data
   FUNC penultimateDatum :             -> Data
AXIOM
   FORALL x:Data, y:Data (
{Daf}   firstDatum = d1;
{Dan1}  next(d1) = d2;
{Dan2}  next(d2) = d3;
{Dan3}  next(d3) = d3;
{Dap}   penultimateDatum = d2;

{Daeq1} eq(penultimateDatum, next(penultimateDatum)) = false;
{Daeq2} eq(next(penultimateDatum), penultimateDatum) = false;
{Daeq3} eq(next(x), next(y)) = false => eq(x, y) = false;
{Daeq4} eq(x, x) = true )
END;


LET DB :=
   IMPORT Data INTO
CLASS
   SORT DB
   FUNC frame          : Data # BOOL -> DB
   FUNC eq             : DB # DB     -> BOOL
   FUNC firstDB        :             -> DB
   FUNC next           : DB          -> DB
AXIOM
   FORALL x:DB, y:DB, d:Data, n:BOOL (
{DBf}   firstDB = frame(firstDatum, false);
{DBn1}  next(frame(d,n)) = if(not(eq(next(d),d)) & eq(n,true),
                              frame(next(d),false),
                              frame(d,true));
{DBp}   penultimateDB = frame(next(penultimateDatum), false);

{DBeq1} eq(penultimateDB, next(penultimateDB)) = false;
{DBeq2} eq(next(penultimateDB), penultimateDB) = false;
{DBeq3} eq(next(x), next(y)) = false => eq(x, y) = false;
{DBeq4} eq(x, x) = true )
END;


LET Events :=
   IMPORT Booleans INTO
CLASS
   SORT Events
   FUNC delta : -> Events         %deadlock
   FUNC tio   : -> Events         %timeout
   FUNC i     : -> Events         %internal action
   FUNC j     : -> Events         %internal action

   FUNC eq               : Events # Events -> BOOL
   FUNC firstEvent       :                 -> Events
   FUNC next             : Events          -> Events
```

```
   FUNC penultimateEvent :                    -> Events
AXIOM
   FORALL x:Events, y:Events (
{Evf}    firstEvent - delta;
{Evn1}   next(delta) - tio;
{Evn2}   next(tio) - i;
{Evn3}   next(i) - j;
{Evn4}   next(j) - j;
{Evp}    penultimateEvent - i;

{Eveq1} eq(penultimateEvent, next(penultimateEvent)) - false;
{Eveq2} eq(next(penultimateEvent), penultimateEvent) - false;
{Eveq3} eq(next(x), next(y)) - false => eq(x, y) - false;
{Eveq4} eq(x, x) - true )
END;


LET InteractionType :-
   IMPORT Booleans INTO
CLASS
   FUNC r : -> IntType                  %receive
   FUNC s : -> IntType                  %send
   FUNC c : -> IntType                  %communicate

   FUNC eq                : IntType # IntType -> BOOL
   FUNC firstType         :                  -> IntType
   FUNC next              : IntType          -> IntType
   FUNC penultimateIntType :                 -> IntType
AXIOM
   FORALL x:IntType, y:IntType (
{ITf}    firstType - r;
{ITn1}   next(r) - s;
{ITn2}   next(s) - c;
{ITn3}   next(c) - c;
{ITp}    penultimateIntType - s;

{ITeq1} eq(penultimateIntType, next(penultimateIntType)) - false;
{ITeq2} eq(next(penultimateIntType), penultimateIntType) - false;
{ITeq3} eq(next(x), next(y)) - false => eq(x, y) - false;
{ITeq4} eq(x, x) - true )
END;


LET Ports :-
   IMPORT Booleans INTO
CLASS
   SORT Ports
   FUNC p1:Ports
   FUNC p2:Ports
   FUNC p3:Ports
   FUNC p4:Ports
   FUNC p5:Ports
   FUNC p6:Ports
   FUNC internal : Ports -> BOOL

   FUNC eq            : Ports # Ports -> BOOL
   FUNC firstP        :               -> Ports
   FUNC next          : Ports         -> Ports
   FUNC penultimateP :                -> Ports
AXIOM
   FORALL x:Ports, y:Ports (
{Po1}    internal(x) - not(eq(x,p1) | eq(x,p2));
```

```
{Pof}    firstP  = p1;
{Pon1}   next(p1) = p2;
{Pon2}   next(p2) = p3;
{Pon3}   next(p3) = p4;
{Pon4}   next(p4) = p5;
{Pon5}   next(p5) = p6;
{Pon6}   next(p6) = p6;
{Pop}    penultimateP = p5;

{Poeq1}  eq(penultimateP, next(penultimateP)) = false;
{Poeq2}  eq(next(penultimateP), penultimateP) = false;
{Poeq3}  eq(next(x), next(y)) = false -> eq(x, y) = false;
{Poeq4}  eq(x, x) = true )
END;


LET D :=
    IMPORT Booleans INTO
    IMPORT DB INTO
CLASS
    SORT D
    FUNC ac :        -> D             %acknowlegde
    FUNC ce :        -> D             %checksum error
    FUNC j  : Data -> D               %embed Dataset
    FUNC j  : DB   -> D               %embed DB

    FUNC eq             : D # D -> BOOL
    FUNC firstD       :        -> D
    FUNC next         : D      -> D
    FUNC penultimateD :        -> D
AXIOM
    FORALL x:D, y:D, d:Data, f:DB (
{Df}     firstD = ac;
{Dn1}    next(ac) = ce;
{Dn2}    next(ce) = j(firstDatum);
{Dn3}    next(j(d)) = if(eq(next(d),d), j(firstDB), j(next(d)));
{Dn4}    next(j(f)) = j(next(f));
{Dp}     penultimateD = j(penultimateDB);

{Deq1}   eq(penultimateD, next(penultimateD)) = false;
{Deq2}   eq(next(penultimateD), penultimateD) = false;
{Deq3}   eq(next(x), next(y)) = false -> eq(x, y) = false;
{Deq4}   eq(x, x) = true )
END;


LET Atoms :=              %Definition of the Atoms
    IMPORT Events INTO
    IMPORT InteractionType INTO
    IMPORT Ports INTO
    IMPORT D INTO
CLASS
    SORT Atoms
    FUNC i        : Events                    -> Atoms  %embed Events
    FUNC do       : IntType # Ports # D -> Atoms
    FUNC has-type : IntType # Atoms       -> BOOL
    FUNC port     : Atoms                 -> Ports  %what port is involved?
    FUNC datum    : Atoms                 -> D      %and what datum?

    FUNC eq                 : Atoms # Atoms -> BOOL
    FUNC firstAtom      :                 -> Atoms
```

```
    FUNC next             : Atoms          -> Atoms
    FUNC penultimateAtom :                 -> Atoms
AXIOM
    FORALL x:Atoms, y:Atoms, e:Events, t:IntType, t1:IntType, t2:IntType,
        p:Ports, d:D (
{At1}   has-type(t,i(e)) = false;
{At2}   has-type(t1,do(t2,p,d)) = eq(t1,t2);

{At3}   port(i(e)) = firstP;                  %default value
{At4}   port(do(t,p,d)) = p;
{At5}   datum(i(e)) = firstD;                 %default value
{At6}   datum(do(t,p,d)) = d;

{Atf}   firstAtom     = i(firstEvent);
{Atn1}  next(i(e))    = if(eq(next(e),e),
                           do(firstType, firstP, firstD),
                           i(next(e)));
{Atn2}  next(do(t,p,d)) = if(not(eq(next(t),t)),
                             do(next(t),p,d),
                             if(not(eq(next(p),p)),
                               do(firstType,next(p),d),
                               if(not(eq(next(d),d)),
                                 do(firstType,firstP,next(d)),
                                 do(t,p,d) )));
{Atp}   penultimateAtom = do(penultimateIntType, next(penultimateP),
                             next(penultimateD));

{Ateq1} eq(penultimateAtom, next(penultimateAtom)) = false;
{Ateq2} eq(next(penultimateAtom), penultimateAtom) = false;
{Ateq3} eq(next(x), next(y)) = false -> eq(x, y) = false;
{Ateq4} eq(x, x) = true )
END;
```

5.3. Sets and Summations
The following sets and summations are needed:

```
LET SetsAtoms :=         %Sets of Atoms
RENAME
    SORT SET        -> SetsAtoms,
    FUNC null-set   -> Atoms-null-set
IN
APPLY
    RENAME
        SORT ITEM       -> Atoms,
        FUNC eq         -> eq,
        FUNC firstItem -> firstAtom,
        FUNC next       -> next
    IN Sets
TO Atoms



LET SumsOverData :=
RENAME
    SORT SET        -> SetsOfData,
    FUNC null-set   -> Data-null-set,
    FUNC FuncsToP   -> FuncsDataToP
IN
APPLY
    RENAME
```

```
        SORT ITEM        -> Data,
        FUNC eq          -> eq,
        FUNC firstItem -> firstDatum,
        FUNC next        -> next
     IN Sum
TO
     IMPORT Data INTO
CLASS
     FUNC DataSet : -> SetsOfData      %The set of all Data-elements
AXIOM
     FORALL d:Data
{SuDa1} is-in(DataSet,d) = true
END;

LET SumsOverDB :=
RENAME
     SORT SET         -> SetsOfDB,
     FUNC null-set  -> DB-null-set,
     FUNC FuncsToP -> FuncsDBToP
IN
APPLY
   RENAME
     SORT ITEM        -> DB,
     FUNC eq          -> eq,
     FUNC firstItem -> firstDB,
     FUNC next        -> next
     IN Sum
TO
     IMPORT DB INTO
CLASS
     FUNC DBSet : -> SetsOfDB       %The set of all DBB-elements
AXIOM
     FORALL d:DB
{SuDB1} is-in(DBSet,d) = true
END;
```

5.4. PAR

Now the processes K, L, S and R are defined:

The channel K waits for input of a frame at port p3. Then three things can happen:

(i) The frame is sent on correctly.

(ii) The frame is damaged, and a checksum-error is communicated at port p5

(iii) The frame is lost, indicated by the occurrence of the internal action i.

This leads to the following equations (cf. equations {PAR5, 6} in the module PARPart1):

$$K = \sum_{f \in DB} r3(f) \cdot K^f$$

$$K^f = (s5(f) + s5(ce) + i) \cdot K \qquad\qquad (f \in DB)$$

The specification for channel L is almost identical, except that the frames are replaced by the acknowledgement atom (cf. equations {PAR7, 8} in the module PARPart1):

$$L = r6(ac) \cdot L^{ac}$$

$$L^{ac} = (s4(ac) + s4(ce) + j) \cdot K$$

The sender S is specified using some auxiliary functions. It reads a data-element (d) from port p1, and sends this element, enriched with some boolean information (n) at port p3. This extra bit enables the receiver to deal with retransmissions, it flips to distinguish successive messages. The process RH^n reads a message (d) from the host. The process SF^{dn} sends frame(d,n) at port p3. The process WS^{dn} waits for something to happen. It can receive an acknowledgement, and after that the sequence can start all over. It can receive a checksum-error, which indicates a failure in the communication, and should be followed by a retransmission. Or, if none of these two events are offered, a time-out occurs, also followed by a retransmission.

$$S = RH^0$$
$$RH^n = \sum_{d \in D} r1(d) \cdot SF^{dn}$$
$$SF^{dn} = s3(dn) \cdot WS^{dn} \qquad\qquad (d \in Data, \ n \in \{0,1\})$$
$$WS^{dn} = r4(ac) \cdot RH^{1-n} + (r4(ce) + tio) \cdot SF^{dn}$$

The receiver R is also defined using extra variables. The process WF^n waits for the arrival of a frame at port p5. If a new frame arrives (as indicated by the extra bit n), the data-element has to be transmitted to the host at port p2 (SH^{dn}), followed by the transmission of an acknowledgement at port p6. There is also a possibility that, due to malfunction of the acknowledgement channel L, a retransmission of the previously arrived frame occurs. Then an acknowledgement has to be transmitted again. If a checksum-error arrives, the receiver just waits until the timer of the sender elapses, resulting in a retransmission.

$$R = WF^0$$
$$WF^n = r5(ce) \cdot WF^n + \sum_{d \in D} r5(d, 1-n) \cdot SA^n + \sum_{d \in D} r5(d,n) \cdot SH^{dn}$$
$$SA^n = s6(ac) \cdot WF^n$$
$$SH^{dn} = s2(d) \cdot SA^{1-n} \qquad\qquad (d \in Data, \ n \in \{0,1\})$$

The communication function is defined by:

$$st(f) \mid rt(f) = ct(f) \text{ for } t \in \{3,4,5,6\}, f \in D$$

```
LET Commerge :=          %Definition of the communication-merge function
    IMPORT Atoms INTO
CLASS
    FUNC _|_ : Atoms # Atoms -> Atoms        %communication merge on Atoms
AXIOM
    FORALL a:Atoms, b:Atoms
{Com1} a|b = if((has-type(s,a) & has-type(r,b))
                                   | (has-type(r,a) & has-type(s,b)),
               if(eq(port(a),port(b)) & eq(datum(a),datum(b))
                                             & internal(port(a)),
                  do(c, port(a), datum(a)),
                  i(delta)),
               i(delta))
END;
```

All unsuccessful communications are encapsulated:

$$H_0 = \{st(f), rt(f) \mid t \in \{3, 4, 5, 6\}, f \in D\}$$

```
LET encapsset :=
   IMPORT SetsAtoms INTO
CLASS
   FUNC H0 : -> SetsAtoms
AXIOM
   FORALL a:Atoms
{enc1}  is-in(H0, a) = if(has-type(r,a) | has-type(s,a),
                          internal(port(a)),
                          false)
END;
```

A priority is defined, to manage the time-outs. By giving time-out the lowest priority, it only occurs when no alternatives are offered, so successful communication is not timed-out.

$$\delta < a \quad \text{for } a \in A - \{\delta\}$$

$$tio < a \quad \text{for } a \in A - \{tio, \delta\}$$

```
LET PO :=                    %partial order on Atoms
   IMPORT Atoms INTO
CLASS
   FUNC sm : Atoms # Atoms -> BOOL        %smaller
AXIOM
   FORALL a:Atoms, b:Atoms
{PO1}    sm(a, b) =  (eq(a,i(delta)) & not(eq(b,i(delta))))
                   | (eq(a,i(tio)) & not(eq(b,i(delta))) & not(eq(b,i(tio))))
END;
```

Furthermore only the external behaviour at ports p1 and p2 is of interest. We abstract from the internal actions:

$$I_0 = \{ct(f) \mid t \in \{3, 4, 5, 6\}, f \in D\} \cup \{tio, i, j\}$$

```
LET abstrset :=
   IMPORT SetsAtoms INTO
CLASS
AXIOM
   FORALL a:Atoms
{abs1}  is-in(I0, a) = eq(a, i(tio)) | eq(a, i(i)) | eq(a, i(j)) |
                       if(has-type(c,a), internal(port(a)), false)
END;
```

Now the PAR-protocol is described by:

$$PAR = \tau_{I_0} \circ \theta \circ \partial_{H_0} (S \| K \| R \| L)$$

Because the systems ACP_t and ACP_θ are not yet integrated into one single system, application of the theta-operator and of the abstraction-operator should be separated in two different modules. In the first module the theta-operator is applied, and in the second module the abstraction-operator. When importing the first module in the second, the theta-operator is hidden.

```
LET PARPart1 :=
EXPORT
    FUNC pre-PAR :       -> process
FROM
    IMPORT Atoms INTO
    IMPORT Base INTO
    IMPORT SumsOverData INTO
    IMPORT SumsOverDB INTO
    IMPORT ACP-Theta INTO
CLASS
    FUNC K        :         -> process
    FUNC K        : DB      -> process
    FUNC L        :         -> process
    FUNC L-ac     :         -> process
    FUNC S        :         -> process
    FUNC RH       : BOOL -> process
    FUNC SF       : DB      -> process
    FUNC WS       : DB      -> process
    FUNC R        :         -> process
    FUNC WF       : BOOL -> process
    FUNC SA       : BOOL -> process
    FUNC SH       : DB      -> process
    FUNC pre-PAR  :         -> process
    FUNC FunK     :         -> FuncsDBToP
    FUNC FunRH    : BOOL -> FuncsDataToP
    FUNC FunWFa   : BOOL -> FuncsDataToP
    FUNC FunWFb   : BOOL -> FuncsDataToP
AXIOM
    FORALL f:DB, d:Data, n:BOOL (
{PAR1}   app(FunK,f)      = i(do(r,p3,j(f))).K(f);
{PAR2}   app(FunRH(n),d)  = i(do(r,p1,j(d))).SF(frame(d,n));
{PAR3}   app(FunWFa(n),d) = i(do(r,p5,j(frame(d,not(n))))).SA(n);
{PAR4}   app(FunWFb(n),d) = i(do(r,p5,j(frame(d,n)))).SH(frame(d,n));

{PAR5}   K               = Sum(DBSet, FunK);
{PAR6}   K(f)            = (i(do(s,p5,j(f))) + i(do(s,p5,ce)) + i(i(i))) . K;

{PAR7}   L               = i(do(r,p6,ac)) . L-ac;
{PAR8}   L-ac            = (i(do(s,p4,ac)) + i(do(s,p4,ce)) + i(i(j))) . L;

{PAR9}   S               = RH(false);
{PAR10}  RH(n)           = Sum(DataSet, FunRH(n));
{PAR11}  SF(f)           = i(do(s,p3,j(f))) . WS(f);
{PAR12}  WS(frame(d,n))  = i(do(r,p4,ac)).RH(not(n)) +
                           (i(do(r,p4,ce))+i(i(tio))).SF(frame(d,n));

{PAR13}  R               = WF(false);
[PAR14]  WF(n)           = i(do(r,p5,ce)).WF(n) +
                           Sum(DataSet, FunWFa(n)) +
                           Sum(DataSet, FunWFb(n));
{PAR15}  SA(n)           = i(do(s,p6,ac)).WF(n);
{PAR16}  SH(frame(d,n))  = i(do(s,p2,j(d))).SA(not(n));

{PAR17}  pre-PAR         = theta(d(H0, (S||K||R||L))) )
END;

LET PARPart2 :=
    IMPORT ACP-Tau INTO
    IMPORT PARPart1 INTO
```

```
CLASS
    FUNC PAR : -> process
AXIOM
{PAR18} PAR = abstr(I0, pre-PAR)
END;
```

6. The OBSW-protocol

6.1. Global Description

The One Bit Sliding Window protocol is a bit more complicated. In contrast to the PAR-protocol, it allows communications in two directions. The process algebra specification is derived by Vaandrager in [22] from a computer program, described in [21]. Using the State Operator, all constructions in the program can be translated to process algebra.

The structure of the system can be visualized as follows:

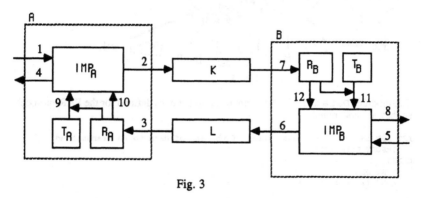

Fig. 3

The two systems A and B communicate using the two channels K and L. Both systems consist of a Timer (T), a Receiver (R) and an Interface Message Processor (IMP), which is the process implementing the computer program.

6.2. Atoms

The description of the way the atoms are built up is analogous to that of the PAR-protocol. Again the interaction-atoms are constructed using three sorts: an Interaction_Type (r, s, c), Ports (p1, ..., p12), and a sort D, containing the items that are communicated. Such an item can be a single Data-element (at ports p1, p4, p5, p8), a data-frame (from DBB), which is some Data-element enriched with two bits of auxiliary information (at ports p2, p3, p6, p7, p10, p12), or it can be one of the events (time-out and frame-arrival at ports p9 and p11, checksum-error at ports p9, p10, p11, p12). Again there is the sort of Simple Atoms, which do not communicate. It contains the internal actions i and j, the deadlock (delta), and for each "action" in the computer program a corresponding atom, which will be interpreted by the State-operator. Because the three events (ce, tio and fa) are also atomic actions in the computer program, the sort Events is also embedded in the sort Simple_Atoms.

The introduction of the extra sort Atoms-Tau is due to the State-Operator, which uses summation over this set. So instead of using the infinite sort process, a new finite sort has to be defined.

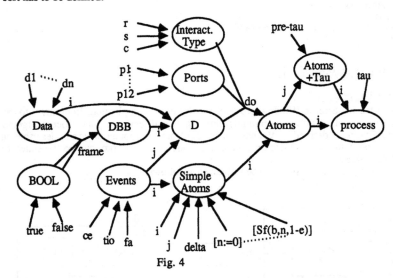

Fig. 4

The modules Data and IntType are equal to the ones defined for the PAR-protocol, so they are not copied.

```
LET DBB :=              %Definition of the set of data to be transmitted
    IMPORT Data INTO
CLASS
    SORT DBB
    FUNC frame : Data # BOOL # BOOL -> DBB

    FUNC eq              : DBB # DBB -> BOOL
    FUNC firstDBB        :              -> DBB
    FUNC next            : DBB          -> DBB
    FUNC penultimateDBB  :              -> DBB
AXIOM
    FORALL x:DBB, y:DBB, d:Data, n1:BOOL, n2:BOOL (
{DBf}    firstDBB = frame(firstDatum,false,false);
{DBn1}   next(frame(d,n1,n2)) = if(eq(n2,false),
                                    frame(d,n1,true),
                                    if(eq(n1,false),
                                        frame(d,true,false),
                                        frame(next(d),false,false) ));
{DBp}    penultimateDBB = frame(next(penultimateDatum), false, true);

{DBeq1}  eq(penultimateDBB, next(penultimateDBB)) = false;
{DBeq2}  eq(next(penultimateDBB), penultimateDBB) = false;
{DBeq3}  eq(next(x), next(y)) = false => eq(x, y) = false;
{DBeq4}  eq(x, x) = true )
END;

LET Events :=
    IMPORT Booleans INTO
CLASS
    SORT Events
```

```
    FUNC tio : -> Events                    %timeout
    FUNC ce  : -> Events                    %checksum error
    FUNC fa  : -> Events                    %frame arrival

    FUNC eq                 : Events # Events -> BOOL
    FUNC firstEvent         :                  -> Events
    FUNC next               : Events           -> Events
    FUNC penultimateEvent   :                  -> Events
AXIOM
    FORALL x:Events, y:Events (
{Evf}   firstEvent = tio;
{Evn1}  next(tio) = ce;
{Evn2}  next(ce) = fa;
{Evn3}  next(fa) = fa;
{Evp}   penultimateEvent = ce;

{Eveq1} eq(penultimateEvent, next(penultimateEvent)) = false;
{Eveq2} eq(next(penultimateEvent), penultimateEvent) = false;
{Eveq3} eq(next(x), next(y)) = false -> eq(x, y) = false;
{Eveq4} eq(x, x) = true )
END;


LET Ports :=                %Definition of the set of Dataports
    IMPORT Booleans INTO
CLASS
    SORT Ports
    FUNC p1:Ports
    FUNC p2:Ports
    FUNC p3:Ports
    FUNC p4:Ports
    FUNC p5:Ports
    FUNC p6:Ports
    FUNC p7:Ports
    FUNC p8:Ports
    FUNC p9:Ports
    FUNC p10:Ports
    FUNC p11:Ports
    FUNC p12:Ports

    FUNC eq             : Ports # Ports -> BOOL
    FUNC firstP         :               -> Ports
    FUNC next           : Ports         -> Ports
    FUNC penultimateP   :               -> Ports
AXIOM
    FORALL x:Ports, y:Ports (
{Pof}    firstP       = p1;
{Pon1}   next(p1)     = p2;
{Pon2}   next(p2)     = p3;
{Pon3}   next(p3)     = p4;
{Pon4}   next(p4)     = p5;
{Pon5}   next(p5)     = p6;
{Pon6}   next(p6)     = p7;
{Pon7}   next(p7)     = p8;
{Pon8}   next(p8)     = p9;
{Pon9}   next(p9)     = p10;
{Pon10}  next(p10)    = p11;
{Pon11}  next(p11)    = p12;
{Pon12}  next(p12)    = p12;
{Pop}    penultimateP = p11;
```

```
{Poeq1}  eq(penultimateP, next(penultimateP)) = false;
{Poeq2}  eq(next(penultimateP), penultimateP) = false;
{Poeq3}  eq(next(x), next(y)) = false => eq(x, y) = false ;
{Poeq4}  eq(x, x) = true )
END;


LET D :=
   IMPORT DBB INTO
   IMPORT Events INTO
CLASS
   SORT D
   FUNC j            : Events -> D          %embed Events
   FUNC i            : DBB     -> D          %embed DBB
   FUNC i            : Data    -> D          %embed Dataset

   FUNC originDBB  : D        -> BOOL       %Is its origin DBB?
   FUNC originData : D        -> BOOL       %Is its origin Data?

   FUNC eq         : D # D -> BOOL
   FUNC firstD     :        -> D
   FUNC next       : D      -> D
   FUNC penultimateD :      -> D
AXIOM
   FORALL x:D, y:D, e:vents, dbb:DBB, d:Data (
{Dor1}   originDBB(i(dbb))  = true;
{Dor2}   originDBB(i(d))    = false;
{Dor3}   originDBB(j(e))    = false;
{Dor4}   originData(i(dbb)) = false;
{Dor5}   originData(i(d))   = true;
{Dor6}   originData(j(e))   = false;

{Df}     firstD      = j(firstEvent);
{Dn1}    next(j(e))  = if(eq(next(e),e), i(firstDBB), j(next(e)));
{Dn2}    next(i(dbb)) = if(eq(next(dbb),dbb), i(firstDatum), i(next(dbb)));
{Dn3}    next(i(d))  = i(next(d));
{Dp}     penultimateD = i(penultimateDatum);

{Deq1}   eq(penultimateD, next(penultimateD)) = false;
{Deq2}   eq(next(penultimateD), penultimateD) = false;
{Deq3}   eq(next(x), next(y)) = false =>  eq(x, y) = false;
{Deq4}   eq(x, x) = true )
END;


LET SimpleAtoms :=
   IMPORT Events INTO
CLASS
   SORT SimpleAtoms
   FUNC delta     :       -> SimpleAtoms     %deadlock
   FUNC i         :       -> SimpleAtoms     %internal action
   FUNC j         :       -> SimpleAtoms     %internal action

   FUNC n-bec-0   :       -> SimpleAtoms     %[n:=0]
   FUNC e-bec-0   :       -> SimpleAtoms     %[e:=0]
   FUNC n-bec-notn :      -> SimpleAtoms     %[n:=1-n]
   FUNC e-bec-note :      -> SimpleAtoms     %[e:=1-e]
   FUNC nn-eq-e   :       -> SimpleAtoms     %[nn=e]
   FUNC ee-eq-n   :       -> SimpleAtoms     %[ee=n]
   FUNC nn-neq-e  :       -> SimpleAtoms     %[nn<>e]
   FUNC ee-neq-n  :       -> SimpleAtoms     %[ee<>n]
   FUNC Fh        :       -> SimpleAtoms     %[Fh(b)]
```

```
   FUNC Sf            :           -> SimpleAtoms        %[Sf(b,n,1-e)]
   FUNC Gf            :           -> SimpleAtoms        %[Gf(bb,nn,ee)]
   FUNC Th            :           -> SimpleAtoms        %[Th(bb)]
   FUNC i             : Events -> SimpleAtoms           %embed Events

   FUNC eq            : SimpleAtoms # SimpleAtoms -> BOOL
   FUNC firstS        :                           -> SimpleAtoms
   FUNC next          : SimpleAtoms               -> SimpleAtoms
   FUNC penultimateS  :                           -> SimpleAtoms
AXIOM
   FORALL x:SimpleAtoms, y:SimpleAtoms, e:Events (
{Sif}    firstS          = delta;
{Sin1}   next(delta)     = i;
{Sin2}   next(i)         = j;
{Sin3}   next(j)         = n-bec-0;
{Sin4}   next(n-bec-0)   = e-bec-0;
{Sin5}   next(e-bec-0)   = n-bec-notn;
{Sin6}   next(n-bec-notn) = e-bec-note;
{Sin7}   next(e-bec-note) = nn-eq-e;
{Sin8}   next(nn-eq-e)   = ee-eq-n;
{Sin9}   next(ee-eq-n)   = nn-neq-e;
{Sin10}  next(nn-neq-e)  = ee-neq-n;
{Sin11}  next(ee-neq-n)  = Fh;
{Sin12}  next(Fh)        = Sf;
{Sin13}  next(Sf)        = Gf;
{Sin14}  next(Gf)        = Th;
{Sin15}  next(Th)        = i(firstEvent);
{Sin16}  next(i(e))      = i(next(e));
{Sip}    penultimateS    = i(penultimateEvent);

{Sieq1}  eq(penultimateS, next(penultimateS)) = false;
{Sieq2}  eq(next(penultimateS), penultimateS) = false;
{Sieq3}  e eq(next(x), next(y)) = false => q(x, y) = false;
{Sieq4}  eq(x, x) = true )
END;

LET Atoms :=              %Definition of the Atoms
   IMPORT SimpleAtoms INTO
   IMPORT InteractionType INTO
   IMPORT Ports INTO
   IMPORT D INTO
CLASS
   SORT Atoms
   FUNC do       : IntType # Ports # D -> Atoms
   FUNC i        : SimpleAtoms         -> Atoms    %embed SimpleAtoms
   FUNC has-type : IntType # Atoms     -> BOOL
   FUNC port     : Atoms               -> Ports    %what port is involved?
   FUNC datum    : Atoms               -> D        %and what datum?

   FUNC eq            : Atoms # Atoms -> BOOL
   FUNC firstAtom     :               -> Atoms
   FUNC next          : Atoms         -> Atoms
   FUNC penultimateAtom :             -> Atoms
AXIOM
   FORALL x:Atoms, y:Atoms, e:SimpleAtoms,
        t IntType, t1:IntType, t2:IntType, p:Ports, d:D (
{At1}    has-type(t,i(e)) = false;
{At2}    has-type(t1,do(t2,p,d)) = eq(t1,t2);

{At3}    port(i(e)) = firstP;       %default value
```

```
{At4}    port(do(t,p,d)) = p;
{At5}    datum(i(e)) = firstD;        %default value
{At6}    datum(do(t,p,d)) = d;

{Atf}    firstAtom = i(firstS);
{Atn1}   next(i(e)) = if(eq(next(e),e),
                           do(firstType, firstP, firstD),
                           i(next(e)));
{Atn1}   next(do(t,p,d)) = if(not(eq(next(t),t)),
                              do(next(t),p,d),
                              if(not(eq(next(p),p)),
                                 do(firstType,next(p),d),
                                 if(not(eq(next(d),d)),
                                    do(firstType,firstP,next(d)),
                                    do(t,p,d) )));
{Atn}    penultimateAtom = do(penultimateIntType, next(penultimateP),
                              next(penultimateD));

{Ateq1}  eq(penultimateAtom, next(penultimateAtom)) = false;
{Ateq2}  eq(next(penultimateAtom), penultimateAtom) = false;
{Ateq3}  eq(next(x), next(y)) = false => eq(x, y) = false;
{Ateq4}  eq(x, x) = true )
END;
```

6.3. Sets and Summations
The following sets, summations and sequences are needed:

```
LET SetsAtoms :=          %Sets of Atoms
RENAME
    SORT SET       -> SetsAtoms,
    FUNC null-set  -> Atoms-null-set
IN
APPLY
    RENAME
        SORT ITEM      -> Atoms,
        FUNC eq        -> eq,
        FUNC firstItem -> firstAtom,
        FUNC next      -> next
    IN Sets
TO Atoms

LET SetsD :=          %Sets of elements from D
RENAME
    SORT SET       -> SetsD,
    FUNC null-set  -> D-null-set
IN
APPLY
    RENAME
        SORT ITEM      -> D,
        FUNC eq        -> eq,
        FUNC firstItem -> firstD,
        FUNC next      -> next
    IN Sets
TO
    IMPORT D INTO
CLASS
    FUNC origin-Data              : -> SetsD
    FUNC origin-DBB               : -> SetsD
    FUNC origin-DBB-ce            : -> SetsD
    FUNC origin-DBB-ce-tio-fa     : -> SetsD
```

```
AXIOM
   FORALL dbb:DBB, d:Data, e:Events (
{SD1}   is-in(origin-Data, i(dbb))  = false;
{SD2}   is-in(origin-Data, i(d))    = true;
{SD3}   is-in(origin-Data, j(e))    = false;
{SD4}   is-in(origin-DBB, i(dbb))   = true;
{SD5}   is-in(origin-DBB, i(d))     = false;
{SD6}   is-in(origin-DBB, j(e))     = false;
{SD7}   origin-DBB-ce             = insert(origin-DBB, j(ce));
{SD8}   origin-DBB-ce-tio-fa      = insert(insert(origin-DBB-ce,
                                            j(tio)), j(fa)))

END;

LET SetsPorts :=        %Sets of elements from Ports
RENAME
   SORT SET        -> SetsPorts,
   FUNC null-set   -> Ports-null-set
IN
APPLY
   RENAME
      SORT ITEM       -> Ports,
      FUNC eq         -> eq,
      FUNC firstItem  -> firstP,
      FUNC next       -> next
   IN Sets
TO
   IMPORT Ports INTO
CLASS
   FUNC pset1         : -> SetsPorts
   FUNC pset2         : -> SetsPorts
   FUNC internalports: -> SetsPorts
AXIOM (
{SP1}   pset1      = insert(insert(Ports-null-set, p3),p7);
{SP2}   pset2      = insert(insert(insert(insert(insert(insert(Ports-null-set,
                     p2),p6),p9),p10),p11),p12);
{SP3}   internalports = union(pset1, pset2) )
END;

LET SumsOverDBB :=
RENAME
   SORT SET        -> SetsOfDBB,
   FUNC null-set   -> DBB-null-set,
   FUNC FuncsToP   -> FuncsDBBToP
IN
APPLY
   RENAME
      SORT ITEM       -> DBB,
      FUNC eq         -> eq,
      FUNC firstItem  -> firstDBB,
      FUNC next       -> next
   IN Sum
TO
   IMPORT DBB INTO
CLASS
   FUNC DBBSet : -> SetsOfDBB
AXIOM
   FORALL d:DBB
{SDBB1}  is-in(DBBSet,d) = true
END;
```

```
LET DBBSeq :=                    %sequences over DBB
RENAME
   SORT SEQ -> DBBSeq
IN
APPLY
   RENAME
      FUNC ITEM -> DBB
   IN Sequences
TO DBB
```

6.4. OBSW

Now a brief discussion on the specification of the OBSW-protocol will be given. The easiest components are the two timers T_A and T_B. They just offer time-outs at ports $p9$ and $p11$.

$$T_A = s9(\text{tio}).T_A$$
$$T_B = s11(\text{tio}).T_B$$

The communication channels K and L are modeled as FIFO-queues with unbounded capacity. The process variables are indexed by the contents of the queue. Frames are received and subsequently communicated correctly, damaged or lost completely.

$$K = K^\varepsilon = \sum_{f \in DBB} r2(f) \cdot K^f$$

$$K^{\sigma*f} = (s7(f)+s7(ce)+i) \cdot K^\sigma + \sum_{g \in DBB} r2(g) \cdot K^{g*\sigma*f}$$

$$L = L^\varepsilon = \sum_{f \in DBB} r6(f) \cdot L^f$$

$$L^{\sigma*f} = (s3(f)+s3(ce)+j) \cdot L^\sigma + \sum_{g \in DBB} r6(g) \cdot L^{g*\sigma*f}$$

$$f \in DBB; \sigma \in (DBB)^*$$

Receiver R_A serves as an intermediate process, which accepts a frame from the communication channel L, and offers this frame to IMP_A via port $p10$, while signaling this offer to the IMP by sending a frame-arrival message at port $p9$. Incoming check-sum errors are also signaled at port $p9$, without using $p10$.

$$R_A = \sum_{f \in DBB} r3(f) \cdot R_A{}^f + r3(ce) \cdot R_A{}^{ce}$$

$$R_A{}^f = s9(fa) \cdot s10(f) \cdot R_A \qquad\qquad (f \in DBB)$$

$$R_A{}^{ce} = s9(ce) \cdot R_A$$

Receiver R_B has the same structure:

$$R_B = \sum_{f \in DBB} r7(f) \cdot R_B{}^f + r7(ce) \cdot R_B{}^{ce}$$

$$R_B{}^f = s11(fa) \cdot s12(f) \cdot R_B \qquad\qquad (f \in DBB)$$

$$R_B{}^{ce} = s11(ce) \cdot R_B$$

The definition of the IMP's follows from the computer program, from [21]. Every IMP takes care of two boolean variables: NextFrameToSend (n) and FrameExpected (e) and one datum-variable DatumToTransmit (b). These three items are packed in a frame, and transmitted over the communication channel. If the other IMP receives a frame, it is unpacked and the items are stored in the variables $\underline{n}$, $\underline{e}$ and $\underline{b}$, and are examined. (In the specification $\underline{n}$, $\underline{e}$ and $\underline{b}$ are denoted by nn, ee and bb)

The program for IMP_A starts with PA. The variables n and e are initialized at 0, while b is initialised by the procedure FromHost (Fh (b)), which accepts a Data-element at port p1. The next state IMP_A enters is SF (SendFrame), in which the three items are packed and transmitted using the procedure Sf (b, n, 1-e). Then we Wait for Something to happen (WS). Either a time-out (tio) or a checksum-error (ce) occurs, or a frame arrives (fa). The first two possibilities indicate some malfunction of one of the communication ports, resulting in a retransmission (SF). The frame arrival indicates that a frame must be accepted and examined (GF). The first test (T1) checks whether this frame has been accepted earlier or not. If not, then the datum-element is offered to the host (Th ($\underline{b}$)) and the expected frame bit is flipped (e:=1-e). In the second test (T2) the need for a retransmission of the previous frame is examined. If our previous frame was received undamaged ($\underline{e}$=n), then a new data-element is fetched from the host, the n-bit is flipped and this new frame is sent. In the other case the old frame is retransmitted.

```
PA = [n:=0] · [e:=0] · [Fh(b)] · SF
SF = [Sf(b,n,1-e)] · WS
WS = tio·SF + ce·SF + fa·GF
GF = [Gf(b,n,e)] · T1
T1 = [n=e] · Th(b)] · [e:=1-e] · T2 + [n≠e] · T2
T2 = [e=n] · Fh(b)] · [n:=1-n] · SF + [e≠n] · SF
```

The program for IMP_B looks the same as the one for IMP_A, except that IMP_B is unable to send a frame before an undamaged frame has arrived from A.

```
PB = [n:=0] · [e:=0] · [Fh(b)] · WF
WF = ce·WF + fa·GF
SF = [Sf(b,n,1-e)] · WS
WS = tio·SF + ce·SF + fa·GF
GF = [Gf(b,n,e)] · T1
T1 = [n=e] · Th(b)] · [e:=1-e] · T2 + [n≠e] · T2
T2 = [e=n] · Fh(b)] · [n:=1-n] · SF + [e≠n] · SF
```

Now we can transform these sequences of atoms into two meaningful processes IMP_A and IMP_B by applying the state-operator to PA and PB.

6.5. Action-Effect

Consider two objects A and B (see the module Objects). With each of them some state is associated, which consists of the values of the six variables n, e, b, $\underline{n}$, $\underline{e}$, $\underline{b}$ (see the module States). Now for each argument the functions action and effect have to be defined. The following definition is too informal, and has to be converted into a more explicit form (see the module ACTION-EFFECT). All relevant instances of the State Operator are given. The notation $\sigma[0/n]$ is used to denote the state that is derived from state σ by substituting 0 for variable n.

For all states σ, all objects m and all events e:

1. $\quad \Lambda^m_\sigma([n:=0]\cdot x) \quad = \tau\cdot\Lambda^m_{\sigma[0/n]}(x)$

   $\quad \Lambda^m_\sigma([e:=0]\cdot x) \quad = \tau\cdot\Lambda^m_{\sigma[0/e]}(x)$

   $\quad \Lambda^m_\sigma([n:=1-n]\cdot x) = \tau\cdot\Lambda^m_{\sigma[1-\sigma(n)/n]}(x)$

   $\quad \Lambda^m_\sigma([e:=1-e]\cdot x) = \tau\cdot\Lambda^m_{\sigma[1-\sigma(e)/n]}(x)$

2. $\quad \Lambda^A_\sigma([Fh(b)]\cdot x) \quad = \sum_{d\in D} r1(d)\cdot\Lambda^A_{\sigma[d/b]}(x)$

   $\quad \Lambda^B_\sigma([Fh(b)]\cdot x) \quad = \sum_{d\in D} r5(d)\cdot\Lambda^B_{\sigma[d/b]}(x)$

3. $\quad \Lambda^A_\sigma([Th(\underline{b})]\cdot x) \quad = s4(\sigma(\underline{b}))\cdot\Lambda^A_\sigma(x)$

   $\quad \Lambda^B_\sigma([Th(\underline{b})]\cdot x) \quad = s8(\sigma(\underline{b}))\cdot\Lambda^B_\sigma(x)$

4. $\quad \Lambda^A_\sigma([Gf(\underline{b},\underline{n},\underline{e})]\cdot x) = \sum_{d\in D}\sum_{p,q\in B} r10(d,p,q)\cdot\Lambda^A_{\sigma[d/\underline{b}][p/\underline{n}][q/\underline{e}]}(x)$

   $\quad \Lambda^B_\sigma([Gf(\underline{b},\underline{n},\underline{e})]\cdot x) = \sum_{d\in D}\sum_{p,q\in B} r12(d,p,q)\cdot\Lambda^B_{\sigma[d/\underline{b}][p/\underline{n}][q/\underline{e}]}(x)$

5. $\quad \Lambda^A_\sigma(e\cdot x) = r9(e)\cdot\Lambda^A_\sigma(x)$

   $\quad \Lambda^B_\sigma(e\cdot x) = r11(e)\cdot\Lambda^A_\sigma(x)$

6. $\quad \Lambda^m_\sigma([\underline{n}=e]\cdot x) = \quad \tau\cdot\Lambda^m_\sigma(x) \qquad \text{if } \sigma(\underline{n})=\sigma(e)$

   $\qquad\qquad\qquad\qquad\quad \delta \qquad\qquad\quad \text{otherwise}$

   $\quad \Lambda^m_\sigma([\underline{n}\neq e]\cdot x) = \quad \tau\cdot\Lambda^m_\sigma(x) \qquad \text{if } \sigma(\underline{n})\neq\sigma(e)$

   $\qquad\qquad\qquad\qquad\quad \delta \qquad\qquad\quad \text{otherwise}$

   $\quad \Lambda^m_\sigma([\underline{e}=n]\cdot x) = \quad \tau\cdot\Lambda^m_\sigma(x) \qquad \text{if } \sigma(\underline{e})=\sigma(n)$

   $\qquad\qquad\qquad\qquad\quad \delta \qquad\qquad\quad \text{otherwise}$

   $\quad \Lambda^m_\sigma([\underline{e}\neq n]\cdot x) = \quad \tau\cdot\Lambda^m_\sigma(x) \qquad \text{if } \sigma(\underline{e})\neq\sigma(n)$

$$\delta \qquad \text{otherwise}$$

7. $\qquad \Lambda^A_\sigma([Sf(b,n,1-e)] \cdot x) \;=\; s2(\sigma(b),\sigma(n),1-\sigma(e)) \cdot \Lambda^A_\sigma(x)$

$\qquad\quad \Lambda^B_\sigma([Sf(b,n,1-e)] \cdot x) \;=\; s6(\sigma(b),\sigma(n),1-\sigma(e)) \cdot \Lambda^B_\sigma(x)$

```
LET Objects :-              %Set of objects to be used with the state-operator
CLASS
   SORT Objects
   FUNC A : -> Objects
   FUNC B : -> Objects
END;

LET States :-              %Definition of the set of states
   IMPORT D INTO
CLASS
   SORT States
   FUNC st: BOOL # BOOL # D # BOOL # BOOL # D  -> States
   FUNC zero-state : -> States

   FUNC subst1 : BOOL # States -> States
   FUNC subst2 : BOOL # States -> States
   FUNC subst3 : D    # States -> States
   FUNC subst4 : BOOL # States -> States
   FUNC subst5 : BOOL # States -> States
   FUNC subst6 : D    # States -> States

   FUNC proj1 : States -> BOOL
   FUNC proj2 : States -> BOOL
   FUNC proj3 : States -> D
   FUNC proj4 : States -> BOOL
   FUNC proj5 : States -> BOOL
   FUNC proj6 : States -> D
AXIOM
   FORALL x1:BOOL, x2:BOOL, x4:BOOL, x5:BOOL, b:BOOL,
          x3:D, x6:D, d:D (
{St1}   zero-state - st(false,false,firstD,false,false,firstD);

{St2}   subst1(b, st(x1,x2,x3,x4,x5,x6)) - st(b,x2,x3,x4,x5,x6);
{St3}   subst2(b, st(x1,x2,x3,x4,x5,x6)) - st(x1,b,x3,x4,x5,x6);
{St4}   subst3(d, st(x1,x2,x3,x4,x5,x6)) - st(x1,x2,d,x4,x5,x6);
{St5}   subst4(b, st(x1,x2,x3,x4,x5,x6)) - st(x1,x2,x3,b,x5,x6);
{St6}   subst5(b, st(x1,x2,x3,x4,x5,x6)) - st(x1,x2,x3,x4,b,x6);
{St7}   subst6(d, st(x1,x2,x3,x4,x5,x6)) - st(x1,x2,x3,x4,x5,d);

{St8}   proj1(st(x1,x2,x3,x4,x5,x6)) - x1;
{St9}   proj2(st(x1,x2,x3,x4,x5,x6)) - x2;
{St10}  proj3(st(x1,x2,x3,x4,x5,x6)) - x3;
{St11}  proj4(st(x1,x2,x3,x4,x5,x6)) - x4;
{St12}  proj5(st(x1,x2,x3,x4,x5,x6)) - x5;
{St13}  proj6(st(x1,x2,x3,x4,x5,x6)) - x6 )
END;

LET ACTION-EFFECT :-     %definition of the action- and effectfunctions
   IMPORT Objects INTO
   IMPORT States INTO
   IMPORT SetsD INTO
   IMPORT SumsOverAtoms-Tau INTO
```

```
CLASS
    FUNC ACTION : Atoms # Objects # States              -> SetsOfAtoms-Tau
    FUNC EFFECT : Atoms # Atoms-Tau # Objects # States -> States
AXIOM
    FORALL a:Atoms, at:Atoms-Tau, sa:SimpleAtoms, m:Objects, st:States,
           e:Events, t:IntType, p:Ports, da:Data, d:D, dbb:DBB,
           b1:BOOL, b2:BOOL (
{Ae1a}  ACTION(i(n-bec-0), m, st)    = tau-set;
{Ae1b}  ACTION(i(e-bec-0), m, st)    = tau-set;
{Ae1c}  ACTION(i(n-bec-notn), m, st) = tau-set;
{Ae1d}  ACTION(i(e-bec-note), m, st) = tau-set;

{Ae2a}  is-in(ACTION(i(Fh), A, st), j(a)) =
        has-type(r,a) & eq(port(a),p1) & is-in(origin-Data,datum(a));
{Ae2b}  is-in(ACTION(i(Fh), B, st), j(a)) =
        has-type(r,a) & eq(port(a),p5) & is-in(origin-Data,datum(a));
{Ae2c}  is-in(ACTION(i(Fh), m, st), pre-tau) = false;

{Ae3a}  ACTION(i(Th), A, st) =
        insert(AtomsT-null-set, j(do(s,p4,proj6(st))));
{Ae3b}  ACTION(i(Th), B, st) =
        insert(AtomsT-null-set, j(do(s,p8,proj6(st))));

{Ae4a}  is-in(ACTION(i(Gf), A, st), j(a)) =
        has-type(r,a) & eq(port(a),p10) & is-in(origin-DBB,datum(a));
{Ae4b}  is-in(ACTION(i(Gf), B, st), j(a)) =
        has-type(r,a) & eq(port(a),p12) & is-in(origin-DBB,datum(a));
{Ae4c}  is-in(ACTION(i(Gf), m, st), pre-tau) = false;

{Ae5a}  ACTION(i(i(e)), A, st) = insert(AtomsT-null-set, j(do(r,p9,j(e))));
{Ae5b}  ACTION(i(i(e)), B, st) = insert(AtomsT-null-set, j(do(r,p11,j(e))));

{Ae6a}  ACTION(i(nn-eq-e), m, st)  = if(eq(proj4(st),proj2(st)),
                                        tau-set,
                                        AtomsT-null-set);
{Ae6b}  ACTION(i(nn-neq-e), m, st) = if(not(eq(proj4(st),proj2(st))),
                                        tau-set,
                                        AtomsT-null-set);
{Ae6c}  ACTION(i(ee-eq-n), m, st)  = if(eq(proj5(st),proj1(st)),
                                        tau-set,
                                        AtomsT-null-set);
{Ae6d}  ACTION(i(ee-neq-n), m, st) = if(not(eq(proj5(st),proj1(st))),
                                        tau-set,
                                        AtomsT-null-set);

{Ae7a}  i(da) = proj3(st) =>
        ACTION(i(Sf), A, st) =
        insert(AtomsT-null-set,
        j(do(s,p2,i(frame(da,proj1(st),not(proj2(st)))))));

{Ae7b}  i(da) = proj3(st) =>
        ACTION(i(Sf), B, st) =
        insert(AtomsT-null-set,
        j(do(s,p6,i(frame(da,proj1(st),not(proj2(st)))))));

{Ae8a}  ACTION(do(t,p,d), m, st) = insert(AtomsT-null-set, j(do(t,p,d)));
{Ae8b}  ACTION(i(i), m, st)      = insert(AtomsT-null-set, j(i(i)));
{Ae8c}  ACTION(i(j), m, st)      = insert(AtomsT-null-set, j(i(j)));
{Ae8d}  ACTION(i(delta), m, st)  = insert(AtomsT-null-set, j(i(delta)));
```

```
{aE1a}   EFFECT(i(n-bec-0), at, m, st)      = subst1(false, st);
{aE1b}   EFFECT(i(e-bec-0), at, m, st)      = subst2(false, st);
{aE1c}   EFFECT(i(n-bec-notn), at, m, st) = subst1(not(proj1(st)), st);
{aE1d}   EFFECT(i(e-bec-note), at, m, st) = subst2(not(proj2(st)), st);

{aE2a}   EFFECT(i(Fh), j(do(t,p,i(da))), m, st)   = subst3(d,st);
{aE2b}   EFFECT(i(Fh), j(do(t,p,i(dbb))), m, st)  = st;
{aE2c}   EFFECT(i(Fh), j(do(t,p,j(e))), m, st)    = st;
{aE2d}   EFFECT(i(Fh), j(i(sa)), m, st)           = st;
{aE2e}   EFFECT(i(Fh), pre-tau, m, st)            = st;

{aE3}    EFFECT(i(Th), at, m, st) = st;

{aE4a}   EFFECT(i(Gf), j(do(t,p,i(frame(da,b1,b2)))), m, st)
                                 = subst6(d, subst4(b1, subst5(b2,st)));
{aE4b}   EFFECT(i(Gf), j(do(t,p,i(da))), m, st) = st;
{aE4c}   EFFECT(i(Gf), j(do(t,p,j(e))), m, st)  = st;
{aE4d}   EFFECT(i(Gf), j(i(sa)), m, st)         = st;
{aE4e}   EFFECT(i(Gf), pre-tau, m, st)          = st;

{aE5}    EFFECT(i(i(e)), at, m, st) = st;

{aE6a}   EFFECT(i(nn-eq-e), at, m, st)  = st;
{aE6b}   EFFECT(i(nn-neq-e), at, m, st) = st;
{aE6c}   EFFECT(i(ee-eq-n), at, m, st)  = st;
{aE6d}   EFFECT(i(ee-neq-n), at, m, st) = st;

{aE7}    EFFECT(i(Sf), at, m, st) = st;

{aE8a}   EFFECT(do(t,p,d), at, m, st) = st;
{aE8b}   EFFECT(i(i), at, m, st)      = st;
{aE8c}   EFFECT(i(j), at, m, st)      = st;
{aE8d}   EFFECT(i(delta), at, m, st)  = st )

END;
```

6.6. OBSW

Now, when $\sigma 0$ denotes an arbitrary initial state, we can define:

$$IMP_A = \Lambda^A_{\sigma 0}(PA)$$
$$IMP_B = \Lambda^B_{\sigma 0}(PB)$$

The communication function (see module Commerge) is defined as:

$$st(f)|rt(f) = ct(f)$$
$$\text{for } t \in \{2,3,6,7,9,10,11,12\}, f \in DBB \cup \{ce,tio,fa\}$$

```
LET Commerge :=              %Definition of the communication-merge function
   IMPORT Atoms INTO
   IMPORT SetsPorts INTO
   IMPORT SetsD INTO
CLASS
   FUNC _|_ : Atoms # Atoms -> Atoms    %communication merge
AXIOM
   FORALL a:Atoms, b:Atoms (
```

```
{Com1}  a|b - if( ((has-type(s,a) & has-type(r,b)) |
                    (has-type(r,a) & has-type(s,b)))
                 & eq(port(a), port(b))
                 & eq(datum(a), datum(b))
                 & is-in(internalports,port(a))
                 & is-in(origin-DBB-ce-tio-fa,datum(a)),

                 do(c, port(a), datum(a)),
                 i(delta)) )
END;
```

The message passing mechanism between L and R_A, respectively K and R_B is modeled as described in [5]. It is possible that before passing the previous frame to IMP_A the receiver R_A is offered a new frame $(s3(f))$ from the communication channel. This frame can get lost. To guarantee that whenever the receiver is able to accept an offer $(r3(f))$, it will not be lost, the following priority is defined (see module PO).

$$\delta < a \qquad \text{for } a \in A$$
$$s3(f) < c3(f) \qquad \text{for } f \in \text{DBB} \cup \{ce\}$$
$$s7(f) < c7(f) \qquad \text{for } f \in \text{DBB} \cup \{ce\}$$

```
LET PO :-                %partial order on Atoms
    IMPORT Atoms INTO
    IMPORT SetsD INTO
CLASS
    FUNC sm : Atoms # Atoms -> BOOL         %smaller
AXIOM
    FORALL a:Atoms, b:Atoms (
{PO1}   sm(a, b) -  (eq(a,i(delta)) & not(eq(b,i(delta))))
                 | ( has-type(s,a)
                   & has-type(c,b)
                   & eq(datum(a),datum(b))
                   & is-in(origin-DBB-ce,datum(a))
                   & ((eq(port(a),p3) & eq(port(b),p3)) |
                        (eq(port(a),p7) & eq(port(b),p7)))
                   ) )
END;
```

After defining (see module encapsset)

$$H1 = \{r3(f) \mid f \in \text{DBB} \cup \{ce\}\}$$
$$H2 = \{r7(f) \mid f \in \text{DBB} \cup \{ce\}\}$$

the following two systems can be defined.

$$\theta \circ \partial_{H1}(L \| R_A)$$
$$\theta \circ \partial_{H2}(K \| R_B) .$$

Now let the sets H_0 and I_0 be defined by (see modules encapsset and abstrset)

$$H_0 = \{st(f), rt(f) \mid t \in \{2, 6, 9, 10, 11, 12\}, f \in \text{DBB} \cup \{ce, tio, fa\}\}$$

$$I_0 = \{ ct(f) \mid t \in \{2,3,6,7,9,10,11,12\}, f \in DBB \cup \{ce, tio, fa\}\}$$
$$\cup \ \{st(f) \mid t \in \{3,7\}, f \in DBB \cup \{ce\}\} \ \cup \ \{i,j\}$$

```
LET encapsset :=
   IMPORT SetsAtoms INTO
   IMPORT SetsPorts INTO
   IMPORT SetsD INTO
CLASS
   FUNC H0 : -> SetsAtoms
   FUNC H1 : -> SetsAtoms
   FUNC H2 : -> SetsAtoms
AXIOM
   FORALL a:Atoms (
{e1}  is-in(H0, a) = (has-type(r,a) | has-type(s,a)) &
                                              is-in(pset2,port(a))   &
is-in(origin-DBB-ce-tio-fa,datum(a));
{e2}  is-in(H1,a) = has-type(r,a) & eq(port(a),p3) &
                     is-in(origin-DBB-ce, datum(a));
{e3}  is-in(H2,a) = has-type(r,a) & eq(port(a),p7) &
                     is-in(origin-DBB-ce, datum(a)) )
END;

LET abstrset :=
   IMPORT SetsAtoms INTO
   IMPORT SetsPorts INTO
   IMPORT SetsD INTO
CLASS
   SORT I0 : -> SetsAtoms
AXIOM
   FORALL a : -> Atoms (
{abs1}  is-in(I0, a) =  eq(a, i(i))
                     | eq(a, i(j))
                     | (has-type(c,a) &
                       is-in(internalports,port(a)) &
                       is-in(origin-DBB-ce-tio-fa,datum(a)))
                     | (has-type(s,a) &
                       is-in(pset1,port(a)) &
                       is-in(origin-DBB-ce,datum(a))) )
END;
```

Then finally the process OBSW is defined by

$$OBSW = \tau_{I_0} \circ \partial_{H_0} (IMP_A \| T_A \| \ \theta \circ \partial_{H_2} (K \| R_B) \ \| IMP_B \| T_B \| \ \theta \circ \partial_{H_1} (L \| R_A) \ )$$

```
LET OBSWPart1 :=
EXPORT
   FUNC pre-OBSW :           -> process
FROM
   IMPORT SumsOverDBB INTO
   IMPORT ACP-Theta INTO
   IMPORT lambda INTO
   IMPORT DBBSeq INTO
CLASS
   FUNC PA      :           -> process
   FUNC SF      :           -> process
   FUNC WS      :           -> process
```

```
      FUNC GF        :              -> process
      FUNC T1        :              -> process
      FUNC T2        :              -> process
      FUNC PB        :              -> process
      FUNC WF        :              -> process
      FUNC Ta        :              -> process
      FUNC Tb        :              -> process
      FUNC Ra        :              -> process
      FUNC Rb        :              -> process
      FUNC Ra        : DBB          -> process
      FUNC Rb        : DBB          -> process
      FUNC Ra-ce     :              -> process
      FUNC Rb-ce     :              -> process
      FUNC K         :              -> process
      FUNC L         :              -> process
      FUNC K         : DBBSeq       -> process
      FUNC L         : DBBSeq       -> process
      FUNC IMPa      :              -> process
      FUNC IMPb      :              -> process
      FUNC pre-OBSW  :              -> process


      FUNC FunRa     :              -> FuncsDBBToP
      FUNC FunRb     :              -> FuncsDBBToP
      FUNC FunK-eps  :              -> FuncsDBBToP
      FUNC FunL-eps  :              -> FuncsDBBToP
      FUNC FunK-s    : DBBSeq       -> FuncsDBBToP
      FUNC FunL-s    : DBBSeq       -> FuncsDBBToP
  AXIOM
      FORALL f:DBB, q:DBBSeq (
{OBS1}    app(FunRa,f)      = i(do(r,p3,i(f))).Ra(f);
{OBS2}    app(FunRb,f)      = i(do(r,p7,i(f))).Rb(f);
{OBS3}    app(FunK-eps,f)   = i(do(r,p2,i(f))).K(seq(f));
{OBS5}    app(FunL-eps,f)   = i(do(r,p6,i(f))).L(seq(f));
{OBS6}    app(FunK-s(q),f)  = i(do(r,p2,i(f))).K(seq(f)+q);
{OBS7}    app(FunL-s(q),f)  = i(do(r,p6,i(f))).L(seq(f)+q);

{OBS8}    PA       = i(i(n-bec-0)).i(i(e-bec-0)).i(i(Fh)).SF;
{OBS9}    SF       = i(i(Sf)).WS;
{OBS11}   WS       = (i(i(i(tio))).SF)+ (i(i(i(ce))).SF) + (i(i(i(fa))).GF);
{OBS12}   GF       = i(i(Gf)).T1;
{OBS13}   T1       = (i(i(nn-eq-e)).i(i(Th)).i(i(e-bec-note)).T2) +
                     (i(i(nn-neq-e)).T2);
{OBS14}   T2       = (i(i(ee-eq-n)).i(i(Fh)).i(i(n-bec-notn)).SF) +
                     (i(i(ee-neq-n)).SF);
{OBS15}   PB       = i(i(n-bec-0)).i(i(e-bec-0)).i(i(Fh)).WF;
{OBS16}   WF       = (i(i(i(ce))).WF) + (i(i(i(fa))).GF);

{OBS17}   Ta       = i(do(s,p9, j(tio))) . Ta;
{OBS18}   Tb       = i(do(s,p11, j(tio))) . Tb;

{OBS19}   Ra       = Sum(DBBSet, FunRa) + i(do(r,p3, j(ce))).Ra-ce;
{OBS20}   Ra(f)    = i(do(s,p9, j(fa))) . i(do(s,p10, i(f))) . Ra;
{OBS21}   Ra-ce    = i(do(s,p9, j(ce))) . Ra;

{OBS22}   Rb       = Sum(DBBSet, FunRb) + i(do(r,p7, j(ce))).Rb-ce;
{OBS23}   Rb(f)    = i(do(s,p11, j(fa))) . i(do(s,p12, i(f))) . Rb;
{OBS24}   Rb-ce    = i(do(s,p11, j(ce))) . Rb;

{OBS25}   K        = K(eps);
{OBS26}   K(eps)   = Sum(DBBSet,FunK-eps);
```

```
{OBS27}  K(q+seq(f))  =  (i(do(s,p7,i(f))) + i(do(s,p7,j(ce))) + i(i(i))).K(q);
                         + Sum(DBBSet,FunK-s(q+seq(f)));

{OBS28}  L            =  L(eps);
{OBS29}  L(eps)       =  Sum(DBBSet,FunL-eps);
{OBS30}  L(q+seq(f))  =  (i(do(s,p3,i(f))) + i(do(s,p3,j(ce))) + i(i(j))).L(q)
                         + Sum(DBBSet,FunL-s(q+seq(f)));

{OBS31}  IMPa         =  lambda(A, zero-state, PA);
{OBS32}  IMPb         =  lambda(B, zero-state, PB);

{OBS33}  pre-OBSW     =  d(H0, IMPa || Ta || theta(d(H2, K||Rb)) ||
                            IMPb || Tb || theta(d(H1, L||Ra)) ) )

END;

LET OBSWPart2 :=
   IMPORT ACP-Tau INTO
   IMPORT SC INTO
   IMPORT SC OBSWPart1 INTO
CLASS
   FUNC OBSW : -> process
AXIOM
{OBS34}  OBSW = abstr(I0, pre-OBSW)
END;
```

7. Final Remarks

7.1. Execution and implementation

One reason for making this algebraic specification is given by the wish to 'execute' or 'implement' systems that are described in terms of process algebra. Two different approaches are possible. The first one is the automatic generation of proofs and the second one is prototyping the specified system.

The former approach originates from the fact that, in many cases, large parts of proofs about specifications in process algebra (e.g. two specification being equal for an external observer) turn out to be straightforward, but long and tedious. The reason for this can be found in the character of the axioms constituting process algebra. Most of them can be viewed, and are often used, as rewrite rules. However, when a proof involves some human ingenuity, which exceeds just using some rewrite rules, an automatic prover may not succeed. This shortcoming is unavoidable, due to the fact that the theory is undecidable. So in the verification of specifications some interaction between man and machine is needed. The computer can be used as an aid in proving. The user can just point out what (sub)term should be expanded or what new process variable should be introduced. Then, after some computations, an equivalent system is displayed.

The latter approach to executing specifications consists of the simulation of the (external) behaviour of the specified system. In interaction with the computer a user is able to check if the specified behaviour conforms to his expectations or intentions. For this purpose the computer should report all (relevant) actions to the user, making appropriate internal choices (e.g. interleaving actions in a merge), and offer external choices (e.g. summation over data-values) to the user. The computer produces a possible trace. Of course the real-time behaviour of the specified system will not be simulated, but it would be a low-cost prototyping technique.

Both approaches explicitly depend on term rewrite systems (TRS's). This requires that all equations can be interpreted as rewrite rules. Equations that are used in only one direction are simple to deal with, but some equations, like the commutativity and associativity of alternative composition, are more difficult. The TRS resulting by adding these rules as a rewrite rule from left to right and from right to left would not be strongly normalizing.

Some equations that could cause problems when being interpreted as rewrite rules are mentioned in the sequel.

In the modules that define the atoms there are no problems, but since the eq-function only tests for syntactical equality, this function could be implemented easier.

In the module Sets only the last equation S8 (s1=s2 when eq(s1,s2)=true)) is not a rewrite rule. The solution is to delete this equation and substitute in the following modules all occurrences of s1=s2 by eq(s1,s2)=true.

In the module BPA, there are three equations that must be implemented directly, not by using rewrite rules. Rule A1 (x+y=y+x) is dealt with by using a "commutative" rewriting system. For rule A2 ((x+y)+z=x+(y+z)) one needs an "associative" system and for rule A3 (x+x=x) an "idempotent" system is needed. Together these three demands state that a process can be represented by the set of its summands. The elements of a set are not ordered (A1 and A2), and a set contains no duplicate elements (A3). Now addition of processes is represented by the union of their defining sets, while removing duplicate summands.

The equations for the communication function C1 (a|b=b|a), C2 ((a|b)|c=a|(b|c)) and C3 (δ|a=δ) simply define some restrictions on its definition. So if the definition is right, these rules can be deleted.

In [1] rewriting systems are given for ACP_τ and ACP_θ. In ACP_τ the rules T2 ($\tau x + x = \tau x$) and T3 (a($\tau x + y$) = a($\tau x + y$) + ax) are deleted because they are used in two directions. Moreover a rule RT2 (x(τy) $\rightarrow$ xy) is added. In ACP_θ two rules are added: RP8 ((x$\lhd$y)$\lhd$y $\rightarrow$ x$\lhd$y) and RTH4 (θ(x) $\lhd$x $\rightarrow$ θ(x))

The equations for Standard Concurrency SC1-SC6 cause some problems that are not simple to deal with.

The most natural way to implement the resulting TRS's seems to be a functional or a logic programming language. Both PROLOG and LISP are candidates. Some programs are already being developed: a PROLOG program that calculates the normal form of finite processes and a PASCAL program that determines the equality of regular processes. There is also an implementation of the sets module in PROLOG.

7.2. Relation to LOTOS

There is some resemblance between the specification language LOTOS [12] and the combination of (the subset of) COLD with the specification of process algebra. LOTOS consists of two parts: the data-definition language (ACT-ONE) (see [13]) and the process specification language (based on Milner's CCS, see [19]). It appears that the COLD-subset and ACT-ONE are much the same. Their syntax is interchangeable and they both use initial algebra semantics.

Some differences between the process specification part and process algebra arise from the fact that in LOTOS it is part of the specification language, while in this approach it is defined by means of the specification language.

1.   LOTOS has a fixed number of primitives, whereas the specification of process algebra could be extended with new primitives any time.
2.   LOTOS supports conditional expressions and variables in a natural way, while in process algebra this is implemented with the State Operator.
3.   LOTOS can deal with (simple) abstraction and encapsulation sets. In this specification a complex sort SETS was needed.
4.   The semantics of LOTOS processes is defined separately from the semantics

of ACT-ONE, while in the specification of process algebra the initial algebra semantics is used.

5. In process algebra a wide range of proof techniques is being developed, while LOTOS is merely used for specification purposes.

6. The information about what process is allowed to use what communication channel is in LOTOS part of the specification. In process algebra this has to be stated in an informal way.

7.3. About the Specification Language

After adding some features from ASF to COLD, the language becomes quite suitable. There are still more features needed to improve the specification of process algebra. A point of comment about the operators is the lack of a mechanism to define the precedence of operators. In the present formalism every equation with some ambiguity has to be expanded with an overkill of parentheses. A method to express the priority of operators would add to the readability of specifications.

The injection functions also produce a lot of brackets. A way to avoid this is the introduction of a new notion: *subsorts*. If some sort A is stated to be a subsort of sort B, then B inherits all elements of sort A. All functions and operators on sort A then become partial functions and operators on sort B. If this construction is considered as a purely syntactical abbreviation, no semantical problems occur. A definition of a subsort could semantically be expanded to a definition of an injection function from sort A to sort B. With these enrichments of the specification language e.g. the equation for timer one would not look like :

```
T1 = (i(i(nn-eq-e)).i(i(Th)).i(i(e-bec-note)).T2) +
     (i(i(nn-neq-e)).T2)
```

but like:

```
T1 = nn-eq-e.Th.e-bec-note.T2 + nn-neq-e.T2
```

7.4. Conclusion

Now we can make some concluding remarks. Transforming process algebra into an algebraic specification is quite easy. The definitions of most operators and functions are in an algebraic form. On account of the modularization it is easy to pick out some modules and join them to form the desired axiom-system. Also adding new operators or processes is easy.

To transform an application of process algebra (e.g. a specification of a communication protocol) into an algebraic specification takes more effort. This is due to the fact that the atoms are often specified quite informally. Giving an algebraic specification forces the specification to be more exact. To facilitate a proper definition of the atoms and other parameters a strong concept of set has to be introduced.

If one wishes to transform a verification into an algebraic specification, problems arise when the proof involves some advanced process algebra techniques. Research in process algebra has to be done to make an algebraic specification possible. This also influences the way to implement or execute a given specification. The most natural way to implement this would be in a term rewriting system, which itself could be implemented in e.g. PROLOG.

Finally the specification formalism could use some more extensions

References

[1] J.C.M. Baeten, *Procesalgebra*, [in Dutch], Kluwer, 1986.
[2] J.C.M. Baeten, J.A. Bergstra & J.W. Klop, *Conditional axioms and α/β calculus in process algebra*, Proc. IFIP Conf. on Formal Description of Programming Concepts - III, Ebberup 1986, (M. Wirsing, ed.), North-Holland Amsterdam, pp.53-75, 1987.
[3] J.C.M. Baeten, J.A. Bergstra & J.W. Klop, *On the consistency of Koomen's Fair Abstraction Rule*, Report CS-R8504, Centre for Math. and Comp. Sci., Amsterdam 1985, to appear in TCS 51 (1/2), 1987.
[4] J.C.M. Baeten, J.A. Bergstra & J.W. Klop, *Syntax and defining equations for an interrupt mechanism in process algebra*, Fund. Inf. IX (2), pp. 127-168, 1986.
[5] J.A. Bergstra, *Put and get, primitives for synchronous unreliable message passing*, CIF report LGPS 3, State University of Utrecht, 1985.
[6] J.A. Bergstra, J. Heering & P. Klint, *Algebraic definition of a simple programming language*, Report CS-R8504, Centre for Math. and Comp. Sci., Amsterdam 1985.
[7] J.A. Bergstra, J. Heering & P. Klint, *ASF - An algebraic specification formalism*, report CS-R8705, Centre for Math. and Comp. Sci., Amsterdam 1987.
[8] J.A. Bergstra & J.W. Klop, *Algebra of communicating processes*, Proc. CWI Symp. Math. & Comp. Sci. (J.W. de Bakker, M. Hazewinkel & J.K. Lenstra, eds.), pp. 89-138, North-Holland, 1986.
[9] J.A. Bergstra & J.W.Klop, *Algebra of communicating processes with abstraction*, TCS 37 (1), pp. 77-121, 1985.
[10] J.A. Bergstra & J.W.Klop, *Conditional Rewrite Rules: Confluence and Termination*, JCSS 32, pp. 323-362, 1986.
[11] J.A. Bergstra & J.W.Klop, *Process algebra for synchronous communication*, Inf. & Control 60 (1/3), pp. 109-137, 1984.
[12] E. Brinksma (ed.), *LOTOS, A Formal Description Technique Based on the Temporal Ordering of Observational Behaviour*, ISO DIS 8807, 1987.
[13] H. Ehrig, W. Fey & H. Hansen, *ACT ONE, an algebraic specification language with two levels of semantics*, TU Berlin, FB 20, Techn. Report 83-03, 1983.
[14] H. Ehrig & B. Mahr, *Fundamentals of Algebraic Specification 1*, Springer verlag, 1985.
[15] L.M.G. Feijs, H.B.M. Jonkers, C.P.J. Koymans & G.R. Renardel de Lavalette, *Formal definition of the design language COLD-K*, Technical Report, ESPRIT project 432, Doc.Nr. METEOR/t7/PRLE/7, 1987.
[16] J.V. Guttag & J.J. Horning, *The algebraic specification of abstract datatypes*, Acta Informatica 10, pp. 27-52, 1978.
[17] C.A.R. Hoare, *Communicating sequential processes*, Prentice Hall International, 1985.
[18] H.B.M. Jonkers, *A concrete syntax for COLD-K*, Philips Research Laboratories Eindhoven, 1988.
[19] R. Milner, *A calculus of communicating systems*, Springer LNCS 92, 1980.
[20] W. Reisig, *Petrinetze*, Springer-Verlag, 1982.
[21] A.S. Tanenbaum, *Computer Networks*, Prentice Hall, 1981.
[22] F.W. Vaandrager, *Verification of two communication protocols by means of process algebra*, Report CS-R8608, Centre for Math. and Comp. Sci., Amsterdam 1986.
[23] H.R. Walters, *An annotated algebraic specification of the static semantics of POOL*, FVI report 86-20, University of Amsterdam, 1986.

Subject Index

Index of Examples

Lecture Notes in Computer Science

Vol. 352: J. Díaz, F. Orejas (Eds.), TAPSOFT '89. Volume 2. Proceedings, 1989. X, 389 pages. 1989.

Vol. 354: J. W. de Bakker, W.-P. de Roever, G. Rozenberg (Eds.), Linear Time, Branching Time and Partial Order in Logics and Models for Concurrency. VIII, 713 pages. 1989.

Vol. 355: N. Dershowitz (Ed.), Rewriting Techniques and Applications. Proceedings, 1989. VII, 579 pages. 1989.

Vol. 356: L. Huguet, A. Poli (Eds.), Applied Algebra, Algebraic Algorithms and Error-Correcting Codes. Proceedings, 1987. VI, 417 pages. 1989.

Vol. 357: T. Mora (Ed.), Applied Algebra, Algebraic Algorithms and Error-Correcting Codes. Proceedings, 1988. IX, 481 pages. 1989.

Vol. 358: P. Gianni (Ed.), Symbolic and Algebraic Computation. Proceedings, 1988. XI, 545 pages. 1989.

Vol. 359: D. Gawlick, M. Haynie, A. Reuter (Eds.), High Performance Transaction Systems. Proceedings, 1987. XII, 329 pages. 1989.

Vol. 360: H. Maurer (Ed.), Computer Assisted Learning – ICCAL '89. Proceedings, 1989. VII, 642 pages. 1989.

Vol. 361: S. Abiteboul, P.C. Fischer, H.-J. Schek (Eds.), Nested Relations and Complex Objects in Databases. VI, 323 pages. 1989.

Vol. 362: B. Lisper, Synthesizing Synchronous Systems by Static Scheduling in Space-Time. VI, 263 pages. 1989.

Vol. 363: A.R. Meyer, M.A. Taitslin (Eds.), Logic at Botik '89. Proceedings, 1989. X, 289 pages. 1989.

Vol. 364: J. Demetrovics, B. Thalheim (Eds.), MFDBS 89. Proceedings, 1989. VI, 428 pages. 1989.

Vol. 365: E. Odijk, M. Rem, J.-C. Syre (Eds.), PARLE '89. Parallel Architectures and Languages Europe. Volume I. Proceedings, 1989. XIII, 478 pages. 1989.

Vol. 366: E. Odijk, M. Rem, J.-C. Syre (Eds.), PARLE '89. Parallel Architectures and Languages Europe. Volume II. Proceedings, 1989. XIII, 442 pages. 1989.

Vol. 367: W. Litwin, H.-J. Schek (Eds.), Foundations of Data Organization and Algorithms. Proceedings, 1989. VIII, 531 pages. 1989.

Vol. 368: H. Boral, P. Faudemay (Eds.), IWDM '89, Database Machines. Proceedings, 1989. VI, 387 pages. 1989.

Vol. 369: D. Taubner, Finite Representations of CCS and TCSP Programs by Automata and Petri Nets. X. 168 pages. 1989.

Vol. 370: Ch. Meinel, Modified Branching Programs and Their Computational Power. VI, 132 pages. 1989.

Vol. 371: D. Hammer (Ed.), Compiler Compilers and High Speed Compilation. Proceedings, 1988. VI, 242 pages. 1989.

Vol. 372: G. Ausiello, M. Dezani-Ciancaglini, S. Ronchi Della Rocca (Eds.), Automata, Languages and Programming. Proceedings, 1989. XI, 788 pages. 1989.

Vol. 373: T. Theoharis, Algorithms for Parallel Polygon Rendering. VIII, 147 pages. 1989.

Vol. 374: K.A. Robbins, S. Robbins, The Cray X-MP/Model 24. VI, 165 pages. 1989.

Vol. 375: J.L.A. van de Snepscheut (Ed.), Mathematics of Program Construction. Proceedings, 1989. VI, 421 pages. 1989.

Vol. 376: N.E. Gibbs (Ed.), Software Engineering Education. Proceedings, 1989. VII, 312 pages. 1989.

Vol. 377: M. Gross, D. Perrin (Eds.), Electronic Dictionaries and Automata in Computational Linguistics. Proceedings, 1987. V, 110 pages. 1989.

Vol. 378: J.H. Davenport (Ed.), EUROCAL '87. Proceedings, 1987. VIII, 499 pages. 1989.

Vol. 379: A. Kreczmar, G. Mirkowska (Eds.), Mathematical Foundations of Computer Science 1989. Proceedings, 1989. VIII, 605 pages. 1989.

Vol. 380: J. Csirik, J. Demetrovics, F. Gécseg (Eds.), Fundamentals of Computation Theory. Proceedings, 1989. XI, 493 pages. 1989.

Vol. 381: J. Dassow, J. Kelemen (Eds.), Machines, Languages, and Complexity. Proceedings, 1988. VI, 244 pages. 1989.

Vol. 382: F. Dehne, J.-R. Sack, N. Santoro (Eds.), Algorithms and Data Structures. WADS '89. Proceedings, 1989. IX, 592 pages. 1989.

Vol. 383: K. Furukawa, H. Tanaka, T. Fujisaki (Eds.), Logic Programming '88. Proceedings, 1988. VII, 251 pages. 1989. (Subseries LNAI)

Vol. 384: G. A. van Zee, J. G. G. van de Vorst (Eds.), Parallel Computing 1988. Proceedings, 1988. V, 135 pages. 1989.

Vol. 385: E. Börger, H. Kleine Büning, M. M. Richter (Eds.), CSL '88. Proceedings, 1988. VI, 399 pages. 1989.

Vol. 386: J.E. Pin (Ed.), Formal Properties of Finite Automata and Applications. Proceedings, 1988. VIII, 260 pages. 1989.

Vol. 387: C. Ghezzi, J. A. McDermid (Eds.), ESEC '89. 2nd European Software Engineering Conference. Proceedings, 1989. VI, 496 pages. 1989.

Vol. 388: G. Cohen, J. Wolfmann (Eds.), Coding Theory and Applications. Proceedings, 1988. IX, 329 pages. 1989.

Vol. 389: D.H. Pitt, D.E. Rydeheard, P. Dybjer, A.M. Pitts, A. Poigné (Eds.), Category Theory and Computer Science. Proceedings, 1989. VI, 365 pages. 1989.

Vol. 390: J.P. Martins, E.M. Morgado (Eds.), EPIA 89. Proceedings, 1989. XII, 400 pages. 1989 (Subseries LNAI).

Vol. 392: J.-C. Bermond, M. Raynal (Eds.), Distributed Algorithms. Proceedings, 1989. VI, 315 pages. 1989.

Vol. 393: H. Ehrig, H. Herrlich, H.-J. Kreowski, G. Preuß (Eds.), Categorical Methods in Computer Science. VI, 350 pages. 1989.

Vol. 394: M. Wirsing, J.A. Bergstra (Eds.), Algebraic Methods: Theory, Tools and Applications. VI, 558 pages. 1989.